A SOLDIER'S STORY

OMAR N. BRADLEY

A Soldier's Story

Foreword by Bill Mauldin

RAND McNALLY & COMPANY
CHICAGO • NEW YORK • SAN FRANCISCO

The author wishes to thank the Editors of Life *magazine for their permission to reproduce the following pictures, which are copyrighted by Time, Inc.: photograph of General Roosevelt by Eliot Elisofon, facing page 108; by David E. Scherman, facing page 109; by Frank Scherschel, facing page 269; by William Vandivert, facing page 460; by Johnny Florea, facing page 492.*

Acknowledgment is also gratefully made to the U. S. Army Signal Corps for permission to use the photographs facing pages 76, 77, 108 (General Terry Allen), 236, 237, 268, 364, 365, 396, 397, and 493.

The cartoon facing page xix is reproduced courtesy of Bill Mauldin.

The photograph facing page 461 is reprinted by kind permission of Acme Newspictures.

The frontispiece photograph is copyrighted by Karsh, Ottawa.

Maps by Rafael Palacios

Hardbound edition: 528-81052-9
Paperback edition: 528-88133-7

First Rand McNally Printing, 1978
Second Rand McNally Printing, 1980

Acknowledgments

IT IS TO A BRIGADIER GENERAL WITH A DISTINGUISHED
name and a no less distinguished record that I am indebted for the
origins of this book. For on his arrival in England for the Normandy
invasion, Brigadier General Theodore Roosevelt, Jr., warned me
that once the war was ended he would exact repayment for the
hazardous mission to which I had assigned him by asking me to do
a book for the publishing house with which he was then associated.
Five weeks after his fourth D-day assault, Roosevelt died in Normandy and the prospect of authoring my memoirs was temporarily
forgotten.

Roosevelt's proposal was not revived until the fall of 1946, two
and one-half years later, when Charles Wertenbaker, *Time* and *Life*
war correspondent and novelist, urged me to write the story of our
land campaign in Europe. Seeking a retreat in wartime reminiscences from my daytime duties as Administrator of Veterans Affairs,
I prepared an initial outline and the project was begun.

During the four intervening years of week-end authorship, I have
enjoyed the devoted and invaluable assistance of Lieutenant Colonel
Chester B. Hansen, my associate and friend through nine eventful
years of war, the V.A., and the Pentagon. Much of the recorded
detail in this volume has been excerpted from the personal diary he
maintained while serving as my aide in those overseas campaigns.
That our joint efforts did at last produce a book is due in large part
also to the able editorial guidance and aid of Theodore S. Amussen.

For his encouragement and assistance in initiating publication, I am obligated to my good friend and counselor, Eugene Meyer, and to his colleague, Louis M. Lowe. In no less measure for the prudence they brought to a final reading, I am grateful to the Arthur G. Newmyers, junior as well as senior.

In the preparation of pertinent background on OVERLORD to which I was not privy during the war, I am grateful to the Historical Division of the United States Army, for the use of documents assembled by it in the writing of official histories. Of particular assistance was the draft of a distinguished study on the invasion written by Gordon A. Harrison for publication by the Army. To Miss Lucy Weidman, too, I am indebted for her many historical document checks and to Mrs. Anne Cosgrove for her week-end labors on the manuscript.

In reconstructing the chronicle on the liberation of Paris, I am grateful to M. Rolf Nordling, a French citizen who accompanied the interventionist delegation through the German lines to my CP. And though space prevents me from listing them by name, my thanks are no less warmly given to the scores of officers and friends who have searched their memories and papers in the preparation of this record.

Conscientiously though we have sought to avoid them, the reader may find errors attributable in part to inaccurate sources and to faulty recollection. To those who may feel themselves wronged, I freely acknowledge that this is in part a book of opinion and that the opinion is my own.

O.N.B.

Washington, D. C.
March 28, 1951

Preface

HOW AND WHY THIS BOOK WAS WRITTEN

ORIGINALLY, THE PUBLICATION OF A SOLDIER'S STORY was scheduled for the fall of 1951, closely following my intended retirement from active duty. But with the outbreak of the Korean war in 1950 I knew that my plans for retirement would be delayed. Rather than defer publication, I requested permission to write and publish the book while on active duty. To avoid embarrassment to those who granted me this permission I have refrained from showing the manuscript to any officer or office, except, of course, for security clearance.

In this book I have tried to achieve one purpose: to explain how war is waged on the field from the field command post. For it is there, midway between the conference table and the foxhole, that strategy is translated into battlefield tactics; there the field commander must calculate the cost of rivers, roads, and hills in terms of guns, tanks, tonnage—and most importantly in terms of the lives and limbs of his soldiers. How, then, did we reach our critical decisions? Why and how did we go where we did? These are the questions I have been asked most often. And these are the questions that give me justification for writing this book.

Despite the enormous quantities of documentation available to historians of this last World War, the real reasons behind many of our decisions are comparatively obscure. For many of our most important moves were decided upon at informal conferences where no memoranda were kept. Many of the most important instructions were given over the telephone protected by a Signal Corps device which scrambled each conversation in transit and unscrambled it at the far end.

To tell the story of *how* and *why* we chose to do what we did, no one can ignore the personalities and characteristics of those individuals engaged in making decisions. For military command is as much a practice of human relations as it is a science of tactics and a knowledge of logistics. Where there are people, there is pride and ambition, prejudice and conflict. In generals, as in all other men, capabilities cannot always obscure weaknesses, nor can talents hide faults.

Even in an Allied command where soldiers of several nations engage in a common struggle for survival, judgments are further complicated by a fierce and sometimes jealous love of country. This cannot be ignored no matter how zealously one may strive to subordinate it to a mutual undertaking. Although this allegiance is keenly developed in the ordinary citizen, it is even more intensively cultivated in the professional soldier who commits his life to the defense of the flag he salutes each day.

This national pride was more evident in the early 1940's than it is today. Some officers of the American army were peculiarly insular in their outlook, never having traveled abroad nor associated professionally with our prospective Allies. As a consequence, some of us were probably unduly sensitive to slights upon our army and our national pride. We were undoubtedly defensive in our attitude toward the British who for three long years had fought the Axis before we took to the field.

I prefer to admit to these difficulties frankly, and to discuss them as fairly and as openly as I can. However, in discussing them, I have been cautioned that any honest examination of such sensitive issues might be deliberately interpreted as a disservice to our North Atlantic alliance. This I dispute. If intelligently examined by intelligent peoples, historical revelations can not only ready them for similar difficulties, should such difficulties arise, but they can likewise help us face those situations, help us resolve them fairly, quickly, and without dissension.

The United States Army has matured greatly since the end of the war against the Axis powers, and its officers have grown vastly more aware of their world-wide responsibilities as military men. Allied command has become the accepted pattern of military operation

among the Western nations, and many of the insular differences
that once caused us to question the motives of our Allies have now
been completely resolved. If we will only remember that from time
to time some difficulties do exist, that they occasionally make cooperation difficult, we shall be better prepared to settle them without exaggerating their dangers.

The American army has also acquired a political maturity it sorely lacked at the outbreak of World War II. At times during that
war we forgot that wars are fought for the resolution of political
conflicts and in the ground campaign for Europe overlooked political considerations of vast importance. Today we are aware that
a military effort cannot be separated from political objectives.

Because military campaigns reflect the limitations as well as the
abilities of individual commanders, it would be foolhardy for me to
assert that every tactical maneuver of the war in Europe was brilliantly conceived and executed. Generals are human; I know of
none immune to error. We may have erred in discretion and in
judgment, but because we were more often right than wrong in
Europe, we can take pride in that campaign and in those colleagues
whose judgments we sometimes disputed but whose achievements
vastly outweighed their mistakes. If a soldier would command an
army he must be prepared to withstand those who would criticize
the manner in which he leads that army. There is no place in a
democratic state for the attitude that would elevate each military
hero above public reproach simply because he did the job he has
been trained and is paid to do.

For critical comments on certain specific tactics of Field Marshal
the Viscount Montgomery of Alamein, I have been warned that I
may offend the British people and thus risk a disservice to the common interests that bind Britain to the United States. This warning
infers that his generalship cannot withstand the critical scrutiny of
a comrade in arms. I do not agree. Montgomery's brilliant record
of achievement in the war against the Axis is too endurable to be
harmed by my few dissenting opinions. Those who would have us
uphold the myth of the infallible military commander are those
who do Montgomery the greatest disservice.

Military science is not an absolute science; it is incapable of absolute judgment on what may be right or wrong. My assertions are
statements of opinion, they can be challenged, and they undoubtedly
will be challenged. If, however, we can profit from such post-mortem

exchanges of military opinion, the arguments that such criticism evokes will be well worth the storm.

For the same reasons, I have attempted to write of my long association with George Patton as fairly and as honestly as I could. General Patton was one of my stanchest friends and the most unhesitatingly loyal of all my commanders. He was a magnificent soldier, one whom the American people can admire not only as a great commander but as a unique and remarkable man. In recollecting our experiences together, I may offend those who prefer to remember Patton not as a human being but as a heroic-size statue in a public park. I prefer to remember Patton as a man, as a man with all the frailties and faults of a human being, as a man whose greatness is therefore all the more of a triumph.

This is the story of a war fought only six years before its publication, unleavened with the passing of time, unseasoned by hindsight judgments. I have tried to tell the story as we lived it, with the prejudices, the obstinacy, the pride, the vanity, and the sensitivity that afflicted us at that time. To avoid falling into the trap of self-justification, I have deliberately refrained from reading any of the books on World War II that were published before this one went to press.

A SOLDIER'S STORY was actually started in 1946 when I prepared an outline of approximately 70,000 words to provide a framework for the final story. During the spring and summer of 1947, with the aid of my wartime aide, Lieutenant Colonel Chester B. Hansen, I recorded approximately one million words of reminiscences on the war. From Colonel Hansen's personal diary of approximately 300,000 words, we then extracted settings, dialogue, and anecdotal background. The first draft of the completed story ran approximately 600,000 words and was subsequently cut to one third of its original length.

Although I would vastly prefer to have written this book while on inactive duty, I could not conscientiously expurgate this story to make it more palatable for the times. If this story was to be told, it had to be told honestly and candidly. And that is the way I have tried to write it.

O.N.B.

Washington, D. C.

March 28, 1951

Contents

Maps

BY RAFAEL PALACIOS

Illustrations

General Bradley was often the subject, but never the butt, of a Bill Mauldin cartoon. In this one, Bradley—asked by Eisenhower to find reasons for the American defeat at Kasserine Pass in Tunisia—consults the GIs who fought in the battle, much to the surprise of the officers involved.

Foreword

O MAR BRADLEY IS ONE OF THE FEW SUPERSTARS IN American military history who never thought of running for President. This is not because he's modest, which he is, or because he's self-effacing, which he is. It's because—brace yourself for this—he doesn't feel that's the job he was trained for.

Sherman put it more colorfully: "I will not accept if nominated and will not serve if elected." Bradley leaves the rhetoric to the Shermans, pulls his chin into his collar, and says he doesn't think military men should mess around in politics.

Besides, being a five-star general is about as good a job as you can get. You remain on "active" status for as long as you live. Although the pay is not exactly astronomical and the perquisites shrink with the size of command, it's worth noting that Bradley's close friend and West Point classmate, Dwight D. Eisenhower, who *did* get into politics, asked for his military rank back after leaving the White House. He preferred to end his days as a General of the Army rather than an ex-President. Ike was no fool.

Incidentally, hearing a general referred to as a superstar might sound odd to the average American who grew up after World War II and has seen nothing but controversial wars since. Nobody, not even a politician, is quite so much a hostage of history as a general. No matter how well he performs, if he's running an unpopular show he's going to get booed.

Our war (General Bradley's and mine) wasn't exactly popular, at least among the men who fought it, but it did have wide national support and is now looked back upon nostalgically by many as the last war where you could tell the good guys from the bad guys without a scorecard. Therefore, anybody who rose to prominence in that conflict (Bradley led more than a million men—the largest individual field command in history) indeed became a superstar.

Being the last living General of the Army (the official designation for wearers of five stars), Bradley might well be the highest-ranking soldier in the world. As such he could put on just about any kind of airs.

Recently I spent a week-end at his home and can report a definite lack of pomp. His aides-de-camp do not have their own aides-de-camp. In fact, there are only three officers—two lieutenant colonels and a major—and a small household staff, including a driver, a cook, and a physical therapist. Something less than a million men. None of this will be a surprise to those who know how Bradley has always operated, but I thought it was worth noting for those who don't.

The General's great joy in his free time has been golf. A recent illness has brought a wheelchair (and the physical therapist) into his life and pretty well screwed up his game, but he still loves to lunch with his regular group of 19th-holers, who tell mildly ribald stories and know they've scored when the old man grins.

A Bradley grin is something to behold. It is rare, it is totally disarming, and it has a gentle quality which somehow removes the sting from any joke without killing the humor.

The late Will Lang, chief correspondent for *Life* magazine during World War II and a Bradley admirer, once told me that this quality of gentleness, set against a background of horrendous, grinding cruel warfare, was the thing he found most fascinating about the General. While presiding over an army involved in this kind of fighting, Bradley was never known to issue an order to anybody of any rank without saying please first.

The man is a straight-arrow. In my days with *Stars and Stripes*, the soldier newspaper which often gibed at the army's ways and its sacred cows, there were several schools of thought about us among the generals. One, typified by Ike, held that soldiers from a democracy were entitled to a taste of free press. Opponents of this attitude, such as George Patton, averred that Ike was merely courting us for the sake of his own political ambitions (we all had fun speculating on what Patton would run for after the war) and that soldiers weren't paid to think.

Somewhere in the middle of all this was Omar N. Bradley. This taciturn, totally honest man had only one concern: *responsibility*. He didn't mind what *Stars and Stripes* said as long as he felt we knew what we were talking about. By the same token, he didn't mind Patton's flamboyant, martinet ways as long as the man didn't start flogging troops.

Ever since World War II, I have itched to ask General Bradley what he thought of my own stuff in *Stars and Stripes*. I knew that Patton didn't like my cartoons (he thought they were downright subversive) and that Ike smiled indulgently at them. But what about Old Taciturn himself? Thirty-odd years later, when I finally got my chance to ask him, I couldn't figure out how to bring it up. Confronted by such massive modesty, your own small conceits tend to wither away.

Anyhow, I think I already know the answer. Bradley probably approved of the raggedy-assed, bearded cartoon characters I drew *when I showed them at the front*. He knew that was the way men looked after they'd been in the line for a few days. But he probably felt I should have cleaned them up when they came back to the rear. That would have been the *responsible*, the accurate way to portray them. (I tried shaving them a couple of times, but trouble was, they immediately lost their identity.)

In this age of anti-heroes and popular apathy, if not downright hostility, toward everything military, it is too bad more kids haven't been exposed to such a man as Omar Bradley. Maybe this book will help spread him around a little once more. To me and to others who served under him, he has always been everything I think an American general should be.

Bill Mauldin
November, 1977

To those soldiers who must often have wondered WHY *they were going where they did. Perhaps this will help answer their questions. . . .*

. . . . and to my wife, Kitty, whom I love.

1: *Summons to the Normandy Invasion*

As THE PLANE BUZZED OVER OUR JEEP, ITS PILOT pulled up on the nose and banked steeply over the bay where the Mediterranean dozed peacefully on the north Sicilian shore.

My driver scowled. "He looks curious," I said. "Maybe our markings scared him off."

But apparently they had not for once more the plane hedgehopped up the road. It was a mottled brown Cub similar to the one I used as an airborne jeep.

Again the plane buzzed us, pulled up, and headed out to sea as the pilot wagged his wings. He had evidently double-checked my red three-star plate on the rear of the jeep. I stood up in the front seat and pointed ahead. "Keep going," I told the driver, "if he wants us he'll land farther up the road."

Around the corner of Cape St. Angelo the cliffs leveled off to a wide sandy beach. The road we traveled was strangely silent. In village after village empty windows stared from fire-blackened brick walls. Here and there the charred frames of *Wehrmacht* trucks lay where our bulldozers had pushed them off the road. Everywhere the bridges had been destroyed by the Germans in their methodical retreat up the north Sicilian coast line. The stream beds were dry and our engineers carved by-passes through their hard, steep banks.

Our jeep lurched into one of these by-passes but we were careful to stay between the white tapes that marked where the path had been cleared of Teller mines in the stream bed. I settled back against the foam-rubber seat that had been scrounged from a German Mark IV tank in Northern Tunisia.

It was September 2, 1943. For three leisurely hours we had been driving up this north coast road toward Messina where Lieutenant General Sir Oliver Leese, commander of the British XXX Corps, had invited me to view General Sir Bernard Law Montgomery's invasion of Italy across the Straits the following morning. Leese and I had commanded adjoining corps during the campaign which had ended just two weeks ago.

Initially, Leese's XXX Corps had been picked by Montgomery to follow up the assault force on Montgomery's Messina crossing. This rapid reinforcement of the beachhead was to have enabled Lieutenant General Miles C. Dempsey to rush his British XIII Corps more quickly up the toe of the boot. But when Montgomery was forced to divert a part of his landing craft to Clark for the Salerno

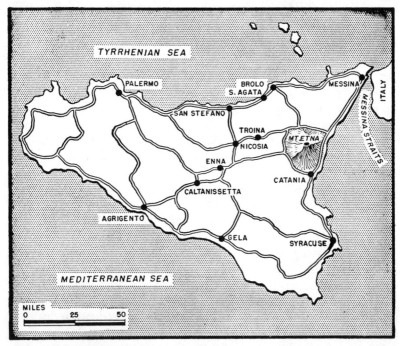

From Palermo on the north and Syracuse on the east the two principal coastwise highways of Sicily lead to the port of Messina across the narrow straits from mainland of Italy.

invasion, he was left with no alternative but to cancel the XXX Corps crossing. As a result Leese was to be a spectator in the invasion. He had selected a vantage point in the hills south of Messina where we could witness the crossing through our glasses.

By the time we rounded St. Angelo the Cub had disappeared. However as the road straightened out, I saw the plane parked near the beach where it had landed. Captain Chester B. Hansen, of Elizabeth, New Jersey, my aide, sat waiting on a stone wall by the roadside. He jumped up and flagged us down.

"Sorry to break in on you, General," he said, "but we've just had a radio from Seventh Army. General Patton wants to see you in Palermo."

Disappointed at the thought of missing the British crossing at Messina, I nevertheless knew something was afoot else Patton would never have called me back. He knew of my plan to meet Oliver Leese at Messina.

During the five-week Sicilian campaign Lieutenant General George S. Patton, Jr., had commanded the new Seventh U. S. Army while Montgomery headed the seasoned British Eighth. My II Corps, a veteran of the Tunisian campaign, was the only one in Patton's Army.

My pilot, Captain Delbert L. Bristol, of Kansas City, Missouri, was waiting by the Cub, on the cowling of which was lettered: "Missouri Mule II." Its battle-worn predecessor had been left behind after an honorable campaign in Tunisia. I climbed in and pulled the throttle, toeing down on the brakes while Bristol turned her over.

Within sight of the bay that sheltered Palermo, we buzzed the II Corps command post and by the time we landed a jeep was waiting by the airstrip. We drove up the sandy road our bulldozers had cut through a vineyard to the top of a hill where the corps had pitched its tent camp in a grove of olive trees. I went directly to the caravan-truck ordnance had built me on the chassis of a 2½-ton truck. This vehicle contained not only my cramped quarters but an office as well. It had been designed like a small ship's cabin with plumbing and fittings that had been ransacked from Oran and Algiers. What the scroungers were unable to locate, ordnance had turned out in its mobile machine shops.

I cranked the field phone on my desk and asked for General Patton.

"Bradley calling," I said. "What's up, sir?"

"Beats the hell out of me. Eisenhower sent a message saying he wanted to see you early tomorrow morning."

"Where am I to meet him—in Africa?"

"Nope. He's coming into that advanced CP AFHQ* set up near Catania. I'll set up my plane to fly you over. It'll be better than a Cub. Stop by here for breakfast before you take off in the morning."

I hung up the receiver in its leather case. "Well that doesn't help," I said to Brigadier General William B. Kean, my II Corps chief of staff. "George doesn't know any more about it than we do. Maybe Eisenhower's going to give us a new job."

During the two weeks that had passed since the last German remnants escaped from Messina to the Italian mainland, we had been resting our troops, replacing their losses, and getting equipment back into combat condition.

From Patton's Seventh Army in its palace headquarters in Palermo to the last rifle company in bivouac on the south shore, we all speculated on where we would be sent next—to Italy or perhaps to England? Nowhere were these rumors more lively than in II Corps. For eight months its more than 100,000 U. S. troops had fought from the cold, wet mountains, or *djebels*, of Tunisia to these arid Sicilian hills. Although 22 months had passed since Pearl Harbor, ours was the only American corps with battle experience against the Germans. The staff had already mounted two large-scale invasions, the first against Oran in North Africa, and eight months later a second in Sicily. It was an experienced staff and an especially good one. No one knew that better than the corps itself.

Because II Corps had not yet been scheduled for Lieutenant General Mark W. Clark's Italian campaign, the hope persisted that it might be reorganized as an Army and redeployed to England for the big invasion of France. As long as Italy held the stage, we had little appetite for the limited objectives of that peninsula campaign.

Not that we were to have anything to say about where we would go, for this choice of strategic objectives was the responsibility of both General Dwight D. Eisenhower as Commander-in-Chief of Allied Expeditionary Forces in the Mediterranean and the Combined Allied Chiefs of Staff. A corps is a lower-echelon tactical unit created to coordinate the fighting of two, three, four, or sometimes five divisions. Ordinarily it operates as part of a field Army. Such an Army

*Command Post, Allied Force Headquarters.

may consist of as many as four corps. Like divisions, these corps are interchangeable. Just as any division may be shifted from one corps to another, so may any corps be transferred—with or without its divisions—from one field Army to another. An Army in the field is a completely self-sufficient organization with the myriad assortment of supply and maintenance units required as overhead in modern warfare. Unlike the Army, a corps is primarily a fighting organization; its combat head is larger than its supporting tail. In addition to infantry and armored divisions, a corps ordinarily contains artillery, tank, mortar, and tank-destroyer battalions. Some of these corps units may be attached to divisions to fight under the division commander's control. Others are retained in corps where they can be readily concentrated at any spot on the line.

It was 4:50 on the morning of September 3 when we turned from the II Corps CP to the hard-topped road that led to Patton's headquarters in Palermo. Always an early riser, especially in the field, George breakfasted at seven during these inactive interludes between campaigns. And although it was only a 30-mile run by jeep, I was careful to be on time.

Patton's command post was surrounded by a dozen light tanks, strategically spotted in the broad piazza fronting the palace where he lived. The palace was a large, gloomy, musty-smelling structure heavily hung with brocades. It was here among this regal bric-a-brac that Patton was doomed to spend the most unhappy and worrisome days of his life.

Still 45 minutes early for breakfast, we parked the jeep and strolled up past the shuttered shops on Via Vittorio Emanuele. While Palermo had not been heavily damaged by air raids, rubble still blocked the side streets. The antiaircraft crews were hurrying off to mess wearing their ties, leggings, and weapons in deference to Patton's notoriously strict uniform regulations.

Precisely at 7 Patton boomed in to breakfast. His vigor was always infectious, his wit barbed, his conversation a mixture of obscenity and good humor. He was at once stimulating and overbearing. George was a magnificent soldier.

Like Eisenhower, Patton ordinarily messed with a small group of intimates from his headquarters. Breakfast was spirited and talkative. Patton picked up the GI holster in which I carried my 30-year-old Colt .45.

"Hell, Brad," he said, "what you need is a social gun. You can't carry that cannon with you everywhere you go."

He showed me the small .32 he carried in a shoulder holster and promised to have ordnance send me one.

Patton drove with me to the airport in his huge Packard limousine, adorned with two noisy chromium-plated horns. His C-47 was a battle-weary bucket seater from the Troop Carrier Command. The pilot had scrounged two sway-backed, overstuffed chairs and wired them to the cargo rings on the floor.

"Real class," Patton gestured, "I wonder where in hell he swiped 'em."

The advance CP of AFHQ where I was to meet Eisenhower scarcely merited so formidable a designation. We drove from the airfield near Catania, where Ike's aide waited, to a huddle of small wall tents screened by a few olive trees in the shadow of Mount Etna. Eisenhower had flown in from North Africa that morning to witness the signing by emissaries from the Badoglio government of a short-term Italian surrender instrument. Standing outside the tent in which Eisenhower was conferring with his airborne commanders were Major General Walter Bedell Smith, Eisenhower's chief of staff, and General Sir Harold Alexander, Army Group commander of Eisenhower's ground forces. Smith looked dour and rumpled after the weary weeks of negotiation that had preceded this surrender. But both were hugely relieved in having accomplished it before Clark's assault on Salerno. At that moment Clark's troops were loading in North Africa for an early morning assault on September 9.

During the middle of July the Combined Chiefs of Staff had scrapped their earlier limited plans for air bombing of Italy in favor of a direct assault on Naples and a full-scale campaign up the boot. For this Eisenhower had been granted an additional 66,000 troops, previously earmarked for England. A later proposal by the British to provide Eisenhower another 50,000 troops had been rejected by U. S. Chiefs of Staff. Anxious to avoid any further drain on the Allied build-up in England, General George C. Marshall had insisted that troop commitments for Italy be cut to the minimum and that the Naples assault be executed as a bold venture. On July 26 the British withdrew their proposal and Eisenhower was left with his slender force for the Salerno attack.

On the assumption that there might still be some fight left in the Italian people, the German High Command made plans in July to reinforce German troops in Italy with additional divisions. We did not anticipate this but believed that the enemy would limit his commitment to the northern plains where a net of airfields lay within reach of Germany's industrial cities. Although General Sir Alan Brooke, Chief of the British Imperial General Staff, had estimated on August 14 that there were but five German divisions in all Italy, he also reported to the Combined Chiefs that there were signs of additional reinforcement. Like most Allied planners, however, Brooke believed that the Germans would not risk troops in the exposed lower boot of Italy. By August 24 Eisenhower's staff estimated that the German divisions then in Italy had been increased to 16. Still the optimists insisted that in the event of attack the German would obligingly fall back to a line on the Po.

Once it had become apparent to the German that we intended to invade the boot north of Montgomery's crossing, the enemy could easily see the necessity of our taking Naples as a supply base for such a campaign. He also realized that a successful landing near Naples would give us the Foggia airfields across the peninsula on the Adriatic shore. From those Foggia bases our heavy bombers could reach southern Germany, Austria, and the strategic Ploesti oil fields. Obviously he meant to do what he could to deny them to us.

General Bedell Smith told me the Italian surrender would be announced on the evening of September 8 to give the Italians time to lay down their arms before Clark's landing. He hoped that this last-minute announcement would delay German reinforcement of the beaches south of Naples until after the Allied landing. Eisenhower and Badoglio were to broadcast news of the surrender simultaneously from Algiers and Rome.

Alexander was elated with the report that had reached him that morning of Montgomery's unopposed crossing of the Straits at Messina. He had spent most of the previous evening in negotiation for the surrender with General Castellano, Marshal Pietro Badoglio's emissary from Rome. Confronted by the prospect of imminent invasion while occupied by the Germans, the Italians were fearfully anxious to salvage what they could by taking up arms on the side of the Allies.

Eisenhower came out of his small wall tent to find me talking with Smith and Alexander. He hurried over, a lively grin on his face.

"Brad, by gosh, I'm glad to see you. How long have you been waiting?"

He took me by the arm into his tent, empty save for a wooden mess table that ran the length of its earth floor. Several C-ration cans stood on the table, half filled with cigarette butts.

"I've got good news for you, Brad. You've got a fancy new job."

I felt startled but tried not to show it.

"We've got orders for you to go to England and command an Army on the invasion of France."

A bare five months before, I had been given command of a corps; now it was to be an Army. After 28 years of snail's-pace, peacetime promotions, I was now finding it difficult to keep stars in stock. As a result of the Tunisian campaign I had become the only U. S. corps commander with battle experience against the Germans. And in Sicily I had cut my teeth on a large-scale amphibious assault. Both assignments were invaluable experience for me for the invasion of Europe.

"When do I leave?" I asked.

Ike laughed. "Just as soon as you can. General Marshall's in a hurry. Apparently Jakie has been after him for sometime now to name an Army commander."

The "Jakie" that Eisenhower referred to was Lieutenant General Jacob L. Devers, commander of the European Theater of Operations. During the last few months he had become concerned lest the British outstrip the U. S. forces on invasion planning.

Devers' worries were not unfounded. At Casablanca in January, 1943, President Roosevelt had initially proposed that a British supreme commander be named to plan and head the invasion of France. At that time he assumed the invasion would come in 1943 and that it would be predominantly British. Churchill, however, suggested they limit themselves at Casablanca to planning and he recommended that the question of command be deferred. Although Churchill agreed the commander should be British, he restated the principle that "the command of operations should, as a general rule, be held by an officer of the nation which furnishes the majority of the force." The Combined Chiefs of Staff thought as Churchill did and they voted to appoint only a chief of staff to the as yet unnamed supreme commander. This British chief of staff was to direct the initial planning until a commander could be named.

Soon thereafter the British named Lieutenant General Sir Frederick E. Morgan as *their* chief staff officer for this planning staff. From the American chiefs there came a protest over this independent action of the British. Finally after an additional month of wrangling both staffs agreed to form a combined planning staff to be headed by Morgan as Chief of Staff to the Supreme Allied Commander (designate). This staff was to be known as COSSAC and took its name from the title of Morgan's new job. Hopes that a supreme commander might soon be named vanished with the prospect of a cross-channel invasion in 1943. With the invasion postponed until 1944, it became obvious that U. S. predominance would necessitate the naming of a U. S. supreme commander.

COSSAC's first task, however, was not to write an invasion plan but to determine whether with the resources expected to be available in 1944 an invasion could be mounted against the Channel coast of Europe. In other words, COSSAC started by planning for a plan. During this period the Commanding General of the European Theater of Operations was to be the American watchdog on COSSAC joint planning, and it was he who was to be consulted on the joint employment of U. S. forces.

As COSSAC planning got under way, the British hurried to form their army, navy, and RAF commands for the invasion. By July, 1943, the Second British Army, the First Canadian Army, and 21st Army Group were all established with operating headquarters in London.

Because there were no comparable American field headquarters in England, Morgan's staff sought guidance on ground-force problems from 21st Army Group. Indeed the only American tactical command in Britain until the arrival of First Army in October, 1943, was Major General Leonard T. Gerow's V Corps. In May, 1943, Devers urged the War Department to establish an American Army headquarters in England to parallel the British and Canadian armies. The War Department, however, demurred. In July Devers urged formation of a United States Army Group to parallel the British 21st Group. Again the War Department waited.

Finally on August 25 General Marshall radioed Eisenhower in Algiers:

Devers and General Morgan have been pressing us since early July to appoint an American Army commander immediately to parallel activities of British army commanders now building up in rather formidable fashion

as to requisitions, requirements, etc. My choice has been Bradley. . . .
Could you release Bradley for this command?

Eisenhower radioed a speedy reply on August 27.

By coincidence, I received your (TWX)* . . . just after I had dispatched a letter regarding the senior commanders in this theater. . . . I
am personally distressed at the thought of losing Bradley because I have
come to lean on him so heavily in absorbing part of the burdens that
otherwise fall directly upon me. This has been so in the past even when
he was only in corps command. This very reason probably makes him
your obvious choice for the other job.

On September 2, the same day Eisenhower radioed Patton while
I was driving up to Messina, a War Department radio reached
AFHQ in Algiers. It was from General Marshall:

Thanks for your generous attitude regarding Bradley. Have him make
preparation to leave for England. Formal orders will be radioed. I am
assuming you will wish to keep his corps headquarters. If not important
to do so find out from him if there is any of the personnel he would wish
to have transferred to England. Tell him that he will head an army headquarters and will also probably have to develop an army group headquarters in order to keep pace with the British planning and requisitions.

General Marshall's invitation to raid II Corps for key members
of my new Army staff was admittedly what I had been waiting to
hear. In extending the invitation Ike was more generous than I
expected.

"Take anyone you want," he said. "You'll need the finest staff you
can get."

Later when I drew up the list Major General John P. Lucas, who
was to succeed me at II Corps, looked up from it and wailed.

"But this will give you a chance," I assured him, "to bring in your
own men."

Lucas frowned.

"I'll make you a deal," I said. "I'll throw in this caravan-truck together with my jeep and its sponge-rubber seats."

"Hell, you couldn't take them with you anyhow. Bradley, you
drive a hard bargain." Lucas gripped me on the shoulder. "But if I
were in your shoes I guess I'd do the same."

*A message sent by teletypewriter. The letters actually stand for teletype-
writer exchange.

For while it may have been unfair of me to strip II Corps of so many of its best officers, I could not in good conscience abandon an experienced staff and risk the Channel invasion to an inexperienced one. Across the Channel there was too much at stake; Lucas realized this as well as I. However competent an officer may be, and however thorough his earlier training, he is always a risky investment until he pays off in combat. Moreover, the planning of an amphibious operation is an intricate and tricky venture. We would have been foolhardy not to have used the men who knew most about it. Eisenhower faced the same problem a few months later when he was named Supreme Allied Commander. Like me, he transplanted a sizable part of his Mediterranean team.

In directing that I organize an Army Group staff while also commanding an Army, General Marshall had doubled the job ahead of me. Although the final decision on command of the Army Group had not yet been made, I was to head them both for nine full months—until the Normandy breakout.

My session with Ike ended with an invitation to lunch. "And it won't be any of those damned Vienna sausages you people always give me!"

Before returning from Palermo to corps that afternoon, I stopped by briefly to see Patton and tell him of my orders. When I told him I was due in England the following Sunday, he offered me his C-47 for the flight to Algiers.

That evening Kean sat up with me long past midnight sifting the corps roster for critical personnel. It was almost one o'clock by the time we had narrowed the list to 30 men. Kean snuffed the cigarette in his holder, looked up from his desk, and smiled.

I spoke what I thought was on his mind. "What a helluva responsibility this is for you and me to be pulling off the biggest invasion of the war."

Kean nodded and stared at the map of Europe on the wall.

"But Bill," I said frankly, "who in the army knows more about it than we?"

Seven months ago that boast would have been an impudent one. For Kean and I were then in Florida with the 28th Division assaulting a half-drowned piece of real estate known to us as Dog Island.

2: *Overseas*

Florida in the winter is a land of many seasons, and the most wintry of them assail the Gulf coast of Apalachicola.

A barren crossroads town despite its singsong Seminole name, Apalachicola bounded the western end of the army's bleak Camp Gordon Johnson. Fifty-five gas-rationed miles farther north, the pleasant capital city of Tallahassee offered some diversion but only on week ends.

It was here on this dismal, damp coast of Florida's panhandle that the 28th Division wintered in early 1943 for invasion training. Early that previous autumn the Amphibious Training Command had shifted its school from Cape Cod to Florida for all-weather training in shore-to-shore assault.

Camp Gordon Johnson had been hacked from the Florida bush along a stretch of empty beach. Offshore a string of keys sheltered the landing beaches on which we trained our troops. Day after day they splashed from the snub-nosed landing craft in mock assaults against the "hostile" beaches of Dog Island.

To the division staff this training brought new and intricate problems in tactics and supply. Although I had studied amphibious tactics before in army schools, this was the first time I had worked with both troops and craft in practice operations. Most of the craft we employed here had been developed since Pearl Harbor.

The 28th Division, originally a unit of the Pennsylvania National Guard, had been given me as the second of my two divisional commands. The first had been the 82d Infantry Division, forerunner of the celebrated airborne division. The assignment to the 82d had come unexpectedly, for at the time I was but a junior brigadier in the army.

In September, 1941, General Marshall visited the Infantry School at Fort Benning where I had been commandant for six months. While walking across the post to my quarters for lunch, he had turned to me and asked, "Bradley, do you have a man to take your place when you leave here to command a division?"

"Not yet, sir," I said, trying not to show my surprise. "But if I could have had Lev Allen when I asked for him he would have been the man."

Several months before, orders had been issued for the assignment of Lieutenant Colonel Leven C. Allen as my assistant at Fort Benning. They were revoked by Brigadier General Gerow, who as head of the War Plans Division in Washington commanded top priority in the selection of choice officer personnel.

The issue was not raised again until three months later. It was just a few days before Christmas, 1941, when Lieutenant Colonel George van W. Pope, an old friend from earlier days at the Infantry School, telephoned from G-1* in Washington.

"Omar," he said, "we're setting up three more divisions and you're slated to get one of them. It will be the 82d. Tell us as soon as you can whom you want for your staff and I'll try to get them for you."

Later that afternoon I called Pope back. "Every man I would want as chief of staff," I said, "seems to be on a key job. Take yourself for example—I don't suppose you could break loose."

"Break out of here?" Pope shouted. "Dammit, there's nothing I'd like better. Let me check around and I'll call you right back. But hold that job for me."

I had known Pope for years as a competent, amiable, and well-rounded soldier. He had been an instructor in my weapons section at Benning where I valued him one of our best-qualified doughboys. Furthermore, with his present assignment to G-1 in Washington, Pope was strategically located in a unique position to help assemble

---

*Army General Staff activities are divided into four classifications: G-1 for personnel, G-2 for intelligence, G-3 for plans, training, and operations, and G-4 for supply. During the war a fifth classification, G-5 for civilian affairs, was added. All other activities are organized under what is known as *special staff* functions.

the division staff I wanted. Within a few minutes he called back. "Omar," he said, "you've got your new chief of staff."

Pope had wrangled an exceptional officer cadre, and the 82d Division was off to a happy start from the day of its activation. By March, 1942, troop trains were backing into the sidings of Camp Claiborne, near the rapidly swelling town of Alexandria on Louisiana's muddy Red River. The troops were draftees, fresh from reception centers.

A soldier's first few weeks in the army ordinarily leave him baffled and homesick. Knowing that these men on their arrival at Camp Claiborne would probably be depressed by the impersonal routine that changes a man into a soldier, we had laid plans to organize them immediately into units they could call home. Teams of officers and noncoms boarded those trains at the reception centers and classified the men for future assignments. Washington learned of our traveling classification teams and the practice later became a standard operating procedure.

As the trains backed into Claiborne, we greeted them with a brass band. Cadres formed the troops into companies and batteries and marched them off to their hutments. There they found clean beds and in the mess halls, hot meals. Laundry services were speeded up to get their travel-soiled uniforms cleaned. Each man was issued the division's All-American shoulder patch.

Across the Red River from us on the other side of Alexandria, the 28th Division was then undergoing the troubles that plagued so many National Guard divisions during mobilization. Like others called into federal service in 1940 and 1941, the 28th Division had been cannibalized again and again for cadres in the formation of new divisions. In addition, hundreds of its finest noncommissioned officers had been sent to officer training schools. Many more of its best-qualified men transferred to the air corps as flying cadets. These vacancies in the divisions were then filled with periodic transfusions of draftees, leaving the division in a constant state of unpreparedness. In June, 1942, I was ordered from the 82d to take command of the 28th, whip those unbalanced units into a trim division, and ready it for the field.

For months afterward the 28th Division continued to be bled both for cadres and officer candidate quotas. The constant turnover in personnel gutted our progress in training, and throughout the entire division we became desperately short of junior officers and noncoms.

Only too often companies were commanded by second lieutenants assisted by sergeants.

Finally when IV Corps called for still another cadre to form a new division, I said, "Fine, we'll send you one. But then suppose you send us a cadre so we can get going here."

At the same time the 28th Division was afflicted with the problem of companies in which home-town cliques still survived. When noncom vacancies developed in those units, the stripes ordinarily went to the home-town boys. Moreover, civilian associations between officers and men in those companies made discipline more difficult to maintain. While commanders disapproved of the favoritism that ensued, they seemed powerless to halt it. I concluded that as long as we tolerated those neighborhood clubs, we could never have a division.

To correct the condition I resorted to a drastic move and in a single order transferred every officer and almost every noncom out of his home-town unit. Later that summer the traffic in divisional transfers slowed down, and shortly before we left for maneuvers in the fall of 1942 we were assigned a complement of brand-new lieutenants fresh from the officer candidate schools. The division took new heart and the 28th soon began to show the keen edge of a trained combat team.

During a routine visit to the maneuver area that fall, Lieutenant General Lesley J. McNair, Commanding General of Army Ground Forces, suggested that I might soon be ready to take command of a corps.

"However, General Marshall wants to make certain you've got the 28th well in hand before he agrees to the move. Don't forget that General Simpson was given the job of straightening out *two* divisions before he got a corps."

When maneuvers proved the 28th qualified for advanced training, orders came in December for the move to Camp Gordon Johnson. I now went on a wartime footing and packed my possessions into two footlockers and a bedding roll. The bulk of our household furniture was crated and shipped home to Missouri and what remained Mrs. Bradley was able to pack into two trunks. I knew then that garrison life had ended, that we could no longer afford the luxury of household moves.

On February 12, 1943, I celebrated my fiftieth birthday at Camp Gordon Johnson. By this time daily newspaper reports on the winter campaign in Tunisia brought closer the realization that our stateside time was running out. At noon that day a TWX arrived from General Marshall.

It is only fitting that your birthday should precede by only a few days your transfer to command a corps which comes as a long-delayed acknowledgment of your splendid record with the 28th Division. Congratulations and best wishes.

Since this was Friday, I estimated that the orders would probably not arrive until Tuesday morning at the earliest. When Tuesday came I stood by at division headquarters instead of going out into the field. Shortly after 10 A.M. Washington telephoned. It was Brigadier General Alexander R. Bolling, G-1 for McNair.

"We're cutting orders on you today, Bradley. You're going overseas on extended active duty."

"Overseas?" I said remembering that General Marshall had spoken of a stateside corps. Something had evidently happened since his TWX three days before.

"Which way do I go?" I asked Bolling, meaning Africa or the Pacific—and hoping for the former.

He paused for an instant. "Remember your classmate?" he said. "Well you're going to join your classmate. I can't say anything more over the phone."

By that I knew he meant Africa. Eisenhower and I had graduated together from the Military Academy in 1915.

"How soon can you leave?"

"Tomorrow," I answered, "I'm all packed to move."

"Good," he said, "we'll make the transportation arrangements here for priorities on air travel from Tallahassee to Washington. Will you call me back at 11?"

I hurried across the duckboards to the single room in which I lived at the end of a neighboring shack. An orderly was cleaning the mud from my infantry boots. "Better pack me up," I told him. "Everything. I'll be back to give you a hand."

Bill Kean, who had succeeded Pope as my division chief of staff when the latter was promoted, was waiting when I returned to the office. "A TWX just came in on your orders. It's being decoded. We should have it in 20 minutes or so."

I told him of Bolling's call. He looked surprised. "Well anything can happen these days," he said.

Twenty minutes later Kean returned. "We've decoded that TWX, General. They're orders to Sherman, Texas. You're to command the X Corps there." I was no less puzzled than he. At 11 I telephoned Bolling in Washington. "Alex, I'm getting a little confused. What do you know about these orders assigning me to the X Corps?"

"Forget them," he replied, "that was yesterday. Today you're going overseas."

I asked Bolling if I was to have a command.

"If it's a staff you're thinking of," he said, "we're limiting you to two aides." Evidently it was no command.

Both aides were out in the field that morning training with troops —Lewis D. Bridge with a company of infantry, Hansen with the reconnaissance troop. I sent a messenger out to get them.

Bridge and Hansen had both entered the army as privates in 1941 and had graduated together from the Infantry Officer Candidate School that previous April where they turned in outstanding records. They reported promptly to the division CP, Bridge sticky with gumbo and Hansen wet to his hips after a landing on Dog Island. "How would you like to get your feet wet?" I asked them. They promised to be packed in 20 minutes.

We cleared camp at 2:30 that afternoon. Because the orders were classified SECRET, I dared not tell even my staff that we were headed overseas.

In Washington I reported directly to General Marshall. The War Department had moved, since I left it in 1941, from the shabby old Munitions Building on Constitution Avenue to the new Pentagon across the Potomac.

The Chief of Staff took only ten minutes to outline my mission. As for background on Africa I was to pick that up as best I could from OPD (Operations and Planning Division) in the Pentagon.

General Eisenhower, as Commander-in-Chief of Allied Forces in the Mediterranean Theater, headed a force that stretched from Casablanca on the Atlantic coast of North Africa 1,200 miles eastward to the Tunisian front. Here the North African colonies of France, previously loyal to Vichy and separated by the Mediterranean from involvement in the war, had been plunged into a political caldron by the Allied invasion. Vichy intrigue, Arab unrest, and French hostility toward the British had presented the Allies with a formidable assortment of explosive problems.

Into this political morass Eisenhower had come as a liberator to some, as an invader to others. Not only was he expected to be chief diplomat of the Allied nations, but he was to be the strategist, logistician, and commander of Allied troops in the field.

As if this were not already enough, Eisenhower's task as an Allied commander called for him to split his loyalty between two flags and devote it instead to a combined command for winning the war. It was a task that demanded objectivity and prudence as a counterbalance to national ties. For however compelling their common cause in war, it is exceedingly difficult for Allies to fuse their forces, to suppress their national rivalries and pride under the authority of an Allied command. Eisenhower was determined to make his Allied command work, to spare no severity in punishing those who tried to shield their insubordinate activities under the flags of their respective nations.

At that time Eisenhower's CP in Algiers was more than 400 miles distant from his Allied troops on the Tunisian front. From that far-off command post he had attempted to marshal the forces of three nations in a shoestring field campaign. Recognizing the danger inherent in any long-distance command of a fighting front he planned to make Alexander his deputy for the ground. But this change-over was not to take place until Montgomery's Eighth Army, then under Alexander's British Middle East Command, crossed the border from Tripolitania into Tunisia near the Mareth Line.

Meanwhile, General Marshall, with a growing army to train in the United States, was anxious to learn more of the battle performance of American commanders and troops and the adequacy of U. S. weapons. To help Eisenhower accumulate this information he had proposed that an American officer be assigned to act as Ike's "eyes and ears" among American troops on the Tunisian front.

On February 12, the day General Marshall radioed his birthday greetings to me at Gordon Johnson, Eisenhower had dispatched a TWX to the chief of staff:

Have been examining the list of general officers to find one suitable for the task you suggest to act as my eyes and ears. I suspect that all those now in the grade of general officer, who could function well in this special capacity, already have very important tasks such as division commanders.

It has occurred to me that in the case of these divisions now being built up in the United States, the commander might get a very valuable experience by reporting to this theater for say a three months tour of duty, after which he could be exchanged for another and this process indefinitely continued.

The nature of the work involved here requires brains, tact, and imagination more than it does thorough acquaintanceship with the theater, so that a man of ability would begin to operate efficiently after a week of indoctrination. If such a scheme would appeal to you at all, there are a number of officers that would be highly acceptable to me. Among them are: Major Generals Hester, Terrell, O. N. Bradley, Brush, Bull, Gerhardt, Ridgway, Ransom, Corlett, Wogan, Prichard and Livesay. One retired officer that I believe could do the job one hundred per cent is General Gasser.

If the idea I have presented does not appear a practicable one to you, could you give me a list of those that might be available for such a task either on a relatively short term or long term basis.

Partly, I imagine, because I was instantly available as a result of the X Corps assignment, General Marshall picked me from among Eisenhower's selections.

For the first time in 32 years as a soldier, I was off to a war.

My long association with General Marshall began in 1929 when I reported to him at the Infantry School in Fort Benning as an instructor in tactics. I was a major at the time and had graduated that June from the Army's Command and General Staff School at Fort Leavenworth. When World War I ended without my getting overseas, I feared my army career had been washed out from the start. As did Eisenhower, I spent the war in stateside assignments. While many of my classmates were distinguishing themselves overseas, I commanded a guard company in the copper mines at Butte.

In 1924 I was sent to Fort Benning as an advanced student in the Infantry School. There I found myself in competition with many combat-experienced officers of my own age. In solving the tactical problems that were given us there, I learned that my judgment was no worse for not having gotten overseas. When I finished second in the class behind Major Gerow, the confidence I needed had been restored; I never suffered a faint heart again.

On graduation from Command and General Staff School I was assigned to the faculty of the Infantry School as an instructor and after a year in battalion tactics was named chief of the weapons section by General Marshall, then a lieutenant colonel and assistant commandant of the school. After once having assigned an officer to his job General Marshall seldom intervened. During the two years I served him as chief of the weapons section in the Infantry School, he sent for me only once to discuss the work of my section. And during that same two-year period he visited me in my office but twice. From General Marshall I learned the rudiments of effective command. Throughout the war I deliberately avoided intervening in a subordinate's duties. When an officer performed as I expected him to, I gave him a free hand. When he hesitated, I tried to help him. And when he failed, I relieved him.

In 1936 Marshall was made a brigadier general. From West Point where I was stationed at the time I sent him a note of congratulations.

General Marshall replied in a brief but prophetic letter:

"I very much hope we will have an opportunity to serve together again; I can think of nothing more satisfactory to me."

The opportunity came in 1940 when General Marshall, then chief of staff, ordered me from G-1 of the War Department to his office as an Assistant Secretary of the General Staff. In this job it was my duty to make oral presentations to the chief of staff on papers that came to him for decision. After the first week General Marshall called me into his office with the other assistants and said, "Gentlemen, I'm disappointed in you. You haven't yet disagreed with a single decision I've made."

"General," I answered, "that's only because there has been no cause for disagreement. When we differ with you on a decision, sir, we'll tell you so."

Although I had then known General Marshall for more than ten years, I was never entirely comfortable in his presence. I boned over each presentation I made. He would instantly absorb the most intricate of staff studies and cross-examine the assistant secretaries while weighing his decisions. If there were a flaw in the study he would immediately detect it and ask why it had not been uncovered before. Rather than search each paper for views that might reinforce his own, General Marshall sought contrary opinions.

"When you carry a paper in here," he told me, "I want you to give me every reason you can think of why I should not approve it. If, in spite of your objections, my decision is still to go ahead, then I'll know I'm right."

In November, 1940, Brigadier General Robert Eichelberger, then superintendent at West Point, asked if I would like to join him there as commandant of cadets. After two years in the War Department I longed to break away from staff work and get back to a command.

But at the time I was still too young for command of a regular regiment.

On a subsequent visit to Washington, Eichelberger spoke to General Marshall. In leaving the Chief's office, he stopped by my desk. "Congratulations, Omar, you've got it," he said, "General Marshall just approved the request."

But a week later as I was leaving his office, General Marshall halted me with a query, "Are you certain that you want to go to West Point as commandant of cadets?"

"Yes, sir," I answered, "it's a command job and it will give me a chance to help develop the officers there. I've had 12 years at West Point, including four as a cadet and I believe I know their problems."

General Marshall looked unconvinced. He turned to the window overlooking Constitution Avenue. "I was thinking of bringing Hodges up from Fort Benning," he said, "to become Chief of Infantry. How would you like to go down there and take his place?"

I caught my breath. Brigadier General Courtney H. Hodges was commandant of the Infantry School, one of the choicest assignments for a doughboy.

"That, sir," I replied, "changes the entire picture."

"Very well, Bradley," General Marshall said, his decision already made, "I'll send you down just as soon as I can bring Hodges to Washington."

Three months later, in February, 1941, I was in General Marshall's office when he said, "Get the Deputy Chief of Staff, Bradley, and come back in here with him." I returned with the deputy and General Marshall issued the orders assigning me to command of the Infantry School.

On February 20 a recommendation for promotion was sent to the Congress on a special list. The next day I left for Benning.

A telegram was waiting for me when I arrived. The Senate had approved my promotion from lieutenant colonel to brigadier general.

When General Marshall had finished outlining my mission with Eisenhower, he handed me two letters to be carried to Algiers. They were marked TOP SECRET and contained instructions to Eisenhower on the Sicilian invasion. He told me to read the letters and be prepared to destroy them should we be forced down en route. The target date for Sicily had been set by the Combined Chiefs of Staff for July 10, only five months off. General Marshall, however, did not doubt that Eisenhower would clear North Africa in time to re-equip his troops there and mount the Sicilian invasion. For Field Marshal Erwin Rommel was withdrawing rapidly across the Libyan desert while Montgomery pushed him toward the Mareth Line. And although Eisenhower had spread his Allied troops thinly on the Tunisian front, it had become clear that the odds lay with him in the

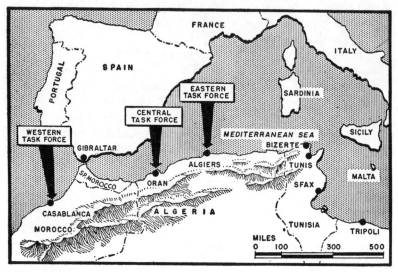

With three separate landings, the TORCH invasion of North Africa in November, 1942, secured French Morocco on the South Atlantic and penetrated the Mediterranean as far east as Algiers.

logistical race for build-up. Allied air strength, though still bogged down on the muddy North African fields, continued to grow as U. S. aircraft production enabled Eisenhower to junk his outclassed P-40's and replace them with P-38's.

To the strategic-minded General Marshall already plotting the cross-channel invasion of Europe, the battle for North Africa had become essentially a battle for time. While the German fought to prolong the African war with reinforcements from Italy, the Allies overextended themselves in an effort to end it in time for the planned Sicilian campaign.

On this morning of my first day in Washington, February 18, 1943, the German seemed to have succeeded in stopping the clock. For as I reported to the brilliantly lighted operations room of OPD in the

Pentagon, radios were streaming in from Algiers with news of an Allied setback at Faid Pass. This was the beginning of what came to be known as the Battle of Kasserine Pass. It was to be our first defeat at the hands of the German.

Let me sketch in some of the background that preceded this. At the time of the African invasion the rich prize at Tunis had justified great Allied risks. For if Eisenhower had been able to seize that port city, he could have cut the line of supply to Rommel's *Afrika Korps* far off in Tripolitania. Tunis lay deep in the Mediterranean. It was too well screened by Axis forces in Sicily to be included as an object in the TORCH amphibious assault against Casablanca, Oran, and Algiers. From Sardinia and Sicily the Luftwaffe pounced on Allied convoys bound through that narrow alley where Sicily abuts the North African coast. RAF units in heavily bombed Malta were too busily engaged in the defense of that island to afford air cover for an Allied invasion in the vicinity of Tunis. Moreover, Allied resources had been strained to mount the widely dispersed TORCH attacks. Those resources could not have been stretched to include a fourth assault.

With scarcely a division of infantry made up from scattered Allied units and an understrength regiment of tanks, Eisenhower struck out for Tunis almost immediately after his landing on November 8, 1942. Tunis lay 560 truck miles away from Eisenhower's easternmost point of landing in Algiers. Ike had played a bold hand at a time when only boldness could bring results. It failed. It failed within sight of its prize when record Tunisian winter rains stalled the advance of his columns.

Meanwhile the German contingent of 5,000 troops in the Tunis area in early November had swelled to three times that size by the end of the month as the Luftwaffe shuttled in reinforcements. By the end of December Eisenhower's hopes for a speedy North African campaign were gone. The Allies settled down to reform their lines in the freezing Tunisian hills. Before he could undertake a new offensive Eisenhower would require a vast build-up in strength.

On January 1, Eisenhower put Major General Lloyd R. Fredendall in command of II Corps and ordered him to concentrate his forces on the south Tunisian front in preparation for an attack toward Sfax. Fredendall's II Corps forces in Southern Tunisia were to consist initially of the 1st Armored Division with infantry support. It was to be concentrated behind a screen of infantry on the rocky north-south mountain range known as the Eastern Dorsal.

With the commitment of II Corps, the Allies found themselves extended over a vast front of more than 250 miles. It stretched all the way from the wild brushwoods of the Sedjenane Valley near the Mediterranean on the north to the bleak edge of the Sahara Desert on the south.

By January this front was divided into three separate national sectors, each under its own flag. In the north the British under Lieutenant General Sir Kenneth A. Anderson, commander of the British First Army, clung to their positions in the mountains that rimmed the port cities of Bizerte and Tunis. In the center a ragged assortment of French battalions held more than 100 miles of the wild Eastern Dorsal with its open passes at Pichon and Faid. And in the south the U. S. II Corps guarded the right flank of the Allied line while stockpiling supplies in Tebessa.

Despite the narrow Tunisian neck to which the enemy was now confined, the Axis continued to bring in troops and equipment in their effort to prolong the African war. A steady stream of huge, slow-flying German transports lumbered into the hard-topped air bases in the vicinity of Tunis. Meanwhile the Allied air force was helplessly bogged down on the muddy Tunisian and Algerian airfields.

By mid-January Eisenhower abandoned his plan for an attack from Tebessa toward Sfax when he learned at Casablanca that Montgomery would not reach the Mareth Line in time to coordinate his offensive with that of II Corps. Eisenhower decided to concentrate on build-up and delay his offensive until the spring. Meanwhile General Jurgin von Arnim, commander of Axis forces in Tunisia, knew that in any race for build-up he would be hopelessly outclassed, for German losses in Russia had drained the Wehrmacht's reserves.

In early January the enemy began to nibble at Eisenhower's position on the Eastern Dorsal. By the end of January these enemy attacks had seriously weakened Eisenhower's grip on that line. With each new crack in the Allied position, troops were shifted to fill it and the reserves on which Eisenhower had counted to withstand an enemy attack were being rapidly depleted. As his front wobbled under von Arnim's recurrent attacks, Eisenhower sensed that the mounting danger justified his overriding French objections to British combined command. During the last week in January he moved to repair his position by consolidating the whole Allied front under Anderson's First Army.

On January 30 the French were attacked by von Arnim, this time at Faid Pass. Although the French held firm on the road beyond it, a critical gateway had been opened through the Eastern Dorsal into the Allied lines.

By February Eisenhower found himself clinging to a shaky and greatly weakened barrier along the entire Dorsal. To make matters worse, Rommel had fallen back from Tripolitania to the Mareth Line. His desert forces were now joined with those of von Arnim in a continuous front for a prolonged holdout campaign in Tunisia.

In early February, Allied intelligence had reported the possibility of a strong enemy attack toward Fondouk and the rear of Anderson's British First Army. Although there were other points along the Allied line where the enemy might also have struck, the Allied command had become convinced that Fondouk was to be the target. This belief came to be a near-fatal assumption.

To satisfy himself that his positions were tightly buttoned up Eisenhower left Algiers at midnight on February 12 to visit Fredendall's headquarters. He arrived at II Corps in Tebessa on the afternoon of the thirteenth. Eisenhower's original instructions to Fredendall called for a mobile reserve to be held in readiness behind a screen of reconnaissance forces and light delaying elements. Instead, he found that American infantry had been lumped on isolated djebels along the line and the mobile reserves were scattered in bits and pieces along the line.

At dawn the following morning German Tiger tanks surged through the gateway at Faid Pass—35 miles south of Fondouk. Fredendall's hope of containing the Pass perished in the first few hours of the attack. For as the enemy swarmed through the Dorsal, he quickly isolated and encircled the American forces on adjoining djebels. Both shoulders were smashed and with them went Eisenhower's chances for blocking the attack.

An armored counterattack against the enemy flank failed near Sbeitla when Stukas pounced on the American tanks. There at Sbeitla the road from Faid divided. One fork ran 80 miles north toward the British dumps at Le Kef, the other 70 miles west toward the American depots at Tebessa. Either offered the enemy a tempting target.

When he learned that his position at Faid had collapsed, Anderson ordered withdrawal to the Western Dorsal, a parallel range behind the barrier on which the Allies had anchored their line. There a narrow three-mile gap, known as Kasserine Pass, opened into the broad,

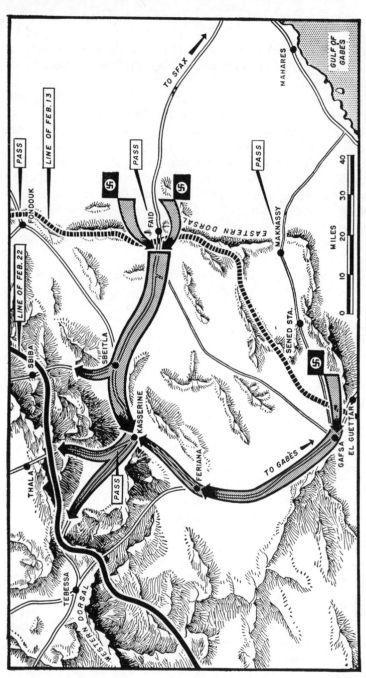

From the Eastern Dorsal, Rommel's panzers raced across the Tunisian plains to break through the pass at Kasserine and threaten the supply base of Tebessa behind the mountain shield that formed the Western Dorsal.

flat bowl that led toward Tebessa. At Kasserine an inept regimental commander had ranged his troops across the gateway on the valley floor as if to halt a herd of cattle. The critical mountain shoulders on each side of that pass were left undefended and the German swept on through. Having dispersed the reserves with which they might have mounted a counterattack, the Allies now spent their strength battalion by battalion. And as quickly as these battalions moved to the attack, the German chewed them up.

Not until the evening of February 21, ten miles from Thala near the Tebessa-Le Kef road, was the panzer attack halted. There tanks of the British 6th Armored Division, rushed south for reinforcement, were joined by artillery from the American 9th Infantry Division. The latter had raced day and night 750 miles from Oran over ice-sheeted mountain roads.

Early on the morning of February 23 the enemy withdrew through Kasserine Pass, planting his rear with Teller mines to discourage Allied pursuit. Montgomery had closed in on the Mareth Line and Rommel was forced to withdraw his panzers to halt the Eighth Army.

Although the German could not hope to win the North African war, in his struggle to prolong the conflict he had won a significant victory at Kasserine Pass.

On the morning that Rommel withdrew his panzers, an American C-54 glided in from the South Atlantic over the harbor city of Dakar on the French North African coast and bumped to a landing on the rough runway of a half-finished air base.

It was a raw, windy day and the spindly-legged Senegalese who trudged by with loads of steel planking pulled their rags tightly about them. I climbed down stiffly from the ship. We had arrived in Eisenhower's theater of war.

CHAPTER

3 : *Tunisia*

O URS HAD BEEN ONE OF THE FIRST SHIPS TO FLY
directly from Natal, Brazil, to the unfinished Air Transport Command (ATC) base at Dakar. Until that field was opened the South
Atlantic air transports flew via Ascension Island, a flyspeck in the
ocean, to the British base at Accra, 1,300 miles below Dakar.

After a 25-cent breakfast of canned bacon and powdered eggs in
a tar-paper shack on the field at Dakar, we boarded our plane for the
1,400-mile flight north to Marrakech in French Morocco. We flew
for hours over the bleak Sahara. But as we passed into Morocco, the
snow-topped peaks of the Atlas Mountains rose steeply out of the
desolate plains and we threaded a course through their passes.
Beyond this mountain barrier, on its fertile northern slopes, Marrakech lay like a crystal city in the center of a green oasis. From
the air its huge white mosques ballooned like giant mushrooms.
We landed there, spent the night at the Arabesque Mamounia
Hotel, and left early the next morning for Algiers in a cargo-loaded
C-47.

Eisenhower's bullet-proof Cadillac was waiting near the hangar
as we splashed into a landing on the bomb-scarred airfield outside
Algiers the afternoon of February 24, 1943. The armored car had
been built in England by a coachmaking firm at the insistence of
intelligence officers who feared for Eisenhower's safety in the narrow streets of crowded Algiers. However, the weight of this armored
body on a standard chassis caused frequent tire blowouts, and **the**

sedan was eventually exiled to the service of VIP's. We dragged our luggage through the mud from the steel-planked runway, and for the first time I understood what Ike meant when he complained to General Marshall of the mud that had bogged down his air force. The heaviest winter rains in years had churned North Africa into gumbo, too sticky to hold even the steel planking that had been rushed forward to improve the airstrips.

Eisenhower's Allied Force Headquarters had been crowded into the sprawling St. George Hotel, high on a palm-covered hillside overlooking the busy harbor of Algiers. Liberty ships jammed the quays teeming with Arab stevedores. Barrage balloons dotted the murky sky. The St. George with its mosaic-tiled corridors had become an African Pentagon, peopled by a brilliantly uniformed assortment of Allied officers. Like all headquarters, AFHQ had mushroomed alarmingly since landing in Algiers. Eventually it was to be staffed by no fewer than 1,100 officers.

On our arrival at the St. George, I was taken directly to Eisenhower's office, adjacent to that of Bedell Smith, his hard-working chief of staff. This was to be my first tour of duty with Dwight Eisenhower and it lasted throughout the war. For 28 years since our graduation together from West Point, we had moved from army post to army post without ever once having served together. Indeed, we had seen one another fewer than a half-dozen times and then only at Army-Navy games and infrequent class reunions.

Eisenhower had entered the class of 1915 at West Point on June 14, 1911. At that time I was still working in overalls in the Moberly, Missouri, shops of the Wabash Railroad. My father, a country schoolteacher, had died when I was 14, leaving my mother, a seamstress, to support me. After graduating from Moberly High School in 1910 I took a job with the railroad, hoping to save money enough to matriculate at the state university the following year.

One Sunday evening in the late spring of 1911 John Crewson, a Moberly house mover and superintendent of the Sunday School of the Christian Church to which I belonged, asked why I did not apply for an appointment to West Point. He knew of my love for the out-of-doors, a heritage left me by my father who took me hunting when I was a child.

"But I couldn't afford to go to West Point," I told him. "If I get to the university, I'll have a hard enough time earning my way."

"You don't pay to go to West Point, Omar," Mr. Crewson explained, "the army pays you while you're there." With that I picked up a freshened interest in a possible career as a soldier.

Knowing no one who knew our Congressman, the Honorable W. W. Rucker of the 2d District in Missouri, I wrote directly to ask him for an appointment. He replied that the principal had already been named, but he would be delighted to have me take the examination as an alternate appointee.

With less than a week in which to study for the examination after almost a year out of high school, I despaired of passing and so declined to give up my job with the railroad that I might study during the day. Only recently I had been promoted to the boiler shop and was now making 17 cents an hour. Furthermore, since the examination was to be given in St. Louis, I was reluctant to waste railroad fare on so hopeless a trip. Even though discouraged, I went to the school superintendent, Mr. J. C. Lilly, a friend of my father's, for advice.

"Go ahead and try it, Omar," he urged me. "Maybe you can get a pass from the railroad to make the trip."

"If I can get a pass, sir, I'll go."

The Wabash Railroad gave me the pass and three weeks later I was notified that the principal appointee had failed his examinations. Orders were sent me to report to West Point on August 1, 1911.

For three years at the Academy Eisenhower and I were friends and in the same cadet company. We played football together until a wrenched knee forced him to quit the squad.

That injury to his knee was afterward aggravated when Eisenhower jumped from his mount in the cadet riding hall. At graduation time a medical board questioned the desirability of commissioning him, fearing he might be limited in service.

During the war Major General Troy H. Middleton, commander of VIII Corps, also suffered an arthritic disability in the knee, and it was suggested to General Marshall that he be sent home rather than given the command of a corps in the field.

"I would rather," General Marshall said, "have a man with arthritis in the knee than one with arthritis in the head. Keep Middleton there."

Happily the West Point examining board felt no less keenly about Eisenhower.

With Bedell Smith my associations had been more constant over a shorter span of years. An intense, tempestuous, and harassed man in contrast to his urbane chief, Smith was already proving himself the most valued member of Eisenhower's staff. A scholarly self-educated soldier, he joined the National Guard at the age of 16. His interests ranged widely beyond his military career and as a result Bedell Smith was admirably equipped to help Eisenhower with the vast administrative and political headaches of his command.

In 1931 Bedell Smith, then only a captain, came to the Infantry School at Benning as a student in the advanced class. Smith showed himself to be an unusual and articulate officer with the intelligence to think clearly and the ability to speak his mind. At the completion of the one-year course I asked for Smith as one of my instructors.

During this time General Marshall had observed a class in which Smith delivered a monograph on his experiences in World War I. So impressed was General Marshall with the recitation that he told an aide, "I want Smith as part of the secretariat here. His was the best monograph I've ever heard."

I promptly relinquished my claim and Smith joined the school staff.

Slumped in a chair before his situation map, a long stick in his hand, Eisenhower outlined my mission.

"Just as quickly as you can," he said, "I want you to get up to the front and look for the things I would want to see myself if I only had the time. Bedell will give you a letter telling Fredendall and the others that you are to act as my eyes and ears."

The American defeat at Kasserine had already raised disquieting doubts in Algiers on the competency of American command, the adequacy of our training, and the worthiness of our weapons. But Eisenhower was not looking for a goat, for the mistakes at Kasserine were too numerous at every echelon of command to be attributed to the dereliction of a single commander. Eisenhower insisted that he was looking primarily for lessons to be learned from the defeat.

If at that time he had lost confidence in Fredendall as commander of II Corps, Eisenhower wisely refrained from intimating it to me. I was to form my own opinions and report them directly to him. And although I had no executive authority to act for Eisenhower, I was free to offer what he called "suggestive corrections" to American commanders on the front. Mine was not altogether an enviable position, for many people thought of me as Eisenhower's agent on the front carrying tales home to the boss outside the chain of command. It was not long before I was to learn that my mission did not endear me to the commander of II Corps.

When Eisenhower asked if I was equipped to travel extensively on the front, I thought ruefully of the 77 pounds of useless blouses and pink trousers I had toted along on the recommendation of my Washington friends. My bedding roll with its down sleeping bag, air mattress, and waterproofed L. L. Bean puptent waited on a pier in Brooklyn for passage on some slow boat. This was the last time during the war that I parted company with my bedroll.

At dinner that first evening in his heavily guarded villa near the St. George Hotel, Eisenhower's amiable manner changed when he spoke angrily of the criticism that had raged in the United States over his deal with Darlan. As though to strengthen his own convictions, he talked eagerly and at length of the circumstances that had led to this expedient deal with Vichy. For though Darlan's assassination on Christmas Eve had provided a convenient way out for Eisenhower, the issue still preyed on his mind.

He had not blundered into the Darlan relationship insensitive to the political hazards of his action. Eisenhower was quick to discern the political nuances of his North African situation. Before approaching Darlan, Eisenhower had shrewdly matched the military advantages of collaboration against the risk of embarrassment to the Allies. Though public reaction to the deal had been more violent than Eisenhower anticipated, he held to the necessity of this compromise as vital to the safety of his North African landing.

Despite his opportunism and his unsavory reputation, Darlan, Eisenhower declared, delivered French North Africa to the Allies as he had promised. It was Darlan's cease-fire order that put an end to French resistance on the invasion. And it was he who persuaded the crusty Admiral Pierre Boisson at Dakar to throw his lot in with the Allies, thus securing this French West African base on the South Atlantic. And although the French fleet at Toulon did not escape to join the Allies, it was effectively scuttled and thus denied the German.

In war, military expediency sometimes compels us to compromise on principles. Collaboration with Darlan was fully as nauseous to Eisenhower as it was to his critics in the United States. But, as Eisenhower insisted, he had not sought Darlan as an ally but as a convenient and useful tool.

For two days I browsed through Eisenhower's headquarters in Algiers seeking additional background on the situation at the front. Within the crowded makeshift offices of AFHQ, British and American staffs had achieved a homogeneity that was already a tribute to Ike's insistence on Allied cooperation. "No one will object," an officer explained to me, "if you wish to call someone a bastard. But the moment you call him a 'British bastard,' then, sir, you'd better watch out!"

Ike was explicit in his orders. Troublemakers who waved the flag were to be sent straight back home—home on a slow boat, unescorted.

In forming an Allied headquarters Eisenhower had organized joint staffs in intelligence, operations, and supply planning. Where a section was headed by a Briton, his deputy was an American. And where an American bossed the operation, a Briton filled in as his Number Two man.

But in the supply and administrative organizations it became necessary to establish parallel British and American staffs because of the disparities that existed in equipment and procedures of both armies.

In their intelligence activities at AFHQ, the British easily outstripped their American colleagues. The tedious years of prewar study the British had devoted to areas throughout the world gave them a vast advantage which we never overcame. The American army's long neglect of intelligence training was soon reflected by the ineptness of our initial undertakings. For too many years in the preparation of officers for command assignments, we had overlooked the need for specialization in such activities as intelligence. It is unrealistic to assume that every officer has the capacity and the inclination for field command. Many are uniquely qualified for staff-intelligence duties and indeed would prefer to devote their careers to those tasks. Yet instead of grooming qualified officers for intelligence assignments, we rotated them through conventional duty tours, making correspondingly little use of their special talents. Misfits frequently found themselves assigned to intelligence duties. And in some stations G-2 became a dumping ground for officers ill suited to line command. I recall how scrupulously I avoided the branding that came with an intelligence assignment in my own career. Had it not been for the uniquely qualified reservists who so capably filled so many of our intelligence jobs throughout the war, the army would have found itself badly pressed for competent intelligence personnel.

On February 26, the day before I was to leave for the Tunisian front, word came to Algiers of a new German offensive against the northern half of the Allied line. Once more the enemy had picked his point of attack with an eye to Allied weakness. For as Alexander reorganized his lines to sort out the scattered American units and concentrate them under II Corps, von Arnim hit British positions in the north with an attack aimed toward their communications center at Beja.

Snug in the Eastern Dorsal that shielded his coastal plains, the enemy could hold Montgomery on the Mareth Line in the south while using his forces nearer Tunis to jab at Western Allies. Not only was he able to hold open the ring we struggled to close by joining our Western forces with those of Montgomery's from the desert, but he sought to defeat us in detail by counterattacking the lightly held sectors of our Western front. Furthermore, with the juncture of Rommel's and von Arnim's forces in Tunisia, the German now gained the advantage of interior lines of communication. This was to permit him rapid shifts in strength from the Eighth to the First Army fronts. As long as the enemy held the initiative, he could continue to torment both Allied fronts.

Authority for my mission as Eisenhower's legman on the Tunisian front was given me in a brief letter addressed to all U. S. commanders:

Major General O. N. Bradley is visiting your headquarters as a personal representative of the Commanding General, North African Theater of Operations, to discuss questions of interest to you concerning American troops under your command. Please give him every possible cooperation and assistance.

Anxious to escape for a few days the frustrations of his desk in Algiers, Bedell Smith volunteered to accompany me as far as II Corps. We flew to Constantine in Eisenhower's armed B-17 while Hansen and Bridge followed in a couple of jeeps. A natural fortress surrounded on three sides by a gorge several times as deep as the one at Niagara, Constantine had been selected as headquarters for the ground force and air commands.

Alexander's ground force headquarters was predominantly British; it contained but a few American liaison officers. Veterans, most of them, of the desert campaign, those British staff officers had affected a picturesque variety of casual uniforms. Sweaters, corduroys, and bush jackets had been substituted for the conventional British battle dress of the First Army. Many of the officers were draped in strong-smelling goatskin greatcoats, a practical garment, I was told, for chill nights on the desert. Alexander's Army Group staff bore the relaxed and easy air of men who had long ago adapted themselves to the inconveniences of war.

While I was still a lieutenant colonel in Washington in 1940, Alexander commanded a division on the evacuation at Dunkirk. From there he had gone to Burma where once again he was forced to beat a retreat. Thus after having been belted by the Axis for three years in opposite corners of the world, Alexander relished the turnabout that had come with superior Allied forces for this Tunisian campaign.

A patient, wise, and fair-minded soldier, it was Alexander who, more than anyone else, helped the American field command mature and eventually come of age in the Tunisian campaign. His was primarily a task of coordination on the Allied front. It was a task that demanded in addition to great generalship, tact and diplomacy, tolerance and discretion. Among all the British officers I was to know, none possessed these qualities in greater abundance than did Alexander.

At Casablanca in January, 1943, Allied planners had foreseen the need for joining Alexander's and Eisenhower's forces in a single command for the final phase of the North African campaign. Accordingly, Alexander's command was to come under AFHQ's direction on the day Montgomery's Eight Army crossed the Tunisian border, and Alexander was then to become the ground deputy to Ike.

The change-over came on February 20 when Alexander not only became Deputy Commander-in-Chief of the Allied Forces but Commander-in-Chief of 18th Army Group as well. The Group consisted of Anderson's First and Montgomery's Eighth Armies, Fredendall's U. S. II Corps, and Juin's French XIX. Designated the 18th Army Group, after the First and Eighth Armies, its principal task was to coordinate the Allied pincer movement on Tunisia, to wall the Axis in its coastal corridor, and then to push the enemy northward into a trap where he could be destroyed.

Just as soon as Alexander established his Group CP at Constantine, Anderson was to relinquish Allied command of the Western Tunisian front and confine himself to the First Army. Both the French and American corps were to have independent status under Alexander's

Army Group control. Alexander's first act was to unscramble the chaotic commitment of units on Anderson's front. The forces of each nation were to be concentrated under their own command and assigned exclusive sectors of responsibility on the front. For the first time, Fredendall on the southern flank of the Tunisian line found himself with the substance as well as the title of a corps commander. Scattered tank battalions of the 1st Armored Division were reorganized into a single powerful force and for the first time since it landed in Oran, the 1st Infantry Division was able to bring together its three regimental combat teams.

Simultaneously with the reorganization of ground forces, Eisenhower concentrated the Mediterranean air and naval forces under deputy commanders-in-chief. On February 19 he created the Mediterranean Air Command under Air Chief Marshal Sir Arthur W. Tedder. Tedder's new command extended Eisenhower's control over all Allied air—British, French, and American—in Northwest Africa, the Middle East, and Malta. To command the key Northwest African Air Force he named Major General Carl A. Spaatz, a deceptively quiet and brilliant airman. Spaatz' subordinate commanders included Major General James H. Doolittle of the Strategic Air Force, Air Marshal Sir Arthur Coningham of the Tactical Air Force, and Air Marshal Sir Hugh P. Lloyd of the Coastal Air Force. Doolittle's heavy B-24's and medium bombers were to destroy strategic targets, pound the enemy's naval bases, drive the Luftwaffe from its Tunisian airfields, and attack the enemy's communications. To Coningham, a native New Zealander, Tedder gave the mission of close support of ground troops. It was a support sorely needed on a front where even the enemy's antiquated and lumbering Stukas harried our ground troops with little fear of interception.

Admiral of the Fleet Sir Andrew B. Cunningham was named Commander-in-Chief, Mediterranean, to include all Allied naval movements from Gibraltar to east of Malta. Thus when I reported to Eisenhower on February 24, his Allied Force Headquarters encompassed the entire Mediterranean from Casablanca to the Middle East. Eisenhower not only was ready to sweep the Axis out of Africa but was already deep in planning for the Sicilian invasion.

From Constantine, Bedell and I headed for the front in a four-year-old Ford sedan that had been commandeered by the Allies shortly after landing. Along the well-paved Algerian highway, busy with truck traffic from Constantine to Tebessa, Arabs huddled singly by the roadside, wrapped in their homespun burnooses, offering eggs for sale. As more and more troops were convoyed to the front, the prices of fresh eggs skyrocketed and these ragged roadside peddlers reaped greater cash incomes than they could have earned in almost a lifetime of farming.

Halfway to Tebessa we shifted at Smith's suggestion from our Ford sedan to an open jeep, which was easier to jump out of in the event of strafing attack. Two 50-caliber machine-gun carriers had been sent along to escort the jeep. The elaborate precautions amused me until Bedell Smith explained that only the week before he had been attacked from the air while driving this road and a member of his party was killed.

Thereafter while traveling by jeep in Tunisia, we conformed to standard precautions. While one rider squinted ahead for enemy air to the front, another maintained a lookout on the rear. Windshields were folded down and kept covered to avoid reflection and the canvas tops were buttoned down. For in the winter of 1943, despite our growing Allied air strength, the Luftwaffe ranged the Tunisian front almost unmolested. The sound of aircraft had become the signal to halt and take cover by the roadside.

II Corps was headquartered in the small phosphate-mining town of Djebel Kouif, 15 miles north of the walled city of Tebessa. Its troops rested in bivouac in the wooded Dorsal behind the rim of hills that guarded their concentrations of supply. As a result of Alexander's reorganization of the front, II Corps now comprised an effective force of four divisions, adequately supported by artillery, antitank, and antiaircraft battalions. Those divisions included the 1st Armored now reassembled under Major General Orlando Ward, the 1st Infantry under Major General Terry de la Mesa Allen, the 34th Infantry under Major General Charles W. Ryder, and the newly arrived 9th Infantry under Major General Manton S. Eddy.

The accumulation of supply at Tebessa for the abandoned attack toward Sfax had left II Corps well heeled with reserves when that attack was abandoned. Meanwhile the matériel losses of Kasserine were being replaced by daily shipments of tanks, trucks, half-tracks, and tank destroyers. Many of these tanks were hurriedly stripped from the 2d Armored Division on guard on the far-off Spanish Moroccan border.

Originally Anderson's supply chief had estimated that 38,000 troops could be supported by existing transportation facilities on the

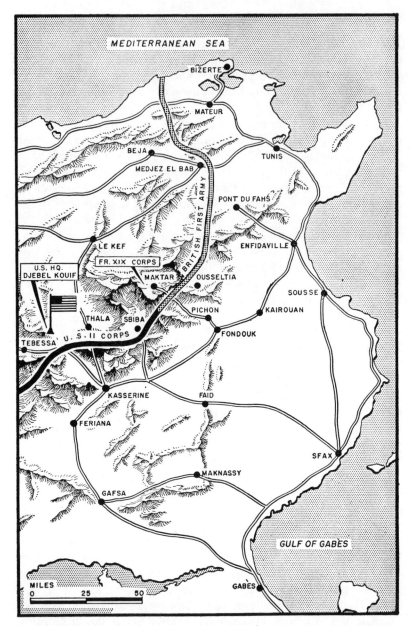

In preparation for its spring offensive in Southern Tunisia, II Corps concentrated its U. S. troops behind the Western Dorsal while the British First Army held in the north before Tunis and Bizerte.

Southern Tunisian front. These estimates, however, had not anticipated either the ingenuity of U. S. railroaders or the astonishing
capacity of U. S. forces to sustain field armies on trucking operations.
To replace U. S. losses and help speed the II Corps build-up, Eisenhower had just ordered an emergency shipment of 5,400 additional
trucks from the U. S. Instead of the 38,000 the British had prescribed
as a limit on this II Corps front, we eventually put in 92,000 troops
and we kept them liberally supplied throughout the offensive.

This inclination of the British to underestimate U. S. efficiency in
logistics was to cause us greater difficulty later in the Tunisian campaign. For in the assignment of forces to a sector on the front, an
army is limited by its ability to support them over the existing roads
and rail lines. Thus logistics become the critical determinant in any
tactical plan.

Later in the war I often explained to my staff that G-2 existed to
tell me what should be done on the basis of his information concerning the enemy. G-4 was to tell me what could be done in view of our
limitations on supply. Then once I made my decision, G-3 was to do
it. Thus a timid G-4 could directly restrict the scope of his commander's operations. And similarly a resourceful G-4 could expand
it. Fortunately, my G-4's were always resourceful.

II Corps had located its CP in the empty, unheated French schoolhouse of Djebel Kouif. The building had long ago been stripped of
its furnishings and plumbing by neighboring Arab looters.

Here at corps, the Anglo-American friendship that had been so
dearly prized at Algiers showed signs of the strain it had undergone
since Kasserine Pass. Still smarting under that defeat, II Corps held
Anderson directly to blame for the dispersion that made it powerless to halt the German attack. His diversion of American forces to
the British and French fronts, they argued, had stripped II Corps
of the mobile reserves it had counted upon for counterattack.

But while it grumbled for fear II Corps would be made the goat
for "Anderson's derelictions," the staff there was not disheartened
over the situation on its front. Though still replacing equipment
losses, it was already laying plans for an offensive to retake the Eastern Dorsal.

Hansen, Bridge, and I were assigned to one room in the mine company's dingy hotel, but with Bedell I left Djebel Kouif immediately
to visit the 1st Armored Division. From it and the other divisions I

hoped to learn what might be helpful to us in the combat training
of troops in the states.

Outside Tebessa where a growth of scrubby aleppo pines screened
the rocky Western Dorsal, Ward had concentrated his heavily reduced 1st Armored Division. In both the December battle for Tunis
and the German breakthrough at Faid, the division had suffered
severe equipment losses. At Faid, alone, more than 90 tanks were left
burning on the valley floor. The surviving tanks were now heavily
daubed with mud for camouflage. And in every bivouac, crews
worked over their vehicles readying them for combat.

Ward was happy to have pulled his division together. For four
months units of the 1st Armored had been fighting as isolated commands in support of British, French, and American troops. The 1st
Armored had not yet been employed as a division and Ward was
anxious to show what a U. S. armored division could do if given a
suitable mission and if supported with adequate supply.

For two days I tramped the division bivouac, talking to officers and
noncoms, asking what they had learned during their first few weeks
of combat. Although they conceded that the enemy was both a crafty
and skilled opponent, they attributed many of their troubles to their
own inexperience. Whereas they had frequently blundered into attack, they spoke of how patiently the German reconnoitered his
routes of advance, how skillfully he employed the wadies or gullies
for cover, and how stealthily he moved in the attack. Initially, our
tankers had galloped like cavalrymen into the offensive, trusting
rashly in the speed of their vehicles and in the thickness of their
armor. Unfortunately neither helped them when the German antitank gunners came within range.

When I asked about equipment, I learned that our gasoline-
driven Shermans had already established a bad reputation among
U. S. troops on the front. Because their high-octane fuel blazed too
easily when the engine was hit, the crews pleaded for diesel engines
to "replace these fire-traps." Sergeant James H. Bowser, of Jasper,
Alabama, a tough young veteran of 23, spoke for his crew. "General,"
he said, "this is my third tank although I've still got my original crew.
We were burned out of the other two. If they were diesels it
wouldn't have happened. But these gasoline engines go up like
torches on the first or second hit. Then you've got to barrel out and
leave 'em burning."

I found the half-track another overrated vehicle, for although effective as an overland personnel carrier, it offered scant protection against enemy fire. When I asked a soldier if enemy machine-gun fire pierced its light armor, he looked up at me and brightened.

"No, sir—" he said. "No, sir, it does not. As a matter of fact bullets generally only come in on one side and rattle around a bit." Actually the American half-track was a competent and dependable contrivance. Its bad name resulted from the inexperience of our troops who attempted to use it for too many things.

Even this early in the war the German 88 had already become the nemesis of infantrymen and the tankers. A dual-purpose gun designed for antiaircraft and for use against tanks, the 88 had already demonstrated the effectiveness of a high-velocity antitank weapon. It easily outranged our Shermans with their 75-mm. guns.

In their first engagement, the American tankers learned that tank for tank their General Grants and Shermans were no match for the more heavily armored and better-gunned German panzers. Two years later in the Battle of the Bulge this disparity had not yet been corrected. Although the Shermans eventually mounted heavier guns, at no time could they engage the enemy's Panthers and Tigers in a direct frontal attack. But it was in dependability that the American tank clearly outclassed the German; its powerful engine could always be counted on to run without a breakdown. This advantage together with our U. S. superiority in numbers enabled us to surround the enemy in battle and knock out his tanks from their flanks. But this willingness to expend Shermans offered little comfort to the crews who were forced to expend themselves as well.

In contrast to the teamwork that flourished between the enemy's panzers and his Stukas, the pleas of American tankers for air support had more often than not gone unanswered. Air-ground staffs had not yet simplified the intricate channeling in which requests for strikes were often delayed until the enemy target had dispersed.

Although I tried to sidestep the issue of command, it became apparent in my first week on the front that Fredendall had lost the confidence of of his division commanders. Along with Ward who could not forgive Fredendall for acquiescing to Anderson's dispersal of his 1st Division, Ryder of the 34th Division was no less critical of corps. He had lost the better part of a regiment in the Kasserine attack as the result of the faulty dispositions he had been ordered to take. This loss of confidence among his division commanders had placed Fredendall in an untenable position. While Kasserine could not be blamed solely upon him, he was deeply enough implicated in the eyes of his subordinate commanders to destroy his future effectiveness with them. Although I was certain that Fredendall should be relieved, I kept this judgment to myself and did not communicate it to Eisenhower.

At Djebel Kouif, Fredendall's staff loyally defended their chief against the mutterings heard round the corps. But confidence had already deteriorated, and the disposition at corps to blame its troubles on the British First Army complicated rather than relieved the situation. Meanwhile the British fidgeted impatiently over what they termed an unnecessary delay in planning by II Corps for its next attack. And in Algiers the suspicion spread that Kasserine had blunted II Corps offensive spirit, that the American command had become too cautious and wary.

Alarmed by these reports of sagging morale in II Corps, Eisenhower visited Tebessa on March 5. Although Alexander as group commander was now busy reorganizing the Tunisian front, command of II Corps still resided in Anderson's First Army. Eisenhower now proposed to place both the French and American corps directly under Alexander on an equal footing with Anderson's Army.

Because Fredendall had neglected to tell me of Eisenhower's visit to the corps, I did not learn of it until a call summoned me from the 9th Division to Tebessa. During a break in the conference Eisenhower asked me to join him outside on the porch of the small European stucco house in which we were meeting.

"What do you think of the command here?" he asked.

"It's pretty bad," I replied. "I've talked to all the division commanders. To a man they've lost confidence in Fredendall as the corps commander."

"Thanks, Brad," he said, "you've confirmed what I thought was wrong. As a matter of fact I've already ordered Patton up from Rabat. He'll report in tomorrow to take command of II Corps."

The news of Patton's coming fell like a bombshell on Djebel Kouif.

4: *With Patton to El Guettar*

W<small>ITH</small> <small>SIRENS SHRIEKING PATTON'S ARRIVAL, A PRO-</small>cession of armored scout cars and half-tracks wheeled into the dingy square opposite the schoolhouse headquarters of II Corps at Djebel Kouif on the late morning of March 7. Even the Arabs plodding through the muddy streets picked up their robes and scurried into the nearest doorways. The armored vehicles bristled with machine guns and their tall fish-pole antennae whipped crazily overhead. In the lead car Patton stood like a charioteer. He was scowling into the wind and his jaw strained against the web strap of a two-starred steel helmet.

Two oversized silver stars on a red plate designated his command car. On either side of its hood the car carried a rigid metal flag. One bore two white stars on a field of red. The other was lettered WTF to signify the Western Task Force, Patton's invasion command on the Casablanca landing. The following day the WTF plate was replaced by one bearing the blue and white II Corps shield.

For almost four months after the North African invasion Patton had fretted restlessly on the French Moroccan coast where with his I Armored Corps he had been posted to discourage any attempt by Franco to close the narrow Straits of Gibraltar and there sever the Allied lifeline into the Mediterranean Sea. His corps consisted of two divisions, the 2d Armored which he had once commanded at Benning and the famed 3rd Infantry. As the likelihood of Spanish intervention on the side of the Axis faded, Patton soon tired of that border watch a thousand miles behind the fighting front. Even though it meant leaving his I Armored Corps for a strange command, Patton snapped at the assignment to Tunisia when Ike offered it to him.

In the words of Eisenhower, Patton was to rejuvenate the jaded II Corps and bring it to a "fighting pitch." By the third day after his arrival, the II Corps staff was fighting mad—but at Patton, not at the German.

For George had set out deliberately to shock II Corps into a realization that the easy-going days were ended. Rather than wait for the effect of this change in command to filter down to the divisions, Patton sought a device that would instantly bring it home to every GI in the corps. He found what he was looking for in uniform regulations.

After several months in combat American front-line troops had affected the British soldier's casual disregard for conventional field dress. While not under fire, an increasing number removed their heavy helmets and wore only the OD beanie that had been issued for wear under the helmet. To Patton this beanie had become the symbol of slovenly discipline within II Corps. He set out to banish the beanie and make it the first of his corps reforms.

The blow fell with an order that prescribed the wearing of helmets, leggings, and neckties at all times in the corps sector. Rear-echelon units were not exempted from the wearing of helmets and front-line companies were not to be spared the wearing of neckties while in combat. To enforce the regulation Patton established a uniform system of fines that ran as high as $50 for officers, $25 for enlisted men. "When you hit their pocketbooks," George used to say, "you get a quick response."

To emphasize how stringently the order was to be enforced, Patton sometimes went out himself to round up a handful of offenders. Seldom did he return from a day out on the road without a collection of beanies confiscated from troops on the front.

This "beanie campaign" marked the start and the ascendancy of Patton's spit-and-polish reign in II Corps. Each time a soldier knotted his necktie, threaded his leggings, and buckled on his heavy steel helmet, he was forcibly reminded that Patton had come to command the II Corps, that the pre-Kasserine days had ended, and that a tough new era had begun.

Though most commanders would have permitted exceptions to the rule on helmets, Patton insisted there be none. The order applied no less to nurses in their hospital tents than it did to mechanics in the ordnance pools.

When ordnance asked General Patton if the order was to be enforced while these mechanics were working on their trucks, George snapped back, "You're goddam right—they're soldiers, aren't they?"

Patton's second reform was applied to the II Corps working staff itself. During field operations a staff ordinarily works from 12 to 16 hours a day, taking time out only to sleep and eat. Because many of the officers were up until after midnight each night correlating their daily reports, breakfast in the corps command post was ordinarily served as late as 8:30 A.M. Until then there was little need for the staff to get to their desks, for first light reports on front-line units did not come in until after nine. These late-morning breakfasts, however, grossly affronted Patton who viewed them as a sign of slovenliness within the corps. Good soldiers, he insisted, always get up before the sun. Within a week of his arrival he ordered the headquarters breakfast hour changed to dawn and at the same time prohibited the serving of any officer after 6:30 A.M.

Though trivial in themselves, these Patton reforms promptly stamped his personality upon the corps. And while they did little to increase his popularity, they left no doubt in anyone's mind that Patton was to be the boss.

With Patton as with Fredendall, I was still a fifth wheel on the wagon, on duty with corps but ranging the front under a directive from Algiers. In the eyes of Patton this unique assignment violated the tenets of sound command. If I was to be in his headquarters, he felt, then I should logically be part of his direct chain of command.

Although George bore me no rancor, he was disturbed by the independence that had been granted me on my mission to corps. "I'm not going to have any goddam spies running around my headquarters," he growled to Lieutenant Colonel Russell F. Akers, Jr., of Gladstone, Virginia, the corps assistant G-3, and with that he rang for FREEDOM, Eisenhower's Allied Force Headquarters in Algiers. General Smith answered the phone.

"Bedell," Patton shouted, "I'm calling you about Bradley and his job up here. Look, we're awfully hard up for a good Number Two man as deputy corps commander. Bradley can fill the bill perfectly. If it's all right with Ike, I'm going to make Bradley my deputy commander. He can help us out and I'd like to have him. Okay? Then clear it with Ike."

Smith queried Eisenhower, and when the approval was phoned back I became Patton's deputy commander of II Corps. This did not mean, however, that I was to cease completely being Eisenhower's legman. The week before at Tebessa he had mentioned he might make me deputy corps commander under Patton that I might pick up some command experience in the Southern Tunisian campaign. I was to continue my observations, however, and report to Algiers anything I believed might directly concern Ike.

Now that I was to be an official part of the II Corps staff, Patton invited me to move down with him into the mine manager's house he had inherited from Fredendall. Until then I had been living with Hansen and Bridge in between visits to the field in one small room on the second floor of the mining company's shabby hotel.

My departure, I learned afterward, disappointed the company of Rangers then posted in Djebel Kouif as part of the headquarters security guard. Hansen and Bridge had invited the Rangers to make use of our beds on the days we went into the field. Almost as soon as our jeep left town, a trio of Rangers would hurry to the room to sleep in a bed with a mattress until we returned.

Patton's command of II Corps brought with it a promotion. When Eisenhower reported that President Roosevelt had recommended to the Senate Patton's promotion as a lieutenant general, George's aides jubilantly unpacked a three-star flag and several sets of the new collar insignia. They had come remarkably well prepared for just such contingencies as these. Indeed had Patton been named an admiral in the Turkish Navy, his aides could probably have dipped into their haversacks and come up with the appropriate badge of rank.

I joshed George and told him the promotion would not become effective until after it had been approved by the Senate.

"The hell you say," he grinned, pinning on the extra star, "I've waited long enough for this one."

Patton had brought with him from I Armored Corps a G-2, G-3, and G-4 in addition to Brigadier General Hugh J. Gaffey, his chief of staff. After viewing the staff work at II Corps, however, he replaced only the G-3. Fredendall's G-2 and G-4 continued in those posts under Patton as they were to do afterward under me.

The II Corps G-2 was a tall, brilliant, and temperamental Philadelphia mainliner. Known in the army as Monk, Colonel Benjamin A. Dickson had graduated from West Point in 1918. After service in

Siberia during World War I he resigned from the army. In 1940 he was hustled back into uniform and assigned to War Department intelligence. In March, 1942, Dickson went to II Corps as an assistant G-2 on that staff.

As G-2 of the corps, Dickson had drawn a group of brilliant and versatile young officers into his operation. His counterintelligence chief, a quiet, pipe-smoking professor of anthropology, Major Horace Miner, of Ann Arbor, Michigan, had trekked across the Sahara from a native hut in Timbuktu to get into the war. Another of Dickson's protegés, Lieutenant Crosby Lewis, of Philadelphia, Pennsylvania, the son of an Episcopalian rector, had joined the Canadian army in 1939 shortly after the outbreak of war. Soon after the United States entered the war Lewis left as a sergeant major in the Black Watch to join the American army in England as a private. On the landing in Oran he was awarded a battlefield commission. While a lieutenant in Tunisia, Lewis learned of Dickson's desperate need for enemy order of battle intelligence. He darkened his skin with shoe polish and in company with an Arab set off across the enemy lines. Several days later Lewis reported back to Dickson with the information. Monk dressed him down for having gone AWOL and awarded him a Silver Star.

While a student at Haverford College before the war Lewis had organized a chapter of the Veterans of Future Wars and was denounced by an angry veteran of World War I as "one of those Reds who will never fight for their country." When Lewis next appeared in the newspapers, it was because of the Silver Star I awarded him for the conspicuous bravery he showed in voluntarily leading assault infantry across a mined Sicilian stream bed to storm and capture the village on its far bank.

Like Dickson the Corps G-4 was also a Philadelphian but there the resemblance ended. For whereas Dickson, the linguist, enjoyed his reputation as a raconteur, the inconspicuous Colonel Robert W. Wilson prided himself on the taciturnity of a conventional businessman. An artilleryman in World War I, he had been called to service as a Reserve officer in June, 1941. As G-4 for II Corps on the Oran invasion he distinguished himself for the improvisation he showed in overcoming the exasperating shortages that harried that landing. Afterward in Sicily and Normandy I came to lean heavily upon the extraordinary executive abilities of this brilliant but modest man. In the complicated business of high-level supply I would unhesitatingly call him the outstanding G-4 in the entire European war.

Another of Dickson's most promising young officers was Captain Leonard M. Bessman of Madison, Wisconsin. After graduating from the University of Wisconsin, Bessman joined the Marine Corps in 1929 to fight as a private in the Nicaraguan campaign. Commissioned after having enlisted in the army in 1941, Bessman was wounded and captured by the enemy while on reconnaissance with Dickson in Tunisia. In Italy he broke out of a PW camp to spend six months with partisans in the hills before making his way back through the Allied lines.

As Montgomery massed his Eighth Army late in that February of 1943 for its assault against the Mareth Line, the Axis renewed its struggle to prevent Alexander from joining his Allied forces and closing a trap around that final corner of Tunisia where the African continent abuts Sicily and Europe. In Northern Tunisia, von Arnim again slashed at the British lines with tanks and Stuka dive bombers to harass Anderson's First Army and drive a wedge into its position. And on March 6 Rommel attempted a desperate spoiling attack from the Mareth Line against Montgomery's forces. Without reconnaissance and without infantry support for his tanks, he sought in a rash mobile movement to turn the British flank. The maneuver was quickly broken up by antitank guns and the enemy retired with a loss of 52 of his dwindling panzers. Not a single British tank was destroyed in the engagement.

Then a sick and disheartened man, Rommel surrendered his Libyan command and returned to Germany.

When in February Rommel withdrew his panzers from the Mareth Line to strike Fredendall at Kasserine, Alexander ordered Montgomery to make a diversionary attack. With that, he sought to worry Rommel into a speedy withdrawal of those forces he had detached for the Kasserine offensive. Montgomery reacted promptly and feinted with his Army. Rommel withdrew his panzers from the high water mark at Thala and sped them back to the Mareth defenses. Alexander now reasoned that by timing alternate attacks between Montgomery's front and ours, he could keep the enemy's armor skidding back and forth across lower Tunisia. Out of this realization there came the diversionary offensive of II Corps at El Guettar.

By the middle of March the Axis was showing the strain of its delaying attacks in the exhaustion of its forces. Allied build-up was now beginning to overwhelm the limited equipment and resources of the German. As the Allied superiority became more and more evident, both von Arnim in the north and Messe on the south were compelled to surrender the initiative once more to the Allied forces. After having regained it we were to hammer the enemy without cessation all the way to Tunis.

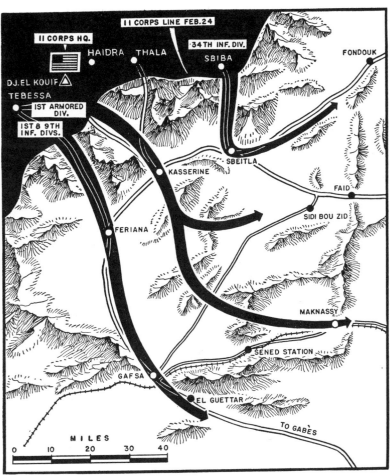

To divert enemy troops from the Mareth Line, II Corps aimed its main force toward El Guettar and Maknassy as though to break through the Eastern Dorsal while the remaining units demonstrated toward Faid and Fondouk.

While Montgomery prepared for his all-out offensive against the Mareth Line, Alexander directed II Corps to attack on the Southern Tunisian front and lure as much of the enemy strength as we could out of those defensive positions. II Corps, it was reasoned, could best threaten the enemy first by securing the Eastern Dorsal and thereafter by pushing beyond it across the coastal plain. For if II Corps could maneuver to within striking distance of the enemy's coastwise route of withdrawal toward Tunis, he would be forced to divert whatever strength might be needed to halt any such hazardous thrust.

Alexander's directive for this diversion by II Corps had been issued on March 2, four days before Patton's arrival at Djebel Kouif. In anticipation of the maneuver II Corps had been readying its attack plans for almost two weeks.

II Corps was to apply its pressure at three points on its Tunisian front. It was to concentrate the bulk of its force near Gafsa, push through the mountains at El Guettar and down the coastal road toward Gabès. This Gafsa-Gabès road led directly into the rear of the Axis defenses on the Mareth Line. It was a sensitive artery and the enemy dared not leave it exposed to Allied attack. Other American forces were to threaten Axis communications farther north from a pass beyond Maknassy where a single rail line pushed through the Dorsal to the Mediterranean coast. The remainder of the corps was to guard our flank on the north and forestall the possibility of a spoiling attack there.

At no time, however, was there any intention of converting this threat into a breakthrough from the Dorsal to the coast. Corps did not possess the force required for so ambitious a mission. Had we overextended ourselves from Gafsa to Gabès, we might have been seriously hurt on the flanks by Axis counterattack. Patton had been ordered simply to divert the enemy on the II Corps front while Montgomery administered the knockout on the Mareth Line.

Terrain in the Gafsa sector where we were to make our demonstration was poorly suited to tank attack. From both sides of the Gabès road steep, rocky hills covered Patton's route of advance. Though stripped centuries ago of all vegetation, those ridges made sturdy redoubts for enemy infantry and antitank gunners hidden in the recesses. On the valley floor centuries of unchecked erosion had covered the path with impassable wadies. And in those small gaps in the sector where nature had neglected to create formidable enough barriers, the enemy had carefully planted belts of antitank mines.

Soon after his arrival General Patton called a conference of division commanders at Djebel Kouif to outline his plan for the Gafsa offensive. Terry Allen's 1st Infantry Division, reinforced with the 1st Ranger Battalion, was to recapture Gafsa and push east through the mountain corridor at El Guettar on the road to Gabès. With the fall of Gafsa, the 1st Armored Division, with a regiment of infantry from the 9th, was to advance over terrain from which it had been expelled in the Kasserine attack, clear the pass at Maknassy, and threaten the coastal plain from that gateway. The remainder of the 9th and 34th Divisions were to hold defensively on the north. Eventually the 9th was to be shifted south to assist the 1st Division when it stumbled into the hornet's nest that lay in the mountains beyond El Guettar.

A month later in writing of this Southern Tunisian campaign some commentators grumbled over the apparent failure of American forces to crash through to the sea and there bag the Afrika Korps in the Mareth Line from the rear. The criticism is undeserved, however, for though Patton was to make noises in that direction, he was not to venture out that far. Indeed, Alexander's directive had specifically stated that "large forces" were not to be passed beyond the Eastern Dorsal.

It is possible that Patton might have hoped for an Allied breakthrough, but certainly his dispositions belied that ambition. For if he were to have broken out to the sea he could more easily have smashed a hole through Maknassy than in the mountains of El Guettar. And yet it was at El Guettar that Patton made his main effort.

In North Africa as in Sicily, Patton was oddly indifferent to the problems of supply. Though a skilled tactician, he had little patience with the logisticians and he habitually shunted supply brusquely aside as too unworthy a detail to merit his attention.

Fortunately, in Southern Tunisia the problems of supply had been solved long before Patton arrived at II Corps. The concentration that had been dumped at Tebessa provided an adequate logistical reserve for Patton's diversionary offensive. Furthermore Wilson had been given free rein on supply planning and he promptly set out to exceed the tonnage he estimated could be shipped to that front.

Later in Sicily Patton—without a Wilson to advise him—fell into such difficulties in supply that he was forced to call on II Corps to assume many of the logistical responsibilities that should properly have belonged to the Army. As a result of this Sicilian experience Patton landed in Europe keenly aware of the limitations which supply could have to his operations.

Patton's offensive started on the night of March 16–17 when the 1st Division walked into Gafsa to retake that French outpost, abandoned only the month before in the Kasserine counterattack. Shortly before the division's arrival, the Italian garrison withdrew down the Gabès road to the hills beyond the date palm oasis of El Guettar. There they were joined by German reinforcements on a line that had been established to safeguard the Afrika Korps' rear.

The evening before this Gafsa attack George had assembled his II Corps' staff for a final briefing.

"Gentlemen," he said, looking about the dimly lighted room, "tomorrow we attack. If we are not victorious, let no one come back alive." With that, George excused himself and retired alone to his room to pray.

These contradictions in Patton's character continued to bewilder his staff. For while he was profane, he was also reverent. And while he strutted imperiously as a commander, he knelt humbly before his God. And while that last appeal for victory even at the price of death was looked upon as a hammy gesture by his corps staff, it helped to make it more clearly apparent to them that to Patton war was a holy crusade.

I still could not accustom myself, however, to the vulgarity with which Patton skinned offenders for relatively minor infractions in discipline. Patton believed that profanity was the most convincing medium of communication with his troops. But while some chuckled delightedly over the famed expletives he employed with startling originality, the majority, it seemed to me, were more often shocked and offended. At times I felt that Patton, however successful he was as a corps commander, had not yet learned to command himself.

The techniques of command vary, of course, with the personality of the commander. While some men prefer to lead by suggestion and example and other methods, Patton chose to drive his subordinates by bombast and by threats. Those mannerisms achieved spectacular results. But they were not calculated to win affection among his officers or men.

During the period of Patton's preparations for the Gafsa attack, I visited Eisenhower in Algiers where he had just completed an exchange of TWX's with General Marshall on American planning for the Sicilian assault. Invasion planning for this Mediterranean bridge had been under way since January when an Allied planning staff was detached from AFHQ to outline the strategy of attack and calculate the resources it would require.

Patton's I Armored Corps had already been designated the American invasion command for Sicily, and detailed planning had been started in its headquarters in Rabat even before George left there to take comand of II Corps. It was intended, of course, that he return on completion of the Tunisian campaign.

Ike asked me if I thought Patton should remain with II Corps for the rest of the Tunisian campaign or return to I Armored Corps for Sicilian invasion planning at the completion of the Southern Tunisian attack. If Patton were to continue with II Corps, then I was to go back to I Armored Corps and substitute temporarily for him in the Sicilian planning.

"Well, I would think George ought to go back," I said, "and resume his Sicilian planning. After all the I Armored Staff is his own. He could get much more out of them than I could."

"That's just the way I feel about it too," Ike answered. "When this Gafsa phase is completed, you'll take command of II Corps and we'll send George on back to Rabat. I've already cleared it with General Marshall."

The news of my command was closely guarded until the day Patton left II Corps. Even then it was censored from the news dispatches until after the capture of Bizerte. For had Patton been publicly withdrawn from the Tunisian fighting front, his departure would have provoked enemy speculation on the next Allied move. And Ike was anxious not to reveal our further intentions in the Mediterranean Sea.

At 10:30 on the evening of March 20, Montgomery touched off the attack against the Mareth Line he had been readying for almost a month. The enemy's main defensive position stretched across a 20-mile neck between the mountains that rimmed the desert and the Mediterranean Sea. To his rear he was protected from II Corps by a long and impassable dry lake. As at El Alamein, the studious Montgomery had meticulously prepared his offensive.

With the deftness he ordinarily employs in a "set" attack, Montgomery had massed four divisions against this major defensive position. But while engaging the enemy on that line, he slipped the mobile New Zealand Corps inland around the "impassable" flank of the French-built Mareth Line defenses. As the line crumbled under this unexpected threat from the flank, Montgomery poured his Eighth Army through and pursued the enemy north up the Tunisian coast.

Meanwhile as Patton pushed beyond Gafsa to El Guettar and the pass that led through that mountain trap across the plains to Gabès, enemy resistance there stiffened. For whatever it cost, the enemy dared not risk a penetration into his rear and across his lines of communication. Consequently, he had no choice but to withdraw his troops from the southern front on which he opposed Monty and shunt them to the flank to halt Patton's diversion.

Unable to pass his tanks through the valleys until first he cleared the surrounding hills, Patton put his 1st Division on the left of the Gabès road, his 9th Division on its right. Both were to clear the enemy out of those ranges and deny him artillery observation. It soon became clear that this was to be a painful advance as American troops struggled down the rocky spine of those djebels, blocked at every boulder, challenged in every wadi, by tough and determined enemy troops.

Unable to endure this harassment on his flank while fighting for his life at Mareth, the enemy struck back on March 23 in a frantic attempt to shake off Patton. To stage the attack he diverted panzer forces desperately needed to hold his main position. The attack started at 6 A.M. just as the sun rose red in the east to bedevil our artillery observation. Mark II and Mark IV tanks crawled across the valley floor seeking shelter in the cover of wadies. They were supported in their advance by infantrymen and by the outdated Stukas overhead. But even though the forward elements penetrated our positions, the attack was halted at 9 A.M.

That afternoon radio intercept picked up German orders for renewal of the attack at 4 P.M. Soon afterward this H hour was postponed to 4:40 and again radio intercept picked it up.

This time our troops were waiting. As the long skirmish lines of German infantry advanced across the valley floor, artillery held its fire until they came within easy range. Then in mass concentrations of fire, it showered them with air burst. General Patton, from a vantage point in the 1st Infantry position, shook his head as the enemy lines thinned and then wavered. "They're murdering good infantry," he said, "what a helluva way to waste good infantry troops."

Eventually the enemy halted and once more withdrew, leaving 32 of his tanks burning behind him. Evidently the enemy had misjudged our intentions on the Gafsa-Gabès road even as we hoped he would. Fearing a breakthrough, he sought to upset our advance, and in the attempt he permitted Montgomery to push on farther in his attack. However much Monty might have helped II Corps at Kasserine with his diversionary offensive, Patton had now evened the score by drawing off those Afrika Korps panzers.

5:

Commanding General,
II Corps

As MONTGOMERY'S EIGHTH ARMY PUSHED UP THE Tunisian coastal plain toward the city of Tunis, Alexander's 18th Army Group completed its plans for the next phase of the Tunisian war.

Instructions had already been sent Patton on March 19 ordering him to transfer the 9th Division to Anderson's Army for deployment north on the British left flank in the attack on Bizerte. This transfer was to be accomplished once the Mareth Line had been cracked and the enemy pushed back north of the Gafsa road.

The remainder of II Corps was to attack at Fondouk between the British First and Eighth Armies. There we were again to demonstrate against the retreating enemy's right rear flank. To redeploy the U. S. forces under this plan it would be necessary only to sideslip II Corps north from Gafsa.

The directive alarmed me when I saw it, however, for it also meant that II Corps would be pinched out of its fair share in the final victory campaign.

For as the British Eighth Army pressed the Axis into the last corner of Tunisia, Anderson was to attack from the west and destroy the enemy's forces. And as both these British Armies converged to close that ring around von Arnim, II Corps would be squeezed out of the line at Fondouk. Thus after having played a supporting role in the preliminary Tunisian campaign, the only American combat command in all of North Africa was to be excluded from its proportionate share in the final battle. I told Patton of my objections to this Army Group plan and he, too, exploded. With Patton's permission I hurried off to Haidra where Alexander's Army Group had pitched its tents near that onetime winter garrison of the Roman legions.

I was told the slight was not intentional. It had been dictated instead by British logisticians who estimated that Alexander would find it impossible to support II Corps over existing roads on that Northern Tunisian front.

Notwithstanding these conclusions of Alexander's staff, I summarized for Patton on my return to Gafsa the three principal reasons for my opposition to the plan.

First: The proposal to pinch out II Corps was tactically unsound for it meant that in his final sledge-hammer drive on the tightly packed enemy before Tunis, Alexander would, by pinching out

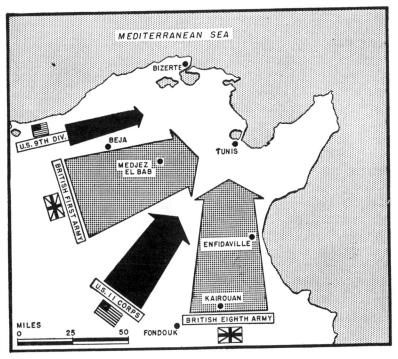

According to Alexander's original plan for the Northern Tunisian offensive, II Corps was to have been pinched out as the British First and Eighth Armies converged in an attack toward Tunis.

II Corps, foolishly forego the power of one entire corps or three full divisions of U. S. troops. I did not believe he could afford to waste them.

Second: The transfer of our 9th Division to the British in the north indicated that we might once more be dismembered into separate American bits for indiscriminate assignment to any Allied command. Not only did this practice threaten to misuse American forces, but it violated the old-time principle that American troops would fight under American command.

Third: I felt that our American troops had earned the right to share in a victory, fighting under their own flag. To deny our troops a share in the enemy's defeat would have been to deny them their only reward for agonizing months under fire. This, I reasoned, could not help, but would irritate friendly relations between our forces.

I could not believe that Eisenhower knew of Alexander's plan or that he would willingly agree to it. With Patton's permission I flew back to Algiers to point out my objections.

As Allied commander in the Mediterranean Eisenhower walked a chalk line to avoid being branded pro-American by the British command. For his command had become a test of Allied unity in the field, and any such label would surely have destroyed Eisenhower's effectiveness as an Allied commander. As a result of these precautions, however, some Americans tended to look on Eisenhower as too pro-British.

It would be foolhardy for us to deny that tense national differences sometimes split the British and American commands. Those differences persisted throughout World War II and will continue to infect any mutual endeavor where troops are banded together under an Allied command. At the outset of the North African war there were some British officers, particularly those on the senior staffs, who regarded the American army with ill-concealed amusement. Their longer experience in the war caused them to look on us as country cousins, unlettered in the intricate arts of combat. And while they cheerfully conceded the superiority of American equipment, they jibed us for having too much of it. As a matter of fact there were few British troops in Anderson's First Army with any more combat experience than the Americans in II Corps. If they looked on us with condescension, the veteran Eighth Army was no less condescending to them.

But by the same token, many Americans viewed the British with undisguised suspicion, as though attempting to uncover Britain's wily hand in every Allied decision. Indeed, not only were many Americans instinctively critical of the British, but they were also far more sensitive to implied rebuffs to their own prestige and pride.

Most British troops respected the capabilities of the U. S. counterparts on the line and they frankly envied our units their equipment. Even the most skeptical British staff officer soon learned to respect American staff practices and the astonishing accomplishments of U. S. logisticians. At the same time, American front-line commands showed their admiration for the great tenacity and courage of neighboring British units. In Tunisia we were both still in the process of getting acquainted. The suspicions and jealousies that split us centered largely in the headquarters commands. The nearer one went to the front the more comradely were our relations.

Eisenhower had not yet heard of Alexander's plan to pinch out II Corps in the Fondouk attack. He listened apprehensively to my explanation.

"The people in the United States want a victory," I explained, "and they deserve one. After playing an important part on the North African invasion and in the early Tunisian campaign, they would find it difficult to understand why the American forces were squeezed out in this final campaign."

"That's probably true, Brad," he replied, surprised by this new turn. "I hadn't thought of it in that light."

"This war's going to last a long time, Ike. There'll be a lot more Americans in it before we're through. I think we're entitled to function under our own command without being farmed out forever from ally to ally. Until you give us the chance to show what we can do in a sector of our own, with an objective of our own, under our own command, you'll never know how good or bad we really are. And neither will the American people."

"What do you have in mind?" he asked.

I gestured toward the map on his wall.

"Move the entire II Corps up north," I said, "—not just the 9th Division. And then let us go after Bizerte on our own."

Ike frowned for a moment over the map. Then after satisfying himself on our ability to move laterally across the British supply lines he called Alexander. Group was directed to give II Corps a sector with an objective in the final campaign. All the American divisions, he said, were to be retained under U. S. command.

The modest diversionary objective that had been assigned Patton on the Gafsa-Gabès road only whetted his appetite for a more active role in the Southern Tunisian campaign. He found it increasingly distasteful to flush the enemy from those hills at El Guettar while acting as a decoy for Monty. And his impatience mounted as the Eighth Army rolled north from the Mareth Line. Toward the end of March Patton's impatience deepened into frustration. He had hurried eagerly to Tunisia at Eisenhower's request and yet he found himself fighting only those leftover troops the German could spare from Montgomery's front. It was hardly a satisfying mission for a man who had once boasted he "wanted to fight the champ."

When on March 25 a directive from Alexander ordered Patton to spearhead tanks through the 1st and 9th Infantry Divisions down the road toward Gabès, he happily put together an armored task force to punch its way to the sea. The order, however, directed Patton to advance carefully phase by phase, first clearing the mountains of enemy before rolling through with his tanks.

For more than a week now Patton's infantry had struggled from ridge to ridge in a costly, slow, and exhausting advance. The enemy had dug in deeply on djebels overlooking the road and from those fortified positions inflicted severe casualties upon the attacking American troops. The battle for El Guettar had become a battle for ridge lines, and the corps advance was ultimately reduced to the advance of individual patrols. Yet before Patton could commit his armored task force down the valley road, the infantry had first to dislodge the enemy from those hills.

To stalemate this flanking effort the enemy had sown his path thickly with pie-shaped Teller mines. Here across the valley floors they could be used with deadly effectiveness as they had in the Libyan war. Not content with Tellers, the enemy also salted his positions with antipersonnel and shoe mines. The most vicious of these antipersonnel mines had already been dubbed "Bouncing Betties" by our troops. The Betty consisted of a canister the size of a No. 10 can of peaches packed with marble-sized steel pellets. Buried in the earth with only a tiny three-pronged detonator exposed, the Betty fired when stubbed by an infantryman's toe or when set off by a trip wire. It bounded into the air and then at a level of four feet exploded with a roar, scattering its can of marbles a radius of 50 feet.

The task force formed by Patton to break through the hills beyond

El Guettar was commanded by Colonel Clarence C. Benson of the 1st Armored Division. This Benson force, as it came to be known, consisted primarily of tanks and armored half-tracks. It was mobile, speedy, and heavy with automatic fire-power.

For three days this Benson force charged into the valley beyond El Guettar. And on three successive days it was thrown back with burning tanks. Until the enemy was first dislodged from those hills, Benson could not force his way through those antitank defenses. Puzzled by the repeated failure of those tanks to break through, Patton asked me to visit the force to make certain that it wasn't for lack of effort or aggressiveness on Benson's part.

It was a warm, sunny day in early spring as I headed by jeep from our *gendarmerie* headquarters in Gafsa to the date palms of El Guettar. Past the wretched Arab huts we drove, through the truck and ambulance traffic headed toward the front, until we reached the reverse slope of an open hill where Benson had parked the cluster of vehicles comprising his command post. Altogether his CP consisted of a dozen tanks and half-tracks huddled together on the treeless terrain under an unlimited sky. The area was dotted with slit trenches hacked out of the hard brown earth. A pair of self-propelled 37-mm. Bofors stood guard against air attack.

After Benson's previous attempts to crash the Gabès road, the enemy had grown increasingly touchy on this sector of his front. The Luftwaffe prowled our lines in growing strength. Stukas hunted our artillery and vehicle concentrations. ME-109's and Focke-Wulf-190's skipped in for hit-and-run raids.

With Brigadier Charles A. M. Dunphie, a British observer attached to II Corps, I stood against a half-track studying Benson's plans when three shrill blasts of a whistle signaled an air attack.

Squinting into the morning sun, I saw a flight of 12 JU-87 twin-engined bombers headed toward our position at almost 8,000 feet. We held fire hoping to escape detection and they floated by overhead. I turned back to the map with Dunphie.

A few minutes later the whistle sounded again. The bombers had circled around and this time they were headed for us. As the AA guns pumped into the sky we made for the trenches. The ground heaved beneath us as a salvo of bombs splashed across our position, tearing the helmets from our heads and searing us with sand. Seconds later a nest of antipersonnel butterfly bombs fell into the CP.

I climbed from my trench to find Dunphie bleeding from a wound in his thigh. With a compress I stanched the blood and fed him my sulfa tablets. Bridge had torn off his own shirt around a blood smudge on his shoulder. A bomb had fallen between two trenches one of which was occupied by Hansen, the other by Patton's aide, Captain Richard Jenson of Pasadena, California. Jenson had been killed and his watch shattered by the concussion. A jeep driver had completely disappeared, probably as the result of a direct hit. By the time ambulances arrived, enemy artillery had zeroed in the position, and as we hurried to evacuate our wounded the first ambulance was knocked out. My own jeep stood riddled on two flat tires.

Later that afternoon Hansen carried Jenson's body into Gafsa on his jeep. Patton climbed into his car and drove immediately to the small French cemetery in the European section of the town. A score of dead lay wrapped in their mattress covers awaiting burial. Patton knelt by the body of Jenson with tears running down his face. He removed a small pair of scissors from his pocket and clipped a lock of Jenson's hair to be sent his mother. Patton folded the lock into his wallet and drove wordlessly back across town.

That afternoon Patton radioed Coningham's air support command to complain of the lack of Allied fighter interception of German air on our front. He was alarmed, as I was, by the demoralizing effect of enemy air on the front-line troops.

And in summarizing the enemy air activity for that day, II Corps G-3 wrote in his sitrep (situation report) for April 1:

> Forward troops have been continuously bombed all morning. Total lack of air cover for our units has allowed German air force to operate almost at will. Enemy aircraft have bombed all division CP's and concentrated on units supporting the main effort.

To Patton there came in reply a tart rebuke from Coningham, commander of the Tactical Air Force. After contesting the accuracy of the II Corps sitrep, he radioed Patton:

> It is to be assumed that intention was not to stampede local American air command into purely defensive action. It is also assumed that there was no intention to adopt discredited practise of using air force as an alibi for lack of success on ground. If sitrep is in earnest and balanced against . . . facts *it can only be assumed that II Corps personnel concerned are not battleworthy in terms of present operations.*[*]

In view of outstandingly efficient and successful work of American air

*Italics mine.

command concerned it is requested that such inaccurate and exaggerated reports should cease. 12 Air Support Command have been instructed not to allow their brilliant and conscientious air support of II Corps to be affected by this false cry of wolf.

Then to make matters worse, Coningham sent a copy of his TWX to every senior commander in the Mediterranean.

No sooner had Patton read the radio than he was on the phone to Algiers. Eisenhower attempted to soothe the now thoroughly enraged Patton and promised him an apology from Coningham for II Corps.

The "apology," however, consisted only of a curt 27-word message to all commands asking that Coningham's previous signal be "withdrawn and cancelled."

Unwilling to either forgive or forget, Patton wrote a letter of record to Eisenhower.

He was, he declared, "quite mad and very disgusted" by Coningham's "altogether inadequate apology to the United States troops, many of whom have marched and fought over hostile country since the 17th [of March]. . . ."

To prevent the incident from further rupturing the Allied command Eisenhower ordered Coningham to corps with a personal apology for Patton. Then to close the issue Coningham radioed the commanders to whom he had sent copies of his original TWX.

The misunderstanding had resulted, he explained, from an error in transmission. Instead of reading "Two Corps personnel concerned," he said, "the TWX should have read 'few corps personnel.'"

Fortunately, episodes such as these were infrequent but they help to illustrate the sensitivity that exists among Allied commands—a sensitivity that can result in bitter misunderstanding under the most trivial of circumstances. No further disciplinary action was taken by Eisenhower against Coningham.

To make certain that we had been thoroughly appeased, Air Chief Marshal Tedder visited Gafsa on April 3 with Tooey Spaatz to explore the need for improvement in Allied fighter cover and air support. They met with us in a small room of the gendarmerie building.

Tedder had scarcely repeated the air force claim of Allied air supremacy in the Mediterranean theater when four Focke-Wulf-190's sped in over the city. Strafing the streets of Gafsa, they stampeded a camel caravan past our door. At the end of the run they dropped their bombs.

Plaster flaked from the ceiling and when we went to open the door, I found that the concussion had wedged it tightly shut.

Tedder packed his pipe, looked up mischievously from the table, and smiled. Tooey looked out the window. He turned to Patton and shook his head. "Now how in hell did you ever manage to stage that."

"I'll be damned if I know," George shouted back, "but if I could find the sonsabitches who flew those planes, I'd mail them each a medal!"

Farther north at Maknassy where Ward was engaged on a secondary diversion, his 1st Armored Division had reached the gateway to the coastal plain. But there his advance was halted under fire from the enemy-held shoulders.

Patton's directive from Alexander had called for a light armored raid against a German airdrome ten miles beyond that pass on the rail line to the coast. Ward did his best to break through but each time his tanks were thrown back. Exasperated by these failures, Patton charged Ward with timidity in the execution of his mission. This was a hasty conclusion hardly substantiated by the facts at Maknassy.

Ward's failure did not derive from his lack of will to attack. Before he could break his tanks through that pass he had first to take the shoulders. Before he could take those shoulders he required more infantry than Patton had allotted him for the task.

One hill held the key to that position and Patton waited impatiently for word from Ward that it had been taken. When none came by March 23 George rang Ward at his CP near the deserted rail depot at Maknassy.

"Pink, you got that hill yet?" he asked, pausing for a moment. "I don't want any goddamed excuses, I want you to go out there and get that hill. You lead the attack personally. Don't come back till you've got it."

Ward put on his helmet, picked up a carbine, and went out to direct a night assault. Once again the infantry stormed up the hill, this time with Ward at its head. But once again the enemy refused to budge and the attackers were driven back. Ward returned at dawn wounded in the eye.

By now Patton's patience was exhausted. But even though he had ordered Major General Ernest N. Harmon up from the 2d Armored in Morocco to take command of the 1st, he could not bring himself to tell Ward that he was relieved.

Finally one morning at breakfast shortly before Harmon arrived, Patton wished the job on me. "Look, Brad," he said, "you're a friend of Pinky Ward's. Go up there and tell him why I've got to let him go."

My news did not come as a surprise to Ward; he had expected it momentarily, for he was convinced Patton could not understand the peculiarities of his position. Although under the circumstances I would not have relieved Ward, there were instances in Europe where I relieved commanders for their failure to move fast enough. And it is possible that some were the victims of circumstance. For how can the blame for failure be laid fairly on a single man when there are in reality so many factors that can affect the outcome of any battle? Yet each commander must always assume total responsibility for every individual in his command. If his battalion or regimental commanders fail him in the attack, then he must relieve them or be relieved himself. Many a division commander has failed not because he lacked the capacity for command but only because he declined to be hard enough on his subordinate commanders.

In the last analysis, however, the issue of relief resolves itself into one of mutual confidence. Though I disagreed with Patton's relief of Ward, the relationship between them had become so demoralized by distrust that it was better severed than patched up.

Ward was returned to the United States and in June, 1943, took command of the Tank Destroyer Center at Camp Hood. In January, 1945, he again went overseas in command of the 20th Armored Division.

In the early morning of April 6 Montgomery attacked again up the coastal plains, this time to dislodge the enemy from the Wadi Akarit, a defensive position to which he had fallen back when driven out of the Mareth Line. With their sharp kukris Gurkhas first infiltrated into the enemy lines and at dawn a barrage of massed guns signaled this final attack against the Axis in Southern Tunisia. From Wadi Akarit the road lay open to Enfidaville in the mountains below Tunis.

On April 7 Alexander sent word to Patton that the time had now come for all-out aid to the Eighth Army. George was to push aggressively down the Gabès road, stab into the flank of the retreating German, and make juncture with Montgomery's forces to close the

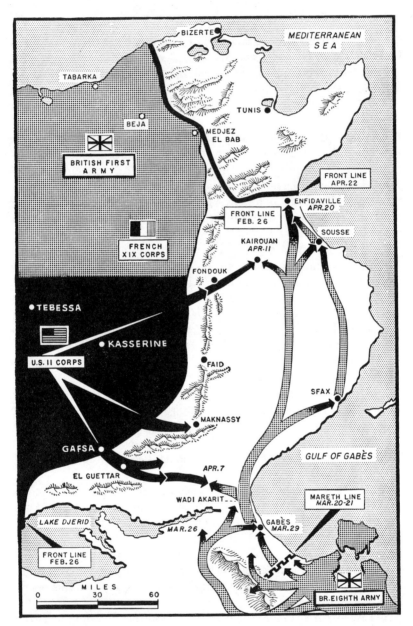

While II Corps prodded the enemy on his flank, Montgomery swept around the Mareth Line to join both Allied fronts together before pushing up the Mediterranean coast to the mountain range that shielded Tunis.

Allied ring. At 9:30 that morning he ordered Benson to "go like hell for the Mediterranean coast"—or until he ran into the enemy falling back from Montgomery's attack.

Within seven hours Benson's tanks had plunged 20 miles across the Eighth Army's boundary, and at 4:10 that afternoon the Eastern and Western Allied forces joined. Alexander had now closed his pincer on the enemy in Tunisia. The Allied forces were drawn into a single front for their final assault against the combined forces of von Arnim and Messe.

Several days before the juncture Alexander had engineered another threat to the enemy's flank and rear. An Allied force was to attack through the holy city of Kairouan, down the road to Sousse on the sea, to cut the enemy off. But to reach Kairouan it would first be necessary to force a pass through the Dorsal at Fondouk. A provisional or makeshift corps was formed for this attack under the British command of Lieutenant General John T. Crocker.

Crocker rejected Ryder's plan for a feint and encirclement of the main enemy position, demanding instead that he take it by frontal attack. As a result, the 34th was rebuffed with heavy losses in its initial assault, and the British suffered severe casualties in attempting to force the pass. Eventually Crocker took Fondouk and pushed on to Kairouan, but by then the enemy had withdrawn north to Sousse into the hills of Enfidaville.

Irritated by the enemy's escape, Crocker went out of his way to criticize the 34th Division, holding it responsible for the failure of his mission. Ryder flatly refuted Crocker's charges of inexperience and excessive caution. The attack failed, he contended, primarily because of Crocker's scheme of attack. Because of Ryder's reputation for excellent tactical judgment I tended to side with him.

As a result of Crocker's outburst, however, the 34th was blacklisted in Alexander's Army Group headquarters and his staff there proposed that it be pulled out of the line for training in the rear. Until now the 34th had been scheduled to join the 9th Division as part of the II Corps' Bizerte campaign.

When I learned of these British plans to scuttle the 34th and run it through a humiliating round of training, I warned Patton that any such withdrawal would dishearten the division and wreck its morale. The 34th was no better and no worse than our other II Corps divisions, but it was in need of self-confidence, the self-confidence that comes from winning battles and killing Germans.

"Just give Ryder an objective he can take," I told Patton, "and no one will have to worry any more about the 34th. If Alexander will give me the division for our push up on the north, I'll *guarantee* him that it makes good."

With George's consent I flew back to Alexander's headquarters at Haidra.

Alexander was no less distressed than we over Crocker's recrimination on the "failure of the 34th." Not only was he anxious to make amends, but as a former division commander himself he instantly saw what I meant when I spoke of the need for self-confidence in a combat unit.

"But my staff tells me the 34th is badly in need of further training," he said.

"Give me the division," I pleaded, "and I'll promise you they take and hold their very first objective. They'll take it if I have to support them with every gun in the corps."

Alexander laughed. "Take them," he said, "they're yours."

The projected move of II Corps to the northern end of the Allied line had originally contemplated the employment of two and one-half divisions on that 36-mile front. The sector extended from the road center of Beja beyond the Sedjenane Valley to the north shore.

It had been held defensively by one British infantry division and two additional brigades. Alexander's staff had estimated the capacity of its roadnet at two and one-half divisions in the attack. They were to consist of the 1st and 9th Infantry Divisions and half of the 1st Armored. By adding the 34th Division to this line-up we could increase our infantry strength by half again as much and greatly enlarge the corps' offensive power.

But when Alexander told his Group supply chief of this decision to give us the 34th, the latter frowned. "I must remind you, sir," he said, addressing Alexander, "that an additional division cannot be supported on that front. The roads won't take any more."

Alexander looked to me.

"Give us the division and we'll supply it," I said, for I was confident that we could beat the British estimate by at least 50 per cent.

Wilson proved me a conservative gambler; we not only exceeded the British estimates, we doubled them instead.

By April 10 the move of II Corps was under way to that northern front, 200 miles across the British line of supply. There was an air of festivity in Gafsa as the troops rolled back from El Guettar, tanned, lean, and cocky. Camel trains dodged the rattling convoys as tens of thousands of troops poured north to pursue the enemy to his escape ports.

During the 25 days of that Southern Tunisian campaign we had suffered a total of 5,893 casualties, of whom 794 were dead. In his afteraction report Patton declined to estimate enemy losses. G-2 had previously indicated we were opposed by 20,000 troops in the El Guettar corridor, while 10,000 held us at the Maknassy gap. Another 7,000 were dispersed elsewhere across the II Corps front. Of these 37,000 enemy troops—most of them from first-class units—a total of 4,680 prisoners were taken, 4,200 of them Italians.

Altogether more than 30,000 vehicles and 110,000 men were involved in this secret move to the Bizerte sector. And to judge by the enemy's surprise in the north, it took him unawares. The intricate maneuver had been worked out in the G-3 section of II Corps. It called for a complex timetable not only in crisscrossing routes of supply but in the relief of British divisions until then assigned to that front. Moreover the shift involved not only the movement of vehicles and men but the transfer of our huge base of supply from Tebessa to Beja. During the El Guettar campaign more than a thousand tons of supply, most of it ammunition, rolled down the road from Tebessa to the front each day.

With this phase of the campaign ended, Patton was to resume command of I Armored Corps where planning for the Sicilian invasion had reached a critical stage. I Armored Corps was now slated to become the American Seventh Army on that invasion, although the change-over would not be made until the ships had put to sea. Meanwhile Mark Clark's headquarters had been designated the Fifth Army for the Salerno invasion.

The evening before he left Gafsa to return to Rabat, Patton spoke of the preparations for the Sicilian invasion. Major General Ernest J. Dawley's VI Corps had just arrived in Africa to command the assault force in Patton's Army.

"Bradley," Patton said, "how would you like to go with me and take II Corps into Sicily?"

"In place of Dawley?" I asked.

He nodded. "I've worked with you and I've got confidence in you. On the other hand I don't know what in hell Dawley can do. If you've got no objection, I'm going to ask Ike to fix it up."

A few days later Eisenhower acceded to Patton's request, and II

Corps was substituted for the VI Corps on the Sicilian landing. Dawley was shifted to Clark's Fifth Army for the Salerno invasion.

On April 15 Patton loaded his staff back into his scout cars for the long trip to Rabat.

At midnight the "deputy" was removed from my title and I became commander of II Corps.

Because the change-over was still secret I dared not write to my wife and tell her of the promotion.

6: *Objective: Bizerte*

THOUGH NOW HOPELESSLY CORNERED IN THE SHRINK-
ing tip of Tunisia, the Axis chose to prolong its costly struggle for
time, hoping to deadlock our Mediterranean forces and thus forestall
a summertime campaign against some other objective.

Persistent reports reached us on the evacuation of Wehrmacht
generals, but for the most part traffic continued in the opposite direction. The Luftwaffe had scraped together its remaining transport
aircraft to haul daily reinforcements into the embattled corner from
fields in Sicily. Huge flights of JU-52's, closely screened by fighters,
risked Allied interceptors to feed the build-up. In desperation the
Axis had even pressed into service the huge six-motored Merseberg
transports. Slow and boxlike, they nevertheless carried 120 men on
each flight. But with their outdated French motors they lumbered
across the Mediterranean at 140 miles per hour and offered easy
pickings for the Allied fighters.

Although Alexander with vastly superior forces had cornered his
quarry, the rough Tunisian terrain partly offset this advantage. For
nature had thrown a perimeter mountain wall around the plains that
stretched toward the ports of Bizerte and Tunis. In the hills of
Enfidaville on the east coast of the Mediterranean Montgomery
found the path of his Eighth Army blocked by a barrier of stony
djebels. To the left of Montgomery three poorly equipped divisions
of General Louis Marie Koeltz' XIX French Corps probed against
that continuing line. Farther left where the line bent north toward the

Mediterranean coast, Anderson's First Army waited with four infantry and two armored divisions for the sledge-hammer blow designed to carry it through those mountains across the plains to Tunis. And to the left of Anderson, II Corps had now deployed its one armored and three infantry divisions across the mountainous belt that led into the thicket of the Sedjenane Valley high up on the Mediterranean north coast.

Estimates of enemy strength within that defensive belt varied from headquarters to headquarters, although none approached the quarter-million PWs we eventually took out of that trap.

On April 14, the day before Patton's departure from II Corps, Alexander called a strategy conference on this final phase of the

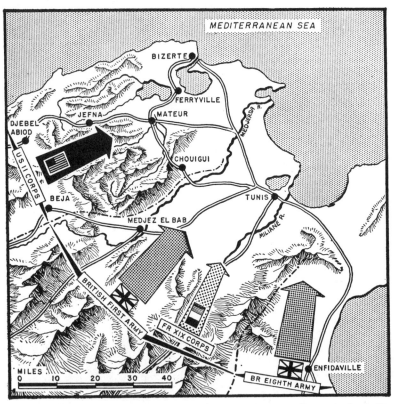

With II Corps assigned to a front of its own north of Beja, Alexander directed his Allied forces toward the last Axis bridgehead in North Africa.

Tunisian campaign at his Group headquarters in Haidra. Eisenhower flew in from Algiers and Anderson came down from First Army. Monty, as was to be his custom, did not attend. Instead, Alexander's chief of staff had called on Montgomery several days before to coordinate his Eighth Army's Enfidaville offensive with that of the Western forces.

Alexander was to concentrate his Western forces in the middle of the line on Anderson's front and strike through Medjez el Bab to the city of Tunis. Thereafter, he was to divide his effort to the north and the south. While one British column headed north to assist II Corps in taking Bizerte, the other was to cut off the escape route into Cape Bon.

Both the Eighth Army and II Corps were to attack primarily in an effort not to seize terrain but to draw off the enemy's strength on Anderson's First Army front. Thus it was not anticipated that II Corps would take Bizerte alone. Instead it was to protect the left flank of Anderson's drive on Tunis and maneuver itself into position for a combined attack with the British on Bizerte. No one, not even Alexander, as yet believed we possessed the strength to take Bizerte alone.

Although II Corps was to remain directly under command of Alexander's 18th Army Group, Anderson asked for authority to coordinate our operations with those of his First Army. But even though this meant my orders were to come through Anderson rather than directly from Alexander, I did not object. Since Anderson was to carry the main effort, I thought him within his rights in asking for authority to safeguard his flanks.

Nevertheless to avoid hamstringing us within Anderson's command Alexander offered me direct access to his headquarters at any time. I was not, he said, to be boxed in a British Army command. Fortunately, I had to take advantage of that invitation only once.

Meanwhile in Washington General Marshall showed increasing concern over the unflattering stories filed by U. S. newsmen following the Gafsa campaign. The Chief of Staff cautioned Eisenhower that the U. S. command was being criticized for failure to break through to the sea and cut off the enemy in the south. General Marshall's letter emphasized the plea I had made to Eisenhower on the prestige value of the coming Northern Tunisian campaign. Two weeks before, while making the proposal, I feared Eisenhower might misinterpret my move as a personal maneuver for a bigger piece of the final

campaign. But now General Marshall's letter had banished any likelihood of Ike's mistaking my motives. My apprehension was further
dispelled in a letter Eisenhower addressed to me on the eve of the
campaign.

The coming phase of . . . operations is of special significance to the
American forces involved. . . . There is no blinking the fact that we
have had certain disappointments. . . . We must overcome these difficulties and prove to the world that the four Amercian divisions now on the
front can perform in a way that will at least do full credit to the material
we have and the quality of our leadership. . . .

In helping Anderson to advance by drawing enemy strength from
his front, we anticipated that we would attract substantially greater
resistance against our offensive toward Bizerte. Initially I was to have
been given but one half of the 1st Armored Division. I pulled the
remaining half of that division up into Anderson's sector. And then
on the pretext of helping Anderson to clear his roads, I moved it the
rest of the way up to my II Corps front.

Thus instead of the two and one-half American divisions originally
allowed us by Army Group, we now had a total of four, with three
on the line and an armored in reserve. With this accumulation of
strength we began to expand on our ambitions.

No one was better pleased than Harmon over the assembly of his
1st Armored Division in reserve for a tank breakthrough. For he was
impatient to prove the aggressiveness of his new division, almost as
impatient as he was with British delay on his move north from
Tebessa.

Harmon had arrived in Beja storming over the delays en route,
complaining bitterly of the British habit of halting for afternoon
tea.

"Relax, Ernie," I told him, "the British have been drinking tea
every afternoon, war or no war, for three hundred years. They'll be
doing it for another thousand. You can't buck all that tradition. Next
time they stop, you stop too, and go up and have some tea with
them."

I remained in Gafsa until the CP had been moved and after a long
day's drive by jeep up the Tunisian valleys now covered in red
blankets of poppies, I pulled into Beja on the evening of April 15.
The CP had been crowded into a grove on the northeast edge of

the town. The tents had been pitched so closely that had enemy air detected our hiding, a single stick of bombs could have cleaned us out. I ordered the commandant to split the headquarters and move half of it up the side of a hill to where the mayor of Beja lived on a handsome farm. There we found that the British had been in residence the previous winter. The garden in which we pitched our tents was conveniently serpentined with trenches. From our tents beneath the flowering figs and rose arbors, we could see the flash of enemy guns on the front.

A neat French colonial city, intersected by a web of strategic roads to both Tunis and Bizerte, Beja stood on the site of an ancient Roman city that had once been sacked by the Vandals. However, typhus had swept the white-stuccoed city with the coming of spring thaws and its bomb-shattered streets were mostly empty. Yellow signs lettered with the word TYPHUS warned our troops to give the town a wide berth.

On the Clos de Beja the mayor and his wife welcomed us into their home. Reluctant to evict them, however, we used only a storehouse room for our war room. The remainder of the offices was set up in conventional staff blackout tents. Officers bunked in the canvas igloos corps had manufactured in Oran and the troops took over the barn.

Two days after his strategy conference at Haidra, Alexander published the Army Group directive to his command. Anderson then summoned us to a meeting of corps commanders on April 18. We were to make oral presentations of our corps plans, after which Anderson would publish his Army order.

British First Army was headquartered on a farm near the mountaintop monastery of Thibar. There I found General Crocker of the IX British Corps, Major General C. W. Allfrey of the V British Corps, and General Koeltz of the XIX French Corps. Each of us carried the large, marked maps to be used in the discussion of our plans. Koeltz, unfortunately, spoke no English. As he traced his plan across a map, I tried to follow him as best I could with my rusty West Point French. When Koeltz apologized for not presenting his plan in English, Anderson waved him airily on. "Of course, everyone here understands French," he said.

I didn't—but I suffered in silence.

Although Bizerte was to be the eventual objective of II Corps, Anderson looked on our initial attack essentially as a diversionary

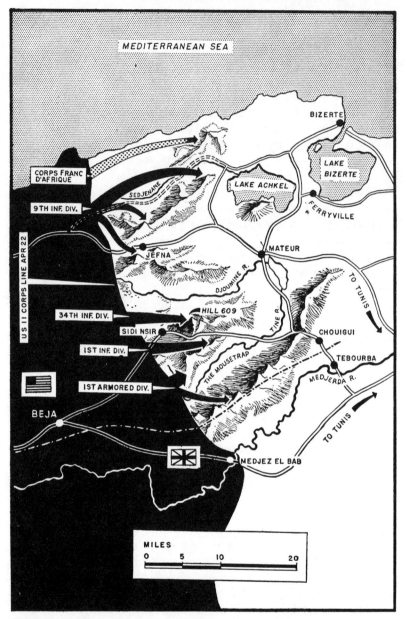

MEDITERRANEAN SEA

BIZERTE

LAKE BIZERTE

CORPS FRANC D'AFRIQUE

SEDJENANE

LAKE ACHKEL

FERRYVILLE

9TH INF. DIV.

JEFNA

MATEUR

DJOUNINE R.

US II CORPS LINE APR 22

34TH INF. DIV.

HILL 609

TINE R.

TO TUNIS

SIDI NSIR

CHOUIGUI

1ST INF. DIV.

THE MOUSETRAP

TEBOURBA

MEDJERDA R.

1ST ARMORED DIV.

BEJA

TO TUNIS

MEDJEZ EL BAB

MILES

0   5   10   20

While the main force of II Corps was to clear the mountains that guarded the Mousetrap Valley in preparation for a tank breakthrough to Mateur, the 9th Infantry Division was to press on toward Bizerte up the Sedjenane Valley.

The Hill that Saved a Division: "From the white crown of Hill 609, the enemy could look down across the Mousetrap Valley to those twin ridge lines that defined it. With the fall of Hill 609, the enemy hastily retreated, and on its summit the 34th Division recaptured the confidence it had lost at Fondouk."

Unconditional Surrender, Tunisia: "I experienced a feeling of great elation on that bright May morning when I drove north from Mateur, past an unending column of trucks and carts loaded with troops of the Afrika Korps heading toward our PW cage on the flats before Djebel Achkel." (May, 1943.)

one, aimed to draw the enemy's strength away from the British main offensive toward Tunis. To be sure, the terrain that blocked our II Corps front was not suited for a speedy advance.

Beyond Beja a valley opened toward Mateur, but like the corridor at El Guettar it was hemmed between parallel ranges of mountains. Farther north our path was blocked by the strong Jefna position where the British that previous winter had splintered an infantry brigade in a vain effort to force it. On the rim of the Mediterranean to the north, the Sedjenane Valley was covered with an almost impassable thicket.

Two principal roads traversed this sector. The first in the north ran from Djebel Abiod through Jefna to Mateur. The other, to the south, skirted the Tine River valley from Beja to Mateur. In addition to these there were two unimproved roads or trails. One led up the Sedjenane Valley toward Bizerte, while the other followed the Tine River. Of the two principal routes, the shorter ran through Jefna, from Djebel Abiod to Mateur on the brink of the salt plain that led to Bizerte. But it ran through that narrow neck where the Green and Bald Hills closed together to form the Jefna position. I knew there was little likelihood of our forcing this path from the front.

Although the one in the south that ran down the Tine River looked the more inviting, it was scarcely less formidable than the one in the north. For the British told us the German had fortified the mountains that rimmed that valley. Any attempt to force it with power could be splintered by antitank guns.

Dickson thereupon dubbed that path the "Mousetrap Valley," and a draftsman in G-2 painted a trap with wide-open jaws on the acetate facing over the map.

Apart from those enemy fortifications, this Mousetrap Valley formed so plausible an approach for tank attack that it attracted Eisenhower's attention. On April 16 he wrote me, " . . . the southern portion of your sector appears to be reasonably suited for tank employment and it is in that area . . . you will be expected to make your main effort, at least in the initial stages."

Unfortunately Ike did not have my intelligence reports on enemy antitank defenses. This route that looked as though it had been made to order could not be used until first we had cleared those hills that rimmed it to the north and south.

At the time of Anderson's meeting near Thibar I had not yet been able to make a reconnaissance of the terrain. As a result, my plans had to be drawn from a searching study of the maps. Hansen had colored in contours to highlight the hills and I spent hours probing the relative tactical importance of those positions. When on April 18 I drove to Thibar, I had already spotted in my mind every important djebel on the II Corps front.

It was apparent from the outset in the mountainous terrain that opposed us that our tactics were to be governed by the character of this terrain. Because the barren djebels commanded unobstructed observation of the treeless plains below them, we could not advance anywhere down the valleys until we first took those commanding hills. And because several key djebels dominated the lesser ones, it became clear that our principal effort would be directed against those strategic positions. I proposed, therefore, to work my way with infantry from djebel to djebel, obtaining artillery observation on each successive hill, until eventually the whole chain of djebels fell, delivering the valleys into our hands.

Though ostensibly slower because this meant scaling each successive djebel, I was convinced on the basis of Patton's campaign at El Guettar that by going after those positions methodically we could eventually press a tank attack up the Mousetrap Valley and gain Mateur.

These tactics meant that the infantry would bear the brunt of attack until Harmon's tanks were committed through a path the infantry had cleared. But while the doughboy would be forced to hike the long way down the spine of those hills, the extra effort might also better his chances of reaching Bizerte alive. In the long run this proved to be true, and we were able to save many lives by these tactics.

Because our attack was to be combined with the British for a jump-off on April 23, I could count on only two U. S. divisions in the initial stages. The remaining two were still en route north. On April 19, I published the II Corps attack order. It was a brief half-page document with a single illustrative overlay map.

The 9th Division on our left was to shun the macadam road that led into the mountain trap at Jefna and instead hack its way through the thicket of the Sedjenane Valley. From there Eddy could outflank the impenetrable Jefna position and train his artillery on its single supply road to the rear. Thus he could force the enemy out of position while pushing on toward Bizerte. On the right of our II Corps sector the 1st Division was to clear the Mousetrap and push across the valley to the Chouigui Hills where we were to join forces with Anderson for the attack toward Bizerte. To Allen's division I attached the regiment of armored infantry from the 1st Armored Division. This regiment was to clean up the south rim of the Mousetrap and keep contact with the British on its right. Meanwhile Harmon's tanks were to be held in reserve at the gate of the Mousetrap until the valley floor was cleared and we could break through to Mateur in a blitz attack.

Realizing that we would have difficulty in shifting our supply lines from Tebessa, Anderson had suggested that we might want to delay our jump-off for a day and follow his starting attack on April 24. One day's delay would not have seriously dislocated the plan but I was determined to get off at the same time as the British if we possibly could.

Every morning at the daily staff meeting Wilson held the key to our plans as he read off the cumulative tonnage trucked to the front the day before. But despite the resourcefulness of G-4, those tonnage totals continued to climb at an agonizingly slow rate.

To speed this build-up we had established a one-way road system to the front from the Mediterranean port of Tebarka. We stripped the divisions of their tactical vehicles and, by doubling the crews on each, ran them for a continuous stretch of 72 hours in convoy without a break. Whereas the British hauled no more than a single one-way load each day, we crowded one round trip, and often two, into each 24 hours.

Until then the threat of enemy attack by air had caused the Allies to restrict night motor movements to slow-moving convoys in blackout lights. This not only slowed our night convoys to a crawl but it resulted in frequent accidents on the steep mountain roads.

"Bob," I said to Wilson one morning after his figures had indicated that we might not reach our supply target by April 23, "let's forget this blackout business and run those trucks at night with lights."

"But what about enemy, sir?" Bill Kean protested.

"We'll lose fewer trucks to air," I said, "than we will through accidents in blackout driving." Wilson agreed. That night the convoys were run with lights, and soon the tonnage levels began to pick up.

It was not until midnight of April 20 that Wilson promised flatly that we would make our supply target in time for the jump-off. He came into my tent as I was studying a captured German map.

"We're going to make it, General," he said. "You can definitely plan to go with the British on April 23."

By this time the II Corps forward echelon had been shaken down to a convenient size. We opened the morning briefings to all officers that each might be cut in on the other's thinking. And we pitched a small mess tent next to the big one where I could discuss operations with Kean and my chief staff officers at mealtimes.

Almost immediately after taking command of the corps I changed Patton's breakfast hour to 8:30 A.M. It vastly improved the efficiency of command at headquarters.

To identify hills, road junctions, and towns without giving our plans away in the event of an enemy tap on the wire, I had key features numbered on my war map and gave copies of those numbers to the division commanders. It was a makeshift private code, lax enough to cause Dickson worry over the security of our plans.

One morning when I called Allen, he referred to an obscure crossroad by its number in this private code.

"Just a minute, Terry," I said. "I can't find that number on my map."

"Well, listen carefully, Brad," he said. "The enemy may be listening in. I'll say the name of the place as fast as I can."

Dickson overheard this conversation and threw up his hands. "Security wouldn't be much of a problem," he said, "if only there were fewer generals in the army."

Before the attack jumped off I went out by jeep to see the division commanders and have a look at their terrain. It was my second visit to Manton Eddy's CP up in the Sedjenane Valley, where the MP's directing traffic wore Arab burnooses so as not to betray his location to enemy air.

A nine-mile gap had been left in the corps line between Eddy's sector in the north and Terry Allen's advance on the south. Although we patrolled this gap with a reconnaissance force, Eddy confessed that he was uneasy over this wide exposure on his right flank.

"Manton," I reassured him, "nothing's going to come through that gap. Why Bill Kean and I will go up with rifles to stop anything that might squeeze through."

Eddy smiled but he was unconvinced. When he protested that the enemy could slip a battalion or even a regiment through that gap in our line, I was forced to admit that perhaps he could.

"But what could he do even if he did get through?" I said. "There's nothing there but mountains and scrub thicket; there's not a single road through the entire gap. Even battalions won't go very far if they can't move their trucks behind them."

We could not have plugged that gap without spreading our attacking forces too thinly elsewhere on the corps front. I took a calculated risk in leaving that gap open. Despite Manton's apprehension, the enemy never made a move to come through. He was far too busy holding his front together.

Terry Allen's combat-wise infantrymen with the Big Red One on their shoulders had headquartered on the Beja-Mateur road in a barnyard piled high with steaming manure. Here, more than anywhere else on the line, an air of easy relaxation hid the tension that comes on the eve of attack. Not only was the 1st thoroughly blooded, but it had come overseas better staffed than most divisions. For unlike the others it had not been stripped for training cadres—it got shipped out too soon.

The initiative of the 1st Division was apparent even in Allen's mess, where his rough table boasted rare roast beef while the other division CO's made do with conventional tinned rations. The meat, Terry explained, was "casualty" beef, from cattle accidentally killed by enemy fire. Despite the warnings of vets on sick cattle, those casualties happened with suspicious frequency. Terry sat with his black hair disheveled, a squinty grin on his face. He wore the same dark green shirt and trousers he had worn through the Gafsa campaign. His orderly had sewn creases into his pants but they had long since bagged out. The aluminum stars he wore had been taken from an Italian private.

Although Terry had become a hero to his troops, he was known as a maverick among the senior commanders. Always fighting to keep his 1st from "being dumped on by the high command," Terry was fiercely antagonistic to any echelon above that of division. As a result he was inclined to be stubborn and independent. Skillful, adept, and aggressive, he frequently ignored orders and fought in his own way. I found it difficult to persuade Terry to put his pressure where I thought it should go. He would halfway agree on a plan, but somehow once the battle started this agreement seemed to be forgotten.

Montgomery's Eighth Army over on the extreme right wing of the Allied line was to break through the hills of Enfidaville on the coast three days before Anderson jumped off in the west. Alexander hoped Montgomery would draw German resistance from Anderson's front and soften the latter's path to Tunis. Montgomery's tough desert forces advanced into the Enfidaville hills, but they found themselves in strange terrain and the attack failed.

Meanwhile the enemy on Anderson's front sensed the growing concentration of British strength on that path to Tunis. Rather than wait for First Army to strike, von Arnim took the initiative and threw his crack Hermann Goering Division supported by Tigers of the 10th Panzer Division into a spoiling attack against Anderson's IX Corps. The offensive had been designed to throw First Army off balance and gain the enemy a few days' more time. The British held stoutly to their position and the German retired after having lost 33 of his badly needed tanks.

Despite von Arnim's interference, the British jumped off as scheduled on the following day.

7 : *End of the Afrika Korps*

EARLY ON THE MORNING OF GOOD FRIDAY, APRIL 23, 1943, I climbed the hill behind the Clos de Beja as the sky to the east exploded in artillery fire.

I waited impatiently for the first light reports and when they revealed little except to confirm that the attack had gone off on time, I browsed nervously through the CP. I dared not leave my headquarters for a closer check in the field for it was at Beja that our communications were centered; it was there that I could best influence the battle.

Two days before the jump-off in this final offensive of the Tunisian campaign, I carted my mapboard off to the press camp nearby to brief the correspondents there on our corps plan. This was my first press briefing and it marked the start of a long friendship with many of those hard-working newsmen. Two years later several of that original band accompanied me to the Elbe to celebrate our juncture with the Russians and the end of the war.

Throughout the war many of these newsmen were better informed on pending operations than some members of my staff. Together they represented the public interest, and they would have been poorly equipped to evaluate our current operations had they not been adequately informed on what was to come. But though they were privy to many of our secrets, not once during the war did a newsman accredited to my command willfully violate a confidence of mine.

As the 1st Division advanced along the rim of the Mousetrap, it found itself raked by artillery fire from a range of higher hills to the north. Before pushing on, therefore, it became necessary for us to drive the enemy out of those higher hills and deny him artillery observation of our movements.

From the 1st Division sector we could look down on a road that ran diagonally from the rail stop at Sidi Nsir, across the Mousetrap Valley to the far-off brown hills of Chouigui. Beyond that road, on the northern rim of the Mousetrap, the bald white face of a djebel soared into the African sky. It was known as Hill 609, since this was its altitude in meters given on our French maps. The djebel was surrounded by a number of lesser hills. By April 26, after only three days of attack, it had become clear that until 609 was taken and the

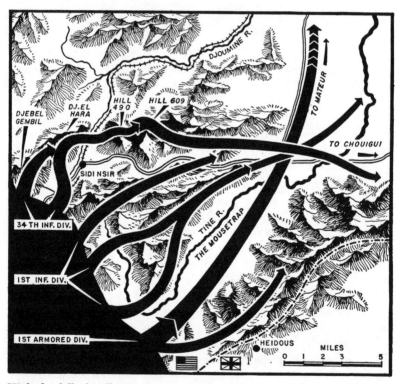

With the fall of Hill 609, the Mousetrap Valley was cleared and Harmon rushed his tanks in the direction of Mateur. Meanwhile the 1st and 34th Divisions crossed each other's path in the U. S. advance toward Chouigui.

enemy driven off its summit the 1st Division could not advance any farther down the rim of the Mousetrap Valley. From 609 the enemy had pinpointed deadly artillery fire on Allen's troops in the unsheltered rocky djebels below it. And yet to take Hill 609 it would first be necessary to clear the outpost positions around it. This massive hill had become the key to any farther advance in the direction of Mateur.

By now Ryder's 34th Division had moved into the II Corps sector after its unhappy experience at Fondouk. Remembering the promise I had made Alexander, I picked the 34th to go after 609.

"Get me that hill," I told Ryder, "and you'll break up the enemy's defenses clear across our front. Take it and no one will ever again doubt the toughness of your division."

To take Hill 609 Ryder had first to take both Djebel el Hara and Hill 490 which covered its approach from the west. He outlined a plan to take both those preliminary barriers in a single attack. On learning of the plan, I worried—for Ryder proposed to take a bigger bite than I could guarantee on a starting attack.

On the evening of April 27 a battalion of the 34th moved out in night attack against Djebel el Hara. It attempted an enveloping movement in the dark over a route that could not be reconnoitered by daylight. When dawn broke over the cold mountains the battalion found itself storming the hill from which it had moved out the night before.

It immediately reorganized and prepared for a fresh daylight assault.

I called Brigadier General Charles E. Hart, my corps artilleryman, to support the 34th with every gun in II Corps that could lay a shell on Djebel el Hara.

"We'll give them a serenade," he promised, "and sweeten it with everything we've got." The firing was to start at 4 p.m. that day.

Shortly after 3:30 on the afternoon of April 28, the 34th signaled that it had taken Djebel el Hara. I met Hart racing down the road in his jeep to turn off the artillery concentration.

With the capture of both objectives the 34th jockeyed into position to assault the rocky face of Hill 609. Just as soon as 609 was cleared we could speed up Allen's advance down the rim of the Mousetrap and set the stage for Harmon's breakthrough.

Perhaps because his drive in the First Army sector to the south was not going as rapidly as he had anticipated, Anderson began to show signs of impatience. On the morning of April 27 he telephoned Kean to urge that II Corps push ahead more quickly toward the Chouigui Pass.

"Never mind the enemy opposing you at Sidi Nsir," Anderson said, ignoring the strategic character of Hill 609 and its surrounding terrain, ". . . when you have him on a hilltop, try always to get around him. . . . I don't want you only to push the enemy back but to get behind him and capture him before he can establish a bridgehead around Bizerte."

Puzzled and shocked by these instructions for they would have upset the strategy of our offensive, Kean answered without committing himself. "We'll put on more steam, sir. I'll get your message through to General Bradley. He's out in the field."

When the message reached me I could not believe that Kean had understood Anderson correctly.

"But it's a stenographic transcript, General," he said, "I had a man on another phone."

If Anderson meant what he said, he was ordering us to call off our attacks down the spine of the hills and crawl instead through the valleys where the enemy had zeroed in every plausible route of approach. Unless the enemy was already withdrawing from our II Corps front, we could not ignore those positions in the hills without running pell-mell into the mouths of his guns. And Dickson denied any hints of enemy withdrawal on the corps front. Rather there was evidence of German reinforcement. For by our advance we had threatened to break through the mountain ring von Arnim had thrown around the plains of Tunis.

Later that day I met with Anderson in Terry Allen's CP. I outlined our plan of attack, showing him how Allen's division had been shot up by fire from Hill 609 on the north. Once again I emphasized the need for our taking those hills if we were to open the valley below them.

"Yet all this depends upon our taking Hill 609," I told him. "It is essential that we get it before pushing on toward Chouigui. Unless we do Terry will have one helluva time trying to cut that road to Chouigui."

Allen grunted in assent. Artillery fire from Hill 609 and its neighboring hills had splashed into the spines of those djebels on which he had advanced, showering his troops with shell fragments and sharp slivers of stone. Many of Terry's rifle companies had already been cut down to the size of platoons.

Anderson squinted thoughtfully at my map in following the II Corps plan. When I had finished he nodded. I ignored the message he had given Kean and Anderson said nothing more about it.

Seldom has an enemy contested a position more bitterly than did the German high on Hill 609. For he knew once that rampart fell, he had no choice but to withdraw to the east and thus open a path to Mateur on the flank of his Tunis line.

After a day of savage fighting up the hill's steep slopes, the 34th Division reached an Arab village under the cliff on the south side of 609. Higher up on the promontory, crack German infantrymen had barricaded themselves in the crevices. From those positions they continued to empty automatic fire on Ryder's troops.

When Ryder spoke to me of the possibility of flanking the hill from the rear, I offered him a company of tanks for mobile artillery support. He looked at me with mild surprise but readily accepted the help. The terrain certainly was not adapted to tanks, and no tactician would ever have recommended storming a cliff with Shermans. Yet their 75's were just what Ryder needed to blast the enemy out of those strong points.

On the morning of April 29, 17 tanks with Ryder's infantry on their tails moved up to Hill 609 from the flank and rear. They rumbled through machine-gun and mortar fire until they sighted the enemy strong points, and soon the hill echoed to their guns as they slammed shell after shell into the enemy's position.

Later a prisoner from the Barenthin Regiment who had defended Hill 609 protested our use of tanks in this attack.

"We could have held out against your infantry for another week," he boasted, "but we didn't expect to see tanks. As a matter of fact you had no right to use them. We had been told that was not tank country and as a result we had few defenses."

With this successful attack against Hill 609 the 34th rid itself of the poor reputation with which it had emerged from Fondouk. The following September Ryder sailed with his division from Tunisia to Italy. In two terrible years of campaigning in the mountains there the 34th Division put in a total of 605 days in the line. Altogether in World War II it suffered approximately 20,000 casualties—almost one and one-half times its full strength.

No longer harassed by enemy artillery fire from Hill 609, the 1st Division pressed forward in its attack up the northern rim of the

Mousetrap. Now outflanked as the result of our capture of that position, the enemy could no longer delay his withdrawal eastward into the hills of Chouigui. Here von Arnim meant to hold a last line of defense on the edge of the broad plain that opened toward the docks of Tunis.

Thus while Anderson hammered at the enemy's frontal position, II Corps in its diversionary offensive, was slipping more rapidly than anyone had anticipated around the enemy's right flank.

Meanwhile as Terry Allen advanced down the rim of the Mousetrap and across the Chouigui road, Harmon's armored infantry pushed on no less aggressively in the south. The inviting path to which Eisenhower had referred was now open to Mateur. Harmon cranked up his tanks in preparation for the breakthrough.

To the north in the Sedjenane Valley where Manton Eddy advanced apace of the Mousetrap offensive, the 9th Division was pushing on through the Sedjenane thicket in its laborious march toward Bizerte.

On Easter Sunday I motored up to the Sedjenane for a conference with Eddy. His CP tent had been dug deeply into the ground near a "Long Tom"* artillery position. Each time the battery fired, his tent top shivered as the shells rushed overhead.

Despite my frequent reassurances Manton still fretted over that open right flank. Thereafter I discovered that he would require an occasional visit from corps to put his mind at rest. For the moment he would accept my logic on the improbability of enemy attack, but within a few days those doubts would recur and Eddy would ask for another visit from corps.

This uneasiness, however, did not slow or hamper the astonishing success of Eddy's attack. With a regiment to contain the Jefna position and harry its defenders from the front, Eddy had maneuvered to the left of the Jefna position to gain a strategic position on its north and rear. By May 2 his guns commanded the solitary enemy exit from that position. The German could either stick to his position and starve or he could abandon it without further resistance. He decided to run out, which he did before Eddy could close the escape road with his infantry.

Eddy's forces in the north included not only his 9th Division but a mixture of Free French expatriates, political refugees, and Berber

*A 155-mm. long-barreled artillery piece.

tribesmen, assembled in a detachment known as the Corps Franc d'Afrique. Along that belt of hills on the Mediterranean coast where the thick cork forests were undergrown with brush to form an almost impenetrable jungle, the Corps Franc hacked a path with machetes in the direction of Bizerte.

This Corps Franc was commanded by a Colonel P. J. Magnan, who had aided Patton in his Moroccan landing. Jailed by General Nogues for aiding the Allies, Magnan was freed when Darlan went over to Eisenhower. His force included three poorly equipped battalions of infantry, another of marines, and a *tabour* or battalion of Goumes. Among his troops were Spanish Loyalists, who had sought asylum in France, and French who had escaped from Vichy. One infantry company, I was told, was commanded by a Spanish admiral, another by a Jewish doctor.

Elsewhere on the Allied line Alexander's giant Tunis offensive had slowed to a disappointing crawl. Montgomery's Eighth Army had stalled in the mountains near Enfidaville and Anderson found his path blocked by strongly emplaced enemy defenses. Faced with a stalemate, Anderson scanned the front for reinforcements that he might strengthen his First Army and break his way through.

First he telephoned me at II Corps. He asked that a regimental combat team be detached from one of our divisions and assigned First Army. At the moment II Corps was heavily engaged on both 609 and Jefna. I could not have pulled even a regiment without seriously dislocating our attack. And any dislocation could easily have forestalled Harmon's later breakthrough to Mateur.

But aside from these tactical objections, I felt that Anderson's request violated a specific agreement we had reached on the employment of American units under U. S. command. By this request he proposed to suspend that agreement and go back to the piecemeal commitment of American troops under British command. I had determined not to give in even if it meant running to Ike. For once that practice started up again, who could tell how it would end.

Anderson undoubtedly guessed the reason for my reluctance, for he insisted that a tactical crisis made it necessary that he seek aid.

"Well let me look into it with my staff," I hedged, hoping to stall for time, "I'll give you a call later."

The corps staff confirmed my fears and I phoned Anderson back.

"We'd like to help you," I told him, "but you're asking me to do something I will not agree to without direct orders from Ike."

Fortunately Eisenhower was due to visit our CP that day. I told him of Anderson's request and my reasons for rejecting it.

"Stand your ground, Brad," Ike said. "I'll see Anderson this afternoon and back you up on it."

The issue did not come up again, for on April 30 Alexander concluded that Montgomery was wasting his strength in the heavily mined hills north of Enfidaville where his Eighth Army had failed to pierce the enemy's defenses.

At that time II Corps and its American divisions still carried a vestigial complement of British officers as "advisers." When we learned of the abandonment of Montgomery's attack in the Enfidaville hills, I spoke good-humoredly to Kean.

"Let's radio Monty and ask if he wants us to send him a few American advisers to show his desert fighters how to get through those hills."

While Anderson regrouped his forces for a renewal of his attack on Tunis, II Corps busied itself with plans for the concluding phase of its campaign. With the loss of Hill 609 and the collapse of his Jefna position, the enemy south of those strong points suddenly found himself in a perilous position. He could do nothing but withdraw eastward to the next hill line, a range running north from Chouigui to the hill mass east of Mateur.

This position was part of the mountain belt that shielded Tunis from the west. If II Corps could pierce those hills at Chouigui or break through them farther north nearer Mateur, it might turn the flank of the enemy army massed between Anderson and Tunis.

Now that the Mousetrap had been cleared the time had come for commitment of Harmon's tanks on a breakthrough. He was to plunge down the Tine River to Mateur where a web of highways opened into the enemy's rear. Once Harmon cleared the Mousetrap, the 1st and 34th Divisions were to turn east, cut across the rear of Harmon's tanks, and attack into the Chouigui range. To take the Chouigui Pass through which a road ran straight to Tebourba, only 15 miles from Tunis, I chose the 34th Division even though it mean crisscrossing Ryder with the 1st, for at that time he was on the left of Terry Allen. The 1st, however, was not only exhausted from its campaign in the hills, but by this time it had absorbed more than its fair share of casualties in the djebels. To lighten its load in this closing phase of attack I assigned it a sector north of the Chouigui Pass to the left of the 34th. There it was to contain the enemy between that vital pass and Mateur.

On May 2, I signaled Ernie Harmon to cut loose with his tanks and get into Mateur. He promptly raced down the valley road to the outskirts of that city. But as he approached a bridge over a river that encircled Mateur, the enemy blew up the structure. Then while Harmon's engineers labored to put in a pontoon span the enemy wheeled up his heavy artillery and the Luftwaffe appeared overhead. The enemy had betrayed his extreme sensitivity to any further advance on this vulnerable flank of his Tunis position. From Mateur, Harmon could thrust deeply into the rear of von Arnim's entire army. The following day Harmon broke through that town.

Because the battle had now outrun Beja, I shifted the Corps CP to Sidi Nsir under the shadow of Hill 609. After a day in the field I returned to find that the commandant had hidden our headquarters far back in a narrow gulch between two steep hills. There it was bottlenecked by a single exit, and only a few enemy bombs could have demolished the installation.

The commandant looked unhappy when I called him to my tent. "Let's get out of this damned canyon in the morning," I said, "and spread the CP on the open side of the hill outside. This place looks as though we're scared to death someone might find us. By golly, I'd be ashamed to be found in such a place."

The shift started at dawn and by 10 we were dispersed on the forward slope of an open hill facing 609. Eisenhower arrived for lunch at noon. He looked approvingly around the landscape where our CP stood boldly on the hill as if to defy enemy air attack.

"Brad," he clasped me on the shoulder, "I'm sure glad to see you spread out like this in the open. Once when I visited Fredendall in his CP near Tebessa I found II Corps dug into the damnedest canyon you ever saw."

Kean glanced my way and smiled. I held a poker face and admitted nothing.

By May 4 Anderson had massed his reinforced First Army on a narrow front preparatory to breaking his way up the Medjerda Valley to Tunis. Two infantry divisions were to start the attack by tearing a 3,000-yard gap into the enemy's lines. Anderson was to plunge through that gap with two armored divisions. After overrunning the enemy's antitank defenses those tanks were to speed on to Tunis. D day for this final attack was set for May 6.

While Anderson was getting ready for this final offensive I devised a plan to have Harmon thrust deep beyond Mateur into the enemy's soft rear. If we could break up those rear-echelon units on the shelf between Bizerte and Tunis, we might seriously demoralize him.

Between Mateur and Ferryville, nine miles farther north, a belt of strongly defended hills dominated Harmon's breakthrough route into the enemy's position. Antitank guns in those hills covered the Mateur-Ferryville road, and from its heights artillery guarded the southern route toward Tunis. There was no way for Harmon to swarm around this position and leave it pocketed in the rear. To get behind the enemy he would have to break through that barrier.

On a field outside Mateur, Harmon and I looked across to this range and the country that lay beyond it.

"Can you do it?" I asked Harmon after we had discussed the several alternate routes of approach into the enemy's rear.

"Yes, but it's going to be expensive," he answered.

"How much?"

Ernie shrugged his shoulders. "I'd guess 50 tanks to finish the job."

This was more than I wanted to pay, but here was a chance to destroy the German in a few bold strokes.

"Go ahead," I told him. "It'll cost us less in the long run if we cut him to pieces quickly." Ernie reminded me one week later that it cost him 47 tanks.

In his attack east from Mateur one column of Ernie's tanks was to drive toward the French naval arsenal at Ferryville on the inner shore of Lake Bizerte. There it would turn east to cut the Bizerte-Tunis road. Another was to strike due east out of Mateur, outflank the Chouigui range, and penetrate the enemy's defensive ring outside Tunis.

As Anderson's First Army swarmed forward in its attack on May 6, the entire corner of Tunisia in which the enemy was trapped reeled under our air and ground blows. Allied fighters and bombers droned overhead all day as Spaatz threw his aircraft into the mightiest tactical strike of the Mediterranean war to date in an effort to soften the path for Anderson's tanks on their breakthrough to Tunis. "During the final drive from Medjez el Bab to Tunis," wrote General Henry H. Arnold in a later report, "we flew 2,146 sorties, the great majority of which were bomber, fighter-bomber, or strafing missions on a 6,000-yard front. We blasted a channel from Medjez el Bab to Tunis." This air attack had been reinforced with the fire of 1,000 guns. Anderson's wedge soon began to pick up momentum as it split the djebels and pointed its way across the plains toward Tunis.

With the enemy's position now trembling almost on the edge of collapse, I was eager to have the 9th Division speed up its attack down the Sedjenane Valley into Bizerte before the enemy demolished that port.

I cranked the field phone for Eddy at his jungle-like CP.

"Manton, the other fellow is beginning to go to pieces. Pick up your tail and get on into Bizerte."

"But we're going as fast as we can," he explained, "and there's still a lot of them out front up here."

"The hell there is," I said. "G-2 tells me the enemy is pulling out everywhere across our line."

"But the road to Bizerte is lousy with mines, Omar. We can't even put a jeep over it until the engineers clear it."

"Well then, get off your trucks and begin walking, but get the hell into Bizerte."

Manton was probably jarred by my curtness. But though I pressed him I understood his caution, for at division headquarters it might have been difficult to judge how imminent was the enemy's collapse. But at corps the signs were unmistakably clear. The German could not hold on much longer.

If the signs of enemy collapse were obscure on Eddy's front they looked clear, perhaps too clear, to Terry Allen. Although he had been ordered to hold on a defensive line in the hills north of Chouigui, the rumbling of gunfire everywhere on the front excited him into an attack. On May 6 the 1st Division pushed brashly into the Chouigui foothills. The enemy struck back with surprising strength and on May 7 Terry withdrew, chastened, and with heavy losses. The gesture was a foolish one and undertaken without authorization. For Allen's path of attack led nowhere. Had he broken through that preliminary range of foothills on his front, he would only have found another range directly beyond them. A commander attacks, I reminded him, to take objectives, not to waste his strength in occupying useless ground.

Allen had been opposed on his front by the elite Barenthin Regiment, the same infantry unit that had held out so long on the summit of Hill 609. In consisted primarily of Luftwaffe volunteers from the parachute school at Witsock and the glider school at Posen. In esprit, intelligence, and tenacity it surpassed every other Axis unit on our front. The regiment had taken its name from its original commander, a Colonel Barenthin. In Tunisia it fought under a Major Baier, a huge legendary hulk of a man, whose shrewdness we grudgingly respected. Baier had parachuted into Crete where he crippled a leg on the jump. This leg, however, did not prevent him from dragging himself over the djebels throughout the Tunisian campaign.

It was in the Chouigui hills that the enemy resorted to one of his few tricks of treachery in the Tunisian campaign. A German platoon, outflanked by the 34th Division in its attack on the Chouigui Pass, advanced under a white flag as though to surrender. When it neared our lines the platoon flung itself to the ground and fired point-blank into our astonished troops. For 24 hours few prisoners came in from the 34th Division's front.

As Anderson's tanks cleared the path to Tunis, the 34th Division on May 7 broke through the Chouigui Pass to the flank of the First Army. With the capture of Chouigui, II Corps had achieved the objective assigned it by Alexander at the start of the North Tunisian campaign. Only now, according to the original plan, were we to join the British in the Battle for Bizerte.

That battle, however, had already been won.

As though irked by my command to get into Bizerte, Eddy had whipped his tank destroyers down the road north of Lake Achkel. At 3 P.M., May 7, the battalion radioed division headquarters: "Believe way to Bizerte wide open. Request permission to proceed. . . ." By 3:30 the TD's were under way and within a half hour the forward half-tracks were clanking into the rubble-laden streets of Bizerte.

Only 20 minutes before we reached that city Anderson's black-bereted Derbyshire yeomanry had raced the 11th Hussars into the outskirts of Tunis. Thus within minutes of each other the last two cities of North Africa were lost to the Axis. Between Bizerte and Tunis, where a coastal shelf carries the highway to link those two port cities, the enemy's service echelons had been completely isolated and cut off.

Although the ports of Sicily lay only 100 miles across the Mediterranean Sea, the enemy had no heart for a Dunkirk. To evacuate even a part of his defeated North African armies the German would have required the guns of the Italian fleet. But the Italian fleet remained prudently at anchor in Spezia and Taranto where it had hidden from the British throughout most of the war. Anxious to destroy the Axis forces should they attempt an evacuation, the British navy swarmed from a dozen Mediterranean ports toward that Tunisian corner. With bitter memories of Norway, Dunkirk, Greece, and Crete, the British had tagged this naval mission "Operation RETRIBUTION." On May 8, the day after Tunis and Bizerte fell, Admiral Cunningham radioed his ships this order: "Sink, burn and destroy; let nothing pass."

But due to the enemy's reluctance to chance a sea battle, RETRI-

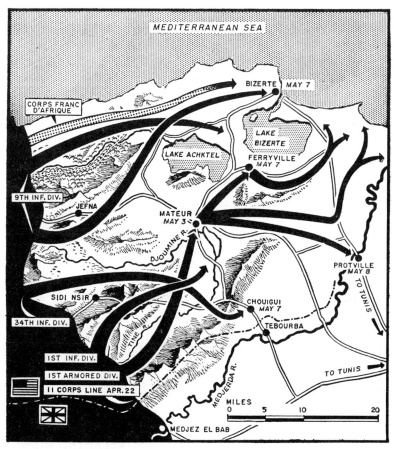

By May 7, both Chouigui and Bizerte had been taken by U. S. forces. Meanwhile the 1st Armored broke out of Ferryville to slash into the enemy's rear between Bizerte and Tunis.

BUTION brought the British only two merchant ships, three small tramps, a barge, a fisherman, and an assortment of rowboats and rubber dinghies. Only 704 fugitives were pulled from the Mediterranean Sea. The remaining quarter-million had chosen the easier life of the prison camps.

By May 8 the enemy command had collapsed into a state of shock. Harmon's tanks on the shelf had slashed through enemy lines of communication to isolate the hopelessly entangled units in confused and disordered pockets. Farther south on the British front a similar debacle had overwhelmed the German forces. Overnight a well-trained army of more than a quarter-million Axis troops disintegrated into a mob. Stunned by the suddenness of this collapse, they seemed drained of the will and resourcefulness to fight.

Some commentators afterward ascribed this collapse to the inability of the German soldier to show initiative in an unanticipated situation. But these critics ignored the disastrous effects of our tank sallies into the enemy's rear. No Allied army could have withstood so paralyzing an attack. For demoralized troops will not struggle against hopeless odds when they have the option of honorable surrender.

On the hillside near Sidi Nsir I awakened early the morning of May 9 to watch the sun come up from behind the distant Chouigui hills across the valley. Its light shimmered across the Mousetrap to chase the purple shadows from the white face of 609. In the stuffy, blacked-out G-3 war tent a duty officer logged the night's TWX's. Across the acetate sheet that covered his large-scale map, the blue lines of Harmon's advance threaded like thin veins into the enemy's sector. Tunis and Bizerte had been ringed heavily in blue to signify that they had been captured.

It was shortly after 11 that morning when Harmon telephoned corps. His gravelly voice rasped noisily over the miles of field wire from his CP near Ferryville.

"A couple of Krauts just drove in under a white flag. They want to talk surrender. What d'ya want me to tell them? Or do you want to come up and handle this stuff yourself?"

"I'll stick by here, Ernie," I said, "in the event something happens elsewhere. Just tell them we have no terms. It must be unconditional surrender."

"You won't have any trouble with this gang," he answered. "They're chewed up pretty badly. They've even asked for an armistice to work things out since they have no communications. I've already stopped my tanks and ordered them to cease fire."

"Good. I'll call the other divisions and tell them to halt in position. No sense in taking any more casualties unless we have to."

"I'm going to send one of my officers back with them to see that they follow our instructions. Suppose I send Maurice Rose?" Rose, then a colonel, was Harmon's brilliant young chief of staff.

"Fine, Ernie," I replied. "but have Rose make certain they don't destroy their weapons. They are to collect their guns in ordnance piles and run their vehicles into pools. Tell them that if we catch them trying to destroy their stuff the armistice is off. We'll shoot the hell out of them."

At 11:40 that May morning Major General Fritz Krause, the poker-faced artillery commander of the Afrika Korps, listened stonily to Harmon's instructions. Twenty minutes later a surrender was nego-tiated for the II Corps front. Thus at noon on May 9, 182 days after the North African invasion, 518 days after Pearl Harbor, the Amer-ican army secured its first unconditional surrender of Axis forces.

At 3 that afternoon Krause was joined in Harmon's CP by a group of senior officer colleagues. In huge Mercedes-Benz staff cars, weighted down with baggage, they had turned out in crisp dress uniforms, as though to stiffen their pride in defeat.

"You would have thought the bastards were going to a wedding," Harmon said in telling me of their arrival.

Ernie in his sweaty OD's pointedly ignored them. When he sat down for dinner his aide tossed the German generals a sack of K-rations. We were to have no truck with the ordinary amenities of civilized surrender. This was not a civilized war.

By mid-afternoon of May 9 II Corps had moved its CP from Sidi Nsir to a farmyard on the worn road west of Mateur. North of the highway, where a sandy plain stretched toward Djebel Achkel, our engineers had strung a barbed-wire cage for the Germans. On the south side of the road a smaller enclosure had been reserved for their Italian allies. We anticipated 12,000 or 14,000 PWs. By nightfall, however, the Germans had overrun our cages. German engineers were conscripted under their own noncoms to expand the enclosure. We doubled and soon tripled that original compound.

For two days, as far as one could see, a strange procession of PWs trailed up the road from Mateur as though on a holiday junket. The Germans spoke confidently of their defeat as a temporary respite; they had earned time for the Reich to gather additional strength. The Italians were pleased to be out of the war, and anxious for a free trip to the United States.

Some came in long convoys of GMC's guarded only by an occasional MP, sprawled atop each cab with a rifle. Others traveled in giant sand-colored Wehrmacht trucks bearing the palm-tree markings of the Afrika Korps. On bicycles, farm carts, motorcycles, gun carriages, even burros, they trailed contentedly toward the cages. By the time this flow thinned down we had counted 40,000.

No other single incident of the war brought me the elation I experienced in viewing this procession of PWs. For until then we had counted ourselves fortunate in capturing a dozen of them at a time.

A carnival air soon pervaded the Italian cages as the PWs squatted round their fires and sang to the accordions they had brought in with them. In contrast, the Germans busied themselves in tidying up the compound. Noncoms issued orders and soon colonies of camouflaged ponchos mushroomed on the desert floor. The men were formed into companies, latrines excavated, cooking areas assigned them, and water rationed from the Lister bags. German quartermasters trucked tons of their own rations into the cages. Troops reached into their haversacks for the black rye loaves they carried wrapped in tinfoil, tubes of Holland cheese, and tins of Danish butter. Unlike the tinned spread shipped to our troops and called "Marfak, No. 1," the Danish butter tasted oddly like butter. We quickly commandeered as much of it as we could find. But at the same time we rejected the British bully beef that had been captured by the Germans a year or two before only to be recaptured by us.

It was almost dark on the evening of May 9 when the German generals arrived at Dickson's tent for interrogation. They came in their own staff cars with a fat entourage of drivers, orderlies, and personal aides. When Dickson asked if I wished to see them I said no and remained buttoned up in my tent. I wrote a letter home to my wife to tell her I was in command of a corps.

Next day Hansen delivered the PWs to First Army.

Across the flats where Djebel Achkel reared in a solitary hump, units of the Hermann Goering Division continued to hold out despite the German surrender. Although isolated in that scrub-covered fortress, they sat within view and range of our PW enclosure on the Mateur-Bizerte road.

Harmon had assaulted that position on May 4 when his reconnaissance battalion stormed the western half and pocketed 80 captives. On the eastern half a stronger force burrowed in for a siege. Rather than waste his time there, Harmon contained the hill and pushed on to Ferryville.

On the morning of May 11, two days after the German's surrender, I instructed Dickson to see that the enemy complied with our terms and put an end to this resistance on Djebel Achkel. He had Major General Gustav von Vaerst, commander of the 5th Panzer Army, scribble a note to "Hauptman Brandenburg (or his successor) of the Hermann Goering Division."

"The 5th Panzer Army," he wrote, "has laid down its arms. You are to do the same."

The message was delivered under a flag of truce to the enemy on Djebel Achkel. The American returned with a German *oberleutnant*—his wounded arm in a sling.

To the battalion commander surrounding his position the German was reported to have said, "This note from von Vaerst. Before we comply, I want to verify it."

"Tell him," the battalion commander said to his interpreter, "tell him to go to hell."

"Well then, before we surrender," the German officer replied, "I want a document from the American army certifying that the Hermann Goering Division was the last to lay down its arms on this front."

"Brother," the battalion commander retorted, "either you'll come down right now and cut out this monkey business or we'll carve that certificate on your headstone."

Three hundred troops marched down with the Hermann Goering flash stitched to their sleeves.

By May 12 the total prisoner count for the Allied armies exceeded a quarter-million, more than half of whom were Germans. Among the prisoners were Generale d'Armata Giovanni Messe, nominal commander of the Axis forces who surrendered the Italian contingent, and General von Arnim who had succeeded Rommel as the German senior commander.

That we might better profit from what we learned in Tunisia, I invited the division commanders and their staffs to a post-mortem on the campaign at II Corps headquarters. Mark Clark sent representatives from his Fifth Army in Morocco; Patton's staff flew in from their new CP near Oran. There in an orchard that shaded our tents we posted a huge map of Northern Tunisia and around it seats for 50. Like an instructor at Benning, I reviewed the plan of maneuver and fitted the divisions into the over-all corps plan.

One week before the opening battle Eisenhower had counseled me to be tough with the division commanders.

"As a final word," he said, "let me offer one item of advice. It is that you must be tough. You must be tough with your immediate commanders and they must be equally tough with their respective subordinates. We have passed the time where we cannot demand from troops reasonable results after you have made careful plans and preparations and estimated that the task can be accomplished . . ."

However, to command a corps of four divisions toughness alone is not enough. The corps commander must know his division commanders, he must thoroughly understand their problems, respect their judgment, and be tolerant of their limitations. For there are few distinguishing characteristics of a successful division commander. Success comes instead from a well-balanced combination of good judgment, self-confidence, leadership, and boldness.

Among the division commanders in Tunisia, none excelled the unpredictable Terry Allen in the leadership of troops. He had made himself the champion of the 1st Division GI and they in turn championed him. But in looking out for his own division, Allen tended to belittle the roles of the others and demand for his Big Red One prerogatives we could not fairly accord it.

In the 34th Division Ryder had confirmed his reputation as that of a skilled tactician. Lacking the dash of Terry Allen, he subordinated himself to the division. His weakness, however, lay in the contentment with which he tolerated mediocrity in his command. For rather than relieve ineffective subordinate commanders, he overlooked their shortcomings and thus penalized the division as well as himself.

The profane and hot-tempered Harmon brought to corps the rare combination of sound tactical judgment and boldness that together make a great commander. More than any other division commander in North Africa, he was constantly and brilliantly aggressive; in Europe he was to become our most outstanding tank commander. Yet like all tankers, Ernie's heart rode with the Shermans and as a result he sometimes failed to make good use of his infantrymen.

But of all these commanders, none was better balanced nor more cooperative than Manton Eddy. Tactically he performed with classical maneuvers such as the one he employed at Jefna. Yet though not timid, neither was he bold; Manton liked to count his steps carefully before he took them.

On May 13 Eisenhower called from Algiers.

"Are you ready to go to work with George?" he said, referring to Allied planning on the Sicilian invasion.

"Any time," I answered. "When shall I report?"

"But how about your PWs?"

"I'll leave a staff detail here to ship them back. We've got the movement under way."

Once again we pulled down the II Corps tents but this time we headed west, west across the long coast of North Africa almost to Oran. Beyond the blue Mediterranean to the north the Axis shore line reached from the Pyrenees to Greece. D day for the Sicilian invasion was now only 57 days off.

8: *Priming for the Sicilian Invasion*

Tʜᴇ ᴀɴᴄɪᴇɴᴛ sᴇᴅᴀɴ ɪɴ ᴡʜɪᴄʜ ᴡᴇ ᴡᴇʀᴇ ʀɪᴅɪɴɢ broke down for the third time and the driver climbed out and tugged at the rusty hood. As we waited by the side of the road a prisoner-of-war convoy sped by, stinging our eyes with dust. The Germans waved at us.

For the triumphal return to Algiers from Tunisia we had chosen a sedan in place of the jeep for what we thought would be a comfortable drive. Now after three breakdowns in as many hours, we were ready to hitchhike a ride in a PW convoy.

We had left Mateur early that morning, May 13. It was dark when we drove into Constantine for black coffee, fried spam, and a night's lodging with the Eastern Base Section.

Unwilling to waste another day driving, I telephoned Tooey Spaatz at his Air Force headquarters.

"Tell me when you want to take off," he said, "and we'll turn out a C-47."

I was annoyed with myself for not having thought of asking for a plane before leaving Mateur. The days were becoming too few to waste, with the invasion of Sicily only seven weeks off.

At Maison Blanche Airfield outside Algiers the mudholes had dried up, and Algiers reflected the growing strength of the North African theater. Hundreds of twin-bellied P-38's had replaced the antiquated P-40's which Eisenhower had used on the TORCH operation. And in Algiers the feverish atmosphere of February had changed to an air of quiet efficiency, so characteristic of all higher headquarters. Meanwhile service troops had brought in more service troops until the palm-shaded boulevards of Algiers overflowed with GI's. This abundance of manpower both astonished and depressed me, for we had just come from a front where rifle companies were down to 20 and 30 per cent of authorized strength. Although Ike had struggled to hold his headquarters down in size, AFHQ had grown the way headquarters commonly do. In an army such as ours where we spend tanks, trucks, guns, and ammunition in an effort to save lives, these huge service echelons are an indispensable part of war. While I often begrudged Services of Supply the manpower it had to employ, my irritation disappeared whenever I saw the startling results of its labor. For in contrast to the enemy who was forced to hoard his supply and equipment, I could spend ours freely to take any objective that merited the cost.

Although Eisenhower's office staff in the St. George Hotel was still answering congratulatory cables that had come with the Tunisian conquest, Ike was hard at work on HUSKY, code name for the Sicilian invasion. The July 10 D day had been selected four months before on the assumption that Tunisia would be cleared of the Axis by April 30.

"How soon can you get your headquarters back?" Ike asked before briefing me on the planning.

"The CP will be on the road tomorrow. But an advance party has already gone back to Patton's headquarters to pick out a place and get it cleaned up."

"Having any trouble with your PWs?" he asked.

"No, not trouble," I answered, "but our troops get mad when they hear we're shipping PWs back to the States."

"How about the Germans?"

"Still cocky. They would just as soon stay here. Afraid their submarines will get them if we ship them back to the States."

Ike walked over to the wall and pulled aside a curtain to expose a map of Sicily.

"Only yesterday the Combined Chiefs approved our new HUSKY plan," he said. "We're going to put everything into this southeast corner of the island."

I nodded and stared at the map.

Sicily abuts the Mediterranean between the tip of Tunisia and the toe of the Italian boot to form a natural bridge across that sea. Only 90 miles separate Sicily's westernmost beaches from the tip of Cape Bon.

Sicily could be used to carry our Mediterranean offensive from Africa to the "underbelly" of Europe. However, even if Allied strategy did not contemplate an Italian land campaign, Sicily would still provide an unsinkable base for an advanced air offensive. Not only would HUSKY deny the enemy a base for his Mediterranean air strikes but the island could be used by us for air bombing of the Italian mainland.

Had General Marshall agreed with the British strategy of opportunism in the Mediterranean, the decision to invade Sicily would have made the Italian campaign a foregone conclusion. Geographically it was the obvious sequel. For Sicily is separated from Reggio on the mainland by the Straits of Messina, only two miles wide.

When the Combined Chiefs of Staff agreed at Casablanca on January 19, 1943, that the Allied summer offensive for that year would be directed against Sicily, General Marshall had little choice but to give his approval. Though believing strongly in the strategy of a *cross-channel* invasion, he knew that limited resources had made it necessary to defer the Channel attack another year.

On the other hand, if Allied armies in the Mediterranean were to be bivouacked during the summer of 1943 we would have failed in one of our primary strategic missions: the containment of German forces which otherwise could be used against the Soviets on the Eastern front. After the setback at Stalingrad the previous winter, the German High Command was busy amassing reserves to mount a heavy summer offensive. Since Russia had to be sustained in the war at all costs, it became necessary for the Allies to contain as many enemy divisions as they could by means of a summer offensive.

Although General Marshall consented to the Sicilian campaign as an unavoidable campaign of containment, he continued to oppose the further Mediterranean advances favored by the British. He feared that the Channel invasion might be compromised even in 1944 if we were to expend Allied resources on indecisive Mediterranean campaigns. Again and again he argued that only by assaulting across the Channel could we secure a decisive victory in the European war.

"Is Sicily," he asked at Casablanca, "to be a means to an end—or is Sicily to be an end in itself?"

In agreeing to the Sicilian campaign General Marshall acknowledged three strong arguments in its favor: (1) to keep Russia in the war by engaging enemy strength, (2) to improve the Allied supply line by shortening the sea route to the Middle East, and (3) to maintain the momentum of the Allied drive.

He never for a moment believed that the Allies could win the war simply by aiding Russia through the distraction of German divisions. Inevitably, he insisted, the mortal blow must be struck across the English Channel.

On January 22, 1943, the Combined Chiefs picked a target date for the Sicilian invasion. It was to be made during the "favorable period of the July moon." This meant that period of the month when the airborne would have a sliver of moon for its drop and that period when the moon would set in time for the amphibious assault.

Later, in their anxiety to prevent Axis reinforcement of Sicily following the collapse of von Arnim's armies in Tunisia, the Combined Chiefs urged Eisenhower to advance HUSKY by a month and go with the June moon. This was almost impossible, for Eisenhower not only required additional craft but needed the extra month in which to ready his embarkation ports.

It was not until April 10 when the Axis withdrew to Northern Tunisia that Eisenhower finally prevailed upon the Combined Chiefs to accept the July D day. With that, Patton submitted his request for the substitution of II Corps on the assault. Had the date been changed to June as the Combined Chiefs proposed, VI Corps would have sailed with Patton to Sicily. And I would probably have taken II Corps on the Salerno invasion. Once in Italy, I might easily have missed the chance to participate in OVERLORD.

As planning for Sicily got under way, Clark relinquished his invasion craft in Morocco to the urgent requirements of HUSKY. Clark's craft had been held in readiness there since the TORCH landing to forestall a German crossing of the Straits of Gibraltar. If Spain were to be used as a bridge for the passage of Axis forces to North Africa, Clark was to attack the Iberian Peninsula on its flank in an amphibious assault. But by the spring of 1943 Germany was much too exhausted from its Russian debacle the previous winter to extend its lines into Spain.

To draw up strategy on the Sicilian assault Ike detached from AFHQ the nucleus of a planning staff. This staff derived its title,

"Force 141," from the room in which it first met in the St. George Hotel. Eventually on May 15 Force 141 was absorbed by Alexander's Army Group to become part of his command. No longer the 18th Army Group, Alexander's command was now to be known as the 15th Army Group, a designation that came from adding together Montgomery's Eighth and Patton's Seventh Armies.

To confuse the enemy and conceal the strength ·of our invasion forces Patton's army-size headquarters in the seaside city of Mostaganem continued to carry the designation, I Armored Corps (Reinforced). Not until the invasion force sailed from Oran, did I Armored Corps become the Seventh Army. Patton later celebrated that change-over from corps to Army in a memorable order of the day which began, "Born at sea and baptized in blood . . . and crowned with victory . . . in battle." Even Montgomery's Eighth Army temporarily dropped its identity for security in Sicilian planning and became the British Twelfth Army.

For two days, while Dickson, Wilson, and Colonel Robert A. Hewitt, II Corps G-3, closeted themselves with their opposite numbers in Force 141, Kean and I reviewed the HUSKY plan with Eisenhower and his staff.

The plan called for simultaneous landings by both the British and American armies. Montgomery was to land with five divisions from the tip of the invasion corner to Syracuse on its east shore. Patton was to land with four in the crescent-shaped Gulf of Gela on the south shore.

Of the 69 miles of sandy coast line assigned Patton on the invasion, 47 were to be allotted us for the II Corps assault.

"That's spreading us pretty thin," I said, knowing that we would have only two divisions for the corps assault. On the left Terry Allen's 1st Division was to take Gela; on the right the 45th Division was to be extended across a 15-mile beach. Our initial objectives on this front were to be the Comiso, Biscari, and Ponte Olivio airfields. All three were to be captured by D plus 2.

After pinpointing the assault, our primary task in corps planning came in fitting troops, vehicles, and tonnage into the lift that had been assigned us. Of the 80,000 troops for which Patton had been provided assault lift, 45,000 were to land on the II Corps beaches. Another 27,000 were to go in with Major General Lucian B. Truscott to the left of Gela, while 8,000 more were to wait offshore as part of a floating reserve. Forty-eight hundred vehicles were to be included

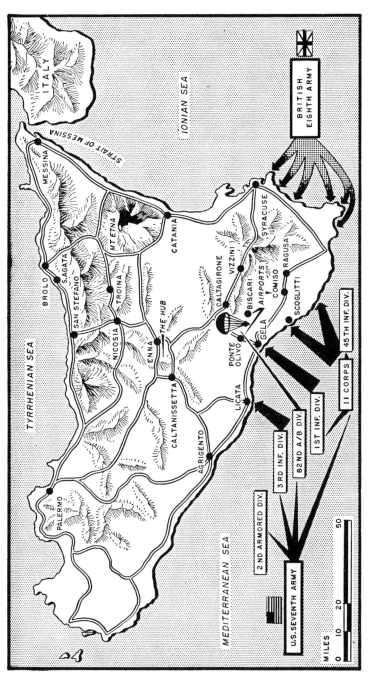

The landing was to be made on the southeast corner of Sicily in preparation for an advance up the east coast road toward the Axis escape port of Messina. Any other point would have been beyond the reach of Allied air support.

in the II Corps force. One hundred and twenty-five tanks were to be divided among the two assault divisions.

However, we anticipated little trouble in loading the 1st Division, for it had gained much experience in the TORCH invasion. And the 45th had sailed from the States already combat-loaded.

Combat loading, as the term implies, differs from unit and convoy loading. For combat-loaded ships carry men, vehicles, and matériel, stowed in the order of debarkation on the hostile shore. Of the three methods of loading it makes the least efficient use of cargo space. In unit loading, ships carry personnel and their unit equipment, but more efficient use is made of the cargo space, as vehicles need not be stowed in the order of their unloading. In convoy loading the emphasis is placed entirely upon effective utilization of a ship's cargo space.

After two days of staff conferences in Algiers, I was anxious to establish my headquarters and get to work. To avoid wasted time in travel I wanted the corps CP near Patton. George had moved his I Armored Corps from Rabat in far-off Morocco to the cool seaside city of Mostaganem, 40 miles east of the staging port at Oran. From Algiers I flew to an airport outside Mostaganem where Patton's heavy black Packard was waiting to take me into that city where George had located his natty CP.

There I found our advance party from corps still searching for a site for the new CP. They had picked one at a modest seaside resort in the dunes east of Mostaganem but Seventh Army had turned it down.

"What's our alternative?" I asked the headquarters commandant.

"Relizane," the colonel replied. "Thirty-two miles farther south, down on the edge of the desert."

I appealed to Patton to overrule his staff. The heat was already becoming oppressive and it was only May. But George refused.

"Why Brad," he said, "if you set up shop on that beach, the Krauts might slip ashore some night, cut your throats, and make off with our plans."

Though unlikely, the possibility nevertheless existed. I ordered my people to clean up Relizane and install the communications.

On May 20 the remainder of II Corps headquarters moved into Relizane. By then hundreds of Arabs were hard at work, scrubbing, screening, and cleaning the city. While the French colony withdrew behind their shuttered windows, we washed the streets, burned the

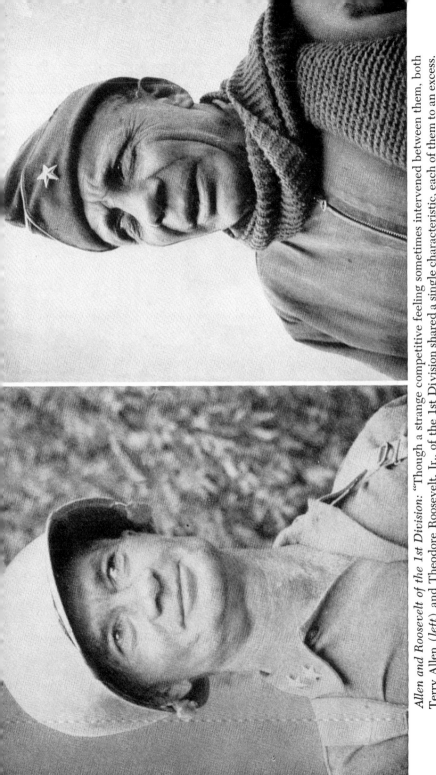

Allen and Roosevelt of the 1st Division: "Though a strange competitive feeling sometimes intervened between them, both Terry Allen (*left*) and Theodore Roosevelt, Jr., of the 1st Division shared a single characteristic, each of them to an excess. So jealous was their devotion to this division they sometimes forgot that the 1st could not singlehandedly win the war."

Planning the Cross-channel Assault: "Shortly after his arrival in England in January, 1944, Eisenhower summoned his Allied Chiefs to Norfolk House in London for a preliminary conference on the Initial Joint Plan for the cross-channel invasion." (*Bradley, Ramsay, Leigh-Mallory, Bedell Smith, Tedder, Eisenhower, and Montgomery, January, 1944.*)

garbage, oiled the nearby stagnant pools, and established our own water purification system. The two schools that we were to use for offices were fenced in with barbed wire. To make life more comfortable during our stopover here the local banker sent me his desk and chair for my office. And the French offered us summertime use of their handsome concrete swimming pool.

To celebrate the North African victory AFHQ staged a parade in Tunis on May 20 to which Eisenhower invited Patton and me. In a B-25 we flew from Mostaganem across the Medjerda Valley and over the plains into Tunis. To the north I could see Hill 609, imperturbable and unchanged. In Tunisia the war had come and gone and the land remained unchanged.

Among the British Empire units parading through the streets that day there marched a battalion of the 34th Division as a token force for the United States. Although the parade had called for only token representation, the French had shrewdly packed the procession with colonial troops. To the impassive Arabs and chastened Italians of cosmopolitan Tunis this parade of French armed strength signified the end of an era of French impotence. For the 120,000 jubilant French in that city of 340,000 persons, the procession celebrated the rebirth of a Fighting France.

Patton, however, was piqued by the spectacle, for Eisenhower had failed to invite either of us to share his reviewing platform with the Allied commanders.

"A goddamned waste of time," he grumbled after we had returned to Mostaganem.

But while the Allies were parading decorously through Tunis, Allen's brawling 1st Infantry Division was celebrating the Tunisian victory in a manner all its own. In towns from Tunisia all the way to Arzew the division had left a trail of looted wineshops and outraged mayors. But it was in Oran, the city those troops had liberated on the TORCH invasion, that the division really ran amuck.

The trouble began when SOS (Services of Supply) troops, long stationed in Oran, closed their clubs and installations to our combat troops from the front. Irritated by this exclusion the 1st Division swarmed into town to "liberate" it a second time.

Because of the brief layover between the Tunisian and Sicilian campaigns, we had previously turned down a suggestion that II Corps troops be issued the summer khaki worn by service units. Not only are khakis impractical for field wear but the change-over would have unnecessarily burdened supply. Furthermore, the change back again into woolens would have given away the timing of our invasion.

Thus the woolen uniform in Oran became the unmistakable badge of troops from the Tunisian front. As long as bands of the 1st Division hunted down khaki-clad service troops in Oran, those sweaty woolens were the only assurance of safe-conduct in the city's streets.

When the rioting had gotten out of hand, Theater sternly directed me to order Allen to get his troops promptly out of town. While the episode resulted partly from our failure to prepare a rest area for troops back from the front, it also indicated a serious breakdown in discipline within the division. Allen's troops had now begun to strut their toughness while ignoring regulations that applied to all other units.

"We'll all play by the same ground rules," I once told Terry Allen, "whatever the patch we wear on our sleeve." I'm afraid Allen gave little notice to my admonition.

Despite their prodigal talents as combat leaders, neither Terry Allen nor Brigadier General Theodore Roosevelt, the assistant division commander, possessed the instincts of a good disciplinarian. They looked upon discipline as an unwelcome crutch to be used by less able and personable commanders. Terry's own career as an army rebel had long ago disproved the maxim that discipline makes the soldier. Having broken the mold himself, he saw no need to apply it to his troops. Had he been assigned a rock-jawed disciplinarian as assistant division commander, Terry could probably have gotten away forever on the personal leadership he showed his troops. But Roosevelt was too much like Terry Allen. A brave, gamy, undersized man who trudged about the front with a walking stick, Roosevelt helped hold the division together by personal charm. His cheery bullfrog voice had echoed reassuringly among the troops in every Tunisian wadi in which his riflemen fought the German.

One night as I stood with Roosevelt watching a blacked-out convoy of the 1st Division move slowly up the road, Teddy turned to me in the darkness and said, "Brad, I'll bet that I've talked to every man in this division. They'd know my voice whether they could see me or not. Listen!"

He shouted hoarsely through the night to a passing truck. "Hey, what outfit is that?"

"Company C of the 18th Infantry, General Roosevelt," a hearty voice called back.

To lighten the lot of his weary troops in the Tunisian djebels Roosevelt liked to tease them on the pleasures that awaited their return to Oran.

"Once we've licked the Boche," he would say in his rough voice, "we'll go back to Oran and beat up every MP in town." This was one of the few admonitions the 1st Division took literally.

While the Oran outbreak demonstrated the need for tightening discipline within the division, it also indicated how woefully we had overlooked a soldier's need for relaxation once he emerges from combat. Had we sped the division into a rest cantonment on the seashore where it might gradually unwind itself, we could probably have avoided this rioting in Oran. Instead, we rushed the 1st into a dreary tent bivouac for the resumption of its strenuous field training. The 9th fared even worse. We trucked it directly from Tunisia to Magenta, a dusty, fly-ridden, sun-baked town 50 miles south of Sidi-bel-Abbes, headquarters of the French Foreign Legion. There it could almost breathe the sands of the Sahara Desert.

With characteristic resourcefulness, however, the Rangers solved their resettlement problems. An advance party preceded the battalion to Nemours in French Morocco. There they staked out a temporary camp on the water's edge. They stocked the camp with extra rations and hauled in a truckload of beer. The beer came from a merchantman in exchange for a truckload of souvenirs. For several days, the battalion banqueted, roistered, and swam in the Mediterranean. After this break they went into bivouac with good morale for a resumption of training.

Behind the barbed-wire concertinas that shielded our planners in their classrooms in the Ecole des Femmes, Dickson and Hewitt papered the blackboards with TOP SECRET and BIGOTED maps. On a portico in the open courtyard we erected a topographical model of Sicily. The map had been constructed in Fort Belvoir and rushed by air under armed guard.

Meanwhile the astonished city of Relizane had adapted itself to the SPEEDY invasion. The word, SPEEDY, a signal designation for II Corps, soon decorated every major building in town. Even the run-down provincial hotel where corps had established its mess had been renamed the SPEEDY HOTEL.

"What is this thing SPEEDY?" the French often asked. When we explained they were only more bewildered.

In Relizane, as elsewhere in North Africa where there were American troops, the Arab bootblack soon upset the economic equilibrium of his community. As the result of lavish GI tipping shines skyrocketed from one franc to 15 francs each. At 50 francs to an American dollar, an enterprising bootblack could earn more in a day than his parents could make in a month of farm labor. These prices, however, brought on a black market in PX shoe polish and the price for polish soon rose to a dollar a can. A few of the more enterprising bootblacks eventually monopolized the trade by cornering the supply of brown polish.

To avoid smothering himself in day-to-day planning Patton had designated Major General Geoffrey Keyes as deputy commander of his force. Consequently it was to Keyes that Patton delegated much of the responsibility for detailed planning of the American assault. Since George intervened directly only in the major decisions, most of our routine business was transacted with Keyes.

By the first week in June our plan had begun to take final form.

As the strong right arm of Patton's Seventh Army, II Corps was to attack in the Gulf of Gela and force three simultaneous landings across a 20-mile strip of the island's soft, hummocked beaches. While two battalions of Rangers slipped into the port of Gela itself, the 1st Division was to land east of that village, push inland across the rolling plains, and seize the airport at Ponte Olivio by daylight of D plus 1. Six miles farther down the coast two regiments of the inexperienced 45th Division were to break a path to the Biscari airfield by dark of D plus 2. And on our right the remaining regiment of the 45th was to push into the hills to seize the airfield at Comiso by daylight of D plus 2. This regiment was also to establish contact with Montgomery near the cliff-like city of Ragusa.

After securing those key airdromes II Corps was to advance 20 miles into that southeast sector of Sicily to gain the arterial highway that linked this corner with the hub of the island at Caltanisetta. Caltanisetta can be well described as the hub for a network of roads radiating to the three corners and intervening sides of the island. Because of the bold mountainous character of Sicily, it was apparent from the start that our campaign was to become a struggle for those roads.

The shortest route to Messina from the invasion corner ran from Montgomery's beaches near Syracuse up the east coast road. Twenty miles north of Syracuse the rolling coastal plains flattened into malarial marshes. Here near the port city of Catania the enemy had located his huge and sensitive Gerbini "complex," a gigantic airdrome with 12 satellite fields.

Beyond Catania on this coastal route of Montgomery's to Messina, the 11,000-foot Mount Etna overshadowed the road where it followed a narrow shelf between that volcano and the sea.

A second coastal road led to Messina along Sicily's scenic north shore. But to reach this road we had first to fight across the midriff of the island. This, too, was a formidable path, straddled by ancient mountaintop towns that dominated the valley roads.

In the assault, II Corps was to contain two forces. The first would comprise the 1st Division and the Rangers, the other the 45th. Meanwhile Truscott's landing to the left of ours was to consist of the 3rd Division and a combat command of the 2d Armored.

Fortunately II Corps was to be spared the ordeal of mounting the air drop. This task was reserved to Army and thus it became Patton's responsibility in the American zone, Montgomery's in the British. We had only to indicate where we wanted the parachutists dropped.

"On the air drop we get 220 C-47's to land four battalions of infantry and another of pack howitzers. Where do you want to use them?" Patton asked me.

"In the high ground behind Gela where they can protect that beach from counterattack by the reserves waiting farther inland," I replied. They were to come in under darkness at midnight, approximately three hours before the amphibious landing.

G-2 had reported the Hermann Goering Battle Group near Caltagirone, only 20 miles up the road from Terry's beaches near Gela. Were this force to counterattack with tanks before Allen could get his guns ashore, it might cause us trouble. I was anxious, therefore, to seize the high ground beyond Allen's beach and use it in defense against this probable counterattack. For where a beachhead is rimmed by high ground, the landing is always imperiled until the invader can take those hills and secure his beach against observed enemy fire.

In addition to Patton's 220 C-47's, air had promised Montgomery another 137 planes to haul a glider brigade into Syracuse and there speed the capture of that port.

In the schoolroom where Monk Dickson worked, scattered red symbols covered the work maps on which he had charted the Axis

ground defenses. Tabbed as enemy divisions, these symbols represented the end product of thousands of items of information,
tediously correlated from agents, interrogations, broadcasts, letters,
photos, newspapers, and the myriad commonplace sources in which
intelligence hunts.

Of the two German divisions then known to be in Sicily both were
pointed toward the invasion corner. "Strictly hot mustard," was the
way Dickson described them. Fortunately however, both were short
on tanks; we estimated only 85 between them.

A total of six Italian static divisions defended the 500 miles of
Sicilian coast line. Known to be understrength and shabbily
equipped, they had grown lazy and indolent on the beaches. "Ersatz
stuff, all of it," Dickson said. "Stick them in the belly and sawdust
will run out."

Somewhat better were the four Italian field divisions drawn back
into reserve in the hills. Of these, only one was posted in the southeast corner. Two held the western end of the island and another was
located in the middle. Altogether this Italian garrison was estimated
by Patton's G-2 to consist of 200,000 men.

"When the going gets tough," Dickson predicted, "the Boche will
pull the plug on the Eyties and wash them down the drain." He
meant the German would ditch his Italian ally to save his own troops.
And that is precisely what happened.

Of all the terrors we faced, however, none seemed more menacing
than the threat of German air. For our army, huddled on a narrow
beachhead, could be severely mauled should the Luftwaffe break
through in strength. And a naval force concentrated offshore would
offer Goering a tempting target for all-out air attack.

I was not to learn how groundless those fears were until after the
invasion. During May and June the Allied air force had decimated
the enemy's Mediterranean air strength. This air offensive began
when Spaatz destroyed the island outposts off Sicily's shores.

Halfway between Tunis and the underside of Sicily a bare out-
cropping of volcanic rock lies in that narrow neck of the Mediterranean. This island of Pantelleria contained an airdrome with underground hangars, enough for 80 fighters. Its defensive force consisted
of 10,000 seedy and second-rate troops.

Even though Pantelleria lay in the middle of the Mediterranean
shipping lanes, it might have been by-passed on the Sicilian invasion
had not the Allies needed additional bases within fighter range of

the assault beaches. Only long-range P-38's could operate over those southeastern beaches from Tunisian airfields. And Malta was limited in its capacity. Pantelleria would provide a convenient base for 80 additional fighters within range of the beaches.

Moreover, until Eisenhower silenced Pantelleria together with the three smaller, nearby islands to the south, he risked enemy detection of the Sicilian-bound convoys. While the Axis held those outposts, it would be foolhardy for us to expect surprise on the HUSKY landing.

On the other hand, an attack on Pantelleria might betray the direction of our next move to the Axis. If large-scale forces were to be committed in the seizure of these outposts, the tie-up in landing craft might force delay of the Sicilian assault.

Eventually Eisenhower reasoned that his compelling need for fighter bases had made it necessary to take Pantelleria. Because that island's steep waterside cliffs contained few landing beaches, he decided first to soften it up by large-scale aerial bombing.

For the task Spaatz could count on approximately 1,000 aircraft including B-17's and RAF Wellingtons. In the Mediterranean at that time the combined Axis air strength amounted to 1,200 serviceable planes, of which almost half were German. But because this aircraft was scattered from Sardinia to Greece, only 900 were believed within range of Pantelleria.

The air offensive opened on May 18 when medium bombers and fighter bombers attacked Pantelleria's underground airdromes. In June the heavy bombers joined the assault. During the days preceding the amphibious attack, planned for June 11, a total of 4,844 bombs were dropped on the island.

On the morning of June 11 as the British assault craft neared the island, a white flag broke out on Semaphore Hill. The only Allied casualty of the invasion occurred when a British doughboy was bitten by a Pantellerian jackass.

Meanwhile in Sicily the 19 scattered airdromes that had worried Eisenhower's planners so much the previous spring had increased to 32 by early May. But as Spaatz aimed the weight of his bombers against those Sicilian objectives, the Axis withdrew its aircraft to safer rearward fields. These extended as far north as Foggia, halfway up the Italian boot. To prevent enemy reinforcement through Messina, Spaatz hammered that port until its peacetime capacity of 4,000 tons each day fell to a small fraction of that. By D day eight Sicilian airports had been put out of operation. Only two fields in the western tip of the island remained operational. By smashing the enemy's air on the ground and by forcing his airfields back, Spaatz had spared us the D-day enemy air offensive we feared the most.

While the 45th Division sailed in convoy from the United States for a practice landing near Arzew prior to the invasion, its planning staff came in by air, after having removed their Thunderbird shoulder patches. The division was commanded by Major General Troy Middleton, who until the war was dean of administration at Louisiana State University. During World War I Middleton gained fame as the youngest regimental commander in the U. S. Army. Recalled to active duty with the 45th, Middleton started on a second spectacular wartime career with the Sicilian campaign. In Europe he was to take command of a corps and lead it from Normandy to the Elbe.

Middleton's artillery commander at this time was Brigadier General Raymond S. McLain, an Oklahoma banker turned soldier. Like his chief, McLain was to end the war in command of a corps.

On June 10, I was advised by TWX from Washington that I had been promoted to lieutenant general. My permanent rank was still that of a lieutenant colonel. Pleased though I was with this additional rank, I would gladly have delayed that third star for an extra consignment of landing craft. Because of this shortage in craft, the U. S. force was to be landed in three successive waves with four-day intervals between them. This would permit a full turn-around trip to the North African embarkation ports. It also meant we had to get along with what we had already landed until those ships returned.

These limitations on craft had caused us to pare to the bone the transportation of all units in the assault wave. Of the 4,500 "vehicles" that had been tabbed to go ashore D day, almost 600 were to be towed guns. But since we did not expect to go very far during those first four days ashore, I had little reluctance in stripping the assault divisions down to their essentials.

When we asked the air forces for their requirements in that initial lift, the Air Support Command requested space for 660 vehicles. Hewitt raised his eyebrows and Wilson stared in disbelief.

"You'll have to cut it down," I told the colonel representing air, "that's almost as much as we can allow for an assault division."

"But these are bulldozers and heavy trucks, General," he answered. "We will need them for repairing the airfields."

"Yes, I know, but we've got to capture those airfields, first, and we'll need vehicles to get to them. If you need any help before your stuff comes in on the second lift, let me know and I'll see that you get some of our combat engineers."

The colonel refused, however, to lower his estimate. "Six hundred and sixty is rock-bottom, sir. We can't go in with anything less."

"Very well then," I answered, losing patience, "you make the assault with your 660 trucks. Clear the beach for us and we'll come in on a later lift. It's either you or the infantry. There's not lift enough for both."

The colonel radioed his headquarters and returned again with the list.

"I'm sorry, General," he said, "but it's either this or nothing. We can't get along on less."

"Very well then, if none of your people will make the decision, we'll make it for you," I said. "You tell me it's all or nothing. Fine. Go back to your headquarters and tell them it's nothing. We'll go in without air."

The next day Patton telephoned from Mostaganem. "Brad," he said, "the air force is up here raising hell. They tell me you're pretty tough to get along with."

"Not half as tough as I will be, George, if they don't come down out of the clouds and play straight with us on this business of lift."

I explained the problem to Patton. "I know what you're up against," he said. "Handle them any way you want. I'll back you up."

Air eventually appealed to Algiers but no one cracked down on me. A week later the colonel returned, chastened and more docile than before. "Can you give us space for 234?" he asked.

"Of course," I told him, "and if you get hard up for engineers before yours come in, give me a call. We'll see that you get what you need."

The distribution of lift among army troops was no less trying. For weeks Hewitt and Wilson bargained and haggled in late night sessions with the special staff. Artillery asked to bring guns ashore even at the expense of engineer troops. Engineers demanded bridging ashore even at the expense of antiaircraft guns. And antiaircraft asked for more guns even at the expense of quartermaster trucks. So it went for weeks, each demanding a larger share of the lift; each contending that if its particular allotment were cut, the whole invasion might fail.

The variety of organizations that would go ashore complicated our problem still further. The II Corps troop list contained 151 units ranging from infantry regiments to engineer well-drilling sections, balloon batteries, MP prisoner-escort companies, auxiliary surgical groups, graves-registration companies, and naval shore battalions.

The first lift had to be delicately balanced for any contingency that might develop on the beachhead. The second was to replace the shortages of the first and put ashore the additional supplies necessary for maintenance. The third was to strengthen the first and second. It was also to provide us extra gas for our tanks and reserve ammunition for our guns.

While unit quartermasters trucked from depot to depot, requisitioning and laying in supply, Terry Allen's 1st Division reverted to its old freebooting procurement habits. Allen had learned his tricks in Tunisia where chicanery helped him secure extra supplies when necessary. This time Allen sent an aide to Eisenhower's headquarters in Algiers to seek help in circumventing the depots on critical items of supply.

When I learned of this I went to Terry Allen. He grinned like a boy caught in a pot of jam. The 1st Division was piratical at heart; regulations were not likely to change it.

To rehearse the assault and try a dry run with the navy, we scheduled practice landings for both assault divisions on the North African shore. Patton, a company of general officers, and I waited in the darkness at Arzew on the morning of June 23 to check the dress rehearsal of Middleton's 45th Division. The convoy, screened by destroyers against submarine attack, had steamed in from the United States to an anchorage offshore. Across the rolling surf we could hear the rattle of davits as the ships lowered their landing craft. A muffled roar of engines drifted across the water as the craft circled in assembly before heading toward the beach.

But as the leading wave reached the beach we learned that faulty navigation had caused two of the three regiments to be landed several miles wide of their mark.

"Good Lord—" I said to Kean, "suppose they miss it by that much in Sicily?" Kean grunted and said nothing. The 45th moved into bivouac for a week of conditioning before reboarding its ships.

The 1st Division also made a practice landing at Arzew where Patton and I viewed the assault. General Marshall and Eisenhower joined us on the beach.

As the first wave stumbled up the beach, Patton stalked off to the water's edge. There he confronted a squad of startled riflemen.

"And just where in hell are your goddamned bayonets," he shouted. While the soldiers stood helplessly before him, George blistered them with his oaths. Eisenhower stood within earshot in embarrassed silence.

Major General Harold R. Bull, an officer on Eisenhower's staff, nodded toward General Marshall and whispered to me, "Well, there goes Georgie's chance for a crack at higher command. That temper of his is going to finish him yet."

George rejoined us a few minutes later having already dismissed the incident from mind. These outbursts were characteristic of him. "Chew them out and they'll remember it," he would say in speaking of the GI's.

Again on Allen's landing the navy missed its mark, this time by half a mile. The British searchlights had blinded them, they said with a reassuring reminder that on the invasion those lights would have been knocked out.

After a last conference with Eisenhower in Algiers I hurried back to Relizane to close out the corps CP. Only a few key staff officers were to sail with me aboard the *Ancon*, flagship for the 45th Division assault. The remainder were to be distributed among five LST's (landing ship, tank). We were to rendezvous on the beachhead at an old castle three miles inland on the 45th Division front. Unfortunately, when our advance contingents arrived there, the German had not yet been forced out.

To explain the corps' sudden departure from Relizane G-2 suggested I make it known in the presence of servants in the home where we were billeted that we were planning to move nearer the coast to escape the summer siroccos that would soon blow in from the Sahara. Within 24 hours the word had spread through town.

With the massing of landing craft in North African ports and the training of troops in amphibious tactics, it had become impossible to conceal from enemy agents signs of preparation for a Mediterranean invasion. Instead we could only hope to keep the four vital secrets of our plan: (1) our objective, (2) the date, (3) the strength and composition of our forces, and (4) the tactical methods we intended to employ.

To confuse both the enemy and garrulous officers on our own staffs, we devised a cover plan for the invasion of Sardinia. It was not an illogical diversion, for at Casablanca a plan for the invasion of Sardinia and Corsica had been quite seriously considered before we finally decided on the HUSKY plan. In the event of a later decision to invade Italy, it was foreseen at Casablanca that Sardinia and Corsica would provide us nearby bases for fighter support. Both islands were only lightly defended with Italian troops and presumably could have been taken with a modest-sized Allied force. However, until Sicily was neutralized, Axis air would continue to terrorize our narrow ship passage through the Mediterranean to the Middle East. Not only would the seizure of Sicily ease Allied shipping shortages but an attack there, it was anticipated, might also push Italy nearer to surrender. These were the reasons that induced the planners to favor Sicily.

When the corps quit Relizane to board its LST's at Bizerte, I moved to Oran where we spent six restless days in an empty house high on the bluffs overlooking that port. From the quartermaster battalions unloading stateside convoys we were able to get several cases of cokes, one of the few things I missed while overseas. Planning had been completed, the decisions had been made; HUSKY was already in motion. There was nothing for me to do but worry and wait.

On the sunny afternoon of July 4 we quit our cliff-top villa and looked down for the last time on the busy quays of Oran. Here ships thronged the piers and jetties, loading troops of the 45th Division. In the outer harbor warships rode serenely at anchor.

We traveled lightly with musette bags into which we had crammed greasy, impregnated woolens to be worn as a precaution against gas attack. The TOP SECRET maps were carried in sealed aluminum containers. I had stored a change of clothes, several cases of K-rations, and two five-gallon jerricans of water in the recon truck to be loaded topside aboard the *Ancon*. After landing we found the ship's crew had rifled those K-rations, why I shall never know. I would happily have swapped them all for a single navy meal.

The *Ancon* was berthed in Mers el Kebir, a French naval base five miles west of Oran. The best natural anchorage on the Algerian coast, Mers el Kebir had long ago been infamous as a pirate's lair. Tied to the mole were two huge British capital ships, the *Nelson* and the *Rodney*. Beyond them was the 23,000-ton aircraft carrier the *Indomitable*. Of Britain's 15 battleships, six had been concentrated in the Mediterranean for the Sicilian invasion. Naval support for HUSKY was to be predominantly British; only six cruisers and eight destroyers could be spared by the U. S. Navy for the operation.

Three years before the British fleet had shelled this harbor of Mers el Kebir in a desperate attempt to prevent the French warships anchored there from falling into the hands of the German.

With the capitulation of France in June, 1940, the British appealed vainly to North Africa to hold out against the enemy. But the colonial administration there declared its allegiance to Petain. With the collapse of French land resistance, Darlan had sailed his fleet to safety in the North African ports. Now unable to chance the surrender of this fleet to the German, the British appeared outside the harbor of Mers el Kebir on the morning of July 3, 1940. After training their guns on the French fleet, the British called on Admiral Gensoul to join them against the Axis or sail to ports where his ships might be disarmed. Gensoul rejected the proposal and the British opened fire. More than a thousand French sailors perished in Mers el Kebir that day.

Three brutal years of German occupation had helped quell French indignation over this British shelling of their fleet. But at Mers el Kebir, across the Mediterranean well away from enemy occupation, sight of the British flag still rankled Frenchmen.

We found the *Ancon* moored to the mole, on the shore side of the *Indomitable*. Originally a luxury ship in the Pan-American trade, the *Ancon* had been converted into a command ship. Atop her masts radar antennae turned like huge reflectors in the sun.

Rear Admiral Alan R. Kirk, naval commander of Middleton's attack force, greeted me at the head of the gangway. I was piped aboard and escorted to a comfortable cabin amidships.

Kirk called on me a few minutes later. "Now General," he said, "is there anything we can get you? You're our guest while you're aboard."

"Anything?" I asked him grinning.

"Anything," he replied.

I ordered a dish of ice cream.

9: *Invasion of Sicily*

AS THE SANDSTONE CLIFFS OF ORAN FELL ASTERN OF the *Ancon,* on the late afternoon of July 5, the voice of Lieutenant John Mason Brown called through the ship's speaker.

A Manhattan drama critic, author, and lecturer, Brown had been called into the navy as an officer on Admiral Kirk's staff. It was his task each day to brief the ship's company with a battle report. For like all able commanders, Kirk knew that men respond more spiritedly to a task they understand.

"We are sailing to Sicily," Brown said. "We are going to land a division of army troops on the southern coast of the island, on the beaches near a small fishing town called Scoglitti." This was the first time the *Ancon's* crew had been told where they and the huge Allied convoy were sailing.

To the *Ancon's* stern the ships fanned out and trailed into the setting sun. Over each of the transports a stubby barrage balloon tugged along in the cloudless sky. Overhead patrols of twin-boomed P-38's searched the horizon for signs of enemy recce.*

Kirk's convoy of 96 ships comprised one of three American assault forces that formed the giant HUSKY invasion armada commanded by Vice Admiral H. K. Hewitt. As naval commander of the Western Task Force, Hewitt was paired off with Patton. It was aboard Hewitt's flagship *Monrovia* that Patton sailed with his Seventh Army staff. Combined command of this amphibious task force lay with

*Reconnaissance aircraft.

Hewitt while the force was at sea. Patton was not to resume control of his Army until it touched down on the beach.

Rear Admiral John L. Hall, Jr., sailed aboard the *Samuel Chase* as task force commander of the DIME assault. Hall was paired off with Terry Allen whose 1st Division was to make the landing near Gela. Attached to Allen's force were two battalions of Rangers loaded aboard British assault craft for the harbor attack on Gela. Light

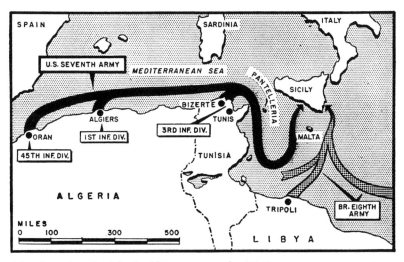

After hugging the North African coast, the U. S. convoys were to turn south toward Tripoli before steaming north past Malta to the beaches of Sicily.

raiding battalions of 500 men each, the Rangers more than made up in aggressiveness what they lacked in battalion size.

As task force commander of the CENT assault Admiral Kirk was paired off with Troy Middleton, whose 45th Division was to land east and west of Scoglitti. Unlike the other two American forces, this one had sailed combat-loaded from the United States. Both the CENT and DIME assaults were to come under my corps command just as soon as they landed.

A third force steering for the JOSS assault beaches in the vicinity of Licata was commanded by Rear Admiral Richard D. Connolly. He was paired off with General Truscott, whose 3rd Infantry Division aided by tanks of the 2d Armored was to shield our II Corps beachhead from counterattack on the west.

Whereas troops in both the DIME and CENT assaults had embarked on ocean-going ships, the first from Algiers, the second from Oran, those in the JOSS attack sailed from Bizerte and nearby Tunisian ports in assault craft across the Sicilian narrows.

Altogether the Allies had assembled more than 3,200 vessels, up to that point the greatest concentration of sea power in World War II. Almost 2,000 were to take part in the initial assault against the southern corner of Sicily.

To protect these landings from the remote chance of surface attack by the Italian Navy, the British had divided their heavy Mediterranean naval units into two battle forces. The first—known as FORCE H—was to rendezvous in the Ionian Sea under the heel of the Italian boot. There it would not only cover the assault of Montgomery's Eastern Task Force, but on D minus 1, FORCE H was to feint toward Greece as though that were our destination.

In the western Mediterranean the U. S. assault was being screened against Italian naval attack by FORCE Z, a British battleship squadron. Initially this force was to block the Tyrrhenian Sea to the north. Thereafter it was to feint toward western Sicily in the hopes of attracting enemy reserves there and so divert them from the invasion corner.

On the second day at sea I was on the bridge scanning the radarscope when a cluster of pips appeared on the glass.

"That must be the UK convoy," the officer on watch explained after consulting his charts. From England the 1st Canadian Division had sailed, combat-loaded, a distance of 3,150 miles to join the British assault on Montgomery's Eighth Army beachfront.

Montgomery's task in mounting his huge force was even more difficult than Patton's. For the American staging ports were limited to Oran, Algiers, and Bizerte. On the other hand, Montgomery's ports ranged all the way to Benghazi, Alexandria, Port Said, Haifa, and Beirut. In preparation for the invasion Montgomery's troops made practice landings as far off as the Red Sea.

In the Allied naval plan the eastbound convoys of Admirals Kirk and Hall, together with the Canadian division from England, were to hug the shore of North Africa and dodge through the Sicilian narrows as though following the Malta convoy route.

After turning south beyond the tip of Cape Bon in an effort to fool the enemy into thinking we were headed for Greece or even

Crete, we were to steam north under cover of darkness past Malta to the Sicilian beaches.

By noon of July 8 we sighted the rubble of Bizerte while passing through that part of the Mediterranean where North Africa is closest to Sicily. There we expected to undergo German air attack from fighters based on the Sicilian airfields, but all day we sailed without a sign of having been detected. I assumed that the enemy must be conserving his air for one massive blow against our ships off the beachhead.

While at sea Admiral Kirk was advised by radio that last-minute submarine reconnaissance of the 45th Division beaches had indicated that sand bars hidden under the surf might ground the assault craft.

"But earlier reconnaissance showed," I said, "that we could count on at least three feet of water over those runnels or sand bars—certainly enough to get the LCVP's* ashore. If we get hung up on them now, we'll not only have a hundred yards to go to the beach, but the water there'll be five feet deep. We'd have one devil of a time getting in."

Kirk studied his charts. "Well, it may not be much to offer," he said, "but there's at least one thing that we can do. We'll pick up every rubber raft in the force and load them with the assault waves. Then maybe if they get hung up on those runnels they can paddle in the rest of the way."

While those rafts might help, they offered no solution. Getting hung on the runnels could delay our beach build-up during the first few critical hours ashore. I was worried that night when I went to bed.

By the morning of July 9, I awakened to find the 10,000-ton *Ancon* bucking a heavy sea. I climbed up to the deck and found Kirk was pacing the bridge in his black foul-weather gear. By late afternoon the wind had reached a velocity of 35 miles an hour. The thin-skinned PC's alongside shuddered as they nosed into the mountainous white-tops. And the barrage balloons bobbed wildly as one by one their cables snapped and they were dashed away.

Although I grew increasingly apprehensive over the excessive danger of landing in so turbulent a surf, I knew the invasion had already gone too far to be recalled—even if threatened with disaster. The Plan was in command, and nothing could have stopped it.

As the ominous day faded into night the convoys turned north past

*Landing craft, vehicle, personnel.

Malta under a forced draft toward the invasion shore. On the bridge I listened to the wind shriek through the rigging and waited fearfully for the TWX that would tell us the air drop had been canceled. The top "safety" limit for paratroopers was a wind velocity of 20 miles per hour. By nightfall it neared 40. Though abandonment of the air drop might not necessarily doom our landing, it would cost us one of the chief instruments on which we had counted in the delay of enemy counterattack. A gale was the last thing we had anticipated on the Mediterranean.

Then shortly before midnight that evening as though in answer to our prayers, the wind dropped and the seas leveled into a broad swell.

While the gale had frightened us badly, it had also helped to keep the secret of our invasion. Axis air recce did not venture out that day and in Sicily the coastal divisions relaxed, certain that we would never sail in such a sea. Even the threat of disaster on the runnels was eliminated by the storm, for the heavier swells lifted our craft over those sand bars and Kirk's rubber rafts remained unused.

On the air drop, however, the freakish weather took a heavy toll. Four airborne battalions totaling 2,700 paratroopers from the 82d Division were to jump near Gela and there grab the high ground behind Terry Allen's beaches. Instead they were scattered along a 60-mile strip the full length of the invasion corner. For more than a week after the drop stray paratroopers crossed over into our lines from the villages and fields into which they had jumped far beyond the drop zone. These losses, however, were confined to the jumpers, for only six of the 226 Troop Carrier aircraft employed in the drop failed to return to their bases.

Although the gale had blown the C-47's off course long before they turned at Malta on the final leg to the drop zone, this scattered drop could not be laid entirely to the Mediterranean weather. Part of the fault lay with Troop Carrier itself where too intricate an operation had been planned for the inadequately trained C-47 crews. They had been directed to fly a tricky overwater course at night with few markers to guide their inexperienced navigators. So difficult was the mission that even today Lieutenant General Matthew B. Ridgway, wartime commander of the 82d, contends we never developed during the war proficiency enough to have executed that drop as it was planned. A share of the failure he ascribed to insufficient training of troop-carrier crews with the airborne troops. This problem of inter-service training had harassed those airborne units since the organization of their first division. It was to haunt them throughout the remainder of the war.

The dispersion that resulted was not wholly without its own reward. For the scattering of U. S. airborne troops throughout that target corner panicked the enemy and caused him greatly to exaggerate our strength. Raiding parties plundered the countryside, demolishing bridges and severing the enemy's communications. Afterward Patton was to estimate that, despite its miscarriage, the air drop speeded our ground advance inland by as much as 48 hours.

In the British drop, Montgomery's airborne troops fared even more disastrously than ours. There they had crowded 1,600 troops of the 1st Airborne Division into 133 gliders. Only 12 of those gliders reached their objective, the bridge over the canal south of Syracuse. Forty-seven others pancaked into the sea and the remainder were scattered wildly inland. Of the eight officers and 65 men who struggled to the bridge, four officers and 15 men were still holding to that position when the vanguards of Montgomery's invasion forces relieved them the afternoon of D day. This decimated British platoon had stood off an enemy infantry battalion reinforced with artillery and mortars.

Although somewhat seasick from the rolling of the *Ancon*, I snatched a few hours' sleep and returned to the bridge at midnight. By that time Kirk had shepherded his vast force with magnificent seamanship into the saucer-like bay off Gela where we now lay undetected. I kept out of Kirk's way, for there was little I could do. During the first few hours of assault I could exercise no control whatsoever over what was happening ashore. Until the division commanders landed and put in their communications, we had to bunk aboard the *Ancon*, trusting in God and the Plan.

From the shore where a previous air bombing had lighted a string of distant fires, a searchlight stabbed through the darkness. Its beam trembled across the water and then as suddenly as it appeared the light disappeared. A thousand fingers relaxed on their triggers throughout the fleet. The enemy had not yet spotted us and he lacked radar to pick us up. Once again that light stabbed nervously across the Gulf of Gela. For an instant the *Ancon* seemed to lie fully exposed in its glare. Then inexplicably the light dimmed and flickered off.

H hour had been set for 2:45 A.M., just after the quarter moon had set and the tide was full. When at last it felt as though the fleet could no longer hold its breath, the navy sounded its opening guns. A sheet of flame seared the sky and two licks of fire soared lazily over the convoy. On the descent they picked up speed and both darts cascaded into a single flash. Seconds later the sound of an explosion thundered back across the water.

By daylight messages were trickling into the *Ancon* with fragmentary reports on the first landings. The 1st Division had grounded precisely as scheduled on H hour. But on the open beachfront of the 45th heavier swells had delayed the landing. Everywhere the resistance had been unexpectedly light except in Gela where the Rangers had aroused a small force of Italian tanks with their bold landing on the quays. When dawn finally lighted the Sicilian coast line and the purple hills behind it, we scanned the streaked sky anticipating that now we would come under an all-out attack by enemy air. Instead of the Luftwaffe, however, we could see only a few Spitfires whistling serenely by with their fat wings. Not until later that day did the Luftwaffe venture out. But even by then it appeared only in fighter pairs assigned to hit-and-run missions. The Luftwaffe had only several days before forfeited its best opportunity to strike our invasion-bound convoys as they filed like sitting ducks through the Sicilian narrows. Now on D day with a thousand ships riding at anchor off the beaches, enemy air had once again failed to hit us with an all-out attack. Either the German was waiting to surprise us or he was far worse off than we knew. As the campaign progressed we learned how exceedingly effective Allied air had been in its preinvasion attacks.

In their simultaneous beach assaults both the 1st and 45th Divisions were supported by radio-directed naval gunfire. Fire support parties with pack radios not only landed with the infantry assault waves but they parachuted into the island with airborne troops of the 82d. How vital to success this naval gunfire was to be we did not learn until D plus 1. Without it the 1st Division might have been thrown back into the sea.

In defending his Sicilian shore line the enemy could not hope to hold in equal strength everywhere. For no matter how intensive beach fortifications may be, an invader coming by sea can concentrate his strength at a point of his own choosing, and force his way ashore. Knowing this, the enemy had screened his beaches lightly with third-rate Italian coastal divisions. We anticipated no trouble in cracking this crust and indeed none developed on D day. The real threat came from behind the beaches where the enemy had concentrated his mobile field divisions as reserves. To the rear of II Corps beachhead, the Hermann Goering Division waited to repel us in a concerted counterattack.

Eager to have a hand in operations ashore before the enemy counterattacked, I left Kirk's flagship on the morning of D plus 1 and headed toward the beach. From the LCVP we thumbed a ride on a passing DUKW* toward Scoglitti. There in the cramped and moldy headquarters of the *carabinieri* II Corps had established its first temporary CP. The *palazzo* we had selected on a map prior to leaving Relizane was still in the hands of the German. And the radio DUKW we had equipped as a mobile communications center had not yet arrived at Scoglitti. While running in to the beach from the *Ancon*, a signal lieutenant had spotted a stray radio jeep awash in the surf where it had been abandoned on the assault. With the aid of a bulldozer we dragged that jeep to the beach, hitched it to a truck, and towed it to Scoglitti where the lieutenant set to work repairing the set.

Off to the west in the sector of the 1st Division I could hear the rumble of guns, too angry and incessant to be dismissed as a routine attack.

"How long will it be before you can get through to the 1st Division?" I asked the signal lieutenant.

"An hour or so, sir, maybe more. I'm going to have to scrounge around Scoglitti for a soldering iron."

"Bill," I said to Kean, "I'm going to run down to see Terry Allen. There's too much noise and dust down there. Maybe he's gotten into trouble."

"But you probably can't get through all the way on the beach. Maybe you'd better take a boat."

"Thanks," I told Kean, "but I'll grab a DUKW somewhere down on the beach."

An invasion beach the morning after a landing is a dismal sight. This one was no exception. More than 200 assault craft wallowed in the surf after having burned out their engines in crossing the runnels while coming ashore. Bulldozers churned through the soft sand, dragging pallets of supply from the water's edge to be piled in dumps behind the grassy dunes. A fleet of more than 700

*A two-and-one-half-ton amphibious six-wheel drive truck. DUKW is a model number used by General Motors; the letters themselves signify nothing.

DUKW's moved from ship to shore, ferrying in the bulk tonnage that would be needed for support. Everywhere along the 15-mile length of beach to Gela belly-wrapper lifebelts littered the sands where they had been discarded by assault troops. Behind the beaches AA crews were digging deeper into the dunes in anticipation of another noisy night of bombing.

Near Gela I found the 1st Division fighting for its life against a panzer counterattack that had almost broken through to the beaches.

Three months before, on April 23, Patton had prevailed on Eisenhower to substitute the veteran 1st Division for the 36th on this invasion. In doing so he may have saved II Corps from a major disaster. As we had anticipated, the burly Hermann Goering Panzer Division lunged down the Gela road with its tanks in a bold effort to throw Allen's division back into the sea. I question whether any other U. S. division could have repelled that charge in time to save the beach from tank penetration. Only the perverse Big Red One with its no less perverse commander was both hard and experienced enough to take that assault in stride. A greener division might easily have panicked and seriously embarrassed the landing.

A dog-tired Terry Allen waited for me in a makeshift CP near the beach. His eyes were red from loss of sleep and his hair was disheveled. His division was still under serious attack.

"Do you have it in hand, Terry?" I asked.

"Yes, I think so," he answered, "but they've given us a helluva rough time." He briefed me on the start of the counterattack.

At 6:40 on the morning of July 11 Roosevelt telephoned from the 26th Regiment to report that panzers had broken through on that front and were headed toward the beach.

"We're going to have a helluva time stopping them," he said, "until we get some antitank stuff ashore."

Allen's artillery and antitank guns were still being dragged ashore from the landing craft. But even the regimental antitank companies had not yet gone into the line. Meanwhile the lightly armed infantry of the 1st Division had already been overrun by tanks. Twenty Mark IV's were reported headed down the road toward Gela where the beachfront bulged with supply. Another 40 tanks had cut across Allen's front toward Gela. If those columns were to converge there and break through to the water's edge, Allen's infantry would not only be cut off, but the whole beachhead would be endangered.

Now in desperate need of artillery pieces with which to fight those panzers, Allen ordered every gun in the division rolled into position to meet the tanks at point-blank range. Trucks raced to the beach to drag up additional artillery as it rolled off the landing craft. At the same time fire-support parties called for help from the naval guns. Though overrun Allen's infantry did not fall back. Instead they burrowed into their foxholes to let the panzer wave wash through while they waited to repel the grenadiers advancing behind it. Fortunately that added artillery enabled the line to hold, and those tanks were stopped on the plains outside Gela. Of the 60 panzers committed to that counterattack more than half were destroyed.

Later that afternoon the enemy resumed his attack, though this time with fewer tanks. However, as salvo after salvo of naval gunfire split their armored hulls, the German panzer commanders wisely concluded that the 26-ton Mark IV is no match for a cruiser. The enemy turned and ran for the hills where the navy could not pursue him. Allen had barely squeaked through, for those tanks had advanced to within 2,000 yards of the beach before they turned. Elsewhere the Allied landings met with only spotty resistance from the demoralized Italian coastal units and casualties were unexpectedly light. The enemy coastal divisions melted away into the hills and soon PWs began to infiltrate back into our cages, preferring asylum with U. S. forces to combat with their German allies. Having landed, we had now only to consolidate our beachheads and get on with the campaign.

That afternoon as we rode back by DUKW into the outskirts of Scoglitti, a soldier in an oversized tin hat called a warning from the side of the road.

"Better watch your step, General," he said, "there's a Kraut sniper in town."

"Thanks, son," I called, and with a carbine under my arm I walked into the village square. There several hundred Italian PWs had been assembled. They stood facing the wall under an MP guard. In the doorways around the square a dozen GI's covered the windows waiting warily for the sniper to show himself.

Walking toward the captain who was directing the PW search, I thrust my carbine to Hansen. In grasping it his hand depressed the safety and tripped the trigger. A shot rang over my head and the soldiers fell to their stomachs as someone shouted "Sniper!"

Hansen looked surprised at the commotion he had caused. "Chet," I said, "be careful with that damned thing, please."

The radio DUKW had arrived, for Kean was waiting at the corps CP with a TWX from Army.

"Matt Ridgway is going to bring in another regiment by air tonight," he said, giving me the penciled message:

Notify all units, especially AA that parachutists 82d Airborne will drop about 2330 tonight July 11–12 on Farello landing field.

"That's the airfield west of Gela?"

Kean nodded.

"Everyone been notified?"

He nodded again. "We've got the AA people checking their units on the beach."

Early in June Eisenhower had approved a plan to speed Patton's build-up on the beaches by flying the two remaining regiments of Ridgway's 82d Division into Sicily and dropping them behind our lines. This would give George all three combat commands of the 82d Airborne to be used as infantry in the first few days ashore. However once the beachhead was safely established and the danger of counterattack had passed, Ridgway's troops were to go into reserve. For paratroopers are too expensively trained to be spent as conventional doughboys unless an emergency warrants their employment in this way.

Alarmed at the prospect of having to fly those reinforcements in by night over the AA guns of the navy, Ridgway had sought an assurance of safe-conduct over the anchorage area offshore. Eisenhower's British airborne adviser replied that the navy could make no promises. For while AA fire could be withheld on the warships, the task would be more difficult on the merchantmen and smaller craft. Every precaution would be taken, he said, but no guarantee could be given the airborne.

This evasive reply worried Ridgway and again on June 22 he repeated his request for a guarantee of safe-conduct, this time in the presence of Ike. But once more the navy insisted that it could promise nothing.

Reluctant to risk a nighttime drop with no further assurance than this, Ridgway hurried to Patton's staff with what amounted to an ultimatum.

Unless given an assurance that his troops would be shielded from "friendly fire," he would protest against this follow-up drop of his division. Unwilling to forego that additional strength, Patton's staff intervened with the navy and coaxed an assurance from them. AA fire would be withheld over previously designated airborne routes.

With that assurance Ridgway agreed to the follow-up plan.

Originally, the initial follow-up drop was to be made after dark on July 10, the evening of D day. But when the assault drop miscarried the night before, the follow-up was delayed for another 24 hours.

On the evening of July 11, 2,000 paratroopers of the 82d Division climbed into 144 C-47's parked on Tunisian airfields. They were to jump near the Farello airdrome in the sector of the 1st Division. Logically there should have been little to worry those parachutists except the ordinary hazards of night-formation flights and the danger of straying off course. For the airmen, however, these were problems enough; the pilots were to fly the same dog-legged course that had caused them such trouble two nights before. Moreover the drop zone lay at the end of a 35-mile strip of beach thickly spotted with guns. But TWX's had been sent out cautioning ships and ground AA to withhold their fire. The C-47's were to come in low over the beach at 700 feet.

Again that evening shortly after darkness the Luftwaffe came in for its nightly raid. From our gloomy carabinieri headquarters, we watched the sputter of AA fire arching into the sky. Hardly had the enemy jettisoned its bombs and those guns ceased their fire when the first flight of low-flying transports roared in over the Gulf and turned toward the drop zone.

It was a cloudless and almost breathless Mediterranean night. Moonlight flecked the sea and offshore the fleet lay motionless after the exertion of that Luftwaffe attack. The lead flight of the airborne formation crossed the shore on time and droned off toward Gela.

Then suddenly somewhere in that vast darkness a lone gun fired into the sky. And while I looked on helplessly from Scoglitti, the sky exploded in AA fire. Soon spent fragments of AA shells clattered on our tiled roof.

Like a covey of quail the formations split as pilots twisted their ships to escape. Ready lights flashed in the darkened cabins and para-chutists tumbled out of the twisting aircraft. Some landed on the division fronts where they were mistaken for German raiders and shot while hanging in harness.

Of the 144 troop-carrier aircraft engaged in that night drop, 23 failed to return. Half the survivors limped back to Tunisia, disabled by fire. Morning revealed the dismal sight of crashed aircraft awash in the surf. Casualties among the airborne troops exceeded 20 per cent.

Although I principally blamed the navy for their laxity in fire discipline that accounted for the tragedy, I was not unmindful that AA guns had also chimed in from the beach. Indeed the trigger gun that set off the debacle was never definitely established as having belonged either to the army or the navy. That the navy was notoriously light-fingered, however, had been demonstrated before on D day when it repeatedly fired on Allied aircraft. It even fired at one of its own gunfire spotters.

AA gunners afterward contended that the Luftwaffe had turned back on the tail of those air transports for a second sneak attack against our ships. Although this report gained wide credence it was never substantiated nor disproved.

The navy's nervousness, however, was afterward "explained" by an officer from Admiral Cunningham's staff.

"Will you gentlemen please remember," he said, addressing the airborne staff, "that up to the present any airship over our naval craft in the Mediterranean has been an enemy ship. And while the navy is now in the transition period, it was extremely difficult to impress upon all 'light-fingered gentry' that there were such things as friendly planes flying over our craft."

As a result of this Sicilian tragedy the embittered air corps concluded that the only way to "guarantee" safe passage over a friendly fleet was to avoid passing over it. Thereafter on airborne drops we gave the navy a wide berth.

The Sicilian campaign was to be divided into several successive phases beginning with the seizure of an Allied beachhead and ending with the capture of the escape port of Messina. Preinvasion planning had provided only for the beach assault. From there the maneuver was to be directed from Alexander's Army Group.

After establishing itself firmly upon the beach II Corps was to move inland and take the three strategic enemy airfields that lay within its sector. From there it was to press on to the Vizzini-Caltagirone road, a highway paralleling the Gulf shore line approximately 25 miles inland. This road marked the "Yellow Line," the limit of the prescribed advance crayoned on our plan for invasion.

After having reached this road, II Corps would have established a firm footing for its further advance to the north. The Vizzini-

Caltagirone road formed one of the vital spoke highways that ran from the shore line of Sicily inland to its fortified hub near Enna. It formed the principal route to that hub from our southeast invasion corner, a fact which I was to learn had not escaped General Montgomery with his canny sense of maneuver.

Comiso airfield, the first of the three to be captured, was overrun by the 45th Division on the late afternoon of July 11. Twenty-five enemy aircraft had been caught there on the ground and the wreckage of 100 more littered the revetments around it. I quickly rushed an AA battalion to Comiso to defend it against enemy air attack while it was being readied as a U. S. base.

The first ship to land at Comiso after its capture was a twin-engined German bomber. As the JU-88 lowered its landing gear and banked into the pattern, our AA fired and missed. Just as soon as he had taxied to a stop, the pilot jumped out shaking his fist at the gunners. Not until then did he learn the field had been captured. Next two ME's swooped in but this time our gunners held their fire and two more pilots were captured. Finally a Spit pounced in low for a quick look over the field but this time the perplexed gunners fired.

The following morning a squadron of Spits was due in to take over the field as a base. Fearful that these Spits might be shot down, I sent Hansen up to Comiso with a message to the AA commander.

"Tell him," I said, and I meant it, "that if a single gun is fired when those Spits come in, he might just as well take off over the hills and give himself up at Messina."

On July 14 as we pressed within easy artillery range of the Vizzini-Caltagirone road that would open a path to Enna, Patton called me to his Seventh Army headquarters in the city of Gela. The road into town was cluttered with oncoming traffic from the beaches and a file of nurses trudged past, their faces streaked with dust and perspiration. I found Patton wreathed in cigar smoke, scanning a map with his G-3.

"We've received a directive from Army Group, Brad. Monty's to get the Vizzini-Caltagirone road in his drive to flank Catania and Mount Etna by going up through Enna. This means you'll have to sideslip to the west with your 45th Division."

I whistled. "This will raise hell with us. I had counted heavily on that road. Now if we've got to shift over, it'll slow up our entire advance."

Originally the contested road had been included within the Yellow Line. I had taken this to mean that we would have it for our advance to the hub. But Monty apparently had the same idea.

"Well, may we at least use that road to shift Middleton over to the left of Terry Allen?" I asked Patton. "It'll be easier to move him around to the left of the 1st rather than shift both divisions over. In that way we can probably keep Terry going and maintain the momentum of our attack. I don't want this other fellow to get set anywhere."

"Sorry, Brad," Patton answered, "but the change-over takes place immediately. Monty wants the road right away."

"But that leaves us in a pretty tough spot. Middleton is now within a thousand yards of that road. If I can't use it to move him over to the other side of Allen, I'll have to pull the 45th all the way back to the beaches and pass it around Terry's rear."

Not only would this tax our transport at a time when it should have been hauling supply, but it meant that we would be forced to suspend our offensive for several days on the II Corps front. The enemy was falling back in disorganization; I didn't want him to regain his balance.

After reading Alexander's directive, I returned it gloomily to Patton. Montgomery was to advance toward Messina on two diverging paths. The first followed the rim of the island up the east coast road, across the marshes, through Catania, and beyond it along the narrow shelf between Mount Etna and the sea. The other ran through the hub, north of Mount Etna toward Messina. This would permit Monty to flank the marshes and avoid the likelihood of a bottleneck on the coastal road. But to gain the hub he would have to use the controversial spoke highway from Vizzini.

It became apparent from Alexander's plan of maneuver that Montgomery was to take Messina while Patton limited his U. S. effort to the western half of the island. Fearful of being trapped there, the German had already started his withdrawal east. He obviously hoped to concentrate his forces in the narrow Messina neck where terrain would enable him to delay overwhelmingly superior Allied forces. With an escape port to his rear to be used at any time he chose, the German could exact a heavy toll there for every step the Allies took.

Altogether only four roads led toward Messina and of these only two ran all the way. Both through-roads followed the shore line, the first through Catania up the east coast of Sicily, the other on the

north. The remaining two were inland routes that ran toward Messina
from the island's hub near Enna. Only ten miles apart, the southernmost of these roads hugged the rim of Mount Etna. The other paralleled it to the north on a path through Nicosia and Troina. Only 15
miles separated the Nicosia route from the coastal road on the north.
Both inland roads converged at Randazzo on the northwest edge of

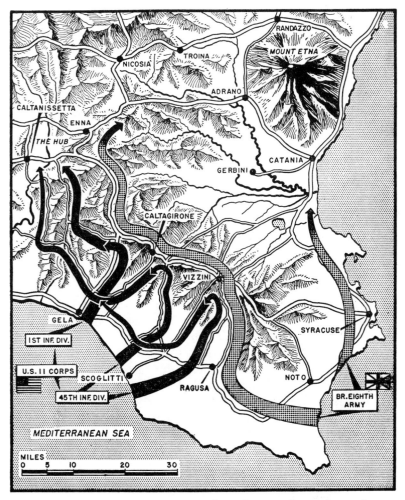

To leave the Vizzini-Caltagirone road to the British in their advance
toward Enna, it became necessary to turn the U. S. columns back almost
to the beaches.

Etna. There one road forked to the Catania highway while the other ran up north. Limited as this road net was, it could nevertheless accommodate two Allied armies in the Messina attack. If Montgomery would limit his flanking movement to the southernmost of those inland roads he could comfortably envelop both the Catania plains and Mount Etna. This would leave the Nicosia road and the coastal highway on the north for a double-pronged offensive by the Seventh Army. I had hoped this was the plan Alexander would follow.

Having been denied the Vizzini road I had no other choice but to shift the 45th by trucking it back to the beaches and placing it into position on the left of Allen's 1st. I was certain that Alexander could not have known how awkward was this movement into which his directive had forced our corps. For want of a day and a night on the Vizzini road, we were forced to disassemble our front and patch it together again.

Weeks later after the Sicilian campaign was ended Patton visited Monty at the latter's CP. During their conversation George complained of the injustice of Alexander's Army Group directive on the Vizzini-Caltagirone road. Monty looked at him with amusement.

"George," he said, "let me give you some advice. If you get an order from Army Group that you don't like, why just ignore it. That's what I do."

Montgomery, of course, had oversimplified his explanation. He was first a good, if sometimes perverse, soldier. He didn't ignore his orders though sometimes he seemed to skirt them, while being careful to avoid a showdown. Basically Montgomery's comment to Patton reflected a common attitude in the British command, a view sometimes difficult for an American soldier to understand. Unlike the U. S. Army where an order calls for instant compliance, the British viewed an order as a basis for discussion between commanders. If a difference of opinion developed, it would be ironed out and the order might be amended. In contrast, we in the American army sought to work out our differences before issuing an order. Once an order was published it could not be changed except by the issuing authority.

Had I known of this British characteristic I most certainly would have appealed to Patton to protest the Army Group decision on the road.

While we were busy shifting the 45th Division, Patton put together a provisional corps under the command of General Keyes to clean up the western tip of the island. To this hastily improvised command he assigned the 3rd Infantry, the 2d Armored, both of Ridgway's combat teams, and two Ranger battalions.

The Rangers had made their initial appearance in the TORCH invasion and soon achieved a unique reputation on the Tunisian front. Comprised of volunteers who welcomed the additional hazards that came with a Ranger's patch, those battalions formed as professional a combat unit as existed in the American army.

The 1st Battalion had been organized in the summer of 1942 by Major William O. Darby, then a 31-year-old major from Fort Smith, Arkansas. While serving in Ireland as aide to the 34th Division commander, Darby sensed the need for a light raiding battalion capable of difficult tasks beyond the endurance of most infantry battalions. He patterned his first group of volunteers after the British commandos. He trained his men so mercilessly at a bleak Scottish commando center that they soon begged for a combat mission to relieve them of those labors.

In choosing their volunteers the Rangers examined applicants first for intelligence, then for motivation, and finally for their agility and endurance. As a result of this selection, the Rangers became so competent that by the war's end I honestly believe there was nothing they could not do.

During the assault on Gela, Darby's Rangers were counterattacked by Italian tanks in the streets of that town. Darby, now a lieutenant colonel and in command of both battalions, raced to the beach in his jeep. There he commandeered a 37-mm. AT gun, hoisted it into the jeep, and sped back into town. With this makeshift "tank destroyer" he engaged the Italian force. Several tanks were soon knocked out and the rest fled in alarm. For his action that day Darby was awarded the Distinguished-Service Cross—only one of many his exploits should have earned him.

When the 45th Division called for a regimental commander to replace one that had been relieved, I asked Patton for Darby. It would have meant a promotion for him and a choice combat command.

George didn't order Darby to the 45th; he propositioned him instead.

"You mean I get a choice, General?" Darby, bald-headed and grinning, replied. "I'm not used to choices in the army."

"Take the regiment and I'll make you a colonel in the morning," Patton said, "but I won't force your hand. There are a thousand colonels in the army who'd give their eyeteeth for this chance."

Darby looked first to me, then to Patton. "Well, thanks anyhow, General," he answered, "but I think maybe I'd better stick with my boys."

On July 16, two days after the order that had given the Vizzini road to Montgomery, Patton received another directive from Army Group. It confirmed my earlier suspicion; only Montgomery was to be turned against Messina. For by its terms the island was to be split into British and American halves. While Patton limited his effort to the soft western end, Montgomery's Eighth Army would drive the German out across the Messina Straits.

Patton was to establish a firm base in the hub of the island where Caltanisetta and Enna lay. From there II Corps would advance in two columns; one pointed to the north coast road, the other northwest toward Palermo. Meanwhile Keyes' provisional corps was to attack north and west from its Licata beachhead.

Although Patton's mission looked the more formidable in terms of real estate, Montgomery's was to be the far more difficult one, for the disintegration of Italian divisions and the withdrawal of the Germans had all but emptied the western half of the island.

To the aggressive Patton, anxious to pursue the enemy up the Messina neck, this confinement to the western half meant only frustration. It was true that Palermo was to become essential to the logistical support of his Seventh Army, but except for that single port there was little to be gained in the west. Certainly there was no glory in the capture of hills, docile peasants, and spiritless soldiers.

The following day 15th Army Group directed Patton to continue his advance to the north and cut the coastal road that ran from Palermo to Messina.

"And then," added an officer on Patton's staff, "we can sit comfortably on our prats while Monty finishes the goddam war." But it was not to be that easy, for Montgomery's Eighth Army was already winded from its struggle on the Catania plains.

By midnight of July 16 the 45th Division had completed its roundabout move from the Vizzini road into position on Allen's left. Middleton lost no time in getting started; he attacked at dawn the next morning.

For six days and nights the 45th Division advanced across the center of the island in one of the most persistent nonstop battles of the Mediterranean war. Confined to a single northbound road, Middleton leapfrogged his regiments one through another to attack both day and night.

Even the hard-pressed enemy could not conceal his admiration for the punishing pace of Middleton's attack. Dickson brought me a letter picked up on a dead German. It had been addressed to the victim's brother on the Russian front.

"These astonishing Americans," he had written. "They fight all day, attack all night, and shoot all the time."

One day as I drove from the corps CP in Pietraperzia (I called it Peter Piper) to the 45th Division, I picked up a hitchhiker on his way to the front. He was wearing the jump boots and high-buttoned tunic of the 82d.

"Where are you headed?" I asked.

"Up to join my outfit, sir."

"But the 82d's out on the other end of the island—"

"Yessir," he replied, "but I parachuted down on the 45th and I thought I'd string along with 'em."

I smiled in spite of myself. "And where are you coming from now?"

"The hospital, sir. I'm AWOL from the hospital but I had to bust out before they ran me through that repple-depple routine. Otherwise I would never have gotten back to my old outfit."

"Wounded?" I asked him.

"Just pinked me. It's all patched up now."

"You know you've probably been reported by the 82d as missing in action when you failed to show up after the jump. Don't you think your folks will be worried?" He shrugged his shoulders.

"Give me your name," I said, "and I'll see to it that you're removed from the missing rolls." I turned it over to corps G-1.

Within a week after the landing Patton's Seventh Army had moved more than 22,000 prisoners through its cages—one fourth of them native Sicilians conscripted into the Italian army. The task of caging and boarding this hungry multitude had become an increasingly heavy chore. Plans had been made for their evacuation by sea to camps in North Africa. From there they would be sent to the United States as prisoners of war, a prospect they did not deplore.

Meanwhile summer grain was ripening on the Sicilian hillsides without manpower to harvest it. Villages had long ago been stripped of all but aged men, their worn-looking women, and children. By caging Sicilian PWs we would deprive those people of the manpower they needed to bring in their crops. Without those crops they would probably become wards of the United States. This could only mean an even greater drain on Allied shipping. It all made little sense.

On our third night ashore Dickson reported that an Italian soldier had been captured near the corps CP wearing civilian clothing.

"Not an agent, I hope?"

"No sir. Not this bird, General. He's just a little *paesano* and he's scared to death. Told us he was home on furlough when the Americans came and it seemed like a good time to stay home on furlough."

"Can't blame him for that," I said.

"No—there are probably thousands of others that would like to change places with him. They don't care about the war. They'd much sooner go home and get to work."

"Then why do we bother to lock them up?"

"Beats me, General."

"Monk, why don't we see what happens if we pass the word around that any Sicilians wishing to desert may go on back to their homes. We won't pick them up as prisoners of war."

"I'll get started on it right away, sir. We can handle it through the local gossips to start with. Let's see how well we do over the grapevine."

I passed the suggestion on to Seventh Army but when higher headquarters learned of this bargain offer, it disapproved the plan. But by then it was too late to halt the desertions that were already mounting in response to the rumor. On July 18 we broke into Caltanisetta, and Monk Dickson called on the local bishop to enlist his aid. Soon the clergy spread the word into the hills and thousands of shabby Sicilians came out of hiding. With this manifestation of good will the Sicilians welcomed us into their homes.

Eventually our recommendation for clemency found its way through channels, and on July 28 legal authority was granted us to parole Sicilian prisoners of war. Of the 122,000 PWs captured on that island by the American army, 33,000 were Sicilians paroled to their homes and farms. In town after town that we entered Fascist slogans had been scrubbed from the walls and the posters of Mussolini defaced. Angry mobs fell on local party headquarters to run their functionaries out of town and make bonfires of their files.

To spearhead his advance up the center of the Messina neck Montgomery chose the 1st Canadian Division of General Sir Oliver Leese's XXX British Corps. The husky brown-legged Canadians in their khaki shorts and flat tin hats were to take the fortress city of Enna in their advance.

South of Enna Leese found the German rooted into the hills for defense of that citadel city. After an attack in which he was thrown back, Leese dodged to the right on a secondary by-pass around Enna. Because the principal roads from Enna ran back toward my unprotected rear-area dumps, I could not afford to ignore the danger of this open flank. Unwilling to chance an enemy raid, I wrote to Leese:

I have just learned you have sideslipped Enna leaving my flank exposed. Accordingly we are proceeding to take Enna at once even though it is in your sector. I assume we have the right to use any of your roads for this attack.

Leese replied so promptly and apologetically that I regretted my brusque note. He assumed that his staff had notified me of his intentions. I was to make use of whatever roads we required for the operation. Then to assure us that no slight was intended he sent two bottles of NAAFI* Scotch along with his message. When Leese visited us a few days later in the heavily ornamented palace of Caltanisetta we reciprocated by serving high tea on china embossed with the crest of the House of Savoy.

With two regiments from the 1st Division we assaulted Enna from the south and west in an early-morning assault. The German, fearful of being pocketed in this mountain fortress, pulled out and fell back to the north. By nine that morning we entered the ancient walled city.

"Not bad," commented Dickson, "not bad at all. It took the Saracens 20 years in their siege of Enna. Our boys did it in five hours."

That night BBC announced the British had captured Enna in their spectacular drive to the north.

*Navy, Army, and Air Force Institute. The British equivalent to U. S. post exchanges (PXs).

10: *Coast Road*

To Messina

AS WE FOUGHT OUR WAY UP THROUGH THE CENTER of Sicily to the north shore, Montgomery found his Eighth Army balked outside Catania on the road to Messina. There, across the hot malarial marshes that stretched from the mountains to the sea, the Hermann Goering panzers had blocked his path in an effort to keep the British out of the Gerbini airfields. Unable to dent the enemy there in his drive up the coastal road, Montgomery considered shifting his force to Oliver Leese's flanking advance through the island's hub.

On July 17 Patton went to Alexander with his proposal to employ the American Seventh as well as the British Army in the Messina neck. His arguments, which all of us held ever since we had been ordered to give the Vizzini road to Montgomery, were briefly these: there is room enough on the Messina neck to fight both Allied armies. The four roads there could easily be split into parallel routes of advance with two roads allotted each army. To break through an enemy concentration in that narrow neck would require the offensive strength of both our armies. Montgomery certainly lacked the strength to do it alone.

By coincidence, George's visit to Group was well timed. For on the morning of July 18 Montgomery failed in a last all-out attempt to crack the Catania road with airborne troops and an amphibious landing. Unwilling to waste further time and strength against that stalemated front, Montgomery effected his shift of force to Leese's inland effort.

By now, Alexander realized that Montgomery had taken on a greater task than he could shoulder alone in the attack toward Messina. A TWX on July 20 confirmed this change of heart. Seventh Army was to be turned east with Montgomery's Eighth Army against Messina. Both Armies were to drive abreast up that strategic neck and drive the enemy across the straits, Montgomery on the south, Patton to the north.

As the right corps of Patton's Army, the turn in direction fell to us. After splitting the island in two by severing the north coast road, II Corps was to turn east in a parallel advance up that and the Troina road.

The offensive was to start with a feeler. First, according to Alexander's directive, we were to explore both routes with strong reconnaissance forces. Thereafter, "if the situation permits," we were to back them up in strength.

Meanwhile the 45th Division advanced rapidly to the northwest against slackening enemy resistance until on the afternoon of July 22 a patrol drove into the outskirts of Palermo. By that time, however, the 45th had exceeded its bounds. For as Middleton's troops raced toward Palermo, Seventh Army changed our boundary, giving that city to Keyes' corps.

Although the 45th had been denied that prestige objective, it welcomed the relief Palermo promised to bring to our overextended lines of supply from the southern invasion beaches. Logistically, however, the situation did not improve as speedily as we anticipated. For in successive weeks, when heavy resistance on the Messina road multiplied our daily ammunition requirements, the line of supply threatened for a time to snap.

Initially, supply across the invasion beaches had been the responsibility of each task force. One week after landing, however, Seventh Army took over. Lacking a base section of the SOS, Seventh Army assigned the supply task to the engineer beach brigade. This improvisation failed, for though beach engineers are trained to get the tonnage ashore, they know little about its distribution and transport to the front. Certainly they were not prepared to operate a chain of depots for the maintenance of Seventh Army.

On the several occasions I appealed to Patton for more supply support, he would respond as though I had come to chide him on a minor detail and he would brush my complaint aside. Although Patton bossed his Army tactically with an iron hand, he remained almost completely indifferent to its logistical needs. In war as Patton knew it then there was little time for logistics in the busy day of a field commander.

Whenever I pressed him on supply, as sometimes I was forced to, George would only gesture impatiently, "Have your people take it up with my G-4. Now let's get back to this scheme of attack—"

In justice to Patton and his Seventh Army staff, however, we must not forget that theirs was the first American Army to take to the field in World War II. From their misfortunes and mismanagement we gained much of the knowledge that was to assist us in the Normandy campaign.

On July 23 Middleton radioed corps at Caltanisetta that his 45th Division had reached the Mediterranean Sea after splitting Sicily in two and cutting the north coast road. Army Group now stiffened its original directive for the U. S. attack toward Messina. We were ordered to "thrust eastward along the coast road and [the] road to Nicosia-Troina-Cesaro . . ." while employing "the maximum strength you can maintain."

With that, II Corps reorganized its front by a 90-degree turn to the east and prepared to attack in force toward Messina by August 1.

In anticipation of this Allied offensive toward Messina, the enemy had wedged three German divisions across the Messina neck. They included the ubiquitous Hermann Goering Division on the Catania front to the east, the 15th Panzer in the middle, and the 15th Panzer grenadiers astride the north coast road. Elements of the 1st Parachute Division were flown in from Italy as reinforcements for the remaining sections of that line which Dickson termed the Etna *stellung.**

Following his shift of British strength to Oliver Leese's left flank, Montgomery resigned himself to a stalemate on the Catania road. There are Americans who still contend that Montgomery despaired too easily at Catania and as a result prolonged the Sicilian campaign. True, had he been able to pierce the east coast road and plug the port of Messina, the enemy might have been trapped on the island and forced to surrender. But confined as Montgomery was to a narrow road with a volcano on one side, the sea on the other, his advance could easily have been blocked elsewhere north of Catania—as, indeed, it eventually was.

After starting the 45th Division toward Messina on the north coast

*Etna position or defense line.

road, I pivoted the 1st Division east on the Nicosia-Troina route. Twenty miles of brush-covered mountains separated those parallel roads and there were few connecting paths between them.

By the end of July our advance had slowed as enemy resistance stiffened. Terry Allen's infantrymen drove on through Nicosia and came to a halt as they ran up against the enemy's defensive line outside the hilltop town of Troina. Meanwhile, the 45th Division on the north coast road found itself blocked by well-placed German defenses at the seaside village of San Stefano. The period of rapid movement had ended, for now we were solidly up against the enemy's Etna stellung.

II Corps had moved its CP into a scanty olive grove on the side of a hill northeast of Nicosia when Hansen came into my trailer one evening.

"I've been talking to Ernie Pyle," he said. "He'd like to trail around with you for a couple of days and do a column or two on you."

At the time I was still wary of newsmen. Thirty-two years in the peacetime army had taught me to do my job, hold my tongue, and keep my name out of the papers.

"Why don't we get out of it if we can without getting Pyle mad. I'd feel better off without all that publicity."

"But General, try looking at it this way," Hansen said earnestly, "how many men do you have in the corps?"

"Oh—about 80,000."

"Well—now for those 80,000 troops you've got better than a quarter-million fathers, mothers, wives, and what-have-you in the United States, all of them worrying about these men. A good many of them are probably asking themselves: What sort of a guy is this Omar Bradley? Is he good enough to take care of my man? They're the American people, General, and they've got a right to an answer. And believe me, Pyle is just the bird to give them a good one."

I threw up my hands and laughed. "Put it that way and I can't turn you down. When does he want to begin?"

For three days Ernie Pyle and I were inseparable. We breakfasted together in the morning on powdered eggs and soybean cereal. After the staff briefing we hung dust goggles round our necks and headed off to see the divisions. Lunches we ate on the road—tinned cheese from the K-ration and a sticky fruit bar for dessert. And in the evenings we cut the dust in our throats with a jigger of Oliver Leese's Scotch.

On the fourth day Pyle returned again to his beat with the GI's. "My friends will accuse me of having sold out to the brass," he explained with a sad smile, ridding himself of the helmet he wore while traveling with me and replacing it with a beanie.

On August 1 Patton substituted Truscott's 3rd Infantry Division for Middleton's 45th on the north coast road. The 45th had been scheduled to go with Clark into Italy and in preparation for that assault required at least a month for rest, refitting, and planning.

Although the 3rd had landed at Licata on D day, its path through the western end of Sicily had been less difficult than that of the 45th. By comparison, therefore, the 3rd Division was in better condition for the last two punishing weeks of this island campaign. While we regretted losing Middleton's plucky 45th, replacement by the 3rd invoked no hardship on II Corps.

Although the retreating German had blocked the port of Palermo with 44 sunken vessels, American engineers opened the harbor six days after its capture to 60 per cent of capacity. The first convoy to be unloaded there carried troops of Eddy's 9th Infantry Division in time to strengthen Allen's offensive on the Troina road. Ridgway's 82d had been withdrawn to Africa in preparation for the Italian invasion. Patton kept his 2d Armored in the far western end of the island for mopping-up operations there. We could not have used its Shermans on the limited roads of the Messina neck.

From the north coast road the enemy's defensive line stretched thinly through the steep, upland hills toward Troina. There it thickened into a strong point astride that vital road center. From Troina the line fell back toward Adrano where once again it thickened to protect the important Etna junction. And from Adrano the line followed the road that hugged the rim of Mount Etna down to Catania on the sea.

A single unimproved road ran between the U. S. front at Troina and the British front at Adrano. And just as Adrano was the key to the enemy's defense before Leese, so Troina was the key to his defenses in our sector. If we could smash Troina at the same time Leese broke through Adrano, the center of the enemy's line would collapse and he would be forced to withdraw speedily up both coastal roads.

The macadam road from Nicosia to Troina twisted through the small, gray, hilltop town of Cerami. Between Cerami and Troina the earth fell away into a brown and treeless depression resembling a giant bowl. The road at the bottom of that bowl disappeared behind

a succession of low hills. On the far side of that bowl Troina clung
to a mountain top like an ancient fortress. And behind Troina lay
the huge crater of Mount Etna.

On August 1 Terry Allen's infantry pushed boldly into this brown
bowl; they were hit by a powerful counterattack and thrown back to
their line of departure.

The following morning I telephoned Terry.

"Troina's going to be tougher than we thought," he said. "The
Kraut's touchy as hell here."

The enemy defending Troina counted on two exit roads from that
mountaintop position. One ran south toward Adrano, the other to
the rear. If we could get around his flanks and cut those roads with-

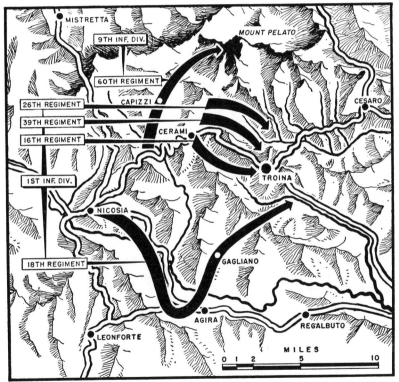

To avoid a frontal assault against Troina, the main attack of the 1st Division was directed toward that mountain city's escape roads to the rear,
while a regiment from the 9th Division went after the enemy's artillery
observation to the north.

out assaulting his main defensive position, he would either be forced to pull out or wait there and be trapped. Allen promptly went after both roads with one pincer from the north, another from the south in a double envelopment.

Terry had located his CP in Cerami in a dank and empty school-house decorated with the Fascist slogan: "Believe, Obey, Fight." I visited him there with Hart to coordinate artillery and air on the Troina attack. A battalion of 155-mm. Long Toms had been rolled into position behind the schoolhouse, and their muzzle blasts rippled the tile roof. Terry listened with amusement as each salvo muffled our conversation until at length I turned to him and asked, "Terry, could you arrange to have those guns shoot over the building instead of through it?" He reached for a phone and silenced the guns.

Air-ground support in Sicily was still hazardous and uncertain. Although we had profited by the Tunisian campaign, the system was still far from effective. Air-support parties with each division radioed for missions directly to the 3rd Air Defense Wing. There the missions were logged and orders teletyped to the fighter fields. A listening post at II Corps monitored the division requests to keep us informed. Too often, however, faulty transmission caused many of those missions to be scratched.

Near the close of the Sicilian campaign air-ground support showed promise of improving with development of mobile ground fighter controls. In jeeps equipped with VHF* radio sets, air-support officers advanced with the ground units to direct fighters assigned to them overhead. Two-way voice communication enabled the pilots to spot enemy concentrations and warn advancing troops. In the II Corps "afteraction" report for the Sicilian campaign, we concluded that "this means of directing fighter bombers warrants further trial." One year later it provided the eyes for our ground forces in their swift liberation of France.

Until we reached the Messina neck II Corps had found little occasion to call for fighter support. For until now the enemy had fought a delaying action, seldom holding long enough to a position to warrant our bombing him out. Here in the Etna stellung, however, he had dug in to stay. This fixed position gave us a remunerative target for air bombing.

In Sicily Allied troops were occasionally harassed by mistaken air identification of their movements on the ground. We stretched lumi-

*Very High Frequency.

nescent panels over our vehicle hoods but even these did not prevent occasional "friendly" bombings.

One afternoon during a conference at Terry Allen's CP a flight of A-36's strafed the position, forcing us to run for cover. Because this was the third U. S. strafing attack that day, I telephoned Patton to call off his air.

"But who told you they're our planes?" he asked. "Maybe they were German."

"General," I answered, slapping the dirt from my trousers, "I just climbed out of a ditch. They're A-36's all right."

On another day a U. S. tank column was attacked by a flight of the same A-36's. The tankers lighted their yellow smoke bombs in a prearranged recognition signal. But the smoke only caused the dive bombers to press their attacks. Finally in self-defense the tanks turned their guns on the aircraft. A ship was winged and as it rolled over, the pilot tumbled out in a chute.

When he landed nearby to learn that he had been shot down by *American* tanks, he bellowed in dismay.

"Why you silly sonuvabitch," the tank commander said, "didn't you see our yellow recognition signal?"

"Oh—" the pilot said, "is that what it was?"

For three days Allen's attack on Troina was thrown back by savage resistance. From a wooded mountain to the northeast of the city the enemy repelled our assaults with observed artillery fire. Each advance was answered with a jarring counterattack until Allen was forced to withstand 24 of them in six days. To strengthen his attack we committed a second regiment from the 9th Infantry Division, increasing to five the total number of U. S. regiments on that front. This last regiment had been ordered to dislodge the enemy from that vantage point where he held a corner on artillery observation. Troina itself was to be bombed until it surrendered or was smashed into dust.

On the late afternoon of August 4, I waited at a bend in the road, high up in Cerami, to witness this air attack, the heaviest to date in our Sicilian campaign. Across the bowl-like depression, now half obscured in dust, the fire from 18 battalions of artillery hammered the enemy's AA positions.

Thirty-six fighters circled high overhead, each loaded with 500-pound bombs. The artillery slackened and the bombers peeled off in a near-vertical dive. Soon the crown of Troina was wreathed in dust.

By the time a second flight of 36 planes had bombed that stricken city, Troina lay half obscured under a column of gray dust that partially hid the cone of Mount Etna. Once more the infantry started forward, but once more the enemy held and slashed back in counter-attack.

The following day we renewed the offensive. This time Major General Edwin J. House, Patton's tactical air commander, accompanied me to Cerami to view the air bombing. H hour passed with no sign of air. As we were about to leave in dismay, a drone sounded far off to the south. There, high in the sky, three A-36's were high-tailing for home.

"Holy smokes," I turned to House, "now just where in hell do you suppose they've dropped their bombs?"

"I'll be damned if I know," he said. "Maybe we'd better get back to your headquarters and see what went wrong."

On our arrival the phone was ringing. It was Oliver Leese from British XXX Corps. "What have we done that your chaps would want to bomb us?" he asked.

"Where did they hit?" I groaned.

"Squarely on top my headquarters," he said, "they've really plastered the town."

But by now the enemy had taken punishment enough on the stellung at Troina. He withdrew and our tanks rolled forward. On the sunny morning of August 6, Allen's 16th Infantry Regiment scaled the steep sides of Troina in the face of desultory rear-guard resistance. Dazed by their week's ordeal, the Sicilians crawled out of their cellars. Already the hot sun had baked the mountains of rubble that clotted the city's streets and a nauseous odor of death settled over the town. But while the bombing had momentarily stunned Troina, few Germans had been killed.

The morning Allen drove into Troina his 1st Division was accompanied by the 39th Regiment of Manton Eddy's 9th Division. At the head of that unit trooped its bold and eccentric commander, the indomitable Colonel Harry A. Flint of St. Johnsbury, Vermont. Stripped to the waist that he might be more easily identified by his men, Paddy Flint wore a helmet, a black silk scarf, and carried a rifle in his hand. The battle at Troina marked the start of his brilliant but brief combat career.

An old-time cavalry crony of Patton, Flint first appeared at the

II Corps CP in Beja to beg a line command that he might get into the shooting war. At the time he was assigned to AFHQ in Algiers. "Hell's bells, Brad," he complained, "I'm wastin' my talents with all those featherbed colonels in the rear—"

Soon after the Tunisian campaign ended Manton Eddy asked for a regimental commander to spark up his 39th Regiment which then showed signs of sluggishness in contrast to its spirited companions.

"What we need in the 39th is a character," Eddy said.

I sent him Paddy Flint.

After landing in Sicily Manton reported to corps at Nicosia with Paddy Flint in tow. The 39th was to be attached to Terry Allen for the Troina attack. The remainder of Eddy's 9th Division had not yet come ashore.

"Brad," Eddy whispered when Paddy ambled off to the G-3 tent for a briefing, "have you seen this?"

He held Flint's helmet in his hand. On its side there was boldly stenciled "AAA-O."

"And just what in hell does that mean?"

"Anything, anytime, anywhere, bar nothing—that's what it means. Paddy has had this thing stenciled on every damned helmet and every damned truck in the whole damned regiment."

I grinned.

"But haven't you issued some kind of a corps order about special unit markings?"

"Manton," I answered, "I can't see a thing today— Nope, not even that helmet of Paddy Flint's."

To help his regiment gain confidence under enemy fire, Paddy would stroll about the front, unconcernedly rolling a cigarette with one hand. With his rifle in the other he would gesture scornfully toward the enemy lines.

"Lookit them lousy Krauts. Couldn't shoot in the last war. Can't shoot in this one. Can't even hit an old buck like me."

These antics of Flint's worried me.

"Someday, Paddy," I once chided him, "you're going to walk around like that and get killed. Then you're going to prove just the opposite of what you're trying to teach your men."

He looked at me strangely for a moment. "Hell's bells, Brad," he said, "you know them Krauts can't shoot—"

Paddy was killed in Normandy when a German sniper shot him in the head. I'm certain he would have called it a lucky shot but even this satisfaction was to be denied him. For though he lived several hours, the wound had impaired his power of speech. Paddy died, a silent Irishman with a grin on his face.

After 24 days of campaigning the 1st Division was painfully reduced in strength. Sergeants were commanding platoons for the lack of officer replacements. To continue the advance on to Randazzo in pursuit of the German I passed Eddy's 9th Division through the 1st Division and halted the latter in place at Troina. Here it had waged its last battle of the Mediterranean war; it was the most severely contested one we fought.

Early in the Sicilian campaign I had made up my mind to relieve Terry Allen at its conclusion. This relief was not to be a reprimand for ineptness or for ineffective command. For in Sicily as in Tunisia the 1st Division had set the pace for the ground campaign. Yet I was convinced, as indeed I still am, that Terry's relief had become essential to the long-term welfare of the division.

A division represents not only the lives of 15,000 men and millions of dollars' worth of equipment, but it also represents a priceless investment in months and years of training. In the 1st Division that investment had been multiplied beyond measure by its long experience in battle. Thus in quality the 1st was worth the equal of several inexperienced divisions. It had become an almost irreplaceable weapon for the Normandy invasion.

In time of war the only value that can be affixed to any unit is the tactical value of that unit in winning the war. Even the lives of those men assigned to it become nothing more than tools to be used in the accomplishment of that mission. War has neither the time nor heart to concern itself with the individual and the dignity of man. Men must be subordinated to the effort that comes with fighting a war, and as a consequence men must die that objectives might be taken. For a commander the agony of war is not in its dangers, deprivations, or the fear of defeat but in the knowledge that with each new day men's lives must be spent to pay the costs of that day's objectives.

Under Allen the 1st Division had become increasingly temperamental, disdainful of both regulations and senior commands. It thought itself exempted from the need for discipline by virtue of its months on the line. And it believed itself to be the only division carrying its fair share of the war.

Yet to fight effectively under corps command a division must always subordinate itself to the corps mission and participate willingly as part of a combination. This the 1st found increasingly difficult to do. The division had already been selected for the Normandy campaign. If it was to fight well there at the side of inexperienced divisions and under the command of an inexperienced corps, the division desperately needed a change in its perspective.

By now Allen had become too much of an individualist to submerge himself without friction in the group undertakings of war. The 1st Division, under Allen's command, had become too full of self-pity and pride. To save Allen both from himself and from his brilliant record and to save the division from the heady effects of too much success, I decided to separate them. Only in this way could I hope to preserve the extraordinary value of that division's experience in the Mediterranean war, an experience that would be of incalculable value in the Normandy attack.

There had also developed in the 1st Division an unintentional rivalry between Terry Allen and Ted Roosevelt, his assistant division commander. This was inevitable in any such association of two strong and assertive personalities. Allen, I realized, would feel deeply hurt if he were to leave the division and Roosevelt were to remain. He might have considered himself a failure instead of the victim of too much success.

By the same token, Roosevelt's claim to the affections of the 1st Division would present any new commander with an impossible situation from the start. Any successor of Allen's would find himself in an untenable spot unless I allowed him to pick his own assistant commander. Roosevelt had to go with Allen for he, too, had sinned by loving the division too much.

Indeed the whole unpleasant situation had been nurtured by a succession of excesses: too much brilliance, too much success, too much personality, and too strong an attachment of two men for the 1st Division.

To break the news as gently as I could—for I knew it would shock them both—I called Allen and Roosevelt to my CP in Nicosia. En route they were ticketed by a corps MP for violation of the uniform regulations.

Terry had been riding in the front seat of his jeep, holding his helmet between his knees while his unruly black hair blew in the wind. An MP flagged him down. He reddened when he saw Allen's two stars. "I'm sorry, General," the MP said, "but my orders are to ticket *anyone* riding without a helmet. My captain would give me hell if he saw you going by."

Allen grinned but Roosevelt objected.

"See here, my boy, don't you know that's General Allen of the 1st Division?"

"Yes sir," the MP replied, "and you're General Roosevelt, sir. But I'm going to have to give you a ticket too, sir, for wearing that stocking cap." Ted shrugged in despair and peeled off the cap.

"Brad," he said on his arrival at corps, "we get along a helluva lot better with the Krauts up front than we do with your people back here in the rear."

The relief came as a severe blow to them. But though it was one of my most unpleasant duties of the entire war, I had to do it. Fortunately, both men rebounded like good soldiers. Allen returned to Europe with a superbly trained 104th Division which he led to the Elbe. And Roosevelt returned to England to win a Medal of Honor on the Normandy assault. There at the age of 56 he made his fourth H-hour landing on a hostile shore.

Among the aggrieved champions of Terry Allen, and he had many, the relief was condemned as completely unwarranted and some of them mistakenly ascribed it to a pique between Allen and Patton. There were no grounds for their suspicion. It is probably true that Patton irritated Allen, but it was Patton who persuaded Eisenhower to give him Allen for the Sicilian invasion. Responsibility for the relief of Terry Allen was mine and mine alone. George did nothing more than concur in the recommendation.

As Allen's successor in the 1st Division we picked Major General Clarence R. Huebner, known to the army as a flinty disciplinarian. Huebner had enlisted in the army as a private in 1910 and was commissioned during World War I. He was no stranger to the Big Red One, for he had already worn its patch in every rank from a private to colonel. In returning to command the division, however, he had come from a desk in the Pentagon, an assignment which did not tend to ease his succession to Allen's post.

On the second day after he assumed command there in the hills of Troina, Huebner ordered a spit-and-polish cleanup of the division. He then organized a rigid training program which included close-order drill.

"Keerist—" the combat veterans exclaimed in undisguised disgust, "here they send us a stateside Johnny to teach us how to march through the hills where we've been killing Krauts. How stupid can this sonuvabitch get?"

But Huebner knew what he was doing, however unpopular his tactics might be. From the outset he was determined to show the division that he was boss, that while the 1st might be the best division in the U. S. Army—it nevertheless was *a part* of the army, a fact it sometimes forgot. Fortunately, the animosity did not perturb him. He had ample time, he reckoned, to win the division to his side.

A more sensitive man than Huebner might have cracked under the strain, for it was not until after the Normandy invasion, one year later, that the last resentful adherents to Terry Allen conceded Huebner the right to wear the Big Red One. When he finally left to command a corps, they missed him almost as much as they did Allen.

At the village of San Fratello on the north Mediterranean shore the German had laid out his defenses on a 2,200-foot peak overlooking the coastal road. Unable to force that position in a frontal attack, Truscott attempted to flank it with a pack-mule maneuver inland. But as his troops moved into the mountains, they came under fire from the enemy's guns on the dry Furiano River bed.

A week before when Middleton found himself stalemated against a similar defensive position at San Stefano, Patton and I had explored the likelihood of outflanking a coastal road block by amphibious envelopment from the sea. If the enemy could be threatened from the rear by a force landed astride its escape route, he must either abandon his frontal position and fall back or hold to that position at the risk of encirclement and capture.

To complete an envelopment from the sea, however, would require skillful coordination with the land attack. For unless the main body can break through the enemy's frontal position quickly enough to relieve those light amphibious forces, the latter may be defeated in detail by the enemy's rear guard.

In mounting this first envelopment by sea at San Fratello, Patton left the delicate problem of timing to II Corps. After consulting with Truscott on the progress of his land attack, we scheduled the amphibious landing for August 8. Early that morning a reinforced infantry battalion landed without opposition at St. Agata, six miles to the rear of Monte San Fratello. Hard pressed by Truscott's assault by land and unnerved by this envelopment from the sea, the enemy evacuated his mountain position and fell back to reform his line.

In that single attack the 3rd Infantry Division advanced 12 miles nearer Messina. More importantly, it picked up 1,500 prisoners and disorganized the enemy's leisurely withdrawal.

Emboldened by this success, Patton called me to his advanced CP and ordered another north-coast landing on August 11. For after having been dislodged from Monte San Fratello the German had skidded skillfully into position again, this time in a range of hills behind the Zappulla River, a sandy, open stream bed.

After checking with Truscott, however, I learned that his division would be unable to crack that position in time to effect a link-up with the seaborne forces on August 11. I asked Patton if we might not delay the maneuver until August 12. "The amphibious attack means nothing," I insisted, "unless we tie in with Truscott's forces by land."

By this time George was anxious to get into Messina. He denied my request for a day's delay and insisted the attack go as scheduled on August 11. Again I remonstrated but George held fast. When I left his command post that day with his final directive, I was more exasperated than I have ever been. As a subordinate commander of Patton's I had no alternative but to comply with his orders.

Shortly before dawn on the morning of August 11 the 2d Battalion of Truscott's 30th Infantry Regiment waded ashore from their landing craft near Brolo, 12 miles to the rear of the German position behind the Zappulla.

Initially the landing passed undetected. However, as Truscott's infantry moved up from the beach to the coastal road, a German motorcyclist chanced along. A squad of jittery riflemen fired and killed him. Within a few minutes flares lighted the sky and sleepy German units were roused for the counterattack. Nevertheless by dawn Truscott's infantry had worked their way into position near the crown of Monte Creole overlooking the tiled roofs of Brolo. Their self-propelled supporting artillery, however, were marooned between the beach and the road, where a network of drainage ditches blocked their passage. Seventh Army had failed to provide Truscott with air photos for the assault. By noon, hard pressed by enemy attack from both front and rear, the infantry on Monte Creole was dangerously low on ammunition. Thirteen of their 15 pack mules were dead and bloating under the sun. Three hours later the marooned artillery on the beach was raked by enemy fire and trapped by tank attack.

Now isolated on its hill, without supporting fire, the battalion clung to its position all that day and night, awaiting relief by the main body of Truscott's troops pushing toward them by land.

Not until 6:00 A.M., August 12, did that relief force reach the battalion's survivors. Unable to afford the time required for an overland flanking attack, Truscott had pushed head-on against the enemy's frontal position. Despite these efforts of Truscott's to relieve it, the battalion had suffered heavy losses.

This misadventure, however, did not inhibit Patton. Despite our steady progress up the north coast road, he ranged the front daily. This prodding was part of Patton's technique of command. He once confided that he had become a successful commander primarily because he was the "best damn ass-kicker in the whole U. S. Army."

With Messina now only 40 miles off George's impatience mounted, for he was determined to precede Montgomery's Eighth Army into that final objective. Like George, I too was anxious to get into Messina before the British. But I was convinced we could make better progress, at less cost, through flanking manuevers rather than by direct attack against the enemy's coastal positions. For by now the speedy capture of Messina was unimportant. However rapidly we pushed into that city, we could not cut the enemy's escape route across to Italy.

As commander of the Third Army in Europe George merited and won the admiration of his troops and the affections of his subordinate commanders. However, this was not true of the Patton that fought the Mediterranean war. In that unhappy part of his career George's theatrics brought him much contempt, and his impetuousness outraged his commanders.

Canny a showman though George was, he failed to grasp the psychology of the combat soldier. For a man who lives each day with death tagging him at the elbow lives in a world of dread and fear. He becomes reproachful of those who enjoy rear-echelon security and safety.

To his troops an army commander is little more than a distant figure who occasionally shows himself on the front. As a consequence the impressions of those men are formed directly from what they see. George irritated them by flaunting the pageantry of his command. He traveled in an entourage of command cars followed by a string of nattily uniformed staff officers. His own vehicle was gaily decked with oversize stars and the insignia of his command. These exhibitions did not awe the troops as perhaps Patton believed. Instead, they offended the men as they trudged through the clouds of dust left in the wake of that procession. In Sicily Patton, the man, bore little resemblance to Patton, the legend.

On August 10 George drove up to call on me at the corps CP. He had stopped on the road en route to visit the patients at a nearby corps evacuation hospital. Few commanders spent more time touring the wards than George did, for he found in the bandaged wounds of those soldiers the recognizable badge of courage he respected most. These were men he could understand. He joked with them, talked to them, shook their hands, and pinned on their Purple Hearts.

As George drove into the CP I walked out to meet him. He jumped down from the high running board of his recon car.

"Sorry to be late, Bradley," he said, "I stopped off at a hospital on the way up. There were a couple of malingerers there. I slapped one of them to make him mad and put some fight back in him."

He spoke of it casually, without remorse and without any evidence of wrongdoing. Indeed I would probably have forgotten the incident had it not been brought to my attention two days later.

That was when Kean came to my trailer with the corps surgeon in tow. He handed me a typewritten sheet.

"Here's a report you should see, General. It came in to the surgeon this morning from the CO of the 93rd Evac."

I read it and turned to the surgeon. "Has anyone else seen this?"

"No, sir," he answered, "no one but me."

I handed the report back to Kean. "Seal it in an envelope," I told him, "and mark it to be opened only by you or me. Then lock it up in my safe."

The paper contained an eyewitness report of what afterward came to be known as the "slapping incident." It had been submitted through channels by the CO of the hospital Patton had visited on his way to corps.

According to the commander, George had strolled unannounced into the receiving tent of the 93rd Evac. There he walked from litter to litter, talking with the wounded and congratulating them on the performance of their divisions.

At length he came to a patient without splints or dressings. George asked what was wrong. The man answered that he was running a high fever. Patton dismissed him without a word.

Another patient was seated nearby, shaking with convulsions.

"And what's happened to you?" Patton asked.

"It's my nerves, sir," the man replied, his eyes filling with tears.

"What did you say?" Patton stiffened.

"It's my nerves," the patient sobbed, "I can't stand the shelling any more."

George raised his voice. "Your nerves, hell," he shouted, "you're just a goddamned coward."

The soldier cried and George slapped him. "Shut up," he said, "I won't have these brave men here who've been shot see a yellow bastard crying."

George struck the man again. His helmet liner fell off and rolled across the dirt floor.

Patton called to the receiving officer, "Don't you admit this yellow bastard. There's nothing the matter with him. I won't have the hospitals cluttered up with sonsabitches who haven't the guts to fight."

Then turning to the patient, he said, "You're going back to the front lines—you may get shot and killed, but you're going back to fight. If you don't, I'll stand you up against a wall and have a firing squad kill you on purpose."

Patton's uproar had alerted the hospital. By that evening an exaggerated version of the tale had started its travels around the island. Within a week it was common gossip.

Eisenhower was told of the slapping, though not through me. The story reached newsmen accredited to Patton's Seventh Army and soon crossed the Mediterranean to the press camp at AFHQ. But though many of these newsmen were critical of Patton, they voluntarily declined to file it.

Reprehensible though Patton's conduct had been, Eisenhower questioned whether it justified his relieving one of the finest ground gainers in the U. S. Army. Instead he reprimanded George and ordered him to apologize not only to the patients and hospital personnel but also to the troops of his Seventh Army.

Inevitably, however, the story leaked to the United States where it touched off a nation-wide dispute that almost cost Patton his career. Although it would have been easy for Eisenhower to dump Patton now that the heat was on, he chose to stand by him.

However, one can rationalize Patton's act without condoning it. To George the war was not so much an ordeal as it was the fulfillment of a destiny to which he shaped his life. He believed war to be a chronic ailment of mankind, destined to pursue civilization to its grave.

Since conflict was to be the inevitable lot of all mankind, George reasoned that man should resign himself to it and indeed welcome it as a manly challenge. Exhilarated as he was by conflict, he found it inconceivable that men, other than cowards, should want no part of war. At the same time he could not believe that men could break under an intense mental strain as a result of the hardships endured in war. To him it was axiomatic that those who did not wish to fight were cowards. If one could shame a coward, George said, one might help him to regain his self-respect.

I cannot believe that George was intentionally brutal in striking the soldier he called a coward. Patton simply sought to purge that soldier of "cowardice" by shaming him.

It is only because this slapping incident had such a significant effect on Patton's later career that I have told it here in detail. During his lifetime George was punished severely for his misstep; he can be hurt by it no longer. The admiration with which we cherish the memory of Patton in Europe is too enduring to be dimmed by this recollection of an incident that in the end made him a better commander.

By August 15 it was apparent that the end would come within a matter of hours. Ferries chugged across the straits from Messina loaded with escaping Germans. Piles of ordnance littered the route of their withdrawal up the coast road.

Determined, nevertheless, that he would beat Montgomery into Messina, Patton ordered a third amphibious envelopment to speed up Truscott's advance. This time, he assured me, we would have craft enough to lift a regiment ashore. The windfall, however, had come too late.

"There's no need for another landing," Truscott declared, "we can outrun an amphibious force by barging straight on up the road. The Kraut's got nothing out front to stop us."

I repeated this conversation to Patton but he would have no part of it.

"Very well, General," I said, "mount this operation if you want to. But we'll be waiting for your troops when they come ashore."

On the evening of August 15 a regimental task force from the 45th Division embarked to outflank the enemy with a landing at the

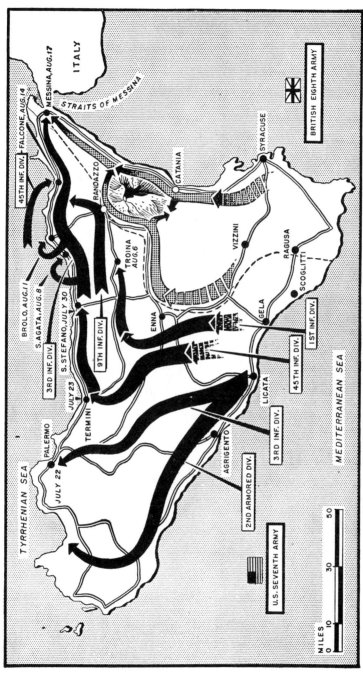

While Montgomery swarmed around Mount Etna in his advance toward Messina, Patton's Seventh Army pushed through the hub to the north and then up the north coast road.

village of Falcone, 32 miles from Messina. In the hushed darkness before dawn of August 16 the regiment waded ashore. Our guides were already on the beach, waiting.

Later that day a battery of Long Toms were wheeled into position on the coast road, and the first of 100 introductory rounds were fired across the Messina neck to the Italian mainland.

By nightfall Truscott's infantry had reached that point on the north shore where the coastal road turns south toward Messina only 12 miles off across the tip of the neck.

At 6:30 on the morning of August 17 a platoon from the 3rd Infantry Division poked warily into the outskirts of Messina. The enemy had made good his escape, leaving only an empty, rubble-strewn city behind him. Months of air bombing had gutted the thousands of reinforced concrete buildings where 34 years before an earthquake had buried 78,000 citizens under their homes.

At 8:25 Truscott's infantry, together with a token patrol from the 45th, reached Messina's City Hall. They arrived there a scant few minutes before a breathless lieutenant colonel raced in from the Catania road to stake Montgomery's claim.

Two hours later Patton entered the city with his Seventh Army staff. Thirty-eight days after our landing the Sicilian campaign came to an unspectacular end. Six weeks before, when questioned by newsmen aboard the *Ancon,* I had estimated 40 days.

11: *Arrival in England*

F ROM AN ALTITUDE OF ALMOST 10,000 FEET WE could barely make out the convoys that trailed across the quiet Mediterranean. A pale blue haze blurred the surface, veiling it from view. Only 20 minutes out of Trapani where the island faded behind us into a brown smudge, we had sighted the outriders of Clark's invasion fleet headed toward Salerno. Nine LST's sailed in a double line while three patrol craft moved alongside them. The pilot rocked the wings of our C-47 and turned off course to avoid them, for he was a veteran of the Sicilian air drop.

By nine that morning—it was September 8, 1943—we had cleared the CP at II Corps and hoisted our baggage aboard the plane for the first leg of an 11,500-mile flight to England with a side trip to the United States. The ship was Patton's, loaned to me for the flight to Algiers. We were to detour by way of Carthage where Eisenhower had established his forward CP for the Italian invasion. Lew Bridge was to wait in Algiers and there join the officers I had hijacked from corps for the voyage to England. Kean and Hansen were to accompany me to the United States where I was to round out my invasion staff.

The night before a chorus had serenaded us with II Corps' campaign song. With a verse for each phase of each new campaign, the tune celebrated the corps' Mediterranean victories. The lyrics were immodest and brash, but then so was II Corps, as good units generally are.

I had hoped to slip out without ceremony early the following morning. Instead, I found an honor guard lining the gravel road from our camp site, through the vineyard to the coast road. The vines were sagging with grapes grown in a soil that had been fertilized with generations of human waste. When eaten without thorough washing they brought on virulent dysentery attacks. If those waiting troops filched those grapes as I once did, their memories of that morning's departure are less pleasant than those I carried away.

Eager as I was to get started on the Channel invasion, I found it hard to leave the corps behind. Like a man's first love, his first field command fills an enduring place in his heart. After seven eventful months with II Corps I now felt like an uncertain young man leaving home to make his way in the world.

As the C-47 rose into the sky I caught one last glimpse of the corps CP where a sign of billboard proportions marked its final Sicilian bivouac. Seventh Army had objected when the II Corps engineers erected so huge a sign. "You might just as well floodlight it at night," they said, "to show the Luftwaffe where you are." But in the end pride prevailed over discretion and the big sign survived. The enemy, we argued, could find far more important targets for bombing than a corps temporarily out of the battle.

After landing on an air base near Carthage we drove through those ruins to a colony of villas high on a hill overlooking the sea. It was to these homes of colonial North Africa's rich Europeans that higher headquarters swarmed in pursuit of plumbing.

Eisenhower did not return to the villa for lunch until almost two. He looked drawn and worried. "Badoglio has gummed up the works," he explained. "We've just had to call off Ridgway's air drop on Rome."

Eisenhower was referring to arrangements for the Italian surrender and his plan to land an airborne division on the edge of Rome. The joint announcement of Italian surrender was to be made at 6:30 that evening. And at 3:30 the next morning Clark was to land at Salerno.

Now with only a few hours left before going on the air, Eisenhower had no assurance that Badoglio would honor his surrender agreement with a simultaneous broadcast from Rome. Unless that broadcast went on the air with Eisenhower's from Carthage, the German would seize the Italian transmitters and brand our statement a hoax.

Badoglio had disrupted the proceedings earlier that morning when in a radio message from Rome he begged Ike to delay the surrender announcement until after the Allied landing.

Eisenhower minced no words in his reply. "I intend to broadcast the existence of the armistice at the hour originally planned," he said. "If you or any of your armed forces fail to cooperate as previously agreed, I will publish to the world the full record of this affair." At the same time, however, he reluctantly ordered Ridgway to cancel the drop of his 82d Division on Rome. Badoglio had indicated that the Italian government could not guarantee a safe landing.

Eisenhower also called for the immediate return to Carthage of Brigadier General Maxwell D. Taylor, then underground in Rome as an emissary from AFHQ. Taylor was to have arranged for safe delivery of the airdromes in the vicinity of Rome.

This hasty switch on the eve of Clark's invasion was to shelve the 82d Division at a time when it was most desperately needed. For there was insufficient time left to shift the 82d back to its original objective at Capua in support of the Salerno landing. As a consequence the 82d almost became the proverbial nail in the horse's shoe at the very moment the Salerno landing wavered on the edge of failure. For the rest of that day Ike waited in Carthage. When it came time for me to leave for Algiers he had not yet received word from Rome that Badoglio would come through on schedule with his proclamation to the Italian people.

After a late-afternoon take-off from Carthage our plane droned up the North African coast toward AFHQ at Algiers. Kean and I napped in the ship's improvised parlor chairs. Behind us the Mediterranean darkened and screened Mark Clark's Army as it neared the Italian boot.

It was 6:34 when Hansen stumbled out of the pilot's compartment, a pair of earphones in hand. "General Eisenhower just came on; he's announcing the Italian surrender. Do you want to hear the rest of the broadcast?" With no prior knowledge of what was in the air, the pilot had tuned in his set on the Armed Forces network. He bounced excitedly in his seat when he heard Eisenhower's voice.

I reached for the earphones and asked the pilot to spin his dial. But there was no hint of Badoglio on the air.

Not until we had landed in Algiers did I learn that Badoglio had conquered his fears, but only after 45 minutes of delay. At 7:15 he came on the air to read his proclamation and urge the Italian people to take up arms against their Axis allies. That evening the King and his government fled for sanctuary behind the Allied lines.

In Algiers I found Bedell Smith tense, tired, and worried while awaiting news on surrender of the Italian fleet. For it was important to Allied operations in the Mediterranean that Italy's powerful surface fleet not fall into the hands of the German. We hoped it need not be scuttled as was the French fleet at Toulon. Admittedly, the situation at sea had vastly improved since 1940 when the British sailed into Mers el Kebir to bombard the French fleet as a precaution against Vichy surrender. Not only were German submarines being hunted in the North Atlantic, but Allied naval strength had multiplied at a staggering rate. Yet the Italian fleet could make up a formidable nuisance force should it fall into German hands. Allied naval units would then have to be deployed in the Mediterranean to contain it. And in 1943 this Allied naval strength could better be used elsewhere. On the heels of Eisenhower's surrender announcement, Admiral Cunningham had radioed an order to the Italian fleet directing its units to steam for Allied ports in compliance with the armistice terms.

Early that evening in Taranto, Spezia, and Genoa the Italian fleet slipped its moorings and headed by night for Malta. In the midmorning of September 9 the Italian flagship *Roma* was sighted by German recce off the Sardinian coast. That afternoon she was attacked by 15 JU-88's. The Italian naval commander-in-chief went down that morning with his ship, guns pointed against the planes of his former ally.

A day later, on September 10, 1943, Admiral Cunningham could wire the Admiralty in London: "Be pleased to inform their Lordships that the Italian Battle Fleet now lies at anchor under the guns of the fortress at Malta."

Cunningham had a right to be proud. For three desperate years he had held the Mediterranean Sea lanes open to Malta and Suez, even though Axis air attack had cost the lives of hundreds of British seamen. Only a year had passed since October, 1942, when Montgomery turned the tide at El Alamein. Now 12 months later, Britain not only controlled the Mediterranean, but Montgomery's Eighth Army troops were advancing up the Italian boot.

For a time Eisenhower had debated the wisdom of withholding from Clark's troops news of the Italian surrender until after they were safely ashore. For he knew that if they went in expecting an unopposed landing, the German might catch them dangerously off guard. Yet were we justified, he asked himself, in withholding such news after the Italians had pledged themselves to fight on our side? In the end Eisenhower thought not. He chose to risk the letdown that would come with the good news.

Not until months later did I learn that it was much worse than we had anticipated that night in Algiers. Clark's troops threw caution to the winds. By the time the German hit them, many were so overconfident that the unexpected resistance caused near-panic in some units.

The German in Italy had not been caught unawares. By the same reasoning that had led Eisenhower to pick the invasion beach at Salerno, the enemy anticipated the target of Clark's assault. He mined and wired the beaches, occupied the strong points, and massed additional Wehrmacht reserves near Naples. Eventually Eisenhower was forced to employ the full weight of his Mediterranean forces to help Clark's troops keep their precarious hold on that beachhead.

Although intelligence had hoped Italian partisan units might slow German reinforcements in the long trip down the Italian boot, Bedell confided that Eisenhower was not banking heavily on their aid. Partisan opposition must come from the heart. Only a sturdy national leader, a symbol of moral rebirth, could have roused the Italian people from their antipathy to war. Not until Italy suffered the brutality of German reprisals did the underground surge to power under the leadership of local chieftains. And not until then did this unhappy nation start on its long way back into the community of its neighbors.

It was Eisenhower who best summarized Italy's tragedy in his report on that campaign. "For three years we strained to break their spirit," he wrote. "We . . . succeeded only too well."

The following day, on September 9, 1943, Kean, Hansen, and I left Algiers in a two-motored bucket seater bound for Marrakech in French Morocco, ATC's Moroccan terminus for the air ferry service to England. A C-54 was scheduled to leave Marrakech that evening on the 1,700-mile ocean flight. The run was made at night over a zigzag course that stretched westward into the Atlantic far from the enemy fighters operating from the coast of Occupied France.

While checking my baggage the dispatcher glanced up briefly at my stars. He looked to the left and right, then whispered across the counter. "This is a bucket seater, General, and it's a nine-hour flight. Why don't you get lost until tomorrow. We'll fix you up with a real plush job that's coming through from the States."

"Sorry," I said, "but I'm in a hurry. Besides your ship can't be much worse than some days I've spent in a jeep." The bucket seats were no worry to me, for I was conveniently calloused from months in the field.

Because my third star rated me as a VIP, we were hustled off to dinner at the Taylor Villa, the fabulous Arabian Nights winter home of a wealthy New Yorker. There in a sunken green tile tub I took my first warm bath since setting sail for Sicily.

Back at the airfield we found the forward section of our ship screened off as a makeshift hospital ward for a wounded British general. It was Major General Percy B. Horrocks, a veteran corps commander from Montgomery's Eighth Army. He had been struck by a falling AA shell during a night bombing of Bizerte just before the Sicilian invasion. Despite the seriousness of his injury, Horrocks later returned to duty as a corps commander in Europe.

After standing all day in the African sun the C-54 was steaming hot as we packed ourselves inside its cabin. One hour out of Marrakech, at 12,000 feet, it felt like a deep-freeze locker. Most of the other passengers were airmen being returned to England after a shuttle bombing raid. Almost before the ship had cleared its runway they scrambled for space on the metal floor to nap their way to England. I corkscrewed across three bucket seats and, blanketed by my trenchcoat, soon fell asleep.

It was dawn when I awoke, stiff and cold but anxious for the first sight of Britain. Ireland sped beneath us with a rich greenness as we turned in from the Atlantic toward Scotland. Our plane freshened with the tart morning air as we glided across the Irish sea, banked over a golf course, and settled on the huge ATC base at Prestwick.

There we were met by an American cavalry major in boots. He had heard of our "mounted troops" in Sicily and for a few minutes welcomed me as the last hope of boots and saddles. The charm was broken, however, when I told him they were pack mules, and he evened the score by sitting us down to a British austerity breakfast.

The waitress, a stocky Scottish girl with a heavy brogue, offered me a choice of two entrees—neither of which I understood. "Let me have the second," I replied nonchalantly. She returned with stewed tomatoes. The first choice had been boiled fish. Prestwick taught me to confine my breakfast thereafter to the U. S. Army mess.

While we waited for the shuttle plane to London, W. Averill Harriman, ambassador to Russia, landed at Prestwick in a special-mission plane. He invited us to fly down with him, and two hours later we broke through the clouds into the barrage balloons that surrounded London.

Devers had motored out to Henley to greet us. A West Point classmate of Patton in 1909, Devers had been picked by General Marshall only four months before to command the ETO.

Eisenhower had become the first ETO commander in June, 1942, when he went to England as a major general. With the invasion of North Africa in November, 1942, Eisenhower went on to Algiers as Commander-in-Chief of Allied Forces there. For several months longer he was also carried as part-time U. S. commander of the ETO. By January, 1943, however, Europe and North Africa had become competitive theaters and Eisenhower could no longer split himself between their diverging interests. As a result the War Department cut the tie and named Lieutenant General Frank M. Andrews, an airman, to be theater commander. Andrews' appointment emphasized the growing importance in 1943 of our strategic air offensive against Germany.

Four months later Andrews was killed when the transport in which he was flying chanced an instrument landing in Iceland and crashed into the side of a peak. Devers was picked by General Marshall to succeed him. Like Eisenhower, myself, and most senior commanders, Devers owed his command to an impression he made on General Marshall earlier in his army career.

In 1940, when General Marshall scanned his list of colonels to fill a number of vacancies for general officer appointments, he broke precedent and reached down into the files to groom a couple of promising men for high command. One was Courtney H. Hodges, then a 53-year-old colonel. The other was Jakie Devers, only one year his junior. At the time Eisenhower and I were lieutenant colonels, too young for even regimental commands. Six months later Devers was made a major general and assigned to Fort Bragg in command of the 9th Division. While there he was ordered to enlarge that cantonment that it might house another division from the National Guard. Devers went after the job with such zest that he was soon known in Washington as a young officer who "could get things done."

My own association with Jakie Devers went back to 1912 when I was a second-year cadet at West Point. Devers reported to the Academy that year as a tactical instructor and was put in charge of the baseball squad. For three years I played on his team.

As senior American commander in the ETO Devers doubled in brass. Not only was he to accumulate troops and equipment for the Channel invasion, but he was also to act as watchdog for the U. S. Joint Chiefs of Staff on combined invasion planning with the British. Issues of major importance were referred, of course, to Washington for decision. But in the hundreds of routine staff agreements that make up an invasion plan, Devers had been charged with seeing that American views prevailed in balance with those of the British.

When in August, 1943, Morgan, as chief of staff at COSSAC, delivered his prospectus on the Channel invasion to the Combined Chiefs of Staff, he completed the task that had originally been assigned his staff. Yes, he concluded, the assault could be made in 1944—even within the stingy limits of resources tabbed for the job. To prove his point Morgan submitted an outline plan. OVERLORD was its code name, coined by no less a phrasemaker than the Prime Minister himself.

At this stage, however, OVERLORD consisted only of an outline. Morgan had narrowed down the choice of Channel beaches; he had scrutinized the ports, calculated tonnage, and reckoned the enemy opposition. With this groundwork he then sketched a plan for the assault. But our troubles were only beginning. To turn that outline into a blueprint would take nine more months of tactical planning.

In Morgan's outline of the OVERLORD plan three divisions were to make the initial assault. One American division was to land on the right; two British divisions on the left. All three were to go in under the field command of a British Army. Once the American divisions built up to a force of Army strength, an American Army headquarters would assume command in that sector. And at that point a British Army Group would take command of both those Armies. This British Army Group was then to direct the ground campaign until capture of the Brittany peninsula, or until the establishment in France of a U. S. Army Group.

In other words, the British were to exercise airtight tactical control on both the Channel crossing and during our first few months ashore.

In their red brick headquarters at 20 Grosvenor Square, American tempers flared and Devers' staff frigidly rejected COSSAC's proposition. It was during this bitter struggle on the OVERLORD chain of command that I arrived in London.

Shortly before I arrived, Devers had sought to break the deadlock with a solution of his own. He recommended that the assault divisions be commanded by British and American corps directly under the thumb of the Supreme Commander. But this was not a practical solution, for Devers would have by-passed the field army, the key logistical element in any chain of command. COSSAC moreover protested that the Supreme Commander could not physically exercise direct command over ground forces in the assault. I was inclined to agree with COSSAC.

When General Marshall radioed Eisenhower that I was to command the American Army on the channel assault, he also disclosed that I was to form a U. S. Army Group "to keep pace with the British planning." A field army ordinarily consists of two or more corps containing six or more divisions. During the last few months of the war in Europe a single field army often contained 12 to 15 divisions. However, where two or more Armies take to the field, their effort must be coordinated by a senior echelon of command. This is the role of the Army Group. By the time we reached the Elbe our 12th Army Group comprised four Armies with a total of 10 separate corps and 43 divisions.

Although General Marshall was not yet prepared to name the Army Group commander, he could no longer delay organization of a group headquarters in the ETO. For as lesser units got under way on their invasion planning, it would become necessary for the Army Group to keep pace on the follow-up. On my stopover in the United States, I was not only to round out the First Army staff, but I was to form an Army Group staff. The assignment was not as difficult as it may have sounded, for Devers had already selected a G-2, G-3, and G-4 for the Army Group.

The day before my arrival in England Devers had radioed General Marshall a proposal for the creation of an American GHQ. This headquarters was to have been similar to Pershing's in World War I. The forward echelon would become the American ground command in the field operating directly under the Supreme Commander. The rear was to carry on as an administrative tail. General Marshall promptly rejected the plan. Not only was he anxious to avoid inter-locking responsibilities between field and administrative staffs, but he wanted to keep them just as far apart as he could. Perhaps be-cause he sensed in Devers' GHQ proposal a scheme to shelter the Army Group within the bosom of ETOUSA,* General Marshall went one step further. He recommended physical separation of the two headquarters.

"I desire," he wrote Devers late in September, "that the organiza-tion of the Army Group headquarters be initially controlled directly by Bradley under your supervision and that it not be merely an off-shoot or appurtenance to ETO headquarters." With this title to autonomy, the fledgling 1st U. S. Army Group staff rolled up its maps and moved to a new home in Bryanston Square, taking over a strip of West End flats two blocks from Marble Arch.

Although I was to be in England for just the week end before continuing on to the United States, Devers suggested that I drive down to Bristol and size up the prospective home of First Army. The decision had already been made at ETOUSA to evict V Corps from that onetime maritime center of the colonial slave trade and make room for First Army. Not only was Bristol a convenient three hours by car from London, but it stood strategically located at the gate-way to southwest England where American troops were to be staged in preparation for the invasion. From there they would be in position to embark from the southwest Channel ports.

This was my first visit to England and I welcomed the chance for a rubberneck tour of the London-Bristol route over which I was to become so frequent a commuter. From the Dorchester Hotel in the fashionable West End of London we turned through Hyde Park, past Albert Hall, and into the busy Saturday afternoon streets of Hammersmith. There queues of housewives, ration books in hand, waited patiently before the boarded shop windows. Here and there an occasional gap in the rows of sooty buildings showed where the blitz had spent its strength only three years before.

V Corps made its home in the Gothic buildings of Clifton College, a British public school, where a statue of Field Marshal Earl Douglas Haig overlooked the rugby field. Until August, 1943, V Corps had existed in England as a lonely tactical outpost in a theater of admin-istrative commands with but a single division to its roster. Since then the 29th Infantry Division had been reinforced by the 3rd Armored

*European Theater of Operations, United States Army.

from the United States and the 5th Infantry from Iceland. By Christmas, 1943, these three had grown to ten. And on the eve of invasion U. S. divisions in England totaled 20.

Commander of V Corps was Major General Leonard T. Gerow, an intimate companion of Eisenhower's ever since their days as lieutenants. I first met Gerow as a promising young officer in 1925 when we were students together at the Infantry School. As the senior field command of the U. S. Army in Britain, V Corps had already been cut into OVERLORD planning. Its 29th Division had already been scheduled as U. S. vanguard on the invasion and maps of the Normandy beachfront were hung in Gerow's war room.

Gerow's billet consisted of a plainly furnished room on the second floor of Clifton's worn administrative building. It was directly over his office and within earshot of his phone. "She's all set up, Brad," he said. "You can move in any time you want to."

"Not for me, thanks, Gee," I answered, "the bed's too damned close to your desk. I've been sleeping under a situation map for almost nine months. Now I want to get away from it at night."

The planning grind in England was to be a long and tedious ordeal. If I were to spend my evenings at the desk, my staff would feel compelled to hang on until I went to bed. I could not see any justification for wearing them out until we got into operations.

While we were breakfasting at Clifton the next morning on eggs beggared from a U. S. naval vessel in port at Bristol, the city's church bells began to ring. Although it was Sunday, Gee's corps staff looked up in surprise.

"First time they've rung since 1940," Gerow explained to me with a grin. "Those bells were to be the signal for alert on the invasion of England. But today they're ringing to celebrate Italy's surrender." I found it difficult to believe that less than a week ago I was sitting with Eisenhower in Carthage wondering if Badoglio would come through.

On our return to London that evening Hansen and I strolled through Hyde Park to see something of the British people. On the mall near Marble Arch, traditional gathering place for street-corner speakers, several orators had attracted the Sunday-evening throngs. One handsome but aged Briton appealed to his listeners to demand that England open "a second front."

On the fringe of the crowd a gray-headed gentleman raised his cane. "Tommyrot," he called to the platform, "why don't you go to work and leave strategy to the military experts?"

"Experts, 'e says," a woman called back, "and now who is 'e to be talking of experts?"

The heckler twisted his head and with icy calmness replied, "Madam, will you please oblige me and go to blazes."

The crowd hooted and the speaker called for order. "May I remind you, dear friends," he said, "that strategy is the decision of the War Cabinet. And the War Cabinet was created by the people's parliamentary government. Therefore, any decision on strategy in this war rightfully and properly belongs to you."

I thought of how little comprehension he had of what the "second front" entailed, of the labors that would be required to mount it. Fewer than five blocks away, in a brick building on the corner of Grosvenor Square, it had already been crayoned on TOP SECRET maps.

An advance guard from First Army headquarters at Governor's Island, New York, had arrived in London several days before to pave the way for that staff. They came anticipating that I would take that stateside staff intact and were crestfallen to learn of the added personnel I had brought with me from II Corps. Of the four principal general staff posts, two were slated for these Mediterranean veterans, Monk Dickson as G-2 and Wilson as G-4. And of the 18 special staff section chiefs, nine were to be filled from II Corps.

My G-3 at First Army was to be Colonel Truman C. Thorson, a doughboy from Benning who reported to corps in Sicily at the tag end of that island campaign. Until the start of the war Thorson was one of those unlucky officers whom Hodges and I referred to as the "forgotten men." Army policy had provided that only officers with superior ratings be sent to the Command and General Staff School. Unfortunately Thorson had served for three years under a commander who denied the literal existence of a "superior" officer. As a consequence, Thorson's record did not include a tour of duty at Leavenworth. He was under orders to leave Benning on an obscure assignment when the Japanese struck at Pearl Harbor.

Inasmuch as Thorson had written the emergency defense plan for Georgia, I asked that his orders be canceled and that he be retained to assist me in executing that plan for the protection of key installations throughout that state. So outstanding was his performance that when I was ordered to form the 82d Division I carried Thorson along as my G-4. Thereafter, when I went to the 28th, I called for Thorson as a regimental commander which brought him a promotion to colonel. Affectionately know to his troops as "Hard Rock Harry," Thorson again showed the versatility that was to make him so valuable in First Army. My good fortune in having "discovered" Thorson illustrates the extent to which chance intervenes even in the most capable officer's career. Thorson became a brigadier general while G-3 of First Army and his star was made a permanent one at the end of the war.

For my G-1 of First Army I chose Colonel Joseph J. O'Hare, then in the same job on Governor's Island. O'Hare was a big red-headed Irishman whom I had known as a cadet when we played football together. Several years after graduation we served together at West Point when O'Hare returned as French instructor and part-time coach of the football squad.

Although somewhat severe in his staff relationships, O'Hare proved himself a wonderfully competent G-1. While at First Army and afterward in the Group he minced no theories on his job.

"People expect G-1 to be a sonuvabitch," he once said, "and I'm just the guy to prove it to them." In the minds of some O'Hare probably did, but from my point of view he was as valuable an officer as I had on my staff. When during the winter campaign Lee's G-1 bungled his job on replacements, it was O'Hare who waded into the mess, carried the issue to Washington, and eventually straightened it out.

After the week end in Bristol we left London for Prestwick on our way back to the States. Red came along to help me sift the First Army staff. After lunch at Prestwick we landed at Iceland for dinner in the famed Hotel de Gink. On our take-off that evening for Presque Isle, Maine, a squadron of P-38's escorted us clear of the island until our pilot suddenly banked around and turned his C-54 back. A mechanic had neglected to replace the cap on our right wing fuel tank and gas was streaming out in a ribbon behind us.

At Maine we refueled while hurrying through a breakfast of ham and eggs and apple pie. Four hours later we landed in Washington after a stopover in New York for a customs inspection. General Marshall's youthful Secretary of the General Staff, the brilliant Colonel Frank McCarthy, had called my wife and daughter and had them waiting on the field. Elizabeth had just started her senior year at Vassar. Meanwhile Mrs. Bradley had settled down at the Thayer Hotel in West Point for the duration. There Elizabeth could visit her mother on week ends while seeing the cadet she was to marry the following June.

I reported to the Pentagon and then went out for a quart of ice cream.

During those two brief weeks in the United States I spent most of my time scouring the Pentagon for personnel. We had no difficulty in tracking down the officers we wanted; the difficulty came in getting them released. For as the army and air corps swelled to over 7,000,000 men by September, 1943, there were many more requests for good officers than there were men with proper qualifications. It was O'Hare who came to my rescue, for better than anyone else he knew the stealthy underground short cuts of a good G-1. In the end he managed to get most of the men I wanted.

For almost a week on my return I waited to see General Marshall. Unable to sandwich me into his tight daily schedule, he invited me to go with him to Omaha where he was to address the American Legion's National Convention. En route in the Chief of Staff's C-47, we reviewed the Sicilian campaign and again General Marshall startled me with his detailed knowledge of it. But nothing was said about future operations and I did not press the point. My information was to come from COSSAC and through the normal chain of command. Another temporary homecomer also accompanied General Marshall on that flight. Lieutenant General Simon Bolivar Buckner had just returned to the United States from Alaska before heading out to the Pacific. It was to be the last time I saw him. Buckner was killed on June 18, 1945, by Japanese artillery on Okinawa.

One afternoon as I sat in the Pentagon leafing through a list of colonels, Colonel McCarthy telephoned from the Chief of Staff's office. "The White House has asked if you will call there tomorrow morning. The President would like to have you report on the Sicilian campaign." This was to be my first and only conference with President Roosevelt.

Uncertain as to whether a soldier saluted his Commander-in-Chief, I played safe and braced inside the office door. The President called hello from across his desk and waved me to a seat. His huge head and massive shoulders overshadowed the cluttered array of knickknacks on the desk top.

I had been told the President was especially interested in hearing how our troops had seasoned in battle. I made my report brief and to the point. He followed me intently with a remarkable understanding of military problems in the field.

Then almost before I was aware of what had happened, the President had reversed our roles and he was briefing me. America's scientific resources, he said, had been recruited in a staggering project to unlock the secrets of nuclear fission. He believed they could produce a weapon that would totally revolutionize warfare.

The President called it an "atom bomb."

At the moment, however, he was worried for fear the Germans might have outstripped us in the development of an atom bomb of their own. Intelligence reports had pointed to Trondheim, Norway, where the enemy was known to be producing "heavy water." He wanted me to know what we were doing in the event we were confronted by a similar German weapon on the invasion of France.

A few minutes later I was ushered out of the President's oval office, past the newsmen in the outer hall. None of them knew me and I went out unaccosted.

That one terse White House warning was all I heard of the atom bomb until I returned to the United States one month after V-E Day. At no time during the war do I recall Eisenhower's mentioning it to me. And during his two visits to our European front, General Marshall never once dropped a hint as to what was afoot.

Of course, during the early 1920's and 30's many of us in the army had speculated on the need for perfecting an explosive mightier than TNT. Although research had produced new explosives, for the most part they were too unstable for military use. Meanwhile enormous strides had been made in the technology of warfare. The development of strategic aircraft had altered the entire pattern of war. But through it all, the explosives we employed were essentially those of World War I. All we had done was to increase the weight and range of our missiles. Now the atom was to fill this gap.

After a week end at West Point, a busy day at Governor's Island, and an evening in New York to see *Oklahoma,* I returned to Washington to complete the selection of key officers on both my Army and Army Group staffs. My choice as Chief of Staff for the Army Group was Leven Allen, the lean and brilliant staff officer who had so expanded the Infantry School's output that by September, 1943, it was commissioning almost 200 second lieutenants a day.

Unlike Kean who was a hard taskmaster and a perfectionist in every move, Allen had a friendly and informal manner. Yet each was competent in his own way and their contrasting personalities fitted their uniquely contrasting staffs. For at First Army the pace was harder, faster, and more rattling than that at Army Group. Moreover, the Army staff was aggressive, touchy, and high-strung. Within the family it performed magnificently, for the Mediterranean contingent had already undergone its hard knocks in the Tunisian campaign. But the II Corps holdovers in that First Army staff had not forgotten the highhanded treatment by Seventh Army during the Sicilian campaign. As a result, in its later relationships with the other Armies and especially with higher commands, First Army was critical, unforgiving, and resentful of all authority but its own. As though from instinct, it closed its ranks and looked upon all outsiders as upstarts intruding in a private war. Yet as much as First Army exasperated me while I was in command of the Army Group, I have never known a finer nor more devoted staff than the one which served with me on the invasion.

At Army Group where the pace was leisurely in contrast to the tenseness at First Army, the staff seemed mild, unhurried, and unworried except during an occasional tussle with Monty. However, if the staff at Group was less tempestuous than that at First Army, its performance was no less efficient.

Eager to get on with planning in England, I left Washington on October 1 aboard a C-54 for the Great Circle winter crossing.

Before plunging into OVERLORD planning on my return, I arranged for billets both in London and Bristol, for it was impossible as yet to determine how much time I would spend with First Army, how much with the Army Group. Since ETOUSA, COSSAC, and 21st Group were all located in London, initially it was important that I be convenient to them. Consequently, I proposed to spend the first part of each week in London, the remainder and week end in Bristol. I based Bridge with the Army Group and Hansen with the staff at First Army. Fortunately, Group was not to enter the actual chain of command over First Army until it became operational in France. Otherwise, I might have been sending directives to myself. Nevertheless an occasional TWX went to BRADLEY, CG, FIRST ARMY, signed BRADLEY, CG, FUSAG. The latter was an abbreviation of the 1st United States Army Group. This designation was later changed to the 12th Army Group as part of our deception plan on the invasion.

In London I was billeted in the Dorchester Hotel, a handsome West End structure on the very edge of Hyde Park. Not only was it just across the street from a U. S. Army mess, but it was less than a brisk ten-minute walk to Group headquarters on Bryanston Square.

"There's another thing you should know, sir," the billeting officer said. "The Dorchester's got a reinforced roof. It'd take a big bomb to get through." I often remembered his reassurance while lying comfortably abed during the winter nighttime raids.

In Bristol, II Corps staff had just landed, yellow-faced from their daily dosage of atabrine in the Mediterranean. Three weeks before I too had landed in England the color of a pumpkin. On our last evening in Sicily, Kean had happily toasted me with what he hoped would be his last atabrine tablet of the war. The next morning, he confessed his toast had been premature. The dosage was to continue for six weeks after leaving the Theater.

V Corps had requisitioned a residence for me beyond the Bristol Downs, a billet spacious enough to house my key staff officers and aides. An English country home with ballroom, greenhouses, and stables, the house, we were told, had been tentatively earmarked as a home for wayward girls. When the first American army truck rolled into its drive, the neighbors were said to have shrugged with resignation, if not relief.

Until the house was readied Kean and I were to be billeted at Bristol's fashionable Grand Hotel, which lay in a corner of the old city. As we approached the desk to register, the room clerk held up his hands.

"Sorry, gentlemen," he said, "but we honestly haven't a vacant chamber. A good many British travelers come to Bristol, you know."

An impasse developed until a hurry-up call brought Colonel Edward Gidley-Kitchen, commander of the Bristol Sub-Area, to our rescue in the hotel lobby.

As I signed my name to the register, the clerk blotted it and looked up. "I hope, sir," he said, "that you won't be staying long."

I hoped so too. For I was in a hurry to cross the Channel and see what awaited us on the other side.

12: *Evolution of*

OVERLORD

To TRACE THE STRATEGY OF OUR CROSS-CHANNEL invasion to the beginning, we must go back to the midnight of June 2, 1940, and to the beach off Dunkirk where a British major general made his way in a small boat through the wreckage of an armada offshore. In the light of fires set by German bombers he searched the harbor and beaches for Allied troops awaiting debarkation. Satisfied that none had been left behind, Major General Harold Alexander, commander of the 1st Division, ordered his skipper to steer for England. He was the last of more than 335,000 Allied soldiers to quit the continent at Dunkirk for the withdrawal to Britain.

Two days before, still another British division commander marched his troops into the surf of the North Sea where they boarded a fleet of rescue craft for the perilous voyage to England. The third son of an Anglican bishop from Tasmania, his name was Bernard Law Montgomery.

Outflanked by the swift German breakthrough and exposed by Leopold's surrender, the British Expeditionary Force of 255,000 troops found itself pocketed on the North Sea coast. There the British navy with the aid of a makeshift holiday fleet, snatched the BEF from its trap and transported it to England only a few hours before the Wehrmacht closed in to the sea. As those British troops straggled up the Thames, weary, hungry, and disheartened, without arms and equipment, and almost without hope, the war seemed all but lost only nine months after it had started.

But as the Wehrmacht closed to the Channel, there it discovered that it had outrun the most ambitious schemes of its staff planners. In not having anticipated the need for so speedy an assault crossing of the English Channel, the German High Command admitted to one of its major miscalculations of the war. Because England had been counted upon to quit with the fall of France, the enemy had failed to provide the craft he would require for a cross-channel invasion. That failure perhaps more than any other doomed Germany to defeat.

Reluctant to risk a makeshift assault against the British navy, the Wehrmacht settled down on the coast until the Luftwaffe softened England. Four years later it was still waiting but this time it was the hunted and not the hunter. Just as the Battle for Britain had become a battle for the English Channel so would the Battle for Germany start with the conquest of that Channel. From the moment Alexander cast off from the beach at Dunkirk, a Channel crossing became the inevitable forerunner to Allied victory in the West.

Even after the RAF had beaten off the frantic attacks of the Luftwaffe during that terrible summer and fall of 1940, it was difficult to see how Britain could long prevail against the uneven odds that had been assembled against her. From Narvik in Norway to the Pyrenees in Spain, Germany commanded the Atlantic coast line. And with the capture of France's Brittany ports, Grand Admiral Karl Doenitz shifted his U-boat bases within easier reach of England's sea lanes. Allied shipping losses mounted catastrophically until by the end of 1940 they totaled more than 5,000,000 tons. And though England had entered the war with a surface fleet that was eventually to prove her salvation, she was unable to replace the shipping losses that threatened to paralyze her merchant fleet.

Germany fed its massive war machine with manpower, food, and other resources from the occupied nations of Czechoslovakia, Poland, Denmark, Norway, Holland, Luxembourg, Belgium, and France. Behind this cordon of occupied countries, German industries expanded in preparation for a renewal of the offensive. By 1941 aircraft production in Germany had increased to more than 12,000 planes each year contrasted to the 8,000 she produced at the outbreak of the war. During the same period tank production rose from less than 1,000 tanks each year to more than 3,600.

The air battle of Britain helped awaken our people to the nearness of the danger and on August 31, 1940, the National Guard was called into Federal Service. Fourteen days later Congress passed the nation's first preparedness draft for war.

As a lieutenant colonel on General Marshall's staff during the critical year of 1940, I watched him patiently nudge Congress step by step in a laborious effort to expand the army from 191,000 men in 1939 to its authorized strength of 280,000. On September 1 when General Marshall took his oath as Chief of Staff of the Army, Hitler's troops had massed for their attack on Poland.

Despite the meagerness of American military resources in the autumn of 1940, U. S. observers in Britain had already concluded that in the event of our involvement, Germany must be the first of the Axis to be defeated. For not only was Germany the ringleader in world aggression, but once having digested her conquests, she alone would possess the power to stalemate or defeat us. In the Pacific where Japan grew more and more belligerent, we could be hurt but not destroyed.

Early in 1941 when the early contingents of draftees trickled into unfinished army camps throughout the United States, British and American military chiefs conferred for the first time secretly in Washington. Out of these conversations there emerged in 1942 a committee to be known as the Combined Chiefs of Staff. With a membership that included the service chiefs of both England and the United States—including Fleet Admiral William D. Leahy, Roosevelt's unofficial chief of staff—the Combined Chiefs became an Allied board of directors in the prosecution of the war. Although the Joint Chiefs of both nations continued to report directly to their commanders-in-chief, the Combined Chiefs answered as a body to the dual authority of Roosevelt and Churchill. The agreement was a happy omen, for it not only established a unity of command but it protected each of the signatories from unjust encroachments by the other.

It was during these conferences in Washington in February and March of 1941 that British and American military chiefs first agreed that should the United States be forced into the war the knockout blow must be aimed at Germany.

On June 21, 1941, Germany attacked Russia. Meanwhile England's situation worsened. In North Africa the Axis armies threatened to drive on through Egypt to the strategic oil lands of the Middle East. And in both Hong Kong and Malaya the emboldened Japanese forced Britain to divert troops she could ill afford from her invasion watch on the English Channel. On the high seas, U-boats continued to prey even more hungrily upon her lifelines until by the end of 1941 Allied shipping losses exceeded 9,500,000 tons. By now Germany's Admiral Doenitz had tripled the undersea craft with which he started the war.

Although Britain had outlined a plan for a cross-channel assault as early as 1941, the proposal was fantastically premature. The eight divisions she had scraped together for defense of her island home were outweighed by the overwhelming strength of the German army. Although Hitler had committed no less than 165 divisions in his attack on Russia, he left another 63 behind to garrison Occupied Europe.

With the threadbare resources left to her, England had little choice for the moment but to pin her hopes for victory on exhaustion of the Reich. If Germany could not be defeated in an armed contest, then perhaps she could be drained of her strength and so weakened as to crumble from within. It had happened before in 1918; might not it happen again? And so in the autumn of 1941, England pitted her hopes for victory on the unlikely assumption that Germany might yet be defeated by naval blockade, by air bombing of her homeland, by resistance in the occupied nations, and last—but undoubtedly foremost—by attrition in her war with Russia.

Although General Marshall could sympathize with the British and the weaknesses that inclined them toward this strategy of exhaustion, as early as September, 1941, he declared to the British Chiefs of Staff that the war could not be won by waiting, that Germany would not be defeated by an indirect approach to what was essentially an offensive problem. To smash Germany's offensive power, he argued, it would be necessary to close with the Wehrmacht and destroy it. These were brave words in 1941 for General Marshall, even with the vast potential that was being mobilized behind him. But Britain could not deal in such abundant expectations for they were not available to her at this time. Instead her strategy had to be realistically fixed to the meager resources she had on hand.

When war came to the United States on December 7, 1941, it came with such suddenness and disaster that our Germany-first strategy was almost abandoned because of what happened at Pearl Harbor. The navy had lost so much of its vital offensive strength that it suddenly found itself hard pressed to keep the sea lanes open. By December 7, 1941, after 15 months of mobilization, the army had expanded to 1,700,000 men or a total of 36 numbered divisions. But few of them were ready for combat. And although the air corps had swelled to 270,000 men, it was still in its infancy.

With the United States actively engaged in the war, the Combined Chiefs' outlook could now be transformed into a realistic strategic plan. Almost immediately Churchill and his military staff hurried to Washington to link their British resources with ours.

In agreeing upon a strategy that would first knock Germany out of the war, the British and American planners had applied an old military axiom: Always concentrate your forces in the attack. Not only would the defeat of Germany make it difficult for Japan to prolong the war, but it was only against Germany that the Allies could concentrate their combined forces in the attack. Neither England nor Russia could have spared troops from their borders to battle the Japanese in the Pacific. If Japan were to be the first target for Allied retribution, the United States would have to undertake that offensive alone. In Europe, on the other hand, Germany lay wedged between the centers of Allied power. Both England and Russia could protect their homelands while engaged in the attack. To these arguments we added the most important of all: if Russia were to survive both as an enemy of Germany and as an ally of ours, she must be given immediate aid. Aid meant the diversion of German troops from the Russian front, a diversion that could be accomplished only by the opening of a second front.

During that disheartening winter of 1941 Providence finally showed itself on the side of the Allies. Outside the gates of Moscow where the German armies had been drawn up on the edge of triumph, a bitter Russian winter suddenly paralyzed the Wehrmacht. Once again, as on the Channel, Hitler's High Command paid dearly for its lack of total preparation. In its elaborate planning for the Russian campaign, no adequate provision had been made for the deadly subzero cold of the steppes. As the Red army halted its withdrawal to dig in on defense, the Germans suddenly found themselves perilously marooned on the icy plains of Russia. With partisans hacking at their exposed lines of communications, the German armies began a strategic withdrawal that would safeguard them until the coming of spring.

And so at Christmas, 1941, the Russians suddenly emerged as the key to Allied strategy during the next two years. Above all it was essential that she be sustained in the war, for nowhere could Germany be bled so desperately as on the Eastern front. With the German withdrawal from Moscow, the Allies had almost miraculously squeaked through their second major crisis of the war.

Almost from the day of our involvement in World War II, American planners set out to explore the only practical method that could bring us to grips with the German army. However difficult the task might be, it called for an assault across the Channel. For not until we had landed in France could we press on to the Ruhr and Berlin. Meanwhile, with the Allied armies approaching his frontiers from the West, Hitler would inevitably be forced to weaken his armies on the Russian front. Anything less could not be decisive.

However, to mount this Channel offensive American planners foresaw the need for resolute long-range planning. They would have to calculate every move, weigh every ton, in terms of its ultimate effect upon that Channel invasion. Every move throughout the world must be subordinated to it.

During the last week of March, 1942, President Roosevelt, fearful of a British defeat in the Libyan desert, startled the Joint Chiefs of Staff with a suggestion that the Channel assault be temporarily sidetracked to permit the commitment of American troops in Syria, Libya, or even northwest Africa.

Although taken by surprise, General Marshall knew that he could not turn the President's proposal aside without an alternative of his own. One week later he presented the White House the first plan for a cross-channel assault in 1943. He was not going to be diverted to a Mediterranean adventure that would be strategically defensive. For while the liberation of North Africa might save the Mediterranean for the Allies, victory there could not be decisive. If the Allies were to waste their troops on indecisive operations, then none would be left for the big push across the English Channel.

In April, 1942, when General Marshall went to England with Harry Hopkins, he carried with him a preliminary outline plan for the cross-channel invasion in 1943. To win approval of his plan from the British Chiefs, General Marshall banked on the inexhaustible resources of the United States. If his plan were acceptable, he said, the United States would put 1,000,000 troops in England by the spring of 1943. With rare enthusiasm the British shelved their reservations on the cross-channel assault and instead laid plans to join the U. S. on the invasion of France.

To provide the build-up General Marshall had pledged for 1943, the planners outlined a logistical project to be known by the code name BOLERO. At the time BOLERO must have seemed more fanciful than real, for while General Marshall was talking of 1,000,-000 troops for 1943, by May of 1942 we had landed but 32,000 in the United Kingdom.

But until the Channel invasion could be mounted, the Allies in 1943 were faced with the more pressing problem of how to help Russia through that intervening year. Despite the German retreat before Moscow, no one underestimated Hitler's capacity to undertake a spring offensive.

To rescue Russia should she be threatened with collapse as the result of that anticipated spring offensive, the Allies agreed on an emergency stand-by plan for a Channel crossing in the summer of 1942. It would be undertaken only to relieve German pressure on the Russian front and would not be staged unless the emergency warranted the great risk. For with the small force available to us in 1942, we could do no more than seize a beachhead in the belief that it might lessen enemy pressure on Russia. This operation had been given the code name SLEDGEHAMMER—TACKHAMMER would have been more descriptive.

Between that April, 1942, and the following June when the Combined Chiefs met again, enthusiasm for ROUNDUP as General Marshall's plan for invasion in 1943 was called, showed signs of cooling on both sides of the Atlantic. After General Marshall had returned to the United States, British skepticism revived, for British planners were not yet totally convinced of the feasibility of a Channel assault. Even in Washington there were some who opposed the priority General Marshall insisted be given BOLERO in preparation for the ROUNDUP crossing. The navy, now totally engrossed in its naval war in the Pacific, shuddered over the prospect of BOLERO interference in its plans for a speedy Pacific build-up.

In the end, however, it was not timidity but the Axis that postponed ROUNDUP. On June 13, 1942, Rommel's Afrika Korps destroyed a British tank force on the Libyan desert and pushed the Empire troops back across the Egyptian border. Near the Arab village of El Alamein, the British dug in only 65 miles from their giant naval base at Alexandria. One week later 30,000 Britons surrendered to Rommel at Tobruk.

Meanwhile, in Russia Hitler had massed 75 German divisions for a fresh summer offensive. This time in deference to Hitler's intuition, they were to be turned away from Moscow toward the Donets industrial basin and the vast oil fields of the Caucasus. At that time few British and American military chiefs believed Russia could hold out until the following winter when cold would once again become her most important ally. Like the German general staff, these officers

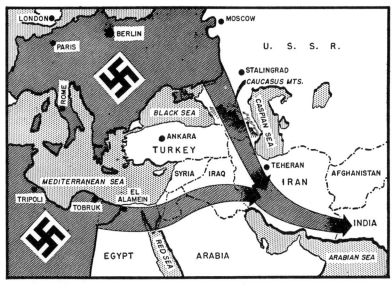

With a pincer through the Caucasus and another across the Arabian desert, Hitler revived a Napoleonic dream for the conquest of India.

had not counted on the vast resources Russia had amassed in the Urals. If by a miracle Russia could survive the summer of 1942, she might, they conceded, squeeze through. (At that time no one could have foreseen the Battle of Stalingrad.) But if the Axis were to break through Egypt, it would sever the Suez Canal and chase the British out of the oil-rich Middle East. Defeat of the British there could set the stage for a disaster of even more telling proportions. For if Hitler were to join his forces from Africa and Russia, he would have realized a Napoleonic dream: the conquest of India and the Middle East by a gigantic double pincer movement through the Caucasus and across the Arabian desert.

Within two months the Axis had wrecked Allied plans for a 1943

Channel crossing. Unless the Allies could fling their few divisions into the conflict in 1942, the war might be lost before the United States could bring its vast power to bear. This was the emergency for which SLEDGEHAMMER had been devised. But when the call came, Churchill balked. He rejected the SLEDGEHAMMER plan for an emergency diversionary landing, declaring that "there should be no substantial landing in France unless we intend to remain." It was impossible for the United States to appeal his decision, for had the assault been made in 1942 it would have been overwhelmingly British. Moreover Churchill was probably justified in his view, for with the forces available to the Western Allies in 1942, there was little prospect of holding on to a permanent beachhead in Europe. If we were to land and thereafter be forced off, the military value of any such diversion would have been more than offset by its disastrous effects upon the morale of occupied peoples. More than anything else, it was essential that the Allies maintain among the peoples of Europe a persevering faith in the certainty of their liberation. Better that this eventuality be delayed than totally despaired of.

Plausible though Churchill's argument might have been, Roosevelt insisted that the Allies could not sit idly by until the summer of 1943. Even a shoestring venture, he declared, would be better than none at all. When the Prime Minister arrived in Washington on June 18, 1942, he came prepared with an answer to Roosevelt. Now that the cross-channel invasion for 1942 had been prevented by the lack of Allied resources, Churchill proposed a Mediterranean diversion to help keep Russia in the war. In his original plan he blueprinted an assault upon the French port of Dakar. But Dakar was separated from the Mediterranean by an impassable desert and the equally impassable Atlas Mountains. Worse yet, it lay 1,600 miles by road from Algiers, 2,200 miles from Tunis, 4,800 miles from El Alamein. Because the capture of Dakar warranted neither the risk nor the resources it entailed, Churchill's plan was replaced by a bolder one that went by the code name TORCH.

TORCH brought the Allies to North Africa on the murky morning of November 8, 1942, when British and American forces landed at Algiers, Oran, and Casablanca in their first large-scale amphibious attack. For TORCH, however, the Allies were to pay a high price. Not only did it force us to cancel ROUNDUP for the following year, but it delayed the ultimate cross-channel attack until 1944. For with this diversion to the Mediterranean, the Allies had branched off on a siding in their strategic offensive. Not until the Combined Chiefs met at Casablanca in January, 1943, was General Marshall able to switch them back to the cross-channel invasion. And even then he was forced to accede to the Sicilian landing. For having once entered the Mediterranean, the British were reluctant to leave. What that sea lacked in military advantage it offered in political opportunity.

Once he had diverted us to the Mediterranean Sea, Churchill wasted no time in championing his pet strategy for a Mediterranean campaign against the "soft underbelly" of the Axis. As early as September, 1942, two months before the TORCH invasion, he had foreseen the possibility of further attacks in that sea. At Casablanca he argued even more vigorously for continuing the Mediterranean campaign.

General Marshall, however, believed so strongly in the strategy of cross-channel invasion that he remained indifferent to the Prime Minister's persuasion. More than anything else General Marshall feared that this British desire for easy victories in the Mediterranean would lure us into a day-to-day war without any long-range strategic plan. This wait-and-see*ism*, he argued, would not win the war.

While the British accepted General Marshall's insistence that strategic planning be aimed at the cross-channel invasion, they nevertheless asked that we exploit our gains in the Mediterranean Sea. For they still hoped that by nibbling at the flanks of the Axis they could defeat it. At Casablanca the British pressed for a Mediterranean sequel to TORCH.

Although ROUNDUP had not yet been formally abandoned, the diversion of Allied resources to North Africa had precluded the likelihood of a successful Channel invasion in 1943. Following the TORCH landing in November, 1942, the BOLERO plan was cut back from 1,147,000 to 427,000 men. Thus even if the Allies were to scrape together an invasion force for 1943, they would be heavily outnumbered by the German. As a consequence the British could argue that a Channel invasion in 1943 could exert but a slight influence on the land battle for Europe.

Meanwhile the strategic situation had once again changed and the emergency that had confronted the Allies only several months before no longer existed. In October, 1942, the British at El Alamein not only blunted Rommel's advance toward the Middle East, but

Montgomery had struck back in a surprising offensive. By January, 1943, when the Combined Chiefs convened at Casablanca, his Eighth Army had reconquered more than 1,400 miles of the North African coast line to rout the Axis forces and drive on to Tripoli.

And in Russia the other half of Hitler's ambitious Middle Eastern pincer had been destroyed in the Caucasus. Not only had the Red army withstood the German offensive at Stalingrad but in smashing Field Marshal Friedrich Paulus' forces, it had shattered the faith of the German people in victory on the Russian front.

Against this strategic background the British could ask at Casablanca with telling effect: Why risk a European invasion in 1943? It could gain no decisive results. On the other hand, might it not expose our forces to disaster? After having gotten off to so successful a start in the Mediterranean Theater why should we abandon our gains now when there is nowhere else to go?

No other alternative presented itself in the summer of 1943 and General Marshall was forced to agree. Accordingly, on January 14, 1943, the Combined Chiefs of Staff directed Eisenhower to invade Sicily during the "favorable period of the July moon."

Had not some offensive been scheduled for the summer of 1943, Allied troops in the Mediterranean might have been forced to spend an idle summer on the North African shore. This inactivity would not help win the war; neither would it have given any aid to the Russians. For even though the Red army had struck back in a winter offensive, Allied planners were fearful that Russia might still negotiate a separate peace with the Germans. They insisted Russia be aided and sustained at all costs. While the Sicilian invasion might not directly relieve the Russian front, it would imperil Italy. And if Italy were to collapse, Germany would be forced to replace from its own reserves the 33 Italian divisions stationed in the Balkans and in southern France.

Of less, though still critical, importance to the Allied planners was the prospect of savings in shipping as the result of a Sicilian campaign. For with the conquest of that island the Luftwaffe would be forced back into the Italian boot and the Mediterranean opened again to Suez-bound convoys. In January of 1943 this was not an advantage to be passed over lightly, for Allied shipping shortages severely restricted offensive operations throughout the entire world.

Since September 4, 1939, when the British liner *Athenia* was torpedoed off the Scottish coast, Axis submarines had accounted for more than 17,000,000 tons of Allied shipping. This was one and one-half times the total tonnage of the prewar American merchant marine. In number of hulls it represented the equivalent of 1,500 Liberty ships. Meanwhile by the end of 1942, despite rising combat losses, the German navy had vastly increased its undersea fleet by the addition of 159 new U-boats. It had started the war in 1939 with only 57 undersea craft. After his surrender in 1945, Admiral Doenitz declared that Germany had lost the Battle of the Atlantic even before it started. In the five and one-half years that Germany was at war, she built 1,105 undersea craft. Had she started the war with only half that number, she might have won it before we turned the tide.

In his effort to hold Allied strategy to a cross-channel invasion, General Marshall labored through the Casablanca Conference to win a flat commitment on it for 1944. But the British chiefs preferred to skirt the issue and hedge their agreements with qualifications. Whereas General Marshall viewed the Channel invasion as a decisive knockout blow, the British preferred to limit it to a final *coup de grâce*, to be administered when the Axis lay exhausted.

Although General Marshall did not win his flat commitment at Casablanca, he gained ground on his objective. Before adjourning, the Combined Chiefs created the cross-channel invasion planning staff, later to be known as COSSAC. At the same time the Chiefs authorized acceleration of the BOLERO build-up in England for 1944. If the British were reluctant to rush into the Channel invasion, at least they were not averse to making a start one year and a half before D day.

When the Combined Chiefs met again, this time in May, 1943, British thinking was still focused on an Italian campaign. Once more the Channel invasion was relegated to the background. The capture of more than 267,000 Axis troops in Tunisia had yielded an unexpectedly rich payoff on the TORCH campaign. By now air was already hard at work preparing a way for the Sicilian invasion. What could be more logical, the British asked, than to jump from Sicily across the Messina Straits to the mainland of Italy? "The collapse of Italy," Churchill said, clearly savoring the prospect, "would cause a chill of loneliness over the German people and might be the beginning of their doom."

From the American point of view, however, Churchill's prophecy was more rhetorical than it was likely. While the collapse of Italy might have had wide psychological effects, Germany would not have been prostrated by the loss of its ally.

Yet chary as the American planners were over the prospect of *another* Mediterranean campaign, they could not easily oppose a 1943 follow-up to the Sicilian venture. Once again troops could not be left to lie idle while there were Germans to be killed. But the Americans were insistent that any further Mediterranean adventures be budgeted on resources. Otherwise, they feared we would dissipate in Mediterranean side campaigns those strategic resources that had been earmarked in BOLERO for the 1944 Channel assault.

Once more—as they had at Casablanca—the British and American planners were eyeing their problem from opposite ends. And like the blind man who sought to describe an elephant by touch, their observations left them with differing reactions. The Americans feared that this persistent search by the British for opportunities in the Mediterranean Sea would eventually exhaust the resources we required for a cross-channel campaign. But the British felt that rigid American insistence on the cross-channel invasion might force them to by-pass more likely opportunities for quick gains in the Mediterranean Sea.

In resolving those opposing views, the Combined Chiefs were sympathetic to both sides. Although unwilling to commit themselves to an Italian invasion months before the Sicilian campaign, they authorized Eisenhower to plan "such successive operations" as might knock Italy out of the war.

At the same time, the Chiefs got down to specifics on the projected Channel invasion. Twenty-nine divisions were allotted for the operation together with the equipment that would be required "to secure a lodgment on the Continent from which further offensive operations can be carried out." They even set a target date; it was to be May 1, 1944.

To establish an indisputable priority for the Channel invasion they earmarked for transfer that fall from the Mediterranean Theater to England four American and three British battlewise divisions.

And finally, as the result of this agreement in May, 1943, the BOLERO build-up was boosted to 1,340,000 men for the spring of 1944. Within several months that target was lifted to 1,460,000.

When the Combined Chiefs convened again, this time at Quebec on August 8, 1943, the Mediterranean investment was yielding even richer dividends than we anticipated it would. Mussolini had been deposed, Sicily was almost swept of the German, and Italy showed signs of a crack-up. Meanwhile an interim decision had been made to invade the boot.

In Russia for the first time it was the Red army and not the Wehrmacht that undertook a summer offensive. Now Germany had begun a retreat that would carry her back to Berlin. And in the Atlantic, Allied shipping losses dropped as the U. S. Navy loosed its escort carriers and patrol craft against the enemy's wolf packs. Even in the far-off Pacific the United States had regained the initiative. By now the Solomons had been retaken and American troops were pushing their way through the jungles of New Guinea.

At Quebec, for the first time, the Combined Chiefs were no longer harassed by the need for emergency operations in Europe. The chain of events that had started with TORCH was now approaching a climax with Italian collapse. No longer could a Mediterranean offensive be justified by the need to maintain Allied momentum. Any further assault against the underbelly of Europe, whether it was to be through southern France or up through the politically desirable Balkans, would call for an immediate showdown on the strategy of cross-channel invasion. At last the days of improvisation were ended; now planning could begin.

Three times before, General Marshall had compromised on the cross-channel assault. The first compromise came with TORCH in 1942, the second with Sicily, the third with Italy. But valuable as these Mediterranean side shows were, they had consumed prodigious quantities of Allied resources. Clearly the time for compromise had ended; any further adventures in the Mediterranean Sea would only set back the Channel invasion.

At Quebec where the American planners pressed for *overriding* commitment on the Channel, the British again demurred and here they split with the Americans on the desirability of day-to-day planning as opposed to the long-range strategic pattern that had been urged by General Marshall. Plagued by shortages and crises almost from the day the war began, the British had been forced to wager their lives on frugal hand-to-mouth operations that promised either instant relief or immediate rewards. In contrast, we Americans had entered the war with boundless confidence in the wealth of our almost limitless resources. Thus while the British, by instinct, played cautiously and safe in their strategic planning, we Americans could afford to bet the works on one climactic invasion.

As the British and American planners collided at Quebec on the issue of how overriding a strategic concept the Channel invasion was to be, this time there was no mistaking the stiffness of the American position. But the policy statement which emerged from Quebec was firm on the outside, soft within. Instead of committing themselves to "overriding priority" on the Channel invasion, as General Marshall had asked, the Combined Chiefs agreed that:

As between operation OVERLORD and operations in the Mediterranean, where there is a shortage of resources, available resources will be distributed with the main object of insuring the success of OVERLORD. Operations in the Mediterranean Theater will be carried out with the forces allotted at TRIDENT [Washington, May, 1943] except as these may be varied by decision of the Combined Chiefs of Staff.

The British had successfully wiggled through another loophole.

Yet despite the unwillingness of the Combined Chiefs at Quebec to commit themselves in so many words to an overriding priority on the Channel invasion, they said almost as much in the three principal decisions to which they agreed. For in August, 1943, they:

1. Approved COSSAC's outline plan for OVERLORD and directed that Morgan go ahead with planning.

2. Spiked a suggestion that seven Mediterranean divisions earmarked for the Channel invasion be diverted to Italy.

3. Recommended that OVERLORD be enlarged over the present COSSAC plan.

Churchill not only concurred in this proposal for the enlargement of OVERLORD but he asked for at least a 25 per cent increase in the prospective assault force of three seaborne divisions. And he proposed an assault landing on the east coast of the Cotentin to widen the base of the invasion. Here the Prime Minister had gone straight to the heart of our problem. For of the two major changes that were afterward to be made in the COSSAC plan, one provided for two additional divisions in the assault, the other for a landing on the Cotentin shore.

With the approval of COSSAC's outline plan, the wheels for OVERLORD were at last set in motion. It would be difficult hereafter to reverse them or even slow them down.

Only one last hurdle was left, for the British were to try once more for the Mediterranean later that fall. It remained for Stalin to arrest that British diversion at Teheran.

13: *Problems of Command*

During the summer of 1943 the Red Army, now strong enough to challenge the invader without the aid of winter, lunged forward in a fresh offensive. Since 1941 the Wehrmacht had held the upper hand during the warm spring and summer months while the Red army yielded and fell back to counterattack with the winter snows. Consequently, as summer faded into fall and the shaken German armies stumbled rearward toward the Polish border, a wave of optimism swept over Britain. It even leaked into the classically designed Norfolk House in London where COSSAC had established its planning headquarters.

Expelled from Africa, hard pressed in Italy, hunted in the Atlantic, and now demoralized in Russia, everywhere the German had lost the initiative. To some it looked as though he had lost the war.

Few were more certain that this was the beginning of Germany's. end than the airmen who flew out of England in day and night raids on the enemy's industrial centers. Now that bombers were no longer being siphoned off to support the Mediterranean war, the strategic air forces in England could concentrate on the expansion of their bomber fleets. Between January and September, 1943, the U. S. Eighth Air Force almost quadrupled its strength from 225 to 881 heavy bombers. As bomb tonnages increased and fires brightened the skies over Germany's industrial cities, most airmen were confident that air might fatally weaken the enemy long before ground forces crossed the Channel.

Key to the Allied air offensive that year, however, lay in the destruction of enemy fighters. For in the spring of 1943 the Luftwaffe awakened to the peril of strategic bombing and hastened to counter the threat by increased production of fighter aircraft. Fearful that enemy fighter production would outstrip their heavy-bomber build-up and drive the big ships from the skies, Allied airmen concentrated their effort against German aircraft plants. But because many of those plants lay deep in Germany behind the Rhine and beyond the reach of fighter escorts, daylight bombers were forced to venture alone into the enemy's heartland. Air losses zigzagged higher and higher on the charts of group commanders at their bases in northern England. In a single raid on October 14 against Schweinfurt's ball-bearing plants, 60 B-17's were shot down. This represented a quarter of the attacking force.

While working to cut down those losses with the aid of long-range fighter escorts, some air commanders still believed that it was only a matter of months until Germany's back would be broken by the Allied bombing campaign.

I withheld judgement on those air claims, for it was apparent that the task of evaluating bombing results was speculative and subject to error. Later re-examination of those claims for the summer and fall of 1943 indicated how extravagantly air had overrated its effectiveness against the German industrial plant. The distortion, however, resulted not from deliberate exaggeration, as some critics supposed, but from the difficulty air experienced in assaying its claims. The airmen had enormously underestimated the astonishing recuperative powers of German industry after bombing.

Yet despite these excessive claims it became increasingly apparent in the fall of 1943 that Germany was beginning to feel the cumulative effects of this intensified heavy-bomber offensive. Air photos of bombed-out plants stacked higher in the A-2* files. And from Italy intelligence reports revealed the anxiety and fear of German soldiers at the front for the safety of their families in air-target towns.

By November, the German line in Russia was split in two by the Pripet marshes. In Crimea the invaders were isolated, and in the scorched Ukraine German troops were threatened with encirclement by the Russian capture of Kiev.

At this time persistent rumors reached us in England of the growing disaffection of those German generals who believed that Hitler's

*Air intelligence.

two-front war had committed the Reich to ruin. If sanity prevailed anywhere in the Reich, this was the time for Germany to escape the certainty of catastrophe by immediate surrender. In London, Allied officers speculated on the depths of this disintegration, and not a few of them predicted that Germany might collapse as it had before in 1918.

Even though there had been no reason for optimism in early 1943, COSSAC had dutifully prepared itself for the chance of German collapse. With characteristic British thoroughness in military planning, COSSAC had tailored its preparations to fit three possible, if unlikely, contingencies: the first was predicated upon German disintegration on the Atlantic Wall; the second, upon a hasty withdrawal to the Siegfried Line; and the third, upon collapse and surrender. These contingencies were to be met by a series of emergency plans known as RANKIN A, B, and C.

Although disintegration on the Atlantic Wall or withdrawal to the Siegfried Line would not have barred some form of an OVERLORD crossing, total collapse would have turned the tables upside down and thrown OVERLORD out the window. To avoid chaos on the continent it would have been necessary for us to mount such forces as we had, cross the Channel at once, move on into Germany, disarm its troops, and seize control of the nation. And so it was that in November, 1943, First Army cut its teeth not on OVERLORD but in emergency planning for RANKIN C. In the event of German collapse that fall, First Army was to provide an emergency force of ten American divisions for immediate movement across the Channel. But because the number of both troops and assault craft swelled each day with new arrivals, RANKIN C required tedious revision of the plan from one week to the next.

However, as the days shortened under Britain's double-daylight saving time without further signs of collapse within the Reich, the short-lived optimism that had swept Britain that fall soon spent itself and vanished. We were not to have another such flap until one year later when our columns dashed from the Seine toward the undefended German border. By November of 1943 not an officer in London would have bet two shillings on the likelihood of German collapse. Though RANKIN C was soon stuffed back into the files, our planning time had not been wasted. Loading tables were developed for later use on the OVERLORD attack. Meanwhile the newly fused First Army staff shook itself down into an operating team and the

planners profited from their growing knowledge of enemy dispositions and terrain.

In November, 1943, while Morgan's staff in London sweated over
its outline of the OVERLORD plan, the Combined Chiefs journeyed
to Cairo. There the British and American staffs were to confer before
flying on to Teheran for the conference with Stalin.

After sidestepping General Marshall's request at Quebec for an
ironclad commitment on OVERLORD, the British were to attempt
once more at Cairo to keep the loopholes open.

It was not that they opposed the Channel invasion; indeed in
England they were up to their ears in preparations for it. But the
British were reluctant to bind themselves irrevocably to it—especially
on so firm a commitment as a specific D day.

For if Britain were to commit herself to an invasion date, she
would have to abandon any hope of a strategic diversion to the
Mediterranean Theater. And this she was no doubt reluctant to do,
for by November, 1943, the Mediterranean offered Britain a choice
of likely opportunities for politically profitable campaigns.

For one thing, Clark had bogged down near Cassino in his drive
on Rome. Eisenhower was in need of resources to mount a flanking
attack by sea if he were to retain the initiative there and contain a
worth-while share of the enemy's effort. In the Dodecanese a British
attempt to grab several island outposts in the Aegean Sea had failed
and the attackers were destroyed. The British argued that if they
were to recover those positions, it was essential that they take Rhodes.
Furthermore, they insisted Turkey had been sitting on the fence too
long. If a fresh Allied offensive in the Mediterranean could draw
Turkey into war, we would have opened a short sea supply route to
Russia through the Dardanelles.

Though enticing, these considerations were too trivial in themselves to warrant abandonment or even delay of the OVERLORD
invasion. Instead it was a report from the American military attaché
in Moscow that added to the reservations of those luke-warm sup-
porters of the cross-channel attack. For the report indicated that
Red army successes in the summer and fall of 1943 might have
altered Russian views on the desirability of a Channel invasion in
1944. The Red army, it was said, might prefer an immediate
offensive now rather than wait for the Channel assault—even if that
offensive were limited to the Mediterranean Sea.

Only one person could say whether OVERLORD was any longer essential. The Combined Chiefs left Cairo and adjourned to Teheran. Stalin settled down to business immediately. After outlining Russian strategy against the German armies he declared that following the defeat of Germany the Soviet Union would join the war against Japan. Then dismissing the Italian front as a flyspeck diversion, Stalin declared that the obvious point for Allied attack lay in the northwest corner of France—across the English Channel. With that the final decision was made, and thus after two years of discussion, evasion, diversion, and confusion OVERLORD became the irrevocable crux of Allied strategy in the European war.

Although First Army set up its headquarters in Bristol on October 16, 1943, its role in the OVERLORD invasion was still fogged in the high command. At that point we did not know whether we were to lead or be led on the assault.

COSSAC's original OVERLORD outline had called for command by a British Army commander of three assault divisions—two British and one American. But this scheme had been rejected by the American chiefs of staff. Devers offered a substitute plan wherein the assault would be led by British and American corps under the direction of the Supreme Commander. But this was in turn rejected by COSSAC as an unworkable device.

Into this impasse came the War Department with a compromise plan of its own. It proposed that the assault be made by a British, a Canadian, and an American corps under the combined command of an American Army. And since our First was the only U. S. Army in England, this, of course, meant us. Thus under the War Department plan I would direct the assault as an Allied ground commander.

Still unanswered was the question as to who was to be my senior commander. There were three possibilities at stake: I could report directly to the Supreme Commander, to an intermediary ground commander-in-chief—or, more probably, to an Army Group commander. The last was the most logical choice because our assault force would be built up on the beach to twin British and American armies. And in the normal chain of command, an Army Group would be echeloned over those assault armies.

The pattern for Allied command in the field had been established in Africa in January, 1943, when army, navy, and air forces were gathered under three service chiefs who performed as "assistant

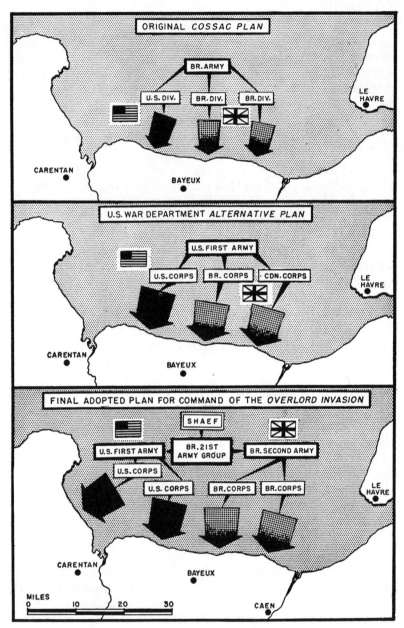

After disposing of several previous proposals, the planners for OVER-LORD prescribed a four-corps assault with ground forces under the command of the 21st Army Group.

commanders" to Eisenhower. As Montgomery's senior commander during the British Eighth Army's drive from El Alamein to the Mareth Line, Alexander became Eisenhower's choice for his deputy on the ground. But since only two Armies were involved in the merger, Alexander was designated as Army Group commander, rather than ground commander-in-chief.

In Europe the situation was drastically changed. Instead of the two modest-sized Armies Eisenhower employed under Alexander in Tunisia, in Europe we were eventually to have eight under the command of three Army Groups.

As a result, persuasive arguments could be given in favor of a ground force commander-in-chief. For one thing, the precedent for Europe had already been established in air and naval commands. At Quebec, the Combined Chiefs had approved Air Chief Marshal Sir Trafford Leigh-Mallory as Commander-in-Chief of the Allied Expeditionary Air Forces and Admiral Sir Bertram Ramsay as Commander-in-Chief of the Allied Expeditionary Naval Forces. Why not complete the triumvirate, some argued, and name a supercommander for the ground?

In Washington, however, War Department planners took a practical view of the problem. If there was to be a ground force commander-in-chief it was desirable that he be an American, for the Americans would eventually outnumber the British more than three to one on the ground. But who, they asked, was he to be? At that time not an American field commander rivaled the stature of either Alexander or Montgomery. If a ground force commander-in-chief were to be named, the odds were heavily in favor of one of these British soldiers. Consequently, the issue was tactfully dropped and hidden away in the files.

Nevertheless, in England we were still to be dogged with the issue of who would head up the ground force chain of command on the Normandy invasion. Certainly someone above the level of the assault army would have to oversee over-all ground planning in conjunction with sea and air on both the assault and follow-up forces. For just as soon as the British forces ashore swelled to Army size, I would revert to single command of the U. S. forces and the beachhead would then be split between two coequal Army commanders. It was essential that they be joined under a single authority for the ground.

This was obviously a task for an Army Group—at least until SHAEF came ashore. Nor was there ever any doubt in my mind that the British should have this Group command. Not only had the British eclipsed us in prestige at this point in the war, but 21st Group had already worked itself into COSSAC's planning. But this was not, as some Americans thought, a demonstration of British connivance. The British had simply gotten there first. Early in the summer of 1943, while Devers besieged the War Department for permission to establish a U. S. Army Group, the British 21st Group had established its headquarters in London. By the time our infant American Army Group had taken possession of Bryanston Square, its British counterpart was deeply rooted in COSSAC's plans and preparations.

By the late fall of 1943 we had not yet overcome this handicap of a tardy start in the establishment of a U. S. Army Group. Meanwhile, the question of command was still left up in the air. A single copy of a TOP SECRET order designating me commander-in-chief of the 1st U. S. Army Group had been hidden away in my office safe but presumably this designation was for "planning purposes only." Devers was thought to be in line for the permanent Army Group post. My job had already been cut out for me in the First Army.

Not until November, when General Morgan returned to England from the United States, did we get a decision on the prospective ground force chain of command. It was explained in a directive from 21st Army Group on November 29. The commander of the British 21st Group would head the over-all ground force planning and thereafter direct the assault as commander of both British and American land forces. That Allied role, however, was to be no more than a *temporary* one, to last only until SHAEF instructed the 1st U. S. Army Group to take over command of American field forces in France. Once we reached that phase of the campaign Montgomery would give up his job as temporary commander-in-chief of Allied ground forces and revert to command of the British and Canadian armies under 21st Army Group. From then until the end of the war both British and American Army Group commanders would fight side by side as equals, each with his own direct line of command to Eisenhower. For SHAEF was to perform as a super ground force headquarters as well as the Supreme Command. This assurance was to become our charter for an equal voice in strategy on the European ground campaign.

Busy as we were throughout that fall, we nevertheless labored under a considerable shadow of frustration. For bravely as Morgan exercised his halfway authority at COSSAC, it was impossible to plan with assurance until the Supreme Commander was named.

The selection of a Supreme Commander for OVERLORD had been under advisement as long ago as January, 1943, during the ANFA conference at Casablanca. At that time, when the cross-channel invasion was being planned for 1943, it was anticipated that the assault would be primarily British. For that reason the conferees proposed that Britain name the Supreme Commander.

When the OVERLORD invasion was later postponed to 1944, British predominance in the assault gave way to the massive man-power reserves of the United States. Churchill stuck by his Casa-blanca declaration and recommended that now an American be named Supreme Commander. At Quebec the Prime Minister sug-gested to President Roosevelt that General Marshall be the man. If ever a man deserved the appointment, that man was General Mar-shall. Yet in the army hierarchy of command the appointment of General Marshall as Supreme Commander would have entailed a stepdown from his post as Army Chief of Staff. But stepdown or no, had General Marshall left Washington to go to Europe, no one—not even Eisenhower—could have taken his place.

In the army we often scoff at the myth of the indispensable man, for we have always maintained that Arlington Cemetery is filled with indispensable men. General Marshall, however, was an exception, for if ever a man was indispensable in a time of national crisis, he was that man.

In the end it was Roosevelt who made the decision to keep General Marshall at home. With characteristic soldierliness the general had declined to state a preference for either post. Roosevelt's choice was an inescapable one, for no one but General Marshall could have allocated manpower and resources between the European and Pacific wars as resolutely as he did. Despite the entreaties of MacArthur and the navy, General Marshall never compromised nor recanted his fundamental conviction that to win the war we must first assure victory in Europe. History traditionally pivots on giants whose per-sistence, stolidity, and courage fashion the events that shape the lives of lesser men. Among the Western Allies three of these giants towered above all others during this last World War—Roosevelt, Churchill, and Marshall. Together they probably influenced the lives of more men than any other triumvirate in the history of mankind.

With General Marshall out of the running, the next logical choice for Supreme Commander fell upon the incumbent of a comparable post in the Mediterranean Theater. For after having defeated the Axis in Tunisia and Sicily, Eisenhower was now forcing his way up the Italian peninsula in that agonizing winter campaign. In terms of experience, tact, and perspective, Ike was admirably equipped for the job. Although some American subordinates thought him too ready a compromiser, especially in Anglo-American disputes, Eisenhower had demonstrated in the Mediterranean war that compromise is essential to amity in an Allied struggle. I confess that at times I thought Eisenhower too eager to appease the British command, but I admit to having been a prejudiced judge. For as the American field commander I more often than not participated as the Yankee partisan in those disputes.

In early December Eisenhower learned from President Roosevelt that he had been chosen at Cairo to become Supreme Commander for the OVERLORD invasion. With only six months to go before D day, Ike wasted no time in forming the beginnings of a SHAEF staff from among his Mediterranean associates. If ever Eisenhower required an experienced and skillfully trained staff, it would be on the cross-channel invasion.

To serve as deputy commander at SHAEF Eisenhower brought his first-ranking Mediterranean airman to England. A taciturn pipe-smoking Briton, Air Chief Marshal Tedder had earned the trust and affection of his American colleagues in Africa by his modesty, skill, and exemplary discretion as an Allied soldier. As an unobstrusive right-hand man to Eisenhower, Tedder had helped forge the spectacularly successful Mediterranean air arm.

As his chief of staff, Eisenhower named the brilliant, hard-working Bedell Smith, then with him in a similar spot at AFHQ in Caserta. Since England in 1942, the two had become inseparable partners. Although neither had grown excessively dependent upon the other, their relationship had been fused into so much an entity of command that it was difficult to tell where Ike left off and where Bedell Smith began.

In contrast to the suave and amiable Eisenhower, Smith could be blunt and curt. Yet like his chief, he was articulate and expressive, sophisticated, and discreet during those diplomatic crises that occasionally erupted at SHAEF. "Bedell, tell them to go to hell," Eisenhower once said in referring to a mission to SHAEF, "but put it so they won't be offended."

Although Eisenhower is ordinarily impersonal, sometimes severe in his relationships with his official staff, Smith's severity greatly exceeded that of his chief.

On the other hand, Bedell's unique capabilities as chief of staff enabled Eisenhower to escape his headquarters and devote a greater share of his time to planning and travel in the field. For Smith possessed the judgment, the strength, and the initiative to go ahead on his own without harassing Eisenhower except on issues of fundamental importance. He possessed that remarkable balance of initiative and restraint so essential to a perfect chief of staff.

To command the British 21st Army Group Eisenhower turned first to his good friend and Tunisian associate, General Alexander. Alexander had accompanied Eisenhower from Tunisia to Sicily to Italy where he commanded the Army Group comprising Clark's and Montgomery's Armies.

The friendship between Eisenhower and Alexander began in February, 1943, when Alexander quit his British Middle East Command to join Eisenhower in Algiers as commander of the 18th Army Group for the last four months of the Tunisian campaign. There he not only showed the shrewd tactical judgment that was to make him the outstanding general's general of the European war, but he was easily able to comport the nationally-minded and jealous Allied personalities of his command. By the fall of 1943, with Tunisia, Sicily, and now Salerno behind him, Alexander occupied a unique position in the Allied high command. He was our only Army Group commander and therefore our only experienced one. At the same time he had demonstrated an incomparable ability to fuse the efforts of two Allied armies into a single cohesive campaign. Had Alexander commanded the 21st Army Group in Europe, we could probably have avoided the petulance that later was to becloud our relationships with Montgomery. For in contrast to the rigid self-assurance of General Montgomery, Alexander brought to his command the reasonableness, patience, and modesty of a great soldier. In each successive Mediterranean campaign he had won the adulation of his American subordinates.

By nature a restrained, self-effacing, and punctilious soldier, Alexander was quite content to leave the curtain calls to his subordinate commanders. As a consequence he was soon eclipsed in fame by the bereted figure of Bernard Montgomery. But while the latter had emerged as a symbol of Britain's comeback in the war, it was Alexander who carried the top rating among Allied professionals who knew them both.

Although I was unaware of it at the time, the British rejected Eisenhower's bid for Alexander and asked instead that he be retained in Italy to spark that peninsula campaign. Stumped on his request for Alexander, Eisenhower turned to Montgomery.

My association with Montgomery up to this time had been limited to two brief encounters: first in Tunis where he came to review our victory parade through that city, again in Sicily when he had us to lunch to celebrate the ending of that campaign. As a result I was poorly qualified to judge him as a soldier. For this reason, if for no other, I would have preferred Alexander as commander of the 21st Army Group. For whereas Montgomery was unknown to me except for the legend that had been woven about him, I was confident that I could work happily and harmoniously with Alexander.

Nevertheless, I had no premonition of difficulty with Montgomery in Europe. Though we often disagreed on plans and tactics, our working relationship was never impaired nor was our personal association unpleasant. While my judgment of Monty's achievements might be less rhapsodical than those of the British people, I shall never deprecate Montgomery's generalship nor his outstanding accomplishments in winning the war.

Monty's incomparable talent for the "set" battle—the meticulously planned offensive—made him invaluable in the OVERLORD assault. For the Channel crossing was patterned to a rigid plan; nothing was left to chance or improvisation in command. Until we gained a beachhead we were to put our trust in The Plan.

Not until we broke out of the beachhead seven weeks after landing did opportunity call for the quick exploitation that is the test of agility in command. In the fluid situation that was to obtain until the end of the war Montgomery's luster was dimmed not by timidity as his critics allege, but by his apparent reluctance to squeeze the utmost advantage out of every gain or success. For Monty insisted upon a "tidy" front even when tidiness forced him to slow down an advance. On the other hand, we Americans preferred to push ahead, unscrambling our troops on the run, in an effort to prevent a fluid front from hardening into a set battle. For each set battle meant that another enemy crust had to be broken and this could only be accomplished with casualties and delay.

Psychologically the choice of Montgomery as British commander for the OVERLORD assault came as a stimulant to us all. For the thin, bony, ascetic face that stared from an unmilitary turtle-neck sweater had, in little over a year, become a symbol of victory in the eyes of the Allied world. Nothing becomes a general more than success in battle, and Montgomery wore success with such chipper faith in the arms of Britain that he was cherished by a British people wearied of valorous setbacks.

But nowhere did the slight erect figure of Montgomery in his baggy and unpressed corduroys excite greater assurance than among the British soldiers themselves. Even Eisenhower with all his engaging ease could never stir American troops to the rapture with which Monty was welcomed by his. Among those men the legend of Montgomery had become an imperishable fact.

As chief of staff for 21st Army Group, Montgomery brought with him to England a cheery Huguenot from the Eighth Army, Major General Sir Francis de Guingand. Like Bedell Smith, a brilliant staff officer dedicated to anonymity and his job, de Guingand went one step further by complementing the personality of his chief. In Freddy, as de Guingand was affectionately known to the American command, we found a ready intermediary and peacemaker. For whenever the distant attitude of Montgomery ruffled a U. S. staff, it was good old cheerful Freddy who came down to smooth things over. An able professional soldier, de Guingand had served Montgomery as chief of staff since El Alamein. He was an able and sympathetic administrator, wise to and unpanicked by the crises and problems of war. Although Freddy's popularity with the American command stemmed partly from the adeptness with which he bridged our good relations, he was uncompromisingly devoted and loyal to his chief. De Guingand earned our affection not because he toadied to us but because he helped to compose our differences with justice and discretion.

At the same time Montgomery brought with him Lieutenant General Sir Miles C. Dempsey whom he had prized as a corps commander in the Eighth Army. To Dempsey he gave command of the British Second Army, counterpart of the U. S. First on the Channel assault.

In Dempsey, Montgomery had found an able and experienced commander who while thoroughly competent to run his Army did not object to Monty's habit of occasionally usurping the authority of his Army commanders. For so fastidious was Monty in the execution of his carefully contrived plans that he frequently intervened in the conduct of a battle to an extent that would never have been tolerated in the U. S. Army. But in his long association with Dempsey, this practice of Monty's had become a normal pattern of command. Dempsey knew how to tolerate it without jealousy or anger. Had Montgomery commanded his American subordinates in this same rigid manner, we would have complained bitterly, for we would never have surrendered the traditional independence of action that is given us within the framework of higher command directives. Monty recognized this distinction and as a result never insisted upon scrutinizing in detail our field operations.

Before quitting the Mediterranean for England to shoulder OVERLORD planning, Eisenhower searched the roster of senior American commanders for a deputy to his British successor, General Sir Maitland Wilson. The task was primarily an administrative chore, for the deputy would become chief housekeeper for Clark's Fifth Army. Thus, while the job did not call for a seasoned battlefield campaigner, it did demand a high-level administrative skill. Had the bill of particulars been prepared with Devers in mind, it could not have fitted him better. Once Eisenhower arrived in England Devers would be automatically ranked out of his job as ETO commander. For when Ike became Supreme Commander he would also double in brass as U. S. commander of the Theater.

On December 23, 1943, Eisenhower radioed General Marshall from the Mediterranean recommending that I be named field commander on the OVERLORD invasion and that Devers be sent south as second in command to Jumbo Wilson. Eisenhower had presumably picked me for commander of the U. S. Army Group primarily because he valued combat experience on so sensitive a high level of planning. The recommendation meant that I was not only to command the 1st U. S. Army Group "for planning purposes," but that I would also head it when Army Group eventually entered the line-up in France.

Command of the Army Group, however, was not to preclude my command of First Army in the Channel assault. Instead, I was to take First Army ashore as First Army commander and build it up on the beachhead. Once our U. S. build-up had been expanded to a force the size of two Armies, I was to relinquish command of the First and step up to Group in command of them both. Until then, I would wear two hats, one as commander of First U. S. Army, the other as commander of 1st U. S. Army Group.

In practice this dual command was not as complex as it may sound, for neither headquarters overlapped the other. For one thing, First Army in Bristol and Army Group headquarters in London functioned as entirely separate establishments more than a hundred miles apart. Furthermore, the command of all U. S. invasion troops had been centered in First Army. At that time Army Group existed simply as a planning headquarters. Despite the confusion it may have caused, there were many advantages to this dual system of command; it permitted excellent continuity between the Army and Army Group. First Army was to schedule its build-up for the first 14 days ashore; thereafter Army Group would phase in the reinforcements. And since Group would pick up where Army left off, it was evident that with one man commanding them both, they could be linked together more securely.

The news that I was to command this Army Group came to me suddenly and indirectly: I read it in a morning paper. On January 18 as I turned through the lobby of the Dorchester Hotel bound for breakfast at the mess across the street, I stopped to pick up a copy of the four-page *Daily Express.*

The clerk at the counter grinned. "This won't be news to you, sir," he said and pointed to a story in which Eisenhower had announced that "51-year-old Lieut.-General Omar Nelson Bradley, who led the U. S. Second Corps in Tunisia and the invasion of Sicily, is to be the American Army's 'General Montgomery' in the western invasion of Europe."

But it was. For this was the first inkling I had that my Army Group command was to be more than a temporary one. Eisenhower had just arrived in England and I had not yet talked with him. In his press conference the day before, the first on his return, Eisenhower had been asked who would command the American ground forces on the invasion. "General Bradley is the senior United States ground commander," was his reply.

For the moment that statement was not clear, for it did not indicate whether Eisenhower meant First Army on the assault or the Army Group as an opposite number to Monty. It was not until later that Eisenhower said he meant the Army Group.

14: *Planning the Assault*

Before leaving the Mediterranean for his roundabout journey to England via the United States, Eisenhower scanned a brief of COSSAC's outline plan for the cross-channel invasion. His frown confirmed the uneasy conclusion we had already come to in England. With only three divisions in the D-day assault and two more afloat as a follow-up force, COSSAC had proposed that we embark on a shoestring in the most decisive assault of the war.

This miserly allocation of troops, however, was not the fault of COSSAC, for Morgan could be no more enterprising than his resources permitted. As had happened in every other amphibious operation of the war, Morgan was hamstrung from the outset by a shortage in landing craft. Lift for five divisions was all that could be spared from world-wide allocations of landing craft. As late as 1944 landing-craft production lagged far behind our needs. As a consequence, OVERLORD was now to be gambled on an undersized landing fleet. For even if the three-division assault force proposed in the plan were to fight its way ashore, it would find itself limited to so narrow a front that it might easily be hurt by German counterattack. Alarmed at so risky a limitation on the OVERLORD assault, I sought comfort in the knowledge that once the Supreme Commander learned how hazardous was the venture he had been asked to undertake, he would move heaven and earth to reinforce it with additional craft even if this reinforcement meant a slowdown in the Pacific war.

As long as the D-day attack remained limited to three assault divisions, I foresaw difficulty in the capture of a major port soon after the landing. COSSAC had banked on an eventual lodgment force of from 26 to 30 Allied divisions. To supply so huge a force would require a major port in addition to the beaches. Meanwhile time

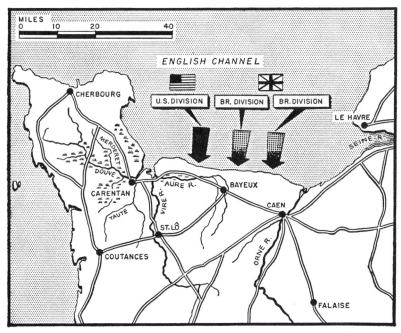

In COSSAC's original OVERLORD plan, the assault was to have been confined to three divisions against the Caen coast.

would be running against us once we got ashore. Unless this port were taken before the advent of dirty weather on the Channel our beach build-up would be slowed down.

In COSSAC's plan, the nearest port of Cherbourg lay dangerously distant from the beachhead. The tentative point for attack had been located on a 25-mile stretch of the shingled Normandy beach, almost midway between Le Havre and Cherbourg.

Though an excellent port, Le Havre was plainly beyond our reach. Naval guns covered its sea approaches and it lay on the far side of the wide mouth of the Seine. Moreover, it could be easily reinforced with German troops from the concentration on the Pas de Calais.

Cherbourg, we assumed, could be taken more easily by envelopment from behind. But there were difficulties that caused me worry. For between Cherbourg and the Calvados invasion beaches an intricate jungle of rivers almost severed the neck of the Cotentin Peninsula. If the German were given time to fortify that marshy neck, I hesitated to estimate how long he might deny us Cherbourg.

Since Cherbourg's harbor defenses precluded envelopment from the sea, our only hope for the speedy capture of that city lay in a simultaneous assault on the Cotentin beaches. There we could land behind any troops the enemy might use to hold the Cotentin neck in an effort to deny us Cherbourg.

This meant we must widen the OVERLORD attack with an extra division or two in the D-day assault. Fortunately Eisenhower came to the same conclusion and ordered Montgomery on ahead to England to see how OVERLORD could be expanded. After several days at COSSAC Monty agreed with us on the necessity for a widened assault to include the Cotentin beaches.

Before recommending that the assault be made against the Calvados coast of Normandy, Morgan's planners had scrutinized the shore line of Europe from the Netherlands to Biarritz. From their intelligence archives the British had culled volumes of patient research on subsoils, bridges, moorings, wharfage, rivers, and the thousands of intricate details that went into this appraisal of the OVERLORD plan.

Characteristic of the enterprise the British applied to this intelligence task was the answer they brought in reply to our inquiry on the subsoil of Omaha Beach. In examining one of the prospective beach exits, we feared that a stream running through the draw might have left a deposit of silt under the sand and shingle. If so, our trucks might easily bog down at that unloading point.

"How much dope can you get on the subsoil there?" I asked Dickson when G-3 brought the problem to me.

Several days later a lean and reticent British naval lieutenant came to our briefing at Bryanston Square. From his pocket he pulled a thick glass tube. He walked over to the map on the wall.

"The night before last," he explained dryly, "we visited Omaha Beach to drill a core in the shingle at this point near the draw. You can see by the core there is no evidence of silt. The shingle is firmly bedded upon rock. There is little danger of your trucks bogging down."

To get this information the lieutenant had taken a submarine through the mine fields off the coast of France. There he paddled ashore one evening in a rubber boat directly under the muzzles of the German's big, casemated guns.

In exploring the Channel and Biscay coasts, COSSAC planners had weighed each of the prospective lodgments against these five critical questions:

1. Could air superiority be maintained over the assault area with fighters based on British fields?

2. How many divisions could be put ashore on D day?

3. How many divisions could the enemy be expected to throw against a landing during its first week ashore?

4. What would the requirements of that area be for naval craft and air transport?

5. How many tons of supply might be transported each day across the beaches and through the nearby ports?

Since all the major ports were known to have been prepared for demolition in the event of Allied attack, we were forced to assume that any we captured would be severely damaged. This, of course, meant added dependence upon sheltered beaches for supply and reinforcement.

With these requisites in hand, COSSAC's planners broke the coast line down into six prospective areas of attack. Those areas included the North Sea coast of Holland and Belgium; the Pas de Calais shore within artillery range of Dover; the mouth of the Seine near Le Havre; the Caen coast and the Cotentin Peninsula with its promising port of Cherbourg; the Brittany peninsula with its girdle of ports including the enemy submarine base at Brest; and lastly the Biscay coast as far south as Bordeaux. The North Sea coasts of Germany and Denmark had been rejected from the start, for both were well beyond the range of Allied fighter aircraft.

In the initial examination, four of those six zones were discarded as prohibitive risks. The coasts of Holland and Belgium were thought too distant from the airfields of Britain. Few passable exits ran from those beaches, and the soft sand dunes there threatened to slow down the movement of supply. If we were to assault the mouth of the Seine near Le Havre, our forces would be perilously split on both sides of that river and as a consequence each might be defeated in

detail. Those beaches under the nose of Le Havre could be brought
under fire from the harbor defenses. And the ones north of the Seine
could be counterattacked by troops from the Pas de Calais.

On the long coast of Brittany the beaches were small, often rocky,
and scattered. But despite its abundance of first-class ports, most of
them strongly garrisoned by the German, Brittany lay more than 200

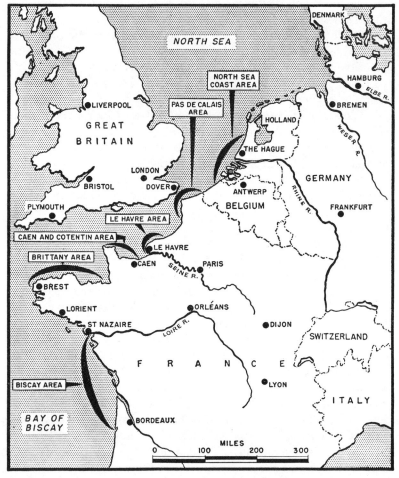

Of the six assault areas surveyed by OVERLORD planners, the Caen-
Cotentin sector offered the broadest advantages with the fewest limitations in fighter support and beach supply.

miles from the fighter fields of England. This in itself was enough to exclude Brittany from the running.

Farther south the Biscay coast was never more than an also-ran, for not only were its beaches hopelessly out of range for Allied fighter cover, but an assault there would have called for a major sea voyage from England. This, in turn, would have excluded many of the smaller craft that might otherwise be employed on the Channel for a shore-to-shore crossing.

The speedy elimination of these four left only two areas eligible for detailed examination. The first was the Pas de Calais, across the narrowest point of the Channel where 20 miles of choppy water separate Calais from the cliffs of Dover. As the German marshaled his troops and poured concrete into his Atlantic Wall, it became evident that he had bet on the Pas de Calais as the point of Allied attack. The remaining area comprised the 60-mile sector that ran from Caen on the east across the Carentan estuary and the Cotentin east shore to within easy reach of Cherbourg. From the enemy's point of view this remote provincial beach, 200 miles from Paris and 400 from the Siegfried Line, seemed to offer fewer inducements for attack than the Pas de Calais. As a result it was left largely unfortified until shortly before the invasion when Hitler intuitively sized it up as a prospective target for Allied attack.

In addition to its scanty fortifications, the Caen area offered an advantage to us in its remoteness from the enemy's concentration of supply and reserves. At the same time, its beaches were ideally suited to amphibious attack. Though not sheltered from the wind, they were not exposed like those on the Pas de Calais. And although these beaches did not possess as many exits as we would have wished, the few that existed were serviceable ones. Moreover, the Seine isolated this sector of Normandy from the Pas de Calais and the Lowlands. If the Seine bridges could be destroyed by air, the enemy might be hobbled in his race for build-up. And since build-up would determine whether the invasion was to stick or be thrown back into the Channel, the opportunity that came to us on the Seine to slow down the enemy build-up was almost significant enough in itself to win Caen the decision.

To airmen an assault near Caen meant a long run to the beachhead and a consequent speedier turnaround. But while this made it difficult to provide air cover over the Caen beaches, the disadvantage was not a prohibitive one. Of the 190 flying fields in England, almost a third were located within 150 miles of this area and many of the others were within a usable range. In other words, a Caen beachhead involved the effort that would be required to screen New York City with Baltimore-based fighters.

From the navy's point of view, an assault against Caen lengthened the cross-channel voyage as contrasted to a landing on the nearer Pas de Calais. But this longer turnaround to England was far preferable to an assault against the Calais guns.

By the time Eisenhower arrived in England on January 15, 1944, Montgomery was waiting with his recommendations that the OVER-LORD plan be strengthened and widened to include the Cotentin coast. I was vastly relieved, for with five divisions in the assault and two more in floating reserve, we could crash our way ashore on both the Caen and Cotentin beaches. Cherbourg would then be taken with a minimum of delay. And the broad beachhead would permit us to pick a soft spot against which to concentrate for the breakout.

One week later on January 23, Eisenhower assembled his SHAEF commanders for the first time in London's historic Norfolk House, birthplace of King George III. In addition to Tedder, Montgomery, Smith, and myself, the commanders included Leigh-Mallory for the Allied Air Forces and Ramsay for the navy. Tooey Spaatz also attended although as chief of the Strategic Air Forces he did not yet come under Ike's SHAEF command. Instead his orders came to him directly from the Combined Chiefs of Staff, except for special operations.

Eisenhower approved Montgomery's recommendations on the widened assault and promptly notified Washington it was essential that the assault force be expanded to five divisions. "Nothing less," he said, "will give us an adequate margin to insure success."

Despite this request for more naval support, Eisenhower was reluctant to postpone D day from its original target date in early May, for he was anxious to get ashore for a full summer's campaign before bad weather set in. Nevertheless, he admitted that this expanded plan might force a delay because of our shortage in landing craft. And he estimated that if increased production did not satisfy his needs for this additional craft, vessels would have to be borrowed from reserves accumulated for other invasions.

At Cairo, only five weeks before, when the Combined Chiefs scrounged around for craft to mount the prospective invasion of southern France, they turned naturally toward the Pacific. Admiral King promptly objected. He did not see why the Pacific should be viewed as an emergency stockpile for the European war. However, craft *had* to be found. No matter how anxious the navy might be to prosecute its war in the Pacific, even the navy would be bound by the Roosevelt-Churchill decision to defeat Germany first.

In Europe the Allies had planned in addition to OVERLORD a secondary invasion of France on the Mediterranean coast. This operation was known by the code name ANVIL; it was later to become DRAGOON.

Although ANVIL was to mount only a two-division assault, even two divisions call for a formidable fleet of landing craft. Meanwhile Anzio had already been scheduled by Eisenhower as an end run around his stalemated Italian front. While Eisenhower was still in the United States en route from the Mediterranean to England, he was cautioned by both Montgomery and Smith that lift for a five-division OVERLORD assault would probably have to come from ANVIL. Cut ANVIL down, they recommended, to a single division assault and divert its lift to the Channel.

However, Eisenhower was reluctant to do this. To save ANVIL he would prefer to take a month's delay on the OVERLORD attack. And even though abandonment of the ANVIL attack would have greatly eased my problems, I hoped desperately that it need not be ditched. For as the air forces bit more deeply into the French transport system, it was apparent that we would have logistical troubles while advancing across France. In addition to cleaning the enemy out of southern France, ANVIL would open up an additional line of supply from the port of Marseilles, up the Rhone Valley, to Alsace.

During the winter and early spring of 1944, ANVIL led a frenetic on-again off-again double life. Not only was it harassed by the OVERLORD shortage in craft, but ANVIL was caught between opposing American and British views.

To American planners ANVIL had become a major pincer in the ground campaign, an integral part of our strategy in Europe.

Meanwhile the British discounted its strategic importance. To them ANVIL was nothing more than a tactical diversion in southern France. While desirable, they thought it less than essential. But this British attitude was unquestionably influenced by the lagging Italian campaign. The Anzio landing on January 22 had fizzled into a bitter disappointment. Under the circumstances they were inclined to ask:

might not ANVIL become too exhaustive a drain on Mediterranean troop resources?

In London the remaining weeks before D day sped by with alarming speed. With OVERLORD competing for ANVIL's craft and with Anzio wearing it out, Ike was urged—and was desperately tempted—to let ANVIL go. Still he hung on in the faint hope he might get by with both.

SHAEF sought a way out of its dilemma by suggesting that we overload existing OVERLORD craft on the assault. Montgomery and I, however, objected, for if we were to overload the craft, we might easily bungle our assault on the beaches. In combat-loading, each boatload becomes a delicately balanced combat team. If we were to disarrange those units we might also unbalance the whole pattern of our attack.

"There's no sense in kidding ourselves," I said to Kean, "we can't pussyfoot around much longer on this shortage in lift. If it means ditching ANVIL, I'd much rather do that than go in with the odds against us."

The showdown on ANVIL finally came on March 21. When SHAEF learned it could not squeeze OVERLORD into its scanty allotment of craft, Eisenhower realized that he could no longer postpone the decision. Reluctantly, he recommended that ANVIL be postponed until after the Channel invasion.

The decision to defer D day from early May to June was made late in January, 1944. When Eisenhower, shortly after his arrival in England, counted up the deficits in landing craft, he grew increasingly concerned over the nearing assault deadline. On January 24, while summarizing his arguments for widening the OVERLORD beachhead, he reported to the War Department that "from the Army point of view" the May D day would be preferable. But in the same message he also said, "Rather . . . than risk failure with reduced forces on the early date, I would accept a postponement of a month if I were assured of then obtaining the strength required."

Now alarmed over the menacing shortage in craft, the British Chiefs seconded Ike's proposal for delay and on January 31 the U. S. chiefs joined them. Although I, too, favored delay while we sought additional craft, I found it difficult to understand why this single, most decisive attack of the entire war should have to compete with the Pacific for its minimum means. Naval bombardment support had been rationed to OVERLORD on an equally tightfisted basis. And while I knew nothing of the navy's commitments in the Pacific war, I was irritated by this disposition of the navy to look on OVERLORD as a European stepchild.

This promise of a month's delay came as good news to the airmen, for the additional weeks would enable us to soften the enemy still more by bombing. Even the far-off Russians welcomed the change in plan. By June, spring thaws on the Eastern front would have dried sufficiently to permit resumption of the Red army offensive.

Even before Montgomery arrived in England, the British staff at 21st Group had initiated the long, detailed planning that was to go into the OVERLORD plan. The first step came in preparation of what was called the "Initial Joint Plan." In this plan 21st Army Group was to work out the ground rules hand-in-hand with the assault Armies. Thereafter each of the Army staffs would draft its own operational orders. Those Army plans would then become directives for the assault corps. At that point each assault division would work out its own detailed plan under the watchful eye of its corps commander. From division to regiment, regiment to battalion, the process would be repeated until at length at the end of the line the company commanders received their missions.

In order to write its "Initial Joint Plan," 21st Group organized the planners into "syndicates" to probe each phase of the invasion. Each of these syndicates or committees included staff officers from Montgomery's Army Group, Dempsey's Second British Army, and my American First. In addition each syndicate was staffed according to its needs with representatives from air, the navy, SHAEF, Whitehall, the ETO, and subordinate units. After six weeks of these syndicate meetings the British and we agreed on a joint plan.

Though shrewd bargainers at the conference table, the British did not abuse the relationship that existed between us. More frequently than not, the British outranked us, but then job for job, they always have. Most of them were more familiar than we with the invasion plan. But this was primarily because they had been working on OVERLORD many months before we entered the picture.

While the First Army staff was locked up in these daily syndicate meetings, a task force was plucked from 1st Army Group and assigned to Montgomery's headquarters. Here they were to collaborate with the British on a schedule for the build-up of follow-up units and supplies. Responsibility for U. S. build-up during the first 14 days ashore fell to First Army. From that point on it was to become the responsibility of the U. S. Army Group.

Originally, I had believed that Army Group might be limited to a small staff of high-level planners without the overhead one ordinarily finds in senior echelons of command. But while Group was still an infant of less than three months, Monty's chief of staff telephoned for 14 engineer officers to be assigned 21st Army Group. At the time we had but three officers on the engineer roster at Bryanston Square. With that I gave up and let the Army Group mushroom. In Wiesbaden shortly after the war ended I was astonished to find more than 900 officers listed as part of the Army Group staff and its special troops. This exceeded the officer strength of a full-strength infantry division. Dismayed over this monster build-up in Army Group overhead, I was relieved to learn from my deputy chief of staff that this staff had handled more than 1,100 mailbags of communication in an average day. Fewer than 30 of those messages came across my desk.

Because most major commands were quartered in London, that restive overcrowded city had become the center for Allied planning. In December the British suggested we pack First Army out of Bristol and move it up to join the others. But rather than tear that establishment up by its roots, I brought only the inner cell of a planning staff to London. Those 30 officers were headed by Bill Kean and they moved into spare offices provided them by our Army Group in Bryanston Square.

First Army located its war room on the second floor of the same row of brick buildings that housed my Army Group office. The structure had been part of a row of fashionable West End flats with fireplaces of Italian marble, ornate rococo ceilings, and a cheery view of the block-long tree-shaded square. Now the windows were curtained both day and night by heavy blackout cloth. An assortment of GI tables and field desks crowded the drawing room. Its walls were papered with TOP SECRET maps, their acetate coverings scrawled with boundary lines, objectives, and phase lines—secrets the enemy would gladly have spent divisions to learn. Into the near corner of this drawing room Dickson had crowded his G-2 staff. The maps were filled with neat red symbols for enemy emplacements and guns. From the enemy-held beaches of France arcs marking the ranges of coastal guns described overlapping ripples far out into the English Channel. At the far end of this crowded room the gaunt, misnamed

Tubby Thorson presided over G-3. There two sergeants typed the troop lists as they were revised endlessly from day to day. Each list required from 25 to 30 pages to list the 1,400 or more American units that would land across the Normandy beaches during the first 14 days.

Outside the room, an MP stood on 24-hour guard at the locked door. Before calling for the door to be opened from inside, he would inspect each entrant's BIGOT card. This BIGOT classification was the most secure in the ETO; it entitled the card-holder to know all details of the invasion including D day itself.

During one of the enemy's intermittent night air raids a string of incendiaries dribbled the length of Bryanston Square and a half-dozen fires broke out in the row of flats housing our headquarters. One of the magnesium bombs crashed through the roof to the floor of my office. Luckily it was a dud. As volunteers swarmed in from the streets to fight the fires with stirrup pumps, our security cordons broke down. Fortunately at the war room the guard stuck to his post and our secrets remained unmolested. Had we been burned out that night, thousands of irretrievable hours of planning would have been lost. But even more fearful was the possibility that our BIGOT room might have been compromised in the confusion.

Of all the secrets in which we dealt, none was more scrupulously guarded than the timing of D day itself. Although our commands were carefully seeded with CIC* agents who rifled desks nightly and rattled safes in search of security violations, only one serious breach was uncovered during the lifetime of the Big Secret.

It was late in April, 1944, when Brigadier General Edwin L. Sibert, the quiet and extremely capable G-2 for Army Group, came to my office one morning in Bryanston Square.

"General," he began, "I wish it weren't necessary for me to come to you with this."

"With what?" I asked.

Sibert explained. The evening before, he had gone to dinner at Claridge's with an American major general and a group of Allied officers. Dinner had been preceded by cocktails. Lamenting over his difficulties in supply, the major general declared that several crucial items would not arrive in England until *after* the invasion. And the invasion, he added, significantly, would come before June 15.

I had known this major general since cadet days at West Point.

*Counter Intelligence Corps.

I respected him and cherished his friendship. But I had no choice. I telephoned Ike.

A speedy investigation proved the officer guilty of indiscretion. He was banished from the Theater within 24 hours and sent home as a colonel. His friends from Claridge's were visited by CIC agents and cautioned to forget the conversation. The prompting was probably unnecessary; by that time all of them had been badly frightened.

There were officers who afterward contended that Ike had acted with unnecessary harshness but I was not among them. For had I been in Eisenhower's shoes, I would have been no less severe. Although no damage had been done, the penalty proved that rank has no privileges where the safety of men's lives is at stake. At the same time this punishment reassured the British that we would not tolerate any loose talk.

Of all the invasion plans, and there were plans for each echelon in the chain of command, none were more intricate, more detailed, and weightier than those of the assault Armies. When on February 25, 1944, we completed the First Army plan for OVERLORD and called for the corps to come into the picture, we stitched together a huge mimeographed volume with more words than *Gone with the Wind*. In all, 324 complete copies of this limited edition were published by First Army.

On D day alone, First Army was to put ashore the equivalent of more than 200 *trainloads* of troops. By D plus 14 the U. S. build-up would more than double the strength of the U. S. Army at the outbreak of World War II in 1939. Within two weeks after crashing the wall we would have landed enough vehicles to form a double column from Pittsburgh to Chicago.

The more than 55,000 men who were to assault the American beaches on D day came from approximately 200 individual units—ranging from a division of 14,000 men to a photographic team of two. Every individual, every vehicle, had become part of a monstrous jigsaw puzzle that was to be disassembled for ferrying across the Channel and then reassembled on the far shore.

The equipment we were to carry varied from 120-foot steel span bridges to sulpha pills. It even included fresh drinking water: 300,500 gallons of it for the first three days ashore.

To Thorson, our G-3, and Wilson, G-4, there fell the onerous task of monitoring priorities on this lift. Thorson controlled the allocation of combat vehicles and personnel while Wilson controlled the supply and service units. Within a month they had become harassed men. For rare was the individual who did not believe that unless he were landed on D day, OVERLORD could not succeed.

To make room for troops, services, and weapons supporting the assault units it became necessary to prune from every command all but its most essential transportation. As a result, even the 1st Division was pared down from its normal complement to fewer than half its vehicles. When an officer of the division complained, Tubby simply growled back, "Look, my friend, you're not going very far on D day. If you find yourself stumped because you're short on trucks, just call for me and I'll piggyback you to Paris."

Even the mild and inoffensive Wilson was being driven to curt replies. When an officer for Civil Affairs demanded D-day tonnage in food for the French, Wilson stared at him across a desk choked with urgent requisitions for ammunition, gasoline, and bridging. "That food's important, is it?" he asked.

"Absolutely, sir," the officer replied.

"Good," said Wilson, "now listen closely. We'll fix you up for lift on D minus 1. There won't be another soul to bother you on the beach. You can feed all the Frenchmen you can find. And on the following morning you can wave a flag for us when we come in." Wilson kept this D minus 1 list at his elbow. He found it the best silencer G-4 had.

When Eisenhower recommended to General Marshall that I command the 1st U. S. Army Group in France, he likewise anticipated the need for someone to take my place as commander of First Army. "One of his Army commanders," Eisenhower wrote, referring to the time I would take over Group in France, "should probably be Patton; the other, a man that may be developed in OVERLORD operations or, alternatively, somebody like Hodges or Simpson, provided such an officer could come over to United Kingdom at an early date and accompany Bradley through the early stages of the operations." When Eisenhower told me of his recommendation, I brightened at the mention of both Hodges and Simpson. Either would have been eminently acceptable. I did not know then that I was to have them both.

A plebe classmate of Patton at West Point in 1904, Hodges was "found" in math in his second year and advised that he was not meant to be a soldier. But the quiet Georgian knew better. He enlisted as a private in 1906 and three years later was commissioned from the ranks.

In February, 1943, when Lieutenant General Walter Krueger was summoned from Third Army to join MacArthur in the Pacific, Hodges moved from command of X Corps to San Antonio for his third star. One month before Third Army sailed for England, Hodges preceded it with orders to First Army. As deputy commander of the First, Hodges supervised the Army's preinvasion training and understudied me on the assault. He took command when I left for Group on August 1, 1944, and led First Army from Avranches all the way to the Elbe. He was still wearing its proud patch four years later when he retired to Texas.

A spare, soft-voiced Georgian without temper, drama, or visible emotion, Hodges was left behind in the European headline sweepstakes. He was essentially a military technician whose faultless techniques and tactical knowledge made him one of the most skilled craftsmen of my entire command. He probably knew as much about infantry and training as any man in the army. But because he was unostentatious and retiring, Hodges occupied an almost anonymous role in the war. Yet as a general's general his stature among our U. S. commanders was rivaled only by that of Simpson. For Hodges successfully blended dexterity and common sense in such equal portions as to produce a magnificently balanced command. I had implicit faith in his judgment, in his skill and restraint. Of all my Army commanders he required the least supervision.

Hodges' claims to greatness as a commander will endure in the achievements of his First Army. Without the flair of Patton's Third Army and the breeziness of Simpson's Ninth, First Army trudged across Europe with a serious and grim intensity. Yet it was the first Army to cross the German border, the first to cross the Rhine, the first to close to the Elbe and join hands with the Russians. En route it ticketed more prisoners than any other American Army. It also buried more American dead in the wake of its long advance.

Now that Eisenhower was firmly committed to the five-division OVERLORD assault, our First Army spearhead was expanded from one to two seaborne divisions, the British assault force from two to three. The first of our U. S. divisions was to land on the Calvados coast to the right of the British, 20 miles west of Caen. The other was to land on the Cotentin east shore in hopes of speeding the capture of Cherbourg. An 18-mile gap separated these two beaches where the Carentan estuary split the neck of the Cotentin Peninsula. It was there that we would join our landings to link the Allied beachhead into a continuous strip. Each of these U. S. assault divisions was to sail under the command of a corps. A third corps would embark with the follow-up forces to take over its own middle sector ashore. The beach to the left of the estuary at Carentan was to be known as Omaha Beach, the one to the right as Utah.

By reason of its early arrival in England, Gerow's V Corps fell heir to the Omaha assault. Indeed Gerow had been working on a plan for assault since COSSAC published its OVERLORD outline. The two additional corps with their incumbent commanders had been ordered by Devers from the United States. VII Corps under Major General Roscoe B. Woodruff was to direct the Utah assault force while XIX Corps under Major General Willis D. Crittenberger would follow Gerow into Omaha beach. Although OVERLORD was to be Gerow's first major combat operation, I had no qualms in entrusting Omaha to him. Not only was he conscientious, self-confident, and steady, but he was thoroughly schooled in the OVER-LORD plan.

However, with Crittenberger and Woodruff both cutting their teeth on the same invasion, Eisenhower and I doubted the wisdom of entrusting the entire U. S. assault to an inexperienced trio. Both Crittenberger and Woodruff had come to England with distinguished records; both had been my long-time friends. But neither had as yet experienced combat command in World War II. This was my only prejudice against them. Certainly they merited tryouts and I would have been happy to have had either or both in a situation where the stakes were less decisive.

While Eisenhower and I were worrying over these reservations, General Marshall radioed SHAEF. There were available in the United States two seasoned division commanders, each with a Pacific campaign to his credit and each capable of taking a corps. He asked if we wanted them; we radioed that we did. Thus Crittenberger and Woodruff were sacrificed that we might better insure success on the OVERLORD landing. Crittenberger went to Italy and Woodruff to the Pacific. Each was subsequently given a corps and both of them proved our apprehensions completely unjustified. They worked out magnificently in combat.

One of the officers suggested by General Marshall was Major General J. Lawton Collins. As commander of the 25th Division on Guadalcanal, Collins had relieved the Marines there and promptly cleaned up that island. Known for many years in the army as one of its bright young men, the Louisiana-born Collins discovered he was far too young for the Pacific. MacArthur, even then a chipper 64, preferred contemporaries in his command. At 48 Collins was little more than a stripling. Youthful for a division, there was little likelihood of his commanding a Pacific corps. In Europe, on the other hand, most of us were nothing but permanent lieutenant colonels wearing temporary stars. Europe was obviously the best place for Collins to get ahead.

One of the most outstanding field commanders in Europe, Collins was without doubt also the most aggressive. With a hand-picked staff to help him he seasoned an unerring tactical judgment with just enough bravado to make every advance a triumph. To this energy he added boundless self-confidence. Such self-assurance is tolerable only when right, and Collins, happily, almost always was.

The second commander to be mentioned by General Marshall was Major General Charles H. Corlett. As commander of the 7th Division in its assault in Kwajalein Island, Corlett had cannily maneuvered his troops ashore. Instead of smashing head-on in a direct assault, Corlett first took a lightly held atoll off the island's toe. There he emplaced artillery to carpet the invasion beaches with fire across a narrow lagoon. During the seven-day campaign Corlett's troops killed more than 8,000 Japanese at a cost of 286 of their own.

As a reward for his ingenuity in that Pacific campaign Corlett stepped into command of the XIX Corps. Unfortunately, he also brought with him an ailing stomach and in December, 1944, after five months of campaigning, Corlett was forced to quit his command for a hospital bed in the United States.

It was not until after we had landed in France that Eisenhower won us permission to pass upon corps and division commanders before they left the States with their commands. Most division commanders we accepted without hesitation, for after having trained their divisions they merited a tryout in combat.

Stateside corps commanders, however, had been sent us from Washington to boss veteran division commanders in the field. As long as these noviates arrived from the United States, each with his own corps headquarters, we would have little opportunity to reward deserving division commanders with well-earned promotions to corps.

"We're not being fair to these division commanders," I once told Ike. "One misstep and we either bust them or hustle them back to the States. Yet when a division commander makes good and shows promise of taking a corps, there's nothing more we can do for him in the way of a promotion."

Ike nodded. "I know what you mean, Brad. If we're going to bust the bad ones, we've got to reward the good ones. Suppose we were to take a look at each corps before it leaves the States and take only those commanders you'd just hate to miss out on. That way you'll get some corps headquarters without commanders. These you can pick from the divisions." This procedure went into effect, and before the war ended 11 division commanders climbed up into corps. Meanwhile in the United States, one corps commander voluntarily stepped down from his post to take a division as the price of getting overseas.

Throughout the fall of 1943, Eisenhower had left George Patton to brood in his requisitioned palace at Palermo. An Army commander without an Army, George had been chastened by Ike's rebuke for the notorious slapping incident. But as the rains of winter continued to darken the Sicilian landscape, the penitent Patton became melancholic. He feared that perhaps he had been left to rot on this island he had conquered.

Ike, however, had not forsaken George, much as he deplored the incident that had brought discredit to Patton. His enthusiasm for Patton as a field commander had not been diminished by it. "Temperament be damned," an officer once said. "Patton pays off in ground gains as well as in occasional headaches." If Patton was sometimes a problem, Ike thought him well worth the while.

I did not learn that Eisenhower had proposed Patton as an Army commander until Ike arrived in England. Had Eisenhower asked for my opinion, I would have counseled against the selection. For not only did I question George's conduct of the Sicilian campaign, but I seriously doubted the wisdom of his forcing Patton to stomach this reversal of roles in command. In Sicily George had commanded my corps from Seventh Army. Now the tables were to be turned and I was to command his Third Army as part of the new Army Group. Ike assured me that George would submit without rancor.

"All he wants is the chance to get back into the war. For a time he thought he was through."

Like Eisenhower, I did not dispute George's brilliant dexterity in gaining ground—and there was much of it to be gained between the Channel and Berlin. But even this striking talent of Patton's could not offset the misgivings I felt in having him in my command. However, I did not speak to Eisenhower of these reservations. If Eisenhower wanted Patton, certainly I would not stand in his way.

To this day I am chagrined to recall how hesitatingly I first responded to Patton's assignment. For when George joined my command in August, 1944, he came eagerly and as a friend without pique, rancor, or grievance. My year's association with him in Europe remains one of the brightest remembrances of my military career.

George arrived in England that March before the invasion with a substantial carry-over in key personnel from his Seventh Army. With Third Army headquarters he settled down inconspicuously in the Midlands, away from the invasion traffic of southern England. Since it was to be an Army headquarters without troops until after its commitment in France, the Third was assigned to the ETO, and as a consequence George became a ward of Ike's until the following August. It was not long before George had put his head into the pillory again. During the dedication of an Allied service club in a nearby British town George unexpectedly was called upon to speak. Instead of playing on the old saw of British-American amity, George expanded his comments.

"The idea of these clubs," he said, "could not be better because undoubtedly it is our destiny to rule the world."

What would have passed for a local boner with anyone less than Patton promptly exploded into a world crisis when it reached the press wires. Unfortunately the censor had passed it—there was no security violation at stake.

Overnight George's unthinking comment had become an affair of state and yet no one was more surprised than the penitent transgressor himself. The Senate tabled his nomination for promotion to a permanent major general. And from everywhere in the United States tart editorials inundated SHAEF.

But again, as in Sicily, Eisenhower fended off the wolves. And once more George offered atonement. This time, however, Eisenhower angrily admitted he had reached the end of his rope.

"I'm just about fed up," he said in speaking of Patton to me. "If I have to apologize publicly for George once more, I'm going to have to let him go, valuable as he is. I'm getting sick and tired of having to protect him. Life's much too short to put up with any more of it."

Fifteen months later Patton invited Eisenhower to keep that promise. As commander of Third Army on an occupation mission, George had sidestepped SHAEF's prohibitions on the employment of former Nazis in the restoration of railroads and public works. Ignoring the political issues at stake, George had recognized that German wartime incumbents were the only experienced employees available for those posts. That they might also have been Nazis seemed of lesser importance to him, for he was primarily concerned with the task of restoring those services.

In explaining his actions to the press, George walked into a buzz saw when he said: "Well, I'll tell you. This Nazi thing. It's just like a Democratic-Republican election fight."

George insisted that he hated Nazis—as much as anyone else. But one of the first things he had learned in military government was that "the outs are always coming around saying that the ins are Nazis. . . . More than half the German people were Nazis and you'd be in a hell of a fix if you tried to remember all the Party members."

Eisenhower fulfilled his threat. George was relieved from command of Third Army and exiled to the Fifteenth, at that time an obscure "paper" staff writing a report on the campaign.

Friends of George Patton contend that until he died he was embittered by this "ingratitude" of Ike. Ingratitude, however, was the last fault with which Eisenhower should be charged. For twice before he had bailed George out when he could more easily and justifiably have dropped him. Indeed Eisenhower showed great personal courage in standing by George Patton. Certainly, he was more forgiving than most commanders would have been in his place.

Few generals could surpass Patton as a field commander. But he had one enemy he could not vanquish and that was his own quick tongue.

It was this unhappy talent of Patton's for highly quotable crises that caused me to tighten the screws on press censorship at the time he joined my command.

"Public relations will cuss me for it," I told Bill Kean, "but the devil with them, I'll take the chance. Tell censorship that they are not to pass any direct quotes from *any* commander without my approval. And I want to see those quotes myself."

So scrupulously was this limitation enforced that during the Battle of the Bulge I was called to the phone shortly after the relief of Bastogne.

"We've got a direct quote from General McAuliffe," the officer at the other end said. "Do you want us to pass it?"

"What did he say?" I asked.

"Nuts," came the reply.

In urging the Cotentin landing to assure early capture of Cherbourg, I had emphasized both to Montgomery and Smith the necessity for an airborne drop behind that beach. For while Utah was broad and flat and therefore suitable for seaborne assault, its exits were limited to several narrow causeways traversing a flooded marshland. As long as the enemy held those causeways he could pin us to Utah Beach.

"Much as I favor the Cotentin assault," I told COSSAC's planners, "I would sooner see it go by the boards than risk a landing on Utah without airborne help."

Moreover to capture Cherbourg and forestall the danger of a delay in build-up it was important that we choke off enemy reinforcement of the Cherbourg defenses. To do this we should have to throw a barricade across the peninsula at its neck. For if the enemy were to pour troops into that peninsula before we broke into Cherbourg, there was no telling how long he might hold out in that port. If the holdout were to last until September, we would be perilously hard pressed by Channel weather on supply across the beaches.

Two principal roads led from Normandy into the Cherbourg peninsula. One ran through the bottleneck at Carentan, the other up the far west coast. Between those two roads the Douve River severed two thirds of the neck. If we were to plug the peninsula, our mission was clear: First, we must seize the bottleneck at Carentan, then hold that east-west river line of the Douve to the west coast road. Finally we would plug the nine-mile gap between that west coast road and the sea. These tasks were to be split between two airborne divisions, the 82d and the 101st.

The 101st was to drop north of Carentan and behind Utah Beach. It was to hold open the Utah exits and prevent the enemy from

blowing those causeways. At the same time it would advance south
to Carentan and there make contact with Gerow's forces from
Omaha Beach.

Meanwhile the 82d was to jump on an even more ambitious venture. It was to cut the Coutances west coast road and block the
western half of the Cotentin neck. Unlike the 101st, it would drop
well beyond the immediate reach of our seaborne forces. However,
unless it were dispersed on landing, we estimated the division could
hold out until our overland forces broke through to relieve it. Each

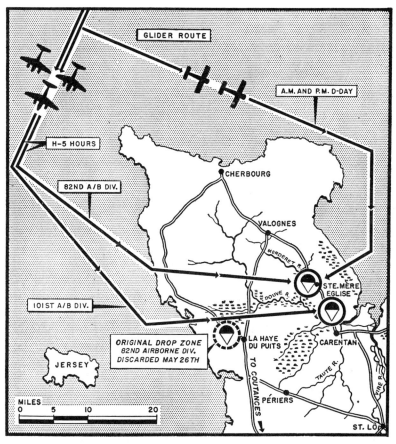

At H−5 hours, the parachute elements of two airborne divisions were to
come in on the Cotentin west coast and cut across the peninsula to the
drop zones behind Utah Beach.

of the airborne division commanders agreed to his task without a murmur.

During the initial airborne planning sessions with Montgomery at St. Paul's School, Leigh-Mallory showed no sign of opposition to the plan. Indeed at one point he even proposed that the 82d Division drop farther south—nearer the road junction at La Haye du Puits. I objected, however, preferring to take a stronger position six miles north.

It was not until later that Leigh-Mallory abruptly shifted his ground to propose that we spike the airborne plan for Utah. He not only aimed his objections at the course to be flown by troop carrier aircraft coming in from the west shore, but he insisted that the risks of an air drop on Utah outweighed the advantages to be gained there.

"I cannot approve your plan," he declared. "It is much too hazardous an undertaking. Your losses will be excessive—certainly far more than the gains are worth. I'm sorry, General Bradley, but I cannot go along on it with you."

"Very well, sir," I replied, "if you insist on cutting out the airborne attack, then I must ask that we eliminate the Utah assault. I am not going to land on that beach without making sure we've got the exits behind it."

Leigh-Mallory stared briefly across the table. "Then let me make it clear," he said, "that if you insist upon this airborne operation, you'll do it in spite of my opposition."

With that he squared himself in his chair, turned to Montgomery, and added, "If General Bradley insists upon going ahead he will have to accept full responsibility for the operation. I don't believe it will work."

"That's perfectly agreeable to me," I answered. "I'm in the habit of accepting responsibility for my operations."

Montgomery rapped quietly on the table.

"That is not at all necessary, gentlemen," he said, "I shall assume full responsibility for the operation." With Monty's approval we went ahead with the Utah airborne plan.

Leigh-Mallory, however, could not conscientiously abandon his opposition to the project. For if he were justified in his apprehensions, the entire Utah assault might be jeopardized by failure of the air drop. With so much at stake he appealed to Ike for a change in the airborne plan. Eisenhower called on me to refute his air chief's predictions.

"It's risky, of course," I agreed, "but not half so risky as a landing on Utah Beach without it."

I conceded that Leigh-Mallory's low-flying C-47's would run into ground fire almost from the moment they made landfall in France. And the Normandy hedgerows would undoubtedly make the glider landings difficult and costly. But those risks, I asserted, must be subordinated to the importance of Utah Beach and to the prompt capture of Cherbourg. Certainly I would not willingly risk the lives of 17,000 airborne troops if we could accomplish our mission without them. But I would willingly risk them to insure against failure on the invasion. This, in a nutshell, was the issue.

Eisenhower debated these irreconcilable views of his ground and air commanders. Then with the fate of OVERLORD dangling over his head, he declared in favor of the Utah drop.

Meanwhile Leigh-Mallory had not yet given up. Having dedicated himself to the task of sparing us a disaster, the air chief made one last appeal to Ike. In the end, however, it was not Leigh-Mallory but the German who forced an eleventh-hour change in the Utah airborne plan.

Late in May, Major Robert Low, assistant G-2 at First Army, brought distressing news of enemy reinforcement in the peninsula below Cherbourg. Agent reports confirmed a shift of three German divisions into this sector rendering Ridgway's drop zone untenable. Unless we were to break through speedily from the beach, the 82d could be destroyed in its far-off exposed position. We had little choice but to shift the 82d nearer the beach in support of the seaborne landing.

On May 26, Matt Ridgway and Max Taylor, commanders of the 82d and 101st Airborne Divisions, flew into Bristol for a last-minute change in plans. The dingy, windowless war room at Clifton was already loaded with crates as First Army headquarters packed its equipment for the invasion.

We hurriedly revised the plan. The 101st was to stick by its original mission, but the 82d was now to drop north of the 101st, within striking distance of Utah Beach. There it would seize the crossroads at Ste Mère Eglise and guard against counterattack from the northwest.

On the very day that revised plan was distributed, Leigh-Mallory again appealed to Ike at the latter's invasion CP in Portsmouth. Abandon the Utah air drop, he urged, and concentrate the airborne on Caen. To go ahead with the drop as planned, he estimated, would cost us 50 per cent casualties among the parachute troops, 70 per cent among the gliders. Eisenhower was disturbed by this reappearance of a problem he had long ago thought settled. If Leigh-Mallory were right, then Eisenhower would carry those losses on his hands. But on the other hand if he took his air chief's advice, he might jeopardize our landing on Utah Beach. Eisenhower retired alone in his tent to sweat out the decision. Later that evening he announced the attack was to go as planned.

I did not learn of this last-minute appeal until afterward in France. Eisenhower's choice, however, had not been one between Utah and Caen. Either the airborne went in on Utah or we could not land on that beach. And in the most portentous invasion of the war, Ike could never have shelved Utah Beach without chancing defeat.

Even before I arrived in England, the 29th Division had staked out squatters' rights on Omaha Beach. The 29th had landed in Britain in October, 1942. It was commanded by Major General Charles H. Gerhardt, a peppery 48-year-old cavalryman whose enthusiasm sometimes exceeded his judgment as a soldier. When OVERLORD was expanded to include Utah Beach, we paired the 4th Infantry with the 29th as the second assault division. But although both divisions had undergone extensive amphibious training, neither had as yet come under fire. Rather than chance a landing with two inexperienced divisions, I looked around for a veteran division to include in the line-up.

In all of England there was only one experienced assault division. Once more the Big Red One was to carry the heavy end of our stick. By this time the 1st Infantry Division had swallowed a bellyful of heroics and wanted to go home. When the division learned that it was to make a third D-day assault, this time in France, the troops grumbled bitterly over the injustices of war. Among the infantrymen who had already survived both Mediterranean campaigns, few believed their good fortune could last them through a third.

Although I disliked subjecting the 1st to still another landing, I felt that as a commander I had no other choice. My job was to get

Omaha Beach, D Plus 2: "Behind Omaha Beach the ground rose steeply to the tableland above it. It was from those bluffs that the enemy poured down fire upon our Normandy assault troops during that first worrisome morning we clung by our fingernails to the beach." (June, 1944.)

Taking Aim with the New Carbine: "While visiting the 9th Division, Churchill confessed to an itch to try out the new American carbine. Targets were promptly put out for Churchill, Eisenhower, and me. Mine was handicapped at 75 yards, Eisenhower's at 50. The Prime Minister's was placed at 25 yards. We each fired 15 rounds in rapid succession. Manton Eddy wisely hustled us away before we could inspect the targets."

ashore, establish a lodgment, and destroy the German. In the accomplishment of that mission there was little room for the niceties of justice. I felt compelled to employ the best troops I had, to minimize the risks and hoist the odds in our favor in any way that I could. As a result the division that deserved compassion as a reward for its previous ordeals now became the inevitable choice for our most difficult job. Whatever the injustice, it is better that war heap its burdens unfairly than that victory be jeopardized in an effort to equalize the ordeal.

The assault force on Omaha was to make contact with the British on its left while at the same time establishing a link with Utah on its right. If one division were to be given both missions, it would have been dispersed across a 25-mile front. And as the follow-up divisions came in, it would have become necessary to reassemble the 1st Division in one corner of Omaha Beach. To avoid the traffic snarl that would otherwise have jammed the beach, I shaped the Omaha attack force with two regiments from the 1st Division, the third from the 29th. Thus while the 1st Division concentrated to the left of the beachhead, the 29th would advance to the right. The follow-up division would then come into the line in the hole between them.

To give the invasion troops the opportunity to see their Army commander and to demonstrate our interest in their training, I toured southwest England that spring, visiting the first 11 divisions scheduled to land in France. From the depressing moors of Dartmoor to the steep green hills of Cornwall I tramped from division to division calling on each company and battery.

To avoid interfering in their training, I had instructed division commanders not to alter their schedules in an effort to impress me. In only one division were these instructions disobeyed. There a battalion commander had rehearsed his troops in a mock company attack. As I watched the men advance in suspiciously pat order, I suspected a rehearsal plan and questioned the battalion commander. When he admitted to having practiced the operation, he was relieved by the division commander. Time was too pressing to be wasted on visiting brass.

While touring the 29th Division I learned that Gerhardt's troops had been infected with a despondent fear of the casualties it was predicted they would suffer in the assault. Some talked of 90 per cent. In my roundup speech to the officers and noncoms of that division, I spoke of our casualty experiences in the Mediterranean campaigns, hoping to allay their exaggerated fears.

"This stuff about tremendous losses is tommyrot," I told them. "Some of you won't come back—but it'll be very few."

Several days later an enterprising reporter from *Stars and Stripes* visited the division and saw a transcript of my statement. Two weeks later it bounded back in press clips from the United States. I was irritated at having been quoted on an off-the-record speech to my troops and I was chagrined to discover that my predictions had been played with raised eyebrows opposite the dolorous warnings of Churchill, Roosevelt, and General Marshall.

One month after landing in France, we published a casualty statement. The American people were relieved to find them less than they had been led to expect. On D day, among the 55,000 U. S. seaborne troops, casualties totaled 4,649. Of these one third were dead, the others wounded and missing.

Several years after the war, the mother of an infantryman who had been training in England recalled my "tommyrot" statement. "I made it only to reassure our troops," I said, "to tell them they would not all be killed on the crossing."

"Well I'm glad it got back home," she replied. "You'll never know how much it helped to relieve the worrying in my family."

To the unfortunate censor whom I asked be skinned for passing that quote to the United States, let this be a footnote to justice.

By the spring of 1944 the hospitable towns of southwest England were thronged with American troops. They filled the cobblestoned streets of Devonshire villages, drained the local pubs of beer, and made an affectionate union of our British alliance. Indeed, nowhere was amity courted with a greater diligence than in the homes of British fathers with pretty unmarried daughters.

The Yankee invasion had come to England well heeled with American dollars. American privates earned three times as much as their British companions. A U. S. staff sergeant's take-home pay equaled that of a British captain. Since a substantial share of this wealth was invested in local courting, it is no wonder that Britain's provincial customs were given a fancy whirl. Indeed, it is a tribute to the civility of the British that they endured us with such good will.

More important than troops, lift, and air power on any invasion is confidence in the certainty of success. When OVERLORD was widened to a five-division assault, skepticism went out the window and our tails went over the dashboard. This time I was afflicted with none of the doubts that had assailed me on the Sicilian invasion, for I had weathered the first and was rid of squeamishness on this second go-round.

On his initial visit to the First Army war room at Bryanston Square, Eisenhower had spoken emphatically on the need for confidence in the undertaking.

"This operation is being planned as a success," he said. "There can be no thought of failure. For I assure you there is no possibility of failure." And as our preparations proceeded, the blandest skeptic would have nodded with him.

I had already cautioned my staff that they were never under any circumstances to hint of doubt or hesitation. For even a trace of skepticism in the high command could be exaggerated to ruinous proportions at division, regiment, and battalion. Yet to muster that confidence in success the plan must genuinely support it. As OVER-LORD shaped up from month to month, we knew we had a winner.

On April 7, Monty called a full-dress rehearsal for air, ground, and naval commanders on the invasion plan. It was to be the first of two such presentations. Both were attended by Eisenhower and Churchill; and on the second they were accompanied by the King. A relief map of Normandy the width of a city street had been spread on the floor of a large room in St. Paul's School. With rare skill, Monty traced his 21st Group plan of maneuver as he tramped about like a giant through Lilliputian France.

In the assault, two U. S. airborne and two seaborne divisions were to be matched by Dempsey's British force of one airborne and three seaborne divisions. After gaining a toe hold on the Normandy shore, First Army was to knit Omaha and Utah together and make contact with Dempsey on its left. Then while First Army cut the Cotentin Peninsula to forestall enemy reinforcement of Cherbourg and thereafter capture that port, the British Second Army was to seize the road center at Caen on D day and expand its beachhead toward the flat tablelands beyond that city. The American forces would then pivot on the British position like a windlass in the direction of Paris. As we whipped our line first to the south and then east, we would isolate the Brittany peninsula with its enemy-garrisoned ports. Third Army would then advance into Brittany to clean up that peninsula.

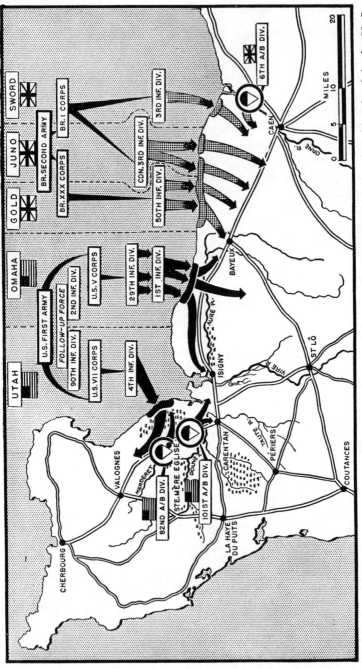

The five assault divisions on the OVERLORD landing were to join forces after securing a beachhead, while the U. S. VII Corps raced toward Cherbourg to seize that port for a speedy build-up.

In the meantime we were to complete our turning movement until the Allied line faced east toward the Seine on a 140-mile north-south front. Its left flank would be anchored on the British beaches, its open right flank on the Loire. From there we would advance to the Seine where it was anticipated the enemy would hold behind that river bank.

During our battle for Normandy, the British and Canadian armies were to decoy the enemy reserves and draw them to their front on the extreme eastern edge of the Allied beachhead. Thus while Monty taunted the enemy at Caen, we were to make our break on the long roundabout road toward Paris. When reckoned in terms of national pride, this British decoy mission became a sacrificial one, for while we tramped around the outside flank, the British were to sit in place and pin down Germans. Yet strategically it fitted into a logical division of labors, for it was toward Caen that the enemy reserves would race once the alarm was sounded.

From the enemy's point of view, a British attack toward Caen was not to be shrugged off lightly. The straight-line distance from Caen to the Seine was less than 50 miles. It was only 120 miles from Caen to Paris, 300 to the Siegfried Line. But even more worrisome to the enemy was the character of the terrain beyond Caen. Open and undulating, it offered an ideal path for tank attack. Faced with the task of defending so tantalizing a route of advance to the Reich, the German could not be blamed for believing Monty might hope to force a breakthrough in the vicinity of Caen.

This was exactly what we wanted him to think. For if the enemy were to throw his reserves against Monty at Caen, we would be free to advance with less opposition on our end of the line.

As Monty discussed this plan for Caen there in St. Paul's School, he became increasingly optimistic. Pointing toward Falaise, he talked of breaking his tanks free on D day "to knock about a bit down there." Falaise lay 32 miles inland by road from the beach; it was to take Monty 68 days to get there.

Monty afterward urged me to explore the possibility of a similar tank knockabout behind Omaha Beach. Although knowing there was scant chance of carrying it through, I nevertheless devised such a mission. As I anticipated, we never even tried it. In contrast to Monty, I had foreseen a hard enemy crust on the Normandy coast.

Throughout that long afternoon at St. Paul's, Montgomery had prohibited smoking. However, as he dismissed us for a ten-minute break late that afternoon, he sniffed the air of the room and grinned. "When we reassemble, gentlemen," he said, "you may smoke if you wish." There was a ripple of laughter in the audience, for both the Prime Minister and Eisenhower were to join us.

My association with Churchill had been limited to two previous encounters. Earlier that spring I accompanied him with Eisenhower on a three-day inspection tour of the U. S. invasion divisions. The 69-year-old correspondent hero of the Boer War tramped happily through the field, mugging under his famed derby for the benefit of the troops. And each evening at dinner on the private train, over a brandy and soda, he lectured his company on the problems and perfidies of war. However dogged his opposition to OVERLORD may once have been, he was now enthusiastic in his support of it.

While visiting the 9th Division, Churchill confessed to an itch to try out the new American carbine. Targets were promptly put out for Churchill, Eisenhower, and me. Mine was handicapped at 75 yards, Eisenhower's at 50. The Prime Minister's was placed at 25 yards. We each fired 15 rounds in rapid succession. Manton Eddy wisely hustled us away before we could inspect the targets.

Once thereafter the Prime Minister invited a half dozen of the senior Allied officers to dinner at 10 Downing Street. Remembering Churchill's eccentric hours, I was resigned to a late evening until I noticed that the invitation had written upon it, "Confidentially, the King is expected."

"Well then maybe," I told Ike, "we'll get to bed early."

However, the King was in no hurry to leave. After dinner we adjourned to the drawing room where the King circulated easily among us discussing the coming invasion. Rank was forgotten for the moment and the King seemed especially appreciative of the informality of the evening. For the first time I realized how lonesome a life a monarch must live, how difficult it must be for him to have friends outside his family.

It was 1:30 A.M. when he finally left.

Unlike the Sicilian invasion where we had attacked at 3:30 A.M. to screen our movements in darkness, the Normandy assault had been timed to touch down after daylight. For in ramming our way ashore against the fortified coast of France, we calculated that firepower would more than compensate for the loss of concealment; stealth could better be sacrificed to more accurate and heavier bombardment. By scheduling H hour after dawn, we reaped double the tonnage from air in softening up the beaches. During the pre-dawn darkness RAF nighttime bombers would saturate the shore defenses. Before that shock wore off, U. S. heavies and mediums would strike at dawn in a daylight attack. By the same token, the navy could use daylight observation to pinpoint the fire of its big guns. This in itself had become a major factor, for naval gunfire was to be our mainstay support.

To exact the greatest advantage from this concentration of air and naval support, we concluded that H hour should come no *sooner* than 30 minutes after daylight, no *later* than one hour and a half. Were it later, the enemy might too quickly recover from the effects of the RAF bombing. Furthermore, each minute of unnecessary daylight would give him an added chance to spread the alarm and bring up reinforcements.

In addition to the overwhelming strength of Allied air and naval forces, we held a decisive advantage in picking the time and place for attack. For while we plotted the assault, the enemy could only wait and speculate where it might fall.

Unable to anticipate where we might strike, the enemy had been forced to spread his strength across 860 miles of European coast line. As he continued to plant more German dead on his long line of retreat from Russia, it became increasingly difficult for him to man that Atlantic Wall. To smash our way ashore we had only to concentrate a force against some single point in his line. With the fire-power at our disposal we could break a hole in that line and pour our follow-up forces through it.

Although the enemy's fortified wall would not halt an intruder, it could slow down an attacking force while Rommel called for reserves. Indeed this was the intended function of his Atlantic Wall. It was to blunt our assault and so split our forces that the enemy might find time to form his reserves and strike back in a counter-attack. When used to screen a mobile reserve in this fashion, the concrete fortifications of a fixed defensive line can be worth many divisions. Without these mobile reserves, however, a fixed defensive line becomes useless. It was for this lack of mobile reserves that the Maginot Line became a trap for the French army.

During the exercise in St. Paul's School, Montgomery had disclosed that Rommel ordinarily committed his reserves just as quickly as he could drag them into the line. If he would only throw them piece-

meal against our break in the wall, we could defeat his forces in
detail and avert the danger of a powerful counterattack.

As Germany dissipated her strength against the Red army, she
sought to economize on troops in the west by strengthening the
fortifications of her Atlantic Wall. The task fell to Rommel, whose
new command now reached from the Frisian Islands of Holland,
400 miles along the Channel coast to Brest, and around that peninsula to the mouth of the Loire. With the energy that characterized
his command, Rommel set out to multiply his casemated guns and
pour thousands of yards of fresh concrete. He also introduced two
wicked innovations that were to cause us trouble on the Normandy
assault. The first device we spotted in February on air photos of the
invasion beaches. Rommel had ordered the construction of underwater obstacles between high and low tide on the beaches to rip
open the bellies of Allied landing craft as they neared the shore.
P-51's from the recce squadrons swooped in low to photograph
those obstructions in detail.

Then to forestall our glider landings, he ordered posts planted in
the most likely Normandy fields. These he wired together and
triggered with Teller mines. Like the beach obstacles, those glider
pickets were first detected on air photos. Ridgway brought them to
me with a worried scowl across his face. At the same time, Rommel
seeded the beaches and the bluffs behind them with Teller mines,
using the same artifice he had shown in the Libyan campaign.

By the spring of 1944, a part of the Allied strategic air effort was
reoriented to our tactical requirements on the ground. Not only was
the enemy to be immobilized by destruction of his industry and
gasoline refineries, but his rail lines were to be bombed, marshaling
yards destroyed, and bridges wrenched from their pilings. The entire
assault area was to be isolated from the body of the continent.

While intelligence continued to speculate on the probable rate
of enemy build-up against the invasion beaches, air undertook the
interdiction campaign that was to knock those calculations galley-
west. To be safe, however, we figured conservatively on the disrup-
tive effect of this bombing. Any slowdown attributable to air we
would count as a bonus. Meanwhile in calculating our build-up we
reckoned on a maximum enemy rate of build-up against us.

At the outset this air campaign was deadlocked by an intramural
dispute among the airmen themselves as to whether priority should
be given the bombing of rail lines or the destruction of synthetic

gasoline plants. In the end it was Tooey Spaatz who carried the day for the refinery campaign—and the results proved Tooey right. For by the time we invaded France the enemy was desperately hoarding his gas. Enemy road movements became more and more restricted until vehicles began to fall into our hands undamaged save by empty fuel tanks. Napoleon's dictum should be revised to fit the modern army: it moves not on its stomach but on gasoline. Tonnage-wise the stomach is more easily satisfied than the thirsty internal-combustion engine. In our pursuit across France an infantry division required six times the tonnage in gasoline that it needed in food. And in an armored division this proportion went up to eight.

On April 14, after a knockdown struggle with the British over the command of strategic air, Eisenhower won command of all Allied air forces for direct support of the OVERLORD invasion. During the next five weeks these air blows mounted with terrifying intensity. In April alone, bombers and fighters of the Eighth Air Force flew a total of 33,000 sorties. And in May more than 1,000 enemy aircraft were shot down over Europe as our pilots taunted them into the air just long enough to draw a bead.

As both the strategic and tactical air forces shuttled daily from their British airfields to France, enemy mobility staggered under the weight of these round-the-clock blows. During the month of May alone, more than 900 locomotives and 16,000 freight cars were listed among claims of the air force. In addition, scores of marshaling yards were hit in daylight precision raids. Even when we discounted the tendency of some airmen to sweeten up their box scores, the record was an impressive one, impressive enough to relieve our minds on the crucial problem of enemy build-up.

In its campaign to isolate the assault area, air forces first chalked off the northwest corner of France and then set out to sever its communications with the rest of the nation. This boundary line encompassed an area approximately the size of Indiana. It ran from Le Havre up the Seine to Paris, across to Orléans on the headwaters of the Loire, and down that river to Nantes on the underside of the Brittany neck. This westernmost corner of France was held by the German Seventh Army, one of the two under Rommel's Army Group. Its force included 17 divisions in addition to the fortress troops stationed in Cherbourg and the Brittany ports. Three of those divisions were panzers, all of them in reserve.

By the late spring of 1944, the German had moved a total of 58 divisions into France. Ten were panzer or panzer-grenadiers; in strength and mobility they varied from good to bad. Seventeen were "field" divisions available to the enemy for counterattack. However most of them had long ago been stripped of all but their rudimentary transport and as a consequence they lacked the mobility required in a war of movement. Another 24 "static" divisions were assigned to coastal defenses. They varied in quality from fair to poor and in transport were even less mobile. The remaining seven were training divisions, staffed primarily with green troops.

By isolating our assault area from the thickly held Pas de Calais and the Bordeaux region of France, the air force intended to close the gate against German reinforcement while we pushed ashore against the Seventh Army. Unless it were speedily reinforced, we calculated that we could lick this Army in the lodgment.

While air was isolating this corner of France, it also struck inside the Normandy sector to tear up railroads and halt all enemy motor movement. This would prevent Rommel from closing a ring around our beachhead before we could force a penetration. So successful was this air mission that one enemy division was forced to walk the last 100 miles into combat.

At the start of this bridge-busting campaign I awaited the results with a patient air. For in Tunisia I had seen Stukas lather themselves in raid after raid while failing to destroy a small Bailey bridge. And in London, despite the blitz of 1940, not a single one of the Thames River bridges was destroyed. However, instead of dumping their bombs upon these pencil-thin bridges in high-altitude raids, the airmen instructed fighter bombers to skip their bombs against the bridge abutments. By June 4 every railroad bridge had been knocked out across the Seine between Rouen and Paris. By June 6 not only had the northwestern corner of France been isolated, but the bombing campaign had demoralized the French railway system. Rail traffic fell to 60 per cent of capacity, an especially serious blow to an army so short of trucks.

To test the assault fire support, check our communications, and drill the beach engineers, we scheduled full-dress rehearsals in late April and early May for both the Omaha and Utah forces. As a stand-in target for the Normandy beach, we chose the Devon coast village of Slapton Sands, a few miles south of the British naval base at Dartmouth. In the meantime, invasion troops had been shifted from their camps and bivouacs in southwest England to concentration areas nearer the Channel on their first shuttle movement toward the embarkation ports. There they waterproofed their vehicles, picked up special equipment, and dropped their administrative tails. From those assembly areas the troops were shifted to forward areas called sausages because of their peculiar oval designations on our maps. These were nearer the hards, or concrete ramps, where troops were to mount their craft.

An entire armored division had been cannibalized to help provide the 54,000 men required for housekeeping in these final marshaling areas. Among them were 4,500 brand-new cooks especially trained for this task. The sausages, moreover, had been sealed inside a barbed-wire cordon, for it was here that many of the troops were to be briefed on their missions. Once briefed, they were to be cut off from the rest of England. Civilian traffic in and out of the coastal area was halted and check-points strung across England. An army of 2,000 CIC agents had been detailed there to prevent security leaks.

These trial assaults created risks themselves for it became necessary for us to bunch the landing craft inside harbors. Yet despite these telltale signs of preparation, we were left almost completely unmolested by German air. The sausage areas had been painstakingly camouflaged, and so carefully had the military traffic been dispersed that our movements escaped detection.

Aboard a 105-foot LCI with its twin assault gangways on either side of the bow, we pitched in the restless English Channel as our craft turned past the transports into Start Bay for a close-up of the Utah rehearsal. Although it was already April 28, the wind bit sharply and a spray wetted our glasses as we searched the misty shore. A cluster of cottages on a narrow white beach marked the village of Slapton Sands half obscured in the haze of a murky morning. Lieutenant General Lewis H. Brereton, commander of the Ninth Tactical Air Force, scrunched deeper into his greatcoat atop the towerlike bridge of the LCI as he sniffed at the overcast sky. The air mission that was to have softened the beachhead was already overdue.

"Do you think they'll get through?" I called.

Brereton shrugged his shoulders.

"Well, if they're on top of this stuff, I hope they go home," I said training my glasses on the craft nosing shoreward. "If they make a pass this late, they may hit our troops."

Brereton's reply was lost in a flash of fire as a ship appeared to explode near the shore. The tails of a flight of rockets screamed through the sky and the gray, muggy beach blinked back. A rumble rolled over the bay. This was the first of our rocket-support craft drenching the beach with close-in fire an instant before the assault wave touched down.

Later that afternoon I was told by Collins that German S-boats had broken through the naval screen offshore to attack his convoy en route to Slapton Sands. A ship—or ships—it was reported, had been hit. I asked if there were any losses. Some, I was told, but no one yet knew how many. Not until the troops were reformed at the completion of the exercise could a thorough count be made.

Meanwhile G-2 was growing uneasy. If survivors of the sinking were to be picked up by the S-boats, the enemy might learn how imminent the invasion was. Deception had been working on a plot to mislead him into thinking it would come in mid-July. Fortunately those troops had not yet been briefed and the secret of where we would strike was presumably still safe. But with this misfortune, the enemy might learn *when* we planned to strike. I now shared G-2's worries.

However, when the week passed and I heard no more of those sinkings, I concluded that the loss had been slight, that there was little likelihood of the enemy having learned anything from it.

While motoring back to Dartmouth following the rehearsal I checked my findings with Kean, Dickson, Thorson, and Wilson. Like me, they were disturbed on two counts. The beach engineer organization had broken down and air support had failed to show. The first failure we could correct, for the faults were easily diagnosed. The second was more perplexing. Brereton had seemed strangely unconcerned with the failure of his air mission.

On a beach assault the engineer brigade performs as longshoreman, trucker, traffic cop, and warehouseman. A breakdown in that beach organization might not only jeopardize the assault but it could most certainly delay our build-up. During that critical period before we secured Cherbourg and before the Communications Zone entered the supply chain, a mismanaged beach could imperil the invasion. I suggested to Collins that he assign a new commander to the Utah beach engineer brigade.

Not until four years after the war did I learn that these engineer troubles during the Utah rehearsal had been caused not by a breakdown in command but rather by the S-boat attack. For what I had been led to believe was a minor brush with the enemy was revealed to have been one of the major tragedies of the European war. Two LST's were sunk in that attack with a loss of more than 700 men. Yet for some unexplained reason the report had been withheld from me. Collins' losses during rehearsal exceeded those of Utah on D day.

If our preinvasion confidence in air support were to be measured by the indifference shown us in England by the Ninth Tactical Air Force, we would have sailed on the invasion with misgivings. Part of our uneasiness stemmed from the brush-off we experienced at the hands of Brereton himself, for in attempting to pin him down on air-ground training, I was told his air force was then too heavily committed in the air battle for France. Certainly if he was aware of our urgent need for combined training with air, he gave no evidence of it. But in fairness to Brereton, it must be remembered that while we were planning and training for the invasion, the Ninth Air Force had joined in the air offensive against the V-1 rocket-launching sites.

The Ninth Air Force had been formed in England in October, 1943, when the tactical air command was separated from the Eighth. In January, 1944, it joined the air battle over Europe under Leigh-Mallory as commander-in-chief of the Allied Expeditionary Air Force. Since the Ninth's ground-support mission would not begin until the invasion, it flew throughout that spring in support of the heavy bombers and helped to drive the Luftwaffe out of its forward airfields.

With discovery of the enemy's rocket-launching sites, much of the effort of the Eighth and Ninth was diverted against that threat. For despite the inclination of intelligence to minimize the V-weapons, we were fearful that these rockets might be used against our crowded ports during the mounting. In the six months before D day air force sorties included 30,000 against these rocket sites.

Finally, just one month before we were to sail, the Ninth Air Force reported that it had at last caught up with its shooting war and could thereafter devote time to training with the ground.

"Too bad," I answered, "but we've completed our training. Troops are already moving into the sausages."

As a result of our inability to get together with air in England, we went into France almost totally untrained in air-ground cooperation.

But we also went in with an offsetting advantage in a breezy young major general named Elwood R. Quesada, chief of the IX Tactical Air Command in direct support of First Army. This 40-year-old airman helped more than anyone else to develop the air-ground support that was to speed us so successfully across France on the heels of the breakout. He succeeded brilliantly in a task where so many airmen before him had failed, partly because he was willing to dare anything once. Unlike most airmen who viewed ground support as a bothersome diversion to war in the sky, Quesada approached it as a vast new frontier waiting to be explored.

During the Channel assault Montgomery was to join the air and naval commanders-in-chief at Eisenhower's headquarters in Portsmouth. There Eisenhower could exercise fingertip control over each of his three principal commanders. Originally, it was planned for me to remain in England until D plus 1, directing the First Army assault from an underground CP near Plymouth. This Plymouth proposal was thereafter dropped and I was ordered instead to stand by with Montgomery at Portsmouth. A crisis, it was explained, might call for joint action. However, this, too, seemed unwise to me and I carried my objections to Ike.

"If we run into trouble on the landing," I told him, "the decisions are going to have to be made aboard Kirk's flagship. Our communications are all tied in there and that's where I belong. If something were to happen on the beach, I could more easily influence the battle from there than I could all the way back here in England." Ike agreed and I made ready to sail.

By May 31 more than a quarter-million ground troops were waiting in their sausages—primed, briefed, and ready for The Day.

15: *D Day, Normandy*

It was 7:15 when I went down to breakfast at my quarters in Bristol on the morning of June 3. We had loitered late over dinner the night before, our last evening together in England. Today we were to board Admiral Kirk's flagship for the invasion. D day had been set for June 5 and the warm summer sun that poured through the leaded glass windows of the Holmes cheered us with the promise of good weather. Tubby Thorson was downing his third cup of coffee. "Morning, General," he called, "how did you sleep with all that brand new rank you've got?" Wilson chuckled.

The day before I had been notified of my promotion to a brigadier general on the permanent list. The commission had been predated to September 1, 1943. Because my rank as a permanent colonel dated from October 1 of the same year, we were not yet certain as to whether I was going ahead or backward. Until the day before I had been a Sears Roebuck general; all three stars were temporary, good for "the duration and six months." Now I was assured at least one permanent one in Arlington.

Most of the First Army headquarters had been evacuated from Bristol several days before to board the army command ship and two additional LST's on the hards at Portland. The rear echelon was to remain in England until priorities slackened on lift. Because space was cramped aboard the *Augusta*, my command group had been trimmed to fit the bunk space allotted us. Besides Kean, it included Dickson, Thorson, Wilson, a fifth officer from signal, five journal clerks and draftsmen. Hodges was to sail as deputy on the army command ship, *Achernar*. While Hansen sailed with us aboard the *Augusta*, Bridge was to remain in London and there frequent the nightspots. His disappearance from London, we feared, might alert the enemy agents.

We knew there were agents in London. In fact several were permitted to operate under secret surveillance by the British, for they could be useful in sending deliberately misleading reports to Berlin. Except for those under surveillance, however, few enemy agents were able to penetrate the security net that had been tightened around England in the spring of 1944. As D day approached, the net was pulled tighter and traffic was even halted to Ireland.

Shortly after 8 we turned south from Bristol across the Avon on the road to Plymouth where we were to rendezvous with Collins. Hansen rode with an aluminum tube of TOP SECRET invasion maps between his knees. Kean and Dickson, Thorson, and Wilson followed in a second sedan. It was a Saturday morning and we slowed down through the market at Taunton where British housewives had already formed their patient queues before the shops. Although the sausages were now packed with invasion troops, so quietly had the D-day force been assembled that Taunton, like those other southern tier towns, remained blissfully unaware that The Day was at hand.

Collins was waiting at a road junction north of Plymouth. He sped us through the MP check-points to the quay where a barge from the *Augusta* was standing by. For the first time since Sicily I buckled on a pistol and bent my neck under the weight of a steel helmet. I tossed my field pack with its greasy gas-protective coveralls to the deck and jumped aboard.

The *Augusta* waited offshore, a rakish beauty among the snub-nosed LST's. Its curved yachtlike bow and eight-inch turrets pointed toward the Channel. Kirk had gone ashore but Rear Admiral A. D. Struble, his chief of staff, welcomed us aboard. I was assigned the skipper's cabin, the one occupied by President Roosevelt in 1941 when he joined Churchill off the Newfoundland shore to draft the Atlantic Charter.

The army war room had been constructed on the afterdeck ordinarily used by the cruiser's spotter aircraft. It consisted of a temporary shed 10 by 20 feet whose sheet-metal walls were to pucker whenever the AA mount above it fired. The three overhead lights were caged and the face of the clock on the wall had been taped against concussion. The outer wall had been papered with a Michelin motoring map of France. Next to it hung a terrain study of the assault beaches, neatly bracketed into letter and color designations. Between them a Petty pin-up girl lounged on a far more alluring beach. On the near wall a detailed map of Normandy described in concentric arcs the ranges of enemy coastal guns. Still another charted the disposition of enemy divisions in blurred red markings. A long plotting table filled the center of the room. There a naval lieutenant traced an overlay of the beach defenses. And on a waist-high shelf the length of the seaward wall stood a row of typewriters for the journal clerks.

I glanced at the weather forecast in the G-2 journal: *Mist from Sunday to Wednesday, with low clouds and reduced visibility in the mornings. Winds not to exceed 17 to 22 knots. Choppy water in the channel with five-foot breakers. A four-foot surf on the beaches.*

"Doesn't look good," I said.

Dickson was more emphatic. "It stinks."

Kirk and I had worked together once before on the Sicilian assault. As naval commander of the Western Task Force he was again my opposite number. But my directives came from Montgomery, while his originated with Ramsay, the Allied naval commander-in-chief.

Kirk's fleet was divided into three forces. The first, Force "O" for Omaha, was commanded by Rear Admiral John L. Hall, Jr., another old friend from the Sicilian invasion. The second, Force "U" for Utah, sailed under the flag of Rear Admiral Don P. Moon. Hall was paired with Gerow aboard the *Ancon,* command ship for V Corps; Moon shared the *Bayfield* with Collins' VII Corps. The third mounted a follow-up force, combat-loaded from the Bristol Channel. It contained the 2d Division bound for Omaha Beach and the 90th Division for Utah.

During spring planning Kirk and I had battled side by side in a strenuous effort to coax additional naval gunfire support from naval operations in Washington. For originally the bombardment fleet assigned the invasion looked woefully inadequate for its task. As late as April, 1944, the U. S. Navy could spare only two battleships, four cruisers, 12 destroyers, and a variety of small craft to support the American landing. We anticipated little resistance from the hit-and-run German navy but we were apprehensive over the coastal guns. Against those fixed shore batteries I would gladly have swapped a dozen B-17's for each 12-inch gun I could wrangle. As in Sicily the American deficit in naval support was to be made up by the British. But because an American destroyer packed almost the fire-power of a British cruiser, while the American cruiser outgunned her British counterpart, I was anxious that our allotment in naval support be tallied in U. S. ships.

By then the preponderance of U. S. naval strength had been concentrated in the Pacific where victory would depend primarily upon sea power. But it had become apparent in 1944 that Japan's expansionist drive exceeded both her power and resources. Ultimately we could defeat her; she could not win the war. In Europe, however, there was no such assurance. For though she had been bled in Africa, Italy, and Russia, Germany had not yet lost her offensive strength. And we could still not free our minds from the fear that Stalin might make a deal and leave us to face the Axis alone. If we were to fail on the OVERLORD invasion, we might never get a second chance. Even at the risk of slowing down its timetable in the Pacific war, I begged the navy to stack the odds more heavily on our side. Eventually Washington agreed and Kirk's bombardment fleet was enlarged to four battleships (two of which were holdovers from World War I), four cruisers, and 26 destroyers. It could not be called a formidable force in terms of Pacific naval campaigns, but at least our pinchpenny days were ended.

On the morning of June 6 we could be thankful that they were. Our forces on Omaha Beach *might* have held even without this additional fire support. But the first message to reach me from V Corps read: "Thank God for the U. S. Navy!"

Despite our disheartening forecast on weather, no word had come from Ike at Portsmouth on the likelihood of postponement. He was to meet at 4 A.M. the following morning on June 4 with his weather officer and the Combined Commanders-in-Chief. Not until then would Eisenhower make the momentous decision that only he could make: whether to go ahead in the face of bad weather or wait for improvement.

Later that afternoon I boarded a barge to visit Hodges and the First Army staff. They were headquartered aboard the *Achernar,* a converted cargo ship now draped with the antennae and radio mounts of a command ship.

Strings of LCT's were already chugging toward the outer harbor, dragging their barrage balloons behind them. In contrast to the

somber, gray LST's, the smaller craft had been daubed in spectacular camouflage paints. Now sealed aboard their cramped craft for
the second day, the troops had wearily reconciled themselves to the
ordeal of waiting. They stretched atop their heavily laden trucks, to
write letters, read, or simply doze in the afternoon sun that still
brightened the windy harbor. Aboard a nearby LCT the assault
ramp had been lowered to the water's edge, and a dozen hardy
soldiers were using it as a diving platform. On still another the
troops had relieved the monotony of waiting by washing. GI laundry
hung from a line that had been strung between the aerials of two
Sherman tanks.

That evening Kirk asked if I would brief the correspondents
aboard the *Augusta* on First Army's assault plans. Only three of
them had been accredited to Kirk's staff. I first outlined the missions
of the airborne and seaborne troops.

"To help the amphibious get elements ashore," I said, "we're going
to soften up each of the beaches with an 800-ton carpet bombing.
Ten minutes before the first wave touches down, we'll drench
Omaha with 8,000 rockets, put another 5,000 on Utah. These rockets
should tear up his wire, detonate his mines, and drive him under
cover the instant before we land." I pointed to the detailed beach
map. "Then promptly at H hour we'll swim 64 tanks ashore . . ."

"Swim them ashore?" someone asked.

"They're DD tanks," I explained, forgetting for the moment how
closely we had guarded this secret.

Another experimental device of the British, the DD, or dual-drive,
tank consisted of a conventional vehicle equipped with canvas
water wings and an auxiliary propeller. After sealing the tank's hull
and fitting the propeller, ordnance had added a tubular frame over
which it stretched a canvas float that completely surrounded the
tank. The driver could spread these wings by a simple mechanical
device as he walked his steel monster off the ramp of an LCT. When
I first saw the invention on the Isle of Wight the previous December,
I blinked as a 30-ton Cromwell tank waded out of the surf and
snarled over the beach, her gun in position to fire. A blast from a
built-in demolition dropped her water wings on the beach. The rig
was easily adapted to our 34-ton Sherman tanks.

Tactically these DD tanks provided the answer to our need for
heavy well-aimed fire against the beach defenses at the moment of
touch-down. Until the DD tanks were developed, we had been

dependent upon the machine guns and mortars the infantry carried ashore.

As soon as possible after breaching the enemy's shore defenses we were to lay down advance fighter bases for our aircraft. By eliminating the 300-mile turnaround from Britain we could almost double the effectiveness of existing fighter craft. By D plus 1 we were to open an evacuation airstrip on each beach. By D plus 14 the schedule called for ten airstrips to base as many fighter groups. And by D plus 35, only five weeks after landing, we expected to have cleared 18 fields through the hedgerows of our American sector.

As in Sicily, the air force grumbled when we reduced the initial allowances on lift for engineer construction battalions. But when Quesada appealed the decision on air force tonnage for D day, we stood our ground. "Pete," I reminded him, "one of your big 14-ton graders displaces a helluva lot of infantrymen. And for the first few hours ashore, I'd rather have doughboys than the stuff with which to build airfields."

One of Kirk's correspondents nodded toward the map where the words *Festung Cherbourg* had been heavily ringed by a red crayon.

"How soon do you expect to take Cherbourg?" he asked.

"I'm going to have to stick my neck out," I told him. "But as of this moment, I'd gladly sell out for D plus 15—yes, or even D plus 20. The D plus 8 estimate you see here on the map is probably much better than we can do."

The rosier estimate had been written into the OVERLORD plan long before Rommel began to thicken his Normandy defenses. Originally the invasion coast had been held by only three static divisions. Now three additional field divisions had crowded into that sector. Dickson had estimated the enemy could mount a total of seven against us on D day.

I pointed toward a map on the wall. "You've got to remember, however, that just as soon as we land this business becomes primarily a business of build-up. For you can almost always force an invasion—but you can't always make it stick.

"We're going to face three critical periods in this invasion. The first will come in getting ashore. It'll be difficult—but we're not especially worried about that part of it. The second may come on the sixth or seventh day when the other fellow gets together enough reinforcements for a counteroffensive. This counterattack will probably give us our greatest trouble. Then once we hurdle the counterattack, our third critical period will come when we go to break out of the beachhead."

It was a bright moonlit night and the harbor waters of Plymouth were almost iridescent. Our first day aboard ship had gone by with few passes from enemy air. Several recce ships had poked toward the harbor but they were chased off by shore-based AA. The watch rang four bells. Naval elements in northern ports had already set sail to rendezvous with Kirk's main force.

OVERLORD had already gotten under way for D day on the morning of June 5. Either Eisenhower would halt it early this morning of June 4 or the invasion would have gone too far to be called back.

At midnight I turned in and fell asleep. It was almost six when I was awakened on Sunday, June 4. The weather in Plymouth harbor was soupy and wet; visibility was down and I shivered as I dressed. Kean came in with a copy of the Admiralty radio to Kirk.

"Postponed?" I asked.

"Twenty-four hours."

Just as soon as Eisenhower had reached his decision the navy rushed fast destroyers to head off the units that had put to sea and shepherd them back to ports. Now the sharp edge of those troops would be dulled and seasickness woud take its toll in another day on the choppy Channel. We checked the weather forecast that had been posted on our journal. It was even less promising that the one on June 3: five-foot waves in the Channel and no sign of a break in the overcast until June 7 or 8.

But unless we adjusted the H hour, tidal conditions on June 8 would rule out that long a postponement. The rising tide would not reach its halfway high-water mark until long after daylight that morning. And while we had planned a daylight invasion at dawn, we backed off at the thought of a late midmorning attack that would enable the enemy to regain his wits after the heavy night bombing.

Thorson ordered his working staff on the *Achernar* to notify all First Army units of the postponements. The code words went out: HORNPIPE to indicate OVERLORD, BOWSPRIT for the one-day delay. The staff there had already been tipped off in a message from Montgomery's headquarters at 5:15 that morning. G-3 had devised a prearranged signal to circulate news of a postponement. Having declared an initial postponement, Eisenhower was left to struggle with the question of whether to go ahead once more. He scheduled another predawn meeting early on June 5 at Southwick House in Portsmouth. For the second time he was to be cornered alone on the single most important yes or no decision of the war. That choice alone might hold the key to success or failure.

On that Sunday afternoon, June 4, I was to go ashore with Kirk to agree on our recommendations in the event of a second postponement. Meanwhile I shuffled impatiently about my cabin. First I sat down with a copy of *A Bell for Adano*. But I was too restless to read it and exchanged it for the previous day's *Stars and Stripes*. Detroit had won a 16-inning game from New York. I tossed the paper aside and went back up to the bridge. A batch of recce photos had just come in. They showed where a battery of six enemy 155's had been smothered by air bombing. G-2 reported them abandoned.

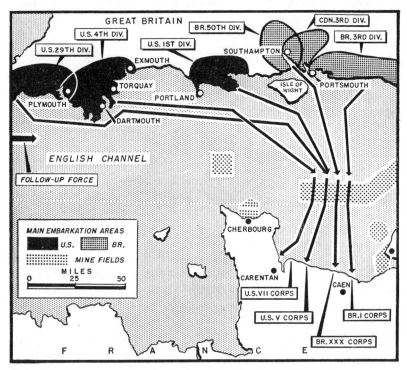

From ports on the southwest coast of England, the U. S. convoys were to converge with those of the British forces off the Isle of Wight before crossing the Channel to Normandy for the assault.

Before going ashore I crossed over once more to the *Achernar* for one last session with the Army staff. For a conference table we used the air filter room where A-2 would track enemy air attacks during our crossing of the Channel. The huge plotting board was painted with naval force channels from the English coast to France. These channels ran from the British ports in the east of England and the American ports in the west to converge in an assembly area off the Isle of Wight. From there they paralleled each other for 50 miles toward the Normandy coast. Within 30 miles of the shore line they fanned out again toward the five invasion beaches.

However, for all the air that ventured out against us on the channel, air filter's room might better have been converted into a pool hall. For improbable though it still seems, Goering's aircraft had failed to detect the approach of our fleet. The bad weather had screened us better than we knew. Even after we had landed, Goering chose to husband his Luftwaffe rather than fling it against our massed ships offshore.

The OVERLORD D day had originally been scheduled by the Combined Chiefs of Staff for the "favorable period of the May moon." Later, on Eisenhower's recommendation, they postponed D day to a "favorable period" in June. The specific date would be left to the discretion of the Supreme Commander. But in choosing the actual D day, Eisenhower was to be at the mercy of the tides. For the lunar cycle left us with only six days each month when tidal conditions fulfilled our requirements on the beaches. The first three fell on June 5, 6, and 7. If bad weather forestalled invasion on all three days, the assault would have to be put off for two weeks. If bad weather again prevented our going during that second June phase of the moon, there was no alternative but to delay the invasion until July. Meanwhile, after having once been briefed on the OVERLORD plan and destination, the assault troops would have to be locked up totally incommunicado. The prospect was a frightening one: 28 days of keeping a secret known to more than 140,000 men.

Even more frightening than the problem of security was the likely effect of a month's delay on Allied operations in France. Not only would that long a postponement shorten by one third the time left for our summer campaign, but it would shove us one month nearer the deadline for seizing a Channel port before the advent of stormy weather. We were told that we could not bank on the Channel for beach unloading after September 1. If the German were to hang on to Cherbourg for 50 or 60 days after a July D-day landing, we might be seriously pressed for wintertime maintenance of our troops ashore. The choice of D day had been limited to six days each month because only during those six days could we satisfy our requirements on morning light and tides. Both air and navy insisted upon daylight as essential to the preliminary bombardment. On the other hand, the army preferred to approach the beach under cover of darkness and touch down at first light. This would have given us concealment on the approach, with just enough light on landing to find our way ashore. To gain the benefit of daylight air and naval bombardment, the army compromised its position on darkness and agreed to an H hour 30 minutes after dawn.

But on the question of tides the army had to be insistent, for there we could not give in. Twice each day the Normandy beach was flooded by a mountainous Channel tide that rose approximately 19 feet from low to high water. At low tide the beach defenses lay exposed more than a quarter mile behind a moist sandy shelf. At high tide the Channel lapped almost to the sea wall behind Omaha Beach.

To get ashore with the fewest losses it would be best to sail in at high tide to within easy crawling distance of the sea wall. At low tide the craft would have grounded more than 400 yards offshore. A quarter mile of open sandy beach could have produced another Tarawa.

The choice, therefore, would have been a simple one in favor of high tide had it not been for the underwater obstacles Rommel had planted on those Normandy beaches. For had we sailed in on a high tide, those obstructions would have pinioned our craft and torn open their bellies. The assault wave might then have foundered in eight feet of surf.

The alternative lay between high and low tide—but it was difficult to say precisely where. To get the answer we experimented with demolitions against underwater obstacles we reproduced on the Channel coast of England. Eventually by trial and error we learned that 30 minutes would be required to blow paths through a belt of underwater obstructions. The engineers could dynamite those obstacles in water up to two feet deep. And since the tide rose at the rate of a foot every 15 minutes, two feet would allow them 30 minutes.

With that, the answer fell into place. We would assault when a rising tide reached the obstacle line and give the engineers 30 minutes to clear it before the water became too deep. Successive assault waves would then ride the rising tide nearer the sea wall through gaps in the obstacle belt.

Of all the days in the month, June 6 would best fit our requirements, for it would have sufficient daylight before the incoming tide would reach the obstacles on Omaha Beach. June 5 would be acceptable with 30 minutes less daylight, June 7 with 30 minutes more. But by June 8 the tide would not reach the obstacles until two and a half hours after daylight. A two and a half hour gap between daylight and touch-down we thought too risky in terms of lost surprise. Ike's first choice for D day had been June 5. For then if weather closed in, he could still choose June 6 or 7. Consequently on May 17 he red-lined June 5 as D day.

By June 4 the weather was such that Ike decided to defer D day to June 6. But in Plymouth on the drizzly afternoon of June 4 there were few signs of a break in the weather. We firmly anticipated a second postponement that night.

But here came the hitch in plan. Ike could not make his decision before the westernmost convoys again weighed anchor on a second start. The first time we had simply turned them back to port. If it became necessary to turn them back once more, they would be forced to put in for fuel. And since refueling called for at least a 48-hour delay, there would be no possibility of getting them off before the morning of June 7.

Consequently in this second go-round on weather Eisenhower could no longer get by with a simple yes or no. The choice had become more complex.

1. He could take a chance on the unpromising weather and go ahead on June 6;

2. He could postpone the assault once more and put it ashore for two weeks to await the next favorable phase of the moon;

3. Or he could accept less favorable tide and daylight conditions and risk June 8 or 9.

Ramsay had put the question to Kirk: in the event of a *second* postponement, how long do you want to delay? It had become a choice between two days, two weeks—or more. Kirk invited me and my staff to sit in council with him. We assembled on the afternoon of June 4 around a giant, felt-covered table in the headquarters of Plymouth's British naval command. Two inscrutable British marines guarded the door. A dozen worn wicker chairs were strewn about the dreary room. At one end a faded dartboard hung on the pin-pricked wall. Admiral Moon had come ashore for the meeting while Hall remained in Portsmouth with his Omaha force.

Faced with the possibility of a two-week delay I immediately withdrew my earlier unequivocal objections to June 8 and 9. At the moment even an overdose of daylight had become infinitely prefer-able to the ordeal of a long delay.

"As far as army is concerned," I told Kirk, "we'll take either the eighth or ninth in lieu of a two-week lay-up. For if we put our troops ashore, we take an awful chance on having this thing leak out. And we can't keep the troops penned up on their craft for two more weeks. But if we're going in on either the eighth or the ninth, I'd rather ride in with the tide as we planned it and take my chances on daylight."

The alternative, of course, would have been to land earlier in the morning, but on a much lower tide.

Kirk doodled on a pad. "Well, speaking for the navy, I know I'd much prefer more daylight to see what I was shooting at. And air would probably like it for bombing. How do you feel, Royce?" Major General Ralph Royce had joined me aboard the *Augusta* as deputy commander for the Ninth Air Force. We studied the tides and calcu-lated prospective H hours for June 8 and 9. To hold to our tidal plan on the beach obstacles we would have to delay the Omaha attack on June 8 until 8 A.M., almost two and a half hours after day-light. On June 9 it would be even worse. To meet tidal conditions that day, H hour would have to come at 8:35.

"Of course, that would make it a lot tougher for the airborne," I cautioned Royce. "They'll have to hold out a couple of hours longer before we can relieve the pressure. But I imagine they can probably take care of themselves if you'll help out on air."

"Don't worry about that," Royce said, "we'll give them all the stuff they can use."

From Portland came word that Hall and Gerow together favored an earlier H hour despite the disadvantage of low tides. But this would put them ashore an hour or more before the British on their left. Because of the rocks on those beaches, the British had no alternative but to go in at high tide.

"Good Lord," I exclaimed to Kirk, "do they know what they're doing? If they land that much earlier on Omaha, they'll pull all the enemy fire from the British beach right down on their heads."

Kirk looked just as disturbed as I.

"Yes, and Jim Hall would come under fire from every coastal gun within range of both beaches," he said. "The enemy could pick us off first and then turn his guns on the British."

From the army's point of view there could be no choice. We would stick with the tides and compromise on daylight, if necessary take a chance on forming our assault waves under daylight observation of the enemy's guns. The disadvantage would have to be overcome by fire-power. So we agreed that, failing to get off on June 6, we would chance either June 8 or 9 in preference to a further delay. That was to be Kirk's recommendation to Ramsay. The meeting broke up and we returned for the last time to the *Augusta*.

At 9:30 on Sunday evening, June 4, Eisenhower gathered his commanders once more at Portsmouth to discuss the weather reports. This time the forecast encouraged a flicker of hope. Rain squalls over the beaches were expected to clear in two or three hours. Visibility, it was thought, might hold up until Tuesday, June 6. Meanwhile the winds were reported slackening, the cloud base lifting. But while the weather report held out hopes for improvement, it did not excite lively enthusiasm for the adventure. Instead it looked barely promising enough to tantalize Ike with the thought of taking a chance. For the clouds that were expected to close in again on June 6 might easily wash out air and spoil spotting for the naval bombardment. Risky though it was, both Eisenhower and Smith welcomed this hazardous break in the weather. Almost anything would have been preferable, they thought, to the ordeal of another delay. Monty was for it. But Leigh-Mallory hung back and Tedder was not sure.

At 9:45 Eisenhower edged reluctantly into a decision. "I'm quite positive we must give the order . . . I don't like it, but there it is . . . I don't see how we can possibly do anything else."

The day for OVERLORD was now set, save for one last look at the weather at 4 A.M., June 5, to make certain the choice need not be reversed.

Aboard the *Augusta* we awaited a postponement signal. But none came and by midnight we heard that Eisenhower had chosen to go. OVERLORD was under way; The Plan had taken over. For the next 24 hours the fate of the war in Europe was to ride not in the big-hulled command ships but in the wet flat-bottomed craft where many GI's were to be seasick on the slippery steel floors as they groaned through the choppy Channel.

"Ike has the forecasters and he undoubtedly knows what he's doing," I confided to Kean, "but by golly, the weather certainly looks lousy here."

The decks were wet from the drizzle, a wind lashed at the canvas curtain to our war room. And the radar antenna on the tip of our foremast washed in and out of the overcast that hung low in the dark sky.

That evening as I fell into bed worrying about the weather, I was quite uneasy on three counts:

1. Unless the wind and surf abated they might swamp our DD tanks in their unsheltered run to Omaha Beach. We had bargained on the shock effect of those tanks. It would hurt badly to lose them.

2. If the overcast were to prevent spotter aircraft from directing naval gunfire, we might lose the effectiveness of our principal weapon in the initial assault. With but slight superiority in ground forces, we had banked heavily on this fire support to help break through the water's-edge defenses. Fear of losing the naval gunfire worried me more than the likelihood of a washout in heavy-bomber missions.

3. The Channel could be distressingly cruel to GI stomachs. A heavy surf might defeat our troops with seasickness before they landed.

But these hazards, I reasoned, must have been equally apparent to Ike. He clearly must have had more pertinent weather forecasts than those available to us. Trusting to Ike's judgment, I went to sleep.

Confirmation came at dawn the following morning when a courier arrived from the *Achernar* with a teletype message from Portsmouth: *D Day stands as is, Tuesday, June 6th*. Soon the waters of Plymouth harbor churned in a tangle of wakes as hundreds of ships turned obediently into line. As the columns uncoiled toward the Channel the *Augusta* put to sea, rapidly overtaking the awkward, slow-moving craft. On the eastern lip of the harbor a weathered pillbox squatted lonesomely on stilts offshore. From the gravelly beach behind it a half-dozen concrete blockhouses faced out across the Channel. They had been constructed as part of Britain's hasty preparations to repel a German invasion in 1940.

Thorson stared at the blockhouses. "Well, after tomorrow Churchill can tear them down."

"I hope he doesn't," I answered. "The British ought to leave them up to remind themselves and the world of the courage they showed when they built those things. That's something you can never take away from them."

At an easy 15 knots the *Augusta* flanked the Utah-bound column out of Plymouth harbor and headed for the Isle of Wight. From the YOKE assembly point there, she would head with the Omaha forces through a mine-swept Channel to the Normandy coast. There she was to fire in support of the initial landing. As far as we could see both fore and aft, ships crowded the British coast line. Overhead their barrage balloons bucked in the wind. Fast destroyers screened us seaward.

Not until several weeks later could we calculate the significance of Eisenhower's decision to dare the Channel in dirty weather. Had he delayed the attack two weeks to catch the tide on its next turn, his caution would have cost us a month's postponement. On June 18 an unseasonable summer storm raged through the Channel. It swamped hundreds of landing craft upon the beaches and taxed us more heavily in matériel than did the enemy guns on D day. In the face of this gale Eisenhower would have had no choice but to delay the invasion another two weeks until the favorable period of the July moon. And by then we would have had to contend with the enemy's V-1 bombardment, for the buzz-bomb campaign opened on June 12 when the first pilotless missiles fell on London. Had they been aimed against our mounting ports on the eve of invasion, those V-1's might have seriously disarranged our preparations.

Even after gaining the continent, however, we would have been seriously hobbled by the month's delay. For it would have been August before we could count on quantity tonnage through Cherbourg, September before we broke out. Instead of wintering on the Siegfried Line, we would have been lucky to have reached the Seine. And France rather than the Rhineland would have been ravaged during the winter campaign. But for the boldness of Eisenhower's decision, even Paris might have been reduced by artillery and air bombardment.

All afternoon, Monday, June 5, the *Augusta* scudded past the Utah-bound convoys, heading for her rendezvous with the Omaha force. High above the cruiser's bridge a radar antenna rotated monotonously under the woolly sky. In the plotting room below an officer bent before the radar screen searching for the telltale pips that would signify enemy air. But day passed and evening came without a bogey report.

"Seems hard to believe," I said to Kirk, "maybe we're going to have a Sicily all over again." There, too, we had held our breaths in anticipation of air attack against the convoys. Yet in Sicily the enemy had slumbered on until we piled up on his beaches. But in the narrow English Channel we could scarcely count on slipping through the enemy's alert without sounding an alarm. On a clear day, aircraft at 10,000 feet over Le Havre could look clear across to Southampton. Enemy radar fringed the French coast and E-boats patrolled offshore in regular nighttime sorties. All that day we waited for signs of enemy recce from across the Channel. First the recce, then probing attacks. On D day we looked for the Luftwaffe to stage a mighty comeback with an attack against our transports in their crowded anchorages offshore. At no time during the European campaign would Goering find a more congested and remunerative target.

We learned later it was nothing less than this dirty weather that spared us enemy detection and air attack. For the enemy could not believe we would venture into the stormy Channel in the face of those weather forecasts available to him. Lacking the weather stations we had established in Greenland and the North Atlantic, German meteorologists had failed to pick up the prospective break that prompted Ike's decision. Because of the high winds and heavy overcast on June 5, German naval patrols were canceled and mine layers restricted to ports. Even the ordinarily vigilant Luftwaffe recce lay grounded on its fields. In this capricious turn of the weather we had found a Trojan horse.

Even in June of 1944 the enemy was not especially alarmed over the imminence of invasion. Indeed there were Germans who viewed the Allied threat as an unlikely, if not impossible, hoax. Our concentration of coastwise shipping had failed to dent their composure and our tightening of the security belt was viewed as another move in the war of nerves. Rommel had returned to Germany for a command visit with Hitler and was now week-ending at his old home near Ulm. In their windowless bunkers on the Normandy coast, enemy troops waited in boredom as they had for so many months.

At 11 that evening I went below, unbuckled my Mae West, and fell into bed with my shoes on. Kirk remained on the bridge, buttoned up in his foul-weather gear, as the *Augusta* slipped quietly past the buoys that marked the mine-swept Channel. Only the lonely wind in the rigging and the wash of water past our sides broke the silence of the night. It was 3:35 A.M. when the clanking bell outside my cabin called the crew to battle stations. I reached for my helmet, scrambled into a Mae West, and hurried to Kirk's bridge. The moon hung misted in an overcast sky and the wind still lashed the Channel. According to the log the breeze had slackened but the change was not yet evident in the seas that washed by the *Augusta*. Off in the Cotentin Peninsula, almost 30 miles to the west, both airborne divisions had already been dropped. In its headquarters near the ancient terraced city of Le Mans, 40 miles behind the Normandy beaches, the German Seventh Army flashed an invasion alarm. But in the comfortable villa that Eisenhower was later to occupy in St. Germain near Paris, von Rundstedt deferred judgment. He feared the airborne drop a diversion preparatory to a main Allied attack against the Pas de Calais.

A faraway roar echoed across the Channel and off our starboard bow orange fires ignited the sky as more than 1,300 RAF bombers swarmed over the French coast line from the Seine to Cherbourg. An enemy AA battery stabbed blindly through the night. A shower of sparks splintered the darkness and a ribbon of fire peeled out of the sky as a stricken bomber plunged toward the *Augusta*. It leveled off, banked around our stern, and exploded into the Channel. By 5:30, first light had diluted the darkness and three Spits whistled by overhead, the first sign of our air umbrella. High above the overcast, relays of American fighters formed a second layer of air cover.

The *Augusta* closed in at five knots to its firing position offshore. High up on the cruiser's open bridge, I squinted toward the shore where it lay blurred in the morning mist. Zero hour had come for the DD tanks on Omaha Beach. They were to be launched from their mother craft at H minus 50 minutes and make their way ashore through paths cleared by demolition teams through the obstacle line. The infantry would swarm ashore on the heels of these DD tanks and push on inland under the cover of their fire.

Thorson stared at the heaving black Channel and shook his head.

"I don't like it, General. The DD's are going to have one helluva time in getting through this sea."

"Yes, Tubby, I'm afraid you're right. But at this point there's nothing we can do."

"Any sign of a letup in the surf?"

"Not yet. Kirk tells me the DD's may be swamped in these seas if they're launched from the LCT's. Either the LCT's cart them ashore —or we'll have to count on getting along without them."

The decision as to whether those tanks would swim or be carted ashore could not be made aboard the *Augusta*. It fell to the commanders of those tank detachments. By now OVERLORD had run beyond the reach of its admirals and generals. For the next few tortured hours we could do little but pace our decks and trust in the men to whom The Plan had been given for execution.

At 5:47 a message appeared on the G-2 journal. Fifteen German E-boats had left the harbor at Cherbourg to engage our fleet. Kean smiled and chewed on a piece of gum. Fifteen E-boats against our armada.

The *Augusta's* eight-inch turrets were turned toward the shore. We plugged our ears with cotton. At 5:50 the ship shuddered as it opened fire upon its predesignated targets among the beach defenses. The salvo coasted over the armada and we followed the pinpoints of fire as they plunged down toward the shore. The targets had been painstakingly picked from thousands of aerial photos, by which each gun, trench, and pillbox was sited on a detailed map.

At 6:15 smoke thickened the mist on the coast line as heavy bombers of the Eighth Air Force rumbled overhead. Not until later did we learn that most of the 13,000 bombs dropped by these heavies had cascaded harmlessly into the hedgerows three miles behind the coast. In bombing through the overcast, air had deliberately delayed its drop to lessen the danger of spill-over on craft approaching the shore. This margin for safety had undermined the effectiveness of the heavy air mission. To the seasick infantry, bailing their craft as they wallowed through the surf, this failure in air bombing was to mean many more casualties upon Omaha Beach.

Meanwhile, of the 32 DD tanks launched off Omaha, 27 had foundered in the heavy surf. Our troops had not yet landed and already two critical supports for the assault had broken down. At 6:45, 15 minutes after H hour, word reached the *Augusta* that the first wave had clambered ashore. It was still too early for news from

Strategy over a Mug of Coffee: "Whenever he could, Ike would slip away from the high-level strategy deliberations of SHAEF to pass the time with us in the field, helping to frame our tactics for subsequent phases of the European campaign."

Breakout through the Hedgerows: "With the steel tusks that had been welded to their noses, our Shermans broke through the hedgerows that had so tightly restricted their movements in the *bocage* country of Normandy to force the St.-Lô Breakout that was to crush the German army in France." (July, 1944.)

the beach. I choked down a scalding cup of coffee. By now it was daylight and because the sun was hidden in a haze overhead, a gray panorama opened about us. So far we had drawn no return fire from the enemy's coastal guns. "I don't understand this lack of counterbattery," Kean said. "He's had time to get us in range."

Thorson squinted toward a bluff that bulged on the shore line. "Maybe the Rangers have gotten in," he said. The 2d and 5th Battalions of Rangers were to knock out the battery of six 155-mm. rifles that covered our Omaha anchorage from the promontory at Pointe du Hoe.

No soldier in my command has ever been wished a more difficult task than that which befell the 34-year-old commander of this Provisional Ranger Force. Lieutenant Colonel James E. Rudder, a rancher from Brady, Texas, was to take a force of 200 men, land on a shingled shelf under the face of a 100-foot cliff, scale the cliff, and there destroy an enemy battery of coastal guns. "First time you mentioned it," Rudder recalls, "I thought you were trying to scare me." To prepare his troops for their mission, Rudder trained them on the stony cliffs of the Isle of Wight. There they experimented with mortar-propelled grapples designed by the British commandos to catapult scaling ropes over the cliffs. In addition to the ropes they trained with lightweight sectional steel ladders which could be quickly assembled and run up the face of the cliff. To these British devices the Rangers then added a new wrinkle of their own. Four long extension ladders were borrowed from the Fire Department in London and mounted on platforms in DUKW's. The DUKW's were to scramble ashore over the shingle shelf and throw their extension ladders up the face of the cliff. In his plan Rudder proposed to lead the assault company ashore himself. Huebner objected, reminding Rudder that as commander of the Ranger force he bore responsibility for the operation. "You can't risk getting knocked out in the very first round," he said.

"I'm sorry, sir," Rudder replied, "but I'm going to have to disobey you. If I don't take it—it may not go."

While Rudder assaulted the cliff, the remainder of his force was to wait offshore for the signal that Pointe du Hoe had been taken. If, after 30 minutes, the signal had not been fired, they were to land with the main Omaha assault force and make for the battery overland.

As Rudder closed in to Pointe du Hoe, 40 minutes behind schedule, enemy artillery raked his LCA's. The Rangers fired their mortars but many of the grappling hooks fell short as their wet ropes trailed sluggishly behind them. The shelf at the foot of the cliff had been pitted with bomb craters and there Rudder's ladder-carrying DUKW's were stalled. The mortar crews fired again and half a dozen ropes were catapulted over the edge of the cliff. But as the Rangers went up them hand over hand, the enemy dropped hand grenades on their heads. A destroyer raced in and swept the top of the cliff with her guns. Within five minutes after they had landed at the base of Pointe du Hoe, the first Ranger had bellied over the top. Seconds later his companions swarmed up behind him.

There they found a desolate tableland bearing the scars of repeated bombings. The big guns, however, were missing; the quarry had skipped. Ranger patrols pushing inland found the guns in an apple orchard 1,200 yards from the cliff. They were mobile, long-barreled French GPF's* with a range of 20,000 yards and they had been sited to fire on both invasion beaches. Quantities of ammunition were stored at the gun sites but the weapons had not been fired. The Rangers killed those remnants of the gun crews that had not yet fled our naval bombardment and disabled the guns by blowing their breeches. By then, however, the enemy had counterattacked on Pointe du Hoe. There the Rangers were to be cut off for two days while reinforcements struggled overland from Omaha to relieve them.

As the morning lengthened, my worries deepened over the alarming and fragmentary reports we picked up on the navy net. From these messages we could piece together only an incoherent account of sinkings, swampings, heavy enemy fire, and chaos on the beaches. By 8:30 the two assault regiments on Omaha had expected to break through the water's-edge defenses and force their way inland to where a road paralleled the coast line a mile behind the beaches. Yet by 8:30, V Corps had not yet confirmed news of the landing. We fought off our fears, attributing the delay to a jam-up in communications. It was almost 10:00 before the first report came in from Gerow. Like the fragments we had already picked up, his message was laconic, neither conclusive nor reassuring. It did nothing more than confirm our worst fears on the DD tanks. *"Obstacles mined, progress slow. . . . DD tanks for Fox Green swamped."*

*Heavy artillery.

Aboard the *Ancon,* Gerow and Huebner clung to their radios as helplessly as I. There was little else they could do. For at the moment they had no more control than I of the battle on the beaches. Though we could see it dimly through the haze and hear the echo of its guns, the battle belonged that morning to the thin, wet line of khaki that dragged itself ashore on the Channel coast of France. Alarmed over the congestion of craft offshore on Omaha Beach, Kirk ordered his gunnery officer in for a close-up view. I sent Hansen with him aboard a PT boat. They returned an hour later, soaked by the seas, with a discouraging report of conditions on the beach. The 1st Division lay pinned down behind the sea wall while the enemy swept the beaches with small-arms fire. Artillery chased the landing craft where they milled offshore. Much of the difficulty had been caused by the underwater obstructions. Not only had the demolition teams suffered paralyzing casualties, but much of their equipment had been swept away. Only six paths had been blown in that barricade before the rising tide halted their operations. Unable to break through the obstacles that blocked their assigned beaches, craft turned toward Easy Red* where the gaps had been blown. Then as successive waves ran in toward the cluttered beachhead they soon found themselves snarled in a jam offshore.

When V Corps reported at noon that the situation was "still critical" on all four beach exits, I reluctantly contemplated the diversion of Omaha follow-up forces to Utah and the British beaches. Scanty reports from both those sectors indicated the landings there had gone according to plan.

With the Omaha landing falling hours and hours behind schedule, we faced an imminent crisis on the follow-up force. There was due to arrive at noon in the transport area off Omaha Beach a force of 25,000 troops and 4,400 more vehicles to be landed on the second tide. However only a portion of the assault force of 34,000 troops and 3,300 vehicles had as yet gotten ashore. Unless we moved both forces ashore on D day, the whole intricate schedule of build-up would be thrown off balance. Whatever the improvisation, our build-up would have to be maintained if we were to withstand an enemy counteroffensive. Despite the setbacks we had suffered as the result of bad weather and ineffective bombing, I was shaken to

*Omaha and Utah beaches were divided into sectors designated by D for Dog, E for Easy, and F for Fox. These sectors were further divided and differentiated by colors, such as Easy Red, Easy Green, Fox Red, and so on.

find that we had gone against Omaha with so thin a margin of safety. At the time of sailing we had thought ourselves cushioned against such reversals as these.

Not until noon did a radio from Gerow offer a clue to the trouble we had run into on Omaha Beach. Instead of the rag-tag static troops we had expected to find there, the assault had run head-on into one of Rommel's tough field divisions.

In planning the assault, originally we had counted upon a thin enemy crust of two static divisions between Caen and Cherbourg. Rommel was known to have concentrated his better reserves behind the beach. Among them was the 352d Division which had been assembled at St.-Lô.

Just before boarding the *Augusta* in Plymouth harbor, Dickson learned that the 352d had been moved from St.-Lô to the assault beaches for a defense exercise. He promptly forwarded this information to V Corps and the 1st Division but was unable to give it to the troops already "sealed" aboard their craft.

Had a less experienced division than the 1st Infantry stumbled into this crack resistance, it might easily have been thrown back into the Channel. Unjust though it was, my choice of the 1st to spearhead the invasion probably saved us Omaha Beach and a catastrophe on the landing.

Although the deadlock had been broken several hours sooner, it was almost 1:30 P.M. when V Corps relieved our fears aboard the *Augusta* with the terse message: "*Troops formerly pinned down on beaches Easy Red, Easy Green, Fox Red advancing up heights behind beaches.*"

Behind Omaha the ground rose steeply up brush-covered slopes from 100 to 170 feet high. At four points along the 7,000-yard beach, lightly wooded draws indented these bluffs to provide exit routes inland. Here the enemy had concentrated his heaviest fortifications and here he had held out the longest. Only one draw was traveled by an improved road; the others contained nothing but cart tracks. Within days these cart tracks were to become the most heavily trafficked roads in Europe.

Reluctant to bank altogether on the laconic reports that trickled in from V Corps, I instructed Kean to go ashore, size up the beach-front congestion, and check on the advance inland that we might calculate our chances on landing a part of the follow-up force that night. With Hansen he sped off in a PT, closed to a thousand yards offshore, and transferred to an LCVP for the final trip through the obstacles. High water had reached its mark and the tide was rolling out, leaving the LCT's and hundreds of craft dried out on the beaches. The *Augusta* had now closed in to within 4,000 yards of the beach and the waters about us were strewn with flotsam from the invasion.

Kean's report was more hopeful than I had dared wish for. Despite the congestion of vehicles on Omaha Beach, our troops had penetrated the enemy's defenses between the well-guarded draws and to the east of Easy Red had pushed one mile inland to cut the first lateral road. Although the strategic draw at Easy Red had not yet been cleared of small-arms fire, bulldozers were already carving a path up its shoulder to the tableland on top of the bluff. And as the tide withdrew from the beach, engineers trailed after it through the debris, blowing new paths through the obstacles as they were uncovered by the Channel.

Despite the improved situation, however, Omaha had fallen seriously behind schedule. The beach was littered with stove-in craft, drowned-out vehicles, and burned-out tanks. Scores of bodies sprawled wet and shapeless in the shingle where they had fallen. Only the lightly wounded could be removed to hospital ships through the heavy surf. The more seriously wounded had been bedded down in slit trenches under the sea wall. And from one end of the beach to the other the tidal shelf was littered with the water-soaked debris that washes in with the surf in the wake of any invasion.

The enormous equipment losses on landing had left Omaha badly in need of replacements. "What do they need most?" I asked Kean.

"Bulldozers," he answered, "bulldozers and artillery. They're badly pinched for both."

Not only were bulldozers needed to clear the debris and obstacles in time for the second tide, but without them our losses mounted as vehicles, ferried ashore on rhino's from the LST's, mired in the soft, low-water sands. Of the 16 dozers that had been sent ashore that morning, only six reached Omaha Beach. Three of these were immediately knocked out by enemy artillery fire.

Although Omaha had squeezed through a crisis, she was still on the danger list. With neither depth, artillery, nor tanks, we might easily be dislodged from our precarious footing and thrown back into the Channel by counterattack. I hurried off to see Gerow aboard the *Ancon*.

However desperate the situation, a senior commander must always exude confidence in the presence of his subordinates. For anxiety, topside, can spread like cancer down through the command.

While splashing toward the *Ancon* aboard a PT boat, I anticipated that Gerow and Huebner might have been unnerved by the prolonged struggle that morning. Both had gone under fire as senior commanders for the first time, and although neither could have averted the crisis, both bore an immediate responsibility for it. Thus while I was eager to check on the situation and push the follow-up ashore, I went partly to stiffen their confidence if confidence was what they needed. I found, however, that Gerow's map showed penetrations at five points on the Omaha Beach defenses. The lateral road had been cut at Vierville and again at Colleville on the left. And a force was pushing toward Pointe du Hoe to relieve the Rangers there. With that we hoisted our tails and went ahead with the original plan to land the follow-up force on Omaha Beach and put five regiments ashore by nightfall.

Huebner was planning to go in and take shore command of his 1st Division that evening.

"How about you, Gee?" I asked, "when can you move V Corps headquarters ashore?"

"Early in the morning, Brad. We'll have our communications in by then."

"To hell with your communications—"

Gerow grinned. "We'll set up on the beach tonight."

At 8:30 that evening V Corps opened its first CP in a ditch atop the bluffs behind Easy Red. I was anxious that Gerow get his teeth into the beach organization and speed up unloading of the 2d Infantry Division on D plus 1.

Across the estuary that slashed into the Cotentin neck, our PT rammed through the surf for Utah Beach at full throttle. With two lookouts hugging the deck to warn him of floating mines, the skipper drove his eggshelled craft through blinding spray. Inside the Utah anchorage we located the *Bayfield* by its topside antennae. As the PT boat pitched to the crest of a six-foot wave, I jumped for the rope net of the *Bayfield* and clambered up its high steel sides. In contrast to Omaha where the shadow of catastrophe had hung over our heads all day, the landing on Utah had gone more smoothly than during rehearsal five weeks before. As G-2 had predicted, the beach was held by second-rate static troops. Except for casemated artillery north of Utah, the resistance quickly collapsed. In tallying up G-1's reports almost a week later, I found that Collins had cracked the wall on Utah Beach at a cost of fewer than 350 casualties in his assault force. This was less than half of what he had lost in the rehearsal on Slapton Sands.

At the outset, however, Utah had gotten off to an unpromising start. In piloting the assault force ashore, the navy had missed its guide point and landed the lead regiment 2,000 yards south of its mark. Apparently Providence had put its hand to the helm. Not only were the underwater obstacles planted less thickly on these beaches but the shore defenses proved less formidable than they were found to be farther north.

Ted Roosevelt, now a spare brigadier with the 4th Division, had volunteered to lead the assault units ashore in the first wave. With the skill and instinct of a veteran campaigner, he quickly improvised an attack to secure an exit across the lagoon that had caused us such anxiety in planning. As the lead regiment pushed across this marshland toward the lateral road three miles inland, it radioed reassuring reports to the 4th Division on the *Bayfield*. Collins promptly passed them on to Army. Thus while we struggled for a toe hold on Omaha Beach, we were at least assured success on Utah. But the ease with which Collins had established his seaborne beachhead bore no similarity to the airborne struggle five miles inland where the Battle for France was already five hours old by the time VII Corps landed. By daylight, paratroopers from both the 82d and 101st Divisions were fighting for their lives deep in the treacherous hedgerows and swamplands of the Cotentin.

The drop had gone awry almost as soon as the 432 troop-carrier aircraft of the 101st Division made landfall on the west Cotentin coast after a midnight flight from England. Cloud banks forced the closely packed nighttime formations to disperse. As the planes neared their drop zones now marked by pathfinder parties, enemy flak scattered the formations still farther apart. Although the drop concentration might have been judged remarkable in the light of our Sicilian episode, the 6,600 paratroopers of Taylor's division were scattered widely behind the causeways they had been ordered to secure. More than 60 planeloads were dumped from eight to 20 miles beyond their drop zones. Others were scattered from Utah Beach through the lagoons. Nevertheless, remnants of the 101st struck smartly toward the causeways that led from Utah Beach while others headed south to seal off Carentan and block that path of enemy reinforcement.

Two thirds of the 82d Division was to have been dropped eight miles inland behind the Merderet River where it parallels Utah Beach. Here it could shield Collins' beaches from the west and harry the enemy in his reinforcement of Cherbourg. The remaining drop zone lay east of that river astride the principal route from Cherbourg to the beachhead. Here Ridgway would block from the north and "establish a firm defensive base" in the village of Ste Mère Eglise.

Like the 101st, however, Ridgway's 82d was badly scattered on landing, especially those elements scheduled to drop west of the Merderet. As a consequence, much of the division's effort on that first day was wasted in the difficult task of assembling combat units. However the division did establish a base in Ste Mère Eglise from among the paratroopers who landed near that tiny dairying town. And like the 101st, it panicked the enemy in most rear areas during those first critical hours of the assault.

Shortly after noon on D day, Collins established contact with Taylor's 101st Division on the southernmost end of his beachhead. But the fate of the 82d still lay obscured somewhere behind the miles of hedgerow that separated it from the beaches.

"No word from Ridgway?" I asked Collins.

"Nope—but I'm not worried about Matt. The 82d can take care of itself. How's Gerow getting along? Has his situation over there cleared up?"

"It looks a lot better than it did at noon. But they've been hanging on all day by their fingertips. The 352d gave us an awful jolt. But the worst seems to be over. Gee is going in tonight. He hopes to get the beach in shape and bring the 2d in tomorrow."

The commander of the 4th Division had gone ashore earlier that afternoon while Collins remained with his VII Corps staff aboard the *Bayfield* to keep a line on communications—and to hold down Admiral Moon. Alarmed over the loss of a few vessels in the assault, Moon had been persuaded by his staff to suspend nighttime unloading on Utah Beach. When Collins learned of Moon's decision, he objected strenuously and the Admiral was hastily dissuaded. "Let the navy expend its ships," I told Collins, "if that's what it takes. But we've got to get the build-up ashore even if it means paving the whole damned Channel bottom with ships—"

I went over the rail of the *Bayfield* as dusk was falling. Below me the PT boat struck savagely at my legs atop each heavy swell. Finally as she reared, I leaped for her wet decks. On the bow, a sailor with a boathook grabbed wildly for balance, lost it, and toppled over the side. He fell into the white water that boiled between our boat and the *Bayfield* as the PT slammed its fenders against the merchantman's steel plates. While the skipper backed off to avoid crushing the man, we threw him a rope and hauled him aboard.

Late that evening as we closed in toward the anchorage off Omaha, a destroyer challenged us with a blinker through the darkness. Slipping into the Omaha anchorage from the estuary near Carentan, we might easily have been mistaken for a German E-boat.

"What in hell's the recognition signal—" the skipper bellowed below as he scrambled for a lantern. "Give it to me quick, or we'll have the whole damn navy sweeping us with a broadside."

"I hope he finds it," I said to Hansen. "This would be a helluva way for a doughboy to end the war—skewered on the end of a five-inch shell in 15 fathoms of water." The skipper got his proper signal and blinked back in reply.

Picking our way through the transport area, we located the *Augusta* just as a star shell broke in the sky. A line of tracers arced skyward. The enemy had come in for its nightly raid.

The skipper grabbed for his megaphone and hailed the *Augusta*. "Ahoy—can we come aboard?"

"Lie off," the deck called back, "lie off until we get an all clear."

I had confessed before to uneasiness in an air raid afloat. But if afloat we were to be, I preferred the 9,000-ton *Augusta* to this sea-going hot-rod. For 20 minutes we idled in a tight circle. When the raid appeared to slacken, we hove to the *Augusta* once more.

"Lie off," the answer came back. "Lie off."

"But we've got passengers aboard," our skipper shouted through the darkness.

"Prisoners?" the deck called; with a note of curiosity. "Stand by to bring the prisoners aboard."

I climbed a rope ladder up the *Augusta's* side and crawled over the rail, cold, wet, hungry, and tired.

The crew pressed forward to see its "prisoners."

"Oh, hell," a sailor grunted, "it's only General Bradley."

Despite the confusion that still existed in many of the smaller isolated units, our situation had materially improved by the morning of June 7.

On the other hand, we were not yet out of danger. On the thin five-mile sliver of Omaha Beach, we had fallen far short of D-day objectives. German artillery still pounded the beaches where traffic had congealed in the wreckage. And we had not yet reached the Caen-Carentan road that was to have strung our Allied landings together. Nevertheless we took some comfort in the fact that five regiments had been put ashore on Omaha by dawn, a miraculous achievement in view of the disordered condition of the beach. But to get them ashore we had sacrificed bulk tonnage. Had it not been for the 90 preloaded DUKW's that waded ashore on D day, we might have been hard put for ammunition.

However, the enemy had paid dearly for our delay on Omaha Beach. His 352d Division had been mauled at the water's edge, depriving Rommel of one more field division. Meanwhile, during our first 12 perilous hours ashore, the enemy had failed to mount a single coordinated counterattack against our beachhead. The omens were better than our progress.

On Utah, Collins had fared better than Gerow. Although unable to extend his beach to the north and overrun his D-day objective, Collins had expanded to the south. There he anchored his landing tightly on the neck of the Cotentin where we were to force a junction between both beachheads. During the night he had linked up Ridgway's 82d Airborne Division.

It was still too early to evaluate the success of the airborne drop. The dispersal had so shaken our confidence in nighttime airborne operations that we never again attempted a nighttime drop. In the initial count casualties looked excessively high and some feared Leigh-Mallory might be vindicated in his prediction. But as "lost" units trickled in through our lines, we discovered that airborne losses for the drop and the first day aground did not exceed 20 per cent. Not until we had turned the Utah force north toward Cherbourg did we learn how effectively those airborne troops had paralyzed the enemy's rear.

On the morning of D plus 1 the enemy's high command in Berlin awaited word from Rommel that the Allied landing had been roped off and would soon be flung into the Channel. But with the passing of D day, the enemy had lost his best chance to destroy us. By the morning of D plus 1 we had not only gotten a tight grip on the beachhead, but Allied build-up was already beginning to swell.

I had long ago anticipated that the enemy would dash his Luftwaffe against our landing with every plane Goering could put into the sky. For it was while we were hanging precariously to a slender beachhead that we could have been most critically hurt by enemy air.

Throughout the daylight hours of June 6 only a few enemy *jabos* broke through our cordon of Allied fighter cover for ineffectual passes at the beach. And during the nighttime raid that had stranded us aboard the PT, a meager force was all that the Luftwaffe could muster against us. Not only had the Allied air forces whittled the German down to 400 first-line aircraft in the west on D day, but the concentrated attack on his French fighter bases had driven him back to the German border. To conserve his fast-waning strength, Goering had flinched at the very moment a bold blow might have saved him.

While planning the Normandy invasion, we had weighed the possibility of enemy gas attack and for the first time during the war speculated on the probability of his resorting to it. For perhaps only then could persistent gas have forced a decision in one of history's climactic battles. Since Africa we had lugged our masks through each succeeding invasion, always rejecting the likelihood of gas but equally reluctant to chance an assault without defenses against it. Even though gas warfare on the Normandy beaches would have brought deadly retaliation against German cities, I reasoned that Hitler in his determination to resist to the end, might risk gas in a gamble for survival. Certainly an enemy that could callously destroy more than a million persons in its concentration camps could not be expected to reject gas warfare as inhumane. When D day finally ended without a whiff of mustard, I was vastly relieved. For even a light sprinkling of persistent gas on Omaha Beach could have cost us our footing there.

Shortly after 6 A.M. on June 7 Montgomery came alongside the *Augusta* aboard a British destroyer. He was anxious that the Allied beaches be joined before Rommel could concentrate his forces against any single beach and there break through. While we per-

spired through the D-day crisis, the British dashed ashore in their
sector and quickly pushed inland for a penetration of seven miles
near Bayeux. Their primary objective at Caen, however, had
eluded them. Sensitive to the British attack against that vital communications center, the enemy had attacked out of Caen in a panzer
counteroffensive.

Eisenhower had signaled that he would arrive in the transport
area at 11. Meanwhile I had slipped ashore on Omaha to prod
Gerow on Montgomery's order for an early link-up of the beaches.
Gerow was to push Gerhardt's 29th to the right toward a juncture
with Collins on the Cotentin neck while Huebner's 1st made contact
with the British on their left.

V Corps had hidden its headquarters in a ditch behind the hedgerow on the exit road from Easy Red. I hitched a ride on a truck up
a road still under construction. A column of infantrymen trudged
up the hill, enveloped in dust from a line of trucks. On the flat top
of the bluff engineers were already leveling an airstrip for the evacuation of wounded to England.

Gerow had gone forward to Huebner's CP and I went on to see
him. The 1st Division had by-passed small enemy pockets in its
advance on D day and was now rooting them out to prevent snipers
from harassing the rear.

"These goddam Boche just won't stop fighting," Huebner complained. He was impatient to clean up the beachhead that he might
drive inland and secure his immediate objectives. "It'll take time and
ammunition," I told him. "perhaps more than we reckon on both."

As Admiral Ramsay's flagship maneuvered into position abreast
of the *Augusta*, the coxswain swung our LCVP under the ship's
Jacob's ladder. I jumped for it and climbed aboard. Ike greeted me
at the rail.

"Golly, Brad," he exclaimed, grasping me by the hand, "you had
us all scared stiff yesterday morning. Why in the devil didn't you
let us know what was going on?"

"But we did." I was puzzled. "We radioed you every scrap of
information we had. Everything that came in both from Gee and
Collins."

Ike shook his head. "Nothing came through until late afternoon—
not a damned word. I didn't know what had happened to you."

"But your headquarters acknowledged every message as we asked them to. You check it when you get back and you'll find they all got through."

Aboard the *Augusta* 20 minutes later I double-checked our journals. Not only had the messages been sent but each had been properly acknowledged. Later I heard that the decoding apparatus had broken down at Montgomery's CP. So heavy was the D-day radio traffic that code clerks fell 12 hours behind in deciphering the incoming reports.

However, Ike's vigil could not have been any more agonizing than the one we suffered aboard the *Augusta*. For the reports, if anything, were no less worrisome than the fears that are spun out of silence. A week later I confessed to Monty that I would never admit to Ike just how worried I was that morning we waited in the mist off Omaha Beach.

Later on the afternoon of June 7 Kirk ferried me to Utah aboard the *Augusta*. I hailed a lift ashore aboard a passing LCM draped with the coxswain's washing. Near shore we spotted a DUKW and I called the driver for a lift dry-shod to the beach.

"Sure, General," he called, "jump aboard."

"Can you run me on to General Collins' headquarters?" I asked.

The driver shook his head. "Like nothing better, General," he answered, "but my captain would give me hell. He told me to hustle right back from this run."

I did not dispute his captain's orders; on D plus 1 rank could not compete with the priority importance of tonnage. Pleased at having avoided a soaking in the surf, I jumped off on the beach and hitched a ride on a passing weasel.

Collins had established his VII Corps CP inside a walled Norman farmyard. He had gone forward leaving behind his deputy corps commander, Major General Eugene M. Landrum. We checked the situation map in a stall in the barn. The 4th Division was pushing north to clear the beach of fire while the 101st shoved south for its link-up with V Corps. Although Ridgway had collected his 82d east of the Merderet, units west of that river were still reported cut off.

"Heard anything from Matt today?"

Landrum showed me a typewritten situation report from the 82d Division.

"Matt must be in pretty good shape. At any rate he's got a typewriter in action."

Ridgway had organized a strong position north of Ste Mère

Eglise. There firmly astride the Carentan-Cherbourg road, he covered the left flank of the 4th Division.

"Well, Gene," I called to Landrum before starting back to the *Augusta,* "you people are going to have to win this war in a hurry if I'm going to make my daughter's wedding."

"When is it?" he laughed.

"Tomorrow—D plus 2."

Landrum threw up his hands.

Our only daughter, Elizabeth, had been graduated the month before from Vassar. She was to marry Henry S. Beukema, son of Colonel Herman Beukema, the Academy's famed political and social scientist, a 1915 classmate of mine. The wedding was to take place on June 8 in the chapel at West Point, two days after young Beukema was to be graduated and commissioned a lieutenant in the air corps. Several days after the wedding an NBC correspondent delivered to me on the beach a chatty account of the ceremony by Mary Margaret McBride, a University of Missouri classmate of my wife. Copies of the cable had been sent to all NBC correspondents "to be handed personally to General Bradley if they should meet him."

On Friday, June 9, army headquarters moved ashore from the *Achernar* to establish its first CP in an orchard behind Pointe du Hoe where the Rangers had tracked down the battery of French GPF's. With communications ashore there was no longer need for me to remain aboard the *Augusta,* and Saturday morning when I disembarked we closed down our floating CP. Kirk's bright young army aide, Lieutenant MacGeorge Bundy of Boston, Massachusetts, reverted to his earlier eminence as the ranking army officer aboard the admiral's flagship. He reminded me the day I came aboard that I had usurped his position.

Monty had called a meeting that morning at the fishing village of Port-en-Bessin to coordinate First Army movements with those of the British Second Army. Dempsey had plotted an attack south of the unspoiled town of Bayeux, partly to extend his beachhead and partly to envelop Caen from the west. I found Monty waiting with Dempsey in a field where British MP's had been posted as outguards. He wore a faded gabardine bush jacket, a gray turtleneck sweater, corduroy trousers, and a tanker's black beret. A map case had been spread on the flat hood of his Humber staff car. Two panzer divisions were dug in before Caen and Dempsey sought to outflank them in his attack from Bayeux. We were to parallel this British attack and drive south in the direction of Caumont. There Gerow was to establish a strong defensive outpost for V Corps. An attack on this end of the lodgment, we estimated, might also help divert enemy reinforcements from Collins' attack toward Cherbourg.

Monty was flying back to his headquarters in Portsmouth that afternoon.

"Anything I can bring you?" he asked.

"Why yes, sir, a newspaper—any one at all." I felt strangely cut off from the news of the world without a paper at breakfast.

By Saturday morning, June 10, Gerow had parlayed his original thin holdings on Omaha into a substantial beachhead. Not only had he linked forces with Dempsey but he had thrust beyond the lateral road that tied their landings together. On his right, the 29th Division had pushed through the burning streets of Isigny to reach the flat-lands of the Carentan estuary. A few miles across the estuary, glider infantry maneuvered in a move to outflank Carentan from the north-east. Meanwhile paratroopers of the 101st advanced toward that pivotal city down the highway that led south from Cherbourg to Carentan. The road ran through a vast marshland, flooded by the enemy in an effort to restrict us to the narrow roads.

"We've got to join up with Gerow just as quickly as possible," I had told Collins, anticipating difficulty in those marshlands. "If it becomes necessary to save time, put 500 or even 1,000 tons of air on Carentan and take the city apart. Then rush it and you'll get in."

Later that afternoon word reached Army that Omaha and Utah had been joined together over a back country route across the estu-ary. The company of glider infantry from Utah had forced its way to the village of Auville-sur-le-Vey where reconnaissance troops of the 29th Division waited a few miles beyond Isigny. With Hansen I drove down through Isigny to see if we could get through on this overland route to Collins.

A small dairying town of 2,800 known for its Camembert cheese, Isigny lay charred from its shelling the day before when the 29th called for naval gunfire to drive the enemy out of town. A few villagers searched sorrowfully through the ruins of their homes. From one, an aged man and his wife carried the twisted skeleton of a brass bed. And down the street, a woman carefully removed the curtain from a paneless window in the remaining wall of what had been the village café. For more than four years the people of Isigny

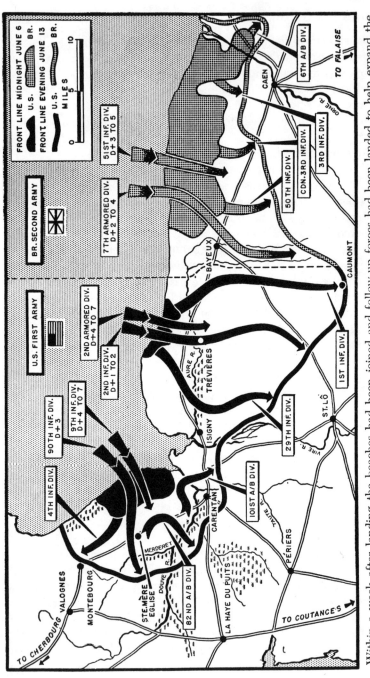

Within a week after landing the beaches had been joined and follow-up forces had been landed to help expand the beachhead. After reaching Caumont, V Corps was to hold, while the VII Corps went after Cherbourg.

had awaited this moment of liberation. Now they stared accusingly on us from the ruins that covered their dead.

Beyond the Vire we pulled up short of Auville-sur-le-Vey. In the intersection ahead an armored car had engaged a sniper with its 37-mm. gun. The ping of his rifle was lost in the crash of the car's cannon.

A jeep pulled up with Brigadier General Edward J. Timberlake, Jr., commander of an AA brigade.

"You're crazy as hell to go through, sir," he said. "The road may be mined. Let me go on in front."

"Nope—but thanks anyhow," I said. "I'm not going to go through."

As my driver wheeled the jeep around I turned back to Hansen.

"Be kinda silly to get killed by a sniper while out sight-seeing," I said. "We'd better stick to the PT boat until Carentan is opened."

By dawn on June 12, Taylor's paratroopers had encircled Carentan in a brilliant pincer movement. At 6 A.M. that day they drove into the city's streets to open the main road between Omaha and Utah. On our seventh day ashore we had linked the Allied forces together in a beachhead 42 miles wide.

We would now force our way across the Cotentin, then choke it off and capture the port of Cherbourg.

16: *Cherbourg Falls*

Nor UNTIL AFTER THE WAR DID WE LEARN THAT BY the evening of June 6, enemy staff officers at the chateau CP of the German Seventh Army headquartered at Le Mans, searched their pencil scorings on the map of France for clues to our intentions. The calm of their long sojourn in Occupied France had ended at 1:30 that morning, when a terse signal from LXXXIV Corps reported Allied airborne landings from Caen to the Cotentin. News of an Allied attack on the Cotentin instantly alerted the German Seventh Army to the probability of an Allied attempt to isolate the port of Cherbourg by sealing the peninsula behind it. But the German High Command declined to rush into so hasty a conclusion. Both at Rommel's Army Group and at von Rundstedt's Western Command, staff officers leafed warily through the first landing reports, hesitant to believe in the all too obvious signs.

Most of them had concluded that an Allied attack would come through the Pas de Calais and so confident were they in this assumption that it became difficult for them to accept our Normandy landing as a major effort. From the start they dismissed it as a "diversion" designed to throw the Fifteenth Army off its guard in the Pas de Calais. The enemy prided himself on the knowledge by which he had discerned our "intentions," not knowing that this "discernment" had been shrewdly encouraged by the OVERLORD cover plan. Thus in rejecting as a Yankee trick our landing in the Cotentin, the enemy fell into the trap we had baited for him on the Pas de

Calais. During the next six weeks while the German Seventh Army lost the Battle for France as a result of its inability to secure reinforcements, the strategists in Berlin persisted in their fatal miscalculation. Not until after the breakout did they realize how completely they had been misled on the Pas de Calais "landing." But by then the Seventh Army had been destroyed and France lay open to the German border. Germany's defeat in France derived in part from its own exhaustion and Hitler's fumbling. But a share of the blame also rests with the German General Staff. For it was German professionals who proved most susceptible to our hoax on the Pas de Calais.

As D day wore on, Seventh Army's trust in its original estimate on Cherbourg wavered. At 6:45 A.M. just 15 minutes after H hour, Army advised Rommel's CP that the naval fire on Omaha Beach might be part of an elaborate diversionary effort to screen a main offensive elsewhere. Shortly before noon, Army made up its mind: the major effort, it reported, had been centered on the British beaches. By then, corps had reported swift British penetrations through the coastal wall toward the rolling tank terrain that led beyond Caen toward the Seine.

Seventh Army's assumption that the British landing now embodied the main threat gained credence that afternoon when corps reported that Allied landings had been smashed from the Vire all the way to Bayeux. This was the sector of Omaha Beach. Indeed, the 352d Division had grown so confident over Gerow's difficulties on that beach that it signaled headquarters at 1:35 P.M. to report that the American assault had been thrown back into the Channel.

Later that afternoon, Seventh Army radioed Group a cautious estimate of the situation. Its fear of an attack on Cherbourg had not yet materialized, for even by 4:20 that afternoon Seventh Army had not yet heard of Collins' Utah landing. Our paratrooper drop had severely scrambled and delayed enemy communications. Army, therefore, concluded that perhaps its fears for the safety of Cherbourg were unjustified. The Cotentin air drop could be viewed as a diversion staged to draw off German forces from the British attack near Caen. Within a few minutes, however, Army hastily recanted. Airborne landings in the Cotentin had been reported reinforced in strength from the sea.

By 6 that evening, the badly disorganized 352d Division amended its exaggerated report of Allied difficulties on Omaha Beach. The

Americans were not only still ashore but they had infiltrated past strong points on the water's edge and were now shouldering their way inland.

Meanwhile, von Rundstedt demanded the Seventh Army destroy the Allied beachhead by that evening. And from Berlin, Colonel General Alfred Jodl chimed in with an order that all available reserve forces be thrown into the battle. But by "available" forces he meant only those in northwest France, not the Fifteenth Army on the Pas de Calais where it searched the Channel for signs of still another Allied fleet.

That night the German Seventh Army took stock of its situation. In the Cotentin, German forces looked strong enough to contain the Allied landing there. By some intuitive reasoning, Hitler had ordered the reinforcement in May of that strategic sector with two additional divisions, bringing its total strength to four. Along the Normandy coast, from the mouth of the Vire to Bayeux, Seventh Army had not yet discovered the true scale of our Omaha landing. But farther to the east near Caen where British tanks were advancing, the enemy sniffed what he thought to be the main Allied effort. He turned his panzers against that penetration and played neatly into our hands. For while the British baited the enemy to confuse him on our intentions, we were to link our American beaches and secure the port of Cherbourg. However, as Collins pushed inland toward the west coast as though to cut off the Cotentin, the enemy rechecked his findings on Cherbourg as a likely initial objective. On D plus 2 he confirmed his speedily growing suspicions when he fished from the Channel waters a copy of VII Corps' field order. What he had originally thought an elaborate diversion he now classified as a secondary main effort. To contain that secondary effort the enemy rushed reinforcements from Brittany into the Cotentin, for at all costs he meant to prevent us from seizing the port of Cherbourg. The German was no less conscious than we of the urgent need for build-up.

We recognized that if the enemy were able to strengthen his defensive ring around Cherbourg, he might seriously delay our capture of that port for weeks. On June 9, therefore, I told Collins to hack through the peninsula to the west coast and seal it off before driving north for Cherbourg. The 82d's bridgehead west of the Merderet had already cut one third of the way across. But this

Cotentin cutoff was not to be started until first we had established ourselves firmly ashore by linking the Omaha and Utah beaches with the capture of Carentan.

On the evening of June 11, Kirk's aide ferried ashore bringing with him a gallon of ice cream and the news that Admiral King and General Arnold would visit us the following day. Later that evening a signal reported that General Marshall would join them. Eisenhower was to escort the Chief of Staff from England. I begged off a 10 A.M. conference with Monty for the following day and unpacked my first clean change of clothes.

The party came in at Easy Red early the next morning. This meeting with General Marshall was to be the third of my four brief conversations with him throughout the war. He jumped down from the DUKW that carried the group ashore, looked up and down the beach, then seaward toward the Channel where a vast armada swung at anchor. Within a week Omaha Beach had been combed of its D-day debris and had become the major port of Europe. Bulldozers had swept beach obstacles, barbed wire, charred trucks, and the flotsam of the assault into a wide antitank ditch behind the high water mark. Unloading points had been flagged and traffic was being routed by MP's in neat columns toward the beach exits. And yet with each successive tide, a dismal ring of D-day refuse was left stranded on the shore. As General Marshall's DUKW waded in it splashed past a broken tennis racket half hidden in the wet sand. Near it a water-soaked boxing glove lay torn in the deep impression made by the tread of a tank.

Offshore a line of Liberty ships and obsolete naval vessels had been scuttled to form a breakwater for unloading by lighter inshore on Omaha Beach. GOOSEBERRY, as the breakwater was called, was the forerunner of a massive artificial harbor that had been contrived by the British and prefabricated in England. Inside the protected anchorage, rhino ferries, loaded to the water's edge with vehicles and guns, chugged peacefully from the gaping prows of the LCT's to the beach where engineers had laid steel matting to form unloading hards.

The bluffs from which the enemy had pinned down Huebner's troops on D day were now honeycombed with foxholes. Here the naval shore parties and beach engineers had burrowed into the sand for protection against the falling flak of the enemy's nightly raids. The more resourceful GI's had roofed their shelters with wreckage and leftovers from the beach. Atop the bluff, the litter-carrying C-47's turned in through a jungle of barrage balloons to pick up the wounded that were to be flown to England. Within two weeks, more than 15,000 wounded were evacuated from Omaha Beach. And on the hill across the draw that identified Easy Red, the dead lay in white mattress covers awaiting burial in a cemetery overlooking the beach.

Although Carentan had fallen that morning to the 101st, the city had not yet been cleared and the arterial road between Omaha and Utah still lay under fire. After touring Omaha by car, we had planned to cross the estuary by PT boat to Utah Beach. Hansen had reconnoitered the route very early that morning, but the traffic that tangled those overloaded roads made it impossible for us to station enough MP's on the route to speed us through. In the cramped Omaha beachhead, a tie-up anywhere on a critical road would back up traffic to the water's edge and slow up unloading. I knew that General Marshall would rather have hiked than displace a truckload of ammunition.

Anticipating that General Marshall might look critically on these tightly packed truck columns, I thought it better to explain the offense soon after we started. Originally we had sought to enforce road discipline on the beachhead by insisting upon the conventional 70-foot interval between trucks. The drivers simply ignored these instructions and herded their vehicles bumper to bumper.

"They're practical soldiers," I explained. "If they're strafed or bombed just once—they'll never again bunch up this way. But if I were to give them the devil now for closing up the way they do, they'd probably look at me and say to themselves: 'Doesn't that damn fool know the Luftwaffe is *kaput?*'"

In a caravan of recon cars we serpentined through traffic that churned the Normandy roads into a trail of choking white dust. It parched our throats, watered our eyes, and chalked King's neat blues. From Omaha we turned toward Isigny, past the dry, malodorous tidal basin at Grandcamp-les-Bains where the enemy had destroyed a dozen fishing craft and damaged the tidal gates. From offshore a salvo echoed across the beach as the battleship *Texas* lobbed its broadsides into the Carentan flats where the enemy had withdrawn behind that city.

After having so persistently badgered the navy for capital ships in the bombardment, I was anxious that King see the effects of his big guns in the streets of Isigny. Hansen had parked two armored cars in the village square to cover our party with their guns. With General Marshall, King, Arnold, and Eisenhower bunched together in three open cars, an enemy sniper could have won immortality as a hero of the Reich.

We lunched on C-rations and biscuits in a mess tent at the First Army CP. After I had outlined our plans for the capture of Cherbourg, General Marshall briefed us tersely on the global war. Later that day he mentioned the navy had asked for me by name to command a Pacific landing. I must have looked startled for he quickly added that he had informed the navy I was already booked for another job. He referred, of course, to the Group command that would become operational after the breakout. After ferrying to Utah for a brief visit with Collins that afternoon, the Chiefs boarded their mine sweeper for the return trip to England.

When Hitler learned in Salzburg of the Allied invasion on June 6, he was reported to have brightened, for he was confident that, before the week was out, Rommel would have punished us by drowning us in the Channel. But by the evening of June 12 we had celebrated our first week ashore without a single threatening counterattack on the American beachhead. Only the British had been hit by panzers in their advance toward Caen and again in their effort to join up with Huebner near Caumont. Meanwhile the German had stiffened his position with reinforcements from other parts of France, especially in the key communications centers of Caen and St.-Lô. But even after a week of frantic build-up of his reserves, Rommel had failed to accumulate strength enough to mount an offensive toward the beaches. Meanwhile we had already doubled our forces in the first week ashore. By the evening of June 12, a total of 16 Allied divisions had been unloaded in France. Seven were British, the other nine ours. And each of us by now had landed the equivalent of one and a half tank divisions.

When Rommel's concrete fortifications on the water's edge were breached on the first day, he found himself hard pressed for the reserves that would dam our penetration. For the lack of infantry, the three armored divisions that Rommel sped toward Caen were thrown into defensive positions in a last-minute effort to save that city. As a result, when Monty increased his pressure against Caen, Rommel was unable to extricate those tanks for use in counterattack without running the risk of a British breakthrough in that position.

A tank is brutally effective in offensive warfare. In the defense it becomes effective only when pooled in reserve behind the line for use in counterattacking an infantry or armored breakthrough. But where the tank is employed in lieu of infantry simply to hold a defensive position, it becomes a wasted and uneconomic weapon.

From the moment we landed, Rommel was beset by a shortage in infantry and artillery reserves. Moreover, each unit that reached the Normandy front bore scars that had been inflicted upon it by Allied air attack during the hazardous movement across France. But while air could harass those reserves, it could neither halt nor destroy them. Each evening when the summer sun went down and our Allied fighters returned to their bases, the enemy stirred out on the roads under a screen of darkness. Difficult and dangerous though these movements were, the German showed astonishing resourcefulness in transporting his troops to the front.

Despite the enemy's difficulties in build-up, I did not discount the probability of a powerful counteroffensive and as a consequence had become increasingly uneasy over two troublesome soft spots in our line. Each was marked by a seam where two sectors had been stitched together—but stitched so loosely as to tempt the enemy to tear them apart. The first of these seams followed the boundary between the U. S. sector and that of the British. The second ran through Carentan where Omaha and Utah had been joined together.

Wherever a pair of Allied Armies join up there exists a point of weakness which the enemy can readily exploit. This weakness lies in the difficulties that may arise in coordinating these two Armies in defense of that sector. Where our beach annexed that of Dempsey's, this weakness was only too obvious. Huebner's 1st Division had plunged boldly through the *bocage** to Caumont, 20 miles south of the coast where it dug into a defensive position at the deepest point in the Allied beachhead. In contrast, the British on Huebner's left had advanced only half as far, leaving the 1st Division with a long open flank exposed toward the enemy concentration at Caen. When Dempsey attacked in an effort to straighten that line, he found himself blocked by panzers. The British fell back to their line of departure, and Huebner was left to fend for himself out on the end of a shaky salient. Between the tip of that salient and the British position he had strung a thin line of troops to cover an eight-mile gap on his

*The hedgerow country in Normandy.

side. When the enemy edged toward that flank with what appeared to be a suspicious intent, I immediately rushed tanks from the 2d Armored to Huebner as a reserve.

Meanwhile at Carentan the enemy had withdrawn deeper into the flats only a few miles behind that city. There he waited, knowing that if he could recapture that position, he would split the U. S. beachhead and make it difficult for our units to move freely between beaches. On the evening of June 12, Dickson broke into my tent with information which indicated a German counterattack against Carentan the next day. Panzer-grenadiers from the 17th SS were to spearhead the offensive. Although Max Taylor had buttoned up his position after occupying the city, his 101st Airborne Division had few heavy weapons with which to blunt a tank attack. I telephoned Gerow and instructed him to get Maurice Rose on the road with a combat command from the 2d Armored and race it to Carentan. Gerow groaned when he heard the order. Without those tanks he could be seriously embarrassed should the enemy strike through Huebner's flank.

"That attack down there might be just a trick to get us to weaken our flank up here," Gerow said.

"Might be—" I agreed, "but we can't let Taylor's house burn down for fear Huebner's might catch fire."

Fortunately the enemy was not so devious as Gerow thought. On the morning of June 13 he struck toward Carentan and drove to within 500 yards of that city before Taylor's paratroopers held him off with rifle and small-arms fire. At 10:30, Rose's tanks sped into the village. With the help of those tanks, the 101st counterattacked the 17th SS and drove them back into the flatlands now sprinkled with German dead.

The following evening I asked Gerow to our CP. He came eagerly for he was anxious to have Rose and his combat command of tanks. Huebner's open flank continued to alarm him. He found me struggling with an oversized mapboard too big for my tent.

"I'll be glad," I told him, "when Joe Collins takes Cherbourg so I can cut this Cotentin hump off the map and move it back inside my tent."

"Me, too," he agreed, "once Joe gets Cherbourg I can stop worrying about the shortages in tonnage coming in over my beach." Gee pulled up a chair to the map and pointed to the hook in the line where his sector adjoined that of the British. Two red squares had been crayoned on the enemy side to the left of Huebner's flank. Both bore the double-X designation of a division and the oval to indicate they were panzers.

"Brad, I'm worried . . ." Gerow began. "Suppose you take a look and see if my situation looks as bad to you here at Army. Until the British push down abreast of us I'm wide open on this flank. The Boche could bust through Huebner's rear and cut me off down here at Caumont. And I don't have enough in depth to stop him if he should come through."

"I know the spot you're in, Gee. And I'm just as worried about it as you are. We took one devil of a chance in pulling those tanks out from behind your flank. But now that Rose is in Carentan, he's going to have to stay there, at least for the night. We've hit tanks there and if the other fellow were to break through with them, we'd have a helluva time holding on at Carentan. If the German should cut the road and isolate us from Collins' forces, he would raise merry hell with our ability to maneuver."

Gerow nodded.

"Let's leave it this way for now, Gee. I'll issue orders to start Rose back tomorrow providing Dickson doesn't come in with any new dope on Carentan. I don't want Rose to have to make another shift on such short notice."

I issued the orders and promptly canceled them the next day. For though defeated, the SS at Carentan showed signs of stirring again. Meanwhile Monty rushed to Gerow's aid with part of the British 7th Armored Division. He massed them on that flank and as a result denied the German his last golden chance to exploit our weakness on that seam.

After only one week ashore we had begun to look beyond the beach to where St.-Lô stood on a rocky hill overlooking the Vire Valley. Once a citadel of Charlemagne, the town lay halfway between our invasion coast and the Cotentin west shore. Not only did its tall, bombed church mark the center of a road junction vital to Rommel, but the town itself straddled a crosscut road that ran from Bayeux on the Calvados coast to Coutances on the west shore thus severing the Normandy shoulder from the main body of France. If we were to take St.-Lô and drive on down to Coutances, we would not only cut off Cherbourg from Rommel's main forces but we would greatly shorten the Allied line and thus help to speed the concentration of U. S. troops for an early breakout.

No less aware than we of the strategic importance of that hill town, the enemy had amassed a substantial share of his scarce infantry reserves on that front. As a result, when the 29th Division drove to within three miles of St.-Lô, German resistance stiffened and Gerhardt was forced to pay for his advance with more casualties than we cared to expend. Cherbourg remained our first principal objective and I had no intention of pinning down forces at St.-Lô until Cherbourg was first safely in hand.

"As a matter of fact," I told Thorson in speaking of St.-Lô, "even if we got the town there's not much chance of our going beyond it. The other fellow's dug in too deep. I'd just as soon settle for the high ground east and west of St.-Lô. If we can get up there and put our artillery on the roads, I don't give a damn if we don't take it. It'll be no good to the German."

"Gerhardt would like to push on and take it," Thorson said.

"If Gerhardt could take St.-Lô without breaking the back of his 29th I wouldn't object. But I doubt very much that he could. Sure, St.-Lô would make good news and give the correspondents something to write about. But we're not going to spend a division just to take a place name. We can get along very nicely without St.-Lô at this time."

Corlett's XIX Corps went into the line on June 15 to take over the Carentan sector and Gerow's front at St.-Lô. Like Gerow, Corlett was eager to break into the town. Faced with the need for conserving U. S. strength, I held Corlett back and ordered him to stand his ground.

Thorson chuckled over my struggle to rein in Corlett. "They're loaded for bear," he observed. "Both Corlett and Gerhardt are aching to get to St.-Lô."

"Well they'll hold their ground," I growled, "even if we've got to take their ammunition away to make them do it. Nobody's going anywhere until Joe gets Cherbourg. I want to see both Pete and Gee dug in solidly on their fronts. The other fellow might still hit them and we're not going to risk his busting through to Omaha Beach." Not until a few days before the breakout did I lift this prohibition on St.-Lô. By then we desperately needed its roads to exploit the attack.

When on June 9, I issued orders to Collins to cut off the Cotentin at its neck before going on to Cherbourg, he was to assign the 82d and 9th Divisions to that mission while the 4th and 90th pushed on abreast toward Cherbourg. Meanwhile, until the 9th was un-loaded ashore, the 90th was to expand the 82d's bridgehead west of the Merderet.

Our choice of the 90th turned out poorly. For three days the division floundered in its starting attack. On the fourth day Collins asked for relief of the division commander. The division had come to England in April, 1944, under the command of Brigadier General Jay W. MacKelvie, its former artilleryman. Shortly before the 90th embarked from the United States, its division commander had been pulled out and reassigned to a corps. Thus MacKelvie found himself saddled with a job for which he had not been adequately trained. Nevertheless, his performance during those two brief months in England convinced me that he warranted a fair tryout as a division commander. Unfortunately, however, his legacy included too many inept subordinate commanders and as a consequence the 90th fumbled in its opening attack.

Across the neck of the Normandy peninsula, the hedgerows formed a natural line of defense more formidable than any even Rommel could have contrived. For centuries the broad, rich flat-lands had been divided and subdivided into tiny pastures whose earthen walls had grown into ramparts. Often the height and thick-ness of a tank, these hedgerows were crowned with a thorny growth of trees and brambles. Their roots had bound the packed earth as steel mesh reinforces concrete. Many were backed by deep drainage ditches and these the enemy utilized as a built-in system of com-munications trenches. To advance from pasture to pasture it became necessary for us to break a path through those ramparts in the face of savage and well-concealed enemy fire. Not even in Tunisia had we found more exasperating defensive terrain. Collins called it no less formidable than the jungles of Guadalcanal.

For the first few days in combat most new divisions suffer a dis-order resulting from acute mental shock. Until troops can acclimate themselves to the agony of the wounded and the finality of death, they herd by instinct in fear and confusion. They cannot be driven into attack but must be led, and sometimes even coaxed, by their commanders. Within a few days this shock ordinarily wears off, the division overcomes its baptismal panic, and troops respond normally to assured and intelligent command.

Where possible we made an effort to relieve the severity of that shock by conditioning each new unit in a "quiet" sector before committing it to attack. But when the 90th came ashore on the heels of the 4th Division across Utah Beach, there were no "quiet" sectors. We had no choice but to fling it into an attack that would have tested the mettle of veterans. But this sudden immersion was not confined to the 90th alone. Other equally green divisions entered the line under even more appalling conditions and most of them weathered the ordeal with distinction. Almost from the moment of its starting attack, however, the 90th became a "problem" division. So exasperating was its performance that at one point the First Army staff gave up and recommended that we break it up for replacements. Instead, we stayed with the division and in the end the 90th became one of the most outstanding in the European Theater. In the metamorphosis, it demonstrated how swiftly a strong commander can transfuse his own strength into a command. But even more than that it proved what we had long contended: That man for man one division is just as good as another—they vary only in the skill and leadership of their commanders.

When Collins assigned Landrum, his deputy at VII Corps, to replace MacKelvie, we cautioned Gene to clean house throughout his new command. A veteran of the Kiska expedition, Landrum had joined Collins in England on the latter's recommendation. Delighted with this opportunity to take a division, Landrum rashly promised me a "salt-water cocktail from the other side of the Cotentin."

However, after three more spiritless weeks, the 90th again fell on its face when two companies surrendered to the enemy and a battalion position fell. Landrum had cleaned house but not thoroughly enough. By now the division's morale had been shaken and its confidence gone. Landrum had failed to furnish the spark that the division needed. He, too, had to go. Although my staff now asked that the division be cannibalized for replacements, I was reasonably certain that it could be rescued by an outstanding commander. On July 30, we found him in Brigadier General Raymond S. McLain, who earned his star in the National Guard. I had discovered McLain in Sicily where he came in as Middleton's artillery commander, and had him brought to England as a spare brigadier for just such an emergency as this.

In Sicily McLain had shown himself to be a soldier who spurned the CP to devote his time to troops on the line where he inspired the aggressiveness so characteristic of the 45th Division. Although I was certain that he could reform the 90th, I thought it only fair to warn him that the division had already jinxed two commanders within a month. We were deliberately putting him on the spot.

"We're going to make that division go," I told him, "if we've got to can every senior officer in it. I'm pretty sure, however, that all it needs is a good stiff shaking-down."

"Can you help me get rid of those officers I may not want and give me replacements?" McLain asked.

"Anything you want, Ray. Go down there and look around for 48 hours. Then come back to me with a list and we'll get rid of every man on it."

McLain returned exactly two days later with a list of 16 field officers. I gave their names to Red O'Hare, told him to transfer them out of the 90th, and give McLain anyone he asked for by name. When McLain left the 90th the following October to take command of a corps, his successor inherited one of the finest divisions in combat on the Allied front.

With the arrival of Eddy's 9th Division, Collins shunted the unhappy 90th aside and paired off Eddy's veterans with those of the 82d in the drive that was to cut the Cotentin and isolate Cherbourg. While Eddy bounded toward the west shore, Ridgway blocked for him on the south behind the Douve River line. Where that river angled north halfway across the peninsula, the lightly armed 82d halted and Eddy split into two columns for his bold dash to the sea.

Eight weeks later Manton Eddy was rewarded with a corps. His change-over came the week after the Breakout and Eddy went 72 miles on his first day as a corps commander. The next time I saw him he grimaced, "Hell's bells, Brad, you guys have been holding out on me—this business of running a corps is a cinch. I've been wasting my time in a division."

As Eddy approached the last lateral road through the Cotentin neck, it became clear that unless the enemy could halt the 9th before it completed that cut, the key port of Cherbourg would be ours. Reinforcements might have helped him to delay the conquest but reinforcements were nowhere in sight, for the enemy lacked enough reserves everywhere to contain our line.

He dared not pilfer troops from the British front near Caen for fear Monty might splash through with a tank attack toward Paris. But neither could he take a chance on St.-Lô. An American breakthrough there would trap his forces in the Cotentin and finish forever his hope for arresting and thereafter destroying our beachhead.

In anticipation of Eddy's attack across the Cotentin, the enemy had blueprinted a plan for dividing his peninsular forces. Two divisions were to fall back to Cherbourg to prolong the defense of that port while the other two were to be turned south to form a defensive line across the Cotentin neck.

Two days after Eddy's jump-off on June 14, Monk Dickson came into the mess tent for dinner whistling. "They call me old kill-joy," he grinned, craning his long neck, "but tonight I bring happy tidings: The Boche is pulling out. He's conceded us the peninsula."

The next day on orders from Hitler, German resistance before Eddy parted according to plan to the north and south. Late that evening of June 17, Collins telephoned to report that the peninsula had been cut. After only 11 days ashore, we had joined the beachheads and Cherbourg was sealed off. There were but nine days to go if we were to take Cherbourg by D plus 20.

The following afternoon we scheduled our first army press conference ashore. O'Hare had compiled U. S. casualties through June 15 and I was anxious they get back to the States. For although we had suffered 15,000 casualties in ten days on the beach, that number fell far below anticipated losses. Prompt release of those casualties, we thought, would help reassure the American people after having been exposed to so many exaggerated estimates before D day. Monty, however, was queried by SHAEF on the desirability of that release. He promptly turned around and rebuked me, contending with evident annoyance that the news was premature, that my hasty release had aided the enemy in estimating our strength. The enemy, I reassured Monty, would simply discredit our figures for they fell far below his claims and told him nothing he did not already know. RADIO BERLIN happily obliged me when it picked up our story from the BBC, terming it a monstrous lie concocted in an effort to conceal from our people the great tragedy we had suffered on the assault. This single altercation marked the only instance in which Monty and I disputed a decision that I had already made. Neither of us ever referred to it again.

Although my fondness for Monty often ran thin during the European campaign, this attitude never impaired the personal and working relationship that existed between us. So scrupulously did we conceal our irritation with Monty that I doubt he was even aware of it. Certainly, had we opposed one another with the asperity some gossipers liked to think existed, Eisenhower would have been justified in sacking us both.

Quite often during the war I disputed Monty's views, challenged his decisions, and questioned the wisdom of his moves. For unlike his British associates, I was never so intimidated by the legend of Montgomery that I could unhesitatingly accept his judgment as infallible. Like the rest of us, Monty is mortal; and being mortal, he has made mistakes.

For his advance on Cherbourg, Collins split the peninsula north of Eddy's cutoff into three north-south alleys. To each of these he assigned a division: Barton's 4th on the heavily fortified right, the

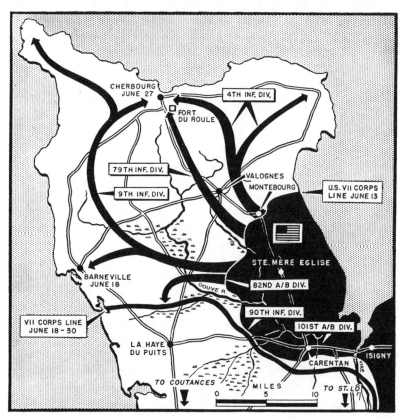

After cutting the peninsula on June 18, Collins pointed his corps toward Cherbourg while three divisions held the enemy off to his rear.

newly landed 79th in the center, and Manton Eddy's 9th on the left. H hour for the attack was set for 3:00 A.M. on June 19. The deadline presented no problem for the 4th and 79th Divisions already in position. But for Eddy's 9th it demanded an unbelievably swift change in direction. Manton had not reached his final objective on the Cotentin west shore until 5:00 A.M., June 18. Within 22 hours he was expected to turn a force of 20,000 troops a full 90 degrees toward Cherbourg, evacuate his sick and wounded, lay wire, reconnoiter the ground, establish his boundaries, issue orders, relocate his ammunition and supply dumps, and then jump off in a fresh attack on a front nine miles wide. Eddy never even raised his eyebrows and when H hour struck, he jumped off on time.

Eddy was entitled to a breather, for his troops were winded after their swift advance. But if we were to prevent the enemy from regaining his balance, it was important that we push on just as speedily as we could. If given an extra day in which to organize his position, the German could have greatly increased the costliness of our subsequent advance. As a result of Eddy's swift turnaround, the 9th Division caught the enemy off balance and thereafter set the fast pace for Collins' advance. After the capture of Cherbourg the enemy confessed that Eddy's swift change in direction had robbed him of the respite he had counted upon to organize that port city's defenses.

In turning his VII Corps north for the attack on Cherbourg, Collins was forced to turn his back on the enemy in the Cotentin neck. To help him protect his rear, I strung Middleton's VIII Corps across the neck. It was not much of a force for the 18-mile front. Both the 82d and the 101st were perilously understrength and the 90th was disheartened. But so long as Middleton remained behind the bogs that flooded the Cotentin neck, he had little to fear from enemy attack. This advantage in safety, however, was counterbalanced by the opportunity that was given the enemy to fortify his defenses there. For the longer we permitted him to dig in beyond those bogs, the greater difficulty we could anticipate in breaking that position. Preferring to risk the present danger of counterattack rather than enable the enemy to entrench, I ordered Middleton to push on beyond those bogs. But because he lacked the strength for a steamroller offensive, he was simply to expand his front and keep it rolling until Collins secured Cherbourg.

As I walked with Troy through his CP after having agreed upon the plan, I clasped him on the shoulder.

"Gosh, I'll be glad when Joe gets Cherbourg and we can get turned around in the direction we should be going. We've got this fellow on the run; we just can't let him rest."

On the morning Collins jumped off for Cherbourg, we awakened to an ominous wind, a leaden sky, and a cold, scaly rain that tore at the tent flaps. Kean trudged with me to the mess tent halfway across the soggy orchard. He scowled at the weather from under his helmet. "Well, this kills Collins' chances for fighter support today."

Two miles beyond our CP, the Channel had broken into white-caps and the surf foamed against the scarred cliffs of Pointe du Hoe. Storm warnings appeared in the weather report. But not until Wilson reported that unloading had closed down on Omaha Beach did we realize how serious was this crisis that had blown in with the storm.

On the eve of the second day of the gale, G-4 reported Omaha Beach strewn with wrecked craft as the Channel tumbled our shallow-draft vessels into junk piles on the shore. On the third day our artificial harbor on Omaha Beach buckled under the pounding of the seas. The giant concrete caissons that had been constructed in England and towed across the Channel to provide an artificial harbor for all-weather unloading were now scattered across the Omaha Beach. The British had designed and prefabricated two of these goliath structures, one for their own beach, the other for ours. Fortunately Monty's survived the storm to prove the project one of the most inventive logistical undertakings of the war.

When on June 22 we went down to the beach to survey the damage, I was appalled by the desolation, for it vastly exceeded that of D day. Operations on Omaha had been brought to a standstill. Even the beach engineers had crawled into their damp burrows to escape the wind and the rain. In four days this Channel storm had threatened OVERLORD with greater danger than had all the enemy's guns in 14 days ashore. Hundreds of craft had piled up on the shingle where they lay mangled beyond the reach of the surf. Where we had landed on Easy Red, a stricken rhino ferry stabbed into the side of another with each swell of the sea. The broken bow of an LCT lurched on a runnel as the seas boiled into its belly. Farther offshore another cowered helplessly as the surf foamed over the abandoned vehicles on its humped deck. A naval lieutenant in a Ranger's jacket ambled over to where we stood. I smiled wryly. "Hard to believe a storm could do all this—"

He looked carefully at my stars. "General," he said, "we would much sooner have had the whole damned Luftwaffe come down on our heads."

But for all the gear and craft that had been lost by the navy, nothing pained us more than the enormous losses we had sustained in tonnage with this shutdown on the beaches. Each day the deficit mounted until we fell thousands of tons in arrears, especially in ammunition. Meanwhile the German had exploited our misfortune. For while Allied airmen cursed the weather that pinned their fighters to the ground, the enemy crammed his roads with reinforcements.

Yet even in the gloom of this disaster we could be thankful that the storm had not struck one week sooner. For without the scanty reserve that had been accumulated during our two weeks ashore, we might have been driven into the sea for the lack of troops and ammunition. Still the loss of ammunition as a result of the storm forced us to pull in our belts. With only a three-day stock in our dumps, we rationed Collins in his attack on Cherbourg and hastily scotched our plans for the expanding offensive on Middleton's front in the Cotentin neck.

I had visited Troy only the day before his jump-off. On the way back to Army, I was stopped by Kean who had Colonel John B. Medaris of Cincinnati, Ohio, with him. Medaris had accompanied me from II Corps to become ordnance officer of First Army.

"Medaris has something you ought to know," said Kean. Ammunition supply had fallen into such critical straits that Army could not support Middleton's attack except at the expense of Collins.

"You're recommending I call off Middleton?"

"Yes, sir."

"You know how important Middleton's attack is to us?"

"Yes, sir—of course I do," Medaris said.

"You know that if we attack down here now—we'll probably save a good many lives later on?"

"Yes, sir."

"And still you say no?"

"That's my recommendation, General. I don't think we can support it."

I turned to Kean. "Call up Tubby Thorson and tell him the VIII Corps attack is off. I'll go back and tell Middleton. Then I'll head up to see Joe."

For two weeks Middleton waited for ammunition supply on that front while the enemy stiffened his defenses on the lower side of the bogs. When eventually we slugged through that neck in preparation for the breakout, we discovered how profitably the German had utilized that time. But however eager we may have been to prevent him from digging in, there was no appeal on a decision forced by a deficit in tonnage.

Although seriously aggravated by the storm, this shortage in ammunition had dogged us from the day we landed. It was to plague us throughout that fall and winter until after we crossed the Rhine. In planning our ammunition requirements, Medaris had amply estimated our needs and Wilson allotted the lift. But in any landing on a hostile beach, tonnage is limited primarily by the capacity of engineers to haul it ashore. The D-day crisis on Omaha Beach upset Wilson's estimates from the start. We were unable to carry ashore any of the 4,600 tons of supply we had scheduled for D day. Before the week had ended we were 35,000 tons in the red. According to Admiral Ramsay, army estimates at the time placed the loss attributed to the gale at 20,000 vehicles and 140,000 tons of stores. Our deficit in U. S. troops alone during this period of shutdown amounted to 83,000 men.

Our situation might have been even more critical had we not beached an emergency reserve in a dozen giant sea-going barges. Several months before the invasion, I had recommended to Ike that he take this precaution and tow a barge-loaded reserve of ammunition across the Channel. Because there were no 1,000-ton barges in England, he wired to Washington for them. General Brehon B. Somervell, Chief of the Services of Supply, sped them to us and we put 12,000 tons on the beaches.

Several years after the war a shipper in New York City mentioned to me one evening that he had been cleaned out of his biggest barges only a few weeks before the invasion.

"Had to tow them across the Atlantic," he said with a smile. "We figured some bright young bird on Eisenhower's staff sold Washington on a cockeyed idea. Was I right?"

"Yes, sir," I colored. "You were."

Responsibility for this shortage in ammunition during our first month ashore lay with both navy and the army service commands in England. For despite their incredible accomplishments on the invasion, both fell down on the significant details that would have made beach unloading far more effective that it was.

In the complex mechanics of supply across a hostile beach, the thousands of tons that are dragged ashore each day must be balanced item for item to fit the on-shore needs. To maintain selective control over the ships we unloaded, we had asked Lieutenant General J. C. H. Lee's Services of Supply to deliver by air the cargo manifests of vessels before they arrived. With those manifests, we could regulate unloading and thus prevent faulty overstockage in unneeded items at the expense of short supply in others. Those manifests, however, failed to arrive and we were obliged to unload ships irrespective of their cargoes. Soon thousands of tons of unneeded supplies were kicking about on the beach while we starved for the want of a few critical items such as artillery ammunition. We repeatedly appealed to SOS. They replied with promises, but no manifests arrived.

The unbalance grew increasingly more critical. I complained directly to Ike.

"Someone had better perform," he replied two days later, "or he will be out of a job." The missing manifests came through without further apologies or explanations.

At this point, however, our troubles in supply shifted to the U. S. Navy. For if the cargo manifests were to be used as aids in unloading, it was essential that we locate each ship as it arrived offshore. Not only did the navy lack accurate lists of the ships in convoy, but once those vessels had anchored, the navy found it almost impossible to locate them offshore. Perhaps he never understood how exasperating the problem had become. At any rate it dragged on without resolution until late in June when Kirk brought Rear Admiral John Wilkes from England to boss the naval installations in France.

No less provoking was the navy's refusal to dry out its LST's on the beach. Although the LST was designed as a flat-bottomed ship for beaching, the navy objected to running them ashore for fear enemy artillery would pick them off. They preferred instead to anchor those LST's in deep water and lighter their cargo ashore via the rhino ferries. Once the beaches were cleared of fire, we urged the navy to stomach its compunctions, beach its LST's, and halve the time spent in unloading.

The appeal, however, fell on deaf ears, for while our tanks were expendable, ships—in the eyes of some skippers—presumably were not. Not until after the enemy had been rolled back from the beaches did an order go out to skippers to beach their LST's.

Rationing on ammunition began just as soon as Gerow reached the line he was to hold on a static front while Collins chased north after Cherbourg. Initially, Gerow was to be limited to 25 rounds per gun per day. If he preferred, he could save that ration for an occasional big shoot. In the event of counterattack the rules on this ration lapsed and he was authorized to fire whatever might be required to drive the enemy off. But when Pete Corlett came into the line with his XIX Corps, he objected to the skinflint ration that had been allotted his guns.

"Pete," I remonstrated, "I hate this rationing just as much as you do. But remember, we've got no choice. Either we ration it now or we shoot what we've got, pack up, and go home."

Ammunition rationing was not to be limited to the beachhead; it harassed our artillery all the way to the Ruhr. Although the shortage passed through four distinct phases and the causes changed with each, the results remained the same: We never had ammunition enough to shoot all we needed.

1. In Normandy our trouble started with the beaches. For even when we boosted unloading to 35,000 tons a day, three times the capacity of Cherbourg in peacetime, there wasn't enough ammunition to go around and the beaches couldn't carry more.

2. As we raced across France on the heels of the breakout, the bottleneck shifted to transportation. Although by now there was plenty of ammunition piled up in the Normandy dumps, even the Red Ball Express* could not carry enough of it to the front.

3. Once we had broken into the Siegfried Line, the bottleneck shifted again, this time back to the ports. Beach unloading was slowed down by the weather and until Antwerp was opened there was insufficient wharfage in the Channel ports to handle Allied tonnage. At one point more than 250 Liberty ships were reported queued up in England awaiting dock space in France.

4. Finally in the winter and spring of 1945, we were made to pay for our optimism of that previous September. The bottleneck shifted this time back across the Atlantic to the United States where rosy

*A one-way road system devised by the Communications Zone for high-speed truck traffic to the front.

estimates on the imminent end of the European war had brought cutbacks in production.

Until the gale struck on June 19, I had been thinking of flying additional infantry into the beachhead. But as ammunition stockpiles fell to three units of fire and Collins was cut back one third on his expenditure in the Cherbourg attack, we went to air in desperation for an emergency ammo lift.

Quesada winced when I told him what we wanted. The heavily laden C-47's would tear up the mesh runways on his fighter fields. But without further hesitation he reached for the phone and the following morning the first troop-carriers flew in. Soon we were getting 500 tons a day by air express.

While First Army struggled with these logistical problems, VII Corps pushed up the rich green Cotentin toward the doomed city of Cherbourg. Wearing a faded salmon-colored trench coat, Collins bustled about his front in an armored scout car, nudging, edging, urging his divisions to speed up the advance. By the evening of June 21, he had tightened a ring around that transatlantic tourist gateway to France.

To hasten the capture of Cherbourg, Collins addressed an ultimatum to the German commander, threatening the garrison with annihilation if he did not surrender by 9:00 the following morning. But with his 30,000 troops, General Karl Wilhelm von Schlieben had been admonished by Hitler to fight to the death. "Withdrawal from present positions is punishable by death," the general declared in an order to his troops. "I empower all leaders of whatever rank to shoot at sight anyone who leaves his post because of cowardice." When news of Collins' ultimatum reached me that evening via the BBC, I called the Army PW chief in for an explanation. "How did BBC get the story of that damned ultimatum?"

"VII Corps released it, General."

I groaned. "Let's see if we can't get Collins' staff to keep those things under their hats. When the German turns that ultimatum down, he's going to look like a hero instead of the fool that he is—"

When 9 o'clock passed with no word from von Schlieben, Collins called for an air bombing to soften his preliminary objectives in the attack on Cherbourg.

This air strike was to be our first large-scale undertaking in saturation bombing. It had been worked out hurriedly in collaboration with Quesada who relayed it to the air forces in England. Ten squadrons of RAF Mustangs and rocket-firing Typhoons were to lead off at 12:40 P.M., 80 minutes before H hour on the ground. They were to be followed by 562 U. S. fighter bombers, together with 387 mediums of the IX Bomber Command. Tooey Spaatz had flown in from England with Robert A. Lovett, Assistant Secretary of War for Air, to witness the operation.

The bad news reached us even before H hour when two of Eddy's regiments and another of the 4th cried back that they were being strafed by friendly aircraft. Several of the fighter bombers had erred in identifying their targets and for the remainder of the war, parts of the 9th Division were doggedly air shy. But while this initial attempt at saturation bombing did not destroy the enemy's defenses, it nevertheless encouraged Cherbourg's defenders to scorn von Schlieben's orders. Cynicism had already set in among the PWs we took, for while Allied air pummeled them on the ground, the Luftwaffe remained conspicuously scarce. "If we are to die for Cherbourg," the prisoners complained, "why doesn't the Luftwaffe come out and die with us?"

More importantly, this air strike encouraged us to think of saturation bombing as an effective tactical weapon. If we could maneuver 1,000 aircraft in a hastily assembled operation against Cherbourg, why not twice or even three times that many in a painstakingly blueprinted attack? I sat up late with Kean that evening pondering the prospects.

The ultimatum that Collins delivered on Cherbourg's commander was symptomatic of the rash of psychological warfare that had broken out on both sides of the line. Before attacking Cherbourg, we feathered the city with leaflets that Dickson labeled *bumpf*. And because the enemy there was already trapped with no hope for escape, we exploited this doleful predicament, offering him a painless escape from death through surrender. Our tag-line on this leaflet read "—And don't forget your mess kit."

Across on Gerow's front, a PW officer from the 2d Armored Division ran his sound truck forward each evening to play Strauss waltzes for the homesick enemy across the lines. At the end of each number he purred in German to ask if the solders remembered their homeland as it was before the war.

"You have fought well," he told them, "and you have conducted yourself honorably before your countrymen. But there is no longer any reason for fighting. Our bombers have destroyed your cities. You are faced with overwhelming strength. Surrender now and return safely to the loved ones you left behind. If you don't surrender and come over, we have no alternative but to give you more and more of this—" With that, the divisional artillery dumped a 48-gun salvo into the German position.

The enemy, too, dabbled in leaflets which he fired across into our lines. What these brochures lacked in effectiveness, they made up in pornography or venom. The text of one was, among other things, brief. "Hey Kid from the USA—" it read, "are you from the wrong side of the street?"

It answered its own question. "FDR's sons are in the army, parading down the streets of London with uniforms and fancy buttons. They come from the right side of the street."

Ike ferried across the Channel on June 24 to check our plans for the turnabout of VII Corps after the capture of Cherbourg. Once he secured that port, Collins was to switch back and join Middleton in the Cotentin neck. We would then drive south across the bogs until our line was stretched across the Normandy shoulder from the Calvados coast to the corner of Brittany. I had long ago rejected the possibility of breaking through St.-Lô to connect with the sea at Coutances, for the enemy there was too strongly entrenched and I had no wish to squander my strength against the strongest point in his line. To make each American life pay off in many more German fatalities, we would concentrate our forces against only those objectives that might most advantageously undermine his strength.

Not until Eisenhower arrived on this late June visit to the beachhead did we learn how unpleasant and damaging the V-1 bombardment of England had become. The pilotless aircraft attack had started on June 15. But because most of the missiles were aimed on London from farther up the Channel coast, we had not yet seen one from the beachhead. As a result we had brushed the V-1 airily aside. "Just another German weapon," we assured one another, "another weapon that has come too late to save Hitler."

When Eisenhower arrived, I bantered with his aide, Lieutenant Colonel Ernest R. Lee of Indianapolis. "What have you come for," I chuckled, "a nice quiet night's sleep on the beachhead away from London?"

My jest, however, contained less whimsy than truth. For although the buzz bomb never threatened England as did the 1940 blitz, it soon proved to Londoners that it was more of a menace than a gadget. In July Churchill was to reveal that 2,752 Britons had been killed by V-1's during the first three weeks of attack. Three times as many more were seriously injured. But terrifying though these missiles were, they had come too late to influence the outcome of the war. Even before the invasion, intelligence had estimated that the enemy could not secure quantity production in sufficient numbers to make them tell.

For most of the 18 days we had been ashore, Eisenhower had paced impatiently inside the confines of that gaudy brass-bound prison known to the world as SHAEF. Now surfeited with high-level strategy, with statisticians, logisticians, and tacticians, Ike was eager to escape the rarified air of SHAEF in England and find reality among the troops in the field.

There are those who contend that the best strategist is the commander most distantly removed from his troops. For where units exist merely as symbols on a map the strategist can perform in a vacuum and his judgment cannot be infected by compassion for his troops. If war were fought with push-button devices, one might make a science of command. But because war is as much a conflict of passion as it is of force, no commander can become a strategist until first he knows his men. Far from being a handicap to command, compassion is the measure of it. For unless one values the lives of his soldiers and is tormented by their ordeals, he is unfit to command. He is unfit to appraise the cost of an objective in terms of human life.

To spend lives, knowingly, deliberately—even cruelly—he must steel his mind with the knowledge that to do less would cost only more in the end. For if he becomes tormented by the casualties he must endure, he is in danger of losing sight of his strategic objective. Where the objective is lost, the war is prolonged and the cost becomes infinitely worse.

Eisenhower found as I did that the well-springs of humility lie in the field. For however arduous the task of a commander, he cannot face the men who shall live or die by his orders without sensing how much easier is his task than the one he has set them to perform.

Throughout the war in Europe Eisenhower frequently escaped SHAEF to tramp into the field and talk with his men. There, like the others of us, he could see the war for what it was, a wretched debasement of all the thin pretensions of civilization. In the rear areas war may sometimes assume the mask of an adventure. On the front it seldom lapses far from what General Sherman declared it to be.

With Ike I drove up into the sector of the 79th Division in the center of Collins' line. There we picked up the division commander and drove on to a regimental bivouac. A captain knelt in his OD undershirt over a helmet full of water, lathering his face for a shave. He looked up in annoyance as we walked into the clearing. His eyes bugged, then rolled in despair as they traveled from the broad smile of Ike to the agonized face of his division commander. The captain stumbled to his feet and, with a towel still tied around his neck, saluted, and reported to the Supreme Commander.

As Eisenhower moved briskly among the troops, the captain fell in behind him. Hands on his hips, head cocked, Ike frowned as he bit off his words in conversation with the men.

"Soldier," he called to a private, "how many experts do you have in your rifle squad?"

"Three, sir—I think."

"You think? Soldier you had better know, dammit. Know exactly what you've got."

He moved to another on down the line.

"And how many experts do you have?"

"Four. I'm one of them, sir."

"Good. That's fine. Where are you from?"

"Kentucky, sir."

"Got a good squad?"

"Best in the company, sir."

"Does the rest of the company think so?"

"Well, sir—"

"Stupid bunch of people, aren't they!" Ike chuckled. The soldier grinned. We climbed back into the jeep.

In his fresh summer worsteds and smart overseas cap, Eisenhower stood out crisply in the monotonous parade of sweaty OD's and bucket-heads that crowded our roads. From their trucks, the troops waved breezily. The bolder ones shouted, "Hey, Ike."

Eisenhower turned around in the front seat of his jeep. "Wish I didn't have to go back," he said. "I'll be mighty glad when we get moved over here with you."

On the fifth day of his Cherbourg offensive, Collins broke through that city's outer rim of defenses, but his path into the port was blocked by a chain of strong points to which the enemy still clung. Flak battalions were rolled into position against us with muzzles depressed against the ground. And from the citadel of Fort du Roule overlooking the harbor, General von Schlieben's forces looked down on our heads. The fort crowned an escarpment that rose steeply behind Cherbourg. From its bluffs the enemy's coastal guns commanded not only the sea approaches to Cherbourg but the streets of the city as well. We could not have by-passed the fort to pinch it out without venturing under the muzzles of its heavy guns.

Unwilling to waste time on a siege when we should have been getting under way on Middleton's front in the neck, I asked Kirk to attack the fort's coastal guns from the sea. Had Kirk told me to go soak my head in the Channel, I could not have held his prudence against him. For Cherbourg had been porcupined with guns that outranged and outnumbered those of his biggest ships.

Knowing that he might take serious losses, Kirk asked, "Is it worth that much to you?"

"It is," I told him. "We must take Cherbourg just as soon as we can."

Kirk accepted without question my measure of the gains to be gambled against the risks to be run and promptly ordered three battleships to sail against the harbor defenses. As they approached within range, the ships were taken under fire and were soon forced to withdraw after an uneven duel with the shore batteries. However, Kirk's willingness to chance the attack even at the risk of losing his ships, caused me to regret the earlier petulance with which we had criticized the navy's handling of our supply on the beaches.

Fortunately, Kirk's valorous gesture did not bring on disaster and the navy retired with light losses. Meanwhile, infantry had scaled the cliffs of Fort du Roule to crack its battlements with satchel charges.

On the evening of June 26—it was then D plus 20—Manton Eddy telephoned to report that von Schlieben and 800 of his troops had been captured alive in an underground fortress. Elsewhere in Cherbourg the enemy continued to hold out. Despite the hopelessness of its position, the garrison had complied with von Schlieben's orders more faithfully than we anticipated it would.

Manton reported that he was sending von Schlieben to Army for interrogation. "Can't you first get him to issue orders and stop the fighting in Cherbourg? You tried? He won't? Well, send him on then. We'll pack him off to Monty."

Major General Everett S. Hughes, Eisenhower's sad-eyed trouble shooter from SHAEF, was seated with me in the CP truck when Eddy's call came in.

"We've got the big boy up in Cherbourg," I explained, "but he won't surrender the rest of his troops."

Hughes scowled. "Going to ask him in to dinner?"

I looked intently at Hughes. "Do you think I ought to have him in for dinner?" I asked.

"Hell, no," he shouted.

"Well if the bastard had surrendered four days ago, I might have asked him in. But since then he's cost us a lot of lives. Now I hope they give him a K-ration and send him back on an LCT across a choppy Channel."

Von Schlieben afterward objected to the "uncivilized" callousness with which we received a captured general of his high rank. He looked coldly on his K-ration breakfast and complained bitterly to G-2 that no shower had been provided in the farmhouse where he was held. As if to content himself in captivity with the memory of better days, he carried with him the menu of a dinner at which he had been the guest of honor in Cherbourg less than a month before: Lobster and hollandaise, *pâté de foie gras*, baked bluefish, roast leg of lamb, peaches and cream, chateau wines, vintage champagne, and Napoleon brandy.

"Wow," Dickson chortled, when he read the menu, "and now he's going to England at the height of the Brussels sprouts season."

Von Schlieben, however, was to suffer a further indignity while in our hands. The vehicle carrying his trunk from Cherbourg collided with a truck en route to the army CP. The general's uniforms were strewn across the road and before the MP's could pick them up, souvenir-hunting GI's had stripped them of braid and rank.

In Cherbourg, the German had destroyed all port installations in an effort to render it useless. Piers, cranes, marshaling yards, bridges, power stations, and transformers were dynamited and burned. The harbor itself was strewn with scuttled ships and heavily seeded with mines. But salvage engineers tramped into the city on the heels of the infantry, and within 21 days the first Allied ships dropped anchor in the harbor. By November Cherbourg was handling 15,000 tons of stores per day. During that month alone it accounted for 433,000 tons.

As the prisoners trekked out of Cherbourg into our hastily expanded cages, the total swelled to 38,000 for our three weeks ashore. Although the younger officers maintained their arrogance, the troops were confused and disheartened. Their punishment at the hands of our air force had left them more frightened than ever for the safety of their families in the Reich. To our queries on the Luftwaffe, they replied with snorts of derision. Had Goering been dropped into their cages, we would have been spared the trouble of bringing him to trial.

Among the troops in Normandy, Cherbourg's strategic worth was soon overshadowed by the wealth of its booty and it was there that the term "liberate" came into popular use in the army. Von Schlieben's forces had thoughtfully stocked their underground shelters for a prolonged campaign—and for what could have been a historic binge. And while they scrupulously complied with orders to demolish the port's installations, their soldiers' hearts rebelled at the sacrilege of destroying or spilling good wine and brandy. As a result we fell heir not only to a transatlantic port but to a massive underground wine cellar as well.

Word of the prize leaked out even before the fighting ended and the scroungers scurried into position for a claims race into those caves. Here was a problem for which the school at Leavenworth had not prepared me and I went to Ike for help. He approved our recommendation that the booty be padlocked for equitable distribution to the divisions. Had we left the distribution to chance, the rear echelons would have made off with those stores, while the divisions that took them went dry. For once, however, the combat troops shared equally in the gratitude of France. My share of the cache was a half a case of champagne which Collins sent me and which I saved and carried home from the war for the christening of my grandson.

17 : *Breakout*

B<small>Y JULY WE HAD NOT ONLY TAKEN THE PORT THAT</small> was to insure the support of our lodgment, but beach build-up was rapidly swelling the strength of our Allied forces ashore. In the three weeks since D day, First Army alone had grown mightier than the combined forces of Patton and Montgomery in the Sicilian campaign. In addition to the two airborne divisions, now overdue for relief, the blue tabs of 11 U. S. divisions had been taped to the G-3 war map: two were armored, the other nine were infantry.

Our 40-mile front in the U. S. sector started with the bulge at Caumont where Gerow joined the British. It fell back behind St.-Lô in an arc that ran through the Carentan marshes before turning across the Cotentin to the west Channel shore. This front was divided into four corps sectors: Gerow occupied the "quiet" front on the left. Corlett held the depression behind St.-Lô. Collins had shifted from Cherbourg to the near half of the Cotentin neck. And Middleton reached across that neck to the west shore where Manton Eddy had cut the peninsula.

In the British sector, Monty's 40-mile front fell off steeply from Caumont toward Bayeux. It bulged out again into the enemy's line just west of Caen, curved behind that besieged city, and arced out into a bridgehead east of the Orne River.

Into this narrow British beachhead Monty had crowded four corps totaling 16 divisions, five of them armored. So rapid had been the Allied build-up that already our combined British-American forces exceeded those on the Italian front. Within 25 days after landing we had ferried ashore more than 1,000,000 Allied troops. And to support this force our navies had delivered through the surf more than 560,000 tons of supply—enough to fill a freight train 190 miles long.

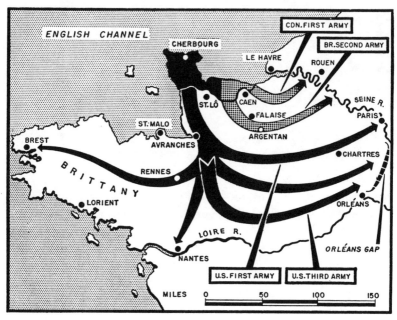

Once they broke out of the lodgment, both U. S. Armies were to turn south to the Loire and east toward the Orléans gap while a tank column raced into Brittany to secure the port of Brest. Meanwhile, the British Armies were to wheel apace of the American advance and push on to the Seine.

But, even this growing lodgment offered scant footing for our mobile armies. Both Middleton's VIII and Collins' VII Corps fronts lay half drowned in the rivers and marshlands of the Cotentin neck. And everywhere the battleground was boxed in by the hedgerows. Only on the British front did this bocage thin into undulating plains near Caen. But there the enemy had substituted panzers for the delaying capabilities of those hedgerows.

Once we had established an all-weather lifeline through the port of Cherbourg, the way was cleared for the Allied offensive that was to be initiated by a breakout. The basic strategy for this attack out of the lodgment had been written into the OVERLORD plan. France was to be liberated in phases and we now stood at the brink of the first: a swift push from the grassy pasture lands of Normandy to the sleepy banks of the Seine.

While Montgomery held the pivot at Caen, the whole Allied line was to wheel eastward. The momentum for this advance was to be generated by First Army with an assault on its westernmost end of the line. We were to sweep south out of the Cotentin past Avranches and there cut off the Brittany peninsula at its neck. After pausing only long enough to secure Brittany and its choice selection of deep-water ports, the American forces were to turn east and, with the right flank on the dry, sandy banks of the Loire, close to the Seine-Orléans gap south of Paris. The remainder of the Allied line was to pivot with our advance and roll eastward to the Seine between Paris and the Channel. Behind the Seine River line, we anticipated the enemy would rally his forces in France while we reorganized and waited for supply to catch up with the advance.

Eisenhower, Montgomery, and I had agreed to the plan without a moment's dissension, for it achieved as no other plan could our two starting objectives in the Battle for France.

The first was apparent from a glance at the map. Until we turned the Allied line east, our front would be facing south as it was when we came in over the beaches. There was no better way to do it than to cartwheel to the left with Monty pivoting on the Channel.

The second objective derived in large measure from the tyranny of logistics that overshadows any tactical movement in war. G-4 had repeatedly stressed the necessity for capturing the Brittany ports before the September gales knocked out our beaches and left us totally dependent upon Cherbourg. At that time Cherbourg's capacity was believed limited to 14 divisions.

Although this offensive that was to carry our Allied line to the Seine had been outlined months before in England, the attack had yet to be fitted to the peculiarities of our situation in France. We were agreed, however, that the main force of the drive should be concentrated on the U. S. end of the line. But we had not yet agreed on how that blow was to be delivered.

From the moment we started on OVERLORD planning, I was determined that we must avoid at all costs those pitfalls that might bog down our advance and lead us into the trench warfare of World

War I. We had fought a fast war of movement in the Tunisian campaign where the terrain militated against us, and I was convinced those tactics could be duplicated in a blitz across France. With the mobility and fire-power we had amassed in both British and American divisions, we could easily outpoint and outrun the German in an open war of movement.

But to exploit this advantage in mobility it was essential that we break a hole through the enemy's defenses rather than heave him back. Only a *breakout* would enable us to crash into the enemy's rear where we could fight a war of movement on our own best terms. As long as the enemy confined us to the bocage of Normandy where we were forced to match him man for man, he could exact a prohibitive price for the few miserable yards we might gain.

How then were we to turn this battle of the bocage into a war of movement?

First, we must pick a soft point in the enemy's line; next, concentrate our forces against it. Then after smashing through with a blow that would crush his front-line defenses, we would spill our mechanized columns through that gap before the enemy could recover his senses.

In selecting this point for the breakout, we were bound by three limitations.

1. It would have to be made beyond the Carentan marshes where they cut through the Cotentin neck. Otherwise our columns might easily be mired even before they cleared the gap.

2. It would have to avoid the enemy's strong points, for there the momentum of an assault could be squandered in too costly an effort to break an initial hole in the enemy's line.

3. And it would have to be made at a point where there were sufficient parallel roads in the direction of the attack to speed our follow-up columns into the enemy's rear.

We had long ago concluded that the best point for breakout lay somewhere along the 16-mile line between St.-Lô and Coutances. But the effort to reach that St.-Lô-Coutances line would have been too great. As we had reluctantly conceded several weeks before, the strength of German resistance at St.-Lô would make the likelihood of a push from there across to Coutances much too costly. On the other hand, if we were to force our way out of the Cotentin neck from the vicinity of Carentan, it would become necessary to cross those troublesome marshes before reaching the breakout line. And while this path looked less difficult than the one at St.-Lô, we could foresee that it, too, would be costly.

A third alternative was one that led straight down the west coast Cotentin road from La Haye du Puits through the moors of Lessay to Coutances. If we could break into Coutances from the west coast road, the enemy would be forced to withdraw across the rest of the Cotentin neck for fear of being cut off by a pincer attack from St.-Lô. After having drawn our line up to the St.-Lô-Coutances road, we would then be set for the main offensive that was to start with an American breakout.

This third alternative was the one we chose, and on June 24, I issued Middleton orders to lead the attack down the west coast road. Collins was to take over part of the VIII Corps front across the Carentan marshes and nudge the enemy out through the neck as Middleton drove on to Coutances. Collins' orders for this deployment reached him even before he broke into Cherbourg. He was to have five days for the turnaround of his corps: one for rest, two for the move, another for reconnaissance, and a fifth on which to issue the attack orders.

It was a tall order even for "Lightning Joe" Collins, a taller one yet for his troops. But I dared not give the enemy more time to dig in on that front. The German had already profited from the ammunition shortage that compelled us to call off Middleton's earlier attack. Each morning brought alarming new signs of defensive preparations. The 82d had discovered widespread mine fields and a patrol from the 90th came in with a disquieting catch of prisoners from the 2d SS Panzer Division.

On June 27, I conferred with Monty on this plan for attack by Middleton down the Coutances road. It came as no surprise to him, for we had explored it once before as an alternative to the St.-Lô route. Three days later Monty published the plan as part of his 21st Group directive. In that directive he carefully reviewed OVER-LORD strategy for the advance to the Seine, emphasizing again for the record that First Army was to deliver the main thrust while Dempsey's Army pinned down the enemy's armor at Caen.

During these operations in the lodgment where Montgomery bossed the U. S. First Army as part of his 21st Army Group, he exercised his Allied authority with wisdom, forbearance, and restraint. While coordinating our movements with those of Dempsey's, Monty carefully avoided getting mixed up in U. S. command decisions, but instead granted us the latitude to operate as freely and as independently as we chose. At no time did he probe into First Army with the indulgent manner he sometimes displayed among those subordinates who were also his countrymen. I could not have wanted a more tolerant or judicious commander. Not once did he confront us with an arbitrary directive and not once did he reject any plan that we had devised.

At 5:30 on the morning of July 3, Middleton started his VIII Corps down the west coast road on the offensive we hoped would secure a line of departure for the breakout. Six days later Middleton had budged only a few miles south and Collins' attack was slowed down in the Carentan marshes. Only the 82d Division had taken its objective but it possessed an uncommon incentive the other units lacked. Upon completion of that mission, Ridgway's troops were to be re-

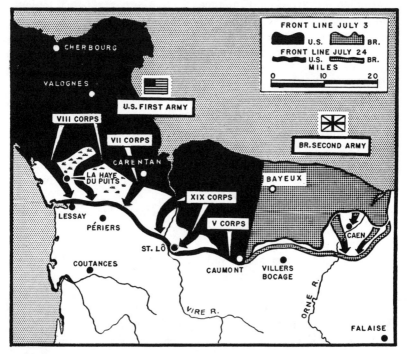

For three weeks troops of the First Army pushed through the Normandy hedgerows and struggled through the Cotentin swamps to reach the St.-Lô road and there establish a springboard for the breakout. Meanwhile Montgomery drove on to capture Caen, his original D-day objective.

turned to England. Incentive is not ordinarily part of an infantryman's life. For him there are no 25 or 50 missions to be completed for
a ticket home. Instead the rifleman trudges into battle knowing
that statistics are stacked against his survival. He fights without promise of either reward or relief. Behind every river, there's
another hill—and behind that hill, another river. After weeks or
months in the line only a wound can offer him the comfort of safety,
shelter, and a bed. Those who are left to fight, fight on, evading
death but knowing that with each day of evasion they have exhausted one more chance for survival. Sooner or later, unless victory
comes, the chase must end on the litter or in the grave.

On July 14, I ordered Middleton to discontinue his Coutances
attack. In 12 days he had advanced only 12,000 yards through mine
fields and against heavy resistance. Although Collins continued to
knuckle forward through the Carentan bogs, it was obvious that the
Coutances-St.-Lô line had become too costly an objective to warrant
our insisting upon it as a starting point for the breakout. We would
settle, I said, for a less desirable springboard somewhere short of
that cross-shoulder line.

On July 1, Eisenhower had crossed the Channel to be with us on
the start of Middleton's unhappy excursion down the Coutances
road. Although correspondents had begun to quip over Monty's recurrent failures at Caen, Eisenhower appeared neither disappointed
in nor distressed by the course of our battle for the beachhead.
While the Army CP displaced forward that day from its farmyard
near the coast to an apple orchard at Colombières, 15 miles behind
St.-Lô, Eisenhower and I drove off to explore future plans with
Monty.

Monty had moved his comfortable caravan CP across into the
U. S. sector where his community of trucks and trailers melted into
the Normandy landscape under their tightly meshed camouflage
nets. At one end of the field a roomy cook tent had been pitched to
house his mess and batmen. Monty lived in a handsome wood-
paneled trailer constructed for an Italian general and captured from
Rommel during the Libyan campaign. Nearby, a British custom-
built truck, fitted to his own specifications, housed an elaborate field
office. Here Montgomery could string his maps the length of two
well-lighted walls and meditate without·interruption in quiet, dry-
ness, and warmth.

Whereas I preferred to live, work, and eat in the field with my staff, Monty sought the solitude of a lonely camp, removed and isolated from his main 21st Group CP. There he lived with his personal staff: one American and two British aides, a Canadian PA —or personal assistant, a British MA—or military assistant. A signal detachment and a security guard equipped with black American jeeps rounded out the tiny caravan camp. It was Sunday morning when we drove into his CP. The bell tolled from a tall stone steeple that rose beyond a line of trees, and from Gerow's front to the south there came a rumble of guns.

Ordnance had dragged two disabled German tanks to Monty's CP for his inspection. One was the squat 63-ton Tiger E Mark VI, the same kind that had outgunned our Shermans in the Tunisian djebels. Next to it stood a 50-ton Panther, Mark V, with the wedge-shaped frontal armor that so effectively deflected the fire of our AT guns. The Tiger carried a long-barreled 88 in its heavy round turret. On its breastplate the armor was seven inches thick. In Europe, as in Africa two years before, the Tiger could both outgun and outduel any Allied tank in the field. Fortunately for us, however, it was inadequately powered with a 650-hp. engine and for that reason it frequently broke down. In fact losses from mechanical failure among these Tiger tanks probably exceeded those attributed to Allied guns in combat.

The lighter Panther or Mark V tank was more evenly powered for its tremendous weight. In lieu of the Tiger's dreaded 88, it mounted a long-barreled high-velocity 75-mm. gun. With this weapon and its tapered hull, the Panther was more than a match for our Shermans.

Originally the Sherman had come equipped with a 75-mm. gun, an almost totally ineffective weapon against the heavy frontal plate of these German tanks. Only by swarming around the panzers to hit them on the flank, could our Shermans knock the enemy out. But too often the American tankers complained it cost them a tank or two, *with crews,* to get the German. Thus we could defeat the enemy's panzers but only by expending more tanks than we cared to lose. Ordnance thereafter replaced the antedated 75 with a new 76-mm. high-velocity gun. But even this new weapon often scuffed rather than penetrated the enemy's armor.

Eisenhower was angry when he heard of these limitations on the new 76. "You mean our 76 won't knock these Panthers out? Why, I thought it was going to be the wonder gun of the war."

"Oh, it's better than the 75," I said, "but the new charge is much too small. She just hasn't the kick to carry her through the German armor."

Ike shook his head and swore. "Why is it that I am always the last to hear about this stuff? Ordnance told me this 76 would take care of anything the German had. Now I find you can't knock out a damn thing with it."

Only the British had found a weapon to pierce the Panther's thick-skinned front in their tough old 17-pounders. To make use of it they mounted those 17-pounders in their lend-lease Shermans. I told Ike that one of our division commanders had seen those guns in action and afterward suggested that they be mounted in our Shermans. But when I queried Monty to ask if the British could equip one Sherman in each U. S. tank platoon with those 17-pounders, he reported that ordnance in England was overloaded on British orders. I offered to compromise on towed 17-pounders but they, too, were in short supply. Obviously, if we were to duel with the Panthers we would have to improvise on our own.

By that time we had hauled ashore eight battalions of long-rifled 90-mm. AA guns. Like the 88, the 90-mm. was a dual-purpose gun and could be deflected for direct fire on ground targets. But like the 88, it was also an awkward weapon, difficult to displace and dig into position. Nevertheless we ordered several battalions of 90-mm. guns into position on the front to form a secondary line of defense behind our Shermans. For the remainder of the war our tank superiority devolved primarily from a superiority in the number rather than the quality of tanks we sent into battle.

At dinner that evening over a captured bottle of good wine Eisenhower relaxed in an evening of conversation. We pulled the blackout flaps on the mess tent and sat until long after dark.

Several days before, Ike told us, he had queried a soldier on his civilian occupation. The youth replied that he was a wheat farmer from Kansas.

"How many acres have you got?" Ike asked with quickened interest at the mention of his home state.

"Twelve thousand, sir."

"Twelve thousand?" Ike said, "and how many do you have in wheat?"

"Nine thousand, sir."

"What's the yield?"

"Forty-one bushels to the acre."

"Mister," Ike replied—and in telling the story he grinned with the recollection of it. "Just remember my name. When the war's over I'll be around for a job."

"When I was a kid," Ike concluded, "250 acres of Kansas wheatland would have represented an honest ambition for any Abilene boy. Yessir, it would have looked mighty good to me—and I guess to you too, Brad."

In Moberly I would have settled for 160.

Before leaving the mess tent to turn in, Eisenhwer questioned me on the progress that was being made in clearing the port of Cherbourg. Lee's engineers had gone to work on the docks and the navy was sweeping the harbor where the enemy had planted the Channel with contact, magnetic, and even acoustic mines. Meanwhile until Eddy took the western tip of the Cotentin, enemy shore defenses had continued to fire on our mine-sweeping craft.

"When are you bringing the 9th Division back down?" Ike asked at my mention of Eddy.

"Just as soon as we can pry them loose. Collins tells me they found a town with four hot-shower heads."

As we walked through the wet grass toward my truck, AA fire riveted the sky over Omaha five miles to the north. Ike stopped to look as the guns echoed over the beachhead.

"A bit noisier than London," I said.

He laughed. "You haven't been back for the buzz bombs!"

Each year at noon on the Fourth of July the army observes the holiday by firing 48 guns in a national salute. While lunching with Gerow two days before, I had suggested we keep the tradition by firing a live salute into the enemy's lines.

"Just 48 guns?" he smiled.

"No, hell no, Gee. We'll fire every gun in the Army."

Eddie the Canon—as Hart, the artilleryman, had been named by Dickson—issued an army-wide order that evening for a TOT salute. TOT to an artilleryman means Time-On-Target. Each gun was to be fired with such split-second timing that every shell would explode on the enemy at the exact moment of 12. And each target, Hart instructed his gunners, was to be a remunerative one.

At precisely noon on July 4 the startled German darted for cover as 1,100 shells from that many guns exploded in a clap of thunder. It was the largest and most remunerative national salute the U. S. Army ever fired.

I returned to the Army CP on the afternoon of July 4 after yanking the lanyard of a 155 to find that Eisenhower had squeezed into the back seat of Quesada's P-51 for a fighter sweep over the Allied beachhead. They grinned like sheepish schoolboys caught in a watermelon patch. Quesada had been cautioned by Brereton to stick to the ground in France where he was worth more to us in a swivel chair than in the cockpit of a fighter. And Eisenhower was frightened for fear word of his flight might leak to the newsmen.

"General Marshall," he admitted, "would give me hell."

And I had no doubt but that he would.

While Collins was hoisting his VII Corps flag over Cherbourg, Montgomery was spending his reputation in a bitter siege against the old university city of Caen. For three weeks he had rammed his troops against those panzer divisions he had deliberately drawn toward that city as part of our Allied strategy of diversion in the Normandy campaign. Although Caen contained an important road junction that Montgomery would eventually need, for the moment the capture of that city was only incidental to his mission. For Monty's primary task was to attract German troops to the British front that we might more easily secure Cherbourg and get into position for the breakout.

In this diversionary mission Monty was more than successful, for the harder he hammered toward Caen, the more German troops he drew into that sector. Too many correspondents, however, had overrated the importance of Caen itself, and when Monty failed to take it, they blamed him for the delay. But had we attempted to exonerate Montgomery by explaining how successfully he had hoodwinked the German by diverting him toward Caen from the Cotentin, we would have also given our strategy away. We desperately wanted the German to believe this attack on Caen was the main Allied effort.

But while this diversion of Monty's was brilliantly achieved, he nevertheless left himself open to criticism by overemphasizing the importance of his thrust toward Caen. Had he limited himself simply to the containment without making Caen a symbol of it, he would have been credited with success instead of being charged, as he was, with failure at Caen. For Monty's success should have been measured in the panzer divisions the enemy rushed against him while Collins sped on toward Cherbourg. Instead, the Allied newspaper readers clamored for a place name called Caen which Monty had once promised but failed to win for them.

The containment mission that had been assigned Monty in the OVERLORD plan was not calculated to burnish British pride in the accomplishments of their troops. For in the minds of most people, success in battle is measured in the rate and length of advance. They found it difficult to realize that the more successful Monty was in stirring up German resistance, the less likely he was to advance.

For another four weeks it fell to the British to pin down superior enemy forces in that sector while we maneuvered into position for the U. S. breakout. With the Allied world crying for blitzkrieg the first week after we landed, the British endured their passive role with patience and forbearing. Eventually, however, the frustration they experienced here at Caen produced an extreme sensitivity to Patton's speedy advance across France. In setting the stage for our breakout, the British were forced to endure the barbs of critics who shamed them for failing to push out vigorously as the Americans did. The intense rivalry that afterward strained relations between the British and American commands might be said to have sunk its psychological roots into that passive mission of the British on the beachhead.

By the end of June, Rommel had concentrated seven panzer divisions against Monty's British sector. One was all he could spare for the U. S. front. The enemy's extreme sensitivity to the British threat at Caen resulted partly from his fear that Monty would break through there in a giant pincer movement calculated to join on the Seine with an Allied sea assault through the Pas de Calais. This assault against the Pas de Calais was the mission for which the German believed Patton waited with an Army in England. The belief had been painstakingly nourished in a shrewd deception plan.

When, at the end of June, Monty sought to lighten our task in the attack on Coutances by threatening the enemy with a British offensive, he discovered that elements of three panzer divisions had been concentrated against a bulge in his line between the U. S. sector and the city of Caen. Another three were reported trundling into the line-up. Of the six, five were SS, sturdily but not fully equipped. Because he was also committed at that time to an offensive beyond the Orne River, Montgomery began to worry over the likelihood of counterattack. He called me and asked for our 3rd Armored Division as a reserve behind his line.

While I did not dispute Monty's need for the 3rd Armored, I needed it even more, for I had only two armored divisions to back up my long front. In addition I knew we would have trouble in reclaiming it once the danger had passed. Even more than the loss of a single division, however, I feared that acquiescence to Monty's request might establish a practice for the assignment of American divisions to British command, for Montgomery was already nearing the bottom of his manpower resources. By the end of our third week ashore, Britain had already committed almost three quarters of all the troops she could spare for this European campaign. By contrast, we had only begun to expand with 11 U. S. divisions. On June 20 an officer flew in from Washington with War Department plans for a build-up to 46 U. S. divisions in Europe by February, 1945.

Although U. S. strength eventually exceeded three times that of the British, we must not forget that England contributed to OVER-LORD to the point of exhaustion. In sacrifice, pain, and deprivation, the British people paid far more dearly than we for the final victory.

With the prestige Montgomery had earned as dean of the Allied field commanders, it was not illogical for both him and the British people to expect that 21st Army Group would carry the lion's share of Eisenhower's ground offensive. But if Monty were to fulfill those ambitious expectations, he would have required a vast infusion of U. S. strength into his British command. There were not enough British troops in the ETO to support a main effort by 21st Army Group.

Remembering General Pershing's troubles in World War I, I was determined to fight any proposal for the assignment of American troops to British field command. Not only were we competent to direct our own battles, but I could not forget the calamitous results of extra-national assignments in the Tunisian campaign. Much as I opposed the assignment of American corps and armies to British army or group command, I objected even more strenuously to the far more perilous practice of assigning individual divisions. For while the larger units could probably retain their integrity, a division might too easily become lost. As a consequence, when I set off for Montgomery's CP to debate this transfer of the 3rd Armored Division, I had made up my mind to oppose his request for its transfer. If necessary, I would appeal to Ike. Monty, however, was reasonable rather than insistent and when he opened the way to a bargain, I offered a compromise proposition.

Gerow was waiting at his V Corps CP when I drove in from my meeting with Monty at 21st Army Group. He had known of Monty's request for the 3rd Armored Division and feared that its diversion would imperil his own open left flank.

"Well, how did you do, Brad?" Gee asked.

I unbuckled my helmet, picked up a crayon, and walked over to his war map. "Maybe I'm a bad horse trader, Gee, but at any rate I got us out for half the price. Look here." I wiped out his V Corps boundary and drew a new one farther to the left in the British sector. "Instead of giving Monty the 3rd Armored, I agreed to take over a piece of his front. Meanwhile, he promised to send over a brigade of tanks to keep an eye on these panzers on your flank."

To pad out V Corps and ease Gerow's worries on that open flank we shipped him a "rubber division." This division consisted of a deception detachment with inflatable rubber tanks and communications net to simulate the radio traffic of a real division. Gerow first learned of the rubber division when an officer reported to V Corps to ask where he wanted to locate an "armored division."

"That youngster must have thought I was crazy," Gerow afterward explained. "But I never even heard of your phony tanks before."

Several days later Monty decided to put an end to the tussle at Caen and improve his position there with an all-out attack on the city. To break a path for his tanks in the assault, he called on Air Marshal Sir Arthur Trevers Harris of the RAF for tactical support by heavy bombers. Shortly before midnight on the evening of July 7 a fleet of 460 night-flying Wellingtons crossed the Channel, picked up the French coast, and turned inland to drop their 500- and 1,000-pound bombs on a carpet Monty had marked 4,000 yards wide and 1,500 deep. At dawn the following morning, Monty's sappers, tankers, and infantry pushed into the stunned and cratered city. More than 14,000 buildings had been damaged and destroyed in the month-long battle for this ancient city which nine centuries before had housed the Duke of Normandy before he became William the Conqueror of England. By July 10 Monty had mopped up enemy resistance. It had taken him 33 days to capture the city he had once hoped to grab on D day.

After having written off the Coutances attack as a dud, I searched our maps for another springboard from which to make the breakout attack. For by then I had been forced to admit we could not reach the St.-Lô-Coutances road without prohibitive cost and as a result I decided to settle for a point somewhere short of that line. But whatever the point we chose, the line of departure would have to be on dry ground. And to reach that point we had no alternative but to club our way through the Carentan marshes. This meant ugly infighting, with slow gains and heavy losses.

"I hate to have to slug through those marshes," I told Thorson, "but I see no other way out, do you?"

Tubby screwed up his long hollow face. "To make money, sometimes you've got to spend it. I don't like slugging any more than you do. But we've got to get a solid footing before we hit him for the breakthrough."

I walked back to the truck to study my maps. Inside my CP truck, map space had become more cramped as the beachhead expanded and we added sheets to the mapboard. By now the daily situation map had overrun the side wall and there was no room for another for planning. I instructed Hansen to have a tent put up next to the CP truck and there mount a detailed map of the lodgment on the biggest mapboard he could find.

Tentage in the CP was scarce and our headquarters commandant roared when Hansen pilfered a mess tent to house the giant new mapboard. Rainy weather had muddied the ground, and when Hansen ordered planking for the new tent, the commandant exploded.

"Now you're pampering the old man. Who ever heard of a wooden floor in a tent in the field?"

For two nights I paced the dry plankings of that floor, scribbling boundaries, penciling roads, coloring the river lines of a giant eight-foot map of the beachhead. When at last one could discern the outline of a plan from those markings, I called in first Hodges—then Kean, Thorson, and Dickson for a preliminary critique.

By July 10 the plan was born and Thorson named it COBRA. But it was destined to become known as the Normandy Breakout—the most decisive battle of our war in western Europe.

The breakout was decisive because it instantly banished any lingering doubt on the outcome of the war. If the enemy could have contained our beachhead, he might still have hoped to negotiate a peace. But once we had broken out of the beachhead to race across France to the German frontier, the enemy could no longer hope for a German victory or even for the prospect of a prolonged stalemate.

From the rubble heap that marked the ancient citadel of St.-Lô, a road ran straight as an arrow for 20 miles through the Normandy bocage to the small gray town of Périers and beyond to the west shore of the Cotentin neck. This St.-Lô-Périers road was to replace the St.-Lô-Coutances highway as the line of departure for our breakout. On the near side of that road the Carentan marshes gave way to dry ground and beyond it the hedgerows thinned toward the corner of Brittany, 25 miles farther south. A few miles outside St.-Lô I marked off a rectangular carpet on the Périers road, three and a half miles wide, one and a half deep. Two principal roads ran south through that carpet together with several unimproved ones.

In this COBRA plan for breakout, the enemy was first to be paralyzed by saturation air bombing of that carpet. Indeed, it was this thought of saturation bombing that attracted me to the Périers road. Easily recognizable from the air, the road described a long straight line that would separate our position from that of the German. *The bombers, I reasoned, could fly parallel to it without danger of mistaking our front line.*

After saturating the carpet with air, we would crash through with two infantry divisions; one on the right to hold open that shoulder, another on the left with its flank on the Vire south of St.-Lô. Just as soon as those shoulders were secured, a motorized infantry and two armored divisions would lunge through that hole in the line. The motorized infantry would push on to Coutances, 15 miles to the southwest, in hopes of bagging the remnants of seven German divisions blocking Middleton on his front. Meanwhile the armor would dash toward Avranches and turn the corner into Brittany.

Since COBRA could not go until first we closed to the Périers road, I concentrated Collins' corps in a narrow sector and pointed it toward the St.-Lô carpet. Corlett was to break into St.-Lô and secure the road junction there for follow-up forces in the breakout while

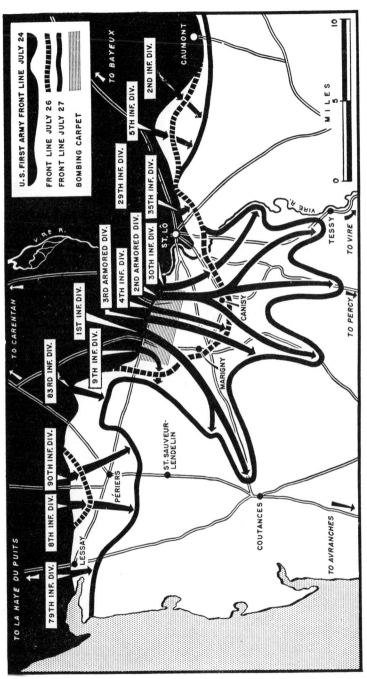

Three infantry divisions were to smash through the St.-Lô carpet immediately after it had been inundated by air bombing. Three more divisions, two of them armored, would then plunge through to exploit that rent in the enemy line.

Middleton was to force the marshes on the Coutances road and be prepared to start forward the instant we plunged through the carpet.

I picked the nervy and ambitious Collins as corps commander for COBRA. To force the carpet and hold open the hole I gave him the 9th and 30th Divisions. Then to make certain the blitz would get off to a fast start, I called on the Big Red One to pace it. By that time the 1st had "rested" for more than a month on the quiet Caumont front. There was no problem in the choice of armored spearheads; we had only two ashore, the veteran 2d and the 3rd Divisions. None of these three divisions was to be shifted into position behind the carpet until just before the attack, and then only at night in a carefully concealed undercover movement.

During a conference the week before COBRA, Eddy spoke irritably of the excessive front that had been assigned his 9th Division. "The carpet's too wide for two divisions," he complained.

"Very well then—how about another," I said, turning to Collins. "You can have the 4th Division." It had just been pulled out of the line for a rest.

Tubby Thorson's face fell and I laughed. "Gosh, I never thought we'd ever be able to give away a division as easily as that!" I said.

"Too easy," he retorted. "Now we've got everything we own in the battle. There isn't a single division left in reserve. The only thing we haven't committed is the Norwegian-American battalion—one battalion in reserve for the whole damned First Army."

"In Tunisia we never had that much," I assured him. "Anything else we can give you?" I said, speaking once more to Collins. "You've got everything now but my pistol."

Collins held out his hand.

It was while Middleton was struggling toward Coutances that the 90th Division took its second dive, this time under Landrum. Faced with the task of finding a successor to Landrum, one who could bounce the division out of its rut, I searched our list of brigadiers for a replacement.

My eye caught two names: MCLAIN, RAYMOND S. and ROOSEVELT, T., JR.

I recalled, however, in thinking of Roosevelt that Eisenhower and I had once agreed in Sicily that Ted's easy indifference to discipline would probably limit him to a single star. "The men worship Ted,"

I had explained to Ike, "but he's too softhearted to take a division—too much like one of the boys." But it was not a disciplinarian the 90th needed now. It called for a man with vitality and courage, a man who could pick up the division singlehandedly and give it confidence in itself. If anyone fitted that description, Ted Roosevelt was his name. With a thick-skinned disciplinarian as his second in command, Ted would have the 90th brawling with the German in a couple of weeks.

It was almost midnight, July 13, when I telephoned Ike at SHAEF to make the recommendation. Ike had gone to bed; I got Bedell Smith over a noisy Channel connection.

"You want to give the 90th to Ted?" he shouted. "Okay, Brad, I'll check it with Ike in the morning." It was Ike who as Theater Commander would forward the recommendation to Washington for Ted's promotion.

Bedell called back early the next morning. I had not yet gone to breakfast. "I've got the answer for you on Roosevelt. Ike said O.K. It's the right thing to do."

"It's too late, Bedell," I answered, "Ted died of a heart attack at midnight last night." The news had been telephoned me from the 4th Division where Ted had been assigned as a spare brigadier. The coronary attack had come unexpectedly and without warning; Ted died as no one could have believed he would, in the quiet of his tent.

After leaving the 1st Division in Sicily on the relief of Terry Allen, Roosevelt had joined General Henri Giraud in time for the French invasion of Corsica. There at the age of 56 he made his third H-hour landing.

Throughout that fall he fidgeted uncomfortably among the brass at AFHQ, longing to get back into the shooting war. When at last he could endure the boredom no longer, he wrote to me in England, begging a job on the invasion.

"If you ask me I'll swim in with a 105 strapped to my back," he said. "Anything at all. Just help me get out of this rats' nest down here."

Because the 4th Division was green to fire, it was difficult to anticipate how it might act on the assault. If Roosevelt would go in with the leading wave, he could steady it as no other man could. For Ted was immune to fear, he would stroll casually about under fire while troops about him scrambled for cover and he would banter with them and urge them forward. I wrote to him what I had in mind: Ted would go in with the first wave on Utah Beach as a spare brigadier with the 4th and show those green troops how to behave under fire.

"You'll probably get killed on the job—" I told him.

Ted never replied to my letter. He broke out of the hospital in Italy where he had been stricken with pneumonia and reported to me in London a few days later with a raging fever.

Roosevelt had earned a division command as few men have but we had waited too long. He braved death with an indifference that destroyed its terror for thousands upon thousands of younger men. I have never known a braver man nor a more devoted soldier.

As we worked to smooth out the lumps in COBRA, a delegation of Russian military observers arrived for a visit to the Allied front. They returned again during the breakout and several times later that fall. Smartly uniformed in their belted tunics, contrasting breeches and jack boots, the Soviet officers pried diligently into our beachhead operations. They were especially interested in our methods of supply; the prodigal quantity of trucking had amazed them. We, in turn, greeted them warmly and held nothing back.

Their British escort was less effusive than we. An old hand from the British embassy in Moscow, he shepherded his charges with discreet distaste. "Whenever we quiz these chaps on the Red army," he confided to Hansen, "they either evade our questions or answer them with lies." At the time we thought the brigadier unduly harsh in his judgment of our Allies.

Acutely conscious of their relative rank and priority, the Soviets reformed their delegation to shake our hands. The ranking officer, a youthful admiral, superseded the two Red army generals. Though keen and conspicuously correct, his face was set in a chilly stare.

The British brigadier nodded toward him and grinned. "Nasty looking chap, isn't he? Probably got those clapboards by pushing his predecessor overboard one night!"

During their first visit the Soviets had asked to see a German PW cage. As they strayed through the camp, one of the Soviets stopped to interrogate a tall hard-muscled German captain wearing the wings of a parachutist.

"And what do you think will happen to Germany after *we* win the war?" the Russian spoke fluent German.

The paratrooper faltered then stiffened. Germany, he assumed, would probably be broken up into little pieces.

"Not Germany," the Soviet officer spoke slowly, "not Germany, *Herr Hauptmann*—but Germans."

By the middle of July we could sense the growing impatience of newsmen who looked critically on the deadlock that seemed to have gripped our beachhead. Middleton's attack toward Coutances had ballooned their hopes, then flattened them even more abjectly. Those who had awaited Monty's assault on Caen as the signal for an Allied breakthrough trooped back disheartened to their gloomy press camps when the British went no farther. Weeks of intermittent rain had shrouded the beachhead with a dismal gray cloud cover, pinning the air forces to the ground while the enemy dragged up reinforcements. As Corlett's XIX Corps bellied forward through the hedgerows toward St.-Lô and Collins crawled through the Carentan swamps, more and more newsmen began to ask if the Allies had learned anything since climbing out of the trenches in France 26 years before.

This melancholy mood was best expressed in a newspaper story that appeared just two days before the breakout. It was written by a well-known correspondent who had succumbed to the gloom of the press camps. He attributed our "stalemate" in the beachhead to an overdose of caution.

"The principal point made by critics of the strategy followed by General Sir Bernard L. Montgomery," he wrote, "is that he is playing safe and in playing safe is turning caution into a vice. The United States Army has consistently followed the policy of doing things the way that costs the least number of lives. This policy has been contagious and has spread to the British command."

For the moment we could do little but grin and bear it. For although COBRA was rapidly taking form, we dared not yet tell newsmen of it. The enemy had already shown signs of apprehension on the Carentan front and by the middle of July had mustered the remnants of 12 divisions against us. Most alarming was the shift of two panzer divisions from Monty's sector to ours.

No one disliked more than I did the disagreeable necessity for inching our way through those St.-Lô hedgerows and Carentan marshlands. For while we sloughed afoot toward the Périers road, our vastly superior motorized equipment lay wasted under its camouflaged nets. Nevertheless, until we reached the carpet and broke through to the terrain beyond it, we could do nothing but belly ahead and swallow those heavy losses.

While aware of this growing criticism from the newsmen, I did not feel that we owed an apology to anyone for our gains. At the end of one week ashore we had linked the beachheads. During the second we cut the Cotentin. In the third we captured Cherbourg. During the fourth we attacked out of the neck. And when the fifth rolled around, we had put together our COBRA plan and were already edging toward the breakout.

Anyone familiar with the tactics of our Mediterranean campaigns could not have believed us so inept as to waste strength deliberately in static or slow-motion warfare. In Tunisia we had cracked an iron-clad position to initiate a war of movement. But there, too, we had found it necessary first to clear a springboard with infantry before committing the armor. Until we cleared the Carentan basin where the marshlands confined us to few roads, it was folly to talk of a blitz. First we must gain the dry ground where our tanks could roam at will.

Besides those critics who thought us too timid to risk the fast stakes of mobile warfare, there were others who searched our tactics for signs of a conspiracy against the Reds. A British columnist asked if our "sitdown" were part of a scheme to exhaust the Russians by leaving them to fight the Reich alone. And an American correspondent cautioned me a week before the breakout that if this were indeed our intent we would default in our right to bargain on the shape of the postwar world. I assured him that we were guileless and suggested he withhold his verdict. "Wait a week or so before you go overboard," I said, wishing it were possible to tell him of COBRA.

The charge that we might have been conspiring against the Soviet was nonsense. I knew no more of the Russian advance than any newspaper reader, indeed probably less, for I saw the newspapers less often. Until we approached the Elbe and came face to face with the problem of joining up with the Red army, I fought the war in total ignorance of Soviet intentions. Even when the Red army had closed to within a hundred miles of ours and the gap between us narrowed daily, we plotted the Soviet advance on our war map from news broadcasts of the BBC. This remained our only pipeline to the Soviet High Command.

While Collins worked over his ground plan for COBRA, Quesada knuckled into the air plan with the zest of any young man anxious to get on to Paris. He had located IX Tac CP in a pasture adjacent to ours and parked the converted machine shop in which he lived on the opposite side of a hedgerow from me.

Although Quesada could have passed for a prototype of the hot pilot with his shiny green trousers, broad easy smile, and crumpled but jaunty hat, he was a brilliant, hard, and daring air-support commander on the ground. He had come into the war as a young and imaginative man unencumbered by the prejudices and theories of so many of his seniors on the employment of tactical air. To Quesada the fighter was a little-known weapon with vast unexplored potentialities in support of ground troops. He conceived it his duty to learn what they were. In England, Quesada first experimented with heavier bombloads for his fighters by hanging their wings and bellies with more and heavier bombs. He even converted a squadron of fast, sleek Spits into fighter bombers. When the British protested this heretical misuse of the fighter in which they took such pride, the imperturbable Quesada retorted, "But they're not your planes any more—they're mine. And I'll do anything I want to with them." This search for more and heavier bombloads reached its climax in England when Quesada hung a pair of 1,000-pound bombs on his P-47 fighters.

Just as soon as Collins' tank and motorized columns broke through the carpet, they were to highball toward Brittany while disregarding both their flanks and rear. To protect these columns from the danger of ambush and to assist them in breaking through the enemy's strong points, air was to put up a dawn-to-dusk fighter-bomber umbrella over the head of each column. Thus air could reconnoiter for the column commander and attack any barrier to his advance. Air and ground were to communicate through an air-support party to be attached to the head of each column.

"You can keep them in radio contact with each other?" I asked Quesada.

"Sure we can," he grinned, "but it may be tough on my boys with your columns. They'll be riding in open radio jeeps while yours are riding in tanks."

"Well, why not put your air-support parties in tanks?"

"Do you mean it, General?" he said. "By golly, that would do it!

But we'll have to check on the radios and see if they can get through from the inside of a tank."

"Fine, Pete. I'll have a couple of Shermans delivered to your CP by noon." Quesada left and I directed ordnance to send two medium tanks to IX Tac at once.

The officer in ordnance looked at the note he had scribbled on my telephone call. "IX Tac?" he thought, "why that's the air force. What in hell would they be doing with tanks? The Old Man's screwy—he must mean Manton Eddy's 9th Infantry Division."

The two Shermans clanked into Eddy's CP, and an officer there shooed them off. "Not us," he told the drivers. "Must be some mistake. We don't need any replacements."

Ordnance called me back. "About those tanks, General—"

"Oh, those two for Pete Quesada," I said. "Yes—did he get them?"

"You mean General Quesada—the Ninth Air Force Quesada?"

"Yep—they're to go to the CP next door."

"Well I'll be damned," someone muttered. The receiver clicked and I hung up.

When at last those tanks sallied into Quesada's CP, an officer there hurried out to turn them away. "This is the air force," he protested, "what the devil would we be wanting with tanks?" It was not until late in the afternoon that those vehicles were finally delivered for testing. The radio worked and Quesada acquired an armored force of his own.

The employment of air power in a carpet bombing to break a path for COBRA was no more novel than the use of artillery in preparation for a conventional attack. The object of both is to pound the path of advance, to kill or demoralize the enemy and force him down under cover. Air bombing, we calculated, would either destroy or stun the enemy in the carpet. Originally Hart had argued against our proposal to use strategic air, preferring instead to break a hole in the line with his guns. Had he ten times the number of guns with which he was to support the breakout, I would probably have sided with him. But it would have been impossible for Hart to saturate the carpet with the intensity that I wanted, for there were neither guns nor ammunition enough for the task. With strategic air in addition to our guns, we could so pulverize the enemy that he could neither take cover nor reinforce that stricken front.

As early as 1939, while some of our contemporaries in the army cherished the illusion that defense had outstripped offense, Bedell Smith and I had argued that the Luftwaffe could break a path through the Maginot Line by thoroughly drenching a narrow strip with bombs through those fortifications. However, this drenching had not been attempted until 1943 when General Anderson massed four divisions on a two-division front in North Africa and with the support of 2,600 tactical air sorties cut a swath to Tunis.

Strategic air was first marshaled in strength against a tactical objective when on March 15, 1944, Mark Clark employed 503 heavy bombers against Monte Cassino. But there Clark sought to take an objective rather than break a path by pulverizing it with air. Not only did that bombing fail to destroy enemy resistance on the position but the reports that reached us in England on accidental spillage within the Allied lines tended to discourage field employment of strategic air power against tactical objectives. Even the carpet bombing at Cherbourg was not notably effective but there we had limited the strike to medium and fighter bombers.

Monty's assault on Caen had provided us the most convincing demonstration on the use of strategic air power in a tactical offensive. But there, too, he had experienced trouble. For the RAF had so completely demolished his path with heavy bombs that Monty's tanks could not get past the craters until bulldozers filled them in.

For several weeks prior to planning COBRA I had been hunting for an enemy concentration where strategic air might be used to wipe out a division. It was while searching for this target that this thought occurred to me one day: Why not combine this mission with the breakout, first smash a division from the air, and then tramp right on through it.

By July 18, Army planning for COBRA had been completed and Montgomery approved the scheme. The following day I flew to Leigh-Mallory's headquarters near London to tie in with strategic air. Hansen had called IX Tac to borrow a C-47 for the cross-channel flight but was turned down by Operations. Rather than pull rank in an appeal to Quesada, I boarded a patched-up C-78 that had been scrounged several weeks before in England by Courtney Hodges' aide. It was a twin-motored ship with a fabric-covered frame that seated four in addition to the pilot. A primary trainer for multiple-engined craft, the plane was known to airmen as a "double-breasted cub with a built-in head wind." I buckled in as copilot with a parachute and Mae West while Hansen sat in the rear with

two of the aluminum tubes that contained our plans and maps for
COBRA. The third I wedged between my knees.

We made landfall over Selby Point and a half hour later skirted
the yard at Harrow to settle on Northholt Field. Brereton had
turned out to greet me with "Mary" Coningham of the RAF. They
looked quizzically on the C-78 as we taxied up to the apron.

Several weeks later Tooey Spaatz assigned me a new C-47 with
a permanent crew from the Troop Carrier Command in England.
Named the *Mary Q* for my wife, this plane remained with me
throughout the war and for several years thereafter until in 1948
it was reassigned for less strenuous duties at West Point. The pilot,
Major Alvin E. Robinson of San Antonio, a former navy pharmacist's
mate and a skilled radio ham, is still with me. I have never flown
with a pilot in whose judgment and skill I have more confidence.

Leigh-Mallory's CP was located at Stanmore, in a neglected man-
sion that overlooked an equally neglected garden and beyond it the
spires of Harrow. In addition to Tedder and Spaatz, Leigh-Mallory
had assembled RAF and U. S. commanders of the strategic and
tactical air commands. At odds among the trimly uniformed airmen
was one tweedy civilian, Solly Zuckerman, bomb expert for the
RAF. It was Zuckerman with whom Spaatz had clashed in the showdown on priority of strategic targets that previous spring. While
Zuckerman urged that the blow be concentrated against rail communications, Spaatz favored a campaign that would knock out the
enemy's petroleum industry, both to limit his air effort and to strain
him on the ground. Tooey's foresight was to be vindicated on the
ground during the Battle of the Bulge when von Rundstedt's panzers
stalled in the Ardennes for lack of gas.

At Leigh-Mallory's invitation, I ran swiftly through our plans for
COBRA, emphasizing our choice of the Périers road as a ground
marker that might guide the heavy bombers to their target. If the
strike were to be made in the morning, air could come in to the
target out of the sun and follow the road west toward Périers. But
if weather were to delay the bombers until late afternoon, air could
just as easily reverse its path and come in from the sun in the west
toward St.-Lô. In either event, the Périers road would furnish the
bombers a flank guide to help air avoid bombing in error American
forces on the upper side of the road. To provide an additional
cushion for safety, Collins' troops were to be withdrawn 1,500 yards
behind this Périers road on the leading edge of the carpet. Manton

Eddy had balked initially at this order to withdraw. After having fought hard for that mile he disliked giving it up with the prospect of having to fight once more to regain it. But I was unwilling to chance a bombing any closer to our lines.

I insisted at the outset, moreover, that air limit its drop to 100-pound fragmentation bombs. Not only would these smaller bombs insure greater density in the carpet but by using them we would avoid the craters that had hampered Monty's advance into Caen. This restriction automatically excluded the RAF from COBRA; their bays were not rigged for such small bombs.

Air's enthusiasm for COBRA almost exceeded that of our troops on the ground, for air welcomed the St.-Lô carpet attack as an unrivaled opportunity to test the feasibility of saturation bombing. Leigh-Mallory proposed a heavier concentration of bombers than the Allies had ever before put into the air. Indeed when he learned of the necessity for excluding the RAF, he was badly disappointed even though he agreed with me on the disadvantages of excessive cratering.

That afternoon when we left Northholt for the return trip to France in Brereton's C-47, I carried air's commitment for a far heavier blitz than I had dared dream of. So skeptical was Collins of this pledge when I told him of it that he confessed afterward he thought I might have been exaggerating the total. For we were to get 1,500 heavy bombers, 396 mediums, and another 350 fighter bombers, altogether a total of 2,246 aircraft for five square miles of Normandy hedgerow.

Each of the 1,500 Liberators and Forts was to carry 40 100-pound bombs, enough to pepper the carpet with 60,000 craters. The battle for COBRA was to start with a 20-minute attack by 350 fighter bombers along a narrow strip on the Périers road. The heavies were then to come in on their tails at 8,000 feet for an hour's drenching of the carpet. When the last box of heavies had dropped its sticks, Collins was to lunge forward with three shock divisions supported by more than 1,000 guns. As Collins advanced to the Périers road, 350 fighter bombers were again to rake the narrow strip on the carpet's leading edge. Once the fighters cleared that congested front, the mediums were to swarm in and hit the back edge of the carpet in a 45-minute attack.

While the airmen in England labored over their slide rules for the split-second timing required in this long parade of bombers over the carpet, a tank sergeant fashioned from the scrap steel of an enemy roadblock the device that was at last to give our tanks an upper hand in the bocage.

The invention came on the eve of its greatest need. For the hedge-rows that had frustrated our tanks in Normandy extended not only through the carpet but beyond it into the path of our blitz. If COBRA were to go, it was essential the armor break free and not be slowed down in the bocage. Previous attempts to force the Nor-mandy hedgerows had failed when our Shermans bellied up over the tops of those mounds instead of crashing through them. There they exposed their soft undersides to the enemy while their own guns pointed helplessly toward the sky.

Less than a week before the planned jump-off, Gerow telephoned early one morning to ask if I could meet him at the 2d Division. "Bring your ordnance officer along," he said, "we've got something that will knock your eyes out."

I found Gerow with several of his staff clustered about a light tank to which a crossbar had been welded. Four tusklike prongs protruded from it. The tank backed off and ran head-on toward a hedgerow at ten miles an hour. Its tusks bored into the wall, pinned down the belly, and the tank broke through under a canopy of dirt. A Sherman similarly equipped duplicated the performance. It, too, crashed into the wall, but instead of bellying skyward, it pushed on through. So absurdly simple that it had baffled an army for more than five weeks, the tusklike device had been fashioned by Curtis G. Culin, Jr., a 29-year-old sergeant from New York City.

Medaris sped back to the CP where he ordered every ordnance unit in the army on round-the-clock production of those antihedge-row devices. Scrap metal for the tank tusks came from Rommel's underwater obstacles on the beaches. Later that afternoon Medaris jumped a plane for England and conscripted the depots there. At six that evening the units in France discovered that more arc-welding equipment would be needed and by eight a plane was en route to England. Trucks were waiting at the airstrip when it returned before breakfast the next morning. Within a week, three out of every five tanks in the breakout had been equipped with the device. For his invention Culin was awarded the Legion of Merit by corps. Four months later he went home to New York after having left a leg in Huertgen Forest.

The COBRA attack had been timed for a July 21 jump-off. The day before, however, an overcast socked in the beachhead and weather forecast more rain. But so eager was Eisenhower to get across for a fill-in on our plans that he slipped through the soup in a B-25. His was the only plane we saw in the air that day.

"You're going to break your neck running around in a B-25 on a day like this," I told him.

Ike snuffed out his cigarette; a tired smile creased his face. "That's one of the privileges that goes with my job," he said, "no one over here can ground me."

But in returning to the airstrip later that afternoon, he scowled disconsolately at the sky. "When I die," Ike told Hansen, "they ought to hold my body for a rainy day and then bury me out in the middle of a storm. This damned weather is going to be the death of me yet."

At midnight that evening AEAF* telephoned from England to report that COBRA would have to be postponed from July 21 to await a more favorable turn in the weather.

Meanwhile the enemy was showing an alarming interest in the point we had chosen for breakout. Two panzer divisions left Monty at Caen and shifted over to our U. S. front. This swelled the German crust before us to nine numbered divisions. But these numbers by now meant little, for the enemy was improvising as best he could with remnants and ragtail pieces.

Five panzer divisions remained in front of Monty where we hoped he would contain them until after the attack. By now, however, the enemy was struggling to extricate those tanks as a reserve and supplant them with infantry as fresh divisions rolled in. In spite of Allied air attack and his critical lack of transportation, the German had shown an astonishing capacity for recuperation. He had increased his 58 divisions in the west on D day to 65. Yet even this remarkable build-up could not conceal the growing seriousness of his position. Although Rommel still talked of smashing the Allied beachhead, it was clear that he spoke primarily for German morale. Von Rundstedt had already been sacked as the goat on the invasion and had been replaced as C-in-C West by Field Marshal Gunther von Kluge, a frosty *Junker*. Von Kluge had scarcely taken over when COBRA struck him. Once again, von Rundstedt was spared defeat by a timely relief; it had happened before, outside Moscow in 1941.

*Allied Expeditionary Air Forces.

While the enemy's Seventh Army, overworked and understrength, struggled to pin us down in the beachhead during July and August, the German High Command declined to reinforce it with troops from the Pas de Calais. There for seven decisive weeks, the Fifteenth Army waited for an invasion that never came, convinced beyond all reasonable doubt that Patton would lead the *main* Allied assault across that narrow neck of the Channel. Thus while von Kluge was being defeated in the Battle for France, fewer than 100 miles away the enemy immobilized 19 divisions and played directly into our hands on the biggest single hoax of the war.

It was not only air power and Allied mobility that defeated the enemy in France. Neither could have brought so decisive a victory had not the German General Staff wasted its Fifteenth Army in this major military blunder.

In the life-and-death race for build-up during the first two weeks ashore, we had counted heaviest on two important factors to overcome the enemy's advantage: First, air was to seal off the lodgment and slow down enemy reinforcement; second, a cover plan was to pin him down in the Pas de Calais while we defeated his Normandy forces in detail. The cover plan involved a monumental scheme of deception. It had been built around known enemy agents, phony radio nets, and a mock-up invasion fleet. Its objective was to delude the enemy into believing that we had collected a full-scale Army Group on the east coast of England for a *main* Channel assault through the Pas de Calais. Dummy headquarters for this fictitious assault was to be the 1st U. S. Army Group. George Patton whose arrival had been freely publicized in England posed as the "assault" army commander of that Army Group.

While British intelligence fed enemy agents in England what we wanted them to believe on this fictitious assault, we established a radio net to simulate the traffic of an Army Group prepping for a Channel assault. In the estuary of the Thames and along the east coast of Britain, engineers fabricated make-believe craft whose only function was to show up well in the air photos of enemy recce. And during the preinvasion bombing of the Channel coast, air saturated the enemy's defenses on the Pas de Calais no less heavily than they did those on the Normandy shore.

In devising this OVERLORD cover plan, we had hoped for no more than a modest delay, a ·week or two at the most, until we hustled sufficient divisions ashore to secure the Normandy landing.

For we had assumed that the enemy would quickly see through our hoax once he calculated the strength of those Normandy landings. But so certain was the enemy of our intentions that by the end of June he still sat on the Pas de Calais, convinced that he had outfoxed us. As we expanded this Normandy beachhead, the enemy denuded Brittany of almost all but its fortress troops to help hold the Normandy front. He ransacked southern France despite the growing threat of ANVIL. He thinned Norway and stripped Denmark in his quest for troops. Yet through it all, 19 divisions waited idly on the bluffs of Pas de Calais.

When in July we made ready to move 1st Army Group headquarters to France for commitment, it became necessary for us to rename the Group lest our hoax be exposed. As a result the 1st Army Group was renamed the 12th and when the 12th sailed for France, the mythical 1st remained behind in England as part of the cover plan.

To head this fictitious Army Group we required a real commander who would lend authenticity to the pose. An appeal to the War Department brought General McNair in the dual role of an observer and decoy commander. By now McNair had almost completed his task in the expansion and training of the stateside army.

Even now I cannot understand why the enemy believed for so long in so transparent a hoax. For once we had landed in Normandy, only a fool could have thought us capable of duplicating so gigantic an effort elsewhere. I can only conclude that the enemy thought us enormously more powerful than we were.

After dinner on the evening of July 20 I rode up the Colombières road to the farmhouse where First Army billeted its newsmen. P & PW* had asked that I give them a preview on the scheme of the coming attack. After grousing through two dull weeks in the Carentan marshes, the newsmen had brightened slightly on July 18 when Corlett finally broke through the last few miles to take the mound of rubble that once was St.-Lô. The correspondents listened quietly to the outline of our plan, craned their necks as I pointed to the carpet, and shook their heads as I tallied the air strength that had been assigned to us. At the close of the briefing one of the newsmen asked if we would forewarn the French living within bounds of the carpet. I shook my head as if to escape the necessity for saying no. If we were to tip our hand to the French, we would also show it

*Publicity and Psychological Warfare.

to the German. The enemy might then move out, leaving us to bomb vacant fields while he collected reserves for a counterattack. The success of COBRA hung upon surprise; it was essential we have surprise even if it meant the slaughter of innocents as well.

Another correspondent pointed good-naturedly to Coutances on the map, 16 miles southwest of St.-Lô.

"How soon do you expect to get there *this time?*" he asked.

I winced at the reference to Middleton's attack and chose to take a flyer. "I'd guess 48 hours."

My questioner looked up startled from the notes he had scribbled. "Forty-eight hours for 16 miles?" I nodded though with a twinge of apprehension, remembering that during the last two weeks we had seldom advanced more than 500 yards a day.

One week later I was told I had failed in my guess by 7 hours and 4,000 yards.

On Sunday morning, July 23, we awakened, as we had for three days before, to a gray and misty sky. By now I had grown edgy, fearful of a leak or a hunch on the part of the German command. "Dammit," I called to Kean, "I'm going to have to court-martial the chaplain if we have many more days like this."

It was either the Sabbath or my ultimatum that appeared to turn the trick, for late that evening Stanmore radioed a promise of clear skies for bombing at noon the next day. Collins alerted his divisions and an imperceptible shudder ran through our U. S. front.

Despite air's prediction of clear weather on Monday, the morning dawned wet and cloudy. With Quesada and Thorson I sped off by jeep for a last-minute checkup with Collins. I had planned to remain there with him during the bombing and the first critical hours of the attack.

By 11:30 a heavy cloud cover still obscured the target. At 11:40, just 20 minutes before H hour for the heavy bombers, a radio signal instructed them to turn back over the Channel. The attack was to be postponed 24 hours more.

It was not until I had returned to my Army CP that I was told a box of heavies had crossed the coast and tripped its bombs through the cloud cover on the target. They had fallen short on the 30th Division, more than a mile behind the carpet.

"*Short?*" I cried, "but how could they? These bombers were to come in on the Périers road parallel to our lines."

"That's not the way they came in, sir," G-3 replied, "they came in on a perpendicular course."

Leigh-Mallory arrived at the CP a few minutes after. Although the casualty count had not yet come in, he was as distressed as I over the accidental bombing.

"But what worries me more than anything else," I told him, "is the fact that those heavies came in *over* our heads instead of parallel to the Périers road. I left Stanmore with a clear understanding they would fly parallel to that road."

Leigh-Mallory could not confirm the agreement, for he had been called out of the conference at Stanmore before it ended.

"If they're to come on a perpendicular course," I said, "we're taking a helluva chance—much more than I want to take with only a mile between my front lines and the target."

He promised to check immediately with the Eighth Air Force on the direction of air attack.

It was not until 11:30 that evening that Leigh-Mallory called back. I had been waiting impatiently for the phone to ring in the cramped cabin of my blacked-out truck, counting the hours on a Signal Corps clock that hung over my bunk.

"I've checked this thing with the Eighth," the Air Marshal said, "and they tell me the course they flew today was not accidental. They're planning to make it a perpendicular approach over the heads of your troops."

"But why," I asked, "when they specifically promised us they would fly parallel to the Périers road? That road was one of the reasons we picked this spot for the breakout."

The planners, Leigh-Mallory replied, had indicated it would take better than two and one-half hours to funnel 1,500 heavy bombers down a narrow path parallel to the Périers road.

"If you insist on that approach," he added, "they tell me they can't make the attack tomorrow." Only a few hours remained before those bomber crews were to be briefed for an early morning take-off.

I was shocked and angered by air's reply, for to me it represented a serious breach of good faith in planning. Five days before when I left Stanmore it was with the understanding that air would follow the Périers road. Had I known of air's intent to chance the perpendicular approach, I would never have consented to its plan. For I was unwilling to risk a corps to the split-second timing required in an overhead drop of 60,000 bombs from 8,000 feet.

Annoyed though I was by this duplicity on the part of the air planners, I had no choice but to consent to the attack or delay it indefinitely. But we had already tipped our hand and could not delay much longer without giving our intentions away.

"Shall I tell them to go ahead in the morning?" Leigh-Mallory asked.

"We've got no choice," I said, "the Boche will build up out front if we don't get this thing off soon. But we're still taking an awful chance. Another short drop could ruin us."

I paused for a moment.

"Let it go that way. We'll be ready to go in the morning."

When I told Quesada of this change in the air plan, he looked no less startled than I. And when the first reports of the vertical approach came in, he refused to believe them. But when several witnesses verified those reports, Quesada radioed Brereton for an explanation.

Brereton did not mince his reply. Yes, that was the plan, he said, and Bradley had been told of it.

Brereton must have been misinformed by his staff. I knew nothing of the change until Leigh-Mallory called, 11 hours after the first bombing. Had I heard of it, I would have pulled my troops farther back.

All morning long on July 25 the air throbbed with heavy bombers while I fidgeted in Collins' CP within easy reach of the telephone. Once again Eisenhower had come across the Channel to be with us on the breakout. After three days of postponement and the previous day's bad bombing, our nerves were tight and stringy.

The thunder had scarcely rolled away when casualty reports began trickling in.

Thorson handed me a TWX. "They've done it again," he said.

"Oh Christ," I cried, "not another short drop?"

He nodded and sifted the messages he still held in his hand. Air had hit the 9th and 30th Divisions a punishing blow. Both units had been rocked off balance and as the bombers floated serenely away, reserves were rushed into the gaps.

Later that afternoon Collins called to report that McNair had been killed in the short bombing. As in Tunisia where he had been seriously wounded while probing about the front, McNair had joined a battalion in the attack to view the results of stateside training. A direct hit on his foxhole had killed him.

For fear news of McNair's death might embarrass our cover plan on the Pas de Calais, we buried him secretly two days later with only senior officers in attendance. The news was suppressed by censorship until a successor could be picked and rushed over to take McNair's place as "commander" of the fictional Army Group.

When Eisenhower took off for England that evening, the fate of COBRA still hung in doubt. Several hundred U. S. troops had been killed and wounded in the air bombing. It had dislocated Collins' advance and there was little reason to believe we stood at the brink of a breakthrough. Rather, the attack looked as though it might have failed.

In a press conference two days later Brereton was to declare that COBRA owed its slow start to the sluggish getaway of our troops on the ground. He neglected to add that the delay had been caused by the removal of those American dead and wounded air had strewn in our way.

Dismayed as I was, Ike was even more dejected. En route to the airstrip that evening with Captain Joseph J. Ryan of New York City, Kean's irrepressible aide, Eisenhower declared that he would no longer employ heavy bombers against tactical targets.

"I don't believe they can be used in support of ground forces," he explained. "That's a job for artillery. I gave them a green light this time. But I promise you it's the last."

It was to be the last until we required another in the winter battles. For although COBRA might have looked like a failure on the evening of July 25, it had struck a more deadly blow than any of us dared imagine.

18: *Encirclement of a German Army*

A S COLLINS STRUGGLED TOWARD THE BOMB-PITTED carpet at St.-Lô on that jittery afternoon of July 25, he broke path for an Army now grown to 21 U. S. divisions. It was as large a force as we dared hitch to a single Army command. For with half again as many divisions as that prescribed in textbooks for a field Army, we had begun to stretch the maintenance and overhead services of First Army.

Earlier in July, Eisenhower had given me authority to split our U. S. forces on the Continent into two field Armies whenever I thought it desirable. I would then relinquish First Army to Hodges and step up to full-time command of the 12th U. S. Army Group. With this shuffle, Monty would surrender his temporary role as Allied ground commander and revert to 21st Group as commander of the British Armies. Thereafter, as dual Army Group commanders, we would report on equal footing to SHAEF.

Initially the limited size of our beachhead militated against this division of American forces into two field Armies. The split would only have aggravated an existing congestion in service units on the beachhead. I had not asked to be freed from Montgomery's British Group command. He had neither limited our authority nor had he given us directives that might have caused us to chafe. As long as Montgomery permitted this latitude in U. S. operations, we were content to remain under his command until the tactical situation necessitated a change.

When Ike flew across for our conference on COBRA, July 20, he looked anxiously on the divisional tabs that now crowded the First Army war map and asked when we planned to bring Group into the picture. Twelfth Army Group headquarters had come ashore and had gone into bivouac on a stand-by order to await commitment of a second U. S. Army. Meanwhile high up in the Cotentin Peninsula behind Middleton's VIII Corps, Patton had located his Third Army CP after a secret move from England. With him there were three corps headquarters awaiting the assignment of troops and commitment with Third Army.

Despite Patton's eagerness to aid us on the COBRA attack, for ease in control I was anxious to restrict it to First Army—at least until after the spearhead divisions had shaken themselves free in the breakout. For as Collins split the German line with a column aimed toward the coast in hopes of pocketing the enemy in the Cotentin neck, Middleton was to smash down the Coutances road and join up with Collins at that intersection. Middleton would then speed on to Avranches and turn into Brittany at the corner. Where VII and VIII Corps converged we anticipated a traffic jam until those columns could be unscrambled and new boundaries assigned them. To speed the advance we were to reorganize on the run without slackening our momentum. I assured Ike we could more easily unscramble a jam alone from the First Army CP than we could in conference between two Armies at an Army Group CP. Once we got safely past that hurdle where simplicity and seconds counted, then we could more easily divide First Army's troops with Patton and at the same time open another echelon in the U. S. chain of command.

"Do you want to set a date for the switch-over?" Ike had asked, leaving the choice to me.

I suggested August 1. That would give me at least a week of fingertip control from First Army immediately after the breakout.

"Fine," he said, "we'll count on August 1."

But even after our U. S. Army Group entered the chain of command, Eisenhower was not yet ready to cut us free from Montgomery at 21st Group. While SHAEF remained in England, Eisenhower could not function as day-to-day commander of ground forces in France. It was for this reason that Monty had been named Eisenhower's deputy for the invasion. Now with the commitment of our U. S. Army Group on an equal footing with that of Monty's, it was anticipated that Eisenhower would take over as *the* ground commander and assume direct responsibility for coordination between the two. Yet the exercise of that direct command from across the Channel involved a risk in communications. If Eisenhower were urgently needed in France for a decision he might find himself grounded in England by weather. Once SHAEF crossed to the beachhead that problem would be eliminated, but we had not yet uncovered a city that would house the activities of SHAEF. Therefore, until SHAEF was permanently established in France, Eisenhower directed that Monty would act as his agent, exercising *temporary* operational control over the U. S. Army Group. The Briton's authority would be limited primarily to coordination and the settlement of boundaries between our Groups. Despite this delegation of powers to Monty, Eisenhower would captain the team.

Although this improvisation did not immediately provide the Group the autonomy we had been promised in England, I did not object to it. After having granted me so free a hand as an Army commander, there was no reason to believe that Monty would now curtail me at Army Group.

SHAEF censored the news of this change-over in the Allied command until August 14, when an AP reporter eluded the restriction and filed a story which said that 12th U. S. Army Group had been granted coequal status with that of Monty's command. It was a harmless story that erred only in anticipating by two weeks the full parity that was to come our way once Eisenhower crossed to France. Yet the report instantly caused a ruckus in England where U. S. parity in command with Monty's 21st Army Group was viewed by some as a deliberate affront to Britain's war hero. Knowing nothing of the original OVERLORD agreement for Anglo-American parity in Army Group command, the British press alleged that Montgomery had been slurred, that his ground command had been undermined by a U. S. bid for "equality." Some writers denounced it as a "demotion" for Monty and a rebuke to the British people. So misinformed were these editorial comments that I favored a full and prompt explanation of the Anglo-American chain of command.

U. S. equality in command with Monty's 21st Army Group had been agreed to in England, months before invasion as part of the OVERLORD plan. At no time was there ever any intention of continuing Montgomery as Eisenhower's deputy for the ground. Had any such arrangement been proposed, I would have vigorously opposed it. For inasmuch as the United States was to provide two thirds of the Continental ground forces, I could see no justification for blanketing us under British field command.

Eisenhower was irritated by the premature disclosure primarily because the angry British press reaction jeopardized the amity he had cultivated so avidly among the Allied forces. But had he met the issue head-on with an announcement of his plan to provide equality for both the British and American field commands, he might have avoided this ridiculous fission. Possibly for fear of offending the British he withheld the explanation.

Eventually, on August 31, 12th Army Group was pulled out from under Montgomery's command and SHAEF granted coequal status to the British and American Groups. General Montgomery's promotion to the rank of field marshal was timed to coincide with the announcement.

Although we remained aloof from this British press fracas, I was puzzled as to why Monty did not squelch it. He could have easily enlightened the British newsmen in an off-the-record explanation of our OVERLORD plans for ground command. At the risk of being unjust to Monty, I could only conclude that he did not wish to.

British prestige had suffered by the middle of August as a result of our glittering U. S. advance. For while we sped around the rim of enemy resistance toward Paris, 21st Group fought in its assigned corner near Caen, accomplishing the task that had been allotted it in the OVERLORD scheme of maneuver. But the comfort to be gained by the knowledge that Montgomery was fulfilling his mission did not satisfy the British hunger for leadership in the ground campaign. Because of their shortage in manpower, the British bid for face in the European campaign depended largely upon Montgomery's retention of his role as an Allied ground commander. While Monty commanded all Allied ground troops, even those of the United States could be properly labeled "Montgomery's forces" for whatever the reference might be worth to the British in prestige. When Third Army monopolized the headlines for a month after the breakout, even First Army became infected with this frustration that afflicted the British. For it, too, was limited by its mission to a less spectacular campaign.

That unfortunate August split never completely healed. It persisted throughout the winter war in a subtle whispering campaign that favored Monty's restoration to over-all ground command. And eventually it came to a head during the Battle of the Bulge when

Montgomery protagonists declared von Rundstedt's breakthrough might have been avoided had Eisenhower echeloned his Army Groups into a single ground command. Those might-have-beens, however, are refuted by the record, for on the eve of von Rundstedt's offensive, Montgomery unwittingly admitted that he was no more occult than the others of us.

Although once again Montgomery could have curbed these backers, he carefully ignored them. Indeed he even intimated during that phase of the campaign from the Seine to the Reich that if ground command were vested in him, he would shorten the span of the war. Monty thought SHAEF too distantly removed from the shooting to direct the day-to-day campaigns of three independent Army Groups. He would remedy the situation and relieve SHAEF of its labors by creating a super ground command to be headed by him as an additional echelon between Eisenhower and the Army Groups.

Because of this attitude, Monty lent substance to the canard that Eisenhower functioned in Europe primarily as a political commander, unfamiliar with the everyday problems of our tactical war. The inference was grossly unfair, for Eisenhower showed himself to be a superb tactician with a sensitive and intimate feel of the front. With Bedell Smith to shoulder a generous share of his administrative duties, Eisenhower directed his major effort to operations in the field. His tactical talents had been demonstrated years before at Leavenworth where he finished at the head of his class in 1926. It is at Leavenworth that the army's most promising officers are schooled in the tactics and logistics of senior commands.

Because Ike's tactical labors were largely confined to private conversations with the Army Group commanders, only Montgomery, Devers, and I could attest to his rare astuteness in this role as field commander. Quite often the working level at SHAEF G-3 was unaware of the issues involved in these private discussions. And similarly the officers of my G-3 staff were cut off from these conversations. After October Eisenhower and I were in almost daily touch by phone and he was fully informed on my every move at Group. Quite frequently our long-range plans evolved during late night conversations at Ike's CP or mine. Sometimes we would sit until two or three in the morning, swapping opinions and discussing plans for successive phases of the campaign. For this reason, historians may find it difficult to ascribe to any individual commander his views or credits for key tactical decisions. Eisenhower contributed more than he benefited from these exchanges; I need not belittle Montgomery nor deny him any of his luster to rate Eisenhower his superior as a field commander.

During the winter campaign Eisenhower was astonished to learn that Montgomery aspired to over-all command of the Allied ground forces. At the same time Monty did not wish to surrender his Army Group command to become Eisenhower's deputy for the ground at SHAEF. He would retain 21st Army Group, and take on the dual role of super ground force commander as an added function.

"Monty," Ike said in exasperation, "wants to have his cake and eat it too."

Patton had crossed the Channel to France on July 6 with the vanguard of Third Army headquarters. He traveled under tight security wraps, for had the enemy learned of his prospective employment on the heels of the breakout, the hoax we had cultivated on the Pas de Calais would have been given away. We assigned George a bivouac in the Cotentin where he was to await commitment under 12th Army Group on August 1—a week after First Army's breakout.

My own feelings on George were mixed. He had not been my choice for Army commander and I was still wary of the grace with which he would accept our reversal in roles. For George was six years my senior and had been my Army commander when I fought II Corps in the Sicilian campaign. I was apprehensive in having George join my command, for I feared that too much of my time would probably be spent in curbing his impetuous habits. But at the same time I knew that with Patton there would be no need for my whipping Third Army to keep it on the move. We had only to keep him pointed in the direction we wanted to go.

George soon caused me to repent these uncharitable reservations, for he not only bore me no ill will but he trooped for 12th Army Group with unbounded loyalty and eagerness. Shortly after the war an officer from Third Army recalled the rancor with which Patton had frequently excoriated his senior commanders. "And yet in all those outbursts," he said, "I never heard the General speak an unkind word of you."

Before many more months had passed, the *new* Patton had totally obliterated my unwarranted apprehensions; we formed as amiable and contented a team as existed in the senior command. No longer the martinet that had sometimes strutted in Sicily, George had now become a judicious, reasonable, and likable commander.

Several months later when George outlined a prospective scheme of maneuver, I showed him several faults in it. Instead of replying huffily as he might have a year before, George merely crinkled his eyes and chuckled. "You're right, Brad," he said, "goddamnit, you're always right."

The reformation, however, was not totally complete, for George was still an impetuous man and even in Europe this impetuous nature continued to make trouble. The first misstep occurred after only 12 days on the beachhead while Third Army was biding its time impatiently in the Cotentin.

Once the COBRA plan was completed, I briefed Patton on it since he was to join the operation once it got under way. On July 18, two days before we were to brief the First Army newsmen, Dickson came to me red-faced with anger.

"We've heard from our correspondents, General," he said, "that Patton has briefed the press at Third Army on COBRA."

"I'll be damned," I said and reached for the phone. But George was not in.

Patton called back that evening with an apology and an explanation. Yes, he had briefed his *staff* on First Army's plan for the breakout but the press was not cut in. His PRO had leaked the plan to the newsmen.

"I'll can him," he promised, "you can bet your life I'll can him— just as soon as we find another." I hung up. George was too contrite for me to argue further. Eventually he did relieve that PRO but for other reasons.

Two days later on July 20 we were cheered by the news that there had been an attempt on Hitler's life. Indeed Churchill spoke for all of us when he was reported to have said, "They missed the old bastard—but there's time yet." Most encouraging from our point of view was the sign that exasperation had driven a clique within the German army into a plot to save the Reich through assassination of its Fuehrer. For several days we waited for the telltale signs of internal crack-up but because the attempt miscarried the opportunity passed. Few of us anticipated the ruthlessness with which Himmler was to clean house in his endeavor to avoid a repetition of the attempt.

Several times later during the European campaign, I wondered why German commanders in the field did not give up their senseless resistance. Prolonged resistance could do nothing but aggravate the disaster that had already claimed the Reich. George Patton offered an answer when he visited Army Group early in August just as we tightened our noose around the German Seventh Army.

"The Germans are either crazy, or they don't know what's going on," I said. "Surely the professionals must know by now that the jig is up."

George answered by telling the story of a German general that Third Army had captured only several days before. He had been asked by G-2 why he had not surrendered before, if only to spare Germany further destruction.

"I am a professional," he replied without emotion, "and I obey my orders."

Most professionals would have made the same reply. For few soldiers are competent to determine at what point military resistance becomes morally wrong and politically suicidal. Petain was one who ventured judgment; the example was not destined to encourage others.

When news of the attempted assassination of Hitler reached Patton in the Cotentin, he bounded down to our CP at Colombières.

"For God's sake, Brad," George pleaded, "you've got to get me into this fight before the war is over. I'm in the doghouse now and I'm apt to die there unless I pull something spectacular to get me out."

I've often wondered how much this nothing-to-lose attitude prodded Patton in his spectacular race across the face of France. For certainly no other commander could have matched him in reckless haste and boldness. Someday a definitive biography of Patton will go into the issue more exhaustively than I. Until then I shall go on believing that the private whose face he slapped in a Sicilian hospital ward did more to win the war in Europe than any other private in the army.

Only 34 days after he had been committed in the Battle for France, George joined me one day in a plea to Ike that he might retain his allotment of tonnage and thus push on to the German frontier.

"If you don't cut us back we can make it on what we're getting," he said. "I'll stake my reputation on it."

"Careful, George," Ike quipped, "that reputation of yours hasn't been worth very much."

Patton hitched up his belt and smiled. "It's pretty good now," he said.

And if one could judge by the headlines, we agreed that perhaps it was.

Just as soon as Collins reorganized his line where it had been lacerated by our own bombing, and closed the gap in front to the Périers-St.-Lô road, he picked up speed through the smoking carpet. The dejection that had settled over us like a wet fog the day of the jump-off was soon burned off by preliminary reports of the destruction that greeted him there. For though air had pummeled us, it had pulverized the enemy in the carpet to litter the torn fields and roads with the black hulls of burned-out tanks, the mutilated bodies of soldiers, and the carcasses of bloated, stiff-legged cattle. By noon on July 26, a bare 24 hours after the jump-off, we sensed that the initial crisis had passed, and that the time had come for bold exploitation of the breakthrough.

On the evening of July 27, the 1st Division broke into the outskirts of Coutances as Middleton picked his way through the mines that had been planted on his Cotentin front. Because VIII Corps was to become part of Patton's Third Army once the latter was committed, I ordered George to trail Middleton's columns and aid in unscrambling them should they became entangled. When on August 1 we split First Army and turned half of it over to Patton, two armored divisions had already rounded the bend at Avranches into the Brittany corner. The speed of our advance had caught the enemy unawares and he was now hastening to retrieve the situation by shifting his armor from Montgomery's front to ours.

When on August 1, I moved up from First Army to direct the 12th Army Group, I had no qualms in leaving the Army to Hodges, an old crony from trap-shooting days at Benning, who had been picked as my successor six months before. A quiet and methodical commander, he knew his profession well and was recognized in the army as one of our most able trainers of troops. Whereas Patton could seldom be bothered with details, Hodges studied his problems with infinite care and was thus better qualified to execute the more intricate operations. A steady, undramatic, and dependable man with great tenacity and persistence, Hodges became the almost

anonymous inside man who smashed the German Seventh Army
while Patton skirted the end. In his way Hodges was as ideally
suited for that mission as Patton was for his.

Leave-taking from First Army ended a memorable period of the

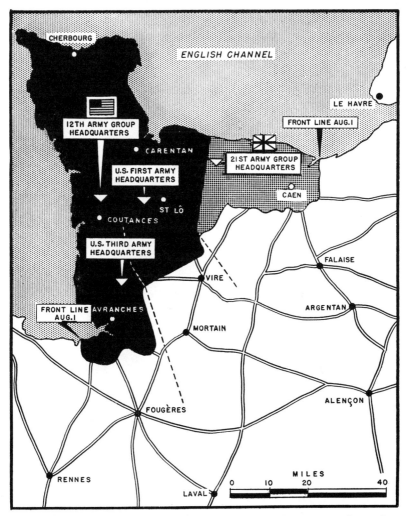

By the time Third Army entered the battle on August 1, six days after
the start of the St.-Lô Breakout, First Army troops had already rounded
the corner past Avranches into Brittany. It was at this point that 12th
Army Group assumed operational control of both U. S. Armies.

war. Most of that Army staff had traveled the long road with me from Tunisia to France. To it I owed much of the good fortune that had attended those campaigns. But because Group, unlike Army, existed as a planning or supervisory unit without logistical operations, there was no place in it for the functional skills of First Army's special staff. And because Group had been delivered to me with a ready-made general staff largely recruited by Devers, there was no need to pad it with imports from the general staff of First Army. But since many of our problems at Group would revolve around the selection of commanders and the procurement of adequate replacements, I did pirate O'Hare for my Army Group G-1. No one knew his way through more official back doors or could run a more efficient shop than Red O'Hare.

When Courtney consented to the transfer of O'Hare, he pulled on his cigarette holder, looked up with a twinkle, and asked, "Anyone else?" I had already arranged to take both Hansen and Bridge.

"One more," I began and Courtney flinched, for he was fearful of losing Bill Kean.

"Any objection to my taking Sergeant Dudley?"

Courtney relaxed. "Now that we're down to sergeants, may I assume that my colonels are safe?"

"They are. Dudley's the last request."

"Well, you found him," Hodges replied, "so I guess we'll have to let him go."

A Manhattan printing executive at the age of 35, Sergeant Richard M. Dudley of Scarsdale, New York, joined our headquarters in Bristol to run the Holmes. We had discovered him there in an MP battalion. In France he soon became one of the war's most resourceful scroungers and his mess achieved an embarrassing fame. As our comforts multiplied, I questioned Dudley on the elegance of this life in the field. "General," he replied in his impatient manner, "you fight the war and I'll worry about your standard of living." Dudley declined a commission until the end of the war when he accepted one shortly before discharge. "It might have knocked me out of my job," he later explained to O'Hare.

In contrast to our primitive quartering at First Army, 12th Army Group had established itself in a camouflaged tent city on a handsome estate a few miles north of Coutances. At first I was alarmed by the enormous spread of that installation. Fearing that the front might easily outrun us, I ordered Major General Lev Allen, the

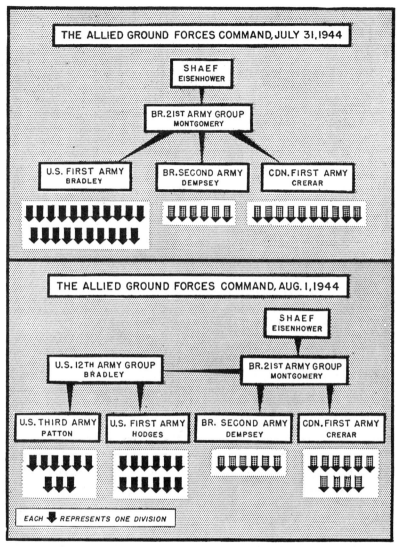

With the change-over in command on August 1, 12th Army Group stepped in over the First and Third Armies. Meanwhile, First Army's 21 divisions were split between the two. For the time being, however, 12th Army Group was to report to SHAEF through Montgomery's command.

Group chief of staff, to put together a tactical headquarters that could race ahead with the Armies. This capsule headquarters was dubbed EAGLE TAC: EAGLE for the code name of 12th Army Group, TAC to distinguish it from the remainder of the headquarters at MAIN and REAR. Except for the essential signal and housekeeping services, EAGLE TAC confined itself to skeletonized G-2, G-3, G-4, and engineering sections. Most of it was mounted in vans for quick and speedy displacement. Altogether EAGLE TAC comprised 65 officers and approximately twice as many enlisted men at the time it started out. Like all headquarters, however, it mushroomed and despite O'Hare's efforts to pare it down, within three months EAGLE TAC had almost doubled in size. But even this swollen TAC headquarters provided an agile base of operations. In contrast to the bewildering complexity of most senior commands in Europe, EAGLE TAC retained the neighborliness of a crossroads village, making it a pleasant place in which to live and work. While EAGLE TAC closely followed its Armies, MAIN and REAR followed more slowly behind it. Until we reassembled the entire headquarters in Wiesbaden at the end of the war, TAC made ten moves forward while MAIN and REAR limited themselves to four.

EAGLE had been picked as the code name of 12th Army Group to designate its seniority in the U. S. chain of command. Standard signal procedure decreed that as commanding general of the Group, I be listed as EAGLE SIX. When Montgomery learned of this designation, he coded 21st Group as LION. To Patton we became The Eagle and The Lion. Other headquarters were no less waggish on their own signal designations. With the vanity that befitted a staff with two campaigns behind it, First Army claimed the code name MASTER. And as if to hex the misfortune that had dogged him in Sicily, Patton name his Third Army LUCKY. When Ninth Army entered the line-up late in August, it acquired the brash code name CONQUER, and SHAEF decided to list itself as SHELLBURST.

As Middleton's VIII Corps carried Patton's colors around the corner at Avranches to head for the Brittany ports, I ordered George to post a strong force on guard in the center of the Brittany neck. There he could stave off any threat from the east while Middleton's columns raced toward St. Malo, first fortress on the Breton north shore. Meanwhile as the rest of the Allied front executed its turning movement toward the Seine, First Army was to hold open a passage at Avranches against the German armor that swarmed hastily toward that point. While visiting Middleton in his CP in the neck on August 2, I found him worried over an exposed left flank and rear. Patton had ignored the Group order to establish a strong force in the Brittany neck and instead had ordered Middleton to race on toward Rennes and Brest. As a result Middleton was left with nothing between his extended columns and the main force of the German Seventh Army to his rear.

Though reluctant to disobey an order given him by his Army commander, Middleton was wary over the likelihood of German counterattack. He pointed to his map. "I hate to attack with so much of the enemy at my rear," he said, "especially while it's so exposed. If the other fellow were to break through at Avranches to the coast, I'd be cut off way out here in Brittany." At that time Middleton had already passed two infantry and two armored divisions through the corner at Avranches. If the enemy were to break through there, he might have marooned a force in excess of 80,000 men.

"Dammit," I said angrily to Middleton, "George seems more interested in making headlines with the capture of Brest than in using his head on tactics. I don't care if we get Brest tomorrow—or ten days later. Once we isolate the Brittany peninsula, we'll get it anyhow. But we can't take a chance on an open flank. That's why I ordered George to block the peninsula neck."

The 79th Division had halted just north of Avranches but at that moment was loading back on the road for its movement into Brittany. I called Patton at his Third Army CP but was told that he was out. Meanwhile Middleton was looking for a way out of his dilemma. "Order the 79th down to Fougères and we'll build up there as George was told to do," I told him. "We can't afford to waste any more time. If the German were to hit us with a couple of divisions on that open flank, we'd all look kinda silly."

Patton had just returned to his CP in a jeep when I drove in later that afternoon. He was stiff and covered with dust after a day on the front. "For God's sake, George," I began, "what are you going to do about this open flank of Troy Middleton's? I just ordered the 79th down there. But I hate to by-pass an Army commander on orders to a corps."

George smiled sheepishly and put his arm around my shoulder. "Fine, fine, Brad," he said, "that's just what I would have done. But enough of that—here, let me show you how we're getting on."

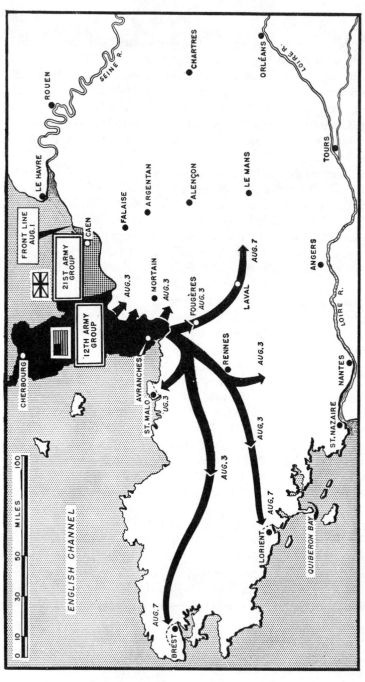

Within a week after entering the battle, Third Army had stabbed toward Brest and Lorient, and east toward the Seine-Orléans gap. Meanwhile, First Army had started to wheel eastward on the massive turning movement pointing toward the Seine.

Bernard Law Montgomery: "A master of the set battle, Montgomery was meticulous in his planning and exacting in his execution of those battle plans. Not only was he an astute tactician, but he was a scholarly soldier, keenly sensitive to logistics, and an inspirational leader of his British troops." (July, 1944.)

Office on Wheels: "On the far end of the map trailer that had been constructed for me in England, ordnance installed a mahogany-paneled office, partitioning it with an 'altar rail.' A telephone mounted on a trolley helped me to follow conversations on the map in any part of this 26-foot trailer."

Brittany derived its strategic importance from the original OVER-LORD assumption that we would be forced to regroup on the Seine and there break a strong German position before pushing on to the Reich. During that halt our lines of communication were to be re-arranged in preparation for stormy Channel weather and the loss of tonnage over the beaches. Cherbourg was to be turned over to Montgomery as a base for British supply while we shifted U. S. logistics to the Brittany ports for convenient unloading of the Atlantic convoys.

Having foreseen that the enemy would destroy Brest before evacuating that port, we planned on developing Quiberon Bay as a logistical base for the U. S. Armies. Quiberon Bay stretched between the ports of Lorient and St. Nazaire. To use it we would have to construct unloading docks. At the same time we would also clear the port of St. Malo on the north for the importation of coal required by the French.

Despite the enemy's drain on Brittany for additional forces to oppose the Normandy landing, the coastal fringe of that peninsula was held by an estimated 50,000 German garrison troops. To prevent them from destroying the railroads and bridges, Patton was to drive them quickly into the fortress areas around the major ports. Thereafter we would smoke them out. Meanwhile in the thinly populated countryside of Brittany, the French *maquis* had become a valuable ally. Nighttime air lift had provided them guns, and even a tiny column of jeeps. With the aid of specially trained Allied detachments that had been parachuted into their hide-outs, the French underground blocked the Brittany roads and drove the Germans into their fortified forts. Meanwhile the enemy had not yet learned the primers of unification among his own forces. When the Wehrmacht commander in Brittany sought to rally a makeshift field force, air and naval garrisons refused to budge from their positions. Hitler had helped create this dissension by ordering all commanders, regardless of the wisdom of such tactics, to hold where they were and above all to yield no ground to the Allies. As a consequence, the enemy was unable to contest our advance but fled instead into his fortified coastal cities. While an infantry division closed in on the rocky port of St. Malo, one armored column sped south toward Nantes. Another raced to the west toward the tip-end fortress of Brest.

On August 6 Patton called me at the Army Group CP to report

that Brest had been taken. I found the report difficult to believe for the enemy did not customarily relinquish so important a prize without a struggle. Patton, however, stood his ground for he had accepted the veracity of the report. It had come, he said, directly from the tank column commander at Brest.

With tongue in cheek, I notified air of Patton's report. The RAF had scheduled a bombing of that port's casemated submarine pens to block the escape of any undersea craft that might still be there. To avoid hitting our own troops, air called the bombing off. Two days later, while seeking confirmation on the report from the column at Brest, we learned that George's call had been premature, for instead of surrendering, the enemy had burrowed into Brest for a siege. Meanwhile the garrisons at Lorient and St. Nazaire had also withdrawn behind their defenses.

Both Lorient and St. Nazaire could be contained until they tired of the siege or ran short on provisions. But Brest would have to be taken if we were to clear the sea lanes that led past it to Quiberon Bay. Eventually three divisions were mounted against Brest in a bitter siege campaign. Not until September 19, 44 days after Patton had reported it taken, did the garrison at Brest surrender its 20,000 troops. By then the siege had taken its toll. Enemy demolitions together with Allied artillery and air had totally destroyed the port.

At Lorient and St. Nazaire the enemy held out until the end of the war. To contain those ports we were forced to sidetrack an entire infantry division. An even greater force would have been required had not the FFI rallied 17 battalions of infantry to assist in pinning down the German. As in Brest, we could have rooted the enemy out, but here it was easier to contain them, for these garrisons were not aggressive like the one at Brest and consequently did not endanger our supply lines.

This costly siege of Brest has since been described by some as a wasteful and unnecessary campaign, executed primarily because of blind obedience to an outdated OVERLORD plan that called for its capture. It is true that OVERLORD's premise on the need for those Brittany ports was invalidated just as soon as our rapid advance uncovered the Channel ports and Antwerp. For with the capture of Antwerp, one of the largest and best ports in the world, we scratched our ambitious plans for the construction of a base on Quiberon Bay and wrote off Brest as surplus. Not a ton was to be delivered through either port.

Why then did we spend three divisions on Brest at a cost of almost 10,000 in American dead and wounded? Why not rope off Brest as we did Lorient and St. Nazaire—or as Montgomery did on the Channel ports? The difference lay in the nature of enemy resistance. For the garrison at Brest was totally unlike those of the other ports. Spiked with troops from the crack 2d Parachute Division, the garrison was commanded by Major General Hermann Ramcke, too aggressive and fanatical a soldier to sit contentedly in that concrete pile. To have contained Ramcke and prevented him from marauding against our lines of supply would have required more troops than we could spare for several months on an inactive front at Brest. Thus the decision to take Brest was not dictated by any outdated OVERLORD plan of maneuver. I went ahead with the costly siege at Brest, with Eisenhower's approval, not because we wanted that port, but because Ramcke left us no other solution. If unable to contain Brest, we had no choice but to take it that we might concentrate our troops on the main front. I cannot agree with those afteraction strategists who now contend that we should have sealed the Brittany peninsula at its neck and pushed eastward with all our remaining strength through the vacuum that had been created in France as a result of the Breakout. To have held a 75-mile gap on the open flank of our main route of supply would have called for many more troops than I could have devoted to the rear if we were to go anywhere on the front.

As Third Army plunged through the provincial villages of Brittany early in August, Churchill suddenly disputed Eisenhower's views on the projected invasion of southern France by Mediterranean forces under the over-all command of General Devers. After an on-again off-again existence the previous winter and spring, the ANVIL invasion had finally been scheduled for August 15. Yet now, as Devers staged his troops in the crowded port of Naples preparatory to an attack on Cannes, Churchill set out to upset Eisenhower's plan with a proposal that the southern landing be abandoned. There was, he asserted, no tactical relationship between southern France and the Normandy front. He calculated moreover that the enemy could probably restrict those forces of Devers to a Riviera beachhead. Divert those troops to Brittany, he argued, where they could be safely landed and there join the Normandy forces. Eisenhower, however, had anticipated that the Brittany ports would probably be blocked by enemy demolitions. For that reason he expected a delay in Brittany tonnage until construction at Quiberon Bay could be completed. But even in the unlikely event Brittany were to produce several usable ports, they would not have solved our fundamental supply problem: how to move the tonnage from those ports to the front. A landing in southern France would yield us the port of Marseilles. From Marseilles Devers could lay a secondary line of supply to the Saar and thus help us out of a logistical corner. For the Saar was nearer Marseilles than it was to the Brittany ports.

Had southern France been left to the German as Churchill had proposed, Eisenhower later would have found himself stretched across the face of France on the north with an open flank of 500 miles from Brittany to the Swiss-German border. To protect this line of communications from enemy raiding parties, he would have had to fence that flank with a line of troops. Eventually he would have had little choice but to turn a corps—or more—into southern France to flush out the enemy.

After having failed to dissuade Eisenhower on this Mediterranean assault, Churchill journeyed into the field to sound out the commanders and perhaps there win adherents to his view. On August 7 he drove into our CP at St. Sauveur Lendelin through a line of poplars that led from the road to the chateau. Inside the trailer I had requisitioned as a temporary map room, the Prime Minister gestured to the large-scale map of Normandy that covered one wall. "It's hard to believe that you were all the way up here when I was last over," he said, pointing with his cigar toward the beachhead near the ceiling. On so large a scale map our COBRA advance showed off to its best advantage.

When I pointed toward the rapid movement of our armored columns toward Brest, Churchill placed a stubby finger on that port city. "The garrison here," he said, "will die like flowers cut off at their stems."

Then with a nod toward the blue tabs that hung from the map beyond the corner at Avranches where we held a 20-mile gap between the German Seventh Army and the sea, Churchill asked, "Divisions?"

"Yes, sir," I answered. "We've passed a dozen of them through."

"Good heavens," he continued, "how do you feed them?" And he pointed to the lone primary road that ran through that narrow gap.

"As a matter of fact, sir, there are two roads," I explained. "The other is a secondary route. We run trucks over both of them bumper to bumper, 24 hours a day."

Churchill called for the black leather dispatch case carried under the arm of his naval aide. He fumbled with a key on his watch chain and opened the case to reveal a box of Havanas. After lighting one, Churchill carefully deposited his used match in a corner and began to talk with animation of a possible diversion of Devers' forces.

"Why?" he growled, "—why break down the back door when the front door has already been opened by your magnificent American army?" Rather than become involved in arguing an issue that was properly the business of SHAEF and the Combined Chiefs of Staff, I listened but did not reply. When at last he finished, the Prime Minister slumped in his chair, looked over his spectacles, and said questioningly, "But of course I'm not at all certain that change at this late date is advisable." Again I did not reply.

Fortunately the change was not made and ANVIL, now renamed DRAGOON, went off on schedule.

COBRA had caught the enemy dangerously off balance with six of his eight panzer divisions concentrated on Montgomery's front. As we splintered the line at St.-Lô, the enemy turned to shift his armor toward the breakthrough. But then as Middleton's advance down the Coutances road unhooked the German line from where it reached to the sea on the west Cotentin coast, the enemy suddenly found his left flank dangling loosely and in distress. And now as Patton pointed his tanks toward the Seine-Orléans gap, and Hodges wheeled against the loose end of that enemy line, the German command was faced with a perplexing decision. For it involved the choice as to where he would seek a showdown on the Western front. *Either* he could withdraw that loose left flank, straighten his north-south line, and hold it intact for an orderly retreat to the Seine, *or* he could gamble an Army by striking for Avranches in an effort to close our gap and peg the loose end of his line back on the sea. No less important than the choice was the speed with which he made it. For as long as the Avranches gap remained open, the German Seventh Army was left with an unprotected flank and rear. The longer von Kluge delayed his decision, the more perilous his position became.

Withdrawal to the Seine would have presented the enemy with a major problem in movement. Not only had the rail lines been wrecked but few German divisions carried sufficient organic transport to make the trek by road. Meanwhile Allied air would harass him bitterly except when he traveled by night. Despite these difficulties, however, he could probably have withdrawn the bulk of his force to safety behind the Seine River line. For though air can harass and delay, it cannot halt or prevent the movement of land forces. Once secure on the right bank of the Seine, the enemy could have strengthened his defenses with troops from the Pas de Calais. By the same token he would have shortened his lines of communications with a position nearer his Luftwaffe bases for better air support.

But in contrast to the difficulties of a forced withdrawal to the Seine, the other alternative offered the enemy an alluring opportunity to attack, regain his balance, and reform his line across the Normandy shoulder.

For if the German could break through our corridor at Avranches to the sea and hook his line back on the coast, he would have reestablished a narrower front where our advantage in mobility could be more easily offset. At the same time he would have confined us to the bocage where terrain became his best ally. Furthermore, if von Kluge could seal the Avranches passage through which we had already poured so many troops, those columns would be cut off from resupply in gas and ammunition. With luck the enemy might bag them before they could be relieved. Thus, while dangerous, this second alternative also offered a tempting objective.

However, before gambling against the considerable risks that such an attack entailed, the enemy should first have calculated the odds that were arraigned against him. For while strategically an attack against the Avranches hinge could have netted the German a bonanza, tactically it lay quite beyond his means. Had this choice been left to the enemy field commanders, they undoubtedly would have chosen to forego the attack in favor of a safe withdrawal across the Seine. They were aware of the vacuum that opened behind them, mindful that disaster on the Normandy front could break a path all the way to the Reich. And far better than Hitler's yes-men in Berlin, they knew how completely outclassed they were on the Normandy front. But it was characteristic of the Nazi regime that even such fateful field decisions as these be divined by the Fuehrer. Thus from his far-off command post on the Eastern front, Hitler peremptorily ordered von Kluge to stand his ground in Normandy and counterattack through the hinge with the objective of re-establishing his line at Avranches. That decision, more than any other, was to cost the enemy the Battle for France.

It was not until 1 a.m. on the morning of August 7 that the enemy collected sufficient strength to launch that fatal attack. He struck toward Mortain, just 20 miles east of the shallow Bay of Mont St. Michel. Five panzer and SS divisions formed the hammerhead of this attack, the German's first great offensive in France, his last until the Bulge. To mount the attack he had drawn his armor from Montgomery's front, reaching back to the Pas de Calais for infantry reinforcements. After two months the enemy was chagrined to learn he had been hoaxed by a cover plan that had immobilized an entire Army during the most crucial hour of his struggle for France.

Only the night before, the 30th Division of Major General Leland S. Hobbs had gone into position on the hinge to relieve the 1st while the latter leapfrogged around the German flank. Under-strength and winded from the two weeks of combat that had followed the Breakout, the 30th dropped wearily into positions vacated by the 1st. These positions had been sited by the 1st while it was still attacking and as a result they lacked sufficient depth for defense. Within several hours the enemy had penetrated Hobbs' forward lines. The 2d Battalion of the 120th Regiment was overrun and cut off from the main force. For six days this lost battalion replied to German demands for surrender with fire and held grimly to its position. On August 8 it radioed for emergency medical supplies. Air answered the call with a flight of C-47's, but in dodging enemy AA fire, those planes spilled more than half their load into the enemy's lines. The 30th then stuffed semi-fixed artillery shells with morphine vials and sulfa and lobbed them over the enemy into the battalion circle. On August 12 this lost battalion was relieved from behind a mound of German dead that ringed its position. For this, one of the epochal struggles of the war, it was awarded a Presidential Unit citation.

In his reckless attack toward Avranches through the 30th Division at Mortain, the enemy challenged us to a decision, the most decisive of our French campaign. It was to cost the enemy an Army and gain us France. Winston Churchill referred to it six months later as "one of the most daring of the war." When the German first struck, only Hobbs' division stood between von Kluge's panzers and the sea. By noon the attack had grown to menacing proportions and Hodges rushed reinforcements from First Army to Hobbs' aid in an effort to stave off the threatened cave-in. Two infantry divisions closed in on the 30th's left and an armored division skirted around on its right to attack the enemy on his open flank.

By now, 12 U. S. divisions had already been passed through the corridor at Avranches. If the enemy were to break through at Mortain, he could cut their line of supply and maroon them deep behind his lines. Of these, four had not yet been committed. From there they were to rush east toward the Seine-Orléans gap and cut off the enemy's route of withdrawal.

Here then was the choice that had been forced upon us:

1. Either we could play safe on the hinge by calling back those last four divisions to strengthen Hodges' defenses at Mortain and thus safeguard the lifeline of our Brittany forces,

2. Or we could take a chance on an enemy breakthrough at Mortain and throw those four divisions against his open flank in an effort to destroy the German Seventh Army.

In betting his life on the success of von Kluge's panzer attack, Hitler had exposed his whole broad flank to attack and encirclement from the south. If we could only plunge eastward in force while the enemy attacked at Mortain, we might thereafter swing north in a pincer movement to cut off his entire army. I resolved to take the plunge and strike for annihilation of the German army in the west.

Within a week this decision brought on the Argentan-Falaise pocket. There in one of the costliest battles of western Europe, the enemy lost his Seventh Army, and with it went his last hope of holding a line in France. He was to flee from Argentan 325 miles to the German frontier.

Unlike Hitler, however, we calculated the odds at Mortain with care. An opportunity for encirclement justified risk but we could not afford to be reckless. For the first 24 hours of enemy attack, I held those four divisions south of Mortain in readiness as reinforcements.

Meanwhile to the right of the 30th Division, a wide gap developed in our line. To plug this hole before the enemy discovered it, I snatched Patton's 35th Division and assigned it to Hodges. Had the enemy sideslipped his panzers several thousand yards south he might have broken through to Avranches that very first day.

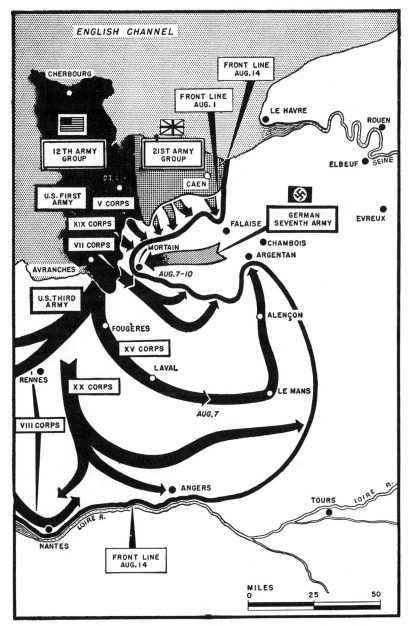

While the Germans tried to break through to the sea at Mortain, the First and Third Armies drew a noose around the exposed flank. Within a week a U. S. column had stabbed north to Argentan, while Montgomery pushed unsuccessfully toward Falaise in an effort to close that trap.

On the morning of August 8, I checked with Hodges and found him holding firm. The German had failed to deepen his early penetrations and the attack appeared to have spent its initial momentum. I concluded the hinge would hold, especially if supported by air. G-2 and G-3 concurred.

We needed only the forecast of good weather to strike east and turn against the enemy's open flank. The forecast came in that morning with a promise of clear skies and good hunting for several days. I handed the report to Lev Allen.

"We'll shoot the works," I told him, "and rush east with everything we've got."

The order went out to Patton. While Middleton chased the enemy into Brittany, Major General Walton H. Walker's XX Corps was to strike out for the Seine-Orléans gap. At the same time, the XV Corps of Major General Wade H. Haislip, now in the vicinity of Le Mans, was to turn north toward the road junction of Argentan and there block the enemy's main route of withdrawal.

As the Caen front loosened with the enemy's diversion of armor toward Mortain, Montgomery issued orders on August 6 to his British and Canadian Armies for their advance to the Seine. Crerar, the Canadian commander on the left, was to drive down the Caen road to Falaise and pivot northeast toward Rouen. Dempsey, on the right, was to travel the arterial road that ran east through Argentan, 25 miles south of Falaise. On this day before the enemy's attack at Mortain, Montgomery's plans were predicated upon the assumption that von Kluge would withdraw from his untenable Normandy position to a defensive line on the Seine.

During the conference several days before in which Montgomery outlined this plan, Dempsey had cheerfully offered to wager that he would beat our U. S. forces to Argentan. I did not challenge Bimbo Dempsey's optimism, for in the wide turning movement that would bring us up to Argentan, we had many more miles than he to travel.

On the evening of August 7—the enemy had attacked at Mortain that morning—Montgomery kicked off his attack and the Canadians rolled down the road toward Falaise in the wake of an air bombing. By noon on the following day, however, they had stumbled into stiff resistance, for the enemy had dug in at Falaise to hold open his communications while concentrating his strength against our corridor at Mortain.

Now that the situation had been changed as a result of the

enemy's attack at Mortain, Montgomery altered his plans. He would join with us in an effort to clamp von Kluge's Seventh Army in the jaws of a double pincer movement. While the American forces drove up from the south, Montgomery would drive down from the north through Falaise to cut off the enemy west of that north-south line and destroy his Seventh Army. As field arbiter on boundaries for Ike, Monty became responsible for coordinating the maneuvers of all four Allied Armies.

Haislip's XV Corps was to form our U. S. pincer on the south, closing north to Argentan. That final objective lay 12 miles inside the British boundary. But because it contained the strategic road junction where our pincers were to converge, Monty happily forgave us our trespasses and welcomed the penetration.

"We'll go as far as Argentan and hold there," I told Patton. "We've got to be careful we don't run into Monty coming down from Falaise."

In closing his half of the jaw from the north, Monty was to rush his attack down the Caen road through Falaise and 12 miles farther beyond to Argentan. Once Monty had closed that gap from Falaise to Argentan, we would have blocked the enemy's last escape route from Mortain. But because it would take time to form our trap and close in on the enemy from the south, we clocked him hourly at Mortain, hoping that he would persist long enough in that fruitless attack to give us the time we required to swing around his flank.

On the second day of the enemy's attack at Mortain, Secretary of the Treasury Henry Morgenthau visited the Army Group front during a routine tour of the Theater. Hobbs' 30th had held nobly on the hinge and with such doggedness we called it the *Rock of Mortain.* Meanwhile rocket-carrying Typhoons of the RAF joined the U. S. Air Force in attacking von Kluge's panzers until the enemy lines were marked by the black plumes of burning tanks.

In briefing Morgenthau that morning, I pointed to where the German line hooked back below Mortain and showed him how we were hemming the enemy in with troops on his open flank. "This is an opportunity that comes to a commander not more than once in a century," I told him. "We're about to destroy an entire hostile army."

While Morgenthau looked on skeptically, I pointed to the German bulge at Mortain and outlined my reasons for that statement. "If the other fellow will only press his attack here at Mortain for another

48 hours, he'll give us time to close at Argentan and there completely destroy him. And when he loses his Seventh Army in this bag, he'll have nothing left with which to oppose us. We'll go all the way from here to the German border."

I'm not certain that Morgenthau believed me. The border was still 350 miles farther east.

On August 11, just 48 hours after Morgenthau's visit, von Kluge at last conceded that he could no longer comply with Hitler's orders at Mortain. He recommended that the foolhardy attack be abandoned and that the line be withdrawn to the Seine.

On the following day Hitler consented to withdrawal but not without a condition: von Kluge was also to clear the enemy from his left flank and rear. Hitler might more reasonably have ordered his field commander to reverse the downstream flow of the Seine. For XV Corps with its two infantry and two armored divisions had neared the road junction at Argentan and was driving hard to close the trap.

Meanwhile Monty labored on the north with slackening success. After five days of attack he had pushed his Canadian pincer only half the way to Falaise. Thus when Haislip reached Argentan on the evening of August 12, he found Monty stalled on the north with an 18-mile gap separating the British and American forces.

Patton telephoned me that evening from LUCKY FORWARD near Laval.

"We've got elements in Argentan," he reported. "Let me go on to Falaise and we'll drive the British back into the sea for another Dunkirk."

"Nothing doing," I told him, for I was fearful of colliding with Montgomery's forces. "You're not to go beyond Argentan. Just stop where you are and build up on that shoulder. Sibert tells me the German is beginning to pull out. You'd better button up and get ready for him."

As though long skeptical of Monty's ability to close the gap at Argentan, Patton had already ordered his XV Corps to push on through that objective to Falaise. Consequently by the time George called me, Haislip's tanks had already started across the gap. So uncompromising were my instructions, however, that George recalled Haislip's troops without a word.

Meanwhile, as we waited impatiently for Monty at Argentan, the enemy reinforced that gap. Already the vanguard of panzers and

SS troops were sluicing back through it toward the Seine. But instead of redoubling his push to close that leak, Monty shifted his main effort against the pocket farther west. Rather than close the trap by capping the leak at Falaise, Monty proceeded to squeeze the enemy out toward the Seine. If Monty's tactics mystified me, they dismayed Eisenhower even more. And at LUCKY FORWARD where a shocked Third Army looked on helplessly as its quarry fled, Patton raged at Montgomery's blunder. George was doubly irritated for having been forbidden to close it himself. But Monty had never prohibited and I never proposed that U. S. forces close the gap from Argentan to Falaise. I was quite content with our original objective and reluctant to take on another.

Although Patton might have spun a line across that narrow neck, I doubted his ability to hold it. Nineteen German divisions were now stampeding to escape the trap. Meanwhile, with four divisions George was already blocking three principal escape routes through Alençon, Sees, and Argentan. Had he stretched that line to include Falaise, he would have extended his roadblock a distance of 40 miles. The enemy could not only have broken through, but he might have trampled Patton's position in the onrush. I much preferred a solid shoulder at Argentan to the possibility of a broken neck at Falaise.

At the same time I was reluctant to chance a head-on meeting between two converging Armies as we might have done had Patton continued on to Falaise. For any head-on juncture becomes a dangerous and uncontrollable maneuver unless each of the advancing forces is halted by prearranged plan on a terrain objective. To have driven pell-mell into Montgomery's line of advance could easily have resulted in a disastrous error in recognition. In halting Patton at Argentan, however, I did not consult with Montgomery. The decision to stop Patton was mine alone; it never went beyond my CP.

Although the enemy's prepared positions on the road to Falaise were undoubtedly thornier than those through which we broke en route to Argentan, I was critical of Montgomery for his failure to close that gap on time. For after having been rebuffed on the Falaise road, he might better have shifted his weight to the east and closed the trap at Chambois—as he was to do one week later.

While Radio Berlin taunted us for what it called a "do or die" attempt at Falaise to destroy the German Army before we succumbed to the flying bombs, Patton paced his LUCKY CP with a fistful of G-2 reports on the enemy's flight from the trap.

"Hell, by now they've all gotten out," he cried. "Instead of waiting here for Monty, we ought to get moving again. There's nothing out front, nothing at all between me and the Seine."

Although I shared the frustration that caused George to fret while waiting helplessly on the Argentan shoulder, I disputed his extravagant claims on the number of Germans that had escaped the trap. With Allied air pounding his movements and artillery interdicting his roads, von Kluge could not in two days and nights have extricated more than a fraction of the 19 divisions then milling in that slowly shrinking pocket.

Having concluded several days before that I could not close the Falaise gap without endangering my Argentan shoulder, I was now left with three courses of action:

1. We could hold in position where we were until the pocket was squeezed dry.

2. We could lighten our force on the shoulder, drive 10 miles northeast to Chambois, and there block one more enemy exit route.

3. Or we could leave a part of our force at Argentan to await a juncture with Montgomery's pincer and race east with the remainder to grab a bridgehead across the Seine.

The first was essentially a do-nothing choice; it offered no dividends whatsoever. The second held out a slight reward. Though we could not close the trap by taking Chambois, we would narrow the neck and perhaps slow down the enemy exodus from the pocket. Of all three, the dash to the Seine offered the greatest tactical promise. For if Patton were to secure a bridgehead there, he would have thwarted the enemy's last bright chance for defense of the Seine River line. But by the same token, we would also be taking a chance. For in striking out for the Seine in preference to the Chambois attack, we might make it easier for the enemy to escape that Falaise trap. Normally, destruction of the enemy's army is the first objective of any force. Was a Seine River bridgehead important enough to warrant our rejecting that military tenet?

George helped settle my doubts when on August 14 he called to ask that two of Haislip's four divisions on the Argentan shoulder be freed for a dash to the Seine. With that, I brushed aside the first two alternatives and sided with Patton on the third. If Montgomery wants help in closing the gap, I thought, then let him ask us for it.

Since there was little likelihood of his asking, we would push on to the east.

In his advance to the Seine, Patton was to split Third Army three ways with one corps on the south headed toward Orléans, another in the center directed on Chartres, while Haislip, on the north, struck toward Dreux, 40 miles this side of Paris. From Dreux, Haislip would turn northeast toward Mantes Gassicourt and there force the Seine, 35 miles north of Paris.

Haislip had scarcely started toward that Seine River crossing when Montgomery called to propose that we extend our pincer from Argentan *northeast* to Chambois. Monty had already diverted his Polish Armored Division toward that objective with a view to closing the trap there.

"I agree with you, sir," I told Monty. "We ought to go northeast. In fact I've just sent two divisions northeast—northeast to the Seine." Mantes Gassicourt was 75 miles farther east than Montgomery's objective at Chambois.

While Monty caught his breath on the other end of the line, I struggled to fight off the doubts that now assailed my earlier decision. For had we not rushed on to the Seine, we might have closed the Falaise trap at Chambois and bettered our PW catch within that pocket. At the time of my conversation with Patton, I had not known of Monty's decision to drive southeast to Chambois. For the first and only time during the war, I went to bed that evening worrying over a decision I had already made. To this day I am not yet certain that we should not have postponed our advance to the Seine and gone on to Chambois instead. For although the bridgehead accelerated our advance, Chambois would have yielded more prisoners.

On August 19, 12 days after the enemy attacked us at Mortain, six days after Patton reached Argentan, Montgomery closed the trap at Chambois, 15 miles to the southeast of Falaise. More than 70,000 demoralized Germans were killed or captured in that pocket. Nevertheless, during the five days Patton had waited for Montgomery at Argentan, thousands of the enemy had escaped. But even this setback could not dim the victory we had achieved as the result of Hitler's stubbornness at Mortain. The bulk of 19 German divisions had been chewed up within the pocket; only their mobile remnants escaped and they slipped through in broken pieces. The enemy west of the Seine had been destroyed and as he fell, the

liberation of France lay only days away. Between the Orne and the
Seine a German force still blocked Monty's 21st Group, but with the
American flank already cleared to the Seine, von Kluge could do
no more than withdraw to save whatever he could.

But while the world gaped over the speed of Patton's spectacular
advance to the Seine, it was Hodges' almost anonymous First Army
that sweated through the laborious in-fighting against the Falaise
pocket. For despite the hopelessness of his position, the enemy did
not easily despair; even division commanders admitted to astonish-
ment over the ferocity of German resistance in the pocket. One day
while visiting a forward battalion engaged against the pocket, a
division commander assured the weary battalion staff that only
"second-rate stuff" opposed them. A red-eyed S-2 lieutenant, gaunt
from the want of rest, eyed his commander dryly. "General," he said,
"I think you had better put the Boche on your distribution list. They
don't seem to realize they're as bad as that."

During the Argentan-Falaise battle Patton measured his successes
in miles; Hodges, in enemy dead. Thus neither can claim to have
excelled the other, for their missions were not comparable ones.
Yet if casualties offer an index to the rigors and ordeal of combat,
First Army can claim to have borne the brunt of our advance. During the 19 days it took Third Army to go from Avranches to the
Seine, First Army suffered 19,000 casualties in rolling up the Argentan pocket. Its casualties were almost twice the number sustained by
Third Army on the enemy's open flank.

As our pincers neared Chambois the dewy morning of August 19,
Montgomery called a meeting to coordinate his advance to the Seine
with ours. We rendezvoused at a midway point between our CP's
and retired with our mapboards to a mound of fresh-mown hay at
the side of the road.

Although by now we stood astride our OVERLORD objective
from Mantes Gassicourt to Orléans, the British had not yet closed
to the Seine. Thinking to trap those units that had escaped through
Falaise and at the same time break ground for the British advance,
I suggested to Dempsey that he haul two British divisions around
through Avranches, over Patton's path to the Seine and there strike
north with a pincer up the left bank.

"We'll get you the trucks to make the move," I promised, assuming that he would require aid on so long an overland haul.

Bimbo pulled a straw through his teeth. "Oh, no thanks, Brad," he objected, "we couldn't pull it off. I just can't spare two divisions for so wide an end run."

Rather than miss this opportunity for a second outside encirclement of the enemy west of the Seine, I proposed that we turn our U. S. forces north into the British sector and cut the enemy off on the left bank.

"If you can't do it, Bimbo," I said, "have you any objection to our giving it a try? It'll mean cutting across your front."

"Why no, not at all," he answered. "We'd be delighted to have you do it. I only wish we could find the troops to do it ourselves." Monty nodded in agreement.

We anticipated beforehand that any such maneuver of U. S. troops across the British line of advance would entail an administrative headache. For the 80,000 troops that eventually marched up north would have to march back down again, this time across the British columns that in the meantime were closing to the Seine.

Nevertheless, so anxious were we to bag the enemy fleeing eastward that we headed four divisions north up the left bank of the Seine. By August 25 they had driven 35 miles across the British front to the vicinity of the Gothic city of Rouen. This unexpected maneuver panicked the enemy retreating before Montgomery's advance. Not only did we close off the Seine between Mantes Gassicourt and Rouen, but we forced the German into a narrow crossing on the north near the mouth of the Seine. As the German columns jammed up there behind the ferry crossings, Allied air rushed in to strafe and bomb them. And for two days our artillery fired on those concentrations until the crossings were marked by pyres of smoke that darkened the summer sky.

Now Dempsey advanced with almost negligible resistance to occupy the front we had cleared for him west of the Seine. And when he reached the river at Mantes Gassicourt, we presented him with a ready-made bridgehead. Then to withdraw our U. S. troops back across the British front now heavily trafficked with east-west supply, Hodges and Dempsey agreed to a system of two-hour clearances on all crossroads. The British and we were to pass our columns through these junctures for alternating periods of two hours each until our forces were unraveled.

Several days later when Dempsey was questioned by the British press on his advance to the Seine, he complained that the movement could have gone faster but for the U. S. traffic that snarled his front.

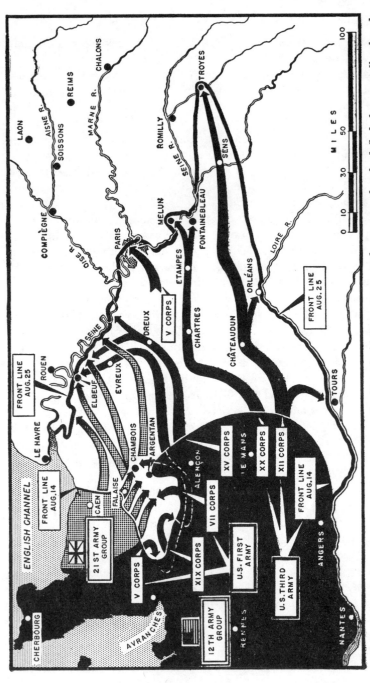

The U. S. First Army struck northeast across the British front to prevent the enemy that had fled the partially-closed Argentan-Falaise trap from escaping across the Seine. Meanwhile, Third Army plunged on east of Paris to Troyes.

Although we were probably unduly sensitive to any reflection on U. S. command, I was piqued to learn that our diversion had been characterized as an obstruction by its chief beneficiary. I reminded Monty that Dempsey's half-time use of roads in a sector cleared by Americans was vastly preferable to a full-time claim on roads still occupied by the German.

Had we not turned that pincer to Dempsey's aid, we could have swept far east of Paris for more spectacular gains in terrain. But once again we were willing to forego ground in an effort to kill Germans.

Monty afterward offered his apologies for Dempsey's comment to the press. "Bimbo," he explained, "tells me that he was misquoted."

19: *Liberation*

of Paris

EﾠARLY IN AUGUST, SOON AFTER THIRD ARMY BANKED east from Laval toward Le Mans, only 110 miles from Paris, a courier from London hurried in one afternoon to our CP near St. Sauveur Lendelin. He clutched a sweaty Manila envelope that had been sealed with a blob of wax. The open pocket of his OD shirt bulged with the high priority credentials that had sped him by air across the Channel.

Hansen tore open the envelope and pulled out a small American flag. A card fell to the ground. "For General Bradley's jeep on the liberation of Paris—" the note attached to it read. The courier had been sent by Major Robert L. Cohen of Boston, the busy little quartermaster officer who had greeted me on my first arrival in London with a tape measure to fit me for any new uniforms I might need.

From his desk in Major General Robert McG. Littlejohn's office in London, Cohen had anticipated the fever that seized the U. S. Army as it neared Paris. To a generation raised on fanciful tales of their fathers in the AEF, Paris beckoned with a greater allure than any other objective in Europe. Yet tactically the city had become meaningless. For all of its past glories, Paris represented nothing more than an inkspot on our maps to be by-passed as we headed toward the Rhine. Logistically it could cause untold trouble, for behind its handsome façades there lived 4,000,000 hungry Frenchmen. The diversion of so much tonnage to Paris would only strain further our already taut lines of supply. Food for the people of Paris meant less gasoline for the front.

Several days before the enemy struck at Mortain, I had reviewed our prospective strategy for the liberation of Paris. Several staff officers had insisted the enemy would declare Paris an "open city" as the French had in 1940 to avert its destruction. I disagreed with their views. The enemy was reported to have cached his supply in Paris; if so, he had no choice but to defend it. This did not mean, however, that we would close in on the city and besiege it. Indeed, we outlined a plan of maneuver to skirt Paris from the south, where we would turn north to join up with an encirclement around the other side and cut off its garrison's escape to the Reich. To seize the Seine-Orléans gap we made plans for an air drop near the cathedral town of Chartres, for we had assumed the enemy would reform his line from Caen on south toward the Loire. After crashing that line Third Army would race up the north bank of the Loire to join up with this air drop at Chartres. By August 10 this airborne plan was on the drafting boards. A week later we asked that it be scrapped. The enemy had not only failed to reform his line but Third Army insisted it could reach the gap without help from the airborne. Abandonment of the Chartres drop left Troop Carrier free to freight tonnage to Third Army and on August 19, 21 C-47's inaugurated the emergency air lift to Patton when they landed 47 tons of rations on the airfields near Le Mans. In the supply crisis that even now had begun to harass our advance, air lift was to become the pawn in a bitter logistical struggle. For within days our rate of advance was to be determined not by enemy resistance but by the tonnage supplied our columns to keep them rolling.

By August 21, Third Army had forced the Seine both north and south of Paris while the enemy still *west* of that river scrambled to escape the skein First Army strung up its left bank toward Rouen. In a last effort to save his disordered troops, von Kluge ordered them to splinter into small parties and infiltrate through our lines. Brokenhearted over the disaster into which he had been forced by Hitler, von Kluge then killed himself.

As Patton crossed the Seine, a delegation of newsmen called on me to ask that Paris be spared artillery bombardment despite the enemy garrison there. Though lacking their affection for a city I had never seen, I assured them that we would not damage so much as a cobblestone in its streets. Instead of hammering down its west gates in a frontal attack, I explained, we would first pinch off Paris and thereafter enter it at our leisure.

"What division will take it?" one of the correspondents asked.

"They've all fought well," I said in an effort to dodge his query. "We'll have a tough time making the choice—"

"If nominations are in order," he laughed, "here's one vote for the 1st."

"Why don't you take it yourselves?" I told him. "You've got enough correspondents here to do it. In fact, you can take it any time you want to and spare us a lot of trouble. For while I wouldn't want the French to know it I might just as well tell you we're not at all anxious to liberate Paris right now."

In the short space of four weeks after Breakout, the U. S. line of supply had stretched from St.-Lô to the Seine. Third Army's bridge-heads southeast of Paris now hung on the end of a 250-mile truck route from the port of Cherbourg. Not only had our advance run through those stops where enemy resistance had been counted upon to give supply a chance to catch up with us, but the force to be maintained on the end of that line increased from day to day with the growth in build-up. This was the interval that preceded the drought—the gasoline drought that was to halt our Shermans a few miles short of the Siegfried Line.

Rail lines had been pushed on to Le Mans, 140 miles east of Cherbourg, but repair of the bombed bridges dragged because of shortages in engineer construction battalions. Meanwhile, despite the critical shortage of war-weary French rolling stock, rail equipment was queued up in England behind high priority cross-channel shipments of trucks. Lacking rail transport, we fell back on the two and one-half ton truck now rolling forward in round-the-clock convoys. To fill the daily demands for more trucks we stripped tactical vehicles from incoming divisions as they landed in Cherbourg and assigned them to supply convoys. But even with such makeshift expediencies, it was only by cutting the army requisitions and resorting to air lift that we were able to hold off the supply crisis until September.

While driving east on this logistical shoestring, I feared that the liberation of Paris might cause our supply line to snap. Each ton that went into that city meant one less for the front, and G-5 of Army Group had estimated the Parisians would require an initial 4,000 tons per day. If Paris could pull in its belt and live with the

Germans a little longer, each 4,000 tons we saved would mean gasoline enough for a three days' motor march toward the German border. Deprived of her milkshed in Normandy and cut off from the grain fields of western France, Paris had exhausted her reserves and the reports that reached us from Allied agents indicated a growing food crisis. To provide emergency stores when the city fell, we radioed SHAEF on August 20 to stand by to send us 3,000 tons by air. However, in spite of this danger of famine in Paris, I was determined that we would not be dissuaded from our plan to by-pass the city. If we could rush on to the Siegfried Line with tonnage that might otherwise be diverted to Paris, the city would be compensated for its additional week of occupation with an earlier end to the war. But we had not reckoned with the impatience of those Parisians who had waited four years for the armies that now approached their gates. My plan to pinch out Paris was exploded on an airstrip near Laval the morning of August 23.

As early as August 7, Paris had begun to show its stringy nerves as the armies of liberation approached. While tanks of the 7th Armored Division clattered through the cobblestone square of Chartres, the Gestapo in Paris loaded its vans and prepared for evacuation.

Raoul Nordling, for 18 years the Swedish Consul General in Paris, had only that morning won the release of 4,213 political prisoners from the city's jails. Fearful that the Gestapo might execute those prisoners rather than leave them behind to the Allies, Nordling had gone as a neutral several days before to call on Otto Abetz, Hitler's ambassador to France. He cautioned the German proconsul that Gestapo atrocities in Paris would only bring on additional world censure once the war was ended.

"Nonsense," Abetz shouted, infuriated by Nordling's inference, "we have never killed political prisoners." Then as if to reprove the Swede for his impertinence, the ambassador added, "the military situation is being re-established. We shall not leave Paris and are making no plans to do so."

Discouraged by the *gauleiter's* angry reply, Nordling appealed to Laval who was then in Paris. But the collaborationist had aged with worry and appeared much more preoccupied with his own fate than with the consul's request. The conversation ended without result, and Nordling left him to his own worries.

With the aid of an Austrian who was reported sympathetic to the French Resistance, Nordling asked to see General Dietrich von Choltitz, commandant of the German garrison in Paris.

The general listened quietly to Nordling. "As a military commander, I cannot interfere in the fate of civilians. They shall probably be sent to Germany for safekeeping."

"But the trains are no longer running out of Paris," the Swedish Consul retorted. "You cannot remove them. Why don't you turn them over either to the Swiss government or to mine? We shall guarantee that they will not take up arms against you."

Von Choltitz twisted uncomfortably. "No," he answered, "I cannot do that. If I am to release those prisoners, I must have an order for them that I may have authority to set them free."

He stared for a moment at Nordling and then spoke more slowly. "If you will give me five military prisoners for each civilian," he said, "I shall release those political prisoners to you."

"But you know I have no military prisoners—" Nordling began.

"Well let's write it down that way."

An exchange, von Choltitz surmised, would pass unquestioned. Thus he could salve his conscience and keep his head. With tongue in cheek, Nordling shrugged and prepared a contract, "pledging" his word as an individual to achieve the exchange of five German military prisoners of war for each Frenchman that was released.

On the evening of August 17, the date set for the "exchange," the German prison commander balked and declined to release his charges. "They'll be violating the curfew if we let them out now," he explained. Nordling agreed to wait until morning.

But once again the prison commander hesitated. This time it was a question of "correctness." The pocket money of his prisoners had been impounded on arrest. They could not be released until it was returned and, unfortunately, he had no funds. Nordling hurried to the bank, withdrew 700,000 francs from Swedish consulate funds and gave them to the German. The commandant paid off his prisoners and opened the cell doors.

Now street fighting started in earnest when underground bands from the French Resistance fired on German patrols. Fearful lest the German commandant be goaded into retaliation, the staff of the loosely organized Resistance sent one of its trusted officers, Alexandre de Saint-Phalle, to the Swedish consul to tell him of their worries. Were the street fighting to get out of hand, they said, Paris might become a battleground and be needlessly damaged. If only the enemy could be induced to concede the hopelessness of his position, an armistice might be arranged and the city would be saved.

When the street fighting showed signs of getting out of hand early on August 19, Nordling went once more to von Choltitz' headquarters at the Hôtel Meurice. The general looked depressed and disheartened.

"The revolution in Paris has begun," he declared, "I must go with my assault guns and attack the Prefecture of Police."

Von Choltitz looked across the Tuileries gardens to the Place de la Concorde and beyond it to where a bridge spanned the Seine. "I'm sorry it's turned out this way," he said. "Since Stalingrad I have been an unlucky commander. It is always my lot to defend the rear of the German Army. And each time it happens I am ordered to destroy each city as I leave it." He grinned sardonically and turned toward Nordling. "Now I shall be remembered as the man who destroyed Paris."

"But it is not your duty to destroy Paris," Nordling rejoined. "The people are revolting, of course—but not against you. It is Petain's government against which they have risen."

Von Choltitz answered dryly. "Against Petain's government, yes. But it is my soldiers they are shooting." The general shook his head and looked again toward the Seine, "This can only end in destruction of Paris."

No longer in doubt as to the German's distaste for his mission, Nordling maneuvered for time. "Don't do it," he begged, "don't do it until first I consult with the Resistance."

Equally alarmed for fear this smoldering underground resistance might force the reluctant von Choltitz to execute Hitler's orders to demolish the city, the French Resistance agreed to a truce to be negotiated by Nordling. The street fighting was momentarily halted, but on Sunday, August 20, it broke out again when isolated bands of the FFI fired on the German troops. This time von Choltitz replied to the French with an ultimatum: either those assaults would be stopped or he would order the bombing of Paris. At the same time he would execute his orders to effect the most extensive destruction possible to the city.

Handicapped by a lack of communications, the Resistance had found difficulty in circulating its cease-fire order. Nordling suggested that public-address trucks be used to tour the city, broad-

casting terms of the truce. In this agreement the German commandant would recognize the insurgent city government of Paris if the
French would only cease firing on German troops. The announcement was greeted by tumultuous crowds and the streets broke out
in Allied flags.

But like the previous agreement, this armistice failed when Communist underground newspapers rushed to the streets demanding
that Parisians reject any truce with *les Boches. Aux barricades!* The
ancient battle cry echoed again through the streets.

Von Choltitz instantly retaliated by shutting off the city's food.
But by now the Resistance was unable any longer to enforce compliance with its truce. Nor could von Choltitz restrain his troops. There
was no alternative, he concluded, but to execute his orders. "For I
shall never surrender," he said, "to an *irregular* army."

The inference did not escape Nordling—if not to an *irregular*
army, perhaps to an Allied one. The Consul volunteered to lead a
mission through the Allied lines, bid the Americans enter the city,
and thus enable von Choltitz to surrender the city with honor. Von
Choltitz not only agreed to this solution, he offered to send an
officer along for safe-conduct through the German lines.

On Tuesday evening, the strange delegation assembled secretly at
the Consulate. The 62-year-old Nordling, meanwhile, had been
taken ill and his brother, Rolf, a French national, was chosen to
head the mission. The four others included de Saint-Phalle as representative of the Committee of National Liberation in Paris, a mys-
terious M. Armoux of the British Intelligence Service, Jean Laurent,
who represented himself as former cabinet secretary to General de
Gaulle, and the Austrian anti-Nazi. Laurent's credentials were
thought suspicious, and he was included only after having been
vouchsafed for by the British agent.

In the Consulate's tiny Citroen with its Swedish and white safe-
conduct flags, the mission motored from Paris through Versailles
followed by a German staff car containing the officer Herman
Bender whom von Choltitz had agreed to send. They arrived at the
German outpost near Trappes on the road to Rambouillet shortly
after 7 P.M. There an SS captain stopped them and listened stonily
to the instructions of their German guide.

"Since July 20," the captain said, "there are some German generals
who are not to be obeyed." He placed the party under surveillance

and drove back to Versailles to confirm the orders. An hour and a half later the wary captain returned. He called to a motorcycle courier and instructed him to inform the German batteries en route to permit the Citroen safe-conduct.

It was dusk when Nordling drove gingerly into the village of Neauphles-le-Vieux. Not a shot had been fired and no one challenged the flag-decked Citroen as it entered the American lines. In the center of Neauphles-le-Vieux Nordling found a U. S. Sherman whose crew was too busily engaged in celebrating the liberation to halt the strange-looking car.

Though mystified by this indifference Nordling hunted down the tank commander. "I have a mission to General Eisenhower," he explained.

"General who—" the sergeant snorted, "—maybe you ought to come with me and see my regimental commander."

Late that night at corps G-2 a duty captain grilled Nordling and his companions. Not until the British agent established his identity did the suspicious captain pass them on. This time Nordling found himself headed toward Patton's Third Army headquarters southwest of Chartres.

At 8 on Wednesday morning Patton listened to Nordling's tale. He telephoned me as I was leaving Laval for Ike's CP. George loaded the mission into a flight of cubs and ferried it back to where I waited on the airstrip.

Just as soon as G-2 had checked the authenticity of Nordling's story, I called G-3 and ordered the French 2d Armored Division to start at once for Paris. It was to be paired with an advance of the 4th U. S. Infantry Division on the south. I buckled into a cub and hurried back to Granville to clear those orders with Ike.

Mustered from among French citizens in North Africa and refugees in Britain and equipped with U. S. tanks, the French 2d Armored had fought gallantly at Argentan where it held Patton's shoulder for two weeks. Its respected and celebrated commander, Major General Jacques Leclerc, had escaped from the Germans after having been captured in 1940. In 1943 during the Libyan campaign, he led a desert striking force across the Sahara from Fort Lamy to join Montgomery's Eighth Army in Tripoli. Leclerc was a *nom de guerre* taken to shield his family then in Occupied France. A magnificent tank commander, Leclerc had already made an unscheduled bid for the liberation of Paris. Shortly after Gerow went into position with his V Corps at Argentan, he spotted French reconnaissance tanks moving eastward outside their sector.

"And just where in hell do you think you're going?" Gerow asked the column commander.

"To Paris—yes?" a French captain answered brightly. Gee bellowed and turned him back with orders not to stir out of position.

Any number of American divisions could more easily have spearheaded our march into Paris. But to help the French recapture their pride after four years of occupation, I chose a French force with the tricolor on their Shermans. Recalling Leclerc's earlier attempt to slip into Paris, Lev Allen laughed. "Those Frenchmen," he said, "will go in on the west side of Paris—and mark my words they'll never come out from the east." Allen's rejoinder almost became a prediction. Within a week we would be rooting Leclerc's Shermans out of every back alley in Paris, even threatening his division with dissolution to get it on the road.

Leclerc was ordered to start immediately on August 22 but it was the following morning before he got under way. For the next 24 hours the French 2d Armored stumbled reluctantly through a Gallic wall as townsfolk along the line of march slowed the French advance with wine and celebration. Although I could not censure them for responding to this hospitality of their countrymen, neither could I wait for them to dance their way to Paris. If von Choltitz was to deliver the city, we had a compact to fulfill.

"To hell with prestige," I finally told Allen, "tell the 4th to slam on in and take the liberation." Learning of these orders and fearing an affront to France, Leclerc's troopers mounted their tanks and burned up their treads on the brick roads. At 10 P.M. on the evening of August 24, a Captain Dronne of the French 2d Armored pulled up to the front of the Hôtel de Ville with a squadron of light tanks and a company of infantry.

On the following morning, August 25, a platoon headed toward the Hôtel Meurice to drive the German commander out of his headquarters. Von Choltitz had assembled his entire staff in a second floor suite with the apparent intention of surrendering. The platoon heaved three smoke grenades into the hotel lobby, and the Germans came out with their hands up. They were driven to the Gare Montparnasse where von Choltitz formally surrendered Paris to the French. He dispatched German officers under safe-conduct flags to round up the garrison troops. That evening Paris started its celebration.

For the first two weeks after commitment on the heels of the Breakout, Third Army had been cloaked under a censorship stop. By hiding the identity and strength of that flanking force, we sought to mislead the enemy on our intentions. For had Hitler known it was Patton's tanks which swarmed around von Kluge's flank, he might have called off his attack at Mortain. I knew how impatiently Patton would chafe under the anonymity forced upon him by this censorship stop and for that reason was eager to lift it just as soon as we could. George was stimulated by headlines, the blacker the headlines the more recklessly he fought.

Earlier I had promised Haislip that a similar blanket would be lifted from his XV Corps when he took Alençon. On August 12, I suggested to Ike that the stop on Patton be removed at the same time, for by then he would have closed his pincer on Argentan. Ike laughed and agreed to the proposal as it applied to XV Corps but he turned thumbs down on Patton. "Not yet," he said, "after all the troubles I've had with George, I have only a few gray hairs left on this poor old head of mine. Let George work a while longer for his headlines." Several days later Ike relented and Third Army flashed into the news. In the United States George had begun to fight his way out of the Sicilian doghouse.

Shortly before Paris fell, we rolled EAGLE TAC 112 miles on up the road from Laval to the tree-shaded city of Chartres in pursuit of the Armies. Signal linesmen had fallen behind the fast-moving columns and at Group we faced the choice between trailing behind to retain telephone communication with Ike while losing it to the Armies or moving on with the Armies and resorting to radio in our communications with Ike. Ike growled over the necessity for snipping the wires to SHAEF but for us there was no other solution; we could not let go of the front. With the break in telephone lines to the rear, 21st Army Group became even more inaccessible than SHAEF. This, however, we did not regret.

Early in August I shifted my mobile field office into a handsomely paneled map van half the length of a Pullman car. A hinged steel deck on its rear formed a veranda that connected to the two and a half ton truck I still retained for living quarters. During his July Fourth visit to the beachhead, Eisenhower had squirmed uncomfortably in the cramped quarters of the small truck in which I lived and maintained an office. "Why don't you give up this damned closet," he said, "and get yourself a map trailer like Monty's?" That was all the authorization we needed.

When completed in England according to Hansen's elaborate specifications, the trailer was so ornate that I often felt it necessary to apologize for the comfort it provided. Four plexiglass astrodomes were fitted into the roof for lighting during the day and a bank of fluorescent lamps illuminated the mapboards that ran the length of its side walls. In the curved front end of the van, mahogany panels covered the walls of a carpeted office not unlike the chancel of a well-appointed church. Indeed when Air Marshal Tedder first entered the trailer, he strode to the railing that separated this office from the map room, knelt on the bench below it, looked up, and said, "I'll have communion, please." In 1947, I made a search through channels for that CP van. But the chaotic pace of demobilization had played havoc with ETO records and no trace of it could be found. The two and a half ton truck I had used for quarters was tracked down to England when a farmer wrote to explain that he had purchased it in a sale of U. S. surplus equipment. It provided a delightful home, he reported, for his sheepherder on the damp moors.

The day after we had liberated Paris I returned from a hurried flight to Brest to find Eisenhower camped on my doorstep in our barnyard CP near Chartres. Although he had come with more pressing issues in mind, Ike suggested we slip quietly into Paris for a glimpse of the city on the following morning. "It's Sunday," he said. "Everyone will be sleeping late. We can do it without any fuss." He radioed Monty an invitation to join us but Monty replied with regrets; he was much too busy pushing his British troops on to the Seine.

It was not yet 8 the following morning when we wedged our column into a convoy trundling through the shuttered boulevards of Chartres. Ike's OD Cadillac with its British, French, and American flags had been placed in between two armored cars; Sibert piloted ahead in a jeep. As we neared the city, bicycles crowded the road until it looked as though half of Paris had pedaled out that morning to forage in the countryside for food. Occasionally we honked past an ancient high-wheeled truck whose charcoal burner fouled its path with a trail of gaseous fumes. Here and there along the road, units of the 4th Division napped in their GI blankets, oblivious to the stir.

Gerow was waiting at a busy streetcorner inside the flag-draped Porte d'Orléans. Through the Montparnasse where air raid shelters had been dug in the uprooted parks, we drove to the headquarters de Gaulle had established in the Prefecture of Police. The Garde Republicaine, in its Napoleonic tunics, red *fourragères,* and black patent leather hats, had been drawn up on the wide stairway from the courtyard to his office. Inside de Gaulle waited. He creased his long mournful face into a smile of welcome. This was my first meeting with France's dour soldier of the Resistance and I could sense nothing in the man but severity and resolution. De Gaulle spoke of the urgent need to reassure the Parisians that this time the Allies had come with forces strong enough to drive the German into his homeland and there destroy him. To impress the people with this strength and give them heart, he suggested that we parade a division or two of troops through Paris.

Ike turned to me and asked what we could do. Since we had already planned to attack eastward out of Paris, I told him that we could probably march a division straight through the Etoile rather than around the city's fringes.

"How soon?" Ike asked.

"Oh, perhaps two or three days—I'll have to check."

With General Joseph-Pierre Koenig, whom de Gaulle had named French military governor of Paris, we drove up the Boulevard des Invalides to where the gilded Dome des Invalides stood over the tomb of Napoleon. After halting briefly at the crypt, we crossed the Seine to the broad Place de la Concorde and drove up the leafy Champs Elysées. A huge Tricolor filled the Arc de Triomphe from its arch to the street. As Eisenhower dismounted to salute France's unknown warrior, a jubilant crowd bore down on him. His way back to the car was blocked and a wedge of MP's struggled to clear a path to its door. But when Ike had closed to within an arm's length of safety, he was collared from the rear by a huge tousled Frenchman who slathered him on both cheeks. The crowd squealed in delight as Ike reddened and fought free. Cut off from the car, I made my way to an escort jeep where a handsome young lady purred over the driver. Later as I rubbed a smear of her lipstick from my cheek, I joked Ike on my better fortune. "I'll leave the accolades to you," I told him, "and take my chances with the crowd."

After having helped tow our dragnet north across the face of Montgomery's front, the 28th Division had withdrawn back into the U. S. sector to reorganize at Versailles for First Army's advance beyond the Seine. There it waited as the logical candidate for our march through Paris.

On the sunny afternoon of August 29 the division's freshly scrubbed columns with loaded guns and full bandoliers swung down the Champs Elysées from the Arc de Triomphe to the crowded Place de la Concorde. There to the division's own tune of "Khaki Bill," the procession parted into two columns, each moving into assembly preparatory to attack. What appeared to the Parisians to be a division on parade was actually a tactical movement into battle. Within 26 hours from the moment it had been alerted for this march, the division had moved up from Versailles to a bivouac in the Bois de Boulogne. There it scrubbed from its uniforms and trucks the encrusted dirt of 36 days in the line, issued instructions for the "parade" and battle orders for the end of the line of march.

Ike stayed away from Paris that day in a discreet effort to avoid offending the British who might look on our parade as a stunt to curry favor with the French. Although we had invited Montgomery to join us, we were not surprised when he declined. Eisenhower's tact, though well-intentioned, did not mollify those Britishers who thought they had been snubbed. A section of the London press pounced upon our U. S. "parade," as we feared it would, and branded it a deliberate affront to British prestige.

Had de Gaulle not asked for an immediate demonstration of force in Paris, I would never have acceded to this parade of U. S. forces. For a liberated Paris had become the symbol of Free France and no one merited a share in the rites more than the British people. The British, however, were not totally bereft of credits in Paris. When Civil Affairs formed a flying column to carry in the first delivery of food, a fleet of British trucks joined the good-will mission. Each carried a Union Jack on its windshield and banners on its sides that read: "Food for the people of Paris." The hundreds of American trucks in that column entered the city in anonymous OD.

It was the middle of August when Monty and I first skirmished over the strategy to be employed in SHAEF's campaign east of the Seine. That skirmishing continued through several major show-

Communications, the Lifeline of Command: "In Europe the war was directed by telephone. Despite the vast distances that often separated units across our front, at no time was any command farther away than the instrument on my field desk." (July, 1944.)

Courtney Hodges and George Patton: "In temperament and tactics, Hodges (*left*) and Patton were quite different, yet each in his own way was no less successful than the other. With Hodges on the inside, Patton on the outside, both sped across France in the speediest blitz of modern war."

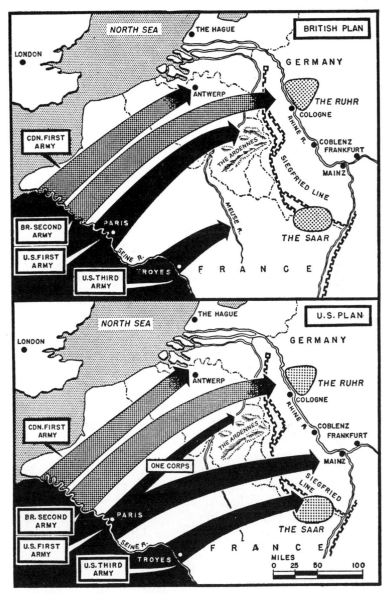

For the campaign beyond Paris to the Rhine, Montgomery proposed a single thrust of three Allied Armies north of the Ardennes toward the Ruhr. A fourth Army was to be held in position on the Meuse, that part of its divisions might be diverted to that main effort on the north. In the alternative plan—or double thrust—recommended by 12th Army Group, Montgomery's main effort was to be supported by only one U. S. corps while the remainder of First Army joined the Third in a secondary drive to the Rhine near Mainz.

downs and did not end until the spring of 1945 when Eisenhower finally turned me loose at Remagen for encirclement of the Ruhr.

Initially, however, our dispute was confined to the issue of an immediate advance beyond the Seine. The issue had come to a head sooner than we anticipated as a result of the enemy's blundering reaction at Mortain to our Breakout. For instead of the river defenses we had expected to find on the Seine, the remainder of France had been laid open from Paris to the Siegfried Line.

Now Eisenhower was forced to choose between two plans in the war beyond the Seine. One involved a predominantly American effort; the other was basically British.

The first or predominantly American plan called for emphasis on a thrust to the Reich straight through the middle of France to the Saar and beyond the Saar to the Rhine in the vicinity of Frankfurt. By August 25 Third Army had opened this path to Troyes, 80 miles southeast of Paris, only 150 from the Reich frontier. Both the First and Third American Armies, we estimated, would be required for this major effort. And it was to be accompanied by a secondary thrust of Montgomery's British and Canadian Armies up the Channel coast to Antwerp.

A second plan recommended by the British proposed that all our Allied strength be concentrated on a drive north through Amiens and Brussels over a path almost twice the distance of the one we proposed through the Saar. The British insisted upon this northern thrust even in the event it were to mean total abandonment of the advance to the Saar.

Principal advantage of the American plan with its primary thrust toward Frankfurt lay in the directness of its route to the enemy's homeland across the undefended front that stretched beyond Third Army. A main effort there would not only carry us past the fortifications of Metz and through the Maginot Line but it might even penetrate the unmanned defenses of the Siegfried Line. And in the event it went all the way to the Rhine, it would deprive the enemy of his important Saar basin.

Its disadvantages stemmed primarily from the weakness of Montgomery whose 21st Group was still opposed by German divisions from the Pas de Calais. Unless Monty could push on abreast of us, we might both find ourselves in salients with dangerously exposed flanks. Even more disturbing was the fear that Montgomery might find his British forces inadequate for the capture of Antwerp. For as weather deteriorated over the beaches, we would rapidly become dependent upon that port. At the same time if Monty were unable to clear the rocket coasts of Belgium and Holland, there were almost certain to be political repercussions in London.

Even though it meant a longer, perhaps even stiffer advance, the British plan offered a variety of undeniable advantages. With two Armies of his own and an American Army, Montgomery could safely guarantee speedy liberation of the Lowlands. This, in turn, would mean:

1. Early capture of Antwerp and the Channel ports. The former was to become a priority project of top-rate importance once we scrapped our plans for the Brittany ports.

2. Seizure of the Belgian airfields for short-range fighter support of heavy bombers engaged in daylight raids.

3. Clearance of the rocket coast from which the enemy harassed London.

At the same time an advance on this northern route would carry the British Armies directly toward the Ruhr—and, as Monty afterward claimed, the best route to Berlin.

In recommending that Eisenhower devote all of his resources to this main effort, Montgomery suggested that Ike might bed Third Army down on the Meuse and there let Patton hold while he raced on to Berlin. The proposal was reminiscent of Monty's tactics during the Sicilian campaign when he recommended that U. S. forces sit out the war on a defensive front while he went on alone to take Messina.

Anticipating Eisenhower's eagerness to secure the Channel coast, I argued for a modified double thrust—one that would encompass the advantages of both British and American plans. Instead of assigning Hodge's entire First Army to Montgomery's advance, I would have Ike limit our support to a corps. "Enough," I contended, "to keep Monty going." The remaining two corps of First Army would then team up with the Third in a direct thrust through the Saar toward the Rhine. Monty, however, declined this compromise; he demanded all of First Army.

In arguing that my support for Monty be limited to a single U. S. corps, I did not challenge the primary importance of his northern thrust. "But why three additional corps?" I asked, "that's two more than he will need!" If only Monty would take a chance and attack without insisting upon an overwhelming preponderance in force, we might use those two remaining corps to reinforce our lower thrust to the Rhine. This lower thrust might then be linked up with that of the Seventh Army to seal off the Germans not yet caught in Devers' advance up the Rhone.

In eyeing the advantages of this American plan, we did not overlook the possibility of reaching the Rhine to knock out the Saar and cut off barge traffic on that river. Beyond that, however, I curbed all speculation. Never in my wildest dreams did I imagine that we could force the Rhine alone. For if we were to gain that river bank, I estimated it would be difficult enough to hold the position without reaching out for more. Those who afterward insisted that Patton could have gone on to Berlin had SHAEF not cut off his gasoline overlook one significant fact in their speculations: inside Germany, beyond the Rhine, there was still a German army. We were to be reminded of that before the month was out and once again on December 16 in the Ardennes.

On August 23 Eisenhower decided tentatively in favor of the single thrust. In a letter to 21st Group he directed that Montgomery make the main effort up the Channel coast. Monty had won the initial skirmish. I was ordered to support the British effort with all nine divisions of First Army.

Third Army was not to be benched but our recommendation for a five-corps thrust in the south through Metz had been watered down to a feint by three. With this priority in troops, Montgomery was also to have top priority in supply. As a result, the First Army was to be given priority over the Third Army in 12th Army Group tonnage.

Meanwhile, Third Army was to push on to the Marne, 70 miles east of Paris. There it would "be prepared to continue the advance on Army Group order to seize the crossing of the Rhine river from Mannheim to Coblenz." However, those Army Group orders were to be governed by the adequacy of our supply. Beyond the Marne, Third Army's tonnage was to be restricted to whatever we could comb from the leftovers of First Army and our Britannic cousins to the north.

Though disappointed, I did not question but as a matter of fact agreed with Eisenhower's choice of emphasis on this offensive to the north. For I could readily understand his desire to secure the Lowlands with their airfields and Channel ports. But I did vigorously dispute his decision to give Montgomery all three corps of First Army. One, I insisted, would have been enough. And I challenged Montgomery's extravagant estimates in his requirements for supply.

Not long afterward, however, I was forced to concede that Eisenhower was probably right in his allotment of those two additional corps for I had underestimated the resistance that confronted Monty. Had the British been limited to support of one U. S. corps as we had originally proposed, Monty could never have advanced speedily enough to exploit the enemy's disorder. As Monty trooped up the coast, he dropped off division after division to bottle up the enemy garrisons in Channel ports. By September 10 more than a third of his forces were pinned down to those rear-area missions.

On the other hand, I do believe that Monty could have delivered his thrust with less extravagance in tonnage. Initially, he maintained that he could not support 21st Army Group without U. S. aid in trucking. To make up this British deficit in trucking we were forced to divert vehicles from Hodges. Then to keep Hodges rolling we hijacked trucks from Patton. As a consequence, George soon found his advance choked off by a shortage in gasoline. Had Monty pared down his ammunition requirements and concentrated instead on gasoline, Patton might have advanced farther. But Monty was reluctant (and he may have been right) to take a chance even on light resistance without fully stocked ammunition dumps. I argued strenuously with Eisenhower on Monty's extravagance in tonnage, but without success, for I was unable to budge him. Meanwhile Patton worried, then moaned and stormed as the growing shortage of QM trucks caused his gasoline supplies to dwindle.

To carry George on to the Marne and as far beyond it as his gasoline would take him, we called on Troop Carrier for an emergency air lift. The lift started on August 23 but even this narrow margin of relief was soon to be denied us. For in the letter in which Eisenhower approved Montgomery's plan, he directed that airborne forces be used to clear a path for that northern thrust. A drop was to be made on Tournai, Belgium, a carpet-manufacturing city 13 miles east of Lille. Eisenhower estimated that this airborne force would help pocket the enemy's Fifteenth Army as it withdrew from the Pas de Calais. I pleaded with Ike to discard the scheme and leave us the aircraft for supply. The drop had been scheduled for September 3. "We'll be there before you can pull it," I warned, but Eisenhower stuck by his guns.

How much of Ike's enthusiasm for this airborne plan could be attributed to Brereton, I do not know. The latter had been transferred from command of the Ninth Air Force earlier that month to head the newly formed First Allied Airborne Army. In addition to Troop Carrier craft, Brereton's command included a British and an American corps, each with two airborne divisions. Almost from the day of its creation, this Allied Airborne Army showed an astonishing faculty for devising missions that were never needed. Yet even apart from the high-pressure entreaties of Brereton's staff, Eisenhower had good reason to favor the Tournai drop. So important was Monty's advance during this period of enemy dissolution that Eisenhower felt compelled to employ every weapon at his disposal. And since we would never discover the full capabilities of an airborne army until one was dropped in a moving situation, here was an opportunity for Eisenhower to try it out.

Day by day C-47's were withdrawn from our air lift to be readied for the Tournai drop until on August 31, airborne supply dwindled to less than 30 tons. Meanwhile of the 400,000 gallons of gasoline requisitioned by Patton the day before, only 31,000 had reached his forward dumps. By now these supply shortages had clamped a stranglehold on Third Army's movements. Without air lift we could not hope to break it.

Patton boomed into TAC the next day from his CP southeast o Paris.

"Dammit, Brad," he pleaded, "just give me 400,000 gallons of gasoline and I'll put you inside Germany in two days." Although George habitually exaggerated even the most optimistic estimates of his Army staff, this time I could not dispute him. He had already passed through Verdun, only 35 miles from Metz, a scant 70 miles from the Saar with nothing to bar his way except the empty fortifications of the Siegfried Line.

But 400,000 gallons of gasoline? George might as well have asked for the moon. Ike's Tournai air drop had now demolished our last faint hope for the support of Patton's offensive.

"When the paratroopers come down," I predicted, "they'll find us waiting on the ground."

On the evening of September 2, a column of Hodges' tanks reached the outskirts of Tournai within view of the five towers of its Cathedral of Notre Dame. Although Tournai lay beyond our boundary, six miles in Montgomery's sector, I had ordered Hodges to push in and take it. "I promised Ike we'd be there," I told him, "and I want to be sure that we are when I call him."

At 5:15 on the morning of September 3, Hansen awakened me with a message from Monty who complained that U. S. troops in Tournai were blocking the British road to Brussels. I called First Army and instructed the officer on duty in G-3 to have them withdraw from the city.

Although we had made good on our boast and Ike's air drop was washed out, even our smugness could not compensate for the critical loss we had suffered in tonnage. For it was not until September 6 that the daily charts of Lieutenant Colonel Harry D. Henshel, staff officer for air movements, showed full recovery of tonnage in air lift. During the six-day stoppage that had resulted from SHAEF's planned drop at Tournai, we lost an average of 823 tons per day. In gasoline, this loss would have equaled one and a half million gallons, enough to run Third Army four days nearer the Rhine.

Although I cannot say that except for this lost Tournai tonnage, Third Army might have reached the Rhine early in September, it is fair to assume that Patton would have gone farther than he did. With it he might possibly have pushed on past Metz and into the Saar. Three months and many casualties later we were to be forcefully reminded that in war, opportunity once forsaken is opportunity lost forever. Not until December 2 did Third Army crack the Saar— and then only after a bitter winter offensive through a heavily fortified line.

When Eisenhower backed Montgomery in the latter's thrust to the north, he also committed himself to the logistical support of 21st Group, and at U. S. expense if necessary. Then to make certain that our principal effort would go in support of Monty, Eisenhower rationed the split in tonnage between my two Armies, requiring me to allot the bulk of it to Hodges. Patton was to go just as far as he could in his advance toward the Reich. But in the event of a logistical showdown, Montgomery and Hodges were to be supplied even if Patton had to be halted.

The logistical crisis that now threatened to halt us where the enemy could not, had come not as the result of a breakdown in supply but as the inevitable consequence of an unexpectedly speedy advance. Despite its achievements, even U. S. logistical know-how could not stretch its lines that fast. By the end of August, Third Army had reached Verdun, 313 miles from Cherbourg. Even the Red Ball Express with its one-way, high-speed columns fell behind the minimum tonnage requirements of our Armies. Turnaround time on the run had increased to five days, meaning that it took five trucks in the pipeline to dump a daily truckload on the front. Beyond Paris the rail system had improved but west of the Seine where the lodgment had been isolated by Allied air, engineers struggled to repair hundreds of bombed bridges and break paths through the gutted yards. Now I could sympathize with the ordeal von Rundstedt had suffered at the hands of Allied air, for we had inherited the terrible devastation he had undergone.

During our late August and September pursuit of the enemy across France, gasoline formed the bulk of our tonnage. For as we rolled on against spotty rather than organized resistance, ammunition expenditures declined. Whereas in Normandy an armored division might ordinarily consume four tons of ammunition for each ton of gasoline it burned, now the proportion was reversed and ammunition tonnage fell to the modest level of that required for food.

As far back as 1942, Lord Louis Mountbatten, then British Chief of Combined Operations, had foreseen this problem of gasoline supply when he proposed construction of an underwater pipeline for cross-channel delivery of fuel to the invasion forces in France. Dubbed PLUTO—for *p*ipe-*l*ine *u*nder *t*he *o*cean—this undersea lifeline pumped its first gasoline ashore in Normandy on August 12. But like the signal construction battalions, pipeline engineers found their overland lines outdistanced by the speed of our advance. By the end of August, they had strung the pipeline no farther than Alençon, then 200 miles behind our front.

Initially, in the campaign east of the Seine, Third Army was to be restricted, on Ike's orders, to 2,000 tons per day. This was barely enough to sustain it in an almost totally uncontested advance. When Patton first learned of this slim ration, he brushed it lightly aside. But once its meaning struck home, he turned back to my CP, bellowing like an angry bull. When I reminded him of the competitive needs of those Armies on the north, George retorted, quite properly, that the problem of balance in supply was a problem for higher headquarters. He would fend for Third Army and let the devil take the hindmost. "To hell with Hodges and Monty," George would roar in good humor. "We'll win your goddam war if you'll keep Third Army going."

Although theoretically immobilized as the result of his scant daily gasoline ration, Patton funneled his driblet of fuel into a few tanks and rolled stubbornly ahead. Within the Third Army he deadlined thousands of vehicles and clamped ironclad conservation measures on the others. Thereafter when George reported to EAGLE TAC,. he would coast in on a jeep with a near-empty tank and instruct his driver to fill it up at our motor pool.

As Patton continued to push on in the face of a gasoline shortage that theoretically should have stopped him somewhere on the Meuse, Montgomery accused me of having hedged on Ike's orders to grant top priority to Hodges. The charge was easily refuted, for it was Eisenhower himself who apportioned the tonnage allotments between them. We had followed those requirements to the letter but at the same time had kept Patton going simply by allocating almost all of his tonnage to gasoline, with very little for ammunition.

Inevitable though it was, this September crisis in supply bred an angry sense of frustration among U. S. combat units. Infuriated by the empty gas tanks that choked off their easy advance, they upbraided the hapless Com Z* for their misfortunes. Although Com Z could not have anticipated the enemy's rapid collapse, it offered fair game to the field forces in search of a whipping boy. For while Com Z had labored heroically to avert the crisis in supply, others of its antics did not endear it to the field commanders. Although I would not hold Com Z at fault for the halt that bogged us down short of the Siegfried Line, neither could I give it a completely clean bill of health. For Com Z was implicated in the failure and Com Z meant General Lee.

As commanding general of the Communications Zone, the fastidious but brilliant Lieutenant General J. C. H. Lee was Eisenhower's chief logistician for all U. S. forces. An energetic and imaginative commander with bold executive talents, Lee suffered however from an unfortunate pomposity that caused others to underrate his skills. Administratively, his was probably the most exacting task in the ETO and although Lee worked at it with the swagger of a martinet, he usually delivered the goods.

In his anxiety to assume personal direction of supply operations in France, Lee had ferried the vanguard of Com Z headquarters from

*Communications Zone.

London to Cherbourg early in August. To house his enormous CP in the field, he built a Nisson hut cantonment that required an extravagant quantity of tonnage at a time when tonnage was tight.

Long before we liberated Paris, Eisenhower had declared he would ban the city to headquarters commands and reserve its hotels for the use of troops on furlough.

Ike's ban apparently did not reach Lee, for on August 30 we heard that Com Z had abandoned its Nisson huts in Normandy for the comfortable boulevards of Paris. In addition to being provoked over Com Z's pirating of these hotels, I was irritated to learn that Lee had picked up his headquarters and dragged it 200 miles during the heat of our supply crisis. However carefully he might have organized the move, the shuffle could not help but disarrange his operations. No one could compute the cost of that move in lost truck tonnage on the front. But whatever the loss, its move to Paris cost Com Z angry reproof in the field. Field forces in combat have always begrudged the supply services their rear-echelon comforts. But when the infantry learned that Com Z's comforts had been multiplied by the charms of Paris, the injustice rankled all the deeper and festered there throughout the war.

20: *Famine*

in Supply

SEPTEMBER, 1944, MARKED THE MONTH OF THE BIG
Bust. But before the bust came the boom and until the German
halted our tanks in the dragon's teeth of his Siegfried Line, we
bounded along on the headiest and most optimistic advance of the
European war.

So complete was the enemy's collapse east of Paris that troops
trucking forward in their GMC's found the front-line scuttlebutt
filled with omens of early redeployment to the CBI.* This optimism
pervaded even the headquarters commands where staffs held their
breath, tallied the tonnage, and talked of getting home by Christmas.

Northeast of Paris where the Picardy roads buckled under the
weight of our heavy columns, organized enemy resistance disintegrated as telephone communications snapped in the frenzy of this
forced withdrawal. The well-drilled Wehrmacht that only four years
before had panicked French refugees along those roads now fled
with no less terror. Lacking the communications with which to
exercise control and unable to form a rear-guard action, the enemy
stumbled blindly toward the Reich and once more blundered into
disaster, this time at Mons.

On September 2 as his VII Corps swarmed across the Belgian
border in flank support of Monty's drive on Brussels, Collins pointed
his troops toward Mons where in 1914 the Kaiser's army had crashed
headlong into the BEF. Approaching Mons from the North Sea

*China-Burma-India theater of operations.

coast were the disjointed elements of 20 German divisions flushed by Monty from the Normandy beachhead and from the Pas de Calais. Fleeing in rout toward the German frontier where it bulges into Belgium near Aachen, the enemy columns collided with Collins near the city of Mons. Neither had been forewarned of the approach of the other and both stumbled into an unforeseen battle. By the time it ended more than 2,000 of the enemy had been killed and another 30,000 were packed off as prisoners to our cages.

This collision at Mons had cost the enemy the last reserves of both his Seventh and Fifteenth Armies, leaving the roads through Belgium virtually unblocked all the way to the Reich border. Not only had Hodges opened a path to Liége and beyond Liége to Aachen but he had destroyed a force the enemy desperately needed to man the empty fortifications of his Siegfried Line. It was this little-known victory at Mons that enabled First Army to break through the Siegfried Line and within six weeks take the city of Aachen.

Elsewhere along the front where our columns threaded eastward, the enemy's withdrawal had fallen into confusion. In the sector of 21st Army Group, a German general was captured in his staff car while rolling north as part of a British convoy. Mistaken for an officer of the RAF, the general had journeyed unmolested in a column of trucks until collared by a bug-eyed MP.

"And just where in blazes do you think you're going?" he asked. The German was headed toward the Somme where he had been ordered to organize a defense of that river line. He was told the British had crossed the Somme two days before.

In the First Army zone of advance where the enemy's route of withdrawal crossed Hodges' path, German traffic flowing through the major intersections had become a highway hazard. In at least one instance, however, our columns crossed as though on an exercise in troop movements. Major General Edward H. Brooks had parked his jeep at a crossroads near Cambrai to look over his 2d Armored as it rolled by. Scarcely had the division's tail cleared that intersection when a French farmer cycled breathlessly up the intersecting road.

"Les Boches, les Boches—" he called, pointing back over the road he had pedaled.

"How many?" Brooks asked as he signaled his radio operator to warm up the transmitter mounted in his jeep.

"Beaucoup, beaucoup—" the man replied breathlessly.

Brooks turned part of his column around in time to nab the enemy procession as it approached the crossroads.

While cheered by these reports of enemy chaos, it was to Brest that I looked for a more meaningful clue to the enemy's will to resist. For despite the futility of its position, the garrison at Brest held out under the pounding of three U. S. divisions. If the enemy could command such stubborn resistance in so hopeless a situation as the one at Brest, I was disinclined to believe in any prediction of collapse until we had reached the Rhine. Perhaps there the enemy would acknowledge the futility of further military resistance and salvage what he could by surrender before we crushed him in a vise between our front and that of the Russian. But if the enemy held out on the Rhine, then we could safely assume that he would fight on to the end.

Thus to end the war we must push on to the Rhine and force the enemy to that decision. But to gain the Rhine it was essential that we maintain the momentum of our St.-Lô Breakout until we had cleared the Siegfried Line. For the enemy could easily deduce from the swift pace of our advance how severely our supply lines had already been strained in support of so rapid a movement. If only he could check that momentum on the Siegfried Line then he might force us to halt for reorganization and supply. Either he halted us there or he fell back across the Rhine.

Logically the enemy should have surrendered during this period of the pursuit, for it was during the succeeding eight months of the war that Germany suffered the most in casualties and air bombing. Moreover, had the army overthrown Hitler before being crushed in defeat before the disbelieving eyes of the German people, it might have preserved the myth of invincibility by attributing its defeat to the Nazis. But rebellion by this time had become a lost hope; Himmler's reprisals for the July 20 attempt to overthrow Hitler had effectively silenced the German army. For the Nazi inner circle, of course, there could be no hesitation—there was no other way out. No one knew better than they that their crimes would not go unpunished. Rather than shorten their lives a few more weeks or months, they chose to drag the nation down with them to destruction.

One bright September morning as I sat in my trailer outside Chartres balancing reports on tonnage against mileage to the Rhine, a stooped figure in wrinkled OD's rapped gently on the door. He carried a scuffed helmet in his hand. A thin smile broke through the weariness on his face. It was Ernie Pyle, our constant companion from the Sicilian campaign.

"Ernie—" I called, "Ernie, come in. What's this I hear about your going home?"

He tossed his helmet on the leather sofa, nodded, and forced a grin. "I just came down from Paris, Brad, to say good-by."

"You'll be back?"

Ernie shook his head and hunched his shoulders in his baggy tanker's jacket.

"Get away from it for a while, you've had enough."

"Too much," he agreed.

Tunisia, Sicily, Italy, and now France—22 months of it. Twenty-two months of too many friendships that ended with the mattress covers in which we wrapped our dead. For a man who suffered it with the intensity of Pyle, it was clearly enough and too much.

During a recent illness Ernie had dipped heavily into his slim backlog of columns until now he was fighting deadlines and crowding a new one each day. Worse yet, he said, he was all written out. Tragedy had at last sponged him dry.

"A couple of months' rest," I told him, "and you'll be back with us on the line."

Ernie forced a wan smile. "They tell me it'll be over by then—"

"Maybe," I agreed. "But if the enemy can command the resistance Ramcke has mustered at Brest, who knows how long it might last? Now is the time to quit but all signs point the other way. If he doesn't fold up on the Rhine, we may have to cut him to pieces before he gives up."

Pyle looked up surprised. "They're a lot rosier than that farther up front, especially at First Army."

I shrugged my shoulders. "Maybe that's because it looks so easy now."

Ernie returned to Paris for lunch; this was to be the last time I saw him. At dinner one evening in Wiesbaden only six days before we closed with the Russians, a TWX was delivered to me from Hugh Baillie of the United Press. Ernie Pyle had been killed on an island near Okinawa by Japanese machine-gun fire. The doughboy had lost his best friend of the war.

Astonished by the ease with which Monty advanced northeast beyond the Seine, SHAEF rechecked its strategy for the east France campaign and on September 4 concluded that Patton's drive toward the Saar need not yet be arrested. Against so demoralized an enemy, SHAEF had estimated that it could supply Patton without handicapping Monty. Although Monty's drive was still to be the *main* Allied effort, this time the pendulum swung nearer our strategy of the double thrust.

Instead of turning all three corps of First Army north of the Ardennes, Hodges was to support Monty's advance with two while straddling that forest barrier to the south, with a third in support of Patton's advance toward Frankfurt. This shift in favor of a double thrust both north and south of the Ardennes brought with it a tactical windfall. No longer was Eisenhower to be committed to a single axis of advance against which the enemy could mass his defenses. Now having spread his offensive across a broad Allied front, Eisenhower could feint and dodge with his double thrust and confuse the enemy on his intentions. If the enemy were to rally his strength on the north to blunt Montgomery's thrust toward the Ruhr, he would be forced to weaken the Saar and expose that front to Patton's Army. On the other hand if he were to shift more weight to the Saar he could do so only by risking a British breakthrough on the north. As long as we held the initiative on so broad a front, the enemy would find his defenses stretched beyond the breaking point.

By the first of September the enemy's June strength on the Western front had been cut down to a disorganized corporal's guard. The total of all German remnants north of the Ardennes equaled only 11 divisions, of which but two were panzers. Meanwhile to oppose Patton's drive to the Saar the enemy could muster the equivalent of no more than five divisions. Another 100,000 troops had fled from the Biscay coast of France, but their field capabilities amounted to no more than a single division. And of the multitude swarming up the Rhone before the U. S. Seventh Army, the enemy could count the equivalent of only two and one-half field divisions. Altogether, his entire force in the West equaled the combat strength of but 20 divisions.

But while the enemy's strength withered, ours grew as the cross-channel build-up continued. By now Monty's Group consisted of 15 divisions while mine had increased to 20. Meanwhile DRAGOON had brought another eight from the Cannes coast up the Rhone Valley. And in England three airborne divisions waited in reserve as part of the First Allied Airborne Army. Four more divisions then in the pipeline from the United States were scheduled to join 12th Army Group by the middle of September.

This margin of superiority, however, would be cut down once we reached the German frontier, for there in a band of fortifications known as the Siegfried Line, the enemy had constructed the equivalent in concrete of many additional divisions. If we were to reach the Rhine before the enemy regained his balance, it was essential we penetrate those Siegfried defenses before he manned them. Otherwise our troop superiority would be largely offset by the enemy's casemated guns and bunkers.

Logistically, SHAEF's change of heart on the double thrust brought a brief new lease on life to Patton. For with the order to resume his advance toward the Saar came equal priority in supply with the First Army.

But despite this promise of parity, Patton's troubles did not end there, for they originated, as did Hodges', not from the inequitable distribution of supply but from inadequate overland shipments. It had become increasingly clear that sooner or later we would be forced to halt, regroup, and re-establish a new line of supply from the deep-water ports on the Channel north of the Seine. Until those new and shorter supply lines were established we dared not even contemplate a major offensive across the Rhine. In the meantime as long as our momentum lasted, we would continue to push on, hoping to forestall the inevitable breakdown until we had cracked the Siegfried Line.

A less aggressive commander than Patton would probably have hoarded the pittance that came his way and halted his line for winter safekeeping behind the Meuse River line. But George plunged boldly on beyond the Meuse 30 miles farther to the Moselle where he promptly grabbed a bridgehead south of the fortress city of Metz.

On the sunny afternoon of September 13, tanks from the 3rd Armored Division of the VII Corps broke across the German border through a soft spot in the Siegfried Line just ten miles south of Aachen. After three successive invasions of western Europe in 74 years, the German army had for the first time been hurled back into its homeland. The news reached me at Dreux, a few miles east of Paris where TAC was about to pull up stakes for the long leap to Verdun.

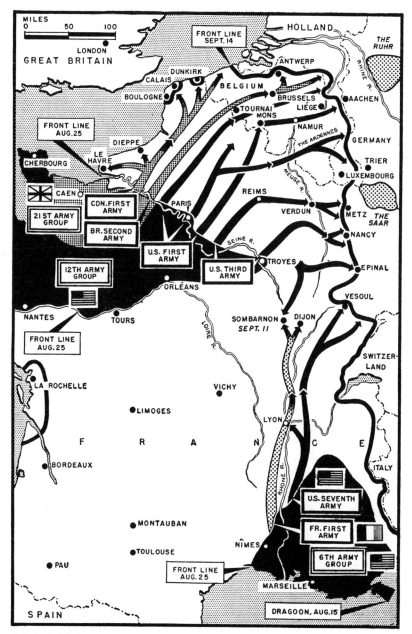

Within 20 days after the capture of Paris, British and American Armies reached the German border, and on September 11, DRAGOON forces from southern France joined Third Army in a continuous front.

But news of this border crossing could not hide the fact that at last we had run out of momentum, for no sooner had our troops crossed the frontier than we jarred to a sudden halt. The six dizzying weeks of Breakout had ended. For the next two months we were to wait on the Siegfried Line until the long supply line that reached back to Cherbourg was replaced by another at Antwerp. With reinforcements brought in from east of the Rhine, the enemy had barely re-established his position. Our dash to the Rhine had failed and with it went our one best hope for an early German surrender.

The morning before Collins crossed the German frontier, I had summoned Hodges and Patton to TAC for a review of their offensive capabilities in the light of our worsening crisis in supply. That evening I summarized the results of this meeting in a letter to Ike. For the previous ten days First Army had averaged 3,300 tons per day compared to Third Army's 2,500, inasmuch as parity for the latter had not been authorized until September 6. Hodges reported that he now had on hand ammunition for five days' fighting and gasoline enough to carry him to the Rhine. On the basis of his current allocation of supply, Hodges estimated that he could support ten days of strenuous fighting on his 120-mile First Army front. Patton reported four days of ammunition and enough gasoline to roll on to the Rhine.

Five days before, Montgomery had complained that this diversion of gasoline to Patton had slowed Hodges in his First Army advance on the right flank of the British. But while Courtney admitted that gasoline shortages might have cost his Army a day's advance, he attributed the delay to difficulty in bridging the Meuse and to a noticeable stiffening of enemy opposition.

By the end of September, Hodges had exhausted his supply of motor fuel in First Army without having broken through the sturdily held Siegfried Line. There he was to be restricted to limited advances until we once again resumed the offensive during the November rains.

On the southern front below the Ardennes forest, Patton's 80th Division had established a bridgehead across the Moselle between Metz and Nancy. But enemy resistance had suddenly grown heavier and George found his crossings strongly opposed as he sought to widen the beachhead. On September 12, I gave him two more days to get the bulk of his forces across the Moselle. If by then he had not succeeded, he was to switch to the defensive from Nancy north to

Luxembourg and thereafter concentrate his effort north of the Moselle where it turns east at Trier. George required no further urging. Still confident that Third Army could push on to the Rhine, he stormed a 50-mile strip of the Moselle and by the evening of September 14 reported four divisions safely across it. But by then George had further depleted his thin stocks of supply. Like Hodges, Patton had finally reached the end of his tether.

Almost two weeks before, Monty and I had agreed on the path to be followed beyond Brussels in our outside thrust toward the Rhine. We were to furnish two U. S. corps in the advance; Monty was to provide one. All three were to strike abreast across the plains of Cologne between Düsseldorf and Bonn. Meanwhile the left corps of Dempsey's Second British Army was to veer off northeast from this thrust while the First Canadian Army pushed up the coast. There it was to capture the Channel ports, clear out the rocket sites, and close in to the Scheldt, the inland waterway that led from the sea to Antwerp.

To the right of this main effort, Hodges' one remaining corps would straddle the Ardennes with a thin line and direct its advance up the Moselle Valley in the direction of Coblenz. Meanwhile, the two northernmost of Patton's corps, below the Ardennes, were to drive toward the Saar. If strength permitted, a third was to attack north of the Vosges Mountains toward the Rhine River city of Karlsruhe.

As Crerar's Canadian Army leapfrogged up the Channel ports, Dempsey's liberated Brussels and Antwerp. From Antwerp it was to push eastward abreast of Hodges' Army toward the Meuse. After flowing east from Namur to Liége, the Meuse turns north again until, renamed the Maas, it flows seaward.

Following the capture of Antwerp on September 4, Montgomery winced as we did over the sudden reappearance of German opposition on his front. The stiffening could be traced to a Prussian, decorated by Hitler the previous summer for stopping the Russians on the Vistula. Field Marshal Walther Model had been ordered to the Western front to re-establish a defensive line after the suicide of von Kluge. In one of the enemy's more resourceful demonstrations of generalship, Model stemmed the rout of the Wehrmacht. He quieted the panic and reorganized the demoralized German forces into effective battle groups. From Antwerp to Epinal, 260 miles south, Model had miraculously grafted a new backbone on the German army.

Early in September Montgomery had reasoned that he could finish the war with a single deft stroke from the Rhine all the way to Berlin across the North Sea Lowlands. Instead of battering ahead toward the Ruhr as part of the three-corps offensive to which we had committed First Army, he would prefer to outflank Model's new line of resistance with a bold dash high to the north. This venture was thereafter to be remembered as the gallant defeat at Arnhem.

Had the pious teetotaling Montgomery wobbled into SHAEF with a hangover, I could not have been more astonished than I was by the daring adventure he proposed. For in contrast to the conservative tactics Montgomery ordinarily chose, the Arnhem attack was to be made over a 60-mile carpet of airborne troops. Although I never reconciled myself to the venture, I nevertheless freely concede that Monty's plan for Arnhem was one of the most imaginative of the war.

Code-named MARKET-GARDEN, it called for a 60-mile salient to be driven up a side-alley route to the Reich. If successful, it would outflank the Siegfried defenses and carry Montgomery across the lower Rhine on the shortest route to Berlin. Five major water obstacles crossed this path between Antwerp and Monty's objective at Arnhem. The first two were canals north of Eindhoven. The third was the Maas—or Meuse—where it coasted seaward 24 miles farther on. Eight miles beyond the Maas, the Waal flows under an arched bridge at Nijmegen. And at the end of the line at Arnhem, the lower Rhine forms a last barrier to the lightly fortified German border only 20 miles farther east.

Three airborne divisions were to roll the carpet across these waterways: the 101st at Eindhoven, the 82d at Nijmegen, and the British 1st at the tip near Arnhem. To thread those air-heads together on the overland advance, Montgomery picked his crack Guards Armored Division.

I had not been brought into the plan. In fact Montgomery had devised it and sold it to Ike several days before I even learned of it from our liaison officer to 21st Group. Monty's secrecy in planning confused me, for although the operation was to be confined to his sector, the move would nevertheless cripple the joint offensive we had agreed upon a few days before. In swerving northeast from the path to which he only recently committed a corps, Monty would

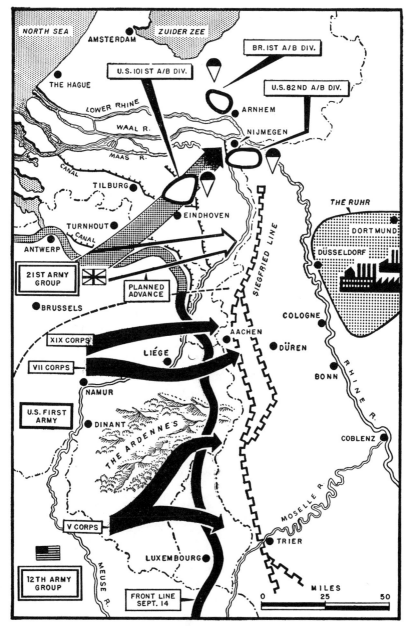

When on September 17, Montgomery swerved northeast to link up the air drop at Arnhem, he opened a gap on the left flank of Hodges' First Army. This unexpected change in direction necessitated an immediate realignment of those U. S. forces on the north.

uncover Hodges' left flank and expose him to counterattack. To protect that flank it became necessary for me to take one of Patton's three armored divisions, turn it north, and give it to Hodges.

Just as soon as I learned of Monty's plan, I telephoned Ike and objected strenuously to it. For in abandoning this joint offensive, Monty would slip off on a tangent and leave us holding the bag. But Ike silenced my objections; he thought the plan a fair gamble. It might enable us to outflank the Siegfried Line, perhaps even snatch a Rhine River bridgehead.

Each division that now came into France increased the margin of U. S. strength over that of the British. By September 15 Monty had completed his build-up except for three Canadian divisions that were to come in from the Mediterranean in April. Apprehensive lest Ike give in to Monty's persistent plea for troops, I was adamant that U. S. troops be retained under U. S. command.

My opposition to the Arnhem operation, however, was not confined to the British diversion of effort. I feared also that Monty in his eagerness to get around Model's flank might have underestimated German capabilities on the lower Rhine. Believing the plan too ambitious a one for the forces at his disposal, I would have preferred that Monty devote his resources to the Scheldt and the opening of Antwerp. For not until that port was cleared for Allied shipping could we undertake an offensive beyond the Rhine.

On Sunday, September 17, the skies over Holland darkened with aircraft as Brereton's Allied Airborne Army jumped into the first *daylight* drop of the war. I flew up to Monty's CP at Brussels later that afternoon where the first few crippled C-47's bellied in on emergency landings. Despite frequent enemy counterattacks against the length of that airborne salient, Monty's armor advanced up the carpet until on September 20 it rammed across the Nijmegen bridge to the east bank of the Waal River.

Between the Waal and Arnhem, however, the Guards Armored bogged down in the face of mounting enemy resistance. Meanwhile on the far bank of the lower Rhine, the British 1st Airborne Division soon found itself pinned in position by furious enemy counterattacks. For five days those red-bereted British airborne troops clung to that embattled bridgehead until on September 25, having despaired of breaking through, Montgomery ordered their withdrawal back across the Rhine. Of the 9,000 British troops who parachuted into that bridgehead, fewer than 2,500 infiltrated back to our lines.

There is a quality to adversity that summons the noblest in British valor and as a result valor often so obscures defeat that a heroic legend is remembered long after the defeat is forgotten. Arnhem followed in that British tradition. Monty had been turned back short of his goal but so valorous was the defeat that the strategic rebuff passed unnoticed.

True, the British had secured a bridgehead across the Waal but it had been won at an incalculable cost. Not until six months later did Monty force the Rhine and then his crossing was made almost 50 miles upstream from the airborne objective at Arnhem. Meanwhile the neglected campaign in the Scheldt was to drag on through October. Not until November 26 would that vital passage be cleared for Allied shipping.

Monty afterward attributed his failure at Arnhem to the perversity of weather; and certainly weather shared in the blame. For on the second day of attack, murky weather over the Lowlands caused Monty's resupply and reinforcement missions to miscarry. With the exception of two days, weather restricted Allied fighter operations and enabled the enemy to form his counterattacks without interference from air. Between September 19 when the Guards Armored reached Nijmegen and October 4 when Monty abandoned the effort, the enemy hit that long salient with 12 separate divisional attacks. Monty ruefully conceded that his "easy" path had concealed a briar patch.

In preparation for a conference of Army Group commanders at SHAEF on September 22, Eisenhower had asked each of us for comment on a strategy for conquest of the Reich itself. At EAGLE TAC we anticipated that Monty would press for overriding support on his northern offensive. For at the time Monty believed that if he were given U. S. divisions to reinforce his British Group, he could leap the Rhine, cap the Ruhr, and force a corridor to Berlin. I felt that he had vastly underestimated the enemy's uncommitted strength beyond the Rhine and was therefore certain that so brash an offensive would be mauled by flanking attack.

For weeks we had been exploring at 12th Army Group an alternate plan of attack for a *double* envelopment of the Ruhr. Whereas Monty would have us close to the Rhine no farther south than Cologne to protect the flank of his crossing, I held that we must

close to the Rhine on a broad front, certainly as far south as Coblenz
and preferably on down to the Swiss border.

In reporting my views to Ike, I prefaced them with three assump-
tions:

1. Not until we had cleared the Scheldt and secured the port of
Antwerp could we hope to sustain any large-scale offensive beyond
the Rhine.

2. Any advance into Germany would have to be made with great
strength in depth to guard the rear areas against counterattack and
sabotage.

3. Wherever the *main* effort might go, it would have to be supported by secondary attacks on the shoulders. For only by pressing
the enemy on a broad front could we prevent him from massing his
resistance against the *main* attack.

Our primary terrain objective lay in the Ruhr where a score of
grimy cities sprawled beneath their tall stacks to form the industrial
heart of Germany's war machine. Nourished by its rich seams of
coal, the Ruhr had grown to supremacy during the First Reich of
Bismarck. Since 1942 the Ruhr had withstood hundreds of Allied
air raids. After each raid it had cleared the rubble, patched the
damage, and gone back into production. Although air eventually
hurt the Ruhr, it had failed to destroy it. Without the Ruhr, Germany would be unable to support its Armies in the field. To snuff
out this industrial furnace I proposed to Eisenhower that we isolate
it with a *double* envelopment. While Monty rimmed the Ruhr from
the north across the plains of Westphalia, we would encircle it from
the south with our U. S. forces.

Although a road running east from Cologne offered the shortest
route for this U. S. encirclement, it twisted through the mountainous
Sauerland where terrain favored the defense. Far preferable was a
southernmost route that ran northeast from Frankfurt through the
rolling hills of Hesse. Both routes would probably be needed, I
wrote, but we would prefer to make Frankfurt the main U. S. effort
and complete our encirclement in the vicinity of Paderborn. This
city lay on the northeast rim of the Ruhr only 145 miles from Berlin.
Six months later when the Ruhr pocket was closed around more than
300,000 troops of Model's Army Group, we knotted it at Lippstadt,
only 20 miles from the point we had chosen that previous September. The campaign had developed precisely according to plan. Yet
seldom has a plan been subjected to so tiring a succession of crises

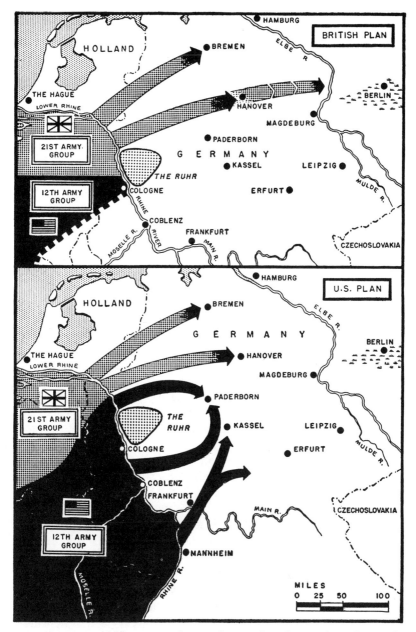

Montgomery would have Eisenhower close to the Rhine only as far south as Cologne, to concentrate American and British strength for his drive north of the Ruhr to Berlin. But 12th Army Group's alternative plan prescribed a double envelopment of the Ruhr.

as those which afflicted this one before Eisenhower gave it a green light.

SHAEF had moved its headquarters from the modest seaport town of Granville to a location around the corner from the palace in Versailles. Ike's office was housed in a small white stone annex behind the stately Trianon Palace Hotel. Inside its glass-walled foyer a bronze bust of Goering had been turned to the wall. A temporary plywood partition divided the huge office originally assigned Ike. "Too elegant," he shuddered, "I'd rattle around in the place and get lost."

Devers had already arrived at Versailles by air from his 6th Army Group headquarters down near the Vosges Mountains. His Group now consisted of two Armies—the U. S. Seventh Army of Lieutenant General Alexander M. Patch and the French First Army of General Jean de Lattre de Tassigny. Mobilized primarily in North Africa from among Free French volunteers, colonial conscripts, and native units, the French Army was equipped with American arms and GI clothing.

Meanwhile 12th Army Group had acquired another U. S. Army when the Ninth came in from England to relieve Patton's Third in its containment of the Brittany ports. The Ninth was green but ambitious and impressively eager to learn. Under the tutelage of Lieutenant General William H. Simpson it matured quickly. Unlike the noisy and bumptious Third and the temperamental First, the Ninth remained uncommonly normal.

The first hint of a hitch in the conference proceedings at Versailles came when Hansen told me that SHAEF's staff was betting Monty would not come. I was not surprised, therefore, when the session opened with Freddy de Guingand, Monty's genial peacemaker, substituting for his chief. Although Eisenhower appeared unperturbed, Monty's absence was viewed by the other commanders as an affront to the Allied chief. The situation at Arnhem was nearing its crisis but I do believe the war could have spared Monty for a few hours that one afternoon. Monty's failure to take part in the conference restricted its effectiveness. Although de Guingand came as a delegate for Monty, prepared to present his views, he lacked sufficient authority to bind his chief on commitments. If Monty's absence exasperated Ike, the latter restrained his irritation with uncommon self-control. I was annoyed myself two days later when Ike instructed me to visit Monty and review the decisions we had agreed to at Versailles. During a bad-weather flight to Monty's headquarters, we lost our way and almost flew into the enemy's lines as the result of a radio failure.

By now SHAEF had become as insistent as we at TAC on the need for a nearby major port to relieve the impossible strain upon our long lines of supply from Cherbourg and the beaches. Although Monty had captured the city of Antwerp 17 days before, he had as yet made little progress in clearing its seaward passage through the Scheldt. And until the Scheldt was cleared, Antwerp would be of no use. In this conference at Versailles, on September 22, Ike had underscored our need for a deep-water port and termed it "an indispensable prerequisite for the final drive deep into Germany." Despite those apprehensions, however, Eisenhower did not direct Monty to clear the Scheldt before undertaking any further offensive but instead granted him overriding logistical support on a British advance toward the Ruhr. Dempsey's Second British Army was to make the *main* effort while Hodges supported him on the right with the U. S. First Army. Eisenhower's decision dealt a blow to Patton's hopes for a speedy advance to the Rhine in the direction of Frankfurt. For after defining the First Army mission, the Supreme Commander had directed "the remainder of the 12th Army Group to take no more aggressive action than is permitted by the maintenance situation after the full requirements of the *main* effort have been met." In plainer language this meant the Third U. S. Army must sit down on the Moselle.

To help Monty concentrate his troops on a narrow front, I was directed to shift our 12th Army Group boundary 40 miles north and clear out the enemy that Monty had by-passed west of the Meuse. Then to lighten our maintenance load on the southern end of the U. S. line, we were ordered to transfer Haislip's corps of two divisions to Devers' Army Group. Because under this plan, Hodges would be extended across a 95-mile front from the Ruhr almost to the Moselle, I wedged Simpson's Ninth Army into the line on his right to take over the Ardennes. The Ardennes covered a quiet unpromising sector opposite the German Eifel, an almost impassable mountainous woodland that lay across the Luxembourg border.

Not until October 9 did Monty finally despair of pushing on swiftly through the Rhineland in his advance toward the northern rim of the Ruhr. After fighting for 20 days in the narrow belt between the Waal and the lower Rhine, Dempsey had failed to crack the enemy's resistance. And from the bridgehead Monty had bypassed west of the Meuse while running off to Arnhem, Model threatened to gnaw into the open British flank. Meanwhile Montgomery's airborne attack on Arnhem had failed to draw the enemy out of the Scheldt where he blocked the vital port of Antwerp.

Late in September von Rundstedt was again brought out of retirement and restored to command on the Western front. Aware of the embarrassing shortage we suffered in supply, he knew that by denying us Antwerp he could probably delay a fresh Allied offensive. And so as the Canadians forced their way up the North Sea coast toward the Scheldt, the enemy ferried across that seaway to dig in on Walcheren Island and there fasten a grip on the peninsula

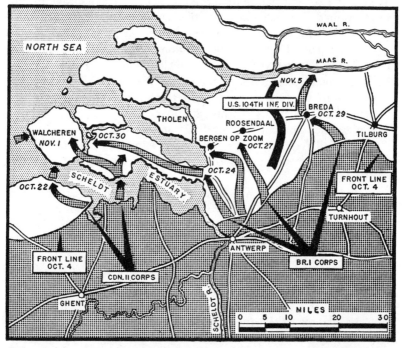

Although Montgomery entered the city of Antwerp on September 5, it was not until almost nine weeks later that he finally cleared the Scheldt for the passage of Allied ships to that key port city. This delay was to account for an irrevocable logistical loss to the Allies.

that joined that island with the mainland. When Monty paused for an inventory on this October position, he reasoned that his commitments now exceeded his means. To avoid overextending himself, he agreed to defer indefinitely his Ruhr offensive until first he cleared the Scheldt and opened the port of Antwerp.

Meanwhile 18 valuable days had been lost since Eisenhower underscored the importance of Antwerp in the September 22 meeting at Versailles. Thirty-five days had passed since the British 11th Armored Division rolled into Antwerp on that terminus of the Scheldt. Had Monty cleared the Scheldt immediately instead of reaching vainly toward Berlin, we might now be hoisting tonnage through that Belgian port. He had wasted a month instead and now we were to wait for another before the first Antwerp convoy came through. Had Monty cleared the Scheldt as SHAEF suggested he do, Antwerp could have been fitted into the scheme of supply much sooner and we might have been spared the famine that immobilized us in October.

Indeed of all the might-have-beens in the European campaign, none was more agonizing than this failure of Monty to open Antwerp. For had sufficient supply been sluiced quickly to our stalemated front through the port of Antwerp, we could have resumed an earlier autumn offensive. Instead we were forced to sit and wait until November for the long-line build-up from Cherbourg. By then the fall campaigning weather was gone; winter had set in. Meanwhile the German had not been idle. Between early September and mid-December he tripled his forces on the Western front to 70 German divisions. And of his 15 panzer divisions, eight were refitted with Panther and Tiger tanks.

When at last Monty unraveled himself from Arnhem to clear the approaches to Antwerp, Eisenhower had become more worried than ever over our urgent need for that port. He thereupon made it clear to Montgomery in no uncertain terms that Antwerp must be opened before we advanced any nearer the Rhine.

The long-deferred cleanup campaign in the Scheldt had been made many times more difficult by Monty's long delays. To take Walcheren Island the Canadians were forced to mount an amphibious assault. Meanwhile air had broken the island's dikes in an effort to flood the enemy positions. As a result the Canadians fought their way through an exceptionally difficult campaign over battlefields inundated with sea water. Finally on November 9, 21st Army Group reported that the Scheldt had been opened and 17 days later, on November 26, the first Allied convoy unloaded in Antwerp. Within a few weeks Antwerp had all but displaced our long and troublesome line of supply to Cherbourg.

The sit-down that was to immobilize our armies for six deadly weeks while supply labored to drag up reserves from Cherbourg began soon after the conference at Versailles, when orders went out to Patton directing him to "Hold present position until supply situation permits resumption of the offensive." Two weeks later on October 9, First Army joined Patton in this sit-down when Montgomery called off his Rhine offensive. With this loss of momentum went our hopes for early conquest of the German army. On September 29, I estimated to Eisenhower that Antwerp would not be cleared by Monty until early November at the soonest, that no appreciable tonnage could be counted on through that port until December 1. The best we could hope for, I concluded, would be a mid-November offensive.

While caching supply for this November attack, Hodges was to exploit his penetration of the Siegfried Line and take the city of Aachen as a foothold inside the Reich. Thereafter when he had stocked his dumps with reserves, he would strike out for the Gothic towers of Cologne on the Rhine.

Although the prospect of victory that autumn had faded, the exuberance of the September pursuit lingered on in the armies. It was still inconceivable to many that the enemy could have rallied sufficient resistance from his torn armies to stand off the strength we had amassed in our seven Allied Armies on the Western front. On September 28, First Army sent me a handsome bronze bust of Hitler with the following inscription upon its base: "Found in Nazi Headquarters, Eupen, Germany. With seven units of fire and one additional division, First U. S. Army will deliver the original in thirty days." Before that 30-day period ended, Hitler had briefed his senior commanders on plans for the Ardennes counterattack.

For a few brief hours one evening First Army thought it might make delivery sooner that even it dared hope. G-2 had run into Hodges' van with a radio intercept picked up by its monitoring detachment. According to a radio broadcast an SS colonel had delivered to von Rundstedt in Cologne orders from the German High Command for an immediate counteroffensive. Von Rundstedt rejected the order and protested that he could not obey it without leading his command to destruction. An altercation followed and the SS colonel was shot. The field marshal, it was reported, had ordered Wehrmacht troops to disarm SS units and at the same time he proclaimed himself military governor of Cologne. He thereupon appealed to the German people in a public broadcast, urging them to rally to his side that he might conclude an honorable peace with the Allies.

The bubble broke when G-2 rechecked its monitoring detachment. The report had originated not from Cologne but from Radio Luxembourg which 12th Army Group used to air its "black" propaganda in an effort to deceive and confuse the German people.

The September restrictions that we had applied to operations of the Third Army were more confining than those with which we later jacketed Hodges. To a man who abhorred defensive warfare with the scorn of George Patton, the shutdown came as a bitter and crushing blow. Until the day he died Patton never recanted on his contention that had priority in supply been given him instead of Monty and Hodges, Third Army could have broken through the Saar defenses to the Rhine. At the same time Monty's proposal that Third Army be halted permanently on the Moselle while he tramped on to Berlin did nothing to appease Patton's unconcealed dislike for the British field marshal. Complete inactivity, however, proved too much to expect of Patton. During October he undertook an unauthorized pecking campaign against the enemy fortress position at Metz. When I found him probing those battlements, I appealed impatiently to him. "For God's sake, George, lay off," I said. "I promise you'll get your chance. When we get going again, you can far more easily pinch out Metz and take it from behind. Why bloody your nose with this pecking campaign?"

George nodded but the diversion went on. "We're using Metz," he explained, "to blood the new divisions." Though I was nettled over George's persistence in these forays at Metz, I declined to make an issue of it. The attacks seldom involved more than a single battalion and I certainly would not forbid an Army commander to mount a battalion attack.

During this period Patton was uneasy and fretful; he padded about his Army like a caged tiger. When a corps commander whom he had disliked as a result of some earlier altercation bivouacked his command in the Third Army sector, George stomped over **to** the CP for a preliminary inspection. The more he saw of the new headquarters the angrier he became. While making his way through a darkened corridor in the schoolhouse CP, George tripped over the inert form of a dozing GI. Awakened by Patton's boot in his side, the soldier spluttered in the darkness.

"Dammit you blockhead, watch your step. Can't you see I'm trying to sleep?"

Patton caught his breath and roared, "Well you're the first silly sonuvabitch around this place that knows what he's trying to do."

By the end of September, Com Z had begun to complain of organized thievery in its long line of supply. Thousands of gallons of gas, tons of food and clothing were being siphoned off each day into the French black market. In despair Lee appealed to Ike for several battalions of infantry to guard his rear-area installations.

Angered by Lee's request when I showed it to him, Patton sped back to his Third Army CP and dictated a letter summarizing his objections. Because he headed it, "My dear General Bradley," I recognized it as one of George's occasional letters for the record. In routine correspondence he always addressed me as "Dear Brad."

As one of your Army Commanders [George wrote], I should consider myself derelict in my duty if I failed to express as forcibly as possible my considered opinion that the use of combat troops, particularly infantry, for any other purpose than fighting Germans would be a mistake of momentous proportions. . . . If the Com Z can use transportation to move soldiers [from the front back] to Paris, the Armies can certainly find sufficient [transportation] to move soldiers from Paris [forward] to the Armies.

Lee afterward apologized for the discomfiture he caused by this request. He satisfied his requirements for security troops by forming limited service battalions from Com Z overhead.

We had scarcely settled down to the dismal prospect of a protracted winter campaign when Ike telephoned from SHAEF to report that General Marshall would visit our front. He arrived in Verdun on October 7 after a low-level flight over the Argonne during which he picked out the terrain features he had remembered from World War I. It was apparent from the Chief of Staff's opening conversations that the chill which had caused us to revise our rosy September estimates on the end of the war had not yet filtered through to Washington and the War Department. While we were now resigned to a bitter-end campaign, he spoke with the cheery optimism we had discarded three weeks before. In approving our plans for a November offensive he predicted that our pressures would force the enemy to quit rather than endure another hard winter. This variation in outlook among distant echelons of command is usually present in any large-scale war where senior commands may be hundreds or thousands of miles removed from the front. Their viewpoints ordinarily trail by weeks those of the field commanders. At no time was this more apparent than during the Battle of the Bulge, when long after we had gotten an upper hand on the front, SHAEF continued in a state of anxiety and fear.

General Marshall had insisted that we not disrupt routine to accommodate his visit, for he proposed to spend his time on the front where he could observe the capabilities of our troops and the adequacy of their equipment. Nevertheless on October 8, I insisted on accompanying him in a C-47 when he called on Hodges and Monty.

Ordinarily we declined fighter escort for the C-47. So thoroughly had Lieutenant General Hoyt Vandenberg's Ninth Air Force scoured the skies that the Luftwaffe had now become a rarity on our front. Even so, Robinson preferred to hug the ground on a hedgehopping course safe from enemy air interception.

Apprehensive for fear German intelligence might have penetrated our flight plan for General Marshall, we called Ninth TAC for a fighter escort. The C-47 was based on a makeshift field in a pasture close to the flooded banks of the Meuse. The escort was to rendezvous with us in the air directly over Verdun. We boarded the plane and Robinson taxied to the end of the field to rev up his engines. Suddenly he skidded his tail and lurched off the runway. The first of the fighters coming in for a landing had almost pancaked on top of us.

Lacking radio contact with the fighter escort, we attempted frantically to wave them off the short mushy runway. But like a column of airborne tanks, the heavy P-47's splashed in, oblivious to our signals. As the fourth attempted to turn off the runway, the seven-ton plane mired down in the soft mud. A truck tried to winch it out but the P-47 only nosed down deeper with its tail straddling the runway at the two-thirds mark. I asked Robinson if he could clear it and take off. Robbie mashed down his brakes, pushed on the throttle, lifted his feet, and we soared off.

In spite of the now dangerously foreshortened field, the three remaining fighters taxied into position for their take-off. The first cleared the mired plane by inches and heaved itself into the air. The second crashed through the tail of the mired fighter, then miraculously climbed into the air with a damaged landing gear. After fighting for altitude it headed for home. The third cleared the wreckage, brushed through a line of trees, and took its position on our wing tip.

At Monty's CP in Eindhoven an overcast of broken clouds hid all but an occasional fogged view of the concrete runway. Robinson made two passes and bounced safely in on the third approach. Our two remaining fighters droned lower and lower. The flight leader made a pass, then another, another, and another. On the fifth turn round he sideslipped in line with the runway. His ship stalled. It pancaked with a shriek of tearing metal. The motor broke loose and the ship skidded to a halt on its back almost at our wingtip. In an instant it had exploded in flames. But the British had alerted a crash truck preparatory to our landing and the explosion occurred almost under the nozzles of its foamite tank. When the flames were smothered, a wrecker righted the ship and a rescue crew pulled back the foam-covered canopy. The pilot climbed out unaided with a grin on his youthful face.

Meanwhile the fourth fighter had been frightened off by the flash of flame. Within an hour our escort had been reduced from four to nothing without as much as a glimpse of enemy air. General Marshall, happily, said nothing.

That evening Hansen telephoned air headquarters to report those losses. "Too bad—" the colonel said, "we'll send you another four."

"No thank you, Colonel," Hansen replied, "I'm sure the general couldn't take another day like this one." We never again called on air for fighter escort for the *Mary Q.*

By early October a familiar specter had reappeared to haunt our front; it was the start of a new ammunition shortage that all but silenced our guns for a month.

Meanwhile gasoline stocks had also dwindled until one day G-4 reported theater levels down to a scant two-days supply. I protested to Lee, and Com Z rushed the construction of extra POL* storage tanks in the Normandy depots.

The ammunition shortage, however, was far more intricate and could not be so easily relieved. For there the crisis had grown out of a lack of wharfage and the remedy lay in opening Antwerp. Unloading across the Normandy beaches had been slowed down with the advent of dirty weather and too few berths could be spared for ammunition discharge in the Channel ports. During the first week of October only one ammunition ship was unloaded while 35 others waited offshore for docking space in France. Com Z meanwhile had exhausted its reserve ammunition stocks and the hand-to-mouth feeding from shipside to the front failed to satisfy even our minimum needs.

On October 2, the day Hodges jumped off for Aachen, we reinstituted ammunition rationing. But a week later we learned that even at this reduced rate of fire we would totally exhaust our ammo stocks by November 7.

Although Com Z could lay the blame to Monty's tardiness at Antwerp, it was not totally blameless itself. Reserves in the Normandy depots had failed to keep apace of the weapons strength of our Armies during their September build-up.

On October 9, I called a supply conference at 12th Army Group to hunt a way out of this crisis that threatened to delay the start of a November offensive. Patton came with his chief of staff and Third Army's G-4. Kean represented Hodges; he was accompanied by Medaris and Wilson. When Patton spotted Medaris whom he had known in II Corps as a shrewd bargainer at the conference table, he put in a hurry-up call for his own ordnance officer.

"Look out for that pair," he cautioned his chief of staff, while nodding roguishly toward Medaris and Wilson. "I know them both. They once worked for me." George's caution was not unjustified, for no one knew better than he that First Army merited its reputation for piracy in supply. While maintaining, as in the adage, that all was fair in love and war, First Army contended that chicanery was part of the business of supply just so long as Group did not detect it.

Bedell Smith had driven up from Versailles with Eisenhower's G-4 in answer to our plea for a showdown on the ammunition shortage. But while Bedell was sympathetic to our plight, he sus-

*Petroleum, Oil, and Lubricants.

pected that a share of our irritation with Com Z reflected the antagonism that normally exists between field and service forces. In order to prevent Com Z from being made the scapegoat for many of our troubles, SHAEF shielded Lee from criticism in the field. First Army was outspokenly intolerant of Com Z's peculiar problems and Patton made no secret of his impatience with Lee.

To accumulate sufficient reserves from Cherbourg for the November offensive, we further restricted expenditures of ammunition in the Armies. They were to squeeze through October on a painfully thin ration. Meanwhile SHAEF was to boost ammunition ship unloadings to 6,000 tons a day and stock the surplus in army dumps. Harsh as the solution seemed, it satisfied Bedell Smith. "Com Z should meet your target levels for attack by October 22," he estimated.

"We'll give them an extra ten days," I said, "and bank on November 2."

Bedell was annoyed with my rejoinder but when October 22 came and passed with an unfulfilled deadline, he telephoned me to apologize. "I didn't know it would take this long," he explained, annoyed over the delay.

"Think no more of it, Bedell," I said. "We've had more experience with those people than you have." In its anxiety to please us, Com Z had again exaggerated its ability to deliver the goods.

On October 14 as Hodges completed encirclement of the roofless city of Aachen, we assembled the U. S. senior command at First Army's CP to greet the King of England then touring the Allied front. Hodges had pitched his CP in the mud surrounding a dilapidated chateau near the Belgian city of Verviers. By then First Army was the only senior headquarters still under canvas, for with the oncoming of winter both Patton and Simpson had quartered their commands in buildings. And only that day EAGLE TAC quit its tents in Verdun for a steam-heated building in Luxembourg, 12 miles from the German lines.

General Hart had motored north to Monty's CP to escort King George across Belgium, down into the U. S. sector. En route over the gutted brick roads after having breakfasted on several cups of tea, Hart squirmed uncomfortably with the knowledge that his jeep outriders would soon require a pause for roadside relief. Uncertain as to how he might explain the necessity for this stop to the King, Hart murmured that he was stopping the convoy "for a sanitary halt."

When the vehicles were once again under way, the King looked to Hart and chuckled, "A sanitary halt, you say?" He turned to his equerry and laughed. "Now be sure to include that in the diary."

At lunch in the barren dining room where MASTER had made a grudging concession to comfort by moving it inside, Patton held the guests with a recital of his experiences in the African campaign. He spoke of the thievery of Tunisian Arabs, sipped his coffee, and declared to the King, "Why I must have shot a dozen Arabs myself."

Ike looked up with a wink toward me. "How many, did you say, George?" he asked.

Patton pulled on his cigar. "Well, maybe it was only a half a dozen—" he replied with a mischievous grin.

"How many?" Ike repeated the question.

George hunched his shoulders, laughed, and turned to the King. "Well at any rate, sir, I did boot two of them squarely in the—ah, street at Gafsa."

That afternoon Eisenhower returned with me to EAGLE TAC in Luxembourg. We motored down through the Ardennes, dank with the dampness of many rains, past the peat bogs of Belgium, and through the village of Bastogne. A mobile baking unit had rolled its ovens into a shed on the edge of town and a tantalizing odor of baking bread hung in the air.

In Luxembourg the mossy stone buildings of that capital city blazed with the Duchy's flag while banners spelled out its bold national slogan: *We wish to remain what we are.* From a thousand cleanly scrubbed shop windows colored lithographs of the Grand Duchess Charlotte looked benevolently out on the decorated streets. Near the Alfa Hotel where we were to be billeted a shopkeeper had decorated his window with a large photograph of President Roosevelt—but the picture was that of T.R. For dinner that evening Sergeant Dudley brought in a huge decorated cake he had ordered from a chef in Paris. It was Eisenhower's fifty-fourth birthday.

Four days later, on October 18, as Aachen crumpled under the First Army's guns, Eisenhower called a strategy conference at 21st Group headquarters in Brussels to draft plans for the November offensive. By convening the conference on Monty's home grounds, SHAEF made it impossible for him not to attend.

With winter approaching our stalemated front, Eisenhower could choose one of two courses of action.

1. He could dig in with his 54 Allied divisions across the 500-mile Allied front that now extended from the North Sea to the Swiss border. By postponing a November offensive he could wait until the following spring when a host of fresh U. S. divisions and a vast reserve of tonnage at Antwerp would insure him sufficient resources to strike a knockout blow.

2. Or he could start a November offensive with the troops he already possessed and bank on adequate logistical support through existing supply lines.

Had Eisenhower chosen to wait for an Allied build-up, he would have risked an even more rapid enemy build-up by the following spring. For the German had already shown startling strength in recuperation. Each week that passed during this autumn sit-down enabled him to refit more panzers, recruit more *Volksturm,* and improve his ground defenses. And each month that dragged by caused Tooey Spaatz greater anxiety over enemy jet-fighter production and German discovery of the proximity fuse. For Tooey had long ago estimated that either might blast our bombers out of the skies.

On the other hand, Allied superiority on the ground was not calculated to inspire long odds on any winter offensive. The enemy had already mustered the equivalent of 32 divisions to oppose us. And except for Collins' penetration at Aachen, his Siegfried Line was intact.

Nevertheless no one entertained seriously the proposal that we bed down for the winter. For apart from the local dangers of this alternative plan, it would surely have precipitated an angry protest from our allies in the Kremlin.

Ike made his choice and predicated it in part on a measure of hope. We would hammer the enemy with all possible force in an effort to splinter his Armies west of the Rhine. Perhaps then when we reached that river, the morale of the Reich would crack and bring the war to an end. General Marshall had previously ventured this same thin hope. Eisenhower and I both clung to it though we sensed it was a fragile reed.

This decision of Eisenhower's to resume the offensive in November resurrected once more the perennial dispute between Montgomery and me over the old issue of a *single* versus the *double* thrust. Again Monty urged that Eisenhower bunch his strength in a concentrated attack toward the Ruhr north of the Ardennes. And again I argued that he split his effort between the Ruhr and the Saar where Patton could overrun that industrial basin in his advance to the Rhine. Though we sparred at this time over the pattern of attack west of the Rhine, both of us knew that this present decision would shape the later offensive east of that river. Monty still argued for the single offensive north on the rim of the Ruhr while I insisted on getting into position for the double envelopment of that industrial heartland. While Monty contended that we need close to the Rhine only from Cologne north, I maintained that we must occupy that river's whole west bank the full length of our Allied line before contemplating any advance beyond it. Eventually Eisenhower would have to choose between one or the other of these views.

My reasoning on the *double* thrust was quite simple. Were Eisenhower to concentrate his November offensive north of the Ardennes, the enemy could also concentrate his defenses there the better to meet that single attack. On the other hand, if we were to split our effort into a double thrust with one pincer toward Frankfurt, we might both confound the enemy and make better use of the superior mobility of our Armies. Patton had the most at stake for if Montgomery's views were to prevail, Third Army would be consigned to the defensive south of the Ardennes and there perhaps wait out the war behind the Moselle River. Could not those divisions be better employed against the Saar, I asked SHAEF?

Ike apparently agreed, for this time he decided in favor of our double-pronged offensive. In his plan, 12th Army Group was to attack north of the Ardennes with the First and Ninth Armies, and south of that wooded barrier with the Third. All three were to push on to the Rhine and seize crossings there if they could. Meanwhile Monty was to clean out his sector west of the Meuse where he had previously by-passed the enemy on his lunge toward Arnhem. Thereafter he was to sweep south from Nijmegen toward the Ruhr down the wedge between the Rhine and Meuse Rivers. Target date for the First and Ninth Armies' offensive was fixed for November 5. Third Army was to go by the tenth.

In preparation for this new offensive I pulled Simpson out of the Ardennes and shifted him north of Hodges adjacent to Montgomery's British front in Holland. When Ninth Army first went into the line in early October, I had moved it into the Ardennes sector that we might employ the more experienced First and Third Armies in our thrusts to the Rhine. But on October 18, I left Brussels with the premonition that sooner or later Monty would wangle a U. S. Army from our line-up to strengthen his British Army Group. By

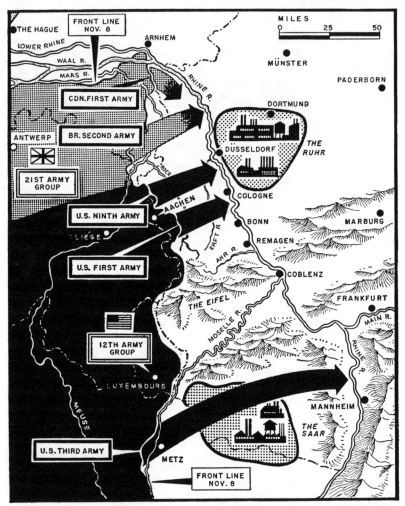

In the November offensive that was to carry the Allies to the Rhine, both American Armies north of the Eifel were to force the Roer River and crash across the plains of Cologne. Meanwhile, Patton to the south was to break through the Saar toward the Rhine north of Mannheim. And Montgomery was to close to that river with two Armies north of the Ruhr.

now we outnumbered him two to one and the proportion was soon to widen. Because Simpson's Army was still our greenest, I reasoned that it could be the most easily spared. Thus rather than leave First Army within Monty's reach, I inserted the Ninth Army between them. Actually this worked to Monty's advantage for the Ninth soon developed into a first-rate fighting unit. And it campaigned for him with less friction than would have either the First or the Third.

To plug the forested Ardennes we brought up Middleton's VIII Corps from Brest, assigned it to First Army, and stretched its three infantry divisions and one cavalry group the length of that desolate front where it extended for more than 90 miles between Hodges' and Patton's offensives. To prop up his thin line we added an armored division and Troy placed it in corps reserve. Trout streams foamed through the steep hills of this quiet middle sector and wild boar roamed its forests. Later the Luxembourg forest warden was to complain that GI's in their zest for barbecued pork were hunting the boar in low-flying cubs with Thompson submachine guns. Inventive, I agreed, but a trifle rough on the game.

Opposite Middleton's Ardennes front lay the scenic and sparsely settled German Eifel with its narrow valleys, steep wooded hills, cratered lakes, and extinct volcanoes. Only a few first-class east-west roads traversed Middleton's sector from the Eifel through the Ardennes and they corkscrewed through the valleys to the Meuse 50 miles to the rear.

To have held Middleton's front more securely would have meant tapping strength for his line from both the projected northern and southern November offensives. As it was, Hodges and Simpson could mass but 14 divisions between them for their combined 55-mile front north of the Ardennes. To the south Patton was spread out over a front of 85 miles with but nine divisions. So pressed were we for troops that the northern offensive had to be delayed for one week until we could reclaim a single division loaned Monty while he cleaned up the Scheldt. And to concentrate the Third Army attack within a narrow path, it became necessary to transfer a piece of Patton's front to Devers' 6th Army Group.

Had we wanted to minimize the risk of enemy attack through Middleton's thin line in the Ardennes, we could have called off Patton's offensive, as Monty had proposed, or even bedded down for the winter the length of our Allied line. As far as I was concerned either alternative was out of the question. We would stretch

Middleton as taut as we dared, willingly take our risks in the Ardennes, and employ every available division in the November offensive to kill Germans. Thus the Ardennes was deliberately thinned to thicken the winter offensive. This calculated risk was mine and I have never regretted having made it. Indeed were I to live through that decision again, I would make no other. To be sure it was not the safest choice but had safety been the byword of our generalship in France, we might have wintered on the Seine within sight of a charred skeleton of Paris.

Initially, the northern offensive was to have preceded Patton's by five days in order that Hodges and Simpson might have first call on the use of strategic air support. For in this *main* effort on the north we were to repeat the saturation air bombing that had paralyzed the enemy at St.-Lô. When I learned that Monty would not return the U. S. division he had borrowed in time for a November 5 jump-off, I postponed the northern offensive five days and gave Patton the starting position.

After waiting three days for clear skies in his rainy CP at Nancy, Patton elected to go ahead without help from the air. With only artillery to support his attack, he stormed off in the rain on the early morning of November 8 with an Army of 220,000 troops. George intended to force the Moselle north of Metz, pinch out that enemy strong point, advance to the Saar Valley, and there break through the Siegfried Line. It was 40 miles from Metz to the Saàr Valley, 80 from there through the Palatinate to the banks of the Rhine.

Weeks of steady rain had swollen the Moselle to a record 50-year flood stage. The torrent washed out Patton's bridges and for five days he supported his Army across the Moselle on rafts and flimsy assault craft. On November 11 when I telephoned George to wish him a happy birthday, he told of an engineer company that had struggled for two days to string a pontoon bridge across the river. On the day it was completed, a tank destroyer started across the steel planking to the far shore. As it neared the end, it suddenly veered off the planking and snapped the cable anchoring the bridge to the shore. In an instant the structure snaked and tumbled off downstream. "The whole damn company sat down in the mud," Patton said, "and bawled like babies."

Up north in the First and Ninth Armies the weather was no

better. Three days past the deadline, air was still socked in. I gave them until November 17. If by then air was still grounded we would decide whether we might have to go on without it and bank on supporting artillery as Patton had done. The heavy bombers were to come from England, the fighter bombers from Belgium. Since weather might not accommodate them both on the same day, we would hitch our plans to the heavy bombers even at the cost of fighter support and delay the jump-off, if need be, until three in the afternoon.

The plan called for Hodges to ram through to Düren with Simpson on his left flank. There he would force the Roer River 15 miles east of Aachen and push on across that barrier to Cologne, 25 miles beyond it. Our primary objective in this offensive was destruction of the enemy's forces west of the Rhine. If we could defeat him there as we had in Normandy, we might hurdle the Rhine on the run as we did the Seine. To slow down reinforcement of the area west of the Rhine, we bombed the Rhine bridges. All of them had already been prepared for demolition in the event of retreat and on November 5 when a fighter pilot scored a near hit on one, the blast detonated those charges. While the astonished pilot blinked, the structure splashed into the river.

I anticipated that we might reach the Rhine within 30 days after jump-off if only the initial attack carried us through the crust immediately outside Aachen. On the other hand, if this offensive were to bog down, I cautioned the staff at Army Group that we might be forced to dig in for the winter and postpone any offensive campaign until the spring. And a spring offensive, I estimated, might easily prolong the war through the summer of 1945.

On November 14, after 13 successive days of dirty weather, I motored from Luxembourg up through Bastogne to Spa, to share the First Army's vigil. The Ardennes were lightly blanketed in the first wet snow of the year. MASTER had only recently moved its headquarters to the fashionable baths of Spa, 12 miles from the German border in the rolling hills of Aachen. Now First Army signs cluttered the streets of Spa. Its trucks tore up the boulevards and its troops tracked red mud into the stately Hôtel Britannique where MASTER set up shop. Field desks were scattered through the casino where Europe's rich had once gambled under the huge crystal chandeliers that hung from its high ceilings. Inside a richly carpeted cocktail lounge, First Army's dispensary had set up its foot-treadle field dental chairs. Instruments were racked across the polished mahogany bar.

Although depressed by the gloomy cycle of weather that had already delayed his attack more than a week and half, Hodges was determined to get off by November 17. "Air or no air," he said, "we're going."

"Don't worry about that, General," Quesada assured him, "our planes will be there when you jump off even if we have to crash-land every damned one of them on the way back."

On the late evening of November 15, I sat up late with Hodges' staff in their Hôtel Britannique war room. Hodges and Kean both chain-smoked. Thorson looked gaunt and fatigued.

"Courtney," I said, "when you get on the Rhine, I want you to send Tubby on leave to England."

Kean looked up disapprovingly. Thorson spotted the frown and called back, "General, maybe you'd better put that order in writing."

It was 1 A.M. when the weather report came in. Our vigil had been rewarded; we would jump off the following noon.

At breakfast the next morning in the Belgian steel baron's home where Hodges billeted his generals, we stared out the plate-glass window that framed the blue hills to the east. Like a curtain in a theater, the dark clouds rolled back and a clear sky showed over the ground mist. Soon the sun nudged up under the clouds.

"Man, look at that ball of fire, just look at it," Hodges cried. "But don't look at it too hard," he called as we pressed against the window, "you'll wear it out—or, worse yet, maybe chase it away."

At 12:45 air thundered in on schedule. Twelve hundred bombers of the Eighth Air Force flying in box-tight formations, an equal number of RAF heavies, flying dispersed in the manner of night bombers. To prevent a repetition of the short drop at St.-Lô, we had posted jeeps with vertical radio beams to mark the front lines by radar. For visual guidance to the target a line of barrage balloons with cerise panels affixed to their backs had been hoisted 1,500 feet into the air. For added insurance the 90-mm. AA guns marked the front with a line of colored flak, 2,000 feet below the bombers. Only two clusters of bombs fell behind our lines, the result of faulty bomb racks. One "friendly" casualty was reported; it was nothing more than a minor wound.

But though the air bombing had shattered an enemy division

and churned up the neighboring terrain, it failed to tear a hole in his line through which our infantry and tanks could be pushed on to the Rhine. The German had skillfully laid out his defenses in depth behind a carpet of mines and field fortifications. With his back to the Rhine, he now fought for each grubby crossroads village as if it were the Brandenburg Gate in Berlin. Meanwhile Goebbels had warned von Runstedt's troops in the Rhineland that this was a fight to the finish, a fight in which weakness would bring defeat and eventual exile to the Siberian labor camps.

As the enemy fell back he left a trail buried in rubble, for he held grimly to each position until we pulverized it. When G-2 interrogated an intelligent young officer of the Wehrmacht to ask if he did not regret this unnecessary destruction of his homeland, the PW shrugged and replied, "It probably won't be ours after the war. Why not destroy it?"

During the first two weeks of that northern offensive, we went less than seven miles. By the time both U. S. Armies had slogged through the bomb-cratered countryside to the outskirts of Düren and Jülich, it was apparent that we had become engaged in a costly war of attrition. But for each casualty our medics carried back in sodden blankets through the rain, we estimated the enemy had lost two or more in killed, captured, and long-term wounded.

Much as the odds favored us in this desperate war of attrition, I hated the butchery we were forced to endure for each mile of this Rhineland advance. Yet since it was here the enemy had chosen to commit his last resources, it was here that we must break his back if we were to force the Rhine. For it followed that if we could destroy him west of that river, he would be powerless to halt us beyond it.

As the northern offensive dragged on through November, intelligence reported an enemy massing of strong panzer reserves across our line of advance. Some of these forces were identified as belonging to the Sixth SS Panzer Army. We deduced that these panzers would probably wait to hit us while we were crossing the Roer, for if they should counterattack while we were astride that river, they might seriously embarrass us there. Thus we resigned ourselves to the prospect of a knockdown drag-out fight between the Roer and the Rhine.

I spoke to Bedell Smith of these gathering concentrations. "If the other fellow would only hit us now," I said, "I'd welcome a counterattack. We could kill many more Germans with a good deal less effort if they would only climb out of their holes and come after us for a change."

At the same time these German concentrations caused me to update my earlier 30-day estimate on the Rhine. If we were to slough through German dead, the advance would take a little longer. But in the meantime enemy losses would compensate us richly for the delay.

Between the Roer and Rhine Rivers, the 30-mile-wide tableland that forms the plains of Cologne offered von Rundstedt an ideal arena for a massed panzer counterattack. If he could catch us astride the Roer, he might hope to stall our drive to the Rhine, perhaps stalemate us through the winter. Certainly the opportunity was worth his examination.

In any counterattack across the plains of Cologne, von Rundstedt could count upon a powerful weapon in the Roer River. As long as he held the huge Roer dams containing the headwaters of that river, he could unleash a flash flood that would sweep away our bridges and jeopardize our isolated bridgeheads on the plains of Cologne. Destruction of the 180-foot-high Schwammenauel Dam, engineers said, would swell the Roer at Düren by 25 feet and create a raging torrent one and a half miles wide. Clearly we dared not venture beyond the Roer until first we had captured or destroyed those dams.

They lay in the uplands of the Schnee Eifel, in a rough woodland area which blanketed our routes of approach. In preparation for his main offensive Hodges had endeavored to grab those dam sites on November 2 with the 28th Division. He came within a hair's breadth of snatching his objective but was downed when the 28th was counterattacked and thrown out of the town of Schmidt. Not until three months later did we finally take those dams and thus secure the Roer for a safe crossing. Had we secured them early in November and pushed across the Roer, the enemy would never have dared counterattack us in the Ardennes.

While Hodges dug into the muddy ridge line overlooking the Roer and turned his First Army attack through Huertgen toward those dams, Patton drove on toward the Saar, whaling the enemy before him. On November 20 he encircled Metz, and as that fortified position fell, George closed to the Saar River. On the evening of December 2 he bridged those chill waters at Saarlautern and

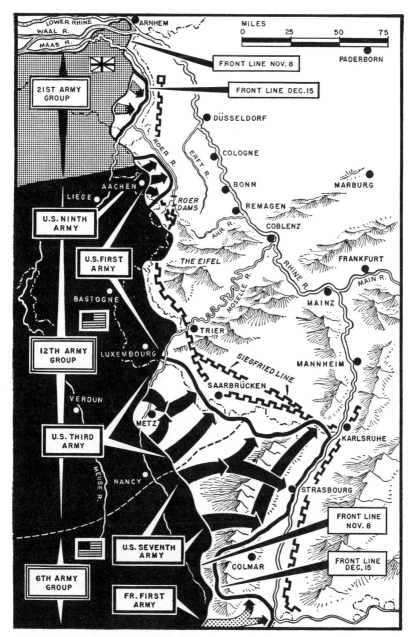

Although Hodges' attack stalled short of the Roer, Patton broke through to the Saar to gain a toe hold in the Siegfried Line. To his right, Devers pushed around the Colmar pocket to the Rhine.

crossed the Lorraine border into the Reich. There Third Army kicked its first toe hold in the Siegfried Line.

It had fallen to Patton in this southern tier offensive to prove the soundness of U. S. strategy for the double thrust. For had he failed to dent the Saar, Montgomery could easily have claimed that this second thrust had been a poorly conceived diversion from the *main* effort. Delighted with Patton's progress after our disappointments in the north, I congratulated him and asked that my good wishes be extended to his division commanders. George cackled in delight. "Hell," he said, "a division commander doesn't have to know anything. He can be as dumb as a sonuvabitch just as long as he's a fighter." I disputed George's disparagement of a difficult job but agreed that what I wanted most were commanders who were fighters.

As November passed into December and U. S. casualties mounted, Com Z's pipeline on infantry replacements began to run dry. Rifle companies were hard pressed on the line for want of reinforcements until in December the average division attacked with but three quarters of its rifle strength. To replenish those losses and halt any further decline in infantry strength, we combed the ETO for emergency replacements. But though truckloads of hastily trained riflemen were bundled off to the front, they could not offset the litter cases that passed them headed rearward. This drain continued until December 15 when G-1 reported the 12th Army Group short 17,000 riflemen among its 31 divisions on the line.

The tempo of attack slowed down with this famine in reinforcements and as a result our northern offensive mired in the mud. Even had I wanted to shift a part of Patton's Third Army north to break Hodges' stalemate, I could not have supported a combined offensive with sufficient reinforcements. Within five short weeks the winter attack had cost us 64,000 casualties, almost half of them on a 12-mile stretch of the First Army front. And as if this were not already strain enough on the bankrupt replacement system, trenchfoot added almost 12,000 more. Though listed as a nonbattle loss, trenchfoot exacted its heaviest toll among riflemen on the line where each casualty sapped our assault strength and thus weakened the offensive. Trenchfoot is caused by persistent dampness or prolonged immersion of the feet in water. It can result in permanent damage to the peripheral vessels of the lower limbs. Of the 12,000 victims of trenchfoot evacuated from our lines, doctors estimated that the greater number could never again be returned to combat. Others would be incapacitated for life.

By the end of January trenchfoot losses had severely crippled our U. S. command. Because the malady had caught us unawares partially as the result of our own neglect, by the time we disciplined troops on the care and treatment of wet feet, the infirmity had fallen upon us with the suddenness of a plague. But in those few divisions where the more alert commanders had set up drying tents for a daily change of socks, the rate of impairment trailed far behind that of the rest of the Group.

When the rains first came in November with a blast of wintry cold, our troops were ill-prepared for wintertime campaigning. This was traceable in part to the September crisis in supply for during our race to the Rhine, I had deliberately by-passed shipments of winter clothing in favor of ammunition and gasoline. As a consequence, we now found ourselves caught short, particularly in bad-weather footwear. We had gambled in our choice and now were paying for the bad guess.

Previous combat had taught us that casualties are lumped primarily in the rifle platoons. For here are concentrated the handful of troops who must advance under enemy fire. It is upon them that the burden of war falls with greater risk and with less likelihood of survival than in any other of the combat arms. An infantry division of World War II consisted of 81 rifle platoons, each with a combat strength of approximately 40 men. Altogether those 81 assault units comprised but 3,240 men in a division of 14,000. In an army of 350,000, fewer than one out of seven soldiers stood in that front line. This does not mean, of course, that none of the other seven fought. Many of them did, but as machine gunners, artillerymen, engineers, and tankers. And in Theater the proportion declined at an even more precipitous rate: one man with a rifle for each 15 men behind him.

Prior to invasion we had estimated that the infantry would incur 70 per cent of the losses of our combat forces. By August we had boosted that figure to 83 per cent on the basis of our experience in the Normandy hedgerows. The appalling hazard of an infantryman's life in combat was illustrated at St.-Lô where in 15 days the 30th Division sustained 3,934 battle casualties. At first glance those casualties would seem to imply 25 per cent losses for the division.

That figure, however, is deceptive. Because three out of every four of those casualties occurred in a rifle platoon, the rate of loss in those platoons exceeded 90 per cent.

Hardly had we gained a foothold in France than the Theater replacement system became a thorn in our side. So wasteful was the effort expended in shifting replacements to the front that we soon overhauled the system, moved it out from under Com Z, and established the Ground Forces Reinforcement Command. Ike then called for Lieutenant General Ben Lear to run this replacement system. Early in the campaign, replacements were filtered directly into their squads, fresh from the "repple depples." Casualties among them greatly exceeded those of battlewise veterans on the line. Many went into the lines at night and perished before the morning. Some were evacuated as wounded even before they learned the names of their sergeants. By the fall of 1944 we had reorganized this procedure and replacements were being indoctrinated by division before being committed into the line.

Among U. S. troops the replacement depots soon developed an infamous reputation for callousness and inefficiency in their operations. Fearful of the damaging psychological effect on troops of this replacement pipeline, Lee had labored in his role as deputy Theater commander to humanize those depots and bring compassion into the operation. He proposed that we make a start by changing the name.

"Colonel Franey, our Theater G-1 feels—and I concur," he wrote in a letter to me, "that the word 'replacement' carries a cannon fodder implication that we could overcome by using another term such as 'specialist.' Would you have any objection to our calling the Replacement System the 'Specialist System' or 'Corps' in which individuals could feel a sense of pride and achievement in their earning 'specialist' designations."

I thought the suggestion a nonsensical effort to solve with words a problem that could be eased by the assignment of better officers to those replacement depots. "The remedy for improving morale among the replacements," I wrote back, "lies not in changing the name but in taking every possible step to see that they are properly taken care of and that they get the feeling that someone is interested in their welfare." Lee reconsidered Franey's suggestion and soon afterward withdrew it.

By December, I was sufficiently alarmed by this growing crisis in infantry replacements that I asked Ike for permission to send my Group G-1 to Washington to go over the problem with his opposite number in the Pentagon. Not only had Washington juggled our quotas to shortchange us on infantrymen but in November at a time when our requirements increased, the War Department cut back our total monthly allotment of replacements from 80,000 to 67,000 men. At the very moment we needed them most, too many men were being diverted to the Pacific.

"Don't they realize," I complained to Ike, "that we can still lose this war in Europe. There'll be plenty of time left after we're finished here to clean up in the Pacific." Though he knew better than I of MacArthur's pressure on the Pentagon for speedier build-up of the Pacific forces, Eisenhower hid his annoyance. Indeed MacArthur and the Pacific were so remote from our daily problems that we became aware of the other war only when shortages reminded us that it was competing for resources.

This manpower shortage was but one in a succession of crises that befell us that fall. Deficiencies in ammunition and tanks had preceded it. "I would suppose," I wrote Patton in December, "that somebody in Washington had made a wrong guess as to the date on which this war will be over." At the same time I cautioned Ike that if no remedy were forthcoming on replacements, we would soon have exhausted the assault strength of our infantry divisions.

During the middle of November, G-2 reported that the Sixth SS Panzer Army had been moved from its assembly point in Westphalia to an area nearer Cologne. Another Panzer Army, the Fifth, was reported to have massed its tanks a little farther north. So conspicuous were these telltale signs of von Rundstedt's apparent intent to nab us astride the Roer, that we should probably have sifted them for evidence of deception. But if anyone on that Western front sniffed in those preparations an intent to mislead us on a German offensive elsewhere, he certainly did not share his suspicions with me.

In estimating von Rundstedt's capabilities, we reasoned that any counteroffensive must necessarily be directed against a limited objective where it could best blunt our threatening advance to the Rhine. Any more ambitious an effort, we estimated, would greatly exceed the enemy's resources. For much as we had been hurt in the November offensive, the enemy had been bled more severely. Intelligence put his casualties, exclusive of PWs, at upward of 100,000, for the five-week campaign. Patton's Third Army alone had picked up 35,000 PWs in its Saar offensive while Hodges and Simpson split another 22,000 between them.

In its G-2 estimate of the enemy situation on December 10, First Army said:

It is apparent that von Rundstedt who obviously is conducting military operations without the benefit of intuition, has skillfully defended and husbanded his forces and is preparing for his part in the all-out application of every weapon at the focal point and the correct time to achieve defense of the Reich west of the Rhine by inflicting as great a defeat on the Allies as possible. Indications to date point to the location of this focal point as being between Roermond and Schleiden, and within this bracket this concentrated force will be applied to the Allied force judged by the German High Command to be the greatest threat to successful defense of the Reich.

The "bracket" to which First Army referred described a 45-mile sector that extended from the Roer dams north of the Ardennes to where the Roer flows into the Meuse high up in Montgomery's sector.

In estimating the enemy's capabilities against the First Army front, Hodges came to four possible conclusions:

1. The enemy could hold where he was on the line of the Roer and southward along the Siegfried Line.

2. He could counterattack "with air, armor, infantry and secret weapons at a selected focal point at a time of his own choosing."

3. He could fall back to the Erft—a narrow river—line between the Roer and the Rhine and thereafter retire behind the Rhine, the most formidable defensive position in western Europe.

4. He could collapse or surrender.

Of these four distinct capabilities, First Army found its weight of evidence pointing toward the second.

It is to be expected, Dickson wrote, that "when our major ground forces have crossed the Roer River, and if the dams are not controlled by us, maximum use will be made by the enemy of flooding of the Roer in conjunction with his counterattack." The vigor with which von Rundstedt had met our attacks against these dams made it clear that he was thoroughly aware of the tactical ace he held.

I accepted First Army's conclusions and therefore anticipated a knockdown battle just as soon as we bridged the Roer. To make certain that we would get replacements enough to absorb these anticipated losses, I instructed O'Hare to ask that replacements be given priority in transport from the United States. He was also to insist that Washington adhere to our quotas on infantrymen and urge that an instant effort be made to replenish our rifle strength.

O'Hare was to leave Luxembourg on December 16 for a preliminary stop-off at SHAEF before boarding his plane at Paris. To impress upon SHAEF the seriousness of his mission as it would affect our January offensive, I agreed to accompany O'Hare as far as Versailles.

A gray pall hung over the city of Luxembourg on Saturday morning, December 16. From my room in the Alfa I stared across the cobblestoned square toward the bomb-damaged depot half screened in a haze. It came as no surprise to me at breakfast when Hansen telephoned to report air socked in for the day. My driver rolled out the Cadillac and stacked four cokes behind the rear seat.

To get an early start on the four-hour drive to Paris, I decided to pass up the nine o'clock briefing in our EAGLE TAC war room, four blocks up the street. Between Verdun and Châlons the high-crowned roadway was iced and we slowed down to 50. A tiny Renault skidded out of a side street almost forcing us into a ditch.

In Paris the streets were deserted. A cold rain washed the leafless trees and the city looked cramped and cold under its lifeless chimneys. At O'Hare's suggestion, we stopped for lunch at the Ritz where the ATC had requisitioned a dining room for its mess.

Eisenhower was waiting at Versailles when we arrived. The day before he had received official notification of his promotion to five-star rank.

The blow fell late that afternoon when a colonel from SHAEF G-2 tiptoed into a room where we sat in conference carrying a message for his chief. Major General Kenneth Strong, Ike's British G-2, glanced at it and interrupted the conversation. At five that morning the enemy had counterattacked at five separate points across the First Army sector.

By evening it had become disconcertingly apparent that this was no demonstration. Eight new German divisions had been identified in the attack. The enemy had centered his blow against Middleton's VIII Corps front—deep in the Ardennes, the most vulnerable point in our entire Allied line.

"Well, Brad," Bedell Smith laid his hand on my shoulder, "you've been wishing for a counterattack. Now it looks as though you've got it."

I smiled wryly at the recollection. "A counterattack, yes, but I'll be damned if I wanted one this big."

21: *Counteroffensive*

THE ARDENNES SECTOR IN WHICH VON RUNDSTEDT had struck was held in the north by two fledgling divisions and in the south by two veteran divisions, both of them badly mauled after a month in Huertgen Forest. Those dispositions, however, were not unintentional. Since Middleton's sector comprised the only quiet front on our line, we used it as a combined training ground and rest area. Altogether those four divisions held a lonely wooded front of 88 miles. Behind them an inexperienced armored division had been parked in reserve.

South of the Ardennes, Third Army had broken into the Siegfried Line where it barricaded the far shore of the Saar River. And to its right, the Seventh Army extended that Saar River line eastward to the Rhine near Karlsruhe. Elsewhere Devers' Sixth Army Group had closed to the Rhine opposite the Black Forest except in the region of Colmar where a substantial enemy pocket had been by-passed this side of the river.

Three days before, on December 13, Hodges had resumed his attack against the Roer dams after having failed to break those giant earthen structures with blockbusters dropped by the RAF. Rather than approach those dams again through the Huertgen Forest, Hodges had moved this time to outflank them from the south through the hills of the Schnee Eifel. Farther to the north, Hodges' front swelled out beyond Aachen to join Simpson's Ninth Army on the banks of the Roer. From there it dropped back into Montgomery's

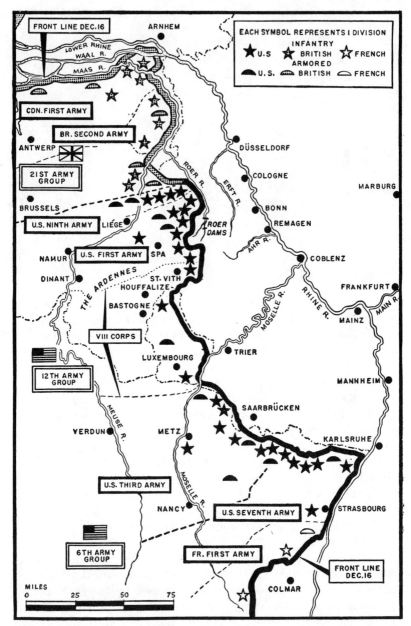

To provide sufficient power for the November offensives on the Roer and in the Saar, U. S. strength had been concentrated in those divided sectors. Meanwhile, Middleton held the Ardennes front with an armored and three infantry divisions.

sector where it followed the Meuse downstream before turning sharply westward to the North Sea.

Of the 63 Allied divisions deployed the length of that 400-mile Western front, 40 were American, and of those, 31 were assigned to 12th Army Group. Montgomery's two Armies comprised 15 divisions while Devers accounted for 17 more.

The 230-mile front of 12th Army Group had been subdivided among three U. S. Armies. In the middle, Hodges' First Army straddled the lion's share of that front with a sector of 115 miles. Two thirds of this First Army front stretched across the wooded Ardennes where Hodges had committed the four divisions of Middleton's VIII Corps. In the vicinity of Aachen Hodges had concentrated his remaining ten U. S. divisions for the Rhineland offensive. North of the First Army sector, Simpson had concentrated the seven divisions of his Ninth Army into a narrow 18-mile front. Thus our combined forces north of the Ardennes totaled 17 U. S. divisions. When added to Monty's British forces they equaled approximately half of all Allied strength in the West.

To the south of the Ardennes, Patton had deployed ten divisions the width of his 100-mile Third Army front, from the Moselle where it formed the Luxembourg border, past Saarbrücken halfway to the Rhine.

While startled by the suddenness of von Rundstedt's offensive, I was even more astonished that he should choose so unremunerative an objective. For in calculating our risks on that lightly held Ardennes front, I had discussed with Middleton the likely inducements that might tempt an enemy to strike there.

"First—" I said, "when anyone attacks, he does it for one of two reasons. Either he's out to destroy the hostile forces or he's going after a terrain objective. If it's terrain he's after then he feels he must either have it himself or deny it to the other fellow."

Neither objective could be attained in the Ardennes, for nowhere were we more thinly dispersed than across that wooded front and nowhere the length of our Allied line was a sector more devoid of industrial resources, transportation facilities, and worth-while terrain objectives.

When I queried Troy on his chances of blunting an enemy attack through that unpromising front, he showed me the hilly, wooded terrain and drove me over the narrow black-top roads that twisted through his sector. "If they come through here," he said, "we can fall back and fight a delaying action to the Meuse. Certainly we could slow them down until you hit them on the flanks."

I reported this reconnaissance to Ike who acknowledged the risks but accepted them as part of the price to be paid for resumption of the winter offensive.

"Why even if the German were to bust through all the way to the Meuse," I said, "he wouldn't find a thing in the Ardennes to make it worth his while."

We were not unmindful that in 1940 Hitler had broken through this same unlikely Ardennes front to overrun France. But if, as some critics say, that precedent should have forewarned us, they would have us ignore, as perhaps Hitler did, a striking change in Allied dispositions between 1940 and 1944.

As a result of the artificial division of nation states in Europe, France is poorly defended by natural geographic barriers from invasion on the east. Yet of the many pathways that lead to France, the least penetrable is through the Ardennes. For there the roads are much too scarce, the hills too wooded, the valleys too limited for maneuver.

However, in 1940, of the four paths for invasion then available to Hitler, the Ardennes was the one least securely blocked. Across the Rhine from the Black Forest, French guns commanded these river crossings. Farther north where the Lorraine hills rolled up to the Saar, the Wehrmacht dared not trifle with the casemated guns of the Maginot Line. And high above the Ardennes where the lowlands of Belgium formed an open path to France, the Belgian army and the British Expeditionary Force waited behind the Meuse.

This left only the Ardennes, north of where the unfortified frontier of Luxembourg paralleled the Siegfried Line. When the enemy struck in the Ardennes and forced a penetration, the static French fortress troops on both sides of that gap lacked the mobility and armor to stab back with a counterattack into the enemy's flanks.

Although lightly held in contrast to those sectors in the north and south where we had massed for the winter offensive, the Ardennes was nevertheless defended by more than 70,000 troops. But of far greater significance was the mobility of our heavily armed strength on the shoulders of the Ardennes. For this was the key factor Hitler had overlooked when he planned his second Ardennes offensive. He had forgotten that this time he was opposed not by static troops in a Maginot Line but by a vast mechanized U. S. Army fully mounted.

on wheels. In accepting the risk of enemy penetration into the Ardennes, we had counted heavily on the speed with which we could fling this mechanized strength against his flanks. While Middleton absorbed the enemy's momentum in a rear-guard withdrawal, Hodges' and Patton's Armies would clamp the invader in a vise.

To the south Patton's Third Army consisted of a quarter-million troops, with its tanks and supporting guns. To the north, the remainder of Hodges' First Army numbered another quarter-million men. Both were equipped with sufficient trucks for speedy redeployment of their forces.

When news of the German offensive reached me at SHAEF, I first thought it a spoiling attack assembled by von Rundstedt to force a halt on Patton's advance into the Saar. For George had hurt the enemy severely in his month-long winter offensive and now, after reclaiming Lorraine for the French, he was about to break through the Siegfried Line.

"The other fellow knows that if he's to hold out much longer," I said, "he must lighten the pressure that Patton has built up against him in the Saar. If by coming through the Ardennes he can force us to pull Patton's troops out of the Saar and throw them against his counteroffensive, he will get what he's after. And that's just a little more time."

Not until after the war when interrogators tracked down the origins of this Ardennes counteroffensive, did we learn how grossly I had underrated the enemy's intentions in thinking the offensive a spoiling attack.

Instead of the tactical diversion I had accused von Rundstedt of staging as an antidote to Patton's advance in the Saar, the German counteroffensive had been marshaled as a master stroke that was to regain the initiative in the West. Antwerp was to be the primary objective, for the enemy reasoned that if he could sever our major supply lines from that port, he would have isolated *four* Allied Armies north of the Ardennes. Though he did not delude himself with dreams of victory in the West, he nevertheless anticipated abundant rewards in Allied losses and disorganization. If successful in the Ardennes counteroffensive, the enemy might stall our Western drive long enough to strike the Red army then massing its strength on the Vistula.

Moreover, it was thought that the psychological effect of a German offensive might stave off the despair that by now had infected so many Germans. For as the Allied Armies neared those cities already devastated by air, the German people began more clearly to comprehend the catastrophe that came with defeat. But it was not primarily for morale that the enemy had devised this Ardennes counterattack. Instead he had chosen to gamble his dwindling resources on the slender chance of achieving a strategic upset.

Planning for the offensive was started in October almost as soon as we had exhausted the momentum of our swift drive across France. It was well under way three weeks before Montgomery had cleared the Scheldt. Before choosing the point of attack, the enemy had calculated his requisite conditions. First, he must at all costs maintain the integrity of his defensive position in the West. For as long as the Maas, the Roer, and the Siegfried Line offered barriers to the Allied advance, he could thin his defenses and refit reserves for the counterattack. At the same time, it was no less essential that he stabilize the Russian front in the East in order that Western resources need not be sidetracked to block an untimely Red army offensive there. Finally, to achieve a large enough build-up, he must allocate absolute priority in personnel and supply to the prospective offensive.

Whereas we ordinarily sought good flying weather for air support on an attack, the enemy reversed this condition. To compensate for his almost total lack of air support, he would delay the offensive until he could count on at least ten days of low cloud cover. With poor visibility he could screen his movements from detection and attack by Allied air. Lastly, he recognized that he must bank on surprise for quick destruction of the opposing forces, for he could not count on sufficient reserves to provide depth in the attack. Enemy success would depend almost entirely upon his ability to achieve a swift breakthrough before we could yank our forces out of the line on either end of the Ardennes and fling them against the flanks of his penetration.

To achieve this swift penetration, the enemy looked for a sector with a tissue-thin front. He found it in the Ardennes where German intelligence had accurately tabbed our troop strength and dispositions. Moreover, as long as he held the Roer River dams, he could safely protect his northern flank from Allied counterattack. For he knew we dared not force that stream while he held the floodgates of its dams deep in the hills of the Eifel. And to the south of the

Ardennes, he could bank on the casemated defenses of his Siegfried Line.

On October 12—as Hodges pushed into the shattered northern limits of Aachen—the German High Command issued its directive for the Ardennes counteroffensive.

Four German Armies were to be employed in the bold undertaking. Two of them, the Fifth Panzer Army and the Sixth SS Panzer, were to break a hole in the Ardennes front and stab through Middleton's lines. To General Sepp Dietrich, commander of the Sixth SS Panzer Army, Hitler entrusted the main effort. Meanwhile to the north and south of this penetration, the Fifteenth and Seventh Armies were to provide flanking support on the shoulders.

Tactical command of the offensive was assigned Field Marshal Model as commander of Army Group "B." But ultimate responsibility for success was vested in the Commander-in-Chief West, Field Marshal Gerd von Rundstedt. The date was tentatively set for November 26–28, contingent—of course—on bad weather and on von Rundstedt's ability to get ready in time.

Von Rundstedt's plan was neatly drafted with the skill and competence of an expert tactician. Indeed had German resources not been so utterly unequal to the task Hitler had assigned him, von Rundstedt might have caused us far more trouble than he did. In spearheading the offensive, Sixth SS Panzer Army was to slash through the Ardennes, cross the Meuse between Huy and Liége, then race northwest toward Antwerp where he hoped to pirate our stores to supply his forces. Meanwhile, a splinter column was to break off north of the Meuse, by-pass Liége and strike for the focal communications center of Ninth Army at Maastricht.

To the left of that major tank thrust, the Fifth Panzer Army was to parallel its breakthrough, bridge the Meuse between Dinant and Namur, and drive on north toward Brussels to protect the left flank and rear of Sepp Dietrich.

On the south, the reconstituted Seventh Army was to storm out of the Eifel, bridge the Sauer River, and hold open a shoulder across Luxembourg from the Moselle Valley on the German frontier to the cliff city of Dinant on the Meuse.

On the northern shoulder where it was anticipated Hodges might form a powerful force for a flank attack, von Rundstedt posted the Fifteenth Army to hold open his Ardennes gap. After breaking a path through our lines for the panzers, Sepp Dietrich's infantry was to turn off into position with the Fifteenth Army on that northern shoulder. So desperate was the enemy's need for speed that only the panzers would rush forward.

Initially, the enemy had contemplated a counterattacking force of between 25 and 30 divisions. But by December 16 he had amassed a surprising total of 36 in all four Armies. Of these, four were crack

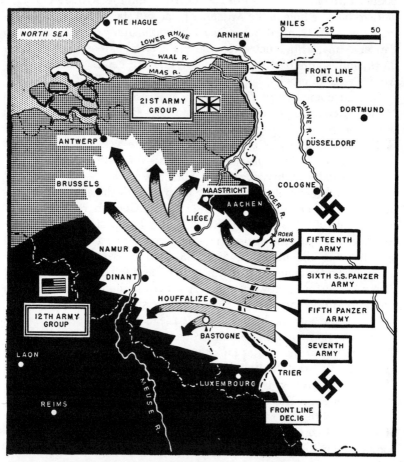

Von Rundstedt's plan for the December counteroffensive called for a slashing drive through the Ardennes with tanks pacing the advance to Antwerp. Two panzer Armies were to carry the main thrust while two others held open the shoulders. If successful, the stroke would have cut off the Allied Armies north of Aachen.

SS panzer divisions assigned to Sepp Dietrich's Sixth Army. General Hasso von Manteuffel's Fifth Panzer Army to the left included three ordinary panzer divisions and four more of infantry. Altogether von Rundstedt had accumulated 600 tanks for the attack.

In the face of this astonishing German build-up, I had greatly underestimated the enemy's offensive capabilities. My embarrassment however was not unique, for it was shared not only by the Army commanders but by Montgomery and Eisenhower as well. Early in December intelligence had counted ten panzer divisions parked behind the Roer; an eleventh, together with six more infantry, down opposite the Ardennes. Although the Ardennes concentration was far heavier than von Rundstedt required for the security of that front, we were too much addicted to the anticipation of counterattack on the Roer to credit the enemy with more fanciful or ambitious intentions. For while we acknowledged the enemy's capability for a knockdown battle there, we could not believe he possessed sufficient resources for a strategic offensive. And unless he sought such strategic objectives as Antwerp and Liége, there was little profit to be gained by his venturing into the Ardennes. On the other hand, if a spoiling attack were to be the limit of his ambitions, we estimated that we could successfully contain it without serious damage or dislocation to our front.

Although we had erred in evaluating the enemy's *intentions,* this estimate of his *capabilities* at the time was nearer right than wrong. For as events in subsequent weeks proved, von Rundstedt lacked the resources necessary to succeed in a strategic offensive against so powerful a force as ours. Instead, he squandered his reserves so recklessly in the Ardennes that two months later when he was charged with defense of the Rhine, he found himself too weak to hold that river line. In his anxiety to stave off for a few more months the disaster that shadowed him in the West, Hitler unwittingly hastened the war to an earlier end.

Earlier that fall von Rundstedt had reached the same conclusion as we on the inadequacy of German forces for the strategic offensive envisioned by Hitler. When the latter disclosed his grandiose plan, von Rundstedt offered a counterproposal. He would attack toward Aachen and restore the Siegfried Line. The dodge, however, failed. Hitler curtly rejected von Rundstedt's substitution, contending that it lacked a strategic objective.

But if the enemy's resources fell far short of Hitler's aspirations, they also admittedly exceeded our conservative estimates on German strength. Representative of the Allied outlook at this time was the Montgomery estimate of German offensive capabilities published at 21st Army Group on December 16. Had I been preparing an estimate of my own on the same day, I would not have changed a word of Monty's, for his appraisal was identical to my own:

> The enemy is at present fighting a defensive campaign on all fronts; his situation is such that he cannot stage major offensive operations. Furthermore, at all costs he has to prevent the war from entering on a mobile phase; he has not the transport or the petrol that would be necessary for mobile operations, nor could his tanks compete with ours in the mobile battle.
>
> The enemy is in a bad way; he has had a tremendous battering and has lost heavily in men and equipment. On no account can we relax, or have a 'stand still,' in the winter months; it is vital that we keep going, so as not to allow him time to recover and so as to wear down his strength still further. There will be difficulties caused by mud, cold, lack of air support during periods of bad weather, and so on. But we must continue to fight the enemy hard during the winter months.

Just as soon as the enemy fell back behind his Siegfried Line, Allied intelligence suffered from a lack of secret-agent reports. No longer, as in France, was the German fighting in a hostile land where French patriots reported his movements and shielded our agents behind his lines. Within the Reich he was at home among his own people where the only informers were traitors and there were far too few of them. As a result, the flow of information from behind German lines thinned to a trickle. More and more we were forced to depend upon PW interrogation, front-line intelligence, and aerial observation.

Since success was predicated largely upon surprise, in massing his troops for the Ardennes offensive the enemy invoked his most rigid security precautions of the war. Pledges were required of all commanders briefed on the operation. Radio communication on the operation was forbidden; correspondence was ordered carried only by trusted couriers and anyone with a knowledge of the offensive was prohibited from flying west of the Rhine. Troops were to be staged in their final assembly areas only in the eleventh hour, and then only at night. Meanwhile, all non-German soldiers were evacuated from the front line. To conceal these elaborate preparations, Armies were to maintain their existing CP's and fake a routine radio

Tanks in the Ardennes: "In the wooded Ardennes, tanks were limited to narrow roads and those sparse fields that had been cleared of forest. When at last the sun broke through the overcast on December 23, the armor was silhouetted for easy observation by air against the snow-covered ground." (December, 1944.)

Eisenhower, Architect of an Alliance: "With Montgomery obviously partisan toward those maneuvers that would benefit or bring prestige to his British troops, I was unabashedly Yankee in my outlook and feelings. To Eisenhower there fell the difficult task of fusing these national differences into an Allied effort."

traffic. And a complete dummy headquarters was established opposite Simpson's Army to divert our attention up north.

When the time came for the enemy's movement of reserves into position for the offensive, the weather on which von Rundstedt had counted closed down on the Western front. For days the sun shone only fitfully and air reconnaissance found its cameras blinded by cloud cover. Meanwhile, the agents that we slipped through the enemy's lines disappeared into the winter and were never heard from again.

In spite of these handicaps, however, intelligence had detected some slight sign of an enemy build-up in the Ardennes. Unfortunately those indications in themselves were not conclusive. What did they mean, intelligence asked? And what should we do about them? Admittedly, there was nothing disquieting, nothing alarming about troop movements in the Eifel. The enemy was using that sector, as we were, to rest his battle-weary divisions and to blood the new ones. For this reason the Eifel might easily echo with more movement than one would ordinarily expect on so "quiet" a front.

In the absence of more conclusive evidence of the enemy's intentions, there were two deductions that could be drawn from this nighttime activity in the Eifel. Either it could be part of an enemy build-up for counterattack behind the Roer, or it could mean the beginning of an enemy threat in the Ardennes. The first conclusion seemed the more rational one, even though it was far riskier for us.

For by chancing the danger of an enemy surprise attack in the Ardennes, we could push on with the winter offensive, secure the Roer dams, and thus force the enemy to commit his reserves in a battle west of the Rhine. But if we were inclined to play it safe by preparing for trouble in the Ardennes, we should have to call off the winter offensive, strengthen Middleton's VIII Corps front, and brace him with reinforcements to meet this danger of counterattack. Clearly there were not enough troops for both a winter offensive and a secure defense everywhere else on the Allied line. To push on in the attack—or bed down until the spring: these were the alternatives we faced.

At that moment nothing less than an unequivocal indication of impending attack in the Ardennes could have induced me to quit the winter offensive. And that did not come until 5 A.M. on December 16 when the enemy opened his artillery barrage.

Our failure to foresee that those signs pointed to an attack through the Ardennes ironically enough spared us heavier casualties when it came. For had we doubled our divisions across Middleton's thin VIII Corps front, we could not have withstood the weight of von Rundstedt's powerful offensive. With the 24 divisions he was to throw into the Bulge, the enemy could have broken a hole anywhere in our line. He may not have been able to advance as far as he did had he dragged through heavier defenses, but he would have undoubtedly inflicted more casualties upon Middleton's troops in the effort.

By the same token I was grateful that Eisenhower had rejected Montgomery's proposal to hold defensively on Patton's Third Army front along the Moselle River. For had we bedded Patton down on that front and diverted part of his troops to Hodges, von Rundstedt might have chosen to break through there rather than through the Ardennes. Had von Rundstedt shaken loose with his panzers west of the Moselle, nothing could have prevented him from rushing headlong to Reims where Com Z's depots bulged with fuel and food enough to shuttle the Wehrmacht to Paris.

It is difficult for Americans who believe so fiercely in the invincibility of United States forces to stomach the reverses a U. S. Army must occasionally suffer if it would fight boldly to the limit of its resources. Setbacks are inevitably blamed upon command or intelligence "failures." We forget that even the U. S. Army is not exempt from miscalculation and error. For unless the enemy is prostrate, or our superiority overwhelming, the initiative in battle must sometimes revert to the enemy's forces. If we would win a war through aggressive campaigning, we must expect to take chances. Even U. S. intelligence is not infallible—and, certainly, neither is command.

As though to compensate for the indignity it suffered when First Army was forced to evacuate its CP at Spa during the Bulge, that staff afterward excerpted its record to "prove" First Army had been clairvoyant in predicting the German offensive but that its "predictions" had been disregarded at higher headquarters—meaning Army Group. First Army's contention is pure nonsense for it was just as neatly hoodwinked by von Rundstedt as was the rest of the Allied command. While I freely accept responsibility for our "calculated risk" in the Ardennes, I do not admit that there were any significant warnings given me which I chose to ignore.

On December 11, I had visited Courtney Hodges at Spa. If, as some officers of the First Army contend, their warnings had been smothered under the complacency that existed at Army Group, certainly they had not yet convinced their own Army commander that disaster lay around the corner. Hodges had been deceived no less than we by the apparent transparency of von Rundstedt's preparations for counterattack on the Roer.

During the four days following that visit, First Army picked up additional signs of enemy activity in the Eifel across from the Ardennes.

On December 12 a PW reported that the elite *Grossdeutschland* Division had moved into that "quiet" sector.

The following day, PW interrogators picked up the scent of another movement, this time that of the 116th Panzer from Simpson's front into the Eifel.

On December 14 a German informant brought Middleton word that bridging equipment was being hauled up to the front opposite Luxembourg on the Our. To this report First Army added the comment: "A very interesting report. Build-up of troops has been confirmed by Tac/R and PW statements. Presence of large numbers of engineers with bridging equipment suggests preparation for offensive rather than defensive action."

But however pertinent these excerpts may seem today, they provoked no more than routine interest when relayed from First Army to Group. For at the time there were scores of contradictory reports of movements elsewhere along the line. If First Army hit the nail on the head, as some staff members now allege, the Army was not yet aware of its good judgment. For on December 15, G-2, First Army, summarized the situation this way:

Although the enemy is resorting to his attack propaganda to bolster the morale of his troops, it is possible that a *limited scale offensive** will be launched for the purpose of achieving a Christmas morale "victory" for civilian consumption. Many PW's now speak of the coming attack between the 17th and 25th of December while others relate promises of the recapture of Aachen as a Christmas present for the Fuehrer.

At this crucial moment weather closed in on Vandenberg's Tac/R and for three days von Rundstedt assembled his troops without fear of detection by air.

While G-2 at First Army did accumulate a few vital shreds of intelligence for the record, he no more evaluated that information to predict the Bulge than did any other of the clairvoyants who after-

*Italics mine.

ward claimed that distinction. Although First Army's observations
could have been read so as to suggest the *possibility* of attack in the
Ardennes, its warnings were not convincing enough to justify postponement of our winter attack to meet this new threat. Monk Dickson was as brilliant and skilled a G-2 as served in the American
army. He functioned as my intelligence officer in Africa, in Sicily,
and on the invasion. But like most G-2's he was often a pessimist
and an alarmist. Had I gone on guard every time Dickson, or any
other G-2, called wolf, we would never have taken many of the
riskier moves that hastened the end of the war.

Nor was my own G-2 at Army Group, Brigadier General Sibert,
sufficiently impressed by these reports to come to me with a warning.
By this time I commanded almost three quarters of a million men
on a 230-mile front. It was impossible for me even to scan the intelligence estimates of subordinate units. As a consequence, I looked
to my own G-2 and to the Army commanders to keep me informed
on the enemy's capabilities. Hodges neither spoke to Middleton, one
of his own corps commanders, of any premonitions in the Ardennes,
nor did he telephone me in advance of the offensive. Indeed no one
came to me with a warning on the danger of counterattack there.

The week after Christmas, in replying to a note of holiday greetings from General Marshall, I wrote, "I do not blame my commanders, my staff, or myself, for the situation that resulted. We had
taken a calculated risk and the German hit us harder than we
anticipated he could."

Time has not altered that opinion. I would rather be bold than
wary even though wariness may sometimes be right.

When the blow fell on December 16, von Rundstedt caught us
fully committed without a division in Army Group reserve. This
plight was not uncommon. Against an enemy as badly beaten as we
imagined the German to be, I could not conscientiously withhold
in reserve divisions better utilized on the offensive. At no time did
my Group "reserve" consist of anything more than a few divisions
assigned to one or another of the Armies where they could be
employed only with Group's consent.

SHAEF's strategic reserve consisted of two airborne divisions, the
82d and the 101st. Both had been assembled at Reims for refitting
after Arnhem. After having been loaned to Monty for what SHAEF
anticipated would be a 48-hour commitment until relieved by British

armor, both divisions were held in the line for 58 days in Holland.

Just as soon as I learned of the Ardennes attack on the afternoon of December 16, I telephoned Patton at Nancy from Eisenhower's office. George's 10th Armored Division, now out of the line, was in reserve near Thionville just south of the Luxembourg-French border. I wanted to use that armor to stab into the enemy's southern flank in the event he broke through on Middleton's front.

"George, get the 10th Armored on the road to Luxembourg," I told him, "and have Morris* report immediately to Middleton for orders."

Patton objected, as I anticipated he would. One less armored division meant lessening his chance of breaking through into the Saar. "But that's no major threat up there," George balked. "Hell, it's probably nothing more than a spoiling attack to throw us off balance down here and make us stop this offensive."

Patton might have been right; it was too soon yet to tell. But I had decided that we couldn't afford to take chances. The risk we had knowingly taken in the Ardennes had been calculated partly upon our ability to counterattack in the event of trouble.

"I hate like hell to do it, George, but I've got to have that division. Even if it's only a spoiling attack as you say, Middleton must have help." Within a few minutes Patton issued the orders by phone.

I then phoned Lev Allen at EAGLE TAC to tell him of my orders to Patton. At the same time I instructed him to have Simpson turn the 7th Armored Division over to Hodges that it, too, might be used like the 10th Armored to hit von Rundstedt on his flank.

Meanwhile Major General Raymond O. Barton had already begun to worry over the wobbly position of his 4th Division on the right end of the Luxembourg line. We had not yet replaced the losses he had suffered in Huertgen Forest, and at the time of attack his division was critically understrength. The following morning as the enemy swarmed across the Sauer River, Barton rushed his cooks, bakers, and clerks into the line. "But we're not stopping them," he warned Lev Allen, 20 miles to the rear in Luxembourg. "If the 10th Armored doesn't get up here soon, Army Group had better get set to barrel out."

On Sunday morning, December 17, I awakened early in the handsome stone villa Ike occupied at St. Germain-en-Laye. The weather

*Major General William H. H. Morris, CG, 10th Armored Division.

had not yet lifted for air and I was anxious to get to my headquarters just as soon as I could. It was midafternoon when we sped into Verdun on the road from Paris. The night before the German had dropped parachutists behind our lines to cut the roads leading into the north flank of his penetration. The drop had miscarried as most night drops do and enemy paratroopers had been scattered widely behind our lines. A machine-gun jeep was waiting at Verdun to escort me the rest of the way.

On the road into Luxembourg a giant American flag hung from the roof of a modest stone cottage.

"I hope he doesn't have to take it down," I said, pointing it out to Hansen.

"You mean we'll stay put in Luxembourg—"

"You can bet your life we will. I'm not going to budge this CP. It would scare everyone else to death."

Eisenhower later challenged the wisdom of that resolution. Fearful that we might lose control should the enemy drive us out and destroy our communications, he recommended that we play safe and pull TAC back to Verdun. I balked but not for pride. Any hint of withdrawal by Army Group, I told him, might easily alarm the command. It might also incite panic in Luxembourg, cause refugees to jam the roads at the very time they were needed for troop movements. A parallel system of Army Group communications tied in Verdun where EAGLE MAIN was located. Even if TAC were to be turned out of Luxembourg at gun point, the switch-over could be made without a break in communications.

We drove directly to the brownstone state railway building in which TAC was located and there found Lev Allen brooding over a map in the war room. G-2 was posting enemy divisions identified in the attack. Already they totaled 14, and half of them were panzers. I scanned the map in dismay. "Pardon my French, Lev, but just where in hell has this sonuvabitch gotten all his strength."

By the following morning, December 18, the center of our line in the Ardennes had been crushed but the shoulders were holding firm. Sepp Dietrich's main thrust had been blocked by First Army at Malmédy. A few miles south of that ridge line the 7th Armored raced into St. Vith to nose out the SS panzers driving hard for that intersection on the road to Liége. Although Barton had been forced to give ground on our right, the timely arrival of the 10th Armored

Division had steadied his position and the shoulder now appeared secure.

In the center, Manteuffel's panzers had smashed through the 28th Division to overrun Middleton's reserves and head for Bastogne almost midway between the city of Luxembourg and Liége. To the north of the unlucky 28th, two regiments of the 106th had already been encircled in position. The remainder of that newly arrived division was fighting for its life at St. Vith.

My decision to hold Bastogne, at all costs, had been anticipated by Middleton even as his front was crumbling to pieces. When I called Troy to give him the order to hold that crucial road junction, he replied that he had already instructed his troops there to dig in and hold. Elements of the 10th Armored Division raced north to Bastogne to reinforce tanks of the 9th Armored in their defense of that key position. That evening the 101st Airborne Division roared into Bastogne after a wild truck ride from Reims while the 82d Airborne continued on north to blunt the pincer that had forced its way between Malmédy and St. Vith.

If we could limit von Rundstedt's penetration to the 35-mile gap between Malmedy and Bastogne while holding firm on the shoulders, we might force the enemy to funnel his strength due west into the Ardennes where the terrain would sponge it up. Between those two points only three mediocre roads meandered westward toward the Meuse.

On the evening of December 18, I had intended to run up through Bastogne to Spa until Hodges' aide telephoned to suggest that I come instead by air. English-speaking Germans in captured American OD's had infiltrated our lines in a brash attempt to panic our rear areas. Captured enemy orders for the recruitment of those "reconnaissance" units had fallen into our hands two weeks before. Volunteers were to be selected and trained by the notorious Lieutenant Colonel Otto Skorzeny, the airborne privateer who the year before had snatched Mussolini out of the Italian hotel in which he had been imprisoned following his fall from power. Most of these GI-uniformed enemy troops were cut down before they reached the Meuse but not until a half-million GI's played cat and mouse with each other each time they met on the road. Neither rank nor credentials nor protests spared the traveler an inquisition at each intersection he passed. Three times I was ordered to prove my identity by cautious GI's. The first time by identifying Springfield as the

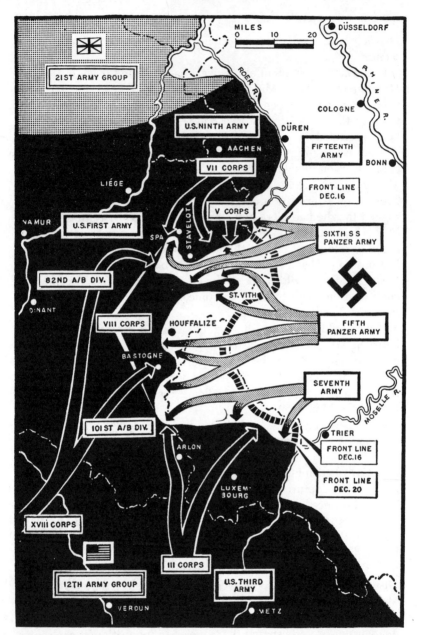

By December 20, after four days of attack, the enemy had failed to score the speedy breakthrough on which he had banked. Not only had Hodges blocked him at Malmédy on the northern shoulder, but the 7th Armored Division at St. Vith had seriously disrupted his tight schedule.

capital of Illinois (my questioner held out for Chicago); the second time by locating the guard between the center and tackle on a line of scrimmage; the third time by naming the then current spouse of a blonde named Betty Grable. Grable stopped me but the sentry did not. Pleased at having stumped me, he nevertheless passed me on.

Within two days it was apparent the enemy had mounted more than a spoiling attack. In an order of the day to his troops, von Rundstedt had declared, "We gamble everything now—we cannot fail." At Army Group we concluded his target lay in the swollen dumps of Liége. I could not yet believe that his ambitions stretched beyond Liége to Antwerp.

As Hodges thinned his Roer River front to fend off the panzers on the right of his line and dig in on a defensive position between the Bulge and the Meuse River, I made ready to call off Patton's offensive in the Saar. While First Army rolled with the German's Bulge offensive on the north, Third Army would slash into its underbelly by wheeling up from the Saar. George was dismayed at the prospect of abandoning his toe hold in the Siegfried Line. "But what the hell," he shrugged, "we'll still be killing Krauts."

I walked out with him to his jeep when he left Luxembourg for Nancy that day. "We won't commit any more of your stuff than we have to," I said. "I want to save it for a whale of a blow when we hit back—and we're going to hit this bastard hard." George grinned and pulled his parka tightly under his chin.

To free Patton for the underbelly offensive it became necessary for Eisenhower to widen Devers' 6th Army Group front and spell Third Army on the Saar. To coordinate this change-over between Army Groups, Eisenhower called a council at EAGLE MAIN in Verdun on December 19. He drove into the chilly caserne from Versailles in a heavy bullet-proof car. CIC had insisted on the precaution after reports reached SHAEF that Skorzeny had dispatched a squad of assassins to hunt down the Supreme Commander. Patton was to pull two of his three corps out of the line in the Saar for the Bulge counterattack while Devers thinned out his front and sideslipped off to the left into Third Army's sector. Like Patton, Devers disliked the need for relinquishing his 6th Army Group offensive to help pull our chestnuts out of the Ardennes. But he, too, had resigned himself to the strategic realignment.

Meanwhile Patton, who in Sicily had brushed off supply as a bothersome detail, demonstrated how well he had learned his lesson during the September drought by stuffing his Third Army dumps with engineer bridging equipment to be used in spanning the Rhine. Fearful lest Devers ransack that hoard should it fall into his hands on the Army Group shift, George insisted that in rearranging his boundary we keep those dumps within his sector. Two months later that foresight paid off when George took the Rhine on the run and jumped Third Army across it on those bountiful engineer stores.

In the chilly squad room of the Verdun caserne where a lone pot-bellied stove helped ease the chill of the moist December, we quickly agreed to an over-all plan for spearing the enemy Bulge on its flanks. Eisenhower had already approved the shift of Third Army; the conference had been called primarily to draft Devers' resources in it. No one proposed an alternative line of action, for the only "alternative" would have involved withdrawal to a winter line on the Meuse. Even the theorists of G-3, whose duty it was to explore the alternatives open to us, shunned withdrawal as too unthinkable to merit consideration.

Although I would have preferred to clamp the Bulge in simultaneous attacks from both shoulders, it was clear that Hodges could not mount an offensive until first he checked the enemy's advance. And on December 19, the harried First Army was too preoccupied in stemming the German offensive to think about a retaliatory blow. Had Hodges been able to gather a force behind his shoulder at Malmédy and strike south from there to St. Vith, he might have narrowed the neck and greatly foreshortened the Bulge. But as fast as he pulled divisions out of the Roer, he was forced to commit them piecemeal to prevent a breakthrough to the Meuse. As the enemy drove deeper into the Ardennes searching for an unblocked road north to the Meuse, Hodges extended his line in a frantic effort to contain him. If Sepp Dietrich's panzers were to break through that wall and drive on to Liége, Hodges would probably have been compelled to slacken his grip on the Malmédy shoulder. And it was there that he saved First Army by holding the enemy's *main* force to a draw.

But if Hodges could not strike back into the enemy's northern flank, there was nothing to deter Patton from counterattacking against the Bulge from the south. Indeed the plight of First Army had become so grave that unless Patton soon hurried to its aid with a diversion, we feared Hodges' line might crack, enabling the enemy to pour across the Meuse.

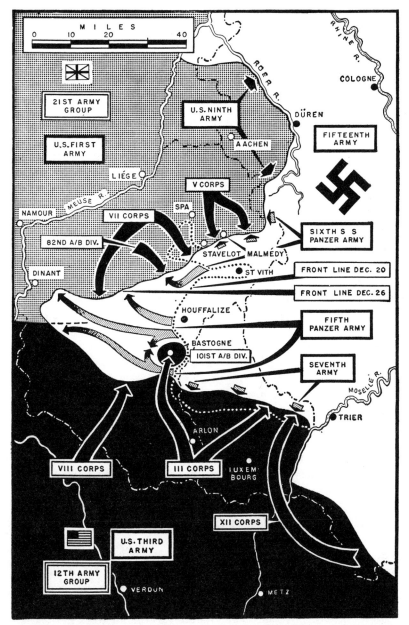

On December 26, near Dinant on the Meuse, the 2d Armored Division stopped the point of von Rundstedt's forces. That same afternoon Third Army broke through to Bastogne. Patton was now engaged in a full-scale attack against the lower flank of the Bulge.

Meanwhile our situation at the crossroads of Bastogne was rapidly shaping into a major crisis. Manteuffel's Fifth Panzer Army, in the center of von Rundstedt's line, had spilled past that isle of resistance to cut its north and south exit roads. With the encirclement of Bastogne foredoomed, I nevertheless ordered Middleton's VIII Corps to hold on to that vital objective. Even though it might cost us heavy casualties in the airborne division and the two armored combat commands* that had reached that outpost, I could not afford to relinquish Bastogne and let the enemy widen his Bulge. But though I did not minimize the ordeal we inflicted upon its defenders, I was confident that the 101st could hold with the aid of those tankers from the 9th and 10th Armored Divisions. They could hold out I thought at least until Patton's Third Army broke through to relieve them. The relief of Bastogne was to be the priority objective in Patton's flanking attack.

"How soon will you be able to go, George?" I asked, knowing how difficult his movement would be over the limited roadnet that connected Luxembourg with his Alsatian front. George estimated 48 hours; any other commander would have held his breath and believed himself taking a chance on 98.

Now totally reconciled to an indefinite postponement of his Saar offensive, George was itching to start the counterattack. He lighted a fresh cigar and pointed to the Bulge where it pierced the thin blue lines on our war map.

"Brad," he exclaimed, "this time the Kraut's stuck his head in a meatgrinder." With a turn of his fist he added, "And this time I've got hold of the handle."

Within two days George had made good on the start of his attack. A week later von Rundstedt dragged to a halt on the high water mark of his offensive. Patton's brilliant shift of Third Army from its bridgehead in the Saar to the snow-covered Ardennes front became one of the most astonishing feats of generalship of our campaign in the West. Even before he left Verdun for Nancy on December 19, George had touched off the movement by phone. Two days later, on December 21, he was attacking toward Bastogne with an armored and infantry division. By Christmas those original two had been joined by four more. Within less than a week Patton had switched the bulk of his Third Army, with its guns, supply, and

*An armored combat command comprises approximately one third of the tanks, infantry, and artillery of an armored division.

equipment, from 50 to 75 miles north into the new offensive. More than 133,000 tanks and trucks joined that round-the-clock trek over the icy roads. From the windows of my office overlooking the gorge where the medieval dungeons and battlements of Luxembourg had been cut into the rock, I could count the double-banked columns as they crossed the arched stone bridge. In heavy greatcoats still caked with the mud of the Saar, troops huddled against the wintry cold that knifed through their canvas-topped trucks. In the turrets of their Shermans, tank commanders had wrapped their faces in woolen scarves as they guided their awkward vehicles through the streets of the city. Day and night those columns rattled over the cobblestoned pavements until on December 21 a new carpet of snow muffled their passage and they glided through like ghosts.

The speed with which Third Army turned its forces north astonished even those of us who had gambled in the Ardennes on the mobility of our army. When movement orders were telephoned the 5th Infantry Division on December 20, two regiments were engaged in an attack against the enemy in Sauerlautern while the third held a defensive sector north of that bridgehead. Twenty-four hours later, two regiments had closed in an assembly area northeast of Luxembourg, while the third was awaiting relief preparatory to moving north.

Until the Battle of the Bulge I did not share George's enthusiasm for his Third Army staff which, unlike those of both the First and Ninth Armies, lacked outstanding individual performers. Indeed, I had once agreed with the observation of another senior commander who said, "Patton can get more good work out of a mediocre bunch of staff officers than anyone I ever saw." His principals were almost without exception holdovers from the Sicilian campaign where their performance could be most charitably described as something less than perfect. However, five months in Europe had seasoned that staff and the greatly matured Patton succeeded in coaxing from it the brilliant effort that characterized Third Army's turnabout in the Bulge.

Although Patton had been understandably reluctant to relinquish his 10th Armored Division during the first day of the Bulge offensive, this remarkable switch-over on his front had caused George very little worry. For despite the enormous complexity of the maneuver, he handled it almost entirely by telephone, improvising from day to day to stretch the capacity of his roads.

While mobility was the "secret" U. S. weapon that defeated von Rundstedt in the Ardennes, it owed its effectiveness to the success of U. S. Army staff training. With division, corps, and Army staffs schooled in the same language, practices, and techniques, we could resort to sketchy oral orders with an assurance of perfect understanding between U. S. commands. Those orders, in turn, were transmitted easily over the most valued accessory of all: the elaborate telephone system we carried with us into the field. From my desk in Luxembourg I was never more than 30 seconds by phone from any of the Armies. If necessary, I could have called every division on the line. Signal corps officers like to remind us that "although Congress can make a general, it takes communications to make him a commander." The maxim was never more brilliantly evidenced than in this battle for the Ardennes.

Although Hodges was fighting a touch-and-go battle on the evening of December 19, I was not perturbed so long as he held tightly to the Malmédy shoulder. Sepp Dietrich had already shattered four first-rate divisions against that position before diverting his *main* effort south through the road center at St. Vith. There where five principal highways intersected in the center of that small Belgian town, Hodges had blocked the German advance with his 7th Armored Division. Dietrich's unwieldy columns piled up in a jam behind. As his panzers forked north and south in an effort to avoid that intersection, they soon lost their precious momentum on the muddy secondary roads that made the Ardennes so treacherous a vehicle trap.

Von Rundstedt had gambled on speed in his offensive, knowing that unless he could score a quick breakthrough, time would react in favor of our motorized Armies as we threw reinforcements in against his flanks. After four days of violent attack the enemy had not yet loosened Hodges' grip on the shoulder at Malmédy nor had he driven the outnumbered 7th Armored Division out of St. Vith. The schedule on which the German had banked his offensive had gone awry and though we could not yet be certain, it looked as though Hodges had already tipped the scales of the Bulge in our favor. Having failed to secure a breakthrough to the Meuse by December 19, the enemy should have despaired of the Bulge and withdrawn his forces.

Although First Army headquarters had been chased out of its CP at Spa when an enemy column approached to within 2,000 yards of that resort city, this threat was dented by the timely arrival of tanks from the 3rd Armored Division. Before quitting its CP, however, First Army had removed more than a million gallons of motor fuel from the enemy's reach. Another 124,000 gallons were ignited to prevent their capture. And a third dump of 2,225,000 gallons was in the process of being removed to the rear. The acute fuel shortages that had followed destruction by air of the enemy's petroleum industry had forced von Rundstedt to mount his attack without adequate gasoline reserves. Without captured American fuel his offensive could not succeed.

Before quitting the office late that evening of December 19 for my billet at the Alfa, I called Middleton at his VIII Corps headquarters. Troy estimated that his corps, though shattered by the offensive, had cost the enemy far more delay than he could afford. For despite the overwhelming weight and surprise of his first day's attack, von Rundstedt had spent four valuable days getting to Bastogne.

Troy was entitled to pride in the VIII Corps, for his divisions had rallied nobly in a furious delaying struggle that emphasized the resourcefulness of the American soldier. Though surprised and disorganized, part of 106th fell back to the crossroads of St. Vith. There it was joined by the 7th Armored Division in the defense of that road junction. In tactical importance that road center was even more valuable than Bastogne itself. On the south end of Middleton's line, where Luxembourg bulges into the vineyards of the Moselle Valley, Barton's 4th Division had buckled but it did not break. In valor, however, neither had outshone the broken and bruised 28th. Though overrun by the first wave of Germans that moved out of the mists of the Eifel, the 28th split into a forest full of small delaying units. For three sleepless days and nights the embattled troops of that division backed grudgingly toward Bastogne buying time for the reinforcement of that anchor position. During the first week of that Ardennes offensive, almost one fourth of the entire division had been reported killed, wounded, or missing.

Although Eisenhower had evidenced no sign of uneasiness during the conference at Verdun on December 19, his staff at SHAEF had shown symptoms of what we at Group diagnosed as an acute case of the shakes. This uneasiness soon spread to the Scribe Hotel in Paris where newsmen accredited to SHAEF echoed the nervousness that came out of Versailles. So exaggerated were their tales of our plight in the Ardennes that I afterward asked Ike's permission to open a press camp at EAGLE TAC where they might get a better picture of the front than they were getting in Paris.

The first evidence of SHAEF's anxiety came in a TWX cautioning us to make certain that no bridge over the Meuse fell into the enemy's hands. "What the devil do they think we're doing," Lev Allen complained, "starting back for the beaches?"

The big blowup, however, came in a telephone call from Bedell Smith the evening of December 19.

"Ike thinks it may be a good idea," Bedell said, "to turn over to Monty your two Armies on the north and let him run that side of the Bulge from 21st Group. It may save us a great deal of trouble, especially if your communications with Hodges and Simpson go out."

This was my first intimation of the change in command that was to put both Hodges and Simpson under Montgomery; the former for a month, the latter until after we crossed the Rhine. Eisenhower had not raised the issue during our meeting at Verdun early that morning nor had he shown concern over my communications to the north. Our lines through Bastogne had been cut but an auxiliary circuit had been run across the western tip of the Ardennes. Still another was being strung for safety's sake behind the Meuse. As long as the enemy was contained within the Meuse, it seemed unlikely that we would lose all our long lines to either the First or Ninth Armies. And as a matter of fact we never did.

The suddenness of Bedell's proposal made me turn it hurriedly over in my mind. "I'd question whether such a change-over's necessary," I said. "When we go to drive him out of the Bulge, it'd be easier to coordinate the attack from here." If Montgomery were to come into the picture as Bedell had suggested, coordination between both Army Groups would have to be directed from SHAEF.

But Smith was for the change-over. "It seems the logical thing to do," he said. "Monty can take care of everything north of the Bulge and you'll have everything south."

"Bedell, it's hard for me to object," I told him. "Certainly if Monty's were an American command, I would agree with you entirely. It would be the logical thing to do." In this moment of decision I could not tell him that what I feared most was the likelihood that this forced change-over would discredit the American command.

For no one could dispute that the change-over would not have been a logical one; there was ample justification for the Army Group on the north taking *temporary* command of all Armies on that side of the penetration. Furthermore, if von Rundstedt were to force the Meuse behind both our U. S. Armies, Montgomery would find his 21st Group seriously jeopardized by the offensive. To protect himself he would undoubtedly want to establish a reserve on that right flank. Yet if his command were to include the U. S. Armies and be extended all the way down to the Bulge, he would probably employ that British reserve against the enemy threat to the Meuse.

"There's no doubt in my mind," I admitted to Smith, "that if we play it the way you suggest, we'll get more help from the British in the way of reserves."

I asked if the change-over was to be a *temporary* one. Bedell agreed that it was and that it would last only as long as the Bulge.

With this assurance that the change-over was to be temporary, my only other objections revolved around the question of face. For unless the change-over were clearly explained by SHAEF, it could be interpreted as a loss of confidence by Eisenhower in me—or more significantly in the American command. If, as a result of the shift, the public were to lose confidence in me, Eisenhower could quickly remedy that situation by sending me home. But if his action were taken to mean repudiation of the American command, if it were inferred that we were bailed out by the British, the damage could be irreparable to our future role in the war.

Although these objections seemed rational enough, I nevertheless distrusted them, fearing they might be too much involved in my concern for my own career. Eisenhower had resolved to fight us together as an Allied command. If there were to be no distinctions between Allies, then I questioned my right to wave the flag for prestige in this particular crisis.

The change-over was to be made at noon on December 20. With this acquisition of the First and Ninth U. S. Armies, Montgomery's command would then be expanded to four. I was to be left *temporarily* with only Patton's Third.

Had the senior British field commander been anyone else but Monty, the switch in command could probably have been made without incident, strain, or tension. Certainly it would never have touched off the Allied ruckus it subsequently did. But Montgomery unfortunately could not resist this chance to tweak our Yankee noses. Even Freddy de Guingand, his chief of staff, was later to chide Montgomery for the manner in which he behaved. And while Eisenhower held his tongue only by clenching his teeth, he was to admit several years after the war that had he anticipated the trouble that was to be caused by it, he would never have suggested the change. Fortunately, the mischief was delayed until after our crisis in the Bulge had passed.

Although Montgomery did not commit more than a *single* brigade of British troops against the Bulge offensive, he backed the First Army's flank with four British divisions. While those British reserves encouraged Hodges to throw everything into the Ardennes, I afterward questioned whether this bargain was worth the misunderstanding that came with the change in command.

Almost as soon as the change-over brought Hodges' and Simpson's Armies under his 21st Group, Montgomery hurried a liaison officer down to the Meuse to ascertain in a firsthand report whether the enemy had anywhere crossed it. Hodges could readily have told him the German had not. The 7th Armored still held to its salient at St. Vith and to the north on the Malmédy shoulder, the veteran 1st, 2d, and 9th Divisions had dug in on that critical shoulder. At the Belgian farm village of Stavelot, only 22 miles southeast of Liége, the 30th Division once more heeled in with the doggedness it had shown at Mortain. Now as the Bulge spilled harmlessly westward through the empty Ardennes, Hodges gathered his VII Corps on the flank in preparation for a counterattack.

This remarkable regroupment of First Army while under attack equaled even the astonishing performance of Third Army. On December 17 alone, it put 60,000 men and 11,000 vehicles in motion on the realignment. During the first nine days of von Rundstedt's offensive, First Army cleared 196 convoys of 48,000 vehicles, 248,000 troops. When during World War I, Marshal Foch raced his famous "taxi-cab" army to halt the Kaiser's troops on the Marne, he shuttled a bare 4,985 troops a distance of 28 miles in 1,200 Paris cabs.

On the eve of Patton's attack toward the U. S. redoubt at Bastogne, Montgomery radioed that he was planning to delay the companion attack from the north for which Hodges had massed Collins' VII Corps. He had chosen instead to "tidy up" the defenses on his front before undertaking a counteroffensive. As a result, the divisions that had been gathered for Collins' attack were dispersed on a retaining wall and the enemy continued to hold the initiative on the northern edge of the Bulge. It was not until January 3, 12 days later, that Montgomery completed his primping and attacked. Meanwhile, the enemy now acknowledged that his main effort had been thwarted on the shoulder at Malmédy where Hodges had fought Sepp Dietrich to a draw. Gone was the element of surprise; von Rundstedt had gambled on speed and lost. Now faced with a major battle instead of the breakthrough he had planned to the Meuse, von Rundstedt shifted the main force of his drive to Manteuffel's Fifth Panzer Army. At the same time he committed his remaining reserves in the gap that had been opened north of Bastogne and attacked due westward. Thus after having been repelled in his advance toward Liége, von Rundstedt, now with no worthwhile objective, could only spend his strength against the Ardennes.

Two days before Christmas the gray cloud blanket that had hung so long over our front lifted for the first time in eight days and a blaze of sunlight silhouetted the enemy against the Ardennes snows. Prior to this, each morning our gloom had deepened as the Ninth Air Force's youthful meteorologist opened the daily briefing with his dismally repetitious report. And each morning Vandenberg, in a chair next to mine, pulled his head a little tighter into his leather flying jacket. On more than 100 socked-in airfields from Scotland to Brussels, an Allied air force of more than 4,000 planes waited for the end of von Rundstedt's conspiracy with the weather.

On the morning of December 23, Vandenberg's meteorologist hurried into the TAC war room with a forecast for good weather across the entire front. Within an hour the air began to pulse with a mighty roar of engines as aircraft swarmed high over Luxembourg to join the attack. Even if von Rundstedt continued to push his famished columns toward the Meuse, he could no longer support the offensive as long as we could pound him from the air. On that first clear day air flew a total of more than 1,200 sorties. The following day, 2,000 bombers escorted by more than 800 fighters went after 31 tactical targets with 4,300 tons of bombs. Fighter bombers splayed out through the Ardennes hunting the enemy where he waited helplessly in clotted columns. At Bastogne where three enemy divisions were attacking that brave pocket, 241 troop-carrier aircraft pinpointed a low-level drop of food, medical supplies, and ammunition.

From Luxembourg we could see the con trails of the heavies as they droned overhead bound for the busy marshaling yards of Trier behind the German border.

Back at SHAEF where the gloom thickened as red tabs marking von Rundstedt's Armies moved across their war maps, G-3 fretted again over the security of those bridges across the Meuse between Namur and Dinant. While not denying that von Rundstedt might yet extend his Bulge to that river, I disputed his ability to cross it even with light reconnaissance forces. The enemy had previously destroyed those bridges during his rout to the Siegfried Line. None had been repaired in that unimportant crook of the river and our pontoon substitutes could be demolished with the stroke of a detonator box. I suggested to Allen that we radio SHAEF to keep its shirt on.

Assured by Patton that he would soon break through to relieve Bastogne, I was eager to have Montgomery hit the enemy from the north. I therefore begged Ike to prod Montgomery in an effort to speed up that counterattack. But Montgomery would not be hurried. Rather than pinch off the enemy at the middle as Patton and I were eager to do, Monty preferred to halt him by denting the nose of his advance. Elsewhere across the flank, Monty was still preoccupied in the task of "tidying" up his front. The 82d Division had been ordered back from its salient on the river line behind St. Vith following the 7th Armored's withdrawal from that position. But when Montgomery proposed a further withdrawal that would have widened the Bulge at that point, both Collins and Ridgway objected so heatedly that Montgomery promptly backed down. In a letter to Hodges I wrote that although he "was no longer in my command, I would view with serious misgivings the surrender of any more ground" on his side of the Bulge.

On Christmas Eve Montgomery suggested I fly up to 21 TAC the next day and there coordinate our respective Group plans for reducing the Bulge. Patton's tanks had now forced an alley to within two and one-half miles of Bastogne. North of that city a 25-mile corridor separated it from the First Army. We could now interdict with artillery the three second-class roads that carried the enemy's lifeline through that narrowing gap.

Fearful that a detachment of Skorzeny's assassins might have penetrated the city of Luxembourg, Sibert had tucked me under an elaborate security wrap. As part of his security precautions, Sibert evacuated my C-47 from the Luxembourg airport where it had been parked, to a night-fighter base, 40 minutes by car to the rear at Etain. To save time on the flight to Montgomery's CP, I instructed Robinson to fly the plane from Etain and pick me up at Luxembourg, only two minutes' flying time from the German line. His crew was to join him there. But, when Sibert got wind of these plans, he protested so strenuously that I abandoned the idea and hurried after the pilot down the road to Etain. Rather than wait for the crew then marooned on the Luxembourg airfield, we took off from Etain in the *Mary Q* on a tree-level course across the corner of the Ardennes. While Robinson piloted, Hansen and I conned the course from a map. An hour later we landed at St. Trond in Belgium, where Hodges' aide, Major William C. Sylvan of Columbia, South Carolina, was waiting with a car. En route to the modest Dutch house in which Montgomery had established his CP, I munched on an apple for lunch.

In the villages through which we sped, the sidewalks were filled with Hollanders in holiday dress.

"What's happening today?" I asked.

"It's Christmas, General—" Hansen replied.

Although I had hoped Montgomery would soon join our counterattack with one from the north, I found him waiting expectantly for one last enemy blow on that flank. Not until he was certain the enemy had exhausted himself, would Montgomery plunge in for the kill. Disappointed at the prospect of further delay, I headed back to St. Trond.

As Robinson revved his engine, the control tower called. "You can't make it before dark—" the dispatcher warned, "you'd better not take off." Pretending that he had misunderstood, Robinson called back into the mike, "Downwind? Thank you, I'll take off downwind." We shot down the runway and climbed into the dusk at full throttle. In the failing light we hedgehopped over the slag piles of Belgium's coal fields, straining to pick up the dim checkpoints. It was dark when we skimmed into Etain. The field lighted its oil torches and we touched down to a feathery landing. That evening Sergeant Dudley sent a plate of turkey up to my room.

It was on December 26 that the Bulge reached its high water mark, 17 miles from where the picturesque city of Dinant guards the rocky gorge of the Meuse. There Ernie Harmon threw his 2d Armored Division across the path of von Rundstedt's 2d Panzer

Division to bring the last enemy thrust to a standstill. For three days those divisions hammered each other without respite. In this head-on clash, Harmon left 81 enemy panzers smoking in the hills. And he halted von Rundstedt's advance.

In reporting to me on the battle several days later, Harmon wrote with characteristic brevity: "We got in front of the 2d Panzer Division on December 23, 24, and 25 and polished them off. Attached is a list of the spoils we took—including 1,200 prisoners. Killed and wounded some 2,500. A great slaughter."

The "spoils" he had listed included 405 of the enemy's fast-dwindling trucks and 81 artillery pieces. After that single historic meeting with its opposite number in the American army, the 2d Panzer limped back with 1,500 frostbitten grenadiers and a handful of surviving Panthers—all that was left of the division that had sallied toward the Meuse.

At 4 o'clock that afternoon Patton called to report that his 4th Armored Division had broken through to relieve Bastogne and end the seven-day siege of that city. At a cost of 482 killed, 2,449 wounded, Tony McAuliffe had withstood the attacks of three German divisions while memorializing the epoch with his single-word rejection of the enemy's demand for surrender.

I telephoned Eisenhower that evening to urge that he now goad Montgomery into an attack against the Bulge on its north flank. However, Eisenhower had headed for 21st Group and I spoke to Bedell Smith instead.

"Dammit, Bedell, can't you people get Monty going on the north? As near as we can tell this other fellow's reached his high water mark today. He'll soon be starting to pull back—if not tonight, certainly by tomorrow."

But Bedell disputed this optimistic appraisal, for SHAEF had been surfeited with the apprehensive estimates of 21st Group. "Oh no, Brad, you're mistaken," he said. "Why they'll be across the Meuse in 48 hours."

"Nuts," I answered, plagiarizing McAuliffe for the lack of any other retort. It was apparent that SHAEF totally lacked our feel of the situation. For by then the enemy's plight was clear. We had all but destroyed his leading division and were holding firmly everywhere on the flanks. Patton's broad advance from the south had joined up at Bastogne and the enemy's three remaining east-west roads were under artillery interdiction.

For two days the enemy held without renewing his advance. On the third day he began to fall back. The following day I drove to Versailles with a plan for resuming the offensive once we had flattened the Bulge. Ike jubilantly declared he would reward me with the rarest treasure in all France. A waiter came in with two steaming bowls. In a pool of rich cream there floated a half-dozen oysters from Chesapeake Bay. I ate them without confessing his treasure gave me the hives.

The New Year began more brightly than the old one had ended when Montgomery reported that he would attack into the north side of the Bulge on January 3. When on New Year's Eve, Bill Walton, a parachutist correspondent for *Time,* toasted the old year out with the doleful farewell, "Never was the world plagued by such a year less worth remembering," I could have added, "—especially the last 15 days." Another 53 days were to pass before we jumped across the Roer to resume the winter offensive that had been halted by German attack. But if our afflictions were heavy, we could take comfort in the knowledge that the enemy's outweighed our own. So severe were his losses that none of those divisions committed in the Bulge was ever effective again.

No sooner had the time of danger ended than the period of recrimination began. During the bitter, strained weeks that followed, the Allied amity that Eisenhower had sought to preserve suffered a severe setback. This setback came as an aftermath to the temporary change in command. For once the enemy had been turned back, Montgomery was depicted as St. George come to save the American command from disaster. As if this were not already irritating enough, the British press suddenly erupted in a rash of comment that attributed the Bulge to our lack of unified ground command. Once again the British revived the proposal that Montgomery be named as deputy to Eisenhower for supercommand of all ground forces.

When Montgomery was pictured in the newspapers as having singlehandedly rescued our shattered American Armies, I protested the distortion to Ike. I feared now as I did when Bedell Smith first phoned to sound me out on the plan that unless this distortion were corrected by SHAEF, my usefulness would be impaired by a loss of confidence among my subordinate commanders. But what alarmed me even more was the fear that this exaggerated story would undermine confidence at home in the field capabilities of the U. S. command.

In an attempt to heal this Anglo-American rift before it widened, SHAEF issued a terse but we thought unnecessarily bland statement of explanation on January 5:

> When the German penetration through the Ardennes created two fronts, one substantially facing south and the other north, by instant agreement of all concerned that portion of the front facing south was placed under command of Montgomery and that facing north under command of Bradley.

SHAEF's statement, however, was too cursory to ease the situation that now threatened to split the harmony of our Allied commands. Two days later Montgomery poured gasoline on the fire in a news conference at 21st Army Group.

"Von Rundstedt attacked on December 16," Montgomery said in describing the Battle of the Bulge. "He obtained tactical surprise. He drove a deep wedge into the centre of First US Army and split the American forces in two. The situation looked as if it might become awkward; the Germans had broken right through a weak spot and were heading for the Meuse.

"As soon as I saw what was happening I took certain steps myself to ensure that *if* the Germans got to the Meuse they would certainly not get over that river. And I carried out certain movements so as to provide balanced dispositions to meet the threatened danger; these were, at the time, merely precautions i.e. I was thinking ahead.

"Then the situation began to deteriorate. But the whole allied team rallied to meet the danger; national considerations were thrown overboard; General Eisenhower placed me in command of the whole Northern front.

"I employed the whole available power of the British Group of Armies; this power was brought into play very gradually and in such a way that it would not interfere with the American lines of communication. Finally it was put into battle with a bang and today British divisions are fighting hard on the right flank of First US Army.

"You thus have the picture of British troops fighting on both sides of American forces who have suffered a hard blow. This is a fine allied picture.

"The battle has been most interesting; I think possibly one of the most interesting and tricky battles I have ever handled, with great issues at stake. . . . The battle has some similarity to the battle that began on 31 August 1942 when Rommel made his last bid to capture Egypt and was 'seen off' by the Eighth Army.

"But then—" he added lamely, "all battles are different because the problem is different."

When Montgomery's statement reached us via the BBC, the acutely sensitive EAGLE TAC staff exploded with indignation. Hansen burst into my office followed by Lieutenant Colonel Ralph M. Ingersoll, editor of New York's now defunct *PM*, and Major Henry E. Munson, Lev Allen's young aide.

"You've got to get something on the record," Hansen said, "that tells the whole story of this change-over in command. Until you do the American people will have nothing to go by except Montgomery's statement which certainly leaves a questionable inference on the capabilities of the U. S. command. SHAEF didn't indicate in its statement when the change-over took place and as a result most newspapers have assumed it was made on December 17. They do not realize that you had the situation pretty well in hand when the change came three days later."

He handed me an editorial from the *Washington Post* of December 28, an editorial asking for an explanation on the Ardennes reversal:

The American people need an authoritative interpretation of what the Rundstedt offensive is all about, how it happened, what its potentialities are. But no authoritative interpretation has been advanced by the War Department. The result has been a babel of voices each with a sovereign explanation of what is going on and with the end result of increasing confusion.

I had no wish to engage Montgomery in a public dispute for fear it might alert the enemy to a tiff in the Allied command. And yet I was no less irritated than my staff over Montgomery's misleading statement. I wanted to have the record cleared. If SHAEF would not do it—then perhaps I should.

"Well, I can do one of two things," I said. "I can take a statement to Ike and ask him to approve it. He may or he may not. If Ike lets me go ahead and we get into trouble over it then he hangs with me. On the other hand, we need not put Ike on the spot. I can release a statement here without clearing it at SHAEF and take the consequences myself—if there are any."

"But you have a precedent," Ingersoll insisted, "after all, Montgomery spoke to the press yesterday."

"Yes, but—"

"Do you suppose Montgomery cleared his interview with Eisenhower?"

"You know darned well he didn't," I said. The decision was difficult primarily because I could not be sure how much my personal feelings affected my judgment as a commander. I stared out through the lace-curtained windows of my office toward the spires of the Luxembourg cathedral. A truck convoy rolled across the bridge.

"Okay," I said, "I'll do it."

The following day we published a statement, my first such document of the war, aiming to repair the mischief Montgomery had caused by his comments two days before. After reviewing the commitments that had induced us to accept a "calculated risk" in the Ardennes, I traced the moves by which we had arrested the breakthrough during those first four critical days—before Montgomery entered the picture.

And in explaining the change in command, I repeated SHAEF's reasoning as Bedell Smith had given it to me.

"The German attack . . ." I said, "cut both our *direct* telephone communication to First Army and the *direct* roads over which personal contact was normally maintained. The weather prevented the making of frequent personal contacts with First Army by plane. It was therefore decided that the 21st Army Group should assume *temporary* command of all Allied forces north of the salient. This was a *temporary* measure only and when the lines are rejoined, 12th Army Group will resume command of all American troops in this area."

This was the first time the change had been publicly described as a *temporary* one. In its all too brief statement of January 5, SHAEF had evaded the issue, calmly ignoring the commonly held belief that British command would now supersede that of 12th Army Group. In view of the clamor Montgomery had incited, I did not want SHAEF to forget its promise that the change-over was to be nothing more than a temporary one.

Not until now had the public been told specifically when the change-over took place, and as a result the British had been too generously credited with reorganization of the U. S. front. During the four days between December 16 and 20 when Montgomery took command on the north, we had already drained von Rundstedt's offensive of the momentum on which it banked for a speedy break-through. For once von Rundstedt lost his momentum, he could never overcome the advantage that quickly accrued to us in the mobility of our forces.

That premise was confirmed soon after the war when Sepp Dietrich under Allied interrogation acknowledged that his offensive in the Ardennes had already slumped fatally behind schedule by December 19. Thus was the offensive doomed to failure—only three days after its start, 24 hours before Montgomery came to our "rescue."

Had SHAEF in its announcement of the change in command pro-tected us with the statement that it was to be but a *temporary* one, Eisenhower might have averted this breakdown of amity in his com-mand. Long afterward Eisenhower stated that this Bulge alter-cation was the most exasperating he experienced during the war. Yet had he only corrected Montgomery's exaggerated report on British intervention, he might easily have nipped the dispute long before it got out of hand.

Although at the time I could not forgive Monty for having ex-ploited our distress in the Ardennes, I am quite certain he never knew just how exasperated we had become, for our personal associa-tion continued cordially throughout the war with never a mention of the fracas.

While we labored to retrieve the integrity of U. S. command, the proposal that Monty be named top ground commander snowballed with the assistance of a part of the British press. And even though General Marshall had once reassured me that we would never be sandwiched under British command, I felt it necessary to state my position uncompromisingly to Ike. When I raised the issue, Eisen-hower fended it off impatiently with a reassuring reply.

"Nevertheless you must know," I said, "after what has happened I cannot serve under Montgomery. If he is to be put in command of all ground forces, you must send me home, for if Montgomery goes in over me, I will have lost the confidence of my command."

Ike flushed. He stiffened in his chair and eyed me hotly. "Well—" he said, "I thought you were the one person I could count on for doing anything I asked you to."

"You can, Ike," I said. "I've enjoyed every bit of my service with you. But this is one thing I cannot take."

Several days previously I had indicated to Patton that I would feel obliged to ask for relief rather than submit 12th Army Group to Montgomery's command.

George clasped me by the arm. "If you quit, Brad," he said, "then I'll be quitting with you."

By this time I could not have temperamentally subordinated myself to Montgomery's command. Not only were we as fully competent as the British but by now the U. S. had committed 50 divisions in the ETO in contrast to the 15 of Britain. So overwhelming a superiority, I argued, strongly supported our insistence that U. S. troops be fought under a U. S. field command.

On this question of a super ground commander, Eisenhower stood firm and the British press relented. Eventually it remained for Churchill to pour oil on the troubled waters. In a speech before the House of Commons on January 18 he said:

I have seen it suggested that the terrific battle which has been proceeding since December 16 on the American front is an Anglo-American battle. In fact, however, the United States troops have done almost all the fighting and have suffered almost all the losses. They have suffered losses almost equal to those of both sides at the Battle of Gettysburg. . . . The Americans have engaged thirty or forty men for every one we have engaged and have lost sixty to eighty men to every one of ours. That is a point I wish to make.

Care must be taken in telling our proud tale not to claim for the British armies undue share of what is undoubtedly the greatest American battle of the war and will, I believe, be regarded as an ever-famous American victory. I have never hesitated to stand up for our own soldiers when their achievements have been cold-shouldered or neglected or overshadowed, as they sometimes are, but we must not forget that it is to American homes that telegrams of personal loss and anxiety have been coming during the past month and that there has been a hard and severe ordeal during these weeks for our brave and cherished ally. . . .

Our armies are under the supreme command of General Eisenhower and we march with discipline wherever we are told to go. According to professional advice which I have at my disposal, what was done to meet von Rundstedt's counterstroke was resolute, wise, and militarily correct. The gap was torn open as a gap can always be torn open in a line hundreds of miles long. General Eisenhower at once gave command to the north of the gap to Field Marshal Montgomery and to the south of it to

General Omar Bradley. Many other consequential movements were made and rightly made.

Judging by the result, both these highly skilled commanders handled very large forces at their disposal in a manner which I think I can say without exaggeration may become a model for military students in the future.

Field Marshal Montgomery, at the earliest moment, acting with extraordinary promptitude, concentrated powerful British reserves at decisive strategic points; and, having been placed in command as he was by General Eisenhower of American forces larger than those he holds from the British Government or from the Canadian, larger than those he holds in the 21st Army Group, he fell unceasingly upon the enemy in the north and fought the battle all the time from that part of the assailed front. The United States First Army, which was one of a group of Armies under General Bradley, was severed by inroads.

It was reinforced with extraordinary military efficiency from the Metz area by General Patton's Army, who hurled themselves on those intruders from outside of Bastogne. All movement of commanders would have been futile but for the bravery of the troops. General Omar Bradley was commanding the American forces and so was Field Marshal Montgomery. All these troops fought in magnificent fashion and General Eisenhower, balancing the situation between his two commanders, gave them both the fairest opportunity to realize their full strength and qualities.

Let no one lend themselves to the shouting of mischief makers when issues of this momentous consequence are being successfully decided by sword.

22: *Breaching the Rhine*

Having failed to reach the Meuse before we stopped him, the enemy could either write off his winter offensive as a failure or prolong the salient in an effort to make it pay off in delay.

In his New Year's message to troops Model pointedly ignored the battle cry with which he had rallied them "on to Antwerp" only two weeks before. "We have succeeded," he wrote while searching for some evidence of success, "in disrupting the enemy's planned offensive against our homeland." But it was too limp an alibi to conceal the costliness of that misadventure in the Ardennes. The enemy had spent the offensive strength of 24 divisions for a "disruption" that could last no more than several weeks at best.

Prompt withdrawal from the Bulge might yet have spared the enemy sufficient reserves for defense of the Rhine River. But rather than yield his gains in the Bulge and take up a position in the Siegfried Line, the enemy chose instead to gamble on his ability to delay us. Except for our 40-mile-wide penetration in the vicinity of Aachen, his Siegfried Line still held intact across the remainder of the Western front. Common sense dictated that he screen us there with the barest minimum of troops while amassing reserves for a later defense of the Rhine River line. But good military judgment was destined to be sidetracked by the fanatical demand of Hitler that each sacred foot of the Reich be defended no matter how vainglorious such tactics might be.

As a consequence, the enemy turned his back on the Rhine, the finest defensive barrier in all western Europe, for a reckless fight to the finish west of that river line. His bid for a few more weeks of delay in the Bulge was to end in the collapse of his Western front. As the German dug into position in an effort to hold on to his Bulge, the terrain, the snow, and the rutted roads that had helped us dent his offensive were now reversed in his favor. But the advantages that the weather and the terrain had given the enemy were more than made up by the advantages that came to us in regaining the initiative. Those two weeks in the Ardennes were my only experience in defensive warfare and I was glad when we finally regained the offensive.

Altogether von Rundstedt had held the initiative for only 11 days, a brief enough spree for so costly an effort. Now that the dream of Antwerp had faded and the hope of an Allied setback was gone, German morale slumped and the enemy fell back dejectedly into his familiar rut of retreat. This time there could be no turning back.

To support his offensive on the limited roadnet available to him in the Ardennes, the enemy had restricted his transport to ammunition and gasoline. Troops had been ordered to forage for food until they reached the dumps of Antwerp where a fabulous concentration of Allied supply awaited their looting. The sparsely populated Ardennes, however, offered scant pickings for foragers and fewer than 40,000 rations were captured in forward U. S. dumps. First St. Vith, then Bastogne, now cold and hunger: it was bitter diet for troops that were to have been rewarded with triumph and rich American stores. An angry PW from the Sixth Panzer SS Army snarled during interrogation at the mention of his Army commander. "Sepp Dietrich," he retorted, "is not even fit to be a good butcher." Dietrich had been an apprentice butcher before joining the German army in 1914. He ingratiated himself to Hitler in 1923 and joined the National Socialist Party five years later. By 1932 he had become a brigadier general in the Waffen SS and commanding officer of Hitler's bodyguard.

In contrast to the enemy's sagging morale, ours was vigorously high despite the beating we had taken at his hands. When the 5th Ranger Battalion called for 50 volunteers among rear-echelon personnel of First Army, it was almost trampled in the rush of a thousand applicants.

On January 16, a little less than a month from the day Houffalize fell to von Rundstedt's columns, Hodges and Patton joined their Armies in the rubble of that tiny town. I had remembered it as a sleepy village on the side of a hill, ten miles north of Bastogne on the macadam road to Liége. In the gully below, a sawmill hummed through the tall, straight timber of the Ardennes. A single inter-section broke through the parallel row of stone cottages that hugged the Liége road. To plug that intersection and deny the enemy its east-west road, heavy bombers had demolished the town. Bulldozers forcing their way north to make juncture with First Army swept the charred rubble of Houffalize into the gaping bomb craters left there by Allied air. Simple, poor, and unpretentious, the village had offended no one. Yet it was destroyed simply because it sat astride an undistinguished road junction. This road junction had made it a more strategic objective than cities 50 times its size.

On the following evening, January 17, First Army reverted to 12th Army Group command. The Ninth, however, remained under Monty, for Eisenhower had promised the field marshal he could have it for the resumption of the Rhineland offensive. I begged Eisenhower to return the Ninth to me if only for 24 hours, that we might complete the cycle and reclaim our command now that the Bulge had been flattened. But Ike replied that he was already ex-hausted in his struggle to block the British on a super ground com-mand for Monty. He would not deliberately harpoon the British now simply to assuage U. S. pride. Ninth Army was to remain with 21st Group until after we crossed the Rhine.

When Simpson learned of Ike's decision, he telephoned me from Maastricht. "Hey, Brad—" he laughed, "what can you do to save us? If this goes on much longer, they'll begin thinking that we were given to them along with a shipment of lend-lease."

"There's nothing we can do," I replied, "Ike's already committed himself. You'd better polish up your British accent. You may be needing it for some time."

As a strategic stroke, the enemy's counteroffensive had been turned into a total failure. Not only had he failed to reach his ul-timate objectives beyond the Meuse, but he had paid an exhorbitant price for the delay he caused in our winter offensive. G-2 estimated enemy casualties in excess of 250,000 for the month-long battle, of whom more than 36,000 had been taken as PWs. More than 600 of his fast-dwindling supply of tanks and assault guns lay rusting in the Bulge.

Remagen Bridge: "With the capture of Remagen bridge, we had opened a gateway for the lower Rhine crossing that was to result in speedy encirclement of the Ruhr and capture of Model's Army Group of 335,000 German troops—a bigger prize than the Russians took at Stalingrad." (March, 1945.)

Highways to the Elbe: "While the defeated enemy trudged rearward under an MP guard, armored divisions raced up the autobahns toward the heart of Germany and our stop-line on the Elbe." (April, 1945.)

Even the Luftwaffe shared von Rundstedt's disaster when it sallied out in one last attempt at ground support. On January 1, Goering mounted the mightiest single enemy air strike of the European campaign. German fighters surprised and destroyed more than 125 Allied aircraft on their Belgian bases. But the Allied fighters that swarmed aloft that day claimed 200 enemy "kills" before the day ended.

As the enemy extricated the mangled remnants of his last reserves of the Western front from the Ardennes, the Red army renewed its winter offensive. The offensive had begun with a tremendous artillery preparation in the center of the line on January 12. Five days later on January 17, the Red army entered Warsaw, now thoroughly destroyed by the Germans in vicious retribution for General Bor's uprising on August 1. More than 250,000 Poles fell to the Germans in Warsaw during the 63-day uprising while the Red army waited impassively in the suburban city of Praga only a few miles east. On January 22 the Red army crossed the Silesian border and on the following day reached the Oder. Hitler now hurriedly disengaged what had been left of Dietrich's Sixth SS Panzer Army to speed it by rail to the threatened German front in Hungary. But while G-2 Battle Order could list Sepp Dietrich's Army as a panzer force of five divisions, the Sixth SS was no more than a skeleton of the one he had committed against us. Those bottom-of-the-barrel reserves that might have slowed the Russian onslaught had been squandered instead against us in the Ardennes. Not only was Hitler's misadventure to speed his defeat on the Western front; it was to hasten his collapse on the Eastern front as well.

Even more significant than its strategic effect upon the new Russian offensive was the impact of this stunning defeat upon the German people. First, the "secret" weapons in which they had so long trusted had failed to alter the course of the war—and now even the blitz had failed them. Although belief in victory had long since eluded all but the most fanatic Nazis, there were Germans who, until the Bulge, believed that if Germany could stalemate the Western front, she might induce the Allies to negotiate a separate peace. Then they hoped, the Wehrmacht might turn its last reserves against the Soviet. But however faintly this hope once glimmered, now even it was gone. Recognizing that their days were numbered, the Germans strove desperately to adjust themselves to the tragedy that had overwhelmed them. Whereas in Aachen and Düren our troops had

moved into empty ghost cities, they were now to advance all the way
to the Elbe under an arch of white flags of surrender. Unlike Hitler,
the Germans had become a desperately reasonable people and
reason dictated they fly their bedsheets in token of their willingness
to give up.

When at the end of January the enemy gave up his last hold on
the Bulge to fall back behind the Siegfried Line, another nine
divisions were shunted off to the Russian front. But even this withdrawal left von Rundstedt 80 numbered divisions against our 71.
Many of his were decimated units, poorly trained, and understrength, but those deficiencies were heavily offset by his Siegfried
Line defenses. Except in that 40-mile gap where we had penetrated the Siegfried Line to the Roer, this cordon remained intact
from Arnhem to the Swiss border. Two months later while lunching
with Churchill at Eisenhower's headquarters in the home of a Reims
champagne king, both Ike and I were to defend the value of this
fixed line of defense. For unlike the French in the Maginot Line,
the German had extracted fair value from his investment in concrete.

Few Americans were aware at this time of the vast array of German land strength still facing us on the Western front. Despite the
enemy's defiance in the Bulge, the September illusion persisted: we
were thought to have whipped what remained of the German army.
When I was asked in January by a visiting delegation from the War
Production Board if the Ardennes offensive would not lengthen the
war, I replied that it would not—except in the minds of some people.

"It may startle those who thought we had the German licked in
September," I explained. "If nothing else the Bulge will show them
he still packs a mighty strong kick."

U. S. casualties for the month-long battle totaled approximately
one fourth of those we had attributed to the German. Of the
59,000 we lost in battle, 6,700 were listed as dead, another 33,400
wounded. The remaining 18,900 were counted as missing though
most were presumed to have been captured when cut off on the
German breakthrough. The majority of them had been trapped with
units of the 106th and 28th Divisions and most were liberated when
their stalags were overrun at the end of the war.

When the War Department announced that battle casualties for
that month in the Ardennes surpassed those of any previous 30 days
in the war, it neglected to add that more divisions were engaged

than ever before. During the month preceding the Breakout, casualties totaled 46,800 with a maximum of 17 divisions engaged in combat. By January 17 we had thrown 27 U. S. divisions against the Bulge. This was almost four times the number of U. S. divisions then committed in Italy; more than the total that had been committed in the whole Pacific war.

But if our casualties were severe, the enemy's were even more critical. Moreover the proportion was better than we could have expected had he struck us on the plains of Cologne, better than if he had withheld his reserves until we reached the Rhine. In stalking us through the Ardennes, the enemy had been forced to expose himself to our fire, especially to the murderous air burst of our proximity fuse. To the 4th Division still nursing its wounds from the Huertgen Forest, this reversal in roles brought a sardonic satisfaction.

"Up there it was our troops who combed the tree bursts out of their hair while the Kraut lay snug in his hole," explained Colonel Charles T. Lanham, the scrappy but scholarly soldier-poet who commanded the 22d Infantry Regiment. "During the Bulge we simply sat on our cans and plugged the Kraut as he came at us. I don't know what happened elsewhere, but in our sector he fought clean. And he certainly showed us that he had guts."

By the end of January we had eliminated the Bulge and were up against the Siegfried Line. First Army was concentrated on a narrow front between Huertgen Forest and St. Vith while Ninth Army had sideslipped to include Hodges' front on the Roer. Patton had drawn the main force of his Third Army up against the enemy's fortifications where they followed the Luxembourg border to the Moselle. A third corps extended Patton's front 32 miles south of the Moselle to the vicinity of Saarlautern where it joined Devers' Group. Of the 47 U. S. divisions then committed on the Western front, 21 had been packed into that narrow sector between the Huertgen and the Moselle.

I wanted to break straight on through without a change in pace, force the Siegfried Line, plunge through the Eifel behind it, and break a path to Bonn on the Rhine. Despite the rough terrain of this route, it offered two significant advantages:

1. By pushing straight through to Bonn, we could avert the loss in time it would take to reorganize an Allied offensive elsewhere.

2. This route through the Eifel would carry us south of the Roer dams and thus enable us to reach the Rhine without becoming entangled in another dam campaign. We already carried the wounds of two previous assaults against those dam sites; I had no wish to add the wounds of a third.

Montgomery, however, put a crimp in our plans. Early in Novem-

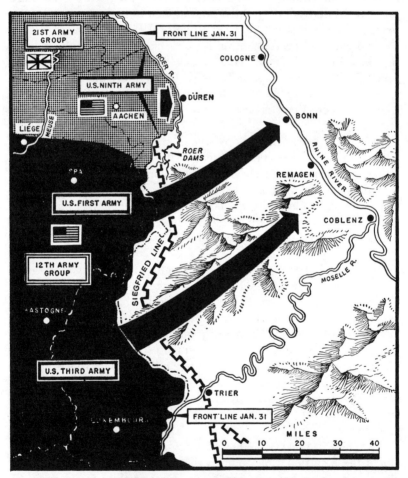

After flattening the Bulge, 12th Army Group proposed to push straight on through the Eifel to the Rhine with its First and Third Armies. The plan was shelved, however, at the insistence of Montgomery who wanted to force the Roer to the Rhine north of Cologne.

ber, Eisenhower had promised at the start of our winter offensive toward the Rhine that if First and Ninth Armies did not break free by the turn of the year, he would pluck Ninth Army out of the 12th Army Group and give it to Monty for his north-of-the-Ruhr offensive. Monty now held Eisenhower to his pledge and in anticipation of this British offensive objected to my proposed "diversion" of First Army through the Eifel. He insisted that Hodges be shifted back to our pre-Bulge sector on the Roer where he would attack to secure those river dams in preparation for Simpson's crossing. After capturing those dam sites, First Army was then to storm the Roer and shield Simpson's right flank during Ninth Army's advance to the Rhine.

Eisenhower had little choice but to accede to Monty's demand. Not only had we failed to meet the January 1 deadline, but our advance toward the Eifel had been slowed by six-foot snow drifts. Furthermore the Siegfried Line showed no signs of yielding to our initial blows. But in the Aachen sector high up on the Roer, that line had already been broken. Consequently on February 4, SHAEF ordered 12th Army Group to cease its Eifel attack and sideslip First Army north to its December position on the Roer.

While I did not relish the dam mission, I could not dispute Ike's choice. By shunting First Army north, we would link our U. S. strength to that of the British in a concerted push to the Rhine just below the Ruhr.

Deprived of his Silesian industry by the Red army advance, the German had become more dependent than ever upon the Ruhr. There the enemy had overcome much of the damage of Allied air raids and by a miracle of improvisation had exceeded his previous peak production in planes and tanks. If Monty could force his way to the Rhine, he would not only deny that arterial waterway to the German, but he could easily unlimber his guns against those industrial plants that crowded a ten-mile belt on the far side of the river.

Since First Army was to attack as an outrider on Monty's offensive, Eisenhower suggested that I shift EAGLE TAC north from Luxembourg to Namur, a citadel city on the bend of the Meuse, 60 miles from the German frontier. In Luxembourg I had been located within ten minutes' driving time of Patton's CP; two hours by road to Hodges. Although Namur was but an hour and a half from First Army, it was three hours by road from Third Army in Luxembourg.

Not much of an advantage, I protested, but Ike was insistent upon the move, for he was anxious that we be nearer Monty's CP in Holland.

During the two months we occupied the handsome Château de Namur overlooking the cliffs of the Meuse, I saw Monty but three times. While we were—as we had always been except while speeding across France—in frequent touch with each other by phone, there was little need for the travel personal visits entailed.

Not until late January when a delivery of U. S. newspapers reached us in Luxembourg did we learn how hysterical the press coverage from SHAEF had been during the Ardennes offensive. Since September, Hansen had been pleading with me for the establishment of a press camp at EAGLE TAC, but I had always put off his proposal. There was little need, I protested, for a situation briefing midway between the eyewitness reporting of correspondents accredited to the Armies and the Theater roundup at SHAEF.

On the other hand in the British sector, Montgomery had consolidated his press at 21st Group rather than disperse it as we had to the Armies. As a result, the efforts of his British and Canadian Armies were welded into a comprehensive frame in the briefing at 21st Group. By contrast, U. S. press coverage had suffered from the failure of newsmen accredited to the Armies to grasp the interrelationship of their respective Army campaigns. In this they received little help from the Armies, for each of the staffs there was intensely chauvinistic and jealous of the others. SHAEF briefings in Paris, I am told, were sketchy and as a result our consolidated Army Group effort during the November and December offensives more often than not emerged in the newspapers as two unrelated campaigns.

To prevent a recurrence of the distorted coverage that had exaggerated our peril during the Ardennes, I reversed my view on an Army Group press camp and notified SHAEF of our intent to open one at TAC in Namur. Eisenhower arrived several days later, mildly suspicious of our intentions. He raised the question late that evening after a desultory game of bridge. I reasoned that Captain Harry C. Butcher, USNR, had probably planted the fear in the mind of his chief, for I am sure Ike would never otherwise have questioned our intentions. As Eisenhower's PRO, Butcher apparently feared that we might utilize the press in a scrap with Monty, or worse yet undercut SHAEF coverage by the press. I assured Ike that we were anxious only to help the newsmen better report the war with a summary briefing each day at TAC. He was satisfied with my explanation and instantly approved the request.

"As a matter of fact," Ike explained, "I wasn't the least bit scared about the Ardennes offensive until I read the U. S. papers."

Montgomery's Rhineland offensive was to be executed in two successive phases. First, Monty's Canadian Army was to push south from Nijmegen down a flat wedge between the Maas and Rhine. Thus it would advance down behind the Siegfried Line where those fortifications fronted the Maas and there cut off the enemy facing the British Second Army. As the Canadian attack gained headway, Simpson was to strike across the Roer and head northeast toward the Rhine where it flowed past the Ruhr. There he would besiege the Ruhr with artillery until Montgomery gathered his forces for a major assault crossing of that river.

While Simpson aimed his blow toward Düsseldorf, we were to protect his right flank with Hodges' First Army. Hodges was to advance first from the Roer River to the high ground between the Erft and the Rhine and there cover Simpson until Ninth Army closed to the bank of the Rhine opposite Düsseldorf. Not until Ninth Army was safely anchored there was First Army to resume its attack south in the direction of Cologne. After taking that cathedral city, it was to move on south along the Rhine and cut off the enemy west of that river. Because the flow of replacements could not yet support a simultaneous offensive by all of my three U. S. Armies, Patton had been ordered to hold in position the length of his front.

On February 7 the First Canadian Army jumped off at Nijmegen in the Allied attack that within 35 days was to destroy the German army west of the Rhine. As Simpson's Army waited in readiness on the Roer, Hodges ordered Gerow to go after the dam sites and gain control of that river. By February 10, V Corps had captured the Roer dams and driven the enemy into the dark forests that stretched beyond them.

But before quitting those dams, the enemy dynamited their floodgates. As the torrent of waters sluiced down the Roer Valley, the river washed three feet above its muddy banks. An unseasonable winter thaw melted the thick snows of the Eifel and soon a score of

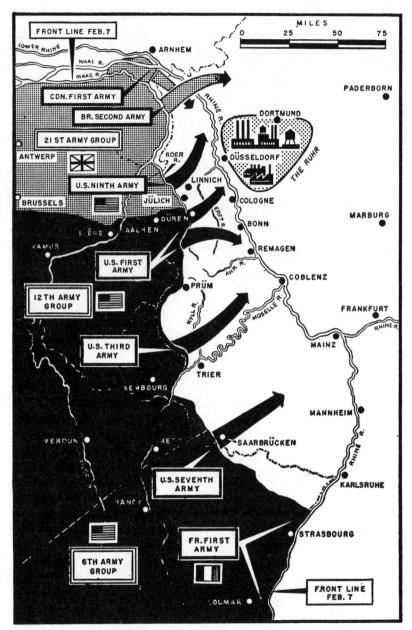

In the Allied plan for the February offensive, Ninth Army was to force the Roer and join the Canadian Army on the Rhine. First Army was to protect Simpson's right flank and close to the Rhine near Cologne.

rushing streams fed the river flood. Division commanders of the First and Ninth Armies, drawn up on the river bank, looked across the muddy torrent and prayed that Group would delay the offensive rather than dare it at flood stage. Not wanting to risk a catastrophe on the river crossing, both Armies settled down to wait for the flood to subside.

By now our intent was apparent and I was fearful the enemy might reinforce this front with troops from the Eifel where Patton had been instructed to hold defensively on his line. There George had been probing the Siegfried Line with small feeler attacks, not in preparation for a major offensive but primarily because he found it impossible to sit still. For Third Army viewed defensive warfare as something to be shunned at all costs. Now with Eisenhower's consent, I ordered Patton to mount an offensive in the Eifel. It was to be strong enough to keep the enemy from shifting his strength to the Roer but not so strong as to arouse the objections of Monty. Replacements for this limited offensive could be spared initially while the First and Ninth Armies fidgeted on the Roer.

Patton was to pierce the enemy's Siegfried fortifications north of the Moselle and advance quietly to the Kyll, a mountain stream that paralleled the Luxembourg border, 12 miles beyond the German frontier. There he was to seize a bridgehead in anticipation of a full-scale advance to the Rhine. But this later phase was not to begin until Monty was safely anchored on the Rhine opposite the Ruhr.

Rather than directly disobey SHAEF's written orders consigning him to the defensive, Patton termed his Third Army operations in the Eifel an "aggressive defense." His staff innocently believed that they were hoodwinking Ike's staff at Versailles. Moreover, it was rumored that I had joined Patton in this conspiratorial offensive. My insubordination however was purely make-believe, for without the knowledge of Patton's staff and mine, Eisenhower had agreed to it.

Against Montgomery's objections, Eisenhower had sided with me on the necessity for closing to the Rhine the full length of our Allied front before attempting to cross that river in strength. Although Ike had not yet rejected our U. S. plan for double envelopment of the Ruhr with a Rhine River crossing near Frankfurt, it was generally assumed in SHAEF that Monty held the inside track on his single-pronged offensive. But even if Monty were to have his way on a single thrust east of the Rhine, my views on closing all the way to the river were valid. For if we were to concentrate our forces on the north and hold lightly to the Swiss border, it was essential that we defend a line where we could not be hurt by enemy spoiling attack. For this purpose, I argued, there was no better barrier than the Rhine. Ike concurred for he was no less anxious than I to rid the west bank of the Rhine of Germans before venturing across it.

No less alluring was the opportunity that beckoned us in the Rhineland for destruction of the enemy there. By February, 85 German divisions had been committed west of the river. If they could be isolated and destroyed, the enemy would be powerless to man the far bank in strength. Our primary objective, after all, lay not in Berlin nor in any other terrain feature; rather we were primarily intent on destruction of the German army. For once the Wehrmacht had been splintered, those other objectives would fall easily into our hands.

While waiting for the Roer to settle, I paced impatiently through the corridors of the baroque palace that housed our CP in Namur. There the provincial governor's ornate drawing room had been converted into an office for me. A huge 20-foot mapboard was mounted on the frescoed wall between two clusters of smirking cherubs. A crystal chandelier hung over my desk and a magnificent oriental carpet padded my footsteps as I paced before the map. The city of Namur had been occupied by ADSEC, a front-line satellite of Com Z, before we arrived. That staff had good-naturedly yielded its priority rights in the town to make room for EAGLE TAC.

"EAGLE TAC?" they exclaimed after we had moved in, exercising the privileges that go with seniority in command. "You should change it to EAGLE TOOK."

Once before I had passed an evening in the ADSEC billet at the Hotel Harscamp in Namur while motoring back to Luxembourg from First Army. I recall the name of that hotel clearly. It was dusk and we had stopped in town to inquire of a GI the way to the *Harscamp.*

"Whores' camp?" At first he looked puzzled but then he brightened with the thought, "say—d'ya mean they really got one here?"

For the Belgians in Namur, 1944 ushered in a disagreeable and chilly winter. The government that had re-established Belgian rule on the heels of the liberating armies immediately instituted a currency reform to weed out the inflated paper with which the enemy had salted the nation and enriched its war profiteers. At the same time emergency wage and price controls were established. Within a year the rewards of this firm stand by Minister of Finance Camille Gutt were apparent. While the rest of Europe floundered in economic chaos, Belgium was already on the way to recovery.

One week passed but the Roer was still too high and we elected to wait another. Meanwhile, there were signs of a growing enemy build-up before Ninth Army. Soon we would be forced to strike a compromise between high water on the river and the risk of more enemy resistance. At the time I was especially sensitive to delay, for each day we waited magnified the illusion that the enemy had hurt us more than he did in the Ardennes counteroffensive.

Strategically, the delay wasted an opportune moment for attack. The Red army was at last gaining headway in its offensive after a three-month layoff that lasted through our Battle of the Bulge. If we could only have attacked concurrently with the Soviet drive, the enemy would have been unable to shuttle reinforcements between the East and West fronts. Although General Bull, SHAEF's G-3, had returned from Moscow in January with an enthusiastic report on the coming Soviet offensive, Eisenhower doubted that this winter attack would carry the Red army beyond the Oder. In the meantime, a report gained credence that these Soviet advances would lessen German resistance on our Western front. That tale was never anything more than wishful thinking; if the German softened in his defense it was not apparent to our front-line troops.

Although dope for our briefings on the Red army still came to us via the BBC, in late February we established a single day's rapport with the Soviet diplomatic service when Moscow's ambassador to France visited us in Namur to award Russian decorations for the OVERLORD invasion. Following the presentation ceremony in the provincial palace, the ambassador, a clerkish looking man, M. Alexander Y. Bogomolov, spent the evening with us in the Château de Namur. The next morning I invited him to accompany me to the staff briefing in the secret war room. We showed him our present troop dispositions and outlined prospective strategy for completion of the Rhineland campaign. En route back to Paris that day with Colonel A. J. Drexel Biddle from SHAEF, Bogomolov spoke delightedly of our guilelessness at the briefing and promised to report my hospitality to Marshal Stalin. That good mark, however, did not spare me five years later when the Soviets listed me high among the Anglo-American imperialist warmongers. Had I been able to anticipate this sequel, I would have been vastly relieved in 1945 when U. S. and British newspapers featured a story on Bogomolov's admittance to our secret staff briefing. For several days I feared my gesture might be misunderstood in Washington. It was finally Lev Allen who said, "Don't worry about it, Brad. When the FBI comes around for a checkup, we won't let you down."

At 10 A.M. on Thursday, February 22, the decision was made to jump the Roer early the following morning. Although the river had not yet fallen to the level we would have preferred for an assault crossing, 22 days had already passed since Eisenhower diverted our *main* effort from the Eifel back to the Roer. Had we been permitted to push on through the Eifel, we might have been much farther ahead on the road to the Rhine. Each day we delayed provided the enemy one more for recuperation until it became increasingly apparent that we could not safely allow him many more. Even now I feared the war would drag on until September, 1945, reaching its climax in a series of summer battles during late July and August. If we were to force the Rhine by late spring, we could dawdle no longer on the Roer.

Meanwhile Monty's Canadian Army was soon stalemated in its drive from Nijmegen down behind the Siegfried Line where it fronted Dempsey's forces. After 14 days of attack the Canadians had advanced fewer than 20 miles against concentrated enemy resistance over terrain that had been soaked by heavy rains and flooded by the German. Not until Simpson struck out across the Roer in the rear of those defending forces could Crerar expect resistance there to slacken.

Between Düren and Jülich where the muddy Roer flowed through a graveyard of rubble, Simpson had massed ten divisions, three of them armored, for his crossing. To his right, Hodges had drawn up three corps, totaling 14 divisions. Collins' VII Corps was to assault the Roer simultaneously with Ninth Army on February 23 while the III and V Corps followed successively from left to right in echelon across that river. Each division was to cross the Roer behind the division on its left by slipping over into the latter's bridgehead.

Once across, it would slip off to the right back into its zone of advance.

We had devised this echelon scheme of attack that Hodges might avoid the need for successive assault crossings of the Roer. He would

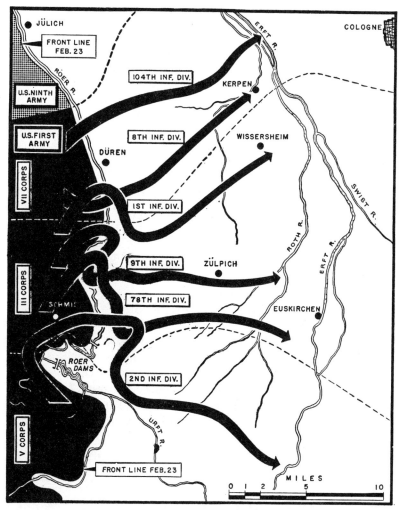

To avoid unnecessary assault crossings of the Roer, First Army echeloned its initial attack on February 23, passing each successive division through a bridgehead already established by the division on its left.

pass the leading division of III Corps through the last one in Collins' bridgehead, roll it off to the right, and thereafter clear successive bridgeheads until they encompassed V Corps. In this pattern of attack, First Army would make its first and deepest penetration in that sector where VII Corps shielded Simpson's flank, while Ninth Army turned toward Düsseldorf to link up with the Canadian advance.

We struck along a 25-mile stretch of the Roer River from Düren up to Linnich and by noon had put in the initial pontoon bridge. Trucks crawled over the corduroy roads that had been laid to the river bank through the woodlands and snaked across the steel ribbons that stretched from shore to shore over a bridge of rubber rafts. A precipitous thaw had come six weeks early after an uncommonly severe winter, and our heavy supply traffic shattered the macadam roads behind us. Miles of hard-topped highways disappeared in the gumbo until even the first-class roads became impassable mires.

Within five days after we had forced the Roer, German resistance showed signs of wilting. On February 28, Simpson broke out of his bridgehead and four days later joined the British Second Army at Venlo, while the remainder of his Ninth Army bulged toward the Rhine. Meanwhile, Collins had advanced to the Erft, a muddy stream between the Roer and the Rhine, where he was to pause before advancing against the savagely bombed city of Cologne.

On March 3, I issued orders to Hodges and Patton for the surprisingly swift campaign that within ten days was to clear the Rhineland north of the Moselle Valley. We captured 49,000 German prisoners during that brief campaign and the enemy never again succeeded in patching up his Western front. Because it was executed with drill-hall precision and split-second timing, this campaign west of the Rhine became a model textbook maneuver. If I were asked what campaign in the war brought me the greatest professional pride, I would point unhesitatingly to this one.

The campaign was to be executed in two successive phases, each of them timed from Army Group.

1. While Hodges closed to the Rhine between Düsseldorf and Cologne, Patton was to ready his bridgeheads across the Kyll.

2. Having seen Simpson safely to the Rhine, Hodges was to turn Collins around toward Cologne and strike swiftly with his whole Army to the southeast where First Army would join Patton's col-

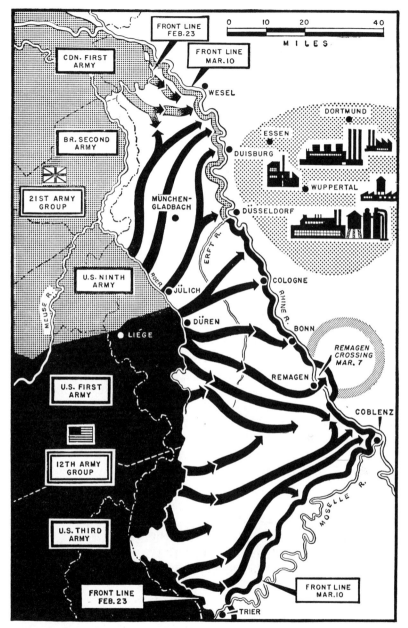

Within two weeks after crossing the Roer, on February 23, the First, Third, and Ninth Armies closed to the Rhine from the Moselle north to the Ruhr. On March 7, First Army seized the Remagen bridge. This speedy Allied advance had not only breached the Rhine but had stampeded the enemy west of that river.

umns as they stabbed toward the Rhine. For Patton was to attack through the mountainous Eifel and bolt for Coblenz where an equestrian statue of Kaiser Wilhelm I marked the confluence of the Rhine and Moselle.

The first phase moved swiftly. By March 5, VII Corps had closed to the Rhine south of Düsseldorf and Patton was waiting the signal to attack from his positions on the far bank of the Kyll. Three armored divisions were held in readiness for Third Army's 50-mile blitz to the Rhine. I signaled the Armies for the start of Phase Two and on the following morning motored down to Reims for an evening of advance planning with Ike. Churchill had been asked to lunch the next day and Eisenhower suggested that I wait over. The Prime Minister arrived shortly before one in the uniform of an army colonel. "I've grown tired of the RAF dress," he explained. He removed a cigar from the leather case he carried in an inner pocket and seated himself with a brandy and soda before we went in to lunch. Churchill had visited Simpson the previous day and now he was elated over the speed of Ninth Army's advance.

For lunch Eisenhower was able again to offer fresh Chesapeake Bay oysters sent to him by Steve Early. When Marshal Brooke and I declined our portions, Ike chortled and speedily divided them among the remaining guests and himself.

Referring to his previous day's visit in the field, Churchill spoke of the astonishing developments in Allied ordnance since the outbreak of this war. Yet his enthusiasm for these new devices was curbed somewhat by his feeling that perhaps we might be using them soon again. "The nation that is defeated and disarmed in this world war," he said, "will stride into the next with an advantage, for it will develop the new arms while we attempt to make the old ones do."

Even Tedder, the airman, nodded at the PM's prediction that "the day is not far distant when the heavy bomber as we know it may become totally obsolete." Rocket weapons, Churchill declared, would someday supplant piloted aircraft.

"And then Britain," he added in a rumbling growl, "shall become one vast bazooka aimed at the aggressors who threaten Europe.

"There may come a day," he continued, "when we shall walk into a cabinet room, break the glass over a switch, dial to the nation to be bombed, and push a button to declare war." President Roosevelt's mention of the atom bomb 18 months before came to mind.

Although I wondered how it had progressed, I hesitated to ask even Eisenhower about it.

Later during the lunch, Churchill defended his policies in Greece where British troops had been committed in support of the Greek government against communist-dominated ELAS opposition. Churchill's action had been vehemently attacked by the London *Times*, the Manchester *Guardian*, "and a significant portion of the American press," he observed, "which took its cue from those two."

"But we shall *never*," he thumped the table, "we shall never sit quietly by and permit a minority to force its will upon a helpless majority anywhere." He spoke scornfully of the rebirth of a communist threat to the West and cautioned us to beware the guile of Stalin whom he referred to as "Uncle Joe." While I, like most Americans, had happily accepted the wartime legend of a heroic Soviet, Churchill snapped with defiance of the communists as he had for so many years before the war. He dismissed Allied critics of his policies with truculence and likened himself to a giant rhinoceros with a sharp tusk and thick hide. That tusk, he promised, would always be pointed against the enemy no matter how many critics pricked his hide.

On March 6, as Hodges threw his 9th Armored Division southeast across the Erft, Patton splintered through the German crust beyond the Kyll. On the war map of our palace CP in Namur a narrow blue finger marking the front line poked recklessly across the acetate toward the Rhine as Hugh Gaffey's 4th Armored Division streaked toward Coblenz. Within two days it had driven a salient, no wider than the road it traveled, through the wooded Eifel, 35 miles into the enemy's rear. In this attack Gaffey had staged the boldest and the most insolent armored blitz of the Western war. Meanwhile to the left of Gaffey's advance Patton pushed out the 11th Armored Division with instructions to advance abreast of the 4th. On March 7, their columns converged a few miles west of the Rhine where they formed a pocket around the troops they had by-passed. Escape to the Rhine had now been cut off north of the Moselle. And in the uplands of the Eifel, enemy units scattered in confusion as U. S. tanks sped through their rear pell-mell for the Rhine.

Farther north, Collins' VII Corps had turned south from Düsseldorf toward Cologne where Terry Allen's 104th Division picked its way into the ruins of that stricken city. Air had miraculously spared its ancient Gothic cathedral and beyond its twin spires, the Rhine washed through the fallen girders of Cologne's Hindenburg Bridge. This mile-long span had been demolished by the retreating German as our troops dodged warily into the outskirts of Cologne. Only its four ugly towers remained standing to mark its demise.

From the grubby mill town of Euskirchen, the 9th Armored Division of Major General John W. Leonard skirted the dark woodlands of Köthen Forest as it sped toward the Ahr where that mountain stream emptied into a bend in the Rhine midway between Coblenz and Cologne. Six miles north of that juncture, a row of stuccoed houses faced the west bank of the Rhine near the town of Remagen. There a single-tracked railway bridge spanned that river.

As the 9th Armored neared the Ahr on the drizzly afternoon of March 7, one of its combat commands sped south to establish a bridgehead across that stream in the V Corps sector. Another, under the command of Brigadier General William M. Hoge, struck out for the Rhine.

By now enemy resistance west of the Rhine had fallen into confusion. Units fleeing toward safety across that river were stranded as their vehicles ran out of gas. In town after town as our tanks rolled through their streets, the villagers shuttered their windows and hung their homes with white sheets. From Düsseldorf to Coblenz a score of heavy bridges collapsed into the Rhine as crews touched off their demolitions. In Düsseldorf the bridges were blown just as American vanguards reached their western approaches. Although eager to secure a Rhine river bridgehead, we had despaired of taking a bridge intact. As far back as England I had resigned myself to the necessity of an assault river crossing.

The blackout blinds were already drawn in my CP that evening when I came in to find that Eisenhower's G-3, Major General Bull, was waiting for me. He had just arrived from SHAEF with a larcenous proposal that would divert four of my 26 divisions to Devers for the latter's breakthrough into the Saar.

Suddenly my phone rang. It was Hodges calling from Spa.

"Brad," Courtney called, with more composure than the good news warranted, "Brad, we've gotten a bridge."

"A bridge? You mean you've got one intact on the Rhine?"

"Yep," Hodges replied, "Leonard nabbed the one at Remagen before they blew it up—"

"Hot dog, Courtney," I said, "this will bust him wide open. Are you getting your stuff across?"

"Just as fast as we can push it over," he said. "Tubby's got the navy moving in now with a ferry service and I'm having the engineers throw a couple of spare pontoon bridges across to the bridgehead."

I pulled the long lead wire from my phone over toward the map-board. "Shove everything you can across it, Courtney," I said, "and button the bridgehead up tightly. It'll probably take the other fellow a couple of days to pull enough stuff together to hit you."

I hung up on Hodges, turned on Bull, and thumped him on the shoulder. "There goes your ball game, Pink," I grinned. "Courtney's gotten across the Rhine on a bridge."

Bull blinked back through his rimless glasses. He sat down before the map and shrugged his shoulders. "Sure, you've got a bridge, Brad, but what good is it going to do you. You're not going anywhere down there at Remagen. It just doesn't fit into *the* plan."

"Plan—hell," I retorted. "A bridge is a bridge and mighty damned good anywhere across the Rhine."

Bull only shook his head. The Plan had been predicated upon a major crossing by Monty north of the Ruhr. If, after satisfying Monty's priority requirements, SHAEF could then support a diversionary offensive, a secondary crossing *might* be made by Third Army between Mainz and Karlsruhe. Indeed this secondary crossing was essential to the Ruhr pincer for which I had fought since the previous September. Although Eisenhower had not yet made a decision to restrict the Rhine crossing to Monty, his British-dominated staff at SHAEF so favored the Montgomery proposal that this single thrust had already become established in their minds as The Plan, SHAEF's irrevocable plan for the assault of the Rhine. But while Bull admitted the desirability of a Rhine crossing in the south, even he shared this British view. As a consequence, he was totally unconvinced there was a place in The Plan for a bridge at Remagen.

"What in hell do you want us to do," I asked him, "pull back and blow it up?" Bull did not answer.

I phoned Eisenhower at Reims to confirm the order I had given Hodges. Ike was delighted with news of the bridge. "Hold on to it, Brad," he said. "Get across with whatever you need—but make certain you hold that bridgehead."

After dinner that evening we returned to the office. Although news of the bridgehead had been greeted as a victory by my staff, Bull did not brighten. To him, Remagen was nothing more than an unwelcome intruder in the neatly ordered SHAEF plan.

"But I don't want you to give up your plan," I told him. "Just let us develop this crossing with four or five divisions. Perhaps you can use it as a diversion. Or maybe we can employ it to strengthen our pincer south of the Ruhr. At any rate, it's a crossing. We've gotten over the Rhine. But now that we've got a bridgehead, for God's sakes let's use it."

"But once you get across, Brad, where do you go? What can you do over there?"

"Here, let me show you," I said, leading Bull to the mapboard where a terrain study of western Germany had been posted under the fluorescent lights. North of the Ruhr in the Rhine basin, engineers had picked the crossing sites where Monty would leap in a massive assault across to the plains of Westphalia. Two hundred miles farther south, between Mainz and Karlsruhe, the banks of the Rhine flattened again and here were the crossings we had chosen for encirclement of the Ruhr from the south. Between those two assault areas the Rhine flowed through a gorge with only occasional sites for single division crossings.

Beyond the Remagen bridge, the steep woodlands of the *Westerwald* posed a barrier to any rapid advance east. But from a point across the river from Coblenz, 25 miles to the south of Remagen, a river valley penetrated those mountains to Giessen where it intersected the path from Frankfurt that we had chosen for envelopment of the Ruhr. If Hodges could gain the *autobahn* that ran six miles beyond the Remagen bridge, he could drive south to that river valley gap and there turn east toward Giessen. At Giessen he would join forces with Patton for encirclement of the Ruhr.

Bull examined the terrain study, tapped it with his finger, and said, "I'll bet you fellows just had it made up."

"Six months ago," I told him, "while we were still in Verdun."

"But you know our plans for the Rhine crossing," he said, referring to Monty's prospective assault, "—and now you're trying to change them."

"Change, hell, Pink," I spoke curtly for by now I was growing impatient. "We're not trying to change a thing. But now that we've had a break on the bridge, I want to take advantage of it."

Bull, however, could not believe that I did not seek a diversion of forces from Monty. "Ike's heart is in your sector," he explained, "but right now his mind is up north." By then it was after midnight; I gave up and went to bed.

Ike's mind might have been up north but it had not yet been made up, for he was not to reach his final decision on the double versus the single thrust until March 15. Meanwhile, he had admitted that an advance north of the Ruhr offered the quickest method of denying the enemy access to his industries there. And he had agreed with Monty that the Westphalian plains on the road to Berlin offered promising terrain for the mobile warfare in which we excelled the Germans. But he knew also that if his offensive east of the Rhine were limited to that northern thrust, the enemy might also concentrate his strength astride that single path. In speaking to Eisenhower I expressed a lukewarm opinion of those Westphalian plains, for while flat they were also crossed by innumerable rivers, streams, and canals. Demolitions, I argued, could easily impede and limit an Allied advance there.

The southern route from Frankfurt to Kassel which I favored for the U. S. pincer was not only hillier than Monty's, but longer. Yet these disadvantages were not overwhelming, for here there were fewer obstacles to oppose our advance.

When all was said and done, despite the preferences of his staff for Monty's single offensive, Eisenhower leaned toward our U. S. plan for double envelopment of the Ruhr. For among other things he saw in it the possibility of an alternative offensive in the event Monty's bogged down in the north. However, it was to Monty's effort on the north that Eisenhower gave the priority in troops, airborne, and river-crossing equipment. If a southern crossing were to be made by Patton in the vicinity of Mainz, it would be limited in strength to the U. S. leftovers of Montgomery's assault.

When the Combined Chiefs of Staff assembled in Malta on January 30, 1945, in preparation for the conference at Yalta, the British challenged Eisenhower's disposition toward our plan for double envelopment of the Ruhr. They proposed that he be *directed* by the Combined Chiefs of Staff to concentrate his strength behind Montgomery on the north. Brooke feared that Eisenhower might divert so much of his strength to our southern crossing that Montgomery's effort would be impaired.

General Marshall, however, rallied to Eisenhower's side and refuted the British contention. He strongly opposed the commitment of all Allied strength into a single path of attack and insisted that Eisenhower be permitted to make the secondary crossing as an alternative one should Montgomery be stalled in the north. For General Marshall anticipated heavy resistance on that northern front and he spoke specifically of the danger of jet aircraft. And at the same time he objected most strenuously to the Combined Chiefs issuing instructions to a field commander on how to accomplish his job. Since the start of the war General Marshall had insisted on virtual autonomy in the field.

As Eisenhower's spokesman, Bedell Smith allayed the British fears with a recital of the Allied strength that would be devoted to Montgomery's major effort. When a 21st Army Group logistical study indicated that Monty could support no more than 21 divisions in that northern offensive, SHAEF had arbitrarily ordered the estimate increased, first to 30—and then 36. Our southern pincer was to be limited to approximately 12 divisions. The remainder of the Allied divisions on the Western front were then to dig in and hold on the near bank of the Rhine.

The day after Remagen was taken, SHAEF ordered me to restrict our commitment in the bridgehead initially to four divisions. No more could be spared if we were to deadline a reserve as Monty had proposed of ten additional divisions to be used by him in the event he smashed through the enemy crust on his northern crossing. I thereupon instructed Hodges to expand his bridgehead approximately a thousand yards each day, barely enough to keep the enemy from mining and entrenching around that foothold. There Hodges was to wait until Eisenhower reached a decision on the southern crossing. If Ike approved our plan for the double thrust, I would have Hodges break out of Remagen and head southeast to join up with Patton's attack through Frankfurt. Both advances could then be turned toward Kassel for encirclement of the Ruhr.

Even before Hoge's bold tankers raced across the planked roadway of the Remagen bridge to yank the wires that ran to the demolitions, that structure had been damaged by a German attempt to blow it up. And almost as soon as we crossed, the German turned his air and artillery against it. To protect the bridgehead and speed reinforcements to the far shore, First Army engineers threw a treadway bridge, then a pontoon bridge across the swollen Rhine. Naval units unloaded LCVP's from the giant trailers that had carried them from the Channel and initiated a ferry service for the transport of supply. AA moved in a concentration of guns half again as dense as that on the Normandy beachhead. Booms were laced upstream across the river to guard against submersibles and radio-controlled mines. And on either end of the bridge, patrols were established to prevent saboteurs from working their way into our columns crossing the bridge. Barrage balloons tugged at their cables from the hills on both sides of the river and depth charges were dropped in the river to prevent frogmen from slipping through.

Enemy fighter bombers attacked the structure each day but fortunately their bombs splashed harmlessly into the Rhine. However, on March 9, long-range artillery scored a hit on the bridge and closed the roadway for five hours. Two days later it was struck again. Finally on March 17 the structure swayed, buckled, and then collapsed into the Rhine. Of the 200 engineers who were struggling to repair it at the time, more than a score were crushed in the crackling girders. Others were drowned as the collapsing bridge flung them into the icy Rhine. Had the structure held just another 24 hours, engineers estimated the span could have been saved. Nevertheless, by now Hodges had established a firm grip on his Remagen bridgehead. He had crowded four divisions into the foothold while expanding it to reach the double-laned autobahn that led toward Frankfurt. Meanwhile the enemy's reaction was slow. As yet he had mustered but 20,000 troops against that open wound in his side. In a communiqué, however, the German did announce that three majors and a lieutenant had been put to death for their failure to destroy the bridge in the first place.

When Bull motored into Namur on the afternoon Remagen was taken, he had come not to oppose our bridgehead but to get additional resources from us for Devers' cleanup of the Saar. Once Patton closed to the Moselle, the enemy would have been cleared from everywhere west of the Rhine except in the Saar basin where Devers had massed Patch's Seventh Army against the Siegfried Line.

While Eisenhower would prefer to close the length of his entire line to the Rhine, he dared not delay Monty's crossing beyond the D day Monty had chosen. As a consequence, SHAEF was eager to allot Devers the strength necessary for a rapid cleanup. However, because Ninth Army could not be tapped for aid in view of the priority that had been assigned it as part of Monty's northern crossing, we suspected immediately that 12th Army Group was again to be the unhappy donor. Soon after the Bulge we had given up three divisions to Devers for his Colmar offensive. Another raid, we feared, would cut us down more than we could afford, perhaps even jeopardize our ability to mount the southern crossing.

Anticipating that Devers might be stalemated in his effort to crash the Siegfried Line, I suggested to Eisenhower that we turn Patton southward across the Moselle to roll up the Saar and cut the enemy off from behind in his fortifications. From a bridgehead below the Moselle near Coblenz, Third Army could race south on the west bank of the Rhine and there block the enemy's supply line. Meanwhile in the vicinity of Trier on the Luxembourg corner, Third Army had cleared a triangle south of the Moselle during its period of aggressive defense. From so convenient a springboard Patton could push south behind the Siegfried Line to flank those fortifications while Devers hammered them from the front. Almost as soon as he heard the plan, Eisenhower ordered me to go ahead.

I immediately flew down to Luxembourg and outlined the scheme to George Patton. He was having his hair cut in a home for the aged in which he had established his CP. George called for another barber and we discussed the plan under steaming towels. Not only did it promise the adventurous type of offensive that appealed instinctively to Patton, but it offered him the chance to pull Devers' Group through the Siegfried Line fortifications.

"At any rate, it'll save us from sitting on our asses," he said, "while SHAEF makes up its mind as to whether we're going to cross the Rhine."

While not hostile, Devers was lukewarm to the plan for he feared a mixup with Patton's Army tramping across his front. Nevertheless, the prospect of wiping out so strong a position as the Siegfried Line was too alluring to be rejected and Devers assented.

With this maneuver already under way among the planners, I was reluctant to yield any further strength to Devers' 6th Army Group. Bull had requested the transfer of three divisions in addition to supporting troops and he looked angry when I demurred.

"It would mean stripping First Army," I told him. "You know we can't touch Simpson while he's with Monty. And George will need all he's got for this mission below the Moselle. I'm sorry, Pink, but we just can't do it."

It was late in the evening and Bull was irritated by the refusal. "By gosh, but you people are difficult to get along with," he said,

"—and I might add that you are getting more difficult every day."

"But SHAEF has had experience," I said, "in getting along with difficult people."

Bull promptly snapped back, "The 12th Army Group is no harder to get along with than 21st Group." He paused. "But you can take it from me, it's no easier either."

Irritated by Bull's asperity, I agreed to the transfer of those divisions he asked for but compromised on the artillery battalions, for we would require them at Remagen. By now I was reduced to a total of 27 divisions for the First and Third Armies. Meanwhile, Monty clung tightly to the 12 that had been allotted Simpson for Ninth Army's crossing of the Rhine. In the south Devers had accumulated 11 U. S. divisions in addition to the French Army of General de Lattre de Tassigny. When Hodges learned of my concession to Bull, he hurried down angrily from Spa. "But they're taking everything I've got, Brad," he complained. "How can I go anywhere out of Remagen if they keep cutting me down?"

"This is the last of it, Courtney," I assured him. "We won't give up another battalion." Fortunately Bull's request was his last. The war accelerated too rapidly thereafter for further harassment from the staff at SHAEF.

As Third Army made ready to bolt south from its bridgeheads below the Moselle and crash down on the Rhine at Mainz, Eisenhower at last came face to face with the long-disputed issue of a single versus a double envelopment of the Ruhr with a second thrust from the south. The question had been simmering for almost six months. In addition to the Canadian First, the British Second, and the American Ninth Armies already allotted him for his major effort on the north, Montgomery had insisted that SHAEF set up a follow-up force in reserve of ten divisions to be "borrowed" from First Army. It was in anticipation of this request that SHAEF had originally limited me to four divisions in the Remagen bridgehead. Had those ten been transferred to Monty as he asked, I would have been left with only the Third Army. And as a consequence Patton and I would probably have sat out the remainder of the war in a holding position on the west bank of the Rhine.

Fortunately Eisenhower called Montgomery's bluff. If those ten divisions of First Army went north, Eisenhower told him, 12th Army Group was also to go north in command of both the First and Ninth

U. S. Armies. Just as soon as Monty learned of Eisenhower's condition on those ten divisions, he promptly dropped the request. Rather than give up the Ninth Army and share the northern thrust with an American Group command, he preferred to go at it with what he had and direct it from 21st Army Group. As a result our six months' struggle was finally won by forfeit and Eisenhower was able to resolve this most contentious tactical dispute of the war. First and Third Armies were directed by SHAEF to encircle the Ruhr from the south. Despite Bull's gloomy objections, Remagen was to form the springboard for First Army's advance to the Elbe.

By March 12, Third Army had closed to the Moselle all the way from the Rhine at Coblenz to the triangle at Trier where Walker's XX Corps had staked out a bridgehead on the flank of the Siegfried Line. Within 18 days from that rainy February morning when Simpson and Hodges hurdled the Roer, we had destroyed the enemy north of the Moselle and west of the Rhine River. Between them, First and Third Armies had caged 51,000 prisoners of war while Montgomery's forces in the north accounted for 53,000 more. Our swift thrust to the Rhine had caught the enemy totally unawares and as our columns carved him into pockets, he surrendered in dejection. The spirited resistance Hitler had hoped to kindle in defense of the homeland now fizzled with the realization that the war was lost. Only the fanatics held to any illusions and their ranks were dwindling fast. So rapid was the dissolution that even the senior German commanders lost touch with their crumbling front. One day a German corps commander drove into a field of listless soldiers and asked why they were not out fighting the Allies. Not until an American MP clasped him on the shoulder and invited him to join the throng, did the general learn that he had stumbled into a PW concentration.

Patton had drawn up nine divisions for his quick thrust into the Saar. Five were strung along the Moselle Valley from Luxembourg to the Rhine and the remaining four were clustered in the hilly triangle southeast of Trier. Within 24 hours after closing to that position on the Moselle, Third Army swarmed down into the Saar. "Tell Devers to get out of the way," Patton said, "or we'll pick him up with the Krauts."

During an earlier conversation with Patton in Luxembourg, I had

asked if Third Army was dragging its bridging equipment behind
it on its advance into the Rhineland.

"Why no, as a matter of fact, we aren't," he said, "but I've got
a helluva lot of it stashed away." I had not forgotten that George
had held onto his bridging during the boundary change that came
with the Bulge.

"Perhaps you'd better get that assault stuff up closer," I said. "I
want you to take the Rhine on the run. We're not going to stop, give
the other fellow a chance to build up and raise hell when we come
across."

Simpson had previously complained of Monty's orders halting
him on the west bank of the Rhine when he could have jumped
across it against light opposition. Since then, Montgomery's spectacular preparations for the assault crossing had drawn vast concentrations of the enemy into that sector.

I had anticipated that on his attack into the Saar, Patton might
run into trouble in the Hunsrück Mountains behind the Moselle.
But this time I had underestimated the slashing speed and flair of
Third Army's reckless advance. Once again, it was Hugh Gaffey's
spirited 4th Armored Division that spearheaded the attack. His tanks
plunged through those wooded Hunsrück Mountains before the
enemy could collect his wits. Within two days Gaffey had pushed
his columns south to the Nahe River near Bad Kreuznach. There
Patton halted his column and brought up additional troops.

At Namur my staff waited nervously for George to push that thin
column beyond Bad Kreuznach to the Rhine only 25 miles farther
east. "Hell's bells," one of them said, "why doesn't the old boy
push on?"

I trusted, however, in George's uncanny feel for the front. "Patton knows what he's doing," I said. "Just keep your shirt on and
you'll see."

Within 24 hours the 4th Armored was hit by enemy counterattack
in that sector. But because Patton had consolidated his spearhead
with reinforcements from the rear, he bounced the enemy off and
went on with scarcely a shrug of his shoulders. Intelligence had not
indicated the imminence of that attack but George had anticipated
it with the curious intuition that helped make him a great field commander.

No less spectacular was the pace of Walker's advance out of Trier
as he rolled down behind the concrete casemates of the Siegfried

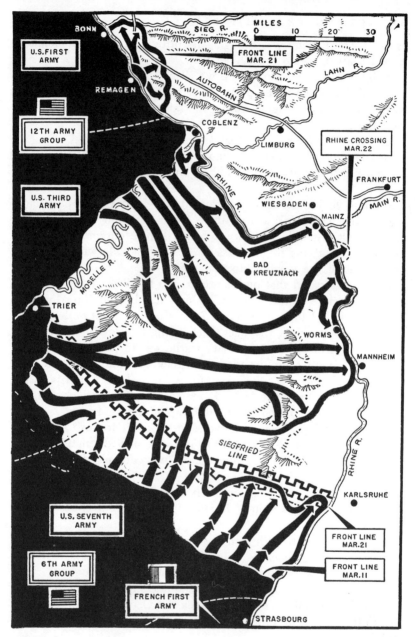

Rather than wait for Devers to break through the Siegfried Line, 12th Army Group proposed that Patton's Third Army be turned south across the Moselle to collapse the enemy position there. Within ten days, Patton had breached that barrier in a nighttime crossing.

Line. Before jumping off, Patton had added two divisions to XX Corps, making it the largest single corps concentration of Third Army during the war. Within six days Third Army had joined those Coblenz and Trier forces together south of the Nahe River. To escape the Shermans that thundered down on his flank and behind his rear, the enemy fled his Siegfried Line, abandoning it to Devers who poured his forces through.

Midway between its headwaters in the Alps and its North Sea delta, the Rhine turns at Mainz before plunging into the gorge that speeds it downstream to Bonn. Between Mannheim and Mainz the river flows through the grassy plains of Hessen with its broad level banks and easy path to the industrial environs of heavily bombed Frankfurt. It was toward these plains that Patton had aimed his armored spearheads.

The vast windows of our dining room in the Château de Namur were flooded with sunlight the morning of March 23 when I came down for breakfast. Below us the Sambre spilled lazily into the broad untrafficked Meuse. To the north a flight of bombers scrawled con trails across the sky as they headed toward the Ruhr. I had just finished my second cup of coffee when Patton telephoned from LUCKY.

"Brad, don't tell anyone but I'm across."

"Well, I'll be damned—you mean across the Rhine?"

"Sure am," he replied, "I sneaked a division over last night. But there are so few Krauts around there they don't know it yet. So don't make any announcement—we'll keep it a secret until we see how it goes."

Confirmation came in the morning's briefing when Lieutenant Colonel Richard R. Stillman, of Paris, Kentucky, Patton's young liaison officer to 12th Army Group, submitted his report. Stillman showed the delight Third Army felt in having slipped quietly across the Rhine under cover of darkness while Monty flexed his muscles ostentatiously farther north. With a smiling allusion to Monty's elaborate preparations, Stillman made his report, "Without benefit of aerial bombing, ground smoke, artillery preparation, and airborne assistance, the Third Army at 2200 hours, Thursday evening, March 22, crossed the Rhine River." With the aid of rafts and engineer assault boats, the 5th Infantry Division had ferried across from the small farming village of Oppenheim to the opposite shore. In this first assault crossing of that river bastion by a modern army, the division suffered a total of 34 dead and wounded.

That evening Patton telephoned again.

"Brad," he shouted and his treble voice trembled, "for God's sake tell the world we're across. We knocked down 33 Krauts today when they came after our pontoon bridges. I want the world to know Third Army made it before Monty starts across."

23: *To the Elbe*

At 3:30 on the afternoon of March 23, Montgomery folded his weather reports, telephoned Dempsey and Simpson where they waited on the Rhine, and ordered them to go that night. As the massed fires of Montgomery's guns arched across the river in search of the enemy batteries that had been moved up to oppose his crossing, four battalions of the 51st Highland Division scrambled quietly into their assault craft and pushed out on the river. Seven minutes later they reported a landing on the far shore.

Although Montgomery had been drawn up on the Rhine for 14 days before crossing, his preparation for that northern offensive had started months before when Second Army outlined its plan and engineers set out to accumulate the bridging. Before leaping the river, Montgomery had insisted upon a fat reserve of stores. Meanwhile Allied air had saturated the far bank as smoke generators screened Montgomery's elaborate preparations against enemy observation.

For the crossing Montgomery had concentrated a force of 26 divisions, four armored brigades, and a separate brigade of commandos. Among them were two airborne divisions to be dropped by daylight after the assault crossing. The nighttime drop had been ruled out, for had Montgomery deposited them on the far shore before daylight, he would have had to forfeit his artillery preparation. Moreover, a daylight drop, it was thought, would demoralize the enemy's rear and speed his disintegration.

By daylight on March 24, the main elements of four divisions had gained the far shore and were rapidly expanding their bridgeheads. At 10 A.M. the air drop began when the first serial of troop carriers soared across the Rhine into the black puffs that dirtied the sky as the enemy AA opened fire. I had flown up to Hodges' CP that morning and we loitered in the air as the long trains of C-47's and a few fat-bellied C-46's swarmed by. Within three hours 1,700 aircraft and 1,300 gliders had landed 14,000 troops of the British 6th and U. S. 17th Airborne Divisions behind the enemy opposing Dempsey's crossing. Losses in this daylight drop were considerably lighter than those of any other airborne operation of the war. Fewer than four per cent of the gliders were destroyed. Fifty-five Allied aircraft were listed missing at the end of the day.

Months before while contemplating an assault crossing of the Rhine, I had anticipated that airborne troops might be needed to gain a bridgehead if the enemy were given sufficient time to prepare his river defenses. But so successfully had we destroyed the enemy west of the Rhine that only a few ineffective units succeeded in escaping across the river.

As a consequence of that debacle west of the Rhine, enemy resistance on the east bank of that river was disorganized and uninspired. Had Monty crashed the river on the run as Patton had done, he might have averted the momentous effort required in that heavily publicized crossing. Fourteen days of preparation had given the enemy sufficient time to dig in with artillery on the far shore. And had it not been for our bridgehead at Remagen, toward which the enemy had diverted a major share of his strength, the German might have massed sufficient resistance to make necessary Monty's use of the air drop.

As Patton sped out of his bridgehead in the direction of Frankfurt and Montgomery joined his river crossings preparatory to a drive north of the Ruhr, I withdrew the order that had confined Hodges to his Remagen bridgehead for more than two weeks. While expanding his bridgehead as I had ordered him approximately a thousand yards each day, Hodges had crowded all three corps of his First Army into the 35-mile strip along the river that extended from either side of the sturdy stone pilings of the collapsed Ludendorf bridge. During the previous week newsmen had queried me on the "timidity" that kept us from breaking out of Remagen and "beating the Russians to Berlin." And in London the pundits once again cried

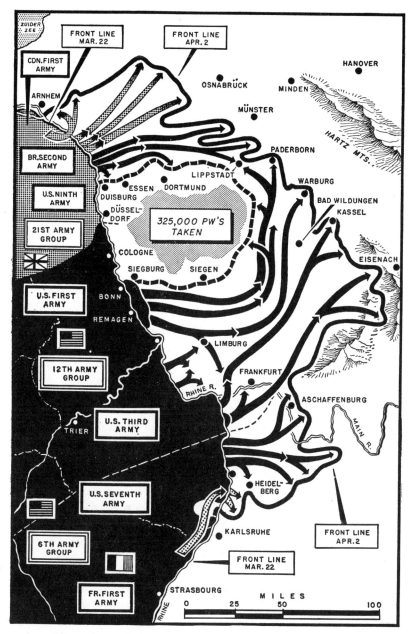

Just as soon as the Allied trap had been forged around the Ruhr, half the American strength was turned against it while the remainder pushed eastward toward the Elbe. With the link-up at Paderborn, Simpson's Ninth Army rejoined the U. S. command.

that we had not yet learned the lessons of blitzkrieg. Rather than reveal our plans, I put off these critics with an assurance that we could and would break out of Remagen any moment we chose.

The plan for breakout from Remagen followed a rudimentary pattern we had devised three months before when Hodges started his attack toward Bonn after having flattened the Ardennes Bulge. At that time we anticipated First Army would be deflected southeast to join the Third Army after it crossed the Rhine. For once Patton jumped the Rhine, he was to be pointed north across the Main River. Together those Armies would outflank the Ruhr and draw a noose around it toward Ninth Army on the north.

Now that Hodges had established the Remagen bridgehead to the south of Bonn, he was to trace that original pattern. First he would speed his tanks down the autobahn where it ran through Limburg on the road to Frankfurt. At Limburg he was to turn east up the Lahn Valley to Giessen. There he would join Patton's pincer coming up from the Main.

The First and Third Armies would then advance abreast of one another in a parallel column with Hodges on the inside, Patton on his flank, up the broad Wetterau corridor toward a union with Simpson. Then while Hodges and Simpson locked themselves around the Ruhr preparatory to cleaning it out, Patton would face his Army to the east and be prepared to advance toward the oncoming Russians.

From his position in the left corner of the Remagen bridgehead, Collins had proposed an advance in the opposite direction. Instead of having us encircle the Ruhr, he recommended we advance to the north up the right bank of the Rhine toward a union with Montgomery's forces. This was precisely what the enemy expected us to do and in anticipation of such a move had organized his defenses on the Sieg River where it crossed that path. When on March 26 Hodges bolted, not north, but to the southeast, he caught the enemy completely off balance.

By the evening of March 26, First Army had raced down the autobahn to Limburg while Patton struggled to tighten his grip on a small but severely contested bridgehead north of the Main. When G-3 telephoned to ask if Hodges' column should be turned off toward Giessen, I instructed them to keep a part of it rolling on down the autobahn in the direction of Wiesbaden. There they could help Third Army get across the Main and at the same time draw a pocket around the enemy in that corner between the Rhine and Main Rivers.

"It'll be good to have the First Army pull the Third out of a pinch," I said. "Patton's people have been getting much too cocky."

There was also a secondary objective to the maneuver. For as the 9th Armored plunged on south, it would isolate Wiesbaden and thus enable us to take that city without breaking it up in a battle. Ever since England where Thorson had reminisced about his World War I visits to that French-occupied city, we had eyed Wiesbaden as a likely spot for our CP. Not until our advance parties raced into the city did we discover that the air forces had preceded us by three months with a bombing that razed many of its best hotels and damaged the magnificent *Kurhaus*.

In anticipation of our advance up behind the Ruhr, Brereton's staff again called on me to support its plan for an air drop on Kassel near Paderborn where we were to join up with Simpson. Brigadier General Floyd L. Parks, the airborne chief of staff, had suggested April 20 as a likely date for the drop.

"But we won't need your drop," I told him. "We ought to be in Kassel by April 10. Besides I'd rather you use your aircraft to help us out on supply. We're going to be mighty pinched until we get a couple of rail bridges across the Rhine."

Even April 10, I afterward explained to Bedell Smith, had been selected to give us a wide margin of safety. Actually, I hoped to be in Kassel by April 1. We made it one day later.

This Kassel drop was to be the last of the airborne army's proposals; we had already rejected a dozen other proposed drops. But I was wary of tying up the air lift as had been done at Tournai, for the engineers were unable to promise us a rail bridge across the Rhine until April 20 at the earliest. Consequently we expected to be hard pressed on supply once our columns stretched out for miles beyond the Ruhr. By then we would desperately need Brereton's aircraft for lift.

By March 30, Maurice Rose had driven his 3rd Armored Division to within sight of Paderborn where he ran into fanatic resistance from SS troops drawn from nearby tank depots. Although Rose soon destroyed the bulk of that makeshift force, its remnants fled to the Harz Mountains where they staged a final holdout. The following day Rose was killed in action.

Meanwhile Simpson still squirmed impatiently in the tight bridge-head to which he was confined east of the Rhine while Montgomery employed his bridges for the priority build-up of Dempsey's Army. To acquaint Simpson with our plans for reduction of the Ruhr once we had joined forces with him near Paderborn, I flew north that day to his CP in the city of München-Gladbach. Since the Bulge, Big Simp, as he was affectionately known, had spent a restless three and a half months under Monty waiting to get back to U. S. command. Yet because his Ninth was the most congenial of all our U. S. Army commands, Simpson had served his indenture without incident or crisis. At the moment, however, he was piqued, first by the two weeks he had been forced to wait before jumping the Rhine, now by the need to wait once more while Dempsey used his bridges.

The priority had been ordered by Monty to speed Dempsey's main British effort up toward Hamburg and beyond that port to the Baltic Sea. Here Dempsey was to block off Denmark from the danger of "liberation" by the Red army. As yet unaware of the astuteness of this British move, we grumbled over the diversion. For despite the nearness of Soviet forces to the North Sea, we were less concerned with postwar political alignments than destruction of what remained of the German army.

Shortly after midnight two days before, the Associated Press had telephoned from Paris to report that the Military Affairs Committee of the Senate had confirmed promotions for Devers, Patton, Hodges, and me to the four-star rank of general. The following morning as I slipped on my jacket preparatory to a visit to SHAEF, I found that my orderly had already affixed the extra stars. Once aboard the plane, however, I removed them. "Let's wait," I told him, "until we get the official orders or better yet until we read it in the *Stars and Stripes*."

As soon as Simpson was permitted to break out of his bridgehead, he threw the 2d Armored across the north rim of the Ruhr and on April 2, just seven days after he had forced the Rhine, joined forces with Hodges in the village of Lippstadt. Two days later Eisenhower returned the Ninth Army to 12th Army Group, swelling to 45 the U. S. divisions in my command. At the same time we moved EAGLE TAC back down to Luxembourg from Namur. There was no longer any need for me to be near Monty in the north.

Within the area we had encircled by the link-up at Lippstadt, Model had gathered his tattered Army Group "B," a force larger than that which Paulus surrendered to Zhukov at Stalingrad. The remnants of three German Armies had been cornered in that trap. Survivors from both the Pas de Calais and the Bulge mingled with teen-age recruits from the *Hitler Jugend,* hastily pressed into shabby, ill-fitting uniforms of the Wehrmacht. Altogether Model's Group consisted of six field corps with the major elements of 17 divisions. To these forces he had added the 100,000 flak troops whose heavy concentration of guns had so long defended the Ruhr. Twice the enemy tried to break through the ring we had forged about him and twice we threw him back.

In anticipation of a prolonged campaign east of the Rhine, we had formed in early January the Fifteenth U. S. Army under the command of Gerow. To Gerow's job at V Corps, we sent the hard-boiled Huebner from the 1st Division. So swiftly had the enemy crumbled west of the Rhine, however, that we now abandoned plans for the commitment of Gerow's Army in the line and ordered it to hold the west bank of the Rhine as a semioccupation army.

Meanwhile as our main body of U. S. forces surged east on a 200-mile front across the undulating hills of Thuringia toward the Russian forces now only 100 miles from the Elbe, I assigned 18 divisions to the reduction of the Ruhr pocket. For 18 days the enemy held out in the Ruhr as we made our way through the forlorn cities that crowded the basin. When on April 18 resistance ended, we learned that 325,000 PWs had been taken. This was more than twice the number First Army had estimated at the start.

Intelligence reported that Field Marshal Model had been trapped with his troops inside that pocket. Remembering how this chilly Prussian had blocked our advance through the Siegfried Line in September, I told G-2 to give a medal to the man who brought him in. But the only trace of Model that came out of the Ruhr was a giant Mercedes-Benz staff car, reputed to be his, which Ridgway presented to me.

Except for the desperate delaying tactics of die-hard Nazis and the SS, enemy opposition slackened as our Allied line bulged from the Bavarian foothills in the south across the flowering mustard fields to Hanover only 150 miles from Berlin. And from behind the lace-curtained windows of their gaily painted homes, the *hausfrauen* looked diffidently on our columns as the vehicles rumbled through their streets in pursuit of the fleeing Wehrmacht.

Only in the Franconian city of Aschaffenburg, 20 miles up the

Main from Frankfurt, did the populace fight back as Goebbels had exhorted them to. But at Aschaffenburg where the enemy in 1934 had constructed a belt of Main River defenses in anticipation of French retaliation for Hitler's remilitarization of the Rhineland, the people fought not out of loyalty to the regime but in response to the entreaties of their local Nazi leader. You fight to live, he told them, for surrender means enslavement; there is no third way out. Troops pushing into the city found German officers hanged in the streets for having advocated surrender. Women and children lined the roof tops to pelt our troops with hand grenades. And from five nearby hospitals wounded German veterans limped in to join the battle. Rather than take the casualties a house-to-house cleanup would have incurred, our troops withdrew and called for an air bombing. After the city's rubble had settled over the bodies of its defenders, the Nazi commander, Major von Lambert, walked meekly out of a bunker carrying a white flag.

As our columns pushed past the storybook houses that huddled in the Hessian hills, they passed the small, decentralized industrial plants that had been scattered outside the Ruhr. Near them stood the ugly barbed-wire stockades that had been used to cage the slave labor. Rubbish littered the empty compounds where prisoners had ransacked the stores before escaping through the broken wire. DPs roamed aimlessly through the streets where Germans had shuttered their windows, and chunky Balt girls pedaled the roads on bicycles taken from the Germans. Small bands of Italians tramped the roads bent under full haversacks, many of them hung with shiny brass kitchen utensils. And in convoy after convoy the sad-eyed poilus in ragged and faded field blues trucked rearward in crowded GMC's toward a France they had not seen since 1940.

The last German illusions of stalemate and the prospects of negotiated peace had been crushed by the weight of our army and the impressive wealth of Allied equipment. Until the week we spanned the Rhine at Remagen, some of the enemy still clung to a last thin hope that the newly developed German jets might yet neutralize the Allied superiority in the air. Top priorities had been assigned the production of jet aircraft and already the enemy was believed to have manufactured in underground plants between 600 and 800 of these fast interceptors. Even in March, 1945, production was estimated at 200 jet aircraft per month. Meanwhile the Luftwaffe had issued recalls for trained airmen from the army, and at a half-dozen airdromes jet pilots were being trained. But like Hitler's V-weapons the jets had come too late. Had von Rundstedt succeeded in stalemating the Allied ground advance in his Bulge attack, the enemy might then have exploited his jet advantage. But as our armies swarmed over the Rhineland, encircled the Ruhr, and headed east, we overran his underground plants before those jets could join the battle. The last illusion was gone; Goebbels could now only harry the people with threats of Russian reprisals.

Soon after we had flattened the Bulge and resumed our offensive toward the Rhine, Eisenhower late one evening asked me how we might prevent an accidental clash in closing head-on with the Red army somewhere in the middle of Germany. Although our forces were then almost 500 miles apart, the Soviet offensive of January 12 showed promise of smashing through Poland, some thought as far as the Oder on Germany's eastern frontier. If Eisenhower were to devise a safe plan for juncture between the East and the West, he dared not defer it much longer. For any recommendation from SHAEF would have to be forwarded to the Kremlin.

Like Eisenhower, I was unwilling to trust in prearranged recognition signals, even less in the use of radio contact with the Reds.

Such signals were likely to be confused and radio contact would be impaired by an impossible language barrier. It was partly this fear of running head-on into a single British division at Falaise that had induced me to halt Patton's forces at Argentan. Now with almost a hundred times as many forces spread from the North Sea to Switzerland, I shuddered at the prospect of a collision that might easily flare into a fight. Not only were our forces totally unfamiliar with each other, but the Russians, I was told, had grown increasingly cocky and rash with each mile they advanced toward the west.

The obvious alternative to so hazardous a head-on meeting lay in a visible line of demarcation, a line on which both forces could be halted and held. Obviously it would have to be some easily recognizable terrain feature. After studying the map Eisenhower and I agreed the Elbe offered the likeliest bet. Not only did it run north and south but it represented the last major obstacle between the Rhine and the Oder. South of Magdeburg where the Elbe bent to the east, the meeting line could be extended along the Mulde River all the way to the Czech border. Eisenhower decided to submit this line as a proposal.

At the time of our conversation the Elbe River line looked almost

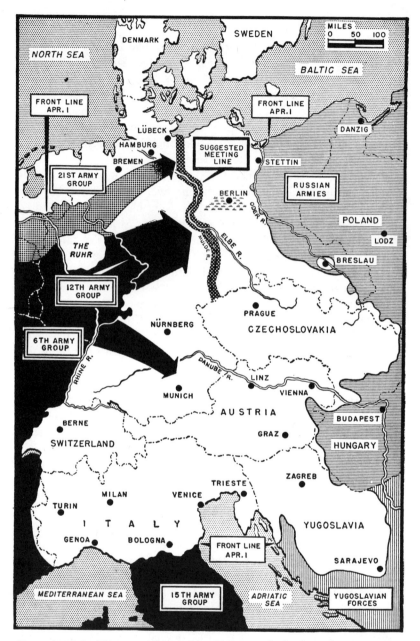

To prevent the Western Allies from colliding with the Russians, a meeting line was designated along the Elbe and Mulde Rivers. To reach this line Eisenhower proposed to center the main effort in 12th Army Group while Montgomery veered off toward the North Sea and Devers toward Munich.

hopelessly beyond the reach of our Allied forces. Where it angled north at Magdeburg, the river flowed only 50 miles west of Berlin. And at its nearest point it lay 220 miles beyond the Rhine at Cologne. If we believed it to be an almost illusory object for the Allied armies, the Soviets must have thought so too, for they accepted the line even though it ran approximately 90 miles inside the western border of their prospective zone of occupation. Indeed if we could reach the Elbe, as we proposed to do, we would have overrun one fifth of the zone allotted the Soviets.

These occupation boundaries had already been drawn by the European Advisory Commission in London. They were haggled over at Quebec, approved at Yalta, and finally forwarded for compliance to us in the field. Russia was to occupy all of east Germany to include the farmlands of Thuringia only 100 miles from the Rhine. In addition to the rich Silesian basin, her zone included the Baltic ports. The British zone in the northwest corner bounded the Russian on the Baltic near the submarine shops of Lübeck. Within it lay the Ruhr, desolate but not yet destroyed, and the long-blockaded North Sea ports. A U. S. enclave at Bremen was established to provide a port of entry for our landlocked zone. For we were to occupy the scenic Bavarian foothills in the south, an area distinguished primarily by its hills and tourist resorts. To the west of us, the French were to occupy the Rhineland south of Remagen to include the industrial Saar. This French zone reached down under the heel of Bavaria to annex the area allotted the French in the occupation of Austria. Like Germany, Austria was to be divided into four parts for the Allied occupation.

Meanwhile, as the result of an agreement reached in London by the European Advisory Commission, Berlin was to be established as a Four Power island in the center of the Russian zone. Thus the capital of the Reich was to be divided equally into four sectors and governed under quadripartite control. When I asked SHAEF how we were to supply U. S. forces in Berlin, I was told that we would be *permitted* to run trains through the Russian zone, 110 miles from the western boundary at Helmstedt to the environs of Berlin. But we were to have no corridor, no assurance, no specific guarantee of passage through the Russian zone. Instead Berlin was to be constituted in trust as a symbol of unity among the Allies. Although I did not dispute the Great Illusion—for I was no less beguiled than the others on the Soviet's friendly postwar intentions—this isolation

of Berlin offended me primarily because it violated one of the fundamental tenets of logistics. In fighting a battle I would never have
assumed responsibility for a sector unless I was certain I could have
supplied it. In the supply of Berlin we were to be totally dependent
upon the good will of the Soviets. And dependence, I learned as
a boy in Missouri, does not make for the very best neighbors.

Five days before Hodges and Simpson closed their trap around

The meeting line on the Elbe lay well inside the prospective Russian zone
of occupation. Although the Western Allies could have driven nearer the
Oder while waiting for the Russians to close to the Elbe, this would have
confronted them with additional problems in vacating the Russian occupation zone.

the Ruhr, Eisenhower radioed Stalin through the U. S. Military Mission in Moscow of his plan to push east with a powerful force in the center to the line of the Elbe. The push was to encompass all three Armies of the 12th Army Group. Meanwhile, Monty's 21st Group on our left was to advance northeast toward the Baltic Sea, cut off the Danish peninsula, and capture the important North Sea German ports. Devers, who had forced the Rhine two days behind Monty against the stiffest resistance of all, was to turn his French and American forces down through Munich toward Austria where the Russians were advancing astride the Danube toward Vienna. By closing off the Alps we would prevent the enemy from retreating into that mountain barrier for a last-ditch stand.

Although Churchill protested Eisenhower's radio to Moscow as an unwarranted intrusion by the military into a political problem, he reserved his angriest vituperation for the plan Eisenhower had proposed. The Prime Minister, according to Eisenhower, was "greatly disappointed and disturbed" that SHAEF had not reinforced Montgomery with American troops and pointed him toward Berlin in a desperate effort to capture that city before the Russians took it.

At the time Eisenhower informed Stalin that he would make his main effort through the middle with the 12th Army Group, Montgomery had just crossed the Rhine and we had only then broken out of Remagen. One hundred and ninety miles lay between Montgomery's Rhine bridgehead and the Elbe. The path we were to take would be even longer, for we were first to encircle the Ruhr. In contrast, Zhukov had massed more than a million men on the banks of the Oder only 30 miles east of Berlin. But even if we were to reach the Elbe before Zhukov crossed the Oder, a 50-mile belt of lowlands separated the Elbe from Berlin. Here the western approach was studded with lakes, crisscrossed with streams, and interdicted with occasional canals. When Eisenhower asked me what I thought it might cost us to break through from the Elbe to Berlin, I estimated 100,000 casualties.

"A pretty stiff price to pay for a prestige objective," I said, "especially when we've got to fall back and let the other fellow take over."

Had Eisenhower even contemplated sending Montgomery ahead to Berlin, he would have had to reinforce that British flank with not less than one American Army. I could see no political advantage accruing from the capture of Berlin that would offset the need for quick destruction of the German army on our front. As soldiers we looked naïvely on this British inclination to complicate the war with political foresight and nonmilitary objectives.

I was eager to clean out the Ruhr and with every division that could be spared from that task push on to the Elbe and Mulde. Once we had closed to that river line, I would spread two of my Armies behind it and turn southeast with the third, down the Danube to link up in Austria with the Red army then nearing Vienna. After having completed that movement we would have cut off the enemy's retreat into his National Redoubt. But if Eisenhower were to divert one of our Armies to Monty as Churchill had proposed for a British push northeast to the Baltic, we would have been forced to write off this Danube offensive. Should the enemy fall back into the Redoubt, we argued, he could greatly prolong the war.

Months before, G-2 had tipped us off to a fantastic enemy plot for the withdrawal of troops into the Austrian Alps where weapons, stores, and even aircraft plants were reported cached for a last-ditch holdout. There the enemy would presumably attempt to keep alive the Nazi myth until the Allies grew tired of occupying the Reich—or until they fell out among themselves.

Troops for the Redoubt, we had been told, were to come primarily from SS units and a swift check of the battle order on both our and the Russian front revealed a suspicious concentration of SS divisions on the southern flanks.

Not until after the campaign ended were we to learn that this Redoubt existed largely in the imaginations of a few fanatic Nazis. It grew into so exaggerated a scheme that I am astonished we could have believed it as innocently as we did. But while it persisted, this legend of the Redoubt was too ominous a threat to be ignored and in consequence it shaped our tactical thinking during the closing weeks of the war.

It was this obsession with the Redoubt that accounted for my gloomy caution on the probable end of the war in Europe. As late as April 24, two days before we joined forces with the Russians, I told a party of Congressmen who had been invited by Eisenhower to view the enemy's death camps that "we may be fighting one month from now and it may even be a year." When a few of them looked alarmed, I told them of our apprehensions on a lingering campaign in the Redoubt.

The Redoubt was finally dismissed as a myth when Lieutenant

General Kurt Ditmar, a German radio commentator known as the "voice of the Wehrmacht," poled across the Elbe in a small boat to surrender to the Ninth Army. When queried by G-2, Ditmar insisted he had not heard of the Redoubt until January, 1945, when he read of it in a Swiss paper. He scoffed at our intelligence reports on elaborate preparations in the Redoubt but conceded an Army might stand there if it wished to continue the fight.

However mistaken our estimate on the Redoubt might have been, this in itself was secondary in our rejection of Churchill's proposal to push on to the Baltic and Berlin. Had the occupation zones not yet been established, I might have agreed that the attack would be politically worth while. But I could see no justification for taking casualties in the capture of a city we would promptly hand over to the Russians. Even prestige could not compensate for those additional heavy losses.

On April 12, as First Army drove into Leipzig, Simpson's Ninth Army, with its 2d Armored Division in front, sped north of the Harz Mountains into which five enemy divisions had withdrawn for a siege. At 8 P.M. on the evening of D plus 309, CC "B" of the 2d Armored Division closed to the banks of the Elbe. I had previously ordered Simpson to snatch a small bridgehead across the Elbe just as soon as he reached its bank. This was not in preparation for an advance on Berlin, as some observers immediately surmised, but only to establish a threat that might draw off German resistance from east of Berlin in front of the Russians. At that time we could probably have pushed on to Berlin had we been willing to take the casualties Berlin would have cost us. Zhukov had not yet crossed the Oder and Berlin now lay almost midway between our forces. However Zhukov's eastern approaches were infinitely more negotiable than the waterlogged path that confronted us in the west.

Simpson was thrown out of his first bridgehead just south of Magdeburg by three German divisions which raced out of Berlin. It was the first time in 30 months of combat that the 2d Armored Division had been thrown back. Farther south, however, a second bridgehead held and there Simpson deepened his foothold to hang on until the end of the war.

On the day Ninth Army troops edged into the environs of Magdeburg itself, I was visiting Simpson in his CP. The phone rang. Big Simp listened for a moment and clamped his hand across the mouth-

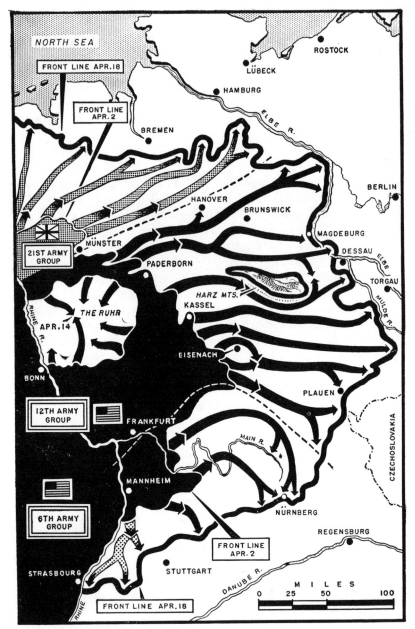

NORTH SEA

FRONT LINE APR.18

FRONT LINE APR. 2

ROSTOCK

LÜBECK

HAMBURG

BREMEN

ELBE R.

BERLIN

HANOVER

BRUNSWICK

MAGDEBURG

21ST ARMY GROUP

MÜNSTER

DESSAU

ELBE

PADERBORN

TORGAU

MULDE R.

THE RUHR

HARZ MTS.

KASSEL

RHINE R.

APR. 14

EISENACH

BONN

PLAUEN

CZECHOSLOVAKIA

12TH ARMY GROUP

FRANKFURT

6TH ARMY GROUP

MANNHEIM

MAIN R.

NÜRNBERG

REGENSBURG

STRASBOURG

STUTTGART

FRONT LINE APR. 2

DANUBE R.

MILES

0   25   50   100

RHINE

FRONT LINE APR.18

Within 16 days after closing the noose around the Ruhr, American forces had driven on to the Elbe and in Simpson's sector had forced a bridgehead to distract the enemy from Berlin. Farther south, Third Army had reached the Czech frontier.

piece. "It looks as though we might get the bridge in Magdeburg. What'll we do if we get it, Brad?"

"Hell's bells," I answered, "we don't want any more bridgeheads on the Elbe. If you get it you'll *have* to throw a battalion across it, I guess. But let's hope the other fellow blows it up before you find you're stuck with it." The existing bridgehead south of that city satisfied our need for a diversion. Another could only cost us extra casualties and trouble.

Thirty minutes later as I was putting on my helmet to leave, the phone rang again. Simpson's bony face split into a broad smile. "No need to worry, Brad," he laughed as he hung up the receiver, "the Krauts just blew it up."

As the war sped into its closing weeks, Eisenhower commuted more regularly between SHAEF and the bombed city of Wiesbaden where we had relocated EAGLE TAC. On April 12 his B-25 slipped into the bombed Luftwaffe base nearby where I joined him for an overnight visit by cub to Patton's and Hodges' CPs.

We flew along the autobahn north to the Third Army headquarters at Hersfield where Patton had moved his CP into a Wehrmacht cantonment. Both lanes of the broad autobahn were crowded with vehicles streaming toward the front while down the grassy center between them a line of refugees straggled toward the rear. Patton was waiting at the airstrip when we landed alongside the road.

Third Army had overrun Ohrdruf, the first of the Nazi death camps, only two days before and George insisted we view it.

"You'll never believe how bastardly these Krauts can be," he said, "until you've seen this pesthole yourself."

The smell of death overwhelmed us even before we passed through the stockade. More than 3,200 naked, emaciated bodies had been flung into shallow graves. Others lay in the streets where they had fallen. Lice crawled over the yellowed skin of their sharp, bony frames. A guard showed us how the blood had congealed in coarse black scabs where the starving prisoners had torn out the entrails of the dead for food. Eisenhower's face whitened into a mask. Patton walked over to a corner and sickened. I was too revolted to speak. For here death had been so fouled by degradation that it both stunned and numbed us. Within a week we were to overrun others and soon the depravity of Buchenwald, Erla, Belsen, and Dachau would shock a world that thought itself inured to the horrors of war.

Glad to be rid of the stench of Ohrdruf, we flew in a line of low-flying cubs to the village of Merkers where three days before the 90th Division had stumbled into an underground cache containing the Reich's last gold reserves. The hiding place was discovered accidentally one evening when an MP accosted two women on the streets shortly after curfew. They explained they had gone to fetch a midwife. To check their story the MP went along. As they walked past the entrance to a salt mine, one of the women gestured and said, "That's where the bullion is hidden." The following day the cache was uncovered. In addition to $100,000,000 in gold bullion, the MP's found three billion *Reichsmarks*. Another $2,000,000 in American greenbacks together with lesser quantities of British, Norwegian, and French currency had been stacked in those dry salt chambers 2,100 feet below the ground.

Eisenhower and I went down in the double-tiered lift with a German workman operating the hoist. The bullion, in 25-pound bars was packed two to a sack and stenciled in black with the imprint of the *Reichsbank*. The custodian explained that these three billion Reichsmarks were the last reserves of that kind in Germany.

"They will be badly needed," he assured me, "to meet the army payroll."

"Tell him," I said to the interpreter, "that I doubt the German army will be meeting payrolls much longer."

In a stack nearby we examined hundreds of crates and boxes, art treasures that had been removed from Berlin for safekeeping.

We joked with Patton on the discovery. "If these were the old freebooting days," I said, "when a soldier kept his loot, you'd be the richest man in the world." Patton only grinned back.

That evening we sat up late with George in the sparsely furnished commandant's house in which he had located his mess. Traffic rumbled past the intersection outside where the Frankfurt autobahn forked toward Hanover and Dresden. Ike was still pale from his visit to Ohrdruf as George poured him a drink.

"I can't understand the mentality that would compel these German people to do a thing like that," Ike said. "Why, our soldiers could never mutilate bodies the way the Germans have."

"Not all the Krauts can stomach it," Patton's deputy chief of staff explained. "In one camp we paraded the townspeople through to let them have a look. The mayor and his wife went home and slashed their wrists."

"Well that's the most encouraging thing I've heard," Ike said slowly. "It may indicate that some of them still have a few sensitivities left."

When news of the gold trove first reached LUCKY, Patton had ordered a censorship stop on the discovery. When a censor passed the story, Patton promptly sacked him. For this he was criticized by the newsmen attached to Third Army. They had not yet been placated when Eisenhower arrived that day.

Patton, however, protested that he was unperturbed by the uproar. "I knew I was right on that one," he exclaimed, spearing a piece of steak.

"Well I'll be damned," Ike snapped, "until you said that, maybe you were. But if you're that positive, then I'm sure you're wrong." George winked at me across the table.

"But why keep it a secret, George," I laughed. "What would you do with all that money?"

George chuckled. Third Army was divided into two schools on the issue, he said. One recommended that the gold be cut up into LUCKY medallions. "One for every sonuvabitch in Third Army—"

The other suggested Third Army hide the loot until peacetime when Congress again cracked down military appropriations. Then whenever funds got particularly tight, the army could dig down into its cave for more money to spend on new weapons.

Ike shook his head, looked at me, and laughed. "He's always got an answer," he said.

It was almost midnight when we turned in. Eisenhower and I had been billeted in adjoining rooms in the commandant's house. Patton walked out to his van which was parked nearby. His watch had stopped and he flicked on the radio to get the time. A voice broke in on the BBC to announce that the President of the United States had died.

George knocked at my door and opened it. I had just climbed in bed.

"Anything wrong?" I asked.

"Better come with me to tell Ike," he said, "the President has died."

We sat up talking in Ike's room until almost two.

At breakfast the following morning George talked moodily of the **failure** of his rescue mission two weeks before when **he dispatched a**

reinforced company of tanks through the enemy line on the Main
to break down the walls of a PW stalag approximately 50 miles to
the German rear. I did not learn of the expedition until it had been
on the road two days. But by then the angry mutterings of division
and corps had traveled the grapevine to Army Group. Out of them
came the story of as brash a venture as Patton dared during the
entire war. It was a story that began as a wild goose chase and
ended in tragedy.

It started on the evening of March 26 when a task force assembled
from the 4th Armored Division, broke out of the Main river bridgehead south of Aschaffenburg to head for the town of Hammelburg,
where G-2 had located a stalag crowded with American PWs. The
column consisted of 50 vehicles including 19 tanks and assault guns.
Its 293 officers and men were commanded by Captain Abraham
Baum, a husky 24-year-old tanker from the Bronx. Major Alexander
C. Stiller, Patton's swashbuckling aide and tank sergeant from
World War I, went along for the ride. From the instant Baum's force
crashed into the village of Schweinheim, beyond the Main, he ran a
gauntlet of enemy fire. Forty-eight hours later, on the afternoon of
March 28, Baum's tanks rammed through the stockade at Hammelburg with a force now reduced to a third of its starting strength.
While the jubilant PWs scurried into the hills, Baum assembled his
sleepless force for the homeward journey. But by now the enemy
had reorganized his rear and he closed in with Tiger tanks to
destroy the raiders. At 9 A.M. on the morning of March 29, after
having exhausted his gasoline and ammunition, the wounded captain surrendered the handful of survivors still with him.

The escapade might easily have been overlooked had not Patton's
son-in-law been a prisoner in that stalag. Although Patton assured
me he did not learn of his son's-in-law incarceration until nine days
after the raid, he was worried for fear the newsmen might draw
their own implications. In his journal George afterward admitted
the folly of this mission when he said, "I can say this—that throughout the campaign in Europe, I know of no error I made except that
of failing to send a combat command to take Hammelburg." A
combat command might have succeeded but it would have meant a
costly diversion from the Third Army drive north to Kassel. His
original mistake had been made in ordering the raid. Certainly had
George consulted me on the mission, I would have forbidden him to

stage it. But while I deplored the impetuousness that had prompted Patton, I did not rebuke him for it. Failure itself was George's own worst reprimand.

With Ninth Army on the Elbe, the First on the Mulde, and the Ruhr shrinking under the pressure of three corps, I was anxious to push southeast, rout the enemy out of Bavaria, and clear the U. S. zone of occupation to the Austrian frontier. From there we would push on down the Danube to head east toward Vienna and cut off the main enemy force from withdrawal into the Redoubt. By now I was especially anxious to occupy all of the U. S. zone of occupation, for though we would be forced by agreement to quit the Russian zone, we had no such assurance that the Red army would get out as willingly if they occupied ours. Rather than make a test of Russian compliance with the zonal agreement, we would sweep up our own U. S. sector without help from the Red army.

Originally, I had told Hodges I would prefer to have First Army close out the war with that final offensive down the Danube. But because the switch-over would have entailed too onerous a rerouting of supply, I diverted the mission to Patton and reinforced his Third Army with First Army divisions as they were drawn out of the Ruhr. On April 16, Devers and Patch joined us in Wiesbaden to work out a dual offensive in which the Third and Seventh Armies would advance side by side. Patch was none too happy at the prospect of teaming up with Patton for he feared his Seventh Army would be diverted into a narrow sector while Patton expanded his Third Army front. The Seventh had assaulted the Rhine in a severely contested crossing and had now advanced to within range of Hitler's colossal stadium in Nürnberg. Patch had fought hard for this sector and he was understandably reluctant to share it.

The following day, as the Russians swarmed across the Oder in their last big offensive of the war, we issued orders for the Danubian offensive. First and Ninth Armies were to spread defensively across our middle front from the Czech border to where the U. S. sector adjoined that of the British on the Elbe. Seventh Army was to advance in the direction of Munich while Patton attacked down the Danube. By now the Red army had overrun Vienna and was pushing west to join forces with us at Linz as though anxious to prevent us from advancing any farther than necessary into Austria.

For almost two weeks we loitered on the Elbe and Mulde awaiting the coming of the Russians. Meanwhile the Army commanders
had grown progressively uneasy over the likelihood of an incident
should the Russian insist on advancing west of the Elbe to occupy
the remainder of his Soviet zone. Although we had no knowledge
of what the Soviet orders might be, I had instructed my Army commanders to hold their advanced positions until we could form an
orderly withdrawal back into the U. S. occupation zone. In the
event the Red army insisted on advancing, however, Army commanders were authorized to negotiate directly with the Soviet
forces on their front and work out a withdrawal.

"Let's put it this way," I told Simpson. "We would prefer to hold
our present line until we can arrange an orderly change-over. But if
the Russian insists on going forward to his line of occupation, we're
not going to start any trouble. Work it out as best you can and
allow him to." In as tense a meeting as the one we anticipated I was
not going to risk an explosion that might bring on a sequel to the
war.

It was not until July 1 that the Russians notified me they would
exercise their occupation rights beyond the Elbe. We were told at
three that afternoon the Red army would move in at daybreak the
following morning.

"You can tell those birds," I instructed our liaison officer, "to keep
their shirts on. We'll require at least 24 hours to pick up our stuff."
The Russian agreed but as we pulled back, he followed closely on
our heels.

By April 14, the British had closed to the Elbe as far north as
Hamburg and the French Army of de Lattre de Tassigny crashed
across the Danube to the Swiss border. Tens of thousands of German refugees streamed tearfully toward our U. S. lines on the Elbe
hoping to escape the Russians. We turned them back. And in the
rear areas G-5 grappled with the fearsome task of rounding up the
more than one million DPs then wandering aimlessly through the
countryside. Initially we had attempted to herd the Balts and Poles
eastward into the zone to be occupied by the Soviets that they
might be more easily repatriated by the Red army. But we were
astonished to find they feared the Russians even more than the Nazis
and they continued to flee westward.

The PW tally had now outrun our ability to keep daily count. In
one cantonment alone we had caged 160,000. The feeding of these

PWs and DPs exerted an additional strain upon our overburdened supply lines and we instructed Army commanders not to accept prisoners streaming westward from the Russians. When a few days later the 11th Panzer Division in Czechoslovakia sent word that it wished to surrender to U. S. forces, we invited them to come in "but only if you bring your own kitchens and can take care of yourselves."

By now our vigil on the Elbe had passed its twelfth day without a sign from the inscrutable Russian. Zhukov was reported to have lunged into Berlin where Hitler was said to have barricaded himself near the Chancellery. And Konev was reported to have crossed the Oder on his advance toward the Elbe. These reports, however, were both fragmentary and unofficial. Even now we had not as yet established direct liaison with the Reds. And though our tank radios crackled with the overlap of Red army communications and air recce spotted the Soviet wagon trains, no one on the ground had as yet sighted a Red Star.

To establish the initial contact Hodges extended his 69th Division on a narrow salient from the Mulde to the Elbe, there to await a link-up on the Elbe's left bank. But as a precautionary measure against accidental air bombing by our planes or those of the Russians, those troops were instructed to conceal themselves from all observation.

P&PW telephoned Wiesbaden on the morning of April 24 to report that a Three Power statement would be issued at noon, Washington time, that day announcing the link-up. "But how the devil can they?" I said. "We haven't made contact yet."

"Oh—" a quiet voice answered.

That afternoon a senatorial delegation stopped off at EAGLE TAC on a swift tour of the ETO.

"How long is your war going to last over here?" one of them wanted to know. I looked up in surprise.

"We need farm machinery in the midwest," he added, "and we're told the priorities are being held up because of your need for steel. How long's this thing going to go on?"

I clenched my teeth until I could compose a civil reply.

The following day the senators were followed by a planeload of touring editors from the United States. They had stopped off at Wiesbaden for a briefing there before continuing on to Luxembourg after inspecting the horror camps.

"Are you ahead or behind schedule?" one of them asked when I pointed to our line on the Elbe.

"Let me put it this way—" I answered, looking back over the 20-foot mapboard to the tip of Normandy on the other end, "if on June 6, one year ago, you had offered me this line as of today I would have taken it and asked no questions."

After dinner that evening I returned for an evening's work in my trailer. It was shortly after dark when Hodges telephoned from his CP at Marburg on the banks of the Lahn River. At 4:10 on the warm afternoon of April 25, a patrol from First Army had established contact with the vanguard of Marshal Konev's First Ukrainian Army Group in the almost empty city of Torgau on the Elbe river.

"Thanks, Courtney," I said, "thanks again for calling. We've been waiting a long time. The Russians certainly took their own sweet time in coming those 75 miles from the Oder."

I took a coke from the cabinet under the bench in my van and circled Torgau on the large wall map. Someone had crayoned a huge broken swastika over the city of Berlin.

After a speedy and skillful regrouping, Patton had jumped off on April 22 in his drive to cut off the Redoubt. Within two days he had crossed the Austrian frontier. From there he plunged on down the Danube toward Linz, almost halfway to Vienna.

Meanwhile the British had been badgering Eisenhower for the attachment of an American corps to Monty's forces on the north for his push beyond the Elbe. Montgomery had insisted he must be reinforced if he was to extend his line to the Baltic and block off Denmark from the Soviets. When Zhukov mounted his Berlin offensive, the British became more vehement in their plea. For unless Monty soon gained the Baltic, they argued, we would awaken to find the Red army in Denmark and the Soviet on the North Sea.

Now that Patton's rapid advance down the Danube had dispelled the likelihood of resistance in the Redoubt, we acceded to Monty's request. Ridgway's XVIII Airborne Corps was shuffled north to 21st Group and on April 29 it struck across the Elbe south of Hamburg toward the Baltic port of Lübeck to save Denmark for the West.

By April 30 the enemy was close to collapse. In Italy Clark's 15th Army Group had wrenched itself free from the Po River line to plunge on to the shores of Lake Como. In Holland Montgomery's

Canadians pushed on to the dikes on the North Sea to isolate Blaskowitz's forces. And in Berlin Zhukov's tommy gunners fought from door to door in the rubble of that doomed city toward the Chancellery where Hitler had barricaded himself in a bomb shelter under the garden.

Germany had now been divided into three shrinking pockets, and air gave up its strategic bombing for the lack of remunerative targets. When Eisenhower telephoned me for a situation report at our new TAC CP in Bad Wildungen, I suggested he have a plane prepared to fly us to our thirtieth class reunion at West Point the first week in June. "It looks now as though we're going to make it," I said. The week before I had been less certain.

To Bad Wildungen's shabby Fürstenhof Hotel where an odor of antiseptic still clung to the rooms that had been used by the Germans as hospital wards, the news of Hitler's death came on the evening of May 2 from Radio Hamburg with three rolls of muffled drums. Six months before that announcement would have called for wild celebration. Now it passed almost unnoticed. For on the eve of Germany's collapse, the death of Hitler had been overshadowed by the greater tragedy of the nation whose destruction he had wrought. Grand Admiral Doenitz, the submariner whose U-boats had sighted victory in their periscopes only three years before, had been named Hitler's successor. He went on the air with a pretentious pledge to continue the war against the Bolsheviks. Himmler's whereabouts were undisclosed although intelligence reported peace feelers attributed to him. When Ditmar, who was then being held at Group for interrogation, was told of Himmler's bid for peace, he dismissed it scornfully. "Himmler," he declared, "could command no following whatsoever in the German army." When told that Himmler was reported first to have announced the death of Hitler, Ditmar smiled wryly. "Herr Himmler," he said, "has a talent for being able to forecast deaths."

Although Third Army had crowded up to the Czech border two weeks before, it was not until 7:30 P.M. on the evening of May 4 that Eisenhower telephoned me permission to cross that border. For weeks Third Army had been begging the mission.

"Why—" I asked Patton, "why does everyone in Third Army want to liberate the Czechs?"

George grinned. "On to Czechoslovakia," he whooped, "—and

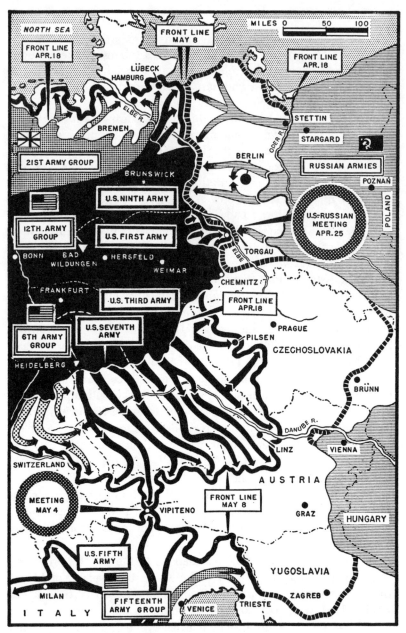

While the U. S. First and Ninth Armies held fast in position after reaching the Elbe, Montgomery (with the aid of a U. S. corps) pushed on northeast to the Baltic Sea to prevent Russian intrusion into the British sector. When SHAEF lifted the stop line that had halted Third Army on the Czech frontier, Patton plunged on to liberate Pilsen but was ordered to halt short of Prague.

fraternization! How in hell can you stop an army with a battle cry like that?"

Because Czechoslovakia had already been earmarked for liberation by the Red army, we were not to advance beyond Pilsen, a few miles inside the border. Patton objected to the stop line, insisting that he could go all the way on to Prague. Indeed had SHAEF remanded its order, he could probably have been in Wenzel Square within 24 hours. But when Eisenhower notified the Soviet command that our troops would move on to Prague "if the situation required," the latter replied that we "should not advance beyond the Budejovice-Pilsen-Karlsbad line."

Soon after our juncture with the Soviets at Torgau, Marshal Konev invited both the EAGLE TAC and Ninth Air Force staffs to a banquet at his Ukrainian Army Group CP on the farther side of the Elbe. In this first flush of companionship with their Western Allies, the Soviets welcomed us with boisterous good humor. For this was the short-lived interlude of good will before the Kremlin put an abrupt end to associations with the West. Russian banqueting on the Elbe had started at division and as the ritual spread, each echelon of command strained to surpass the one beneath it in the variety of its food and drink.

Wary of the vodka victory toasts that had already felled several previous U. S. staffs, including part of First Army, I prepared for our trip on May 5 with a heavy breakfast of buttered wheat cakes and a tumbler of canned milk. Before leaving, Dudley issued each of us a small bottle of mineral oil.

"Swallow this on the way," he said, "and you can drink anything they put before you."

It was a sodden gray day when we drove out to the wrecked airdrome at nearby Fritzlar for the flight to Leipzig in two C-47's.

I was unhappy over the need for making the trip and the weather did not improve my disposition.

Vandenberg scowled at the sky. "How's Leipzig?" he asked the pilot.

"Closing in fast, sir."

"What's your out if you can't get in?"

"We'll turn around and go to Paris."

"What the devil, if there's a chance of getting to Paris as an alternate field, we might as well start off toward the Russians," I said. "I don't want to have to go through this business again."

"Just like a doughboy," Van smiled, "he's too damned dumb to know when it's not safe to get off the ground."

Collins met us at Leipzig and convoyed us through the corridor to Torgau. He had made the trip himself almost a week before and while en route to the Soviet lines was asked if he would object to seeing a division commander.

"Of course not," he answered and the column turned off to where a Soviet division occupied a position facing us.

The division commander was apologetic. "May I ask you a question?" he said.

"Go ahead," Collins replied.

"Are your people digging in opposite us?"

"Digging in?" Collins looked startled, "why of course not. After all, we're Allies, you know."

The Red commander called for a staff officer. "Cancel that order to dig in," he said. "We'll stay right where we are."

On the river front of the desolate city of Torgau where a bombed railroad bridge slumped across the Elbe, a company of Russian officers waited to convoy us to Konev. A crude bridge had been thrown across the river and teamsters were snaking timber from the nearby forests to repair the railroad span. A crudely fashioned pile driver chugged in the middle of the stream. Except for the steam engine on that pile driver, Russian methods had not changed since the time Peter the Great of Russia had massed his armies at Torgau almost 200 years before to march with the Austrians against Frederick the Great.

On the far bank of the Elbe, red banners had been draped across the road with brightly lettered signs of welcome. Three huge lithographs of Roosevelt, Churchill, and Stalin decorated a roadside building. The towns and villages through which we sped had been mysteriously cleared of Germans, and only once during the 20-mile drive did a frightened face look out from behind a shuttered window. Russians in grimy uniforms stared curiously at our American cars as we sped past their bivouacs. On the intersections stocky Russian girls in boots and skirts waved us on with elaborate hand signals reminiscent of those employed by British MP's.

A horse-drawn Soviet column passed us moving up to the Elbe. Its column commander rode in a surrey, handling the reins of his team through a black weather curtain similar to those I remembered as a boy in Missouri. Behind him a train of heavy farm wagons carried his troops and equipment. Here and there a kerchiefed head showed among the sleeping soldiers.

Konev was waiting with his staff outside the gloomy villa he had commandeered for a CP. A powerfully built man with a huge bald head, Konev took me first to his office for a moment of private conversation through our interpreters. I gave him a map I had prepared for the occasion, showing the disposition of every U. S. division across his group front. The marshal started in surprise but did not volunteer to show me his own dispositions. Had he wanted to, he would probably have had to ask permission from the Kremlin. American lieutenants were delegated greater authority on the Elbe than were Russian division commanders.

Pointing to Czechoslovakia on the map I had given him, Konev asked how far we intended to go. He frowned as the interpreter translated his query.

"Only to Pilsen," I told him, "see it's marked here with a line. We had to go in to protect our flank on the Danube."

Konev replied with the trace of a smile. He hoped we would go no farther.

The banquet table had been banked lavishly with fresh caviar, veal, beef, cucumbers, black bread, and butter. A row of wine bottles filled the center. Vodka decanters were spread liberally about for the toasts which started as soon as we sat down. Konev arose and lifted his glass. "To Stalin, Churchill, and Roosevelt—" he said, not yet having learned of Truman's succession.

After seating himself Konev shifted to a smaller glass which he filled not with vodka but with white wine.

"The marshal has stomach trouble," his interpreter explained. "He can no longer drink vodka." I smiled and reached for the wine myself, relieved to know there would be no need for the mineral oil I had already swallowed.

After dinner Konev led us into the great hall of his house. A chorus of Red army soldiers broke into the "Star-Spangled Banner" and their resonant voices filled the room. Konev explained that the chorus had memorized the anthem without knowing a word of English. Then to the accompaniment of a dozen balalaikas, a ballet troupe danced into the room.

"Why, that's splendid," I exclaimed.

Konev shrugged his shoulders. "Just a few girls," he explained, "from the Red army."

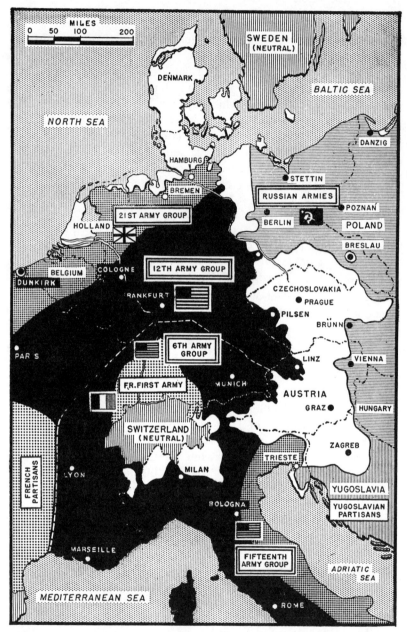

When the war ended at midnight, May 8–9, German forces had been split into northern and southern pockets. Although the Western Allies had closed everywhere to their stop line, the Soviets had not yet liberated Prague nor had they overrun Austria.

Two weeks later when Konev repaid our call with one to our CP, he was enthralled with the violin virtuosity of a thin khaki-clad man.

"Magnificent," the marshal cried in delight.

"Oh that," I said. "Nothing, nothing at all. Just one of our American soldiers."

We had pirated the violinist from Special Services in Paris for the day. His name was Jascha Heifetz.

As we left Konev's villa that afternoon, the marshal accompanied me into the garden. An orderly led out a Don Caucasus stallion whose saddle blanket bore a Red army star. Konev handed me the bridle and a handsomely carved Russian pistol. Anticipating this exchange of gifts, I had carried along in the rear of the *Mary Q* a new jeep just unloaded from Antwerp. Across the cowling we had painted this inscription in both English and Russian: "To the Commander of the First Ukrainian Army Group from Soldiers of the 1st, 3rd, 9th and 15th American Armies." A holster was affixed to the jeep with a brightly polished new carbine. And we stuffed the tool compartment with American cigarettes.

"I'll probably get stuck by the comptroller and have to pay for this thing 20 years after the war," I told Hansen when he ordered the jeep from Antwerp, "but what the dickens, I don't suppose we can go up empty-handed."

While Alexander accepted the surrender of Kesselring's forces in Italy and Montgomery denied terms to Admiral Hans Friedeburg on the Luneberg Heath, we continued to press on into Austria, killing those Germans who still resisted, capturing those who had given up.

Reports reached us of a surrender mission that was rumored en route to SHAEF but Eisenhower had not called to confirm them. On May 6, I went to bed shortly before midnight after writing a letter home to my wife.

It was not yet 4 A.M. when the telephone rang on my bedside table in the Fürstenhof Hotel. I sat up and switched on a lamp. It was Eisenhower calling from Reims.

"Brad," he said, "it's all over. A TWX is on the way."

Jodl had signed for the German army; Friedeburg for the navy. The surrender had taken place at 2:41 that morning in the schoolhouse SHAEF had requisitioned near the marshaling yards of Reims.

I buzzed the operator for LUCKY SIX and roused Patton from his trailer in Regensberg. "Ike just called me, George. The Germans have surrendered. It takes effect at midnight, May 8. We're to hold in place everywhere up and down the line. There's no sense in taking any more casualties now."

Hodges was asleep in the ornate home he had requisitioned in Weimar. Simpson occupied the commandant's quarters of a Luftwaffe headquarters at Brunswick. I repeated the message to both. By the time I had reached Gerow, then in bed with a cold near Bonn, it was almost 6:30. I could hear the mess kits rattling in the chow line outside the hotel. I crawled out of bed and dressed.

A canvas map case lay under my helmet with its four silver stars. Only five years before on May 7, as a lieutenant colonel in civilian clothes, I had ridden a bus down Connecticut Avenue to my desk in the old Munitions Building.

I opened the mapboard and smoothed out the tabs of the 43 U. S. divisions now under my command. They stretched across a 640-mile front of the 12th Army Group.

With a china-marking pencil, I wrote in the new date: D plus 335.

I walked to the window and ripped open the blackout blinds. Outside the sun was climbing into the sky. The war in Europe had ended.

Appendix

Glossary

Index

Appendix

ORDER OF BATTLE

12th ARMY GROUP
May 7, 1945

NINTH ARMY	Lieutenant General William H. Simpson
XIII Corps	Major General Alvan C. Gillem, Jr.
35th Infantry Division .	Major General Paul W. Baade
84th Infantry Division .	Major General Alexander R. Bolling
102d Infantry Division .	Major General Frank A. Keating
XVI Corps	Major General John B. Anderson
29th Infantry Division .	Major General Charles H. Gerhardt
75th Infantry Division .	Major General Fay B. Prickett
	August, 43 – January, 45
	Major General Ray E. Porter
	January, 45 – June, 45
79th Infantry Division .	Major General Ira T. Wyche
95th Infantry Division .	Major General Harry L. Twaddle
XIX Corps	Major General Charles H. Corlett
	March, 44 – October, 44
	Major General Raymond S. McLain
	October, 44 – May, 45
2d Armored Division .	Major General Edward H. Brooks
	April, 44 – September, 44
	Major General Ernest N. Harmon
	September, 44 – January, 45

	Major General Isaac D. White
	January, 45 – August, 45
8th Armored Division .	Major General Wm. M. Grimes
	April, 42 – September, 44
	Major General John M. Devine
	October, 44 – August, 45
30th Infantry Division .	Major General Leland S. Hobbs
83rd Infantry Division .	Major General Robert C. Macon

FIRST ARMY   .   .   .   General Omar N. Bradley
                            October, 43 – July, 44
                            General Courtney H. Hodges
                            August, 44 –

78th Infantry Division .	Major General Edwin P. Parker, Jr.
VII Corps	Lieutenant General J. Lawton Collins
3rd Armored Division .	Major General Leroy H. Watson
	August, 42 – August, 44
	Major General Maurice Rose
	August, 44 – March, 45
	Brigadier General Doyle O. Hickey
	March, 45 – June, 45
9th Infantry Division .	Major General Manton S. Eddy
	August, 42 – August, 44
	Major General L. A. Craig
	August, 44 – May, 45
69th Infantry Division .	Major General Charles L. Bolte
	May, 43 – September, 44
	Major General Emil F. Reinhardt
	September, 44 – August, 45
104th Infantry Division	Major General Terry M. Allen
VIII Corps	Major General Troy H. Middleton
6th Armored Division .	Major General Robert W. Grow
76th Infantry Division .	Major General William R. Schmidt
87th Infantry Division .	Major General Frank L. Culin, Jr.
89th Infantry Division .	Major General Thomas D. Finley

THIRD ARMY   .   .   .   General George S. Patton, Jr.

4th Infantry Division .	Major General Raymond O. Barton
	July, 42 – December, 44
	Major General Harold W. Blakeley
	December, 44 – October, 45
70th Infantry Division .	Major General John E. Dahlquist
	June, 43 – July, 44

	Major General Allison J. Barnett July, 44 – July, 45
III Corps	Major General John Millikin October, 43 – March, 45
	Major General James A. Van Fleet March, 45 – February, 46
14th Armored Division .	Major General Vernon E. Prichard November, 42 – July, 44
	Major General Albert C. Smith July, 44 –
99th Infantry Division .	Major General Walter E. Lauer
V Corps	Major General Leonard T. Gerow July, 43 – January, 45
	Major General Clarence R. Huebner January, 45 – September, 45
9th Armored Division .	Major General John W. Leonard
16th Armored Division .	Major General Douglass T. Greene July, 43 – August, 44
	Brigadier General John L. Pierce September, 44 –
1st Infantry Division .	Major General Clarence R. Huebner July, 43 – December, 44
	Major General Clift Andrus December, 44 –
2d Infantry Division .	Major General Walter M. Robertson May, 42 –
97th Infantry Division .	Brigadier General Milton B. Halsey
XII Corps	Major General Gilbert R. Cook October, 43 – August, 44
	Major General Manton S. Eddy August, 44 – April, 45
	Major General Stafford LeRoy Irwin April, 45 –
4th Armored Division .	Major General John S. Wood May, 42 – December, 44
	Major General Hugh J. Gaffey December, 44 – March, 45
	Major General William M. Hoge March, 45 –
11th Armored Division .	Brigadier General Charles S. Kilburn March, 44 – March, 45
	Major General Holmes E. Dager March, 45 –

5th Infantry Division .	Major General Stafford L. Irwin June, 43 – April, 45 Major General Albert E. Brown April, 45 –
26th Infantry Division .	Major General Willard S. Paul
90th Infantry Division .	Brigadier General Jay W. MacKelvie January, 44 – July, 44 Major General Eugene M. Landrum July, 44 – August, 44 Major General Raymond S. McLain August, 44 – October, 44 Major General James A. Van Fleet October, 44 – February, 45 Major General Lowell W. Rooks February, 45 – March, 45 Major General Herbert L. Earnest March, 45 –
XX Corps	Lieutenant General Walton H. Walker
13th Armored Division .	Major General John B. Wogan October, 42 – April, 45 Major General John Millikin April, 45 –
65th Infantry Division .	Major General Stanley E. Reinhart
71st Infantry Division .	Brigadier General Robert L. Spragins July, 43 – October, 44 Major General Eugene M. Landrum October, 44 – November, 44 Major General Willard G. Wyman November, 44 –
80th Infantry Division .	Major General Horace L. McBride
FIFTEENTH ARMY . .	Lieutenant General Leonard T. Gerow
66th Infantry Division .	Major General Herman F. Kramer
106th Infantry Division	Major General Alan W. Jones March, 43 – November, 44 Brigadier General Herbert T. Perrain December, 44 – January, 45 Major General Donald A. Stroh February, 45 –
XXII Corps	Major General Henry Terrell, Jr. January, 44 – November, 44 Vacant November, 44 – January, 45

	Major General Ernest N. Harmon
	January, 45 –
17th Airborne Division .	Major General William M. Miley
94th Infantry Division .	Major General Harry J. Malony
XXIII Corps	Major General Louis A. Craig
	January, 44 – July, 44
	Vacant August, 44 – September, 44
	Major General James I. Muir
	September, 44 – November, 44
	Vacant December, 44 – January, 45
	Major General James A. Van Fleet
	February, 45 – March, 45
	Major General Hugh J. Gaffey
	March, 45 –
28th Infantry Division .	Major General Lloyd Brown
	January, 43 – July, 44
	Brigadier General James E. Wharton
	July, 44 – August 12, 44
	Major General Norman D. Cota
	August, 44 –
XVIII Corps (Airborne) .	Major General Matthew B. Ridgway
(*Attached to 21st Army Group*)	
5th Armored Division .	Major General Lunsford E. Oliver
7th Armored Division .	Major General Lindsay M. Silvester
	March, 42 – November, 44
	Major General Robert W. Hasbrouck
	November, 44 –
82d Airborne Division .	Major General Matthew B. Ridgway
	June, 42 – August, 44
	Major General James M. Gavin
	August, 44 –
8th Infantry Division .	Major General William C. MacMahon
	February, 43 – July, 44
	Major General Donald A. Stroh
	July, 44 – December, 44
	Major General William G. Weaver
	December, 44 – February, 45
	Major General Bryant E. Moore
	February, 45 –

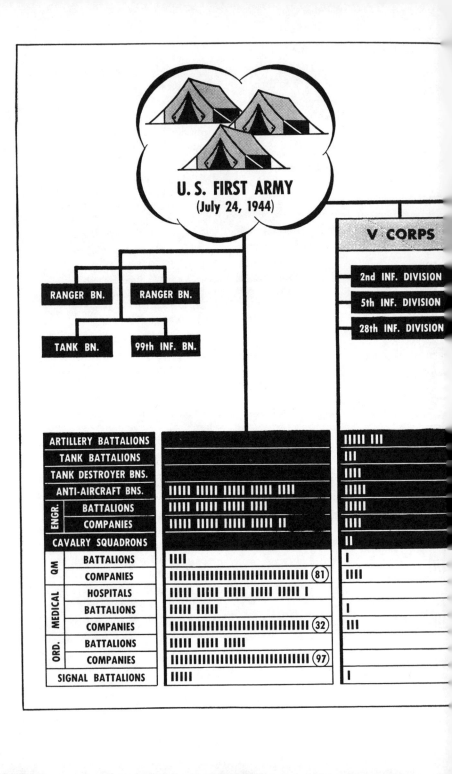

U.S. FIRST ARMY
(July 24, 1944)

RANGER BN.

RANGER BN.

TANK BN.

99th INF. BN.

V CORPS

2nd INF. DIVISION

5th INF. DIVISION

28th INF. DIVISION

			V CORPS
ARTILLERY BATTALIONS			IIIII III
TANK BATTALIONS			III
TANK DESTROYER BNS.			IIII
ANTI-AIRCRAFT BNS.		IIIII IIIII IIIII IIIII IIII	IIIII
ENGR.	BATTALIONS	IIIII IIIII IIIII IIII	IIIII
	COMPANIES	IIIII IIIII IIIII IIIII II	IIII
CAVALRY SQUADRONS			II
QM	BATTALIONS	IIII	I
	COMPANIES	IIIIIIIIIIIIIIIIIIIIIIIIIIIIIIIIIIIIIII (81)	IIII
MEDICAL	HOSPITALS	IIIII IIIII IIIII IIIII IIIII I	
	BATTALIONS	IIIII IIIII	I
	COMPANIES	IIIIIIIIIIIIIIIIIIIIIIIIIIIIIIIIII (32)	III
ORD.	BATTALIONS	IIIII IIIII IIIII	
	COMPANIES	IIIIIIIIIIIIIIIIIIIIIIIIIIIIIIIIIII (97)	
SIGNAL BATTALIONS		IIIII	I

ORGANIZATION OF A U. S. FIELD ARMY

SHOWING MAJOR COMBAT AND SUPPORT ELEMENTS

| HEADQUARTERS ELEMENTS | COMBAT ELEMENTS | SUPPORT ELEMENTS |

 **VII CORPS**

 VIII CORPS

XIX CORPS

VII CORPS	VIII CORPS	XIX CORPS
1st INF. DIVISION	8th INF DIVISION	29th INF DIVISION
4th INF. DIVISION	79th INF DIVISION	35th INF DIVISION
9th INF. DIVISION	83rd INF DIVISION	
30th INF. DIVISION	90th INF DIVISION	
2nd ARMD. DIVISION	4th ARMD. DIVISION	
3rd ARMD. DIVISION		

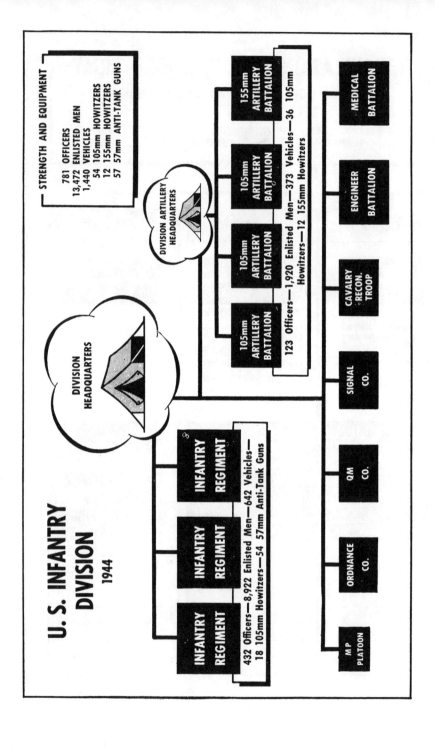

U. S. INFANTRY DIVISION
1944

STRENGTH AND EQUIPMENT

781 OFFICERS
13,472 ENLISTED MEN
1,440 VEHICLES
  54 105mm HOWITZERS
  12 155mm HOWITZERS
  57 57mm ANTI-TANK GUNS

DIVISION HEADQUARTERS

DIVISION ARTILLERY HEADQUARTERS

INFANTRY REGIMENT

INFANTRY REGIMENT

INFANTRY REGIMENT

432 Officers—8,922 Enlisted Men—642 Vehicles—
18 105mm Howitzers—54 57mm Anti-Tank Guns

105mm ARTILLERY BATTALION

105mm ARTILLERY BATTALION

105mm ARTILLERY BATTALION

155mm ARTILLERY BATTALION

123 Officers—1,920 Enlisted Men—373 Vehicles—36 105mm
Howitzers—12 155mm Howitzers

MP PLATOON

ORDNANCE CO.

QM CO.

SIGNAL CO.

CAVALRY RECON. TROOP

ENGINEER BATTALION

MEDICAL BATTALION

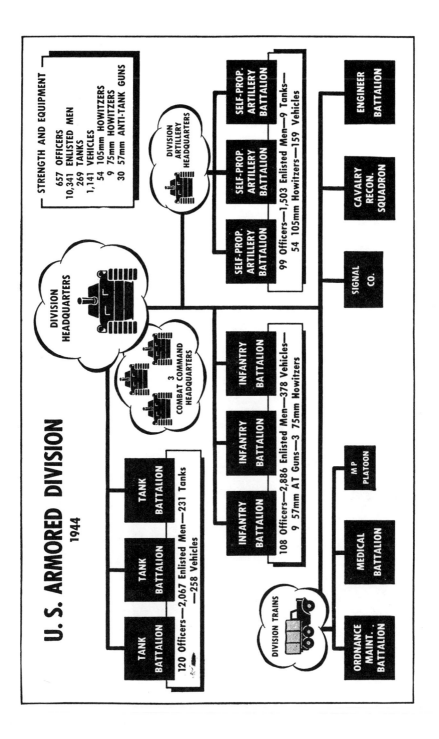

U. S. ARMORED DIVISION
1944

STRENGTH AND EQUIPMENT

657	OFFICERS
10,341	ENLISTED MEN
269	TANKS
1,141	VEHICLES
54	105mm HOWITZERS
9	75mm HOWITZERS
30	57mm ANTI-TANK GUNS

DIVISION HEADQUARTERS

COMBAT COMMAND HEADQUARTERS

DIVISION ARTILLERY HEADQUARTERS

TANK BATTALION   **TANK BATTALION**   **TANK BATTALION**

120 Officers—2,067 Enlisted Men—231 Tanks—258 Vehicles

INFANTRY BATTALION   **INFANTRY BATTALION**   **INFANTRY BATTALION**

108 Officers—2,886 Enlisted Men—378 Vehicles—9 57mm AT Guns—3 75mm Howitzers

SELF-PROP. ARTILLERY BATTALION   **SELF-PROP. ARTILLERY BATTALION**   **SELF-PROP. ARTILLERY BATTALION**

99 Officers—1,503 Enlisted Men—9 Tanks—54 105mm Howitzers—159 Vehicles

ENGINEER BATTALION

CAVALRY RECON. SQUADRON

SIGNAL CO.

MP PLATOON

MEDICAL BATTALION

ORDNANCE MAINT. BATTALION

DIVISION TRAINS

PRINCIPAL PERSONS

Alexander, General Sir Harold (later Field Marshal the Viscount Alexander of Tunis)
Commander-in-Chief, 18th Army Group, Tunisia; 15th Army Group, Sicily, Italy; later, Supreme Allied Commander, Mediterranean Theater of Operations.

Allen, Major General Leven C.
Chief of Staff, U. S. 12th Army Group.

Allen, Major General Terry de la Mesa
Commanding General, 1st Infantry Division, Tunisia, Sicily; later, Commanding General, 104th Infantry Division, Europe.

Anderson, General Sir Kenneth A.
Commander-in-Chief, British First Army, Tunisia.

Brereton, Lieutenant General Lewis H.
Commander, U. S. Ninth Tactical Air Force, Europe; later, Commander, First Allied Airborne Army.

Bridge, Captain Lewis D. (later Lieutenant Colonel)
Aide to General Bradley, Tunisia, Sicily, Europe.

Bull, Major General Harold R.
Special Assistant to General Eisenhower, Tunisia; Assistant Chief of Staff, G-3, SHAEF, Europe.

Choltitz, General Dietrich, von — German Military Commander, Paris.

Clark, Lieutenant General Mark W. (later General) — Commander, U. S. Fifth Army, North Africa, Italy; later, Commander, 15th Army Group, Italy.

Collins, Major General J. Lawton (later Lieutenant General) — Commanding General, U. S. VII Corps, Europe.

Coningham, Air Marshal Sir Arthur — Commander, Tactical Air Force, Tunisia, Sicily; Commander-in-Chief, Second Tactical Air Force, Europe.

Crerar, General Henry D. G. — Commander-in-Chief, Canadian First Army, Europe.

Dempsey, Lieutenant General Sir Miles C. — Commander, British XIII Corps, Tunisia, Sicily; Commander-in-Chief, British Second Army, Europe.

Devers, Lieutenant General Jacob L. (later General) — Commanding General, European Theater of Operations; later, Commander, U. S. 6th Army Group, Europe.

Dickson, Colonel Benjamin A. — Assistant Chief of Staff for Intelligence, U. S. II Corps, Tunisia, Sicily; later, U. S. First Army, Europe.

Dietrich, General Sepp — German Commander, Sixth SS Panzer Army.

Dudley, Sergeant Richard M. (later Lieutenant) — Mess Sergeant; later, aide to General Bradley, Europe.

Eddy, Major General Manton S. (later Lieutenant General) — Commanding General, 9th Infantry Division, Tunisia, Sicily, Europe; later, Commanding General, U. S. XII Corps, Europe.

Eisenhower, General Dwight D. (later General of the Army) — Commander-in-Chief, AFHQ, Tunisia, Sicily; Supreme Commander, Allied Expeditionary Forces, Europe.

Flint, Colonel Harry A.	Commanding Officer, 39th Infantry Regiment, 9th Infantry Division, Sicily, Europe.
Fredendall, Major General Lloyd R.	Commanding General, U. S. II Corps, Tunisia.
Gaffey, Major General Hugh J.	Chief of Staff, U. S. II Corps, Southern Tunisia; Commanding General, 2d Armored Division, Sicily; Chief of Staff, U. S. Third Army, Europe; Commanding General, 4th Armored Division, Europe; Commanding General, U. S. XXIII Corps, Europe.
Gerow, Major General Leonard T. (later Lieutenant General)	Commanding General, U. S. V Corps, Europe; Commander, U. S. Fifteenth Army, Europe.
De Guingand, Major General Sir Francis	Chief of Staff, British Eighth Army, Sicily; Chief of Staff, British 21st Army Group, Europe.
Haislip, Major General Wade H. (later Lieutenant General)	Commanding General, U. S. XV Corps, Europe.
Hansen, Captain Chester B. (later Lieutenant Colonel)	Aide to General Bradley, Tunisia, Sicily, Europe.
Harmon, Major General Erńest N.	Commanding General, 1st Armored Division, Tunisia; Commanding General, 2d Armored Division, Europe; Commanding General, XXII Corps, Europe.
Hodges, Lieutenant General Courtney H. (later General)	Commander, U. S. First Army, Europe.
Huebner, Major General Clarence R.	Commanding General, 1st Infantry Division, Europe; Commanding General, V Corps, Europe.
Kean, Brigadier General William B., Jr. (later Major General)	Chief of Staff, U. S. II Corps, Tunisia, Sicily; Chief of Staff, U. S. First Army, Europe.

Kirk, Rear Admiral Alan R.
(later Vice Admiral)

Commander, CENT Naval Force, Sicilian invasion; Commander, Eastern Task Force, Normandy invasion.

Kluge, Field Marshal Gunther, von

German Commander-in-Chief, West, during the Falaise-Argentan battle.

Lattre de Tassigny, General Jean, de

Commander, French First Army, Europe.

Leclerc, Major General Jacques

Commanding General, French 2d Armored Division.

Lee, Lieutenant General J. C. H.

Commanding General, Communications Bone, Europe.

Leese, Lieutenant General Sir Oliver

Commander, British XXX Corps, Sicily.

Leigh-Mallory, Air Chief Marshal Sir Trafford

Commander-in-Chief, Allied Expeditionary Air Force, SHAEF.

Marshall, General George C.
(later General of the Army)

Chief of Staff, United States Army.

McLain, Brigadier General Raymond S. (later Major General)

Artillery Officer, 45th Infantry Division, Sicily; Artillery Officer, 30th Infantry Division, Europe; Commanding General, 90th Infantry Division, Europe; Commanding General, U. S. XIX Corps, Europe.

Medaris, Lieutenant Colonel John B.

Ordnance Officer, U. S. II Corps, Tunisia, Sicily; Ordnance Officer, U. S. First Army, Europe.

Middleton, Major General Troy H.

Commanding General, 45th Division, Sicily; Commanding General, U. S. VIII Corps, Europe.

Model, Field Marshal Walther von

Commander, German Army Group B.

Montgomery, General Sir Bernard L. (later Field Marshal the Viscount Montgomery of Alamein)

Commander-in-Chief, British Eighth Army, Tunisia, Sicily; Commander-in-Chief, British 21st Army Group, Europe.

Morgan, General Sir Frederick E.	Chief of Staff, COSSAC.
Nordling, Raoul N. A.	Swedish Consul General, Paris.
O'Hare, Colonel Joseph J. (later Brigadier General)	Assistant Chief of Staff for Personnel and Administration, U. S. First Army, Europe; Assistant Chief of Staff for Personnel and Administration, U. S. 12th Army Group, Europe.
Patton, Major General George S., Jr. (later General)	Commanding General, U. S. II Corps, Tunisia; Commander, U. S. Seventh Army, Sicily; Commander, U. S. Third Army, Europe.
Quesada, Major General Elwood R.	Commanding General, IX Tactical Air Command.
Ramsay, Admiral Sir Bertram	Commander-in-Chief, Allied Naval Expeditionary Force, SHAEF.
Ridgway, Major General Matthew B. (later Lieutenant General)	Commanding General, 82d Airborne Division, Sicily, Europe; Commanding General, U. S. XVIII Airborne Corps, Europe.
Rommel, Field Marshal Erwin	German Commander, Afrika Korps, Tunisia; Commander, German Army Group B, Europe.
Roosevelt, Brigadier General Theodore, Jr.	Assistant Division Commander, 1st Infantry Division, Tunisia, Sicily; attached to 4th Infantry Division, Europe.
Rose, Colonel Maurice (later Major General)	Chief of Staff, 1st Armored Division, Tunisia; Commanding General, 3rd Armored Division, Europe.
Rudder, Lieutenant Colonel James E. (later Colonel)	Commanding Officer, 2d Ranger Battalion, Europe; Commanding Officer, 112th Infantry Regiment, 28th Infantry Division, Europe.

Rundstedt, Field Marshal Karl Rudolf Gerd, von — German Commander-in-Chief, West.

Ryder, Major General Charles W — Commanding General, 34th Infantry Division, Tunisia.

Sibert, Brigadier General Edwin L. — Assistant Chief of Staff for Intelligence, U. S. 12th Army Group.

Simpson, Lieutenant General William H. — Commander, U. S. Ninth Army.

Smith, Major General Walter Bedell (later Lieutenant General) — Chief of Staff, AFHQ, Tunisia, Sicily; Chief of Staff, SHAEF, Europe.

Spaatz, Major General Carl A. (later General) — Commanding General, Northwest African Force, Tunisia, Sicily; Commander, U. S. Strategic Air Forces, Europe.

Taylor, Brigadier General Maxwell D. (later Major General) — Commanding General, 101st Airborne Division, Europe.

Tedder, Air Chief Marshal Sir Arthur W. — Allied Air Commander-in-Chief, Allied Air Forces, AFHQ, Tunisia, Sicily; Deputy Supreme Allied Commander, SHAEF, Europe.

Thorson, Colonel Truman C. (later Brigadier General) — Assistant Chief of Staff for Operations, U. S. First Army, Europe.

Vandenberg, Major General Hoyt S. (later Lieutenant General) — Commander, U. S. Ninth Tactical Air Force.

Van Fleet, Colonel James A. (later Major General) — Commanding Officer, 8th Infantry Regiment, 4th Infantry Division, Europe; Assistant Division Commander, 2d Infantry Division, Europe; Commanding General, 90th Infantry Division, Europe, Commanding General, U. S. III Corps, Europe.

Walker, Major General Walton H. (later Lieutenant General)   Commanding General, U. S. XX Corps, Europe.

Ward, Major General Orlando   Commanding General, 1st Armored Division, Tunisia.

Wilson, Colonel Robert W. (later Brigadier General)   Assistant Chief of Staff for Supply, U. S. II Corps, Tunisia, Sicily; Assistant Chief of Staff for Supply, U. S. First Army, Europe.

Glossary

A-2—Air intelligence or principal air intelligence officer for a Group or higher command.

AA—Antiaircraft artillery.

ADC—Aide de Camp.

ADSEC—Advance Section, Communications Zone, logistical organization in direct support of U. S. Channel-based troops.

AEAF—Allied Expeditionary Air Forces, senior air command for SHAEF.

AFHQ—Allied Force Headquarters, combined command for the Mediterranean Theater.

ANFA—Term applied to the Casablanca Conference, January, 1943. Conference headquarters were located in the Anfa Hotel.

ANVIL—Code name applied to the Allied invasion of the Mediterranean coast of France. Changed to DRAGOON prior to the landing on August 15, 1944.

AT guns—Antitank guns.

ATC—Air Transport Command.

Autobahn—Four-lane super highway, Germany and Austria.

AWOL—Absent without leave.

Beanie—Woolen headgear for winter wear under a steel helmet.

BEF—British Expeditionary Forces.

BOLERO—Code term applied to build-up of American forces in the United Kingdom for the cross-channel invasion of France.

BOWSPRIT—Signal code word devised to notify U. S. invasion troops of a 24-hour delay in the OVERLORD assault.

C-47—Douglas (DC-3) twin-engined transport aircraft designed to carry cargo and personnel.

CBI—China-Burma-India Theater of Operations.

CC "B"—Combat command of an armored division. Usually contains from one third to one half of the division's strength.

CENT Force—Gela assault force on the Sicilian invasion. Consisted of the 1st Infantry Division, the 1st and 4th Ranger Battalions, the 505th Parachute Regiment, and a battalion of the 504th.

CG—Commanding General.

Chott—Arabic term for a beach or any land next to water. Often used in reference to a dry lake.

CIC—Counter Intelligence Corps.

C-in-C—Commander-in-Chief.

Com Z—Communications Zone, senior U. S. logistical echelon in support of the field armies.

CONQUER—Signal code term used to designate the U. S. Ninth Army.

Con trails—Vapor trails left in the wake of aircraft passing through atmosphere heavy with supercooled water particles.

COSSAC—Forerunner of SHAEF for OVERLORD planning. Name is derived from title of the Chief of Staff to the Supreme Allied Commander. (Designate.)

CP—Command Post.

Davits—Cranes used to lower small craft over the side of a ship and pick them up again.

DIME Force—Scoglitti assault force on the Sicilian invasion. Consisted of the 45th Infantry Division and the 753rd Tank Battalion.

Djebel—Arabic word for mountain or hill.

DRAGOON—Replacement code name for ANVIL, the allied invasion of the Mediterranean coast of France.

DUKW—Dual-drive, 2½-ton, amphibious truck.

EAGLE—Signal code designation for the U. S. 12th Army Group.

Easy Green—Beach sector, English Channel assault.

Easy Red—Beach sector, English Channel assault.

E-boat—German naval attack craft, enemy counterpart of the U. S. PT boat.

EVAC—Evacuation Hospital, normally serving an Army corps, contains from 400 to 750 beds.

FFI—Forces Français de l'Intérieur (French Forces of the Interior) engaged in underground resistance during the German occupation of France, 1940–45.

Focke-Wulf—German single piston-engined fighter aircraft.

Fox Green—Beach sector, English Channel assault.

Fox Red—Beach sector, English Channel assault.

FREEDOM—Signal code designation for Allied Force Headquarters in Algiers.

FUSAG—First United States Army Group, predecessor to the U. S. 12th Army Group.

G-1—Personnel and administrative section of the general staff or principal staff officer heading that activity in a division or higher command.

G-2—Intelligence section of the general staff or principal staff officer heading that activity in a division or higher command.

G-3—Operations and training section of the general staff or principal staff officer heading that activity in a division or higher command.

G-4—Supply and maintenance section of the general staff or principal staff officer heading that activity in a division or higher command.

GMC's—A six-wheel, six-wheel-drive, 2½-ton truck built to transport cargo and personnel.

GOOSEBERRY—One of the five artificial harbors constructed off the coast of Normandy for the OVERLORD invasion. Together they formed the two major harbors known as MULBERRIES.

Goumiers—Moroccan tribesmen from the Atlas Mountains serving with the Regular French African Infantry Forces.

GPF's—French heavy artillery.

Hards—Concrete ramps constructed in England from the high to low water mark to facilitate the loading of vehicles on assault craft for the invasion.

HORNPIPE—Code designation for OVERLORD in the message sent to notify units on 24-hour delay of the Normandy assault.

HUSKY—Allied invasion of Sicily, July 10, 1943.

Jabos—Jagdbomber, German term for fighter bombers.

Jacob's ladder—A rope or wire ladder with wooden or iron rungs commonly used to board a ship at sea.

JOSS—Licata assault force on the Sicilian invasion. Consisted of the 3rd Infantry Division, the 2d Armored Division, and the 3rd Ranger Battalion.

JU-88—Junkers 88, a German twin-engined medium bomber.

LCA—Landing craft, assault. Designed to carry approximately 35 troops.

LCI—Landing craft, Infantry (large). Designed to carry 200 troops or 75 tons of cargo.

LCM—Landing craft, mechanized. Designed to carry one 30-ton tank or 100 troops.

LCT—Landing craft, tank. Designed to carry four Shermans.

LCVP—Landing craft, vehicle, personnel.

LION—Signal code designation for the British 21st Army Group.

"Long Tom"—155-mm. long-barreled artillery piece (U. S.).

LST—Landing ship, tank. Designed to carry 1,600 to 1,900 tons of vehicles or cargo.

LUCKY—Signal code designation for the U. S. Third Army.

MA—Military assistant, a British term.

Mae West—A pneumatic life jacket.

MARKET—Airborne operation designed to seize a bridgehead across the lower Rhine at Arnhem, September 17, 1944.

MARKET-GARDEN—*See* MARKET. GARDEN was used to designate the land operation mounted in conjunction with the MARKET air drop.

MASTER—Signal code designation for the U. S. First Army.

ME-109—Messerschmitt 109, a speedy and versatile German piston-engine fighter.

NAAFI—Navy, Army, Air Force Institute, British counterpart of the U. S. post exchanges and ships' stores.

OD's—Olive drab uniform of the U. S. Army.

OKW—Oberkommando der Wehrmacht, German High Command.

OMAHA—Designation given U. S. invasion beach on the Calvados coast of Normandy between Isigny and Bayeux.

OPD—Operations and Planning Division of the War Department, U. S. brain center of World War II.

OVERLORD—Plan and operation for the English Channel invasion of France in the spring of 1944.

PA—Personal Assistant, a British term.

Parka—Three-quarter-length hooded jacket, lined with woolen pile for winter wear.

PLUTO—Pipeline-under-the-ocean for the cross-channel delivery of gasoline to Allied troops in Normandy.

PM—Prime Minister (of Great Britain).

POL—General supply term applied to petroleum, oil, and lubricants.

P&PW—Publicity and Psychological Warfare, a special staff section.

PRO—Public relations officer.

PT boat—Motor torpedo launch, a high-speed attack boat of the U. S. Navy.

PW—Prisoner of War.

QM—Quartermaster.

RANKIN "A"—Plan for a cross-channel landing on the Continent in the event of a breakdown in German morale and resistance prior to the OVERLORD invasion.

RANKIN "B"—Plan for a cross-channel landing on the Continent in the event of German withdrawal from France and/or Norway.

RANKIN "C"—Plan for the swift occupation of western Europe in the event of unconditional surrender of Germany.

Recce—Abbreviated term for reconnaissance.

Recon—Term commonly used to designate the three-quarter-ton reconnaissance car.

RETRIBUTION—British naval concentration designed to prevent the escape of Axis forces from Tunisia to Sicily.

Rhino ferry—Steel raft-like craft used to lighter vehicles from landing ships offshore to the beach.

ROUNDUP—Planned operation for an English Channel assault against the coast of France, predecessor to OVERLORD.

Runnel—Term used by the British to designate a sand bar or shoal.

Sausages—Term applied to oval-shaped assembly areas in southern England for Normandy invasion troops.

SHAEF—Supreme Headquarters, Allied Expeditionary Force.

SHELLBURST—Signal code designation for the advance headquarters of SHAEF in Normandy.

Sitrep—Situation report prepared by G-3 at 24-hour intervals.

SLEDGEHAMMER—Plan for a premature English Channel invasion of the Continent to secure a limited beachhead in the event imminent collapse of Russia made it necessary to divert German troops from that front.

SOS—Services of Supply.

SPEEDY—Signal code designation for U. S. II Corps, Tunisia and Sicily.

Spit—Spitfire, a British high-speed fighter aircraft.

Stalags—Prisoner of war compounds, German term.

Stellung—Defense position, German term.

Stuka—German single-motored dive bomber with fixed landing gear. Also known as a JU-87. Used extensively in direct support of German ground troops during the early years of the war.

TAC—Advanced tactical headquarters.

Tac/R—Tactical reconnaissance aircraft.

Teller Mine—German antivehicle mine.

TORCH—Allied landings on the South Atlantic and Mediterranean coasts of North Africa, November 8, 1942.

Trident—Washington Conference: Roosevelt, Churchill; May, 1943.

TWX—Teletypewriter exchange, term commonly applied to all electronically transmitted messages.

UTAH—Westernmost of the Allied invasion beaches in Normandy, located on the Cotentin east shore.

VHF—Very high frequency radio equipment used principally for air-to-air and air-to-ground communications.

Wadi—Arabic term for an arroyo or gully caused by erosion.

Wellingtons—British twin-engined bombers.

Index

546; Montgomery's Rhineland offensive, 492; Montgomery's super-ground command conspiracy, 492; Mousetrap Valley, 77; Ninth Army command return, 492, 528; North African campaign, 23–24, 29; North African victory parade, Tunis, 109; November offensive strategy conference, 433–35; occupation mission prohibitions, 231; officer competency, 11; officer indiscretion, punishment, 224; official staff, 207; Pantelleria, importance of, 115; Paris capitulation, 391; Paris headquarters commands, 406; Paris visit, 394–96; Patton, 42, 45–46; Patton censorship stop, 393; Patton slapping incident, 161, 229–31; Patton-Coningham incident, 62–63; Patton's Allied Service Club speech, 230–31; Patton's Battle for France, 357–58; Patton's supply restrictions, 427; Patton's temper, 119; *photographs, opp.* 109, 268, 461; Prague advance, 549; press conference (1st), England, 211; promotion to five-star rank, 449; Quesada, 325; radio messages, 280–81; Reich conquest strategy, 419–22; Reich morale cracking, 434; Reims conference, 508; Remagen bridge taking, 510; replacement system, 446, 447; Rhine supply problem, 413; Rhineland offensive, 497–98, 501–02, 504, 508, 511–18, 527–28, 539; Roosevelt, F. D., death, 541; Roosevelt, Theodore, Jr., evaluation, 332–33; St. Germainen-Laye, 465; Seine, war beyond the, 398; Sfax project, 24; SHAEF, rarefied air at, 310–11; SHAEF command, 218; SHAEF staff, 511; SHAEF trouble-shooter, 313; SHAEF-Wiesbaden commuting, 539; Sicilian invasion, 130, 132, 156, 192; Sicilian invasion instructions, 21; Sicilian invasion planning, 101, 103–04, 115, 118–19; Sidi Nsir CP location, 91; Siegfried Line, defense value, 494; Siegfried Line forcing plan, 497; single versus the double thrust, 434–35; soldier's civilian occupation, query, 323–24; Southern France by Mediterranean invasion, 367–69; Soviet winter attack (1944), 503; Soviet-Allied juncture plan, 531–33; Stalin, Elbe line radio, 535; strategic objectives responsibility, 4; supply conference, 431; supply manifests, 305; Supreme Commander, 205–06; surrender mission, 553–54; tactician, 354; Tebessa visits, 25, 42, 91; telephone communication, 393; 3d Army gasoline, 404; tonnage allotments, 405; troops, 311; trouble makers, 33; Tunis, capture, 23–24; Tunisian campaign, 18, 23–29, 39, 42, 53, 57–61, 63, 67–70, 73–74, 77, 89, 91, 100, 103; Tunisian front information TWX, *quoted*, 18–19; unannounced fighter sweep, 325; UTAH assault, 234–36; Verdun conference, 469, 475; Versailles conference, 422–23, 427; Versailles headquarters, 422; weather, *quoted*

on, 343; West Point, 16, 29–30, 547; World War I, 19

El Alamein, Egypt, 188, 190–92; *map,* 189

ELAS opposition, Greece, 509

Elbe River, 523–54; Allied-Soviet juncture, 531–33, 535–36; Armored Division (2d), 537; Army (1st), 226; Eisenhower-Stalin wire, 535; *maps,* 216, 421, 532, 534, 538, 548; 104th Division, 156; Russian banqueting, 549; Russian front, 529; Russians, waiting for, 543–46

El Guettar offensive, Tunisia, 48–51; Benson force, 61; corridor, 77; enemy opposition, 52, 68–69; *maps,* 26, 49, 66; Patton, 51, 54, 60, 78; supply, 69; troops, 68

Enfidaville, Tunisia: hills, 67, 90; *maps,* 38, 57, 66, 72; Montgomery advance, 73, 82, 89–90; terrain, 71; Wadi Akrit, 65

England: air forces, 197; barges, 304; blitz *1940,* 310; blockhouses, 265; bombing (1940), 183; border troops, 186; Bradley, 10; civilian traffic, 247; coastal area, 247; embarkation areas, *map,* 258; enemy agents, 344; flying fields, 217–18; German invasion in 1940, 265; homeland protection, 186; *map,* 216; marshaling areas, 247; optimism, 199; rail equipment, 386; resources, 185, 186; rocket bombs, 309–10; shipping losses, 183; situation (1941), 184; "strategy of erosion," 185; U. S. parity in command, 352; V-1 bombardment, 309–10; victory hopes, 185; weather, 352; Yankee invasion, 238

English Channel invasion, 251–85, 286–314; American attitude, 193–94, 195; beachheads, 214–18, 257, 292; BOLERO plan, 188, 191; Bradley, 8, 11; Brest, capture of, 366–67; British attitude, 193–96, 200; British intelligence, 214; British outline plan, 185; Brittany ports, 366; Chief of Staff, 206–07; Combined Chiefs, 196; command, 197–211, 352; cover plan, 344–45; D-day postponement, 220–21, 259, 261, 264; deception plan, 344–45; delay causes, 190–91; deputy commander, 206; Devers, 8, 172; divisions unloaded, 291; France, liberation plan, 317; German army advantage, 344; German army retaliation, 287–88, 291–95, 298; Germany, collapse of, 199; ground force commander, 211; H hour, 243, 255, 257, 260, 262, 267–68; importance, 183; landing craft, 212, 218–20; *maps,* 202, 213, 216, 233, 240, 258, 284, 300; Marshall's position on, 104–05, 187, 191, 193, 195–96; planning (OVERLORD), 175, 182–96, 197–211, 212–50; planning staff, *see* COSSAC; plans rehearsal, 240–41; postponement, 257–58, 261–62, 264–66; radio traffic breakdown, 281; ROUND-UP, 187–88, 191; Russian attitude, 201; seasickness, 257, 264, 268; shoestring policy,